BAILOUTS OR BAIL-INS?

Responding to Financial Crises in Emerging Economies

Praise for *Bailouts or Bail-ins?*

"Roubini and Setser bring valuable experience from the policymaking process to their analysis of responding to 21st century financial crises in emerging economies. *Bailouts or Bail-ins?* will prove to be a useful tool for those confronting these crises, and a clear, accessible overview for those studying global markets."

—Lawrence Summers, former US treasury secretary, president, Harvard University

"*Bailouts or Bail-ins?* is masterful. It is by far the best book written in recent years on the vexing subject of how the international community should address international financial crises of emerging market economies. Roubini and Setser put it all together: a masterful overview of theoretical issues, a skilled and accurate account of recent crises, and a wise, balanced, and judicious discussion of the policy debates. They don't shy away from reaching clear policy recommendations. Even when one disagrees with one or another these recommendations, the reader is bound to feel that the issue has been treated with care, forthrightness, thorough empirical knowledge, and good judgment. This book will be read with enormous benefit by students, scholars, policymakers, and financial market participants."

—Jeffrey D. Sachs, director of the Earth Institute, Columbia University

"This is the most intelligent and comprehensive analysis yet of how the international community should respond to financial crises. Its analyses of the theoretical literature on the causes of crises, the evolution of official doctrine, and recent experience with crisis management are especially strong. It will be the definitive work on this subject for some time to come."

—Barry Eichengreen, George C. Pardee and Helen N. Pardee Professor of Economics and Political Science, University of California-Berkeley

"A fluid and deeply informed synthesis of the recent debate on how to improve sovereign debt workouts. Roubini and Setser's book will likely be a standard reference for many years to come."

—Kenneth Rogoff, Thomas D. Cabot Professor of Public Policy and Professor of Economics, Harvard University

"The Rubin-Summers era policy wonks take on financial architecture, matured by distance, turbocharged with academic authority."

—Jeromin Zettelmeyer, International Monetary Fund

INSTITUTE FOR INTERNATIONAL ECONOMICS

BAILOUTS OR BAIL-INS?

Responding to Financial Crises in Emerging Economies

Nouriel Roubini and Brad Setser

Viva Books Private Limited

New Delhi • Mumbai • Chennai • Kolkata • Bangalore • Hyderabad

First Indian Edition 2006

VIVA BOOKS PRIVATE LIMITED

- 4262/3, Ansari Road, Daryaganj, New Delhi 110 002
  E-mail: vivadelhi@vivagroupindia.net, Tel: 23258325, 23283121
- 215-216 New Apollo Estate, Mogra Lane, Andheri (E), Mumbai 400 069
  E-mail: vivamumbai@vivagroupindia.net, Tel: 56997844,56997845
- Jamals Fazal Chambers, 26 Greams Road, Chennai 600 006
  E-mail: vivachennai@vivagroupindia.net, Tel: 28290304, 28294241
- B-103, Jindal Towers, 21/1A/3 Darga Road, Kolkata 700 017
  E-mail: vivakolkata@vivagroupindia.net, Tel: 22836381, 22816713
- 7, Sovereign Park Apartments, 56-58, K. R. Road, Basavanagudi, Bangalore 560 004
  E-mail: vivabangalore@vivagroupindia.net, Tel: 26607409, 26607410
- 101-102 Mughal Marg Apartments, Narayanguda, Hyderabad 500 029
  E-mail: vivahyderabad@vivagroupindia.net, Tel: 27564481, 27564482

Published by arrangement with

Institute for International Economics
1750 Massachusetts Avenue, NW
Washington, DC 20036-1903

This publication is part of the overall program of the Institute, as endorsed by its Board of Directors, but does not necessarily reflect the views in individual of the Board or the Advisory Committee.

The council takes no institutional position on policy issues and has no affiliation with the US government. All statements of fact and expressions of opinion contained in its publications are the sole responsibility of the author or authors.

ISBN 81-309-0092-0

Published by Vinod Vasishtha for Viva Books Private Limited, 4262/3 Ansari Road, Daryaganj, New Delhi 110 002. Printed & bound at Raj Press, R-3 Inderpuri, New Delhi - 110 012.

Contents

Tables

Figures

Boxes

Preface

The international financial system, and especially the problems of international debt, have long been a focal issue at the Institute for International Economics. In 1999, Morris Goldstein produced *Safeguarding Prosperity in a Global Financial System: The Future International Financial Architecture* (as project director of an Independent Task Force Report sponsored by the Council on Foreign Relations). We have published comprehensive systemic analyses by two outstanding visiting fellows: *Toward a New International Financial Architecture* by Barry Eichengreen (1999) and *The International Financial Architecture: What's New? What's Missing?* by Peter Kenen (2001).

Over the past decade, a number of major emerging economies have encountered serious financial trouble. The International Monetary Fund (IMF) and the IMF's major shareholders often faced a sharp choice: Barring a major rescue loan or an agreement—which was always difficult to achieve—with the crisis country's creditors to defer payments, the country would default. Few international economic issues have generated more controversy among policymakers than deciding what to do in such circumstances.

This book breaks new ground on that issue in several ways. It provides a comprehensive analysis of the series of crises that started with Mexico in 1994–95, looking at recent large IMF loans to Argentina, Turkey, Uruguay, and Brazil (in 2001–02) as well as IMF lending to Mexico, the Asian-crisis countries, Russia, Brazil (in 1998–99), and several smaller cases. It integrates analysis of large IMF loans with analysis of attempts to convince private creditors to provide emergency financing to crisis countries, whether alongside the IMF or as a substitute for large-scale IMF lending.

Authors Nouriel Roubini and Brad Setser argue that private creditors have contributed far more emergency financing in recent crisis cases than is commonly realized—and hence that the story of crisis response since Mexico is not one of all bailouts and no bail-ins. They also emphasize that sovereign bonds have not been the most important source of financial pressure on crisis countries, that the absence of formal protection from external litigation is not the most important problem that arises in a sovereign debt restructuring, and that the recent success of efforts to introduce collective action clauses into sovereign bond contracts is unlikely to significantly reduce pressure to bail out crisis countries.

It is not surprising, then, that Roubini and Setser argue that the end of the recent efforts to create a new international bankruptcy regime for sovereign borrowers should not end the debate on how best to respond to financial crises. There remains much that can be done, but making progress requires moving beyond a policy framework based on calls to limit IMF lending at some unspecified point in the future—calls that lack credibility, as recent experience suggests they will be ignored in the heat of crisis. Far better, the authors argue, is to define the set of problems that large-scale IMF lending should and should not address. There is also a need to examine whether IMF financing can help soften the blow associated with a sovereign debt restructuring: Roubini and Setser suggest that a debt restructuring is not necessarily a substitute for IMF lending and that, in some cases, the two can work as complements.

The Institute for International Economics is a private, nonprofit institution for the study and discussion of international economic policy. Its purpose is to analyze important issues in that area and to develop and communicate practical new approaches for dealing with them. The Institute is completely nonpartisan.

The Institute is funded largely by philanthropic foundations. Major support for this study was provided by the GE Foundation. Major institutional grants are now being received from the William M. Keck, Jr. Foundation and the Starr Foundation. A number of other foundations and private corporations contribute to the highly diversified financial resources of the Institute. About 23 percent of the Institute's resources in our latest fiscal year were provided by contributors outside the United States, including about 8 percent from Japan.

The Board of Directors bears overall responsibilities for the Institute and gives general guidance and approval to its research program, including the identification of topics that are likely to become important over the medium run (one to three years), and which should be addressed by the Institute. The director, working closely with the staff and outside Advisory Committee, is responsible for the development of particular projects and makes the final decision to publish an individual study.

The Institute hopes that its studies and other activities will contribute to building a stronger foundation for international economic policy around the world. We invite readers of these publications to let us know how they think we can best accomplish this objective.

C. FRED BERGSTEN
Director
June 2004

INSTITUTE FOR INTERNATIONAL ECONOMICS
1750 Massachusetts Avenue, NW, Washington, DC 20036-1903
(202) 328-9000 Fax: (202) 659-3225

Acknowledgments

We would like to thank Fred Bergsten and the Institute for International Economics for all their support in this project. The Council on Foreign Relations enabled Brad Setser to spend a year as an international affairs fellow writing this book and financed a research trip to Argentina. Ngaire Woods and the Global Economic Governance Programme at University College, Oxford, provided additional support during the home stretch.

This project benefited enormously from the input and constructive criticism provided by many close colleagues during our successive iterations. We are grateful to Anna Gelpern, Arend Kapteyn, and Peter Kenen for thoughtful comments on our initial, rather rough draft. Carole Setser and Don Setser helped us in our efforts to communicate to an audience not already immersed in the vocabulary of emerging-market debt. Ted Truman provided us with the detailed, expert comments that those who have worked for him have come to expect. Sergio Schmukler and two other anonymous referees helped strengthen our final draft with their insightful comments. We benefited from the skilled counsel of Jeremy Pam and Anna Gelpern on legal issues. Rich Kelly helped track down some hard-to-find data. Anjela Kniazeva and Diana Kniazeva at the Stern School of Business at New York University and Khalid Nadiri and Helen Harris at the Council of Foreign Relations provided excellent research assistance. Madona Devasahayam performed Herculean labor during the copyediting.

We also received valuable comments and suggestions from the participants of two study groups at the Institute for International Economics in Washington, DC, and one at the Council on Foreign Relations in New York.

We would be remiss not to thank Tim Geithner for his consistent support and feedback over the years and Robert Rubin and Larry Summers for creating a fertile intellectual environment for thinking about crises in emerging economies during their tenure at the US Treasury.

Many friends and colleagues exchanged ideas with us over the years and helped shape our thinking on the topics in this book. They include Lewis Alexander, Mark Allen, Thanos Arvanitis, Caroline Atkinson, Jeff Baker, Ed Bartholomew, Fred Bergsten, Andy Berg, Amer Bisat, Patrick Bolton, Lee Buchheit, Charles Calomiris, William Cline, Giancarlo Corsetti, Barry Eichengreen, Martin Feldstein, Stan Fischer, Matthew Fisher, Jeffrey Frankel, Kristin Forbes, Mark Giancola, Mary Goodman, Bernardo Guimaraes, Sean Hagan, Andy Haldane, Ricardo Hausmann, Brett House, Olivier Jeanne, Michael Kaplan, Christian Keller, Ken Kletzer, Clay Lowery, David Lipton, Anthony Marcus, Alan MacArthur, Matt McBrady, Mauro Mecagni, Zanny Minton-Beddoes, Steve Morris, Mike Mussa, Jens Nystedt, Paolo Pesenti, Richard Portes, Arturo Porzecanski, Steve Radelet, Ken Rogoff, Christoph Rosenberg, Jeff Sachs, Anne Salladin, Michele Shannon, Mark Siegel, Hyun Shin, Mark Sobel, Louellen Stedman, Benn Steil, Dan Tarullo, Ramin Toloui, Dan Zelikow, and Jeromin Zettelmeyer.

We also have benefited from the steady exchange of views and ideas over the years with colleagues—too numerous to thank individually on this page—in the academic and international financial policy worlds, the markets, the International Monetary Fund, the US Treasury Department, the White House's Council of Economic Advisers, the Council on Foreign Relations, the Institute for International Economics, and other research institutions and think tanks.

The usual disclaimer applies with force: The views and opinions in the book are strictly those of the authors and not of the current and past institutions that they have been affiliated with. No individual cited above is in any way implicated in the conclusions that we ended up drawing.

1

Introduction

Roughly once a year—if recent history is any guide—the managing director of the International Monetary Fund (IMF), the US treasury secretary, and in some cases the finance ministers of other Group of Seven (G-7) countries get a phone call from the finance minister of a large emerging-market economy. The precise details of each conversation differ, but the core does not. The emerging-market economy's finance minister indicates that the country is rapidly running out of foreign reserves, that it has lost access to international capital markets, and that it has perhaps even lost the confidence of its own citizens. Without a large rescue loan, the country will be forced to devalue its currency and either default on its government debt or be unable to help its banks avoid a payments standstill.

This book is about how to answer that phone call.

The list of countries that have asked the official sector[1] for help since 1994 is long and covers all parts of the globe. It includes major emerging economies like Mexico, Thailand, Indonesia, Korea, Russia, Brazil, Turkey, and Argentina—as well as smaller economies like Ukraine, Pakistan,

1. The IMF, World Bank, regional development banks, G-7, Group of Ten (G-10), and the group of bilateral creditors that meet in the Paris Club are collectively known as the official sector. The G-7 countries are the United States, Japan, Germany, the United Kingdom, France, Italy, and Canada. Belgium, the Netherlands, Sweden, and Switzerland join the G-7 in the G-10. Like the Big 10 conference, the G-10 has 11 members. The G-10 countries provide the bulk of the funds that the IMF, World Bank, and other multilateral development banks (MDBs) lend to emerging economies and have a correspondingly large say over how those funds are used. Regional development banks include the Inter-American Development Bank, Asian Development Bank, European Bank for Reconstruction and Development, and African Development Bank.

Ecuador, Uruguay, and the Dominican Republic. The call rarely comes as a total surprise, at least when the phone rings. It is bad form to call the IMF's managing director, the US treasury secretary, or the finance minister of another G-7 country without giving their staff a heads up. But it is hard at times even for the flotilla of economists at the IMF, Treasury Department, Federal Reserve, and other G-7 finance ministries and central banks to predict with certainty who will call in the next six months.

Whether the call comes as a surprise or not, those receiving the plea for help almost always face the same core choice. One option is a rescue loan from an international financial institution (IFI), such as the IMF, or from a major country like the United States. The loan has to be big enough to enable the crisis country to make payments on at least those debts that are coming due immediately. The country uses the financial reprieve to take steps to correct its macroeconomic problems. If all goes well, it regains access to financing from private markets, money starts flowing back, reserves rise, and it can repay the IMF. Official rescue loans are not gifts: IMF loans have to be repaid with interest, as do loans from the G-7 or G-10, the World Bank, and other multilateral development banks (MDBs).

The other option is to encourage the country to ask its creditors to agree to roll over or reschedule their maturing claims. The debts coming due can be the obligations of the crisis country's government—for example, a maturing international sovereign bond. They also can be cross-border loans to private borrowers—most often banks—in the crisis country. In either case, convincing the country's creditors to defer payments, whether through a bond exchange or an agreement to roll over maturing bank loans, requires at least the implicit threat that the country will halt payments if the creditors do not agree. The IMF, G-7, and others can tell the country that it must reach agreement with its creditors in order to receive an IMF loan, or they can go one step further and help the country organize a rollover agreement or a bond exchange.

Both an IMF loan and a debt restructuring are ways of giving a crisis country time to put its economic and financial house in order. Neither typically works if the country does not take advantage of the financial breathing space to make the policy changes (adjustments) needed to address the major economic imbalances that gave rise to the crisis. A country with a current account deficit needs to let its exchange rate adjust to shrink its trade deficit and reduce the amount it borrows from the rest of the world. Countries with profligate governments running large budget deficits need to put their fiscal accounts in order. At the same time, agreement on a set of policy changes rarely is enough to stop all financial pressures. A financial rescue typically does not work without policy changes, but policy changes also often will not work without emergency financing.

There are no silver bullets: No option for providing a country with emergency financing is attractive. IMF loans—*bailouts* to their critics—are given to help the country honor its contractual commitment to pay its debts.[2] But they also help the country's creditors, particularly those who are lucky enough to have claims coming due soon after the country gets the rescue loan. Former US Treasury Secretary Paul O'Neill often speculated about the wisdom of spending the tax dollars of American "plumbers and carpenters" to bail out creditors who lent at high spreads to shaky emerging economies. Former US Treasury Secretary Robert Rubin has said that if he had his druthers, he would not have lent a "nickel" to bail out private creditors. He also has noted that it is often hard to help a country—or to avoid a default that spills over and damages other countries—without also helping those who lent to it (Rubin and Weisberg 2003; Rubin 1998).

A *bail-in*—either an agreement by creditors to roll over their short-term claims or a formal debt restructuring[3]—also can give a country some time to right itself. But it requires that the country, with the implicit backing of the IMF, break its contractual promise to pay creditors in full and on time. Doing so risks triggering a broader loss of confidence in the country's currency and banking system. Moreover, there is no guarantee that the country will be able to reach agreement with its creditors on a consensual rollover agreement or restructuring to avoid an outright default. Even if a restructuring were to leave both the country and its creditors collectively better off, every individual creditor would prefer to get paid in full while others agree not to demand full current payment on their debts.

No market can work if debt restructuring becomes a habit and if debtors do not take their promises to repay seriously. On the other hand, the additional return emerging-market debt offers over safer financial assets like US treasuries implies at least the occasional restructuring, if not outright default. Many look to the corporate bond market and dream of a world where sovereign governments—or, for that matter, the banking system of a major emerging-market economy—can go under without

2. Throughout the book, we use the terms "rescue loans" and "bailouts" as shorthand to refer to the IMF's financial support to crisis countries. Other terms sound too bland or too euphemistic. Analytically, though, we do not want to endorse fully either the positive connotation of the term "rescue loans" or the negative connotation of the term "bailout." Some "rescues" have failed to save the crisis country. And IMF "bailouts," as we will discuss later, differ fundamentally from many taxpayer-subsidized bank bailouts, like the bailout of the US savings and loans industry in the 1980s.

3. We use the term "debt restructuring" broadly to denote any change in the country's contractual payments profile. A restructuring could aim to do little more than defer principal payments on maturing debts, without any reduction in the contractual interest rate the country must pay. Such restructurings are often called a rescheduling. Alternatively, a restructuring could both defer principal payments and reduce interest payments. The loss associated with such restructuring terms is a function of both the length of time repayment of principal is put off and the interest rate on the new debt. Finally, a restructuring can reduce the face value of the country's debt. A restructuring may occur before a formal debt default and thus preempt it (as in the case of Uruguay) or after the country has formally defaulted on its obligations (as in the case of Ecuador).

drawing the IMF into the country's decision to default or into the often messy restructuring process that follows. To those opposing any official intervention, IMF or G-7 efforts to catalyze a consensual restructuring are just as bad, if not worse, than large bailouts: The involvement of the IMF tarnishes the official sector with the country's decision not to pay on time. It is not surprising that some would prefer a world where the IMF, MDBs, and governments of the G-7 and G-10 countries simply refuse to supply financing and make no effort to help the country get through its troubles. Letting nature take its course is an alternative to both an IMF bailout and an IMF sanctioned bail-in.

The debate on reforming the international financial architecture that followed the 1997–98 Asian and global crises has primarily focused on proposals for grand institutional reforms, often motivated by a desire to make decisions during crises easier. One notable example is the proposal for an international bankruptcy regime as an alternative to bailouts. Anne Krueger (2001a), the first deputy managing director of the IMF, has suggested a new treaty to provide some bankruptcy-style protections to sovereign debtors. Joseph Stiglitz (2002) has suggested a "super" Chapter 11 regime to facilitate an across-the-board restructuring of private borrowers' debts in the event of macroeconomic shocks. Stanley Fischer (1999) has suggested that the IMF be transformed into a lender of last resort able to put enough money on the table to be sure that it could stop runs on countries. Back in 1995, Jeffrey Sachs laid out the case for both an international lender of last resort and a sovereign bankruptcy regime.[4] Others have suggested new binding rules to substantially scale back the amount the IMF can provide in all crises. The International Financial Institutions Advisory Committee (IFIAC 2000), more commonly called the Meltzer Commission, suggested that the IMF get out of the business of lending to countries that discover macroeconomic virtue only when they are close to default and that instead it lend large sums only to countries with good policies that qualified in advance for extra protection—assuming those policies could be defined.[5] Adam Lerrick and Allan Meltzer (2001) have called on the IMF to support the secondary market for a country's sovereign bonds rather than to lend directly to the crisis country. To date, these calls for major reforms have not significantly changed the international financial system. Some grand proposals fail to address the real problems of

4. Sachs (1995) put particular emphasis on a bankruptcy regime's ability to provide administrative priority to new financing, since he envisions new private money as the solution to underfinanced IMF programs. For a history of the idea of a sovereign bankruptcy regime, see Rogoff and Zettelmeyer (2002b).

5. The International Financial Institutions Advisory Committee (IFIAC) specifically recommended that the IMF lend large sums for short-term loans—120 days with only one possible rollover—to countries that prequalified for support. The IFIAC also suggested that the strength of a country's banking system be the key criterion for determining eligibility. Others have proposed less draconian forms of prequalification.

crisis resolution. Others are just impractical or inappropriate ways to resolve crises.

A long, hard slog through the details of past financial crises suggests that there is no easy, glamorous institutional change to dramatically transform the options for resolving financial crises in emerging-market economies. More could be achieved by aiming a bit lower. The real challenge is not so much redesigning existing institutions as finding ways of using existing institutions and tools more effectively. We therefore focus on practical ideas for improving the official sector's capacity to respond to emerging-market financial crises. Some institutional reforms might make a bond restructuring or an interbank rollover easier. However, no institutional reform will either eliminate the need for those on the receiving end of pleas for help to make hard choices or make it substantially easier for them to tell a country that it has no choice but to seek a debt restructuring.

Why Crisis Resolution?

It is worthwhile to focus on how to respond to crises for three main reasons. First, IMF decisions matter. Refusing to give rescue loans to countries that have temporary financial difficulties risks pushing them into an economic and financial abyss. Often these are countries where the United States and the other G-7 countries, which provide the bulk of the IMF's funds, have strategic as well as financial interests at stake. Moreover, the economic and financial losses from an uncontained crisis typically spill over beyond the crisis country's borders, and its policy choices will influence expectations about how other countries will act when they get into trouble.

Yet spending large amounts of the IMF's ammunition on an *unsuccessful* attempt to help a country avoid a debt restructuring leaves almost everyone worse off. A few creditors get paid in full, and a few investors can sell their local currency for a foreign currency at a better price than otherwise would have been possible. But the need to repay the IMF will likely require that other creditors take larger losses in the subsequent debt restructuring.[6] The already-exposed IMF will not be able to lend more to try to avert a deeper crisis. Rather than being in a position to help shape the country's policies during its restructuring, the IMF is left negotiating to get its money back as the crisis country falls off a financial and economic cliff.

Second, the emerging economies' ability to borrow reserves in a crisis from the IMF is a form of "insurance" against a liquidity crisis, just as holding reserves can be viewed as a form of insurance. The analogy to

6 Payments to the IMF are traditionally given priority over payments to other unsecured creditors. Using an IMF loan to repay existing private debts therefore substitutes debt that can be restructured with debt that by tradition is not restructured—in formal terms, it makes the country's debt structure more rigid.

insurance is imperfect. The size of the IMF's insurance policy and its price—the policy changes linked to the loan—that the IMF charges a country for its insurance are set during a country's crisis, not in advance. Still, the expectation that the IMF will try to prevent a temporary shortage of liquidity from producing a deep crisis means that the IMF, like all insurance companies, has to worry that its lending will alter the incentives of the country and its creditors alike. If countries are spared the costs of running dangerous policies and if creditors do not pay any price for financing sketchy countries, then risky policies and bets become more likely. Because of this risk of moral hazard, the IMF cannot just worry about the case in hand. It also has to worry about how its actions will shape the expectations of other countries and their creditors.

Third, the choice between a bailout and a bail-in, one that is often discussed under the euphemistic banner of whether "to involve" the private sector in crisis resolution,[7] has rightly been called the most difficult issue in the entire debate on international financial architecture reform. Policymakers, academics, and private-sector participants all continue to debate how to respond most effectively to crises. Despite recent efforts to clarify the IMF's access policy, its major shareholders—the countries that control the majority of the voting power on the IMF's Executive Board—simply don't agree on the right approach to resolving financial crises in emerging economies.

The key questions of crisis resolution are a source of near continuous disagreement. Should the IMF help a country avoid a crisis triggered in part by a creditor panic, even if it means letting some of the country's creditors off the hook? Or should priority be placed on the imposition of payment standstills that lock creditors in, even if it may hurt the crisis country? Is large-scale IMF lending acceptable only if it is balanced by a commensurate commitment by private creditors to restructure their claims to help the crisis country? If the IMF is going to lend less, should the IMF—or the G-7 countries—do more to help the country get a debt restructuring agreement with its creditors? Could protection from litigation substitute for official lending or, at least, make it easier for the IMF and the G-7 to refuse the country asking for a large bailout?

The official sector remains uncomfortable both with providing large financial bailouts to emerging economies and with the consequences of not providing large bailouts. The result is a policy framework that is in disar-

7. Private-sector involvement (PSI) in crisis resolution became the accepted jargon to describe the official sector's efforts to obtain crisis "financing"—deferring scheduled payments counts as emergency financing—from the private creditors of a crisis country. Other terms were also tried. Initially, some spoke of the need for "burden sharing." However, this term was considered too heavy-handed: No private creditor happily takes on a burden. At the other extreme, there was talk of the need for "constructive engagement" with private creditors. For the sake of directness and simplicity, we have opted to use "bail-ins" and "debt restructurings" rather than "PSI."

ray, with growing gaps between the rhetoric describing the official sector's goals and its actual actions. The G-7 countries agree in principle that IMF financing should be less forthcoming if a country's debts are unsustainable, yet they continue to support large bailouts for countries whose debt levels put their sustainability—and their ability to quickly repay the IMF—at risk. Bailouts that were reserved for countries with relatively modest overall debt levels have become the policy tool of choice to bring countries with substantially higher debt levels back from the brink.[8] There is much talk of the need to make IMF loans that exceed the IMF's normal access limits the exception, not the rule, but there is little desire to scale back the size of IMF loans during actual crises.

Confused signals are being sent on other issues as well. For example, there is no agreement on the role the IMF and the G-7 should play when a country needs to restructure its debts to avoid sinking deeper into crisis. The Bush administration believes that sovereign debt problems should be left to the markets to resolve, with minimal official interference. Yet the Bush administration encouraged the IMF to put money on the table—admittedly, too little way too late—to catalyze a private debt restructuring in Argentina and linked Uruguay's rescue loan to a restructuring of Uruguay's bonded debt. The major European members of the G-7 are no more consistent. They argue that financial contributions from private creditors should always accompany large rescues to avoid distorting private markets, but they often still support IMF programs that lack binding financial commitments from the country's private creditors.[9]

Purging Unhelpful Myths

The IMF and its major shareholders face difficult choices when an emerging economy may be close to default. But a number of myths have inhibited a clear, honest debate on the options. The biggest myth is that less talk about the theoretical virtues of large bailout packages has somehow made large bailout packages go away (see table 1.1 and figures 1.1 and 1.2). But

8. Argentina received $13 billion of its $22 billion IMF credit line (8 percent of precrisis GDP) before defaulting. Turkey has received $23 billion from the IMF, around 11 percent of its precrisis GDP. It also recently reached agreement to get an additional $8.5 billion low interest rate loan directly from the United States. Brazil has borrowed over $30 billion from the IMF, around 5 percent of its precrisis GDP. Uruguay's $2.7 billion IMF credit line was 13 percent of its precrisis GDP. Argentina, Turkey, Brazil, and Uruguay all have substantially more debt relative to GDP than countries like Mexico or Korea that received large IMF rescue loans of a comparable size in the past.

9. Brazil's recent program did not contain any requirement to seek commitments from private creditors, and—after the dismal success of efforts to coordinate the rollover of interbank lines in Turkey—recent programs for Turkey have also excluded a requirement that the country seek private cofinancing. Neither program includes a meaningful bail-in.

Table 1.1 IMF financing

	Amount agreed			Total disbursed			Disbursed in the first year		
	As percent of quota	In billions of dollars	As percent of GDP	As percent of quota	In billions of dollars	As percent of GDP	As percent of quota	In billions of dollars	As percent of GDP
Mexico (1995)	688	18.0	4.4	500	13.1	3.2	500	13.1	3.2
Thailand (1997)	505	3.9	2.2	470	3.7	2.0	366	2.8	1.6
Indonesia (1997)	557	11.3	5.0	555	11.3	5.0	245	5.0	2.2
Korea (1998)[a]	1,938	20.8	4.0	1,802	19.4	3.7	1,757	18.9	3.6
Brazil (1998)	600	18.4	2.3	436	13.4	1.7	363	11.1	1.4
Russia (1998)	186	15.1	3.5	63	5.1	1.2	63	5.1	1.2
Argentina (2000–01)	800	22.1	7.8	461	12.7	4.5	461	12.7	4.5
Brazil (2001)	400	15.6	3.1	375	14.6	2.9	261	10.2	2.0
Brazil (2002)	752	29.3	5.7	567	22.1	4.3	566	22.1	4.3
Brazil (combined)	900	35.1	6.9	770	30.1	5.9	340	13.3	2.3
Uruguay (1999–2001)	694	2.7	14.5	560	2.2	11.7	434	1.7	9.1
Turkey (1999–2001)	1,560	20.7	10.4	1,218	16.2	8.1	900	11.9	6.0
Turkey 2002	1,330	17.6	8.9	1,154	14.8	7.7	1,030	13.7	6.9
Turkey (combined)	2,548	33.8	17.0	1,709	23.1	11.4	900	11.9	6.0

a. Korea's quota was unusually small in relation to its GDP.

Note: Combined programs = Outstanding disbursement plus new commitment; however, some of the new commitment was intended to refinance the IMF's existing exposure. Special drawing rights (SDR) are converted into dollars at the SDR/dollar exchange rate at the time of the initial program.

Sources: Financial data from International Monetary Fund, www.imf.org/external/fin.htm. GDP data from Moody's Investor Service.

Figure 1.1 IMF loans outstanding, 1993–2003

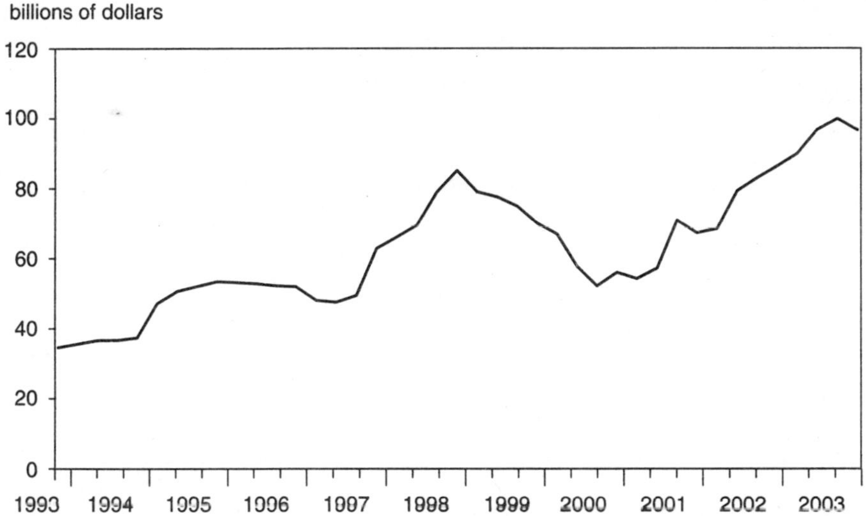

Note: Data are for April, August, and December of the years indicated. Data for 1993 are for December only.

Sources: International Monetary Fund data and authors' calculations.

perhaps more pernicious is the myth that a better way of restructuring sovereign bonds would significantly reduce demand for large bailout packages. Eight myths have far more influence than they should.

Myth 1

The era of large bailouts has ended. Some date the end to Lawrence Summers's departure from the US Treasury, others to Argentina's default. In reality, bailouts have not gone away. Turkey, Uruguay, and Brazil all have obtained very large rescue packages after Argentina's default. Moreover, Argentina went through a large "bailout"—nearly $15 billion—before it defaulted. Between mid-1996 and the end of 1998, the IMF increased its outstanding credit by $38 billion in response to the crises in Asia, Russia, and Brazil. Between September 2000 and September 2003, the IMF increased its outstanding credit by $48 billion in response to the crises in Turkey and a series of Latin American economies.[10]

10. As important, three years after the Asian crisis, the crisis countries made large net repayments to the IMF. In June 1997, the IMF had $48 billion in outstanding loans. That rose to a peak of $85 billion at the end of 1998 before falling back to $58 billion in June 2000. The IMF had $97 billion outstanding at the end of 2003 with no clear prospects of a major reduction in its exposure to its largest borrowers in the near term. All data are from the IMF and refer to its nonconcessional (general resources account) lending.

Figure 1.2 IMF lending, 1997–98 versus 2000–02

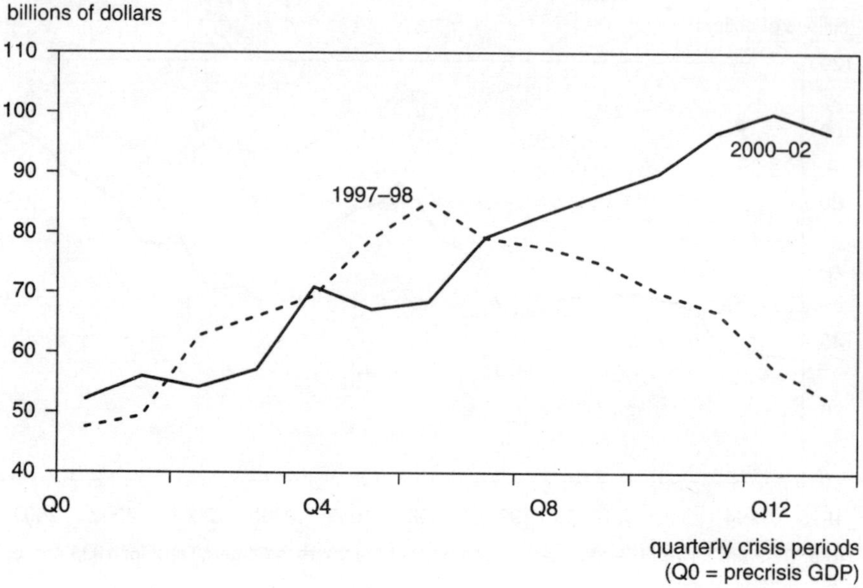

Source: International Monetary Fund data.

Myth 2

The IMF—and the official sector more generally—is small in relation to the international bond market. The IMF's total "usable" resources are around \$200 billion. A reasonable estimate of the amount of outstanding international sovereign bonds issued by emerging economies is \$370 billion.[11] Bonds are long-term obligations, so the IMF can usually put more money into a country than international bondholders can take out in the short run. The IMF, for example, provided more money to Turkey in two years than it had ever borrowed from the international bond market. Of course, maturing international bonds are not the only source of financial pressure on crisis countries. The pressures that can come from cross-border bank lending and the roll-off of domestic debts and bank deposits can overwhelm even large IMF packages.[12]

11. The IMF (September 2003a) estimated the stock of original sovereign bond issues outstanding at \$290 billion. The stock of outstanding Brady bonds and the bonds that emerged from Russia's 2000 restructuring are not included in this total.

12. International bonds are governed by the law of an external state or country (usually the law of New York state, England, Germany, or Japan, with New York state and England the two most important jurisdictions), and domestic bonds are governed by domestic law. Other definitions of external debt are discussed later in this chapter and in chapter 7.

Myth 3

The bond market has displaced banks as the key source of emerging-market financing. It is true that in the 1990s banks got out of the business of providing medium- to long-term external financing to sovereigns. But they did not get out of the game of providing short-term external financing to other banks or firms. Because bank lines are usually short-term, they can roll off faster than longer-term credits. Local banks often use short-term loans from international banks to finance the purchase of the high-yielding sovereign debt of an emerging economy, even though this combination is particularly risky. At the end of 2000, banks held $530 billion of a total of $875 billion in external claims on nine major emerging economies; bonds held abroad accounted for $345 billion. At the end of 2001, total exposure had fallen to $809 billion, bank claims to $477 billion, and the stock of outstanding bonds to $331 billion.[13] Cross-border bank claims remain an important source of financing.

Myth 4

A better means of restructuring international bonds would eliminate the need for bailouts.[14] As former US Treasury Assistant Secretary Edwin Truman has noted, the international bonds of sovereign governments were at the center of one of the past eight major emerging-market financial crises (Truman 2002). Mexico had difficulty refinancing the government's domestic dollar-linked debts (tesobonos), not the government's international bonds. Russia also had difficulties mostly with the government's domestic debts—the ruble-denominated GKOs. Short-term cross-border bank loans—from international banks to local banks and other financial institutions and, in some cases, to local firms as well—were the source of difficulty in Indonesia, Korea, and Thailand. In 1999, Brazil had problems with international cross-border bank lines and prospective problems with the government's domestic debts. Turkey had difficulties with the government's domestic debt and the roll-off of short-term interbank loans. Only in Argentina were international bonds a major source of financial distress, but even there, a domestic bank run put more pressure on reserves.

13. Data are from the World Bank's *Global Development Finance* (2003). Bond data include bonds issued both by the public and private sectors, and bank loan data include bank loans to both the public and private sectors. The nine countries are Mexico, Thailand, Indonesia, South Korea, Russia, Brazil, Turkey, Argentina and Uruguay. Since these numbers include bonds issued by private borrowers as well as emerging-market governments, they cannot be directly compared to the earlier data that only count sovereign bonds.

14. See, among others, Taylor (2004a).

Myth 5

The IMF responded to the crises of the 1990s and the first part of the 21st century with large bailouts that let private creditors entirely off the hook. In reality, getting through these crises required both large bailouts and, in some instances, large concessions from the country's private creditors. The second Korean program was built around the rollover of bank lines. The official sector refused to support the country in the absence of a bond restructuring in Ecuador, Ukraine, Pakistan, and Uruguay. Private creditors have also contributed when rescue programs failed. Russia, Argentina, and Indonesia defaulted well before the majority of private creditors could get out.

Myth 6

Concerted bank rollovers are a feature of the 1980s, not the 1990s. In reality, in Korea at the end of 1997 and with less success in Indonesia during the course of 1998, commercial bank creditors were "bailed in," and interbank credits were restructured. In Brazil, a program was put in place to monitor banks' commitment to roll over their interbank positions in 1999, though unlike in Korea, monitoring did not morph into a formal restructuring. Turkey also put in place a system to monitor the rollover of interbank credits in 2001, though the program hardly prevented international banks from dramatically reducing their lending to Turkey's banks.

Myth 7

International sovereign bonds cannot be restructured, either because bondholders are dispersed and difficult to contact or because many bonds lack collective action clauses.[15] In reality, bonds and other widely traded debt instruments can and have been restructured by Pakistan, Ukraine, Russia, Ecuador, and Uruguay. Ecuador, Ukraine, and Uruguay all restructured some bonds that lacked collective action clauses.

Myth 8

Restructurings were easy and orderly in the bank-dominated 1980s. In reality, in the 1980s, hundreds of different banks initially had exposure to indebted countries, and many banks wanted to reduce, not increase, their exposure. Getting agreement among them to both roll over maturing

15. Collective action clauses allow a supermajority of bondholders to amend the bond's financial terms. Some bond contracts also include provisions that make it difficult for an individual creditor to initiate litigation and keep all the proceeds of the litigation for itself.

principal and provide "new money" to help the country make interest payments on its existing debt was difficult from the beginning and became more difficult with time. Banks were also reluctant to recognize the need for some debt forgiveness: It took a very long time for serial restructurings to give way to the Brady plan, which restructured bank loans into long-term bonds.[16]

Summing Up

Many of these myths are both pervasive and pernicious. The IMF is widely perceived as being in the business of bailing out bondholders, despite the reality that relatively little of the IMF's lending has gone directly into the hands of international bondholders.[17] This should not be a surprise: Holders of long-term bonds who sell their claims in a crisis put pressure on the bonds' market price, not on the country's reserves. Holders of short-term debt, in contrast, have a contractual right to exchange their claims for the country's scarce cash the day their debt comes due.

The "bailing out bonds" debate paints a misleading picture of the largest beneficiaries of IMF lending and postulates a solution—making bonds easier to restructure—that would only marginally impact on the demand for IMF loans. Debates these myths have framed result in a set of false and oversimplified choices that have hindered a real debate about the IMF's role in resolving emerging-market financial crises.

Closing the Gap Between Rhetoric and Reality

A better starting point would be to both clearly examine the full range of financial vulnerabilities that give rise to demands for rescue loans—demands that come only in part from the sovereign's international bonds—and honestly examine the options the country, the IMF, and the IMF's major shareholders face when a country needs a large loan to avoid defaulting on its debt.

This, alas, requires defining a number of often poorly understood terms. "Bailout" sounds pejorative. But there is a meaningful difference between the type of "bailouts" the IMF has provided to crisis countries

16. For details of the IMF's role in these debt restructurings and in the development of the Brady plan, see Boughton (2001) and Cline (1995).

17. A strict definition of "international bondholders" would exclude international investors in domestic instruments like Mexico's dollar-denominated tesobonos or Russia's ruble-denominated GKOs. However, even with a looser definition of "bonds" that includes all traded securities bought by international investors, bonds have not been as large a source of pressure as international banks and domestic residents seeking to move their savings abroad. See chapter 4.

and the type the US government, for example, provided to the savings and loan industry. An IMF loan no doubt lets some of the crisis country's creditors off the hook, just as a loan from a domestic lender of last resort lets a troubled bank pay off its depositors. However, most domestic bank "bailouts" do more than just provide the bank with emergency liquidity from a lender of last resort. They also typically require giving a troubled bank a government bond—a new financial asset—to make up for its bad loan portfolio. This bond is a true financial loss to taxpayers, but it also avoids the need for depositors (and sometimes even the shareholders) in the bad bank to take losses. To be sure, international taxpayers put up the money needed to make an IMF loan. But they also expect to get repaid in full. The IMF lends at rates that are often lower than the market rate, but this does not imply the IMF lends at a subsidized rate. It can lend at lower rates because crisis countries, by long-standing convention, pay the IMF even if they are not paying their other creditors. We use the term "bailouts" as shorthand because terms like "official crisis lending" sound bland and bureaucratic, not because we want to imply that IMF loans are costing taxpayers' money.[18]

The use of IMF loans can also cause confusion. Does the IMF "bail out" a country or the government of that country? The correct answer is both. The IMF helps a crisis country by lending to its government. An IMF loan often does rescue a country in trouble because its government is having difficulty repaying its own debt. The additional reserves from an IMF loan are used to avoid a default on the government's foreign-currency debt. However, an IMF rescue loan has other potential uses. IMF lending to a crisis country's central bank can finance emergency lending to support a country's banking system, which otherwise would have had trouble paying domestic depositors or international bank credits. The foreign exchange the IMF supplies also can be sold to prop up the value of the crisis country's currency, which helps all those who had faith in the financial assets denominated in that currency, as well as those who need to buy foreign currency to pay off their external debts. Foreign-currency reserves borrowed from the IMF can be used in as many different ways as the government's own reserves.

One additional term warrants discussion, if not a precise definition: a country's debt. Let's consider an actual country like Argentina to make the discussion more concrete. The classic meaning of "the debt of Argentina" is the external debt of Argentina's banks, firms, and government. External means debt sold to foreigners—nonresidents, in neutral economic language. A country can get into trouble on the back of the external borrowing of private firms even if its government has borrowed little

18. See chapter 3 for detailed discussion. Klingen, Weder, and Zettelmeyer (2004) found that the ex post return on IMF lending was similar to the ex post return on private lending.

from abroad, as the world learned in Thailand, Indonesia, and Korea. Another common meaning of "the debt of Argentina" is the externally issued debt of the government of Argentina. Most emerging-market economies can sell debt abroad only if a trusted foreign law—usually the law of New York state or England—governs the debt contract. Economically, what matters is that the debt is owed to foreigners. In a debt restructuring, however, the governing law of the debt instrument becomes crucial.

A final meaning of the term "the debt of Argentina" is the domestic and external debt of the government of Argentina. A statement like "Argentina has too much debt" can, depending on the context, mean that Argentines—private banks and firms as well as the government—have borrowed too much from abroad, that the government of Argentina has borrowed too much from abroad, or that the government of Argentina has borrowed too much both at home and from abroad.

We focus on the financial difficulties experienced by countries that are able to borrow from private banks and private capital markets at home and from abroad when times are good but that cannot always access capital markets when financial trouble emerges. They are not the advanced economies—such as the G-7—whose government debt is considered to be a nearly risk-free asset and who can count on market access at a reasonable price in bad as well as good times. Nor are they the poorest of the poor: Such countries can almost never access private international capital markets and depend exclusively on concessional lending from other governments and institutions like the World Bank. These countries often do end up with too much debt, but the resolution of their debt problems does not typically require the restructuring of debts owed to private creditors. It simply requires a decision by taxpayers of wealthy countries to forgive their claims on the poorest countries.[19] Emerging economies are stuck in the middle. They do not necessarily have more debt than advanced economies, but they do lack the policy credibility advanced economies have built over time. They tend to finance themselves in ways that create financial vulnerabilities—whether by relying on short-term debt, foreign currency–denominated debt, external debt, or all three.[20]

19. See "Debt Relief under the Heavily Indebted Poor Countries (HIPC) Initiative: A Factsheet" (IMF April 2004) at www.imf.org/external/np/exr/facts/hipc.htm for a summary of the process of forgiving the debts the poorest countries owe to other governments. Critics of this process, like Jeffrey Sachs, argue that the HIPC process is too slow and does not provide enough debt relief. Sachs has called for full debt forgiveness and a major increase in concessional, multilateral development aid to jumpstart growth in the poorest countries (Jeffrey Sachs, "Doing the Sums on Africa," *The Economist*, May 20, 2004).

20. Eichengreen, Hausmann, and Panizza (2003) argue that emerging markets cannot borrow abroad in their own currency because they suffer from "original sin." Goldstein and Turner (2004), in contrast, emphasize that sound policies sustained over time can allow a country to build a market for its own local-currency debt.

Different Countries, Different Crises, Different Solutions

A surge in demand for foreign currency, at a time when private markets are unwilling to provide the crisis country with access to foreign currency it needs, marks all crises. Indeed, private creditors are usually looking to get back the money they have already lent to the country in a crisis, not supply more funds to it. Nonetheless, countries are exposed to a wide range of potential sources of financial difficulties.

Countries can sustain current account and budget deficits only so long as they have the capacity to issue new debt. Trouble often starts when they lose market access and draw on their reserves rather than taking steps to reduce the size of their current account or fiscal deficits. Countries need to raise money not only to finance current account and budget deficits but also to refinance their existing debt as it matures. Financial trouble quickly develops if a country's government cannot raise the needed money in private markets to pay its own maturing debt or if private firms and banks that borrowed from abroad have trouble refinancing their existing debts.[21]

Countries that lack reserves to cover their maturing foreign-currency debts are vulnerable to a run. Concerns that other creditors will want to get out and therefore won't roll over their short-term debts as they come due can lead all creditors to demand payment as soon as possible. Such runs usually don't happen entirely by accident. Creditors are understandably reluctant to lend to countries with poor macroeconomic policies or weak financial systems with long maturities. Moreover, growing doubts about a country's policies—or the disclosure that it has fewer liquid reserves than creditors thought—often trigger the run. As the run intensifies, a country can be pushed toward default well before it has time to show whether it can make the policy changes to ensure its long-run solvency.

A country that is not running a current account deficit and has little maturing external debt—and thus little need to borrow from abroad—can still get in trouble if its citizens want to shift their savings abroad. Depositors in the banking system can decide to pull their funds out of the local banks (a local asset) and deposit them abroad. The depositors need foreign currency to purchase foreign assets. Consequently, the shift from domestic to foreign assets places enormous pressure on the country's reserves under a fixed exchange rate, on its exchange rate under a float, or if the country has a managed float, on both reserves and the exchange rate. Sergei Dubinin, the chairman of Russia's central bank in the 1998 crisis observed, "We can play games against the market, against the banks

21. The government's own debt was central to the crises in Mexico, Russia, Brazil, Ecuador, Pakistan, Romania, Ukraine, Turkey, Argentina, and Uruguay; private-sector debt was the obvious source of weakness in Thailand, Indonesia, and Korea as well as in other cases.

even, but we can't do anything if the entire population wants to change rubles into dollars" (Blustein 2001, 266–67).

Just as the precise source of the surge in demand for foreign currency that marks a crisis will vary, so too will the country's underlying ability to emerge from the crisis. Some countries have more debt relative to their GDP (or relative to other measures of their ability to pay, such as exports or government revenues) than others. Countries with the same overall amount of debt can differ in other ways. Those with lots of short-term debt risk losing reserves because short-term debt can roll off quickly. Those with lots of foreign-currency debt risk seeing the burden of their debt in local currency increase sharply after a large devaluation. Those that depend on oil for most of their revenues often are vulnerable to adverse oil-price shocks. The ability of countries with the same level of debt to deliver on promises to change their economic and financial policies also will differ. All these variables will influence the country's ultimate ability and willingness to pay and its chances to avoid a catastrophic crisis.[22]

No matter what the precise cause of a crisis is, getting out of it almost always requires a combination of policy adjustment and emergency financing, whether from an official loan or a restructuring of private debts. Policy adjustment—less spending, higher taxes, or both to close a fiscal deficit and more exports, fewer imports, or both to close an external deficit—serves two purposes. First, it directly reduces the overall amount of new financing that the country needs to raise, whether from official or private creditors. Second, steps to make the country a better long-term credit can help raise private financing, or at least help convince existing creditors to roll over their claims—though the improvement in long-term solvency has to be balanced against the fact that adjustments may be contractionary in the short run.[23] Runs on countries with no policy weaknesses are rare: Those that get into trouble usually need to take steps to correct their underlying macroeconomic policy weaknesses.

Yet policy changes, while necessary, are unlikely on their own to close a country's financing gap—the difference between what a country needs to raise to pay its maturing debts and to cover any ongoing deficits and what it is projected to be able to raise from private investors and creditors. Closing the financing gap usually requires combining economic policy

22. A more precise definition of solvency is provided in chapter 2.

23. The precise set of policy conditions that should be associated with an IMF program has been the subject of intense debate. Sachs and Radelet (1998) in particular criticized the IMF for putting too much emphasis on structural conditionality in Asia. Stiglitz (2002) has criticized the IMF's call for fiscal and monetary tightening in Asia and elsewhere. We do not directly tackle the debate on the details of IMF conditionality or assess how individual countries have performed on each and every element of their IMF program. However, we clearly believe that countries with overvalued exchange rates need to let their exchange rates adjust, and countries with large government debt stocks and large fiscal deficits going into a crisis will need to adjust their fiscal policies as well.

changes with some form of bailout or bail-in. However, not all bailouts or bail-ins are alike. It is also important to distinguish among different types of bailouts and bail-ins.

- A full bailout provides the country with enough money to cover all debts that are coming due. This is how a domestic lender of last resort usually handles a bank run: It promises to lend the bank as much money as it needs to honor its existing deposits in full and on time.
- A partial bailout provides the country with a substantial sum of money but not enough to cover all its maturing debts. The hope is that the policy changes that accompany the lending and the financial vote of confidence from official lenders will lead most external creditors to agree to refinance the debt they hold and most domestic investors to keep their funds in the country. One might call this strategy "lend and pray." The IMF and the official sector call it the "catalytic" approach. If all goes well, policy adjustment and official lending will catalyze the private financial flows the country needs.
- A partial bail-in limits the scale of possible outflows by convincing some creditors to agree not to ask for immediate payment on their maturing debts, thus reducing the overall amount the country needs to raise to service its debts. A country can always bail in some creditors by not paying them as the claims come due (a formal standstill or default). However, this works only if creditors and domestic investors that are not locked in opt not to flee. Creditors and investors who have not been forced to defer payments need to be convinced that the partial bail-in, combined with policy changes and official financing, will solve the country's problems so that it will be a worthwhile place to continue to invest in. One might call this strategy "restructure and pray."
- A full bail-in comes only from a comprehensive standstill on all external debt payments—and often capital and exchange controls that limit the ability of those with domestic assets and domestic currency to trade them for foreign assets and foreign currency. This eliminates the need to raise external financing but also severely disrupts economic activity.

Much of the academic debate has focused on the relative merits of a full bailout from a lender of last resort and a full bail-in from a comprehensive debt standstill. But actual policy decisions often amount to choosing among a small partial bailout, a large partial bailout, a small partial bail-in, and a large partial bail-in. Full bailouts and full bail-ins are both very unusual.

The IMF rarely provides enough funds fast enough to cover all maturing payments for more than a short period. For example, Mexico received enough money to cover payments on the government's maturing tesobonos and to help Mexican banks repay their external debt for several months but not enough to cover all potential sources of capital flight. A rescue loan typically covers only the most obvious sources of payment difficulties. It works only if additional sources of financial pressure do not materialize.

Countries are also extremely relucant to impose a comprehensive standstill that locks in everyone who has invested in or lent to the country at the early stages of a crisis. A total standstill—full suspension of sovereign payments, comprehensive capital controls on private payments, suspension of currency convertibility, and a bank holiday—is only imposed at the very end of the day, when total loss of confidence has eliminated all other options. Targeted restructurings are more common.

Academic models often try to clarify the core choice between a bailout and a bail-in. In practice, however, it is often possible to combine a partial bailout with a partial bail-in. For any set of debts, there is a binary choice between a bailout and a bail-in. But sources of existing or potential financial pressure on a crisis country are usually diverse. Consequently, it is possible to bail out some creditors and bail in others.

Agenda for Reform

Our willingness to defend a world where partial bailouts and partial bail-ins are linked to policy changes in the crisis country—and our doubts about grand institutional reforms—does not mean that we have a Panglossian view that we live in the best of all possible worlds. Three critiques of the current framework for crisis resolution stand out:

- The G-7 needs to stop pretending that a return to low levels of access is just around the corner. The gap between the rhetoric of limits and the actual practice of continued large loans impedes policymaking.
- There has been too little differentiation in the official sector's response to different crises.
- The IMF should be more willing to use its lending capacity to soften the blow during a debt restructuring. Lending to a country that is going through a debt restructuring is one way to limit the risk of the decision to seek restructuring of some debts triggering a broader run. It also gives the official sector more leverage over the policies of the restructuring country.

First, the stated goal of limiting IMF lending over time has failed to provide a useful framework for deciding how to respond to actual crises. A new framework for IMF lending is needed, one that focuses less on limits and more on defining the circumstances when IMF lending can play a constructive role in crisis resolution. The IMF needs a game plan that helps it do a better job of using its limited capacity to provide "liquidity insurance" to emerging economies, not a game plan for getting out of the business of providing liquidity insurance altogether.

Insisting that limits are around the corner has become a way to avoid carefully considering whether current lending decisions are setting precedents that should be emulated if other countries encountered similar problems. The new roles the IMF has assumed recently, including the use of the IMF to backstop domestic banks and the de facto use of the IMF to provide medium- and long-term financing to help Turkey cover large budget deficits, can not be dismissed as temporary aberrations. Attempts to ground IMF lending decisions, not on a desire to return to old lending norms but rather on an assessment of the country's debt sustainability, have not been significantly more successful. The recent trend has been for IMF lending programs to increase in size as countries' debt levels—and resulting financing needs in the absence of a debt restructuring—increase in size, despite the IMF's very real effort to improve the analytics behind its assessment of debt sustainability.[24] The IMF is paying more attention to debt sustainability than before: It is lending larger sums to countries that are substantially more indebted than before.

Second, a policy that in practice, though not in theory, provides every country with a large loan to try to avoid any debt restructuring is not the best way of using the substantial financing that the official sector provides to crisis countries. The IMF's initial response to crises in major emerging economies has generally been the same—a large IMF loan to try to avoid any restructuring—even though not all countries that get into trouble have the same chance of getting out of trouble. As one former policymaker noted, the standard response to a crisis is to provide liquidity and hope that the country truly just has a problem of "illiquidity." The IMF's organization as a credit cooperative, political pressure from the G-7, the impossibility of determining with certainty if any given level of debt is unsustainable with enough adjustment, and the consequences of demanding a restructuring result in pressure to give almost all countries the benefit of the doubt.

24. Debt sustainability involves more than just the size of a country's debt in relation to its economy—the average coupon on the debt, the amount of debt coming due in the near term, amount denominated in foreign currency, and the country's ability to deliver the adjustments it needs also matter. However, many of these variables tend to be correlated with the overall debt level. Countries with large debts tend to be able to borrow only at high rates and for a short period. Countries with large debts also tend to need to promise investors protection from exchange rate movements in order to attract funds. The difficulty in sustaining the political support for the effort required to pay also tends to increase as the amount of effort that is required increases.

Similar crises should be treated similarly, but not all crises should be treated the same way. Countries that get into trouble despite modest deficits and accumulated debts are better financial bets than those that get into trouble with larger debts and little proven ability to reduce their deficits. A policy that does not differentiate on the basis of an upfront judgment about a country's prospects is risky: Countries with more debt tend to need more money to have a reasonable chance of avoiding restructuring, yet even large sums may not be enough. If the rescue fails, the country literally has nothing left in reserve—it is in a deeper financial hole, with no further capacity to borrow from the IMF and fewer options to limit the trauma of the inevitable restructuring. Differentiation need not be based entirely on the size of IMF lending to crisis countries: The IMF also needs to insist that its financing be used to avoid a broader economic and financial collapse while the country seeks agreement with its creditors to restructure some of its debts.

Third, the IMF needs to be both tougher and more generous when a country's debt levels and policy track record suggest that there is a high risk that the traditional catalytic IMF lending won't work. Tough because the IMF should be willing to make an upfront judgment that a country won't be able to avoid a restructuring and thus be willing to refuse the country's request for help unless the country is willing to develop a credible plan to restructure its debts (and to change its exchange rate regime, if needed). More generous because the IMF should also be more willing to provide meaningful financial support to a country undergoing a restructuring. This is particularly true if the country, encouraged by the IMF, decides to restructure early on, before digging itself into a deeper hole. Restructuring a country's external debt carries the risk that the decision to seek a restructuring will prompt the crisis country's population to pull their savings out of the country's banks at the same time and trade their rubles, pesos, or baht for dollars en masse. A key argument of this book, in a nutshell, is that the signal of international support and money from an IMF loan can do far more to limit these risks than outright legal protection.

These three suggestions are not radical, but they are controversial. Lending new money to a country that has to seek a restructuring because, in part, it already has too much debt is counterintuitive. It still offers the best way to help cushion the blow to the domestic economy likely to result from decisive action by an emerging-market government to address its debt problem. A run on the currency that leads the country's exchange rate to overshoot or a run on the domestic banking system that leads the financial system to collapse can make the debt problem worse. Creditors need to make concessions, and the country needs to adjust its policies, but a cooperative win-win outcome is still possible if the country avoids a bigger fall in output, and its creditors avoid bigger losses. Of course, any steps to soften the blow of a restructuring could, at the margin, reduce a country's incentives for prudent policies. We think that this risk is manageable, though, and it is better to step in and help than run the risk that a crisis will end in an Argentine-style implosion and stalemate.

Structure of the Book

The details of a crisis matter, which is one reason this book is long. The mix of economic policy adjustments by the debtor country, official lending (bailouts), and commitments from private creditors (bail-ins) that is most likely to work depends on the nature of the crisis. Abstract discussions of either debt restructuring or IMF lending tend to oversimplify. But not every reader will want to read each and every chapter. Some will be more interested in the chapters that focus on the mechanics of debt restructuring; others will be more interested in the theory and practice of large-scale IMF lending. Each individual chapter can be read as a standalone essay on a particular topic, though the whole is also, we hope, more than just the sum of its parts. Our goal is to draw on both the growing body of experience with "21st century financial crises" and the analytical literature on crisis resolution to explore in some depth the choices the official sector faces in a crisis.

Chapter 2 examines the reasons many emerging-market economies have experienced financial crises in the last decade. A key theme in chapter 2 is that financial vulnerability stems from the interaction between ongoing budget and current account deficits, the way these ongoing deficits are financed, and the way the country has financed itself in the past. Chapter 3 focuses on academic models of the choices the IMF and other official creditors face once a crisis strikes. These analytical lenses inform the chapter's discussion of the arguments for and against payments standstills, the market failures that would arise in the absence of an international lender of last resort, the risk that an international lender of last resort could trigger moral hazard, and the case for—and against—partial bailouts.

Chapter 4 looks at the lessons that can be drawn from the actual experience in the last decade with bailouts and bail-ins. Rather than offering a chronological account of what happened in each case, the chapter is organized around the official sector's experience with different policy tools. Chapter 5 reviews the evolution of "official" G-7 and IMF policy. It highlights the reasons for shifts in policy as well as the private sector's reaction to official policy initiatives. Above all, it accesses whether the official sector has been able to send signals that were consistent with the policy decisions it took in subsequent crises.

Chapters 2 through 5 in some sense summarize and analyze the current state of play. Chapters 6 through 8 examine the difficult and still controversial open issues in the debate on crisis resolution—issues marked by the continued absence of consensus either within the official sector or among the official sector, crisis-prone countries, and market participants.

Chapter 6 examines in detail the options for providing emergency financing to countries facing shortages of foreign exchange as well as the challenges that arise when the country's private sector, not the government, is the initial source of the country's financial difficulties. Chapter 7 asks if sovereign debt restructurings could be made less disorderly and costly if claims against a sovereign could be ranked according to a more precise system of priorities, as well as the practical obstacles to establishing an enforceable priority structure.

Chapter 8 focuses on the case for creating a stronger legal basis for overcoming collective action problems in a sovereign debt restructuring. The key policy question is whether legal reform can reduce the economic disruption that can accompany a sovereign debt restructuring without upsetting the balance between the rights of creditors and of the debtor needed for the sovereign debt market to work.

Chapter 9 concludes with our critique of the current policy framework and our recommendations for reform. The debate on crisis resolution has two components. First, are the institutions needed to respond to a wide range of crises in place? Second, does the current policy framework match the available tools of crisis resolution to a country's specific problems? We argue that the institutions for crisis resolution, what we call the system's hardware, are in better shape than the current policy framework—the system's software.

Throughout the book, we make the case for a policy that recognizes that (1) there are enormous differences among different crises, and (2) different cases need to be addressed within an overall framework that provides some consistency and predictability to borrowing countries as well as to those who invest in emerging-market debt. One way to respond consistently to a range of crises is to provide all countries that get into trouble with a certain sum of money, appropriately scaled to reflect differences in economic size, to be used as the country sees fit. In our view, though, a policy that tries to treat all countries with similar problems in the same way is likely to be more effective. Making such a policy predictable, though, requires agreement on how to identify and respond to a range of crises.

2

New Nature of Emerging-Market Crises

Back in 1997, then US Treasury Deputy Secretary Lawrence Summers liked to compare modern finance to a jet plane. The technology of modern finance, like a jet plane, lets you get to your destination faster than older transportation technology. But the rare crashes that occur along the way are also more spectacular. To Summers, the occasional crash was not sufficient cause to abandon the technology of modern finance.

This analogy now seems to suffer from one problem. Emerging-market economies crash more frequently than 747s. The jet planes flown by major airlines are a mature technology, safer than the piston-powered planes they replaced. After "financial" crises in Mexico, Thailand, Korea, Indonesia, Malaysia, Russia, Brazil, Turkey, and Argentina—as well as crises in smaller economies like Ecuador, Ukraine, Uruguay, and the Dominican Republic—it seems clear that emerging economies are still at the early stages of understanding how they can best benefit from global financial markets.[1]

The collapse of an exchange rate peg, whether a soft peg or a currency board, has marked almost all recent crises.[2] A currency crisis, though, is

1. See the recent IMF study by Rogoff et al. (2003) for an examination of whether or not capital account liberalization has brought benefits to emerging-market economies. The debate on capital account liberalization is highly contested: Stiglitz (2002) and Rodrik and Kaplan (2001) offer a skeptical perspective of the benefits of capital account liberalization.

2. Mexico, Thailand, Korea, Indonesia, Malaysia, Russia, Brazil, and Uruguay all had had soft pegs or pegged but adjustable exchange rates before the crisis. Turkey had a regime with a programmed rate of depreciation well below the current inflation rate (formally a forward looking crawling peg) reinforced by a "quasi currency board." Argentina had a currency board. Most countries moved toward a more flexible exchange rate during their crisis.

not quite the same as a payments crisis, which requires an IMF rescue loan or a debt restructuring. Industrial countries—like the United Kingdom in 1992—have been able to let their currencies float, reduce domestic interest rates, and move on without experiencing further financial distress. Emerging economies generally are not so lucky: Currency crises usually are associated with severe banking, corporate, or sovereign payments crises.

Several reasons exist for the strong correlation between the collapse of an exchange rate peg—or for that matter sharp falls in the value of a floating currency—and payments problems. The need to let the currency float from a previous peg usually indicates a broader loss of confidence in the crisis country's economic policies and a sharp fall in international capital flows into the crisis country. This fall in capital flows, in turn, often creates financial difficulties for banks, firms, and sovereign governments, which count on continuous access to market financing both to cover ongoing current account and budget deficits and to refinance existing debts. Moreover, exchange rate stability often leads to excessive foreign-currency borrowing. In turn, the increase in the burden of these foreign-currency debts after the exchange rate collapses makes it harder for banks, firms, and the government alike to service their long-term debts, let alone convince creditors to refinance maturing short-term debt.

When crises struck Thailand, Korea, and Indonesia, private banks, financial institutions, and corporations experienced the most acute payment difficulties. The external borrowing of private banks and firms, not the government, had financed current account deficits in Asia before the crisis.[3] In Mexico, Russia, Brazil, Ecuador, Argentina, and Turkey, the sovereign was at the center of the country's financial difficulties. These countries either averted a sovereign payments crisis with IMF lending or had to seek a sovereign debt restructuring. Uruguay combined a banking system vulnerable to a cross-border and domestic run with a heavily indebted sovereign.

However, clean lines between corporate, banking, and sovereign payments crises are hard to draw. The systemic collapse of the corporate sec-

Malaysia and Ecuador are the exceptions. Malaysia repegged its exchange rate at a lower level after floating for a year and bolstered its new peg with capital controls. Ecuador's currency fell into a free fall early in its crisis, well before its government defaulted in 1999. After the government default, it formally adopted the US dollar as its currency to restore its monetary stability. Also, most floats are heavily managed, both in Asia and other emerging economies, which may be in part due to what Calvo and Reinhart (2002) refer to as the "fear of floating."

3. Malaysia also experienced a currency crisis but of a slightly different kind. It ran a large current account deficit before 1997 and financed it largely with foreign direct investment (FDI) and portfolio equity, not debt. While it shared many of the characteristics of other Asian economies, Malaysia had a much lower level of short-term external debt. Therefore it was able to avoid both a debt restructuring and an IMF program but not a sharp currency depreciation and a major fall in output.

tor typically bankrupted the banking sector, and the cost of saving the banking system increased the government's own debt. In some crises, domestic banks borrowed from abroad to purchase the government's domestic debt, blurring the lines both between a domestic and an external crisis and between a sovereign and a banking crisis. Most sovereign debt crises contaminate the banking system in some way (often because banks hold large amounts of government debt) and trigger large falls in the currency's value that create payments problems for many firms. Argentina is a case in point. Table 2.1 provides an overview of the most salient characteristics of recent crises in a cross-country format that helps identify commonalities and isolate differences.

These crises not only force the IMF and the G-7 to decide how to respond to a request for help but also have serious economic consequences. Output fell sharply in almost every crisis country, and, by advanced-economy standards, these output contractions were extraordinarily steep: Falls of 5 percent of GDP were common, and falls of 10 percent of GDP or more marked the worse crises.[4] Brazil in 1999 is a partial exception: With the IMF's help, it was able to avoid both a sovereign and a banking crisis when it let its currency float and only experienced a mild fall in output. Russia is the true exception: Its economy was contracting before its financial crisis in 1998 and started to rebound after the crisis.

This chapter explores the reasons why many emerging markets have experienced severe financial crises. The first section explores the sources of vulnerability common to most recent crises. The second section reviews the specific vulnerabilities that, in our view, contributed to major recent crises. However, no relatively brief overview can cover individual countries in enough depth to explore all the policy weaknesses that contributed in one way or another to the country's vulnerabilities.[5] Our goal is to provide readers with the basic background on each country's crisis and, in some cases, to highlight specific financial weaknesses of broader interest. Chapter 4 picks up the case studies of the individual countries as it evaluates the success of efforts to contain and resolve their crises.

4. The output contraction in the crisis year was severe in all countries but Russia, Ukraine, and Brazil. In the year following the crisis, output fell 8 percent in Mexico, 6.7 percent in Korea, 13.1 percent in Indonesia, 10.2 percent in Thailand, 7.4 percent in Malaysia, 6.3 percent in Ecuador, 7.4 percent in Turkey, 10.9 percent in Argentina, and 10.8 percent in Uruguay. In Argentina, the cumulative fall in output, relative to the precrisis peak, was over 20 percent, as the output fall started before the crisis and persisted longer.

5. These vulnerabilities have been studied in a very large body of literature; for comprehensive analyses and surveys of the causes of last decade's financial crises, see the volumes edited by Feldstein (2002), Dooley and Frankel (2003), and Edwards and Frankel (2002). See also Roubini and Uzan (2004) for a collection of readings on the crises of the last decade and crisis resolution.

Table 2.1a Crisis countries' aggregate balance sheet vulnerabilities

Indicator	Mexico 1994	Korea 1996	Thailand 1996	Indonesia 1996	Malaysia 1996	Russia 1997
Stock imbalances						
Liquidity/rollover risk						
Short-term foreign debt (percent of reserves)	203	289	136	158	49	255
M2/reserves	High	6.2	4.0	6,6	3.5	6.2
Country solvency risk						
External debt (percent of GDP)	33	31	60	43	38	35
External debt (percent of exports)	196	104	150	164	42	140
Sovereign solvency risk						
Public debt (percent of GDP)	35	12	5	24	35	53
Public debt (percent of revenues)	155	58	27	186	154	148
Currency mismatch risk						
Net foreign currency external debt (percent of GDP)	Medium	Medium	Medium	Medium	Medium	Medium
Foreign-currency government debt (percent of total government debt)	53	n.a.	12	100	14	60
Dollarization vulnerability indicator (liability dollarization in banks)	n.a.	n.a.	1.1	89	n.a.	56
Capital structure mismatch						
Equity/FDI (percent of foreign liabilities)	Medium	Low	Medium	Medium	High	Low
FDI (percent of GDP)	2	–0.3	2.6	2.1	7.2	0.4
Flow imbalances						
Current account deficit (percent of GDP)	–7.1	–4.4	–8.1	–3.4	–4.4	0.5
Fiscal deficit	–0.2	n.a.	1.7	1.6	2.4	–7.6
Primary balance	2.1	0.6	2.6	2.9	4.7	–2.8
General government interest payments (percent of general government revenue)	n.a.	n.a.	1.8	11	10	13
Other relevant issues						
Exchange rate regime	Soft peg	Soft peg	Soft peg	Soft peg	Soft peg	Peg
Currency overvaluation	High	Modest	High	Modest	Modest	High
Banking sector fragility						
Government debt as percent of banks' assets	n.a.	<10	<10	<10	<10	31
Liquidity ratio relative to BIS banks	140	232	507	251	64	76
Overall banking system fragility	High	High	High	High	Medium	High
Political/electoral instability	High	Medium	Medium	High	Medium	High
Domestic financial repression	Low	Low	Low	Modest	Modest	Low
Capital account controls (before the crisis)	Open capital account	Open capital account	Open capital account	Open capital account	Open capital account	Open capital account

Brazil 1998	Ecuador 1998	Pakistan 1998	Ukraine 1998	Turkey 2000	Argentina 2000	Uruguay 2001	Brazil 2002
126	181	189	327	246	149	320	142
5.7	2	14.7	7.8	3.9	3.7	3.3	3.1
31	68	68	29	60	51	81	41
369	267	347	66	203	376	365	300
48	67	103	41	53	45	38	73
143	486	646	113	203	226	191	211
Medium	High	Medium	Medium	Medium	High	High	Medium
n.a.	n.a.	52	68	50	91	83	25
0	High	168	64	96	123	132	0
High	Medium	Medium	Medium	Low	Low	Low	Medium
3.7	3.7	0.7	1.8	0.1	1.3	1.7	3.7
–4.3	–8.6	–3.6	–3.1	–4.9	–3.1	–2.6	–1.7
–6.3	–4.1	–6.2	–2.7	–10.4	–2.4	–4.4	–5.2
0	–1.3	0.5	–0.4	5.4	–1.0	–2.2	3.9
20	29	40	7	62	17	13	21
Peg	Managed and float	Heavily managed	Heavily managed	Quasi currency board	Currency board	Peg	Managed float
High	Modest	Modest	Modest	Modest	High	High	No
n.a.	High	30	14	n.a.	21	n.a.	n.a.
70	48	58	141	70	70	49	
Medium	High	Medium	Medium	High	High	High	Medium
Medium	High	High	Medium	High	High	Medium	High
Low	Low	Significant	Significant	Low	Low	Low	Low
Open capital account	Open capital account	Capital controls	Capital controls	Open capital account	Open capital account	Open capital account	Open capital account

Table 2.1b Policy adjustment, bail-ins, bailouts, and other policies to resolve crises

Indicator	Mexico 1994	Korea 1997	Thailand 1997	Indonesia 1997	Malaysia 1997	Russia 1998
Output fall	Large	Large	Large	Very large	Large	Small
Currency crisis	Yes	Yes	Yes	Yes	Yes	Yes
Banking crisis	Yes	Yes	Yes	Yes	No	Yes
Fiscal costs of banks' bailout (percent of GDP)						
Corporate financial crisis	Yes	Yes	Yes	Yes	Some	Yes
Fiscal/domestic policy adjustment during the crisis	Large	Large	Large	Large	Modest	Modest
Domestic bank run	No	No	No	Yes	No	Some
Cross-border bank run	No	Yes	Yes	Yes	Yes	No
Deposit freeze	No	No	No	Some	No	No
Default or coercive restructuring of sovereign debt	No	No	No	No	No	Yes, domestic and external debt
Default on private corporate external debt	No	Some	Some	A lot	No	No
Capital controls after crisis	No	No	No	No	Yes	Yes
IMF package (bailout)	Large	Large	Large	Large	No	Large but stopped
Bail-in or PSI	No PSI	Coercive on interbank loans	Coercive on some interbank loans	Coercive on some interbank loans	No PSI (apart from capital controls)	Default on GKO and London Club debt
Paris Club debt restructuring	No	No	No	Yes	No	Yes

BIS = Bank for International Settlements
FDI = foreign direct investment
M2 = money supply
n.a. = not available
PSI = private-sector involvement

Brazil 1998	Ecuador 1998	Pakistan 1998	Ukraine 1998	Turkey 2000	Argentina 2001	Uruguay 2001	Brazil 2002
Small	Very large	Modest	Modest	Large	Very large	Large	Small
Yes	Yes, from a float	No	No	Yes	Yes	Yes	No
No	Yes	No	No	Yes	Yes	Yes	No
No	Yes	No	No	Yes	Yes	No	No
Modest	Large	Modest	Modest	Large	Large	Large	Modest
No	Yes	No	No	No	Yes	Yes	No
Yes	Yes	No	No	Yes	Yes	Yes	No
No	Yes	Some	No	No	Yes	Some	No
No	Yes, domestic and external debt	Yes, external debt	Yes, external debt	No	Yes, domestic and external debt	Yes, domestic and external debt	No
No	Yes	No	No	No	Yes, a lot	No	No
No	No	Yes, pre exist	Yes, pre exist	No	Yes	No	No
Large	Small	Small	Small	Large	Large but stopped	Large	Large
Soft PSI; agreement to rollover interbank loans	Coercive default and debt reduction	Restructuring of external debt but no principal haircut	Restructuring of external debt but no principal haircut	Very soft PSI Interbank Rollover	Soft PSI at first, then full default on domestic external debt	Restructuring of external debt but no principal haircut	Very soft PSI; voluntary interbank rollover
No	Yes	Yes	Yes	No	No	No	No

Note. Data for Asian countries' current account and primary balance are for 1996, as the onset of the crisis affected the 1997 data.

Sources: Most data are from Moody's Statistical Handbook, Country Credit, October 2003. Data for Mexico are from IMF datasets, and primary deficit data are from IMF sources.

Sources of Vulnerability in Emerging-Market Crises

Some sources of vulnerability are common to most recent crises, even though every crisis also has its own specific causes. These common sources include the following:

- large macroeconomic imbalances, such as current account, fiscal deficits, or both, that led to the accumulation of large stocks of public and foreign liabilities;
- financing these deficits in ways—with short-term debt, foreign-currency debt, and with debt rather than equity—that made countries vulnerable to liquidity runs and increased the risk of a fall in the exchange rate leading to a debt crisis because of the depreciation's "balance sheet" effect;
- doubts about the credibility of a country's commitment to take the policy steps to assure its long-term creditworthiness;
- fixed or semifixed exchange rates, which increased both the risk of a large current account imbalance and the risk that borrowers would underestimate currency risk and rely too heavily on foreign-currency debt;
- poor banking regulation, implicit and/or explicit government guarantees, and other microeconomic distortions, which can lead to excessive investment and overreliance on dangerous forms of borrowing;
- political shocks—whether from elections, weakening governments, scandals, or political violence—that increase policy uncertainty and make investors trigger-happy; and
- external shocks—commodity price shocks that deteriorate a country's terms of trade, interest rate changes in the world's major financial centers, and sudden changes in the willingness of domestic and international investors to invest in risky financial assets—that tend to hit emerging economies more frequently and harder than advanced economies.

Emerging economies tend to be more exposed than advanced economies to shocks and also must pay more to borrow in ways that insulate them from various risks. Those that have not carefully managed their finances generally have little capacity to respond to shocks by borrowing to defer the need to adjust. They also can be punished severely for macroeconomic policy errors, as rapid swings in the willingness of domestic and international investors alike to roll over existing debts can trigger a vicious circle where growing financial distress overwhelms belated efforts to make needed policy changes.

Large Macroeconomic Imbalances. Most crisis countries had significant macroeconomic imbalances going into their crises. A country running a current account deficit necessarily either is attracting foreign direct investment (FDI) into its economy and net inflows of portfolio investment into its stock market or is borrowing from the rest of the world. Budget deficits typically have to be financed by selling government debt, either at home or abroad. The ongoing need for *new* net financing to cover fiscal and current account deficits is a potential source of vulnerability: Access to the needed new financing can disappear, or the cost of new borrowing can increase suddenly.

Most crisis countries had significant current account deficits before their crises (Russia is the major exception). The Asian-crisis countries demonstrated that a booming private economy could lead to current account deficits and the accumulation of external liabilities even in the absence of budget deficits.[6] However, outside of Asia, persistent fiscal deficits typically contributed to the creation of "twin" current account deficits and added to the country's vulnerability: Government borrowing competes with private investment unless additional financing is obtained from abroad, and public spending often leads to the real appreciation of the local currency.[7]

Risky Financing of Budget and Current Account Deficits. The way ongoing budget and current account deficits are financed can exacerbate a country's financial vulnerability.

An enormous difference exists between financing a current account deficit with short-term interbank borrowing and with long-term bonds or FDI and between financing a budget deficit with 90-day foreign currency–linked paper and with 10-year maturity local-currency bonds. After a few years of financing substantial current account deficits with short-term borrowing, a number of Asian countries found that they had accumulated a large stock of short-term external debt. Similarly, gov-

6. The East Asian countries—China, Hong Kong, Singapore, and Taiwan—that avoided a severe financial crisis in 1997–98 despite coming under pressure all had persistent current account surpluses and, as a result, had less need for net new financing and had not accumulated large stocks of foreign debt. The Philippines also avoided a severe crisis but for different reasons: It had a financial and banking crisis earlier in the decade and had not experienced a large precrisis boom.

7. The current account deficit is equal to a country's capital account surplus, net of reserve accumulation. The current account balance is determined by the difference between national (public plus private) savings and investment. A budget deficit is equal to public dissavings (excess of public spending including interest payments over its income—i.e., revenues) and, unless private saving rises or private investment falls, it will lead to a current account deficit. Government spending is usually biased toward domestic and nontradable goods. Excessive budget deficits thus lead to an increase in the price of domestic goods relative to foreign goods or to an increase in the relative price of nontraded goods—i.e., a real appreciation.

ernments that financed their fiscal deficits by issuing short-term debt (Mexico, Russia, Brazil, Turkey, and to a lesser degree, Argentina) quickly found that their financial health depended on the creditors' willingness to roll over large amounts of their debt at reasonable interest rates.

Borrowers that depend on short-term debt are in effect giving their creditors an option to exit at par when these debts mature. Countries typically assume that they can refinance their existing debt rather than pay the debt as it matures. However, investors are—unsurprisingly—more inclined to exercise their option to get out in bad times than in good times. Consequently, in a crisis, an emerging economy finds not only that it cannot raise new funds to cover ongoing deficits (let alone run larger deficits to minimize its need for immediate adjustments) but also that it must come up with money to pay off its existing debts. At a minimum, a country is likely to find that its costs of funds go up, even as an adverse shock may reduce its ability to pay.

Countries that finance themselves by issuing foreign currency–denominated debt are selling investors protection against the risk that the country's own currency will depreciate—and, in the process, increasing their own vulnerability. Often, the easiest way to adjust to a shock—domestic or external—is to let the exchange rate adjust to reduce the country's external imbalance. However, a large stock of debt denominated in foreign currency—either external debts owed to nonresidents or domestic debts denominated in foreign currency—complicates the exchange rate adjustment. The real burden of foreign currency–denominated debts goes up in the face of a real depreciation of the local currency (this effect is often called the "balance sheet effect").[8] The risk that short-term creditors will run and the risks of borrowing in foreign currency are interrelated. Difficulties refinancing short-term debts often result in a sharp depreciation in the currency that increases the real burden of foreign–currency debt. A shock to the real exchange rate that increases the real burden of foreign-currency debts, in turn, increases the risk that short-term creditors will run (box 2.1).

Michael Pettis (2001) has noted that the true costs of both short-term and foreign-currency debt are masked when times are good, growth is

8. If the real depreciation is large enough, negative balance sheet effects can push a borrower into technical insolvency: The borrower's larger liabilities formally exceed its assets. This "insolvency" does not necessarily trigger an automatic financial crisis. In the short run, the borrower only has to cover the payments on maturing debts as well as make ongoing interest payments. If the short-term payments are small enough, a technically insolvent borrower may remain liquid and still operate in the hope that over time the real exchange rate will bounce back (the real exchange rate often overshoots its long-run value at the peak of a currency crisis), restoring the borrower's solvency. On the other hand, even a technically solvent borrower can default if the combination of higher interest on maturing debts, larger payments on maturing debt due to a real devaluation, and reduced cash flows due to an economic contraction (and lack of other liquid assets) leave the borrower unable to cover its debt payments.

Box 2.1 Recent academic literature on currency and financial crises

The recent experience with capital account crises has led economists to thoroughly rethink the causes of currency and financial crises. Until the mid-1990s, the standard "first generation" model explained a currency crisis on the basis of fundamental macroeconomic weaknesses. Poor policies—in early models, borrowing from the central bank to finance a fiscal deficit—mechanically led to the loss of foreign exchange reserves and the abandonment of the exchange rate peg once reserves fell below a critical level (Krugman 1979, Flood and Garber 1984). Over time, the set of macroeconomic weaknesses that could trigger a crisis was expanded to include current account imbalances, real exchange rate misalignments, borrowing to defend a pegged exchange rate, and a projected increase in the government's debt-servicing costs after an expected devaluation.

The 1992 exchange rate mechanism (ERM) crisis and, more important, the 1994–95 Mexican crisis led to "second generation" crisis models. Early second-generation models argued that a crisis was not triggered by the mechanical fall in reserves but by authorities who were constantly assessing the trade-off between defending the peg by raising interest rates and floating. For example, in the 1992 ERM crisis, some European governments chose to devalue when the costs of using high interest rates to defend an overvalued exchange rate—lower growth and higher unemployment—became too great. In other cases modeled in the literature, high interest rates lead to an unsustainable increase in fiscal deficits that prompts the government to abandon the peg.

These models added the insight that some crises may stem in part from self-fulfilling shifts in investor expectations as well as from fundamental weaknesses. If investors doubt the government's commitment to the peg, the (output and fiscal) costs to the government of defending the peg increase. These costs may become so high that they can trigger a crisis that would not have occurred if investors had not expected a crisis in the first place. Doubts about the government's commitment to the peg make the costs of defending the peg higher than the government wants to bear, and the government's decision to abandon the peg, in turn, validates ex post the investors' ex ante doubts. In formal terms, crises could be the result of the endogenous policy choice of an authority assessing the benefits and costs of maintaining the peg rather than the automatic result of reserves reaching a critical level (Obstfeld 1994, Drazen and Masson 1994, Cole and Kehoe 1996).[1]

The possibility of multiple equilibria in many of these models was extended to examine how liquidity mismatches, either in the government or the private sector, could lead to a currency crisis in the event of a self-fulfilling rollover crisis. Vulnerability to this kind of self-fulfilling crisis of expectations stemmed directly from an excess of short-term claims relative to the liquid assets (foreign reserves) of the country. This emphasis on the risk of runs stemming from gaps between short-term debts and liquid reserves was further developed in many "third generation" models.

The "third generation" models were developed after the Asian crisis, in part because clearly the fiscal imbalances the first generation models emphasized did not cause the 1997–98 Asian crisis. Rather, imbalances in the private sector were at the core of the crisis, and currency and banking crises ("twin crises") were clearly connected. Some interpreted the Asian crisis largely as a self-fulfilling "liquidity run" and built on earlier work that emphasized the risk of short-term debt by formally modeling the role liquidity mismatches play in triggering runs on banks and governments. Others emphasized, in various ways, the vulnerabilities in the corporate and financial sectors of these economies. Certain third generation models stressed how the balance sheet effects of private-sector currency mismatches can contribute to runs and how the erosion of capital that

(box 2.1 continues next page)

Box 2.1 Recent academic literature on currency and financial crises *(continued)*

follows a currency depreciation can lead to the loss of external market access, credit constraints, and large losses in output. Others emphasized how implicit and explicit government guarantees, poor corporate governance, and absence of a credit culture distort economic and investment decisions (moral hazard distortions) and showed how these distortions can lead to overinvestment, a private sector–driven boom, and eventually a currency crisis. This literature has looked generally at different financial mismatches and distortions to broadly analyze "capital account" crises, "twin crises," sovereign debt crises, or all, not just currency, crises. (See Dornbusch [2001] for an early interpretation of the 1990s crises as "capital account" crises.)

1. Note that, formally speaking, multiple equilibria and fundamental crises can occur both in first (Obstfeld 1986) and second generation models, while some second generation models have unique equilibria (Drazen and Masson 1994) rather than multiple equilibria. What distinguishes the first and second generation models is not whether multiple equilibria can occur but rather whether the policymaker is passive and a mechanical rule (i.e., reserves falling below a certain threshold) triggers a peg's collapse or whether the policymaker actively decides to drop a peg based on a payoff function (for example, the relative costs and benefits of a move to float that increases output but may also increase inflation). Many loosely interpret first generation models as models of fundamental crises and second generation models as models of self-fulfilling multiple equilibria.

strong, and capital inflows are plentiful. Short-term debt rolls over not only without difficulty but also often at a lower interest rate. Expectations that interest rates will fall over time make economic actors reluctant to lock in today's interest rates. Large capital inflows fuel a real appreciation of the currency, which in turn reduces the real burden of foreign-currency debt. The positive dynamic feeds on itself.[9] Unfortunately, the same factors also work in reverse. Forms of financing that let emerging economies benefit strongly from a virtuous circle also leave them particularly exposed to the risk of a vicious circle.

Doubts about Policy Credibility. A close relationship exists between "stock" problems—the difficulties a large stock of external or government debt creates—and ongoing "flow" deficits—the current account and fiscal deficits. A large stock of debt usually is the product of large past deficits, and countries with important macroeconomic imbalances often have difficulty financing themselves in ways (long term and local currency) that limit their risk of crises. Moreover, ongoing fiscal and current account

9. A country that has found a model for successful growth often attracts additional capital from abroad, fueling faster growth and a bigger boom. The desire to profit from Asia's economic miracle, for example, fueled capital flows in the mid-1990s. A successful exchange rate–based stabilization program and the introduction of economic reform also can usher in a period of high growth and booming credit. See Calvo and Vegh (1999).

deficits eventually lead to concerns about the country's ability to reduce these imbalances in time to avoid an unsustainable accumulation of debt.[10]

Long-term solvency requires, at a minimum, that the country's external debt to GDP ratio—or the government debt to GDP ratio for public-sector solvency—not increase without bound over time. It does not require that the current account or the overall fiscal balance go into a surplus. A stable external debt to GDP ratio, however, does require the country to run a surplus in its noninterest current account (for most countries, the country's trade balance plus any remittances or transfers).[11] Similarly, a government has to be able to generate large enough primary surpluses over time—the primary balance is the gap between what a government collects in revenue and what it spends on items other than interest—to stabilize its debt ratio. A large existing stock of debt, slow growth, or a high average real interest rate all increase the size of the primary or trade surplus that eventually will be needed to avoid an ever-increasing debt burden.[12]

This analysis of long-run solvency raises a broader point. Because a country's—or a government's—solvency hinges on fairly intangible assets—its future ability to run trade and primary surpluses—policy credibility is often a policymaker's most important asset. A credible government can run larger fiscal deficits in the face of a temporary adverse shock without creating concerns about its future solvency. A government with large debt stocks, large fiscal deficits, and a primary balance insufficient to assure long-term debt sustainability may be able to lower its borrowing

10. A broad econometric literature exists on the determinants of sovereign debt crises which is based heavily on data drawn from the 1980s debt crises. However, a new generation of studies is starting to look at episodes of default and near defaults in the 1990s. Detragiache and Spilimbergo (2001) were the first to note the role of liquidity measures, in addition to traditional measures of debt sustainability, in explaining recent debt crises. Manasse, Roubini, and Schimmelpfenning (2003) found that external debt ratios (measuring solvency and debt sustainability), measures of illiquidity or refinancing risk (such as short-term debt relative to reserves), and other measures of external imbalance (current account deficits) all influence the probability of entering into a debt crisis. Some studies—namely Reinhart (2002)—have found a direct correlation between currency and debt crises.

11. Intertemporal solvency formally requires that the discounted value of trade balances (or undiscounted sum of current account balances) be at least as large as the initial stock of a country's foreign liabilities and that the discounted value of primary balances (or undiscounted sum of fiscal deficits) be at least as large as the stock of net government debt. This is a necessary, but quite loose, condition for solvency; closing primary or resource gaps is a sufficient, but more binding, condition for solvency. See Roubini (2001c) for a more detailed analysis of solvency and debt sustainability.

12. The primary balance needs to be at least equal to the public debt ratio (to GDP) times the differential between the real interest rate and the growth rate of the economy for the government's debt-to-GDP ratio not to increase over time. On the external side, the noninterest current account—typically close to the trade balance—must be at least equal to the external debt ratio (to GDP) times the differential between the real interest rate and the growth rate of the economy.

costs if it can credibly commit to future fiscal adjustments that will assure its long-term solvency. On the other hand, doubts about a country's commitment to future adjustments can immediately increase borrowing costs, and higher borrowing costs in turn make future solvency more difficult. If a country loses market access because creditors doubt its commitment to make the adjustments needed to service its debts, it almost always will eventually run out of funds and be forced to default, absent a rescue loan or emergency restructuring.

Fixed and Semifixed Exchange Rates. There is little doubt that fixed—or heavily managed—exchange rates have contributed to the vulnerabilities that have led to recent financial crises.

Exchange rate pegs and other heavily managed exchange rates often contributed to the emergence of current account deficits. Many emerging economies adopted pegged exchange rates as part of a program to reduce high inflation—so-called exchange rate–based stabilization programs.[13] However, inflation typically fell slowly—or at least more slowly than the programmed rate of depreciation, if any, in the exchange rate. Domestic prices rose, and the exchange rate was either fixed or did not depreciate by a comparable amount, leading to real appreciation, loss of competitiveness, and current account deficits. Countries that peg their currency to a single anchor currency also can experience a currency appreciation when the anchor currency appreciates relative to a range of other currencies. For example, many countries pegged their currencies to the US dollar and saw them rise when the dollar appreciated relative to the yen, the euro, and the euro's precursors between 1995 and 2001. The eventual currency crisis has many potential triggers: a fiscal deficit that cannot be financed by selling new debt and that has to be financed by printing money, leading to an unsustainable reserve loss; a current account deficit that is no longer financed by inflows from external investors; or a country that simply concludes that the costs of raising interest rates to defend the peg exceeds the benefits of currency stability (see box 2.1 for a review of the standard models of currency crises).

Pegs also can create financial vulnerabilities by distorting the borrowing decisions of private firms, banks, and households, as a period of currency stability can lead economic actors to underestimate future currency risk and borrow too much in foreign currency. For example, a period of nominal exchange rate stability in Asia led many firms (and the banks who lent to them) to conclude that the lower nominal interest rate on dollar, yen, or euro debt was worth the additional exchange rate risk. Similarly, most Argentines effectively bet that the one-to-one parity between the dollar and peso, which was embedded in Argentina's currency board,

13. See Calvo and Vegh (1999) for an analysis of such exchange rate–based stabilization programs.

would last indefinitely, and so they borrowed in dollars, not in pesos. Private firms and banks often interpret the government's promise to maintain a fixed rate as a promise to protect the private borrower from currency risk either by selling currency at a fixed rate or by providing a financial hedge or an effective bailout in the event of a currency crisis.[14] The free insurance against currency risk can be revoked at any time, but the promise itself often seems to result in the excessive accumulation of foreign-currency debt.

Pegged exchange rates can lead to crises in more subtle ways as well. Governments often believe that their exchange rate peg is the pillar of their macroeconomic policy framework, the anchor of financial stability, and the source of their economic success. Consequently, they defend a peg that comes under pressure. Raising domestic interest rates alone may not work: Higher rates on domestic–currency deposits and debts alone may not be enough to induce foreign capital to return to the country or to convince domestic residents to keep their money in domestic currency–denominated assets rather than seek the safety of a foreign currency (Berg et al. 2003). While higher interest rates increase the return on some local financial assets, their negative impact on the government's budget and on the health of the financial system as well as the risk that higher rates will lead to a politically unacceptable slowdown in economic activity all can undermine the credibility of an interest rate defense.[15] Governments often respond to pressure on the exchange rate in two additional ways: They sell their reserves to defend the exchange rate and increase their issuance of debt denominated in a foreign currency, often the dollar. Such debt is a form of indirect foreign-exchange intervention: By increasing the supply of local dollar-linked or dollar-indexed debt, the government hopes to persuade its own citizens to opt for local dollar-linked assets rather than move their funds abroad.[16] Such intervention, however, risks creating

14. Formally, a fully credible peg should lead to less borrowing in foreign currency, as debts denominated in local currency should be as safe as those denominated in foreign currency. If the peg is not fully credible, it should not lead firms to borrow in foreign currency, as the lower rate on foreign-currency relative to local-currency debt represents the expected depreciation risk (Krugman 1998a). Thus, if all economic actors were perfectly rational, an implicit guarantee of a bailout in the case of a currency crisis that reduces the cost of borrowing in foreign currency would be needed to explain the high reliance on foreign-currency debt. An alternative explanation is that economic actors are myopic and infer the future by looking at the past: A period of exchange rate stability consequently leads borrowers to expect the same in future.

15. See Vegh and Lahiri (2000) on whether interest rate defenses of pegs can work.

16. Foreign-currency assets issued by a local government are not a perfect substitute for true foreign assets (for example, the debt of the US government). First, exchange controls risk blocking the conversion of local payments on foreign currency–denominated local assets into foreign exchange. Second, the government may default—or forcibly restructure—its local debt.

additional financial weaknesses, as investors holding foreign-currency debts—whether foreign-currency debt of the government or short-term claims on the banks—start worrying about whether the government has sufficient reserves to cover its short-term debts. Mexico, for example, both increased its issuance of dollar-linked debt (tesobonos) and spent its reserves trying to defend the peso in 1994, laying the foundations for its subsequent debt crisis.

Microeconomic Distortions. Poor banking regulation, large implicit and explicit government guarantees, and other microeconomic distortions can create macroeconomic and financial imbalances that can contribute to crises. For example, such distortions can lead to excessive borrowing and investment by private borrowers, resulting in the accumulation of short-term, foreign currency–liabilities.

Particularly in Asia, the expectation of government guarantees encouraged domestic banks to take risks that they otherwise would have shied away from, whether lending to favored firms and sectors (directed lending) or taking on the risks associated with short-term external debt. Such guarantees can combine with poor regulation and supervision to fuel excessive borrowing and reckless lending. Distorted incentives in the financial sector can be particularly dangerous when combined with the early stages of capital account liberalization, as the opportunity for domestic financial and nonfinancial institutions to borrow from abroad can result in lending/credit booms[17] and asset price bubbles.

Poor corporate governance and cronyism, while never immediate triggers of crises, can distort incentives and otherwise contribute to a financial environment that creates financial risks and vulnerabilities.[18] Connected lending—large corporations who borrow from financial institutions they control—can fund investment activities with low returns. Crony capitalism and weak corporate governance more generally can lead investors to prefer debt to equity (since insiders can exploit equity investments by outsiders) and short-term to long-term debt.

These microeconomic and structural distortions were an important source of vulnerability in Asia,[19] but they do not fully explain Asia's cri-

17. See Gourinchas, Valdez, and Landerretche (2001) for evidence of excessive credit booms and eventual busts in many crisis episodes.

18. For "third generation" models of crises that emphasize how microeconomic distortions and moral hazard from bailout guarantees generate crises, see Krugman (1999); IMF (1998); Corsetti, Pesenti, and Roubini (1999a); Burnside, Eichenbaum, and Rebelo (1999, 2001); and Schneider and Tornell (2000). See also the evidence in Wei (2001) of how domestic crony capitalism affects capital flows and their composition.

19. See Corsetti, Pesenti, and Roubini (1999a, 1999b) for analytical models and empirical evidence supporting the view that government policies exacerbated such structural problems, which caused the Asian crisis.

sis. China had and still has some of the same underlying domestic financial weaknesses as other Asian economies—a very shaky banking system, large domestic debts, and cronyism. Yet China's large reserves, current account surpluses, limited external debt, and tightly managed capital account insulated it from a crisis. Moreover, structural weaknesses did not inhibit an enormous increase in external bank lending to Asian economies in the mid-1990s; thus, they cannot be held solely accountable for the reversal of these flows.[20]

Yet even if these structural weaknesses do not fully explain Asia's crisis, they clearly sapped the resilience of Asian economies when the tide turned. High debt-to-equity ratios imply that firms have a smaller buffer against all shocks, including capital account shocks. Heavy reliance on short-term interbank borrowing rather than on equity at the national level similarly fails to provide a built-in buffer against shifts in capital flows. It increases the country's risk of facing a rush to exits and a rollover crisis. More subtly, the scale of the government's contingent liabilities from weak banking systems heavily exposed to overleveraged firms made it difficult to assess the fiscal health of most Asian countries and thus may have made it harder for a government guarantee to stop bank runs. So long as the ultimate cost of bailing out weak financial systems was substantially uncertain, it was hard to assess the government's own solvency.[21]

Political Shocks. Unexpected political developments have often been the immediate trigger for trouble. Doubts about a government's commitment to the policies to maintain macroeconomic stability will result in an increase in the premium that investors demand to hold the country's financial assets; falls in the prices of the country's stocks, bonds, and currency; a desire to shift funds into safer foreign assets; and an inclination not to roll over claims as they mature.

Consequently, it is not surprising that crises are often closely correlated with elections, which raise doubts about policy continuity. Mexico's 1994 crisis, Korea's 1997 crisis, and Brazil's crises in 1998 and 2002 all coincided with elections. Conversely, the introduction of a new government that demonstrates the ability to define and carry out a coherent economic pol-

20. Short-term lending by international banks to Thailand, Malaysia, Korea, and Indonesia nearly doubled from $89.4 billion to $167.2 billion between mid-1994 and mid-1997, even though most of the structural weaknesses present in 1997 were also present in 1994 (data from the *Quarterly Review: International Banking and Financial Developments*, Bank for International Settlements, 1998).

21. In retrospect, the underlying solvency of Korea's government hardly seems to have been at risk. Yet it was hard to know the true scale of Korea's potential contingent liabilities in the midst of a crisis. Both Korea and Indonesia were widely considered to be in better shape than Thailand at the early stages of Asia's crisis. While Korea turned out to be fine, Indonesia did not.

icy often plays a key role in ending the crisis. For example, fears that a left-leaning presidential candidate would be unwilling to make the primary fiscal adjustment Brazil needed to honor its debts led to a sharp fall in the Brazilian real's value in 2002, but President Luiz Inacio Lula da Silva's subsequent commitment to fiscal stability contributed to a rally in 2003.

Elections, though, are not the only sources of political turmoil and uncertainty. Political violence (the Chiapas revolt and two political assassinations) played a role in the Mexican peso crisis. Doubts about the continued viability of Suharto's regime fueled a vicious circle of economic and financial decline in Indonesia. Argentina's 2001 crisis was marked by persistent doubts about the central government's ability to reign in provinces controlled by the opposition and about a fragile coalition's ability to deliver appropriate policies. Turkey's crawling peg collapsed in February 2001 after a public spat between the president and the prime minister. Ecuador's class cleavages and divisions between the coast and the highlands have made it very difficult to govern.

External Shocks. Many shocks—like the failure to pass needed legislation or the belated disclosure of bad news—are in part self-inflicted. Yet there is little doubt that many emerging economies are also exposed to shocks stemming from events beyond their control. Certain emerging economies depend heavily on the export of a single commodity—often oil—and thus are exposed to commodity price shocks. Many emerging economies also depend on access to external capital markets, whether to fund a current account or a fiscal deficit or to refinance a portion of their existing debt stock. International investors are more willing to lend to emerging economies or buy their existing bonds when interest rates in the largest economies are low than when they are high. Emerging economies are also at risk if a crisis in one emerging economy triggers a broad reduction in investors' willingness to hold the financial assets of a broad range of emerging economies, not just those of the crisis country. This phenomenon, referred to as contagion, itself has a number of potential triggers (box 2.2).

However, emerging economies are not passive victims of external shocks. Their resilience is determined in part by their own policies—both the choices they make in the face of the shock and their past policies. Countries running large current account deficits will likely have less scope to borrow and to run a larger current account deficit in the face of an adverse commodity price shock. Countries running large fiscal deficits before an adverse shock in the capital markets will have less scope to absorb higher interest costs by running a larger budget deficit, just as countries with large accumulated debts will have less scope to take on additional debt in the face of an adverse shock. Countries that have financed themselves with short-term debt may find that their borrowing costs increase sharply precisely at those points in time when their capacity to pay is reduced, just as

Box 2.2 Contagion

Contagion is notoriously difficult to define and measure.[1] Clearly, crises do not arise unless an underlying financial weakness leaves the country vulnerable to various capital account shocks. Yet international contagion, in some form, can play a role in the transmission of crises. A crisis in one country can trigger difficulties in another for several reasons:

- *Trade linkages and pressure for competitive devaluations.* If country A devalues, its trading partner, country B, will lose competitiveness. Investors will put pressure on B's currency as well, or policymakers in country B may decide that they need to devalue to prevent losing export market share. Such pressures were present in Asia in 1997–98, in Argentina after Brazil's devaluation in 1999, and in Uruguay after the Argentine peso collapsed in 2002.[2]
- *Wake-up calls.* A crisis in one country can highlight the risks a certain financial vulnerability poses. Investors, like countries, learn from experience. They may decide to preemptively seek to reduce their exposure to countries with similar financial vulnerabilities, such as a similar dependence on short-term interbank debt. If the country is not prepared for such an adjustment, it can be tipped into a vicious circle.
- *Common creditor linkages.* A bank, portfolio manager, or hedge fund may have exposure to many different emerging markets. Losses in one country may lead the financial institution to pull back from others for a host of reasons. Losses—or its prospects—may eat into a bank's capital and lead the bank to cut back on its exposure to other risky borrowers (including other emerging economies). Losses in an emerging market may lead investors to pull their money out of emerging-market bond funds, forcing fund managers to sell their holdings of other emerging markets. Losses by a leveraged hedge fund may lead its creditors to call in their loans and demand that the hedge fund deleverage. To raise the needed cash, the hedge fund may need to sell its most liquid assets. Selling drives prices down and spreads up. This produces losses for all financial institutions with similar positions and may therefore trigger further selling. Japanese banks which were already fragile given the economic crisis in Japan, felt these common creditor effects during the Asian crisis; so did US banks after the Mexican peso crisis. Similarly, dedicated emerging-market debt fund managers may cut back their exposure to a wide range of emerging markets if they incur losses in one emerging market. Russia's collapse led to a sell-off of Brazil's debt in 1998.
- Sophisticated models of risk management, paradoxically, tend to lead investors to respond to turmoil in one market with rapid cutbacks in exposure to other markets. The "value-at-risk" (VAR) models used by many banks and fund managers imply that a loss in the portfolio should be associated with an immediate increase in capital or reduction of risk. Investors who mark-to-market and book losses immediately are more inclined to sell losing positions rather than exercise 1980s-style forbearance.
- The risk of contagion increases if investors have difficulty picking out a buying opportunity from a warning signal. If a sophisticated but leveraged investor is forced to dump its holdings of Brazilian assets to raise funds to meet a margin call after taking losses in a country like Russia, the price of Brazilian assets should not change, in spite of this margin-triggered sale. Nothing fundamental has happened to Brazil, and other investors should be prepared to step in and buy. But uninformed investors may not know whether the informed investor is dumping Brazil because of a margin constraint or because he or she has superior information and knows that Brazil is

(box 2.2 continues next page)

Box 2.2 Contagion *(continued)*

also in trouble.[3] Thus, Brazilian asset prices fall even if, based on fundamentals, they should not. Investors may rationally decide not to acquire costly information about a country's conditions because portfolio diversification tends to reduce the portfolio's overall risk.

Portfolio adjustments by one market participant—or by a set of market participants with similar positions—will have an immediate impact on the secondary market price of long-term bonds and the country's ability to roll over its short-term debt. If the country is prepared to weather temporary periods of instability and capital-market droughts, such portfolio adjustment will not have an enduring economic impact. Lower prices mean higher yields, and other investors will eventually move in. But if the country's balance sheet is shaky, the initial portfolio adjustment may trigger a cascading crisis—the unwillingness of one group of creditors to roll over their maturing debts leads others to pull out, pushing a country into a deep crisis.

1. See Claessens and Forbes (2001) for a systematic overview of contagion.

2. See Corsetti et al. (2000) for a formal model.

3. See Calvo (1999) and Calvo and Mendoza (1999) on the role of information asymmetries.

countries that finance themselves with foreign-currency debt will find that an adverse shock that leads to a real depreciation in their currency increases their overall debt burden.

Take, for example, an emerging economy that depends on oil both to finance imports and to cover the government's own expenses. A negative oil price shock is a direct shock to the country's income: The country will earn fewer dollars on its exports, the government's revenues will fall, and its currency will likely depreciate. The effect of that shock, though, will be magnified if the country has borrowed in a foreign currency, as the country's debt servicing burden will increase as a result of the depreciation even as its revenues are falling.

The "Balance Sheet" Framework

A formal way of thinking about the risks of an emerging economy experiencing a "capital account" crisis is to look in an organized way at the strengths and weaknesses of its financial balance sheet. Balance sheet analysis adds to traditional economic analysis—which typically emphasizes flow variables like the size of current account and fiscal deficits—a focus on the risk created by mismatches between a country's existing debt stock and its assets. The size of a country's—and its government's—outstanding debt is an obvious "stock" variable. But two countries with identical government debt-to-GDP ratios will not be equally vulnerable to crises if all of one country's debt is short-term and denominated in a foreign currency and all of the other country's debt is long-term and denominated in the local currency. Balance sheet analysis therefore emphasizes the debt's maturity structure, the currency in which the debt is denominated, and the availability of equity-like buffers that may help cushion against some shocks.

Maturity Mismatches. The amount of short-term debt determines how much existing debt a country needs to refinance, how quickly the interest rate the country has to pay on its debt can increase during financial distress, and how quickly investors can run if they lose confidence. Assessing a country's—or a government's—full maturity mismatch, though, requires looking at both the structure of the country's liabilities and its assets. A maturity mismatch arises when there is a gap between the term structure of debts and the term structure and liquidity of the corresponding assets. If short-term debts exceed liquid assets, a government, bank, or firm risks not being able to roll over its short-term debt, thus being forced to seek a restructuring or default.[22] Mexico faced default at the end of 1994 because it had nearly $29 billion in dollar-linked short-term debt (tesobonos) maturing over the next year and only $6 billion left in reserves, and Korea got into trouble because its banking system's short-term external liabilities largely exceeded the government's foreign-currency reserves.

Currency Mismatches. A currency mismatch arises when the currency that debts are denominated in differs from the currency that the firm, government, or household earns revenues in, or has assets in, or both. Usually, a mismatch arises because a firm or government borrows in foreign currency but earns revenue in domestic currency. Standard textbook economics teaches that a currency depreciation stimulates the local economy: Exports increase and imports fall as locally produced goods substitute for foreign goods. This dynamic, however, only dominates in the short run if the debts of local firms and the local government are denominated in the local currency. If a substantial portion of debts is denominated in foreign currencies, as is often the case in emerging economies, a mismatch be-

22. Many recent "third generation" models of currency crises build on the emphasis that "second generation" models place on self-fulfilling, "nonfundamental" crises by stressing the role of maturity mismatches in triggering crises. These papers and models (for example, Chang and Velasco 2001, Sachs and Radelet 1998, and Rodrik and Velasco 1999) reinterpret the financial crises of the 1990s as international variants of "bank run" models (Diamond and Dybvig 1983). An insight from some of these models is that the feedback between the depreciation of the currency and the deterioration of the balance sheet of the bank or the government (if it has not matched foreign-currency assets and liabilities) or those who have borrowed from the bank can contribute to the risk of a self-fulfilling run (Jeanne and Wyplosz 2001, Schneider and Tornell 2000).

tween foreign-currency debts and revenues can lead to an increase in real debt burdens without a commensurate increase in the ability to pay.[23]

This balance sheet effect does not mean that the currency depreciation is not needed: Exchange rate adjustment is almost always necessary to close a current account deficit that can no longer be financed by borrowing from abroad. But the process of exchange rate adjustment is likely to be more contractionary in economies that have lots of external—or domestic—debt denominated in a foreign currency. Currency mismatches have been a consistent source of financial fragility in emerging economies. Many governments have encountered financial difficulty after a currency depreciation increased the local currency value of their foreign-currency debts, as did private borrowers throughout Asia and in Argentina.

Capital Structure Mismatches. A country that has financed itself in a way that "shares" downside risk (as well as upside gains) with its creditors and investors will be in better shape than one that itself has assumed all the downside risk. For example, debt payments are fixed even in bad times like recessions while dividends on equity can be reduced in bad times. Equity consequently acts as a buffer against shocks while debt does not, though in principle it is possible to design debt contracts that have "equity-like" features, such as state-contingent coupon payments (i.e., coupons that are lower in bad times and larger in good times). In the corporate or financial sector, capital structure risk arises when debt is large in relation to equity, or in the case of banks, loans are large in relation to capital. For the government, capital structure risk arises when senior debt is large in relation to junior debt or if privatization revenue is not used to reduce the accumulation of public debt. For the country as a whole, capital structure risk arises when the country relies on debt rather than FDI and equity portfolio investment to finance a current account deficit.[24] Many Asian economies, for example, financed external deficits with debt

23. Much of the "third generation" literature on crises has stressed the role of balance sheet imbalances deriving from currency mismatches (Krugman 1999; Cespedes, Chang, and Velasco 2000; Gertler, Gilchrist, and Natalucci 2000; Aghion, Bacchetta, and Banerjee 2000 and 2001; Cavallo et al. 2002). Some of these models posit that concerns about the impact of a depreciation on balance sheets can create a self-fulfilling crisis of expectations. Fears that a depreciation will devastate private-sector balance sheets lead to a run on the currency, and the resulting collapse in output and investment validates the loss of confidence. Other models emphasize shocks to fundamentals that in turn prompt adverse balance sheet effects. Any overshooting of the real exchange rate (beyond what fundamentals warrant) exacerbates the balance sheet effects of foreign-currency liabilities.

24. Balance sheet analysis draws heavily on corporate finance theory in order to better explain the vulnerability of emerging markets to financial crises. Pettis (2001) puts particular emphasis on "inverted" capital structures that magnify a shock: Debt-servicing costs increase as payment capacity decreases. Gray's (2002) "macrofinance" approach also draws on corporate finance theory, particularly on "contingent claims analysis" to assess the risk of a banking crisis leading to a sovereign crisis.

rather than equity, and at a micro level, firms and financial institutions were extremely highly leveraged with very large debt to equity ratios.[25]

Maturity, currency, and capital structure mismatches all increase the risk of a shock leaving a firm, bank, household, government, corporate sector, banking sector, or even the country with more debt than it can pay. Of course, a company that borrows to invest in a project that fails to generate enough revenue will also go bankrupt, and a government that borrows to invest in an economic model that fails to generate growth will also likely experience trouble. Weaknesses in a firm's—or a government's—financial structure are not the only source of risk. But recent experience suggests that balance sheet weaknesses can be an important independent source of risk, and that financial weaknesses can overwhelm other sources of strength.

Balance sheet weaknesses also can augment the economic contraction associated with a shock. For example, the balance sheet effects of a devaluation, particularly when there is excessive reliance on debt relative to equity, often lead to a real economic contraction. Aggregate supply falls as firms with weakened balance sheets are unable to borrow to finance production, and aggregate demand falls as the credit crunch limits the ability of consumers and firms to borrow to finance consumption and investment.[26]

The Dynamics of Crises

Balance sheet analysis is particularly helpful for understanding the dynamics of crisis. It explains both how a crisis in one sector of the econ-

25. FDI is usually considered among the most stable sources of financing. But FDI stability can be deceptive at times. FDI investors cannot close factories or halt fixed investments overnight. But they can take steps to hedge their exposure, which can add to pressures on the country during times of crisis. For example, FDI investors who are producing goods for the local market are taking on currency risk. They may not hedge this currency exposure in normal times. But as the risks of a crisis builds, FDI investors who do not usually hedge that risk ex-ante may have a strong incentive to hedge, whether by covering forward their local-currency positions, by buying local foreign currency–denominated debt that would pay off if the exchange rate fell, or by making outright purchases of foreign currency. This can add to the speculative stampede against the crisis country's currency. A recent example is that of Brazil, where new FDI dried up during the 2002 crisis, and legal capital outflows through "C5A accounts" were a source of significant pressure.

26. In many recent "third generation" models, financing constraints that capital structure mismatches generate interact with currency mismatches to generate crises after a real devaluation. In some models, a "financial accelerator effect" magnifies the impact of a currency depreciation on investment, as investment depends on the net worth of the firm/country, and a real depreciation interacts with foreign-currency debt to reduce the borrowers' capital and ability to borrow to invest (see, for example, Cespedes, Chang, and Velasco 2000; and Gertler, Gilchrist, and Natalucci 2000). In other models, when the stock of external debt relative to capital hits a binding constraint, a "margin call" is triggered, and assets/capital need to be liquidated in a "fire sale" to reduce the debt to equity ratio (Mendoza and Smith 2002; Cavallo et al. 2002; and Mendoza and Arellano 2002).

omy can snowball and lead to a broader crisis and how the financial weaknesses created by large stocks of short-term debt and foreign-currency debt or the twin negatives of large stocks of short-term foreign currency–denominated debt interact in a dynamic way with policy weaknesses as stress mounts. The risk that a crisis will spiral out of control depends both on the country's willingness to make needed policy adjustments early on and on the size of the imbalances on a country's financial balance sheet.

How Intersectoral Linkages Transmit Financial Vulnerabilities across Sectors. Understanding how trouble in one sector of the economy can lead to trouble in other sectors requires looking beyond the maturity, currency, and capital structure risks of a country's overall balance sheet and looking at the risks that arise from domestic debts and the financial links between the economy's major sectors.[27] The domestic debts of one sector are the assets of another sector. These debts do not show up in the country's overall balance sheet, yet they create financial linkages between the key sectors, notably the government, financial, and private nonfinancial (firms and households) sectors. These financial interlinkages increase the risk of one sector's difficulties snowballing and leading to a deeper and more generalized crisis.

Looking closely at intersectoral linkages inevitably highlights the importance of the *domestic banking system* in the propagation of a crisis. This is not surprising. Banks are highly leveraged institutions and thus inherently vulnerable to financial instability. Moreover, their financial health is highly correlated with the financial health of the sectors that they lend to, whether the corporate and household sectors or the government. An imbalance on the balance sheet of a country's private firms can create problems for the banking system, just as the banking system's need to match the currency denomination of its assets and liabilities can create difficulties for firms. In many emerging economies, for example, the domestic banking sector takes in domestic foreign-currency deposits. It needs to make foreign currency–denominated loans to limit its direct foreign-currency risk. However, if it lends to firms that lack export revenues, a currency depreciation risks bankrupting the country's corporate sector. The

27. Constructing sectoral balance sheets requires more data than constructing national balance sheets. A sectoral balance sheet provides more information about potential sources of vulnerability than just the country's external balance sheet. The needed data are often available for the government and the financial sectors (at least the regulated banking sector), and the data on the financial sector usually provide important information about the balance sheet of firms and households. The aggregated balance sheet of the financial, corporate, household, and government sectors net out debts between, say, various financial institutions. They do show, though, how a financial sector that borrows (by taking deposits) from the households lends those funds to the corporate sector, the government, back to households (through the mortgage market), or to nonresidents.

distress of the country's firms, in turn, creates problems for their creditors: Currency risk gets turned into credit risk for the banks. A government that borrows heavily from the domestic banking system similarly puts the system at risk if the government should ever prove unable to honor its debts.

One result of these financial interlinkages is that it is often difficult to distinguish between a domestic and an external financial crisis. When residents lose confidence in domestic dollar debt—or in the domestic banking system's ability to honor its dollar deposits—they typically do not move in mass into other local assets. They move into external assets. It is equally difficult to prevent an external crisis from spilling over into the domestic economy. Domestic banks often hold large amounts of the country's external-law debt, so an external debt default leads directly to a domestic banking crisis. Efforts by domestic residents with most of their assets in domestic currency to diversify their financial holdings during an external debt crisis only adds to pressure on the country's reserves and the exchange rate. A domestic crisis rarely remains purely domestic, and an external crisis almost always becomes a domestic crisis.

To illustrate how weaknesses in one sector of the economy eventually give rise to some form of external vulnerability, suppose a government budget deficit does not crowd out domestic investment and therefore leads to a current account deficit of equal magnitude. The government could finance the country's budget and current account deficits directly by selling long-term foreign currency–denominated bonds to foreign investors (nonresidents). The government takes on the currency risk and directly raises the financing needed to cover the current account deficit. Alternatively, the government could finance its fiscal deficit by selling long-term domestic currency–denominated bonds to the domestic banking system.[28] In our thought experiment, though, all domestic savings is already financing private investment, so the banking system has to borrow from abroad to finance its acquisition of government bonds. If the banks take out short-term, cross-border, foreign-currency interbank loans to lend to the government, they are assuming the currency risk that the government would have otherwise taken. The country as a whole now has a large maturity mismatch: The banking system is raising the needed external funds with short-term debt. Should the government ever be unable to honor its debts to the banks, it may make the banking system insolvent.[29]

28. Domestic bank regulation and, at times, capital controls often either make government bonds an attractive asset or restrict other assets that the banks can buy or both.

29. This example—quite relevant for the cases of Argentina and Turkey—shows why the development of domestic capital markets does not mechanically reduce the vulnerabilities that foreign-currency external debt borrowing generates. If local capital markets become a way of forcing the financial system to intermediate the financing needs of the government via international markets (rather than the government relying more on direct financing from nonresidents), they may increase intersectoral financial vulnerabilities.

Interaction Between Policy and Financial Weaknesses in a Crisis. If a country does not have a large buffer of reserves, the unwillingness of some short-term creditors to roll over their debt can lead other creditors to decide to pull out as well. Once a run starts, creditors may pay more attention to the country's declining reserves than to its efforts to improve its macroeconomic policies. If all creditors believe others will stay in, they won't run, and a good outcome is possible. If all creditors run, a bad outcome is guaranteed (Sachs 1995). In the extreme case, fears of a crisis may trigger a race among short-term creditors to get out, which itself causes the crisis.[30]

However, runs usually don't happen entirely by accident. Investors run in part when they have reason to worry about the country's capacity to take the actions to assure its long-term solvency. Moreover, the speed of the run—and the time the country will have to take corrective action—depends on the extent to which the country has relied on short-term debt for financing. Countries with close-to-perfect policies and little debt sometimes can get away with lots of short-term debt. The credibility of a country's policies allows it to retain the confidence of investors even in times of stress, preventing potential financial weaknesses from transforming into serious problems. Conversely, countries with truly awful policies usually cannot survive for long if they rely on short-term financing. The biggest risk comes from countries with real but correctable problems—problems that may only come to light in the face of adverse shocks—that have relied heavily on short-term debt. Here, a run can overwhelm a country before it has the time to take action to reestablish its policy credibility.

Heavy reliance on foreign currency–denominated debts also can trigger a self-reinforcing downward spiral that turns an otherwise manageable problem into a deep crisis. As in the case of a run, these pressures can be strong enough to overwhelm even a significant effort to improve policies. For example, firms that borrowed in foreign currency without having offsetting foreign-currency assets (as well as FDI investors that made unhedged local-currency investments financed from abroad) often will want to take steps to protect themselves, or hedge, as the risk of the currency

30. The dynamics of a run are captured in many models that allow for multiple equilibria. Both the good no-run equilibrium and the bad-run equilibrium are possible. Such models, however, usually fail to explain what leads investors and creditors to start to run. Recent analytical contributions suggest that the risk of a run is directly linked to the strength of the country's economic fundamentals: the weaker the signals that investors receive about the strength of the country's fundamentals, the greater the fraction of investors who run rather than roll over their claims and the higher the likelihood of a crisis. In the technical jargon of economic models, an economy can end up in the region where a self-fulfilling currency or bank run is possible only if economic fundamentals and policies are weak enough. See Corsetti, Guimaraes, and Roubini (2003) and Morris and Shin (2003).

peg breaking increases. If firms start hedging by buying foreign exchange before the exchange rate peg breaks, they put additional pressure on the government's reserves. If they wait until after the peg breaks, they put additional pressure on the nominal exchange rate and can contribute to the overshooting of the exchange rate. The net result can be very sharp and disruptive moves in the currency, massive financial difficulties in sectors with foreign-currency debts, a severe banking crisis, a credit crunch, and a very sharp fall in economic activity.[31] The same destabilizing dynamics can also occur, though typically with less virulence, if a floating exchange rate comes under unexpected pressure. The steps private banks and firms take to protect themselves from further falls themselves put more pressure on the exchange rate.[32]

Labels abound for the complex dynamics of flow imbalances, accumulation of stocks of liabilities, and financing of these stocks in forms—short-term, in foreign currency, and debt rather than equity—that make countries vulnerable to sudden stops and capital flow reversals.[33] Former Treasury Secretary Lawrence Summers and other officials talked of "21st century financial crises" to differentiate the 1990s' crises from the 1980s' bank debt crisis. The IMF prefers the greyer term "capital account" crises, noting the difference between pressures that stem from rapid swings in capital flows rather than those that stem from a slow increase in a current account deficit.[34]

31. See Kaminsky and Reinhart (1999) for a seminal empirical contribution to this "twin" currency and banking crisis literature. See Cavallo et al. (2002) for a study of the output effects of financial distress after currency crises: They find that output contraction are larger when balance sheet effects from large stocks of foreign-currency debt are more significant.

32. Brazil's recent experience is an obvious example. A fall in inflows and difficulty refinancing debt before the 2002 election led to a real depreciation that made all of Brazil's financial indicators look worse. Conversely, a return of confidence and the resumption of (limited) inflows, together with a large catalytic IMF package, triggered a currency rally in 2003 that made all financial indicators look better.

33. See Dornbusch (2001) for an early academic study of how the "capital account" crises of the 1990s differed from the previous decade's crises.

34. Calvo (1998) has called these sharp swings "sudden stops," alluding to the saying that it is not speed that kills but the sudden stop. The term "sudden stop" is often used to suggest that the change in capital flows is justified not by any fundamental weaknesses in the emerging economy but rather by investors' fickleness, contagion, sudden changes in investors' appetite for risk, and more generally conditions in the financial markets of advanced economies. This suggestion is way too strong. Investors can overreact, but usually the crisis country's own macroeconomic weaknesses and policy mistakes play a key role in creating its underlying vulnerability. For a fuller discussion of sudden stops and models combining a number of financial vulnerabilities to explain financial crises, see Calvo (1998), Calvo and Mendoza (1999), Mendoza (2001), and Schneider and Tornell (2000).

Interpreting Recent Crises

This section draws on the analytical framework described in the previous section to look at how policy weaknesses and financial vulnerabilities interacted in major crisis cases. We highlight what we think were the key sources of the country's vulnerability, paying particular attention to the financial imbalances that gave rise to the need for a bailout or a debt restructuring (see part A of table 2.1 for a summary of such vulnerabilities). This section both illustrates many of the key themes of this chapter and provides the background for the later chapters. In several cases, we take time to go through particularly interesting examples illustrating how interlinked domestic balance sheets gave rise to crises.

Mexico

The elements of Mexico's 1994 crisis are familiar:

- An effectively fixed exchange rate resulted in significant real appreciation of the peso and a large and growing current account deficit. Fiscal deficits were moderate and not the primary drivers of the current account deficit, though a tighter fiscal policy might have helped restrain the domestic boom and election-driven quasi-fiscal credit expansion in 1994 that exacerbated the credit cycle.
- A number of political shocks buffeted the country: the Chiapas revolt; the assassination of the anointed presidential candidate of the government, Luis Donaldo Colosio Murrieta, on March 23, 1994; the electoral uncertainty; and another high-profile political murder (of José Francisco Ruiz Massieu) in the fall of 1994.
- External shocks, notably, a sharp increase in US interest rates reduced investors' willingness to finance the current account deficit.
- The government exacerbated the country's vulnerability to crises during 1994 by replacing domestic peso-denominated debts (cetes) with domestic dollar-linked bonds (tesobonos), in part because it was having difficulty selling peso debt in the face of concerns that its exchange rate was overvalued. As discussed, dollar-indexed tesobonos provided a substitute for dollar-denominated foreign assets, and thus increasing tesobono issuance acted as a kind of hidden intervention in the foreign exchange market. The stock of tesobonos increased from 6 percent of domestic debt in early 1994 to 50 percent at the end of November, just before the devaluation.

Mexico compounded the problems it created by shifting into dollar-indexed debt by selling off most of its reserves to avoid a peso devaluation, thus creating a large maturity mismatch on the government's balance sheet. Reserves fell from around $30 billion at the beginning of 1994 to about $17 billion in early November and to $6 billion at the end of December. By the end of 1994, a clear mismatch existed between Mexico's $6 billion in reserves and around $29 billion in tesobonos coming due in 1995. With nearly $10 billion coming due in the first quarter of 1995, Mexico was facing imminent default—even though Mexico's overall government debt, at about 25 percent of precrisis GDP, was not exorbitant.

Mexico also illustrates how balance sheets interconnect. Some tesobonos were sold directly to foreign investors, but domestic Mexican banks held many tesobonos. However, many of the banks borrowed in the international interbank market to finance tesobono purchases: International banks lent short term in dollars to Mexican banks, and Mexican banks used these dollars to finance the purchase of short-term domestic dollar-linked securities. When international banks wanted to reduce their exposure to the Mexican banks, the Mexican banks needed to liquidate their offsetting tesobono positions. Consequently, Mexico's rollover crisis has aspects of both an international and a domestic rollover crisis. International banks did not want to roll over their loans to Mexican banks (as well as their own tesobono holdings), and Mexican banks did not want to roll over their domestic claims on the government.

Mexico's currency was doubtless overvalued before the crisis, and a fall in the real value of the peso was needed to balance the current account. However, households with foreign currency–denominated mortgages, as well as firms that had dollar liabilities but lacked export revenues, were not able to service their foreign-currency debts after the devaluation. The financial distress of many private borrowers was one reason why Mexico's banking system had a severe crisis: The resulting bank bailout cost Mexico's taxpayers over $50 billion. Fortunately, the Mexican government went into the crisis with a relatively low level of debt, and it was able to bear the costs of the bank bailout and the higher real burden of its own foreign-currency debt after the devaluation.

East Asia

In East Asia, fiscal deficits and the governments' own debts were clearly not the source of the crisis: A private sector–led investment boom fueled Asian current account deficits. The specific vulnerabilities of each East Asian crisis country differed, but all shared certain common characteristics. The crisis hit Thailand, Indonesia, and Korea the hardest; Philippines, Singapore, Taiwan and Hong Kong saw their rates of growth slow but avoided a widespread payments crisis. Malaysia was something of an intermediate case. All Asian-crisis countries had effectively, even if not formally, fixed or semi-fixed exchange rates. Most of them favored financing these deficits with debt rather than equity: The external borrowing, often at short maturities and in foreign currency, of domestic banks and firms provided the capital inflows needed to finance ongoing current account deficits.

Close ties between banks and firms and expectations that well-connected banks would not be allowed to fail created distorted incentives, with too much borrowing from abroad and too much investment in marginal projects. These distorted incentives became particularly dangerous when combined with partial capital account liberalization in the 1990s, as domestic banks neither had the skills nor the incentives to manage the new risks that they were free to take on, and domestic supervision and regulation were poor. Finally, a credit boom, financed in part by external borrowing, contributed to a broader asset price bubble.

Thailand

Thailand provides a particularly compelling example of both how maturity, currency, and capital structure mismatches in the country's private sector created serious vulnerabilities in the country's balance sheet and how financial linkages between different sectors of the economy can lead to a cascading crisis. Thailand was running an unusually large current account deficit before its 1997 crisis, and its domestic economy showed clear signs of overheating. Many questioned the sustainability of Thailand's exchange rate peg. But relatively few predicted how the subsequent crisis would unfold. In retrospect, this is surprising because Thailand's national balance sheet suffered from every imbalance in the book.

Thailand increased its outstanding stock of short-term external interbank borrowing to finance its current account deficit: Between June 1994 and June 1997, Thailand's stock of short-term debt increased from $27.2 billion to $45.6 billion-an increase of $18.4 billion.[35] Thailand's short-term external debt exceeded 25 percent of GDP—an unusually high ratio.[36] Thai domestic banks—and very loosely regulated finance companies—typically borrowed foreign currency from abroad and then matched their short-term external liabilities with short-term foreign-currency loans to domestic Thai firms. The net result: The financial sector's short-term debt

35. Thailand's reserves increased at a much slower pace, rising from $27.4 billion only to $31.4 billion. The $18.4 billion increase in short-term debt during three years financed a large fraction of the cumulative current account deficit during the same period.

36. Countries like Chile that had financed comparable current account deficits with FDI, not by a surge in cross-border borrowing, were in much better financial shape. Chile's short-term debt increased by only $2.1 billion over the same period, rising from $5.5 billion to $7.6 billion. Chile's reserves increased by much more, going from $10.8 billion to $17 billion (data from the *Quarterly Review: International Banking and Financial Developments*, Bank for International Settlements, 1998).

exceeded the liquid foreign-currency reserves of the government (as well as the banks' own liquid reserves), creating a classic maturity mismatch, and heavy overall reliance on debt rather than FDI to finance current account deficits left Thailand as a whole with a smaller buffer against adverse shocks.

The Bank of Thailand compounded this maturity mismatch by selling its dollar reserves forward (in effect, offering investors insurance against the risk of devaluation) to defend the baht-dollar peg. This scale of its forward book was hidden from the public. In the end, the central bank's commitment to sell dollars in the future exceeded the amount of dollars that it actually held in reserve.

Thailand's external borrowing ended up creating a substantial currency mismatch as well. Local Thai banks and finance companies needed to offset their external borrowing with dollar-denominated loans to local companies. Some loans went to companies with export revenues, but many went to companies that were constructing office buildings and investing in local real estate (a part of the nontraded goods sector).[37] This created a real estate bubble. When Thailand could no longer finance its large current account deficit by taking out additional short-term loans—or by selling its reserves—it had to abandon its peg. As the real value of the baht fell and the real value of foreign-currency debts increased, much of the economy fell into deep financial distress.[38] When Thai firms went belly-up, the banks and financial institutions that lent to them also experienced financial distress.

The end result was substantial pressure on the finances of Thailand's government, even though the government itself entered the crisis with relatively little domestic or external debt. The government guaranteed payment on the cross-border liabilities of commercial banks, though not the finance companies, during the crisis. This guarantee, combined with the size of the Bank of Thailand's forward sales, put pressure on the government's reserves. The cost of protecting depositors from the banking system's large losses also significantly increased the government's domestic debt.

---

37. Allen et al. (2002), drawing on the Bank of Thailand's work, estimate that the Thai banking system held $7.6 billion in foreign assets ($2.6 billion in liquid foreign assets) against its $32 billion in short-term foreign loans. The banking system's domestic lending to Thai firms in foreign currency closed the "gap" between its external liabilities and external assets.

38. Allen et al. (2002), drawing on the Bank of Thailand's work, estimate that $94 billion of the Thai nonfinancial sector's $268 billion in precrisis total liabilities were denominated in foreign currency—$62 billion in loans to nonresidents and $32 billion in loans to domestic banks. The baht's devaluation dramatically increased the burden of these debts. The debts were fixed in dollar terms, but Thailand's GDP fell from $182 billion in 1996 to $151 billion in 1997 and $112 billion in 1998.

Indonesia

Indonesia's current account deficit and currency overvaluation were not large relative to those of Thailand and Malaysia. Indonesia's banks also had comparatively little external debt, not because they were unusually virtuous but because their weaknesses were widely known. Most international banks preferred to lend directly to Indonesian firms. The state banks in particular had accumulated large, unrecognized losses before the crisis.

Consequently, the core mismatch in Indonesia arose in the corporate sector. International banks lent, in foreign currency and at short term, to many Indonesian firms,[39] creating a large maturity mismatch both in the corporate sector and on the national balance sheet. Indonesia was a major exporter, but during the period of currency stability that preceded the crisis, many firms without export earnings took out foreign-currency loans. For example, an infamous Indonesian taxi firm that Suharto's daughter owned took on large dollar debts. The firms with export revenues were not necessarily the ones with the dollar debts.

Indonesia offers a powerful example of two phenomena: (1) the pressure on the currency that can come from firms' hedging demands and (2) the broad economic collapse that is possible if an external crisis is combined with a domestic bank run and political instability leading to policy uncertainty. After Indonesia let its currency float, Indonesian firms—as well as some banks that also needed foreign exchange—entered the currency market to buy dollars both to hedge against further falls in the rupiah and to repay their short-term debts, which put additional pressure on the currency. This hedging demand fueled a vicious circle: in thin markets, the demand for hedges resulted in large currency movements, which made hedging imperative. Finding a solution to these problems was more difficult than in Korea: An outright government guarantee would have made negotiating a rollover easier, since it would have avoided the need to negotiate agreements with a number of different firms with different financial positions. It also would have been an enormous bailout of Suharto's cronies who had borrowed from abroad. This is discussed in more detail in later chapters.

Domestic capital flight added to the pressure that the need to hedge foreign currency debt placed on the exchange rate. Initial bank closures were handled poorly and no doubt contributed to the development of a domestic bank run (Sachs and Radelet 1998).[40] Indonesia's problems, how-

39. Indonesian firms owed $39.7 billion to external creditors, roughly thrice the $12.4 billion banks owed. In contrast, Korean banks had taken out $67.3 billion in external loans, more than twice the $31.7 billion nonbanks owed (see Sachs and Radelet 1998).

40. The Independent Evaluation Office of the IMF (IEO 2003) concluded that the risks of bank runs were not properly assessed.

ever, were more profound: The crisis called into question the continued viability of Indonesia's political and economic model, which was based in large part on close ties between the president, the president's family, and a group of wealthy and often ethnically Chinese businessmen. Concerns about the political viability of Suharto's government and growing ethnic tensions contributed to large-scale domestic capital flight as well—those who had profited most from the old political and economic order wanted to move their savings out of the country.[41]

The Bank of Indonesia lent large quantities of rupiah to distressed banks facing pressure from the domestic run, fueling the currency's collapse. A substantial real depreciation was necessary to swing the current account from a deficit to a substantial surplus, but the rupiah went into free fall and ended up overshooting its equilibrium value. This increased the real burden of the debts of Indonesian firms that had borrowed from abroad and the real burden of the government of Indonesia's own debts, owed largely to the multilateral development banks. Widespread corporate distress augmented the preexisting weaknesses in the banking system and resulted in an extremely costly (56 percent of GDP) bailout, further adding to the government's debt. Indonesia's public debt to GDP ratio rose from 25 percent of GDP in 1997 to over 83 percent of GDP by 2002.

Korea

Korea had a smaller current account deficit than Thailand, and its currency was less overvalued. Korea's external debt burden was also substantially smaller than that of either Thailand or Indonesia. Korea had two core sources of financial fragility. First, its domestic banks had lent heavily to often overleveraged *chaebol*, threatening the banking system with large losses: By mid-1997, even before the currency crisis and investor run exacerbated the crisis, 7 out of the top 30 *chaebol* were bankrupt or in severe financial distress. Second, Korea, like other Asian economies, had financed current account deficits with short-term external debt, not through equity or FDI. The bias toward debt and against FDI was a product of policy: The government of Korea had opted to allow local banks to borrow from abroad before it lifted restrictions on FDI, a particularly dangerous way of sequencing capital account liberalization. The result was a clear mismatch between the short-term external borrowing of the financial sector and the liquid foreign-currency reserves of both the financial sector and the government.

When foreign creditors began cutting back on their interbank lines in the fall of 1997, the central bank started depositing its foreign-currency

41. See Chua (2002) on the role of economically dominant ethnic minorities in some financial and political crises.

reserves in the local banking system. These deposits supplied the banks with the foreign currency they needed to avoid default for a while. However, the government lacked the reserves to back all maturing bank lines on its own and, as more of the government's reserves were committed to the banking system, the run only accelerated. At the end of 1997, Korea had only $5 billion in reserves and more than $20 billion in remaining short-term interbank debts. The fact that most external borrowing was channeled through the banking system, however, did make it easier to resolve Korea's crisis. A government guarantee of all cross-border lines allowed the government to negotiate for the entire banking system. This experience is covered in detail in Chapter 4.

Malaysia

Like other East Asian crisis countries, Malaysia had a soft peg, little public debt, a large current account deficit without a large fiscal deficit, and a domestic credit boom. However, in other ways, it was somewhat less vulnerable than other East Asian crisis countries. A larger fraction of its current account deficit had been financed with FDI and portfolio equity investments rather than with external debt, and less external debt meant both a smaller currency mismatch and a smaller maturity mismatch. Malaysia's ratio of short-term debt to reserves was 94 percent, well below the ratios in Thailand, Indonesia, and Korea.

While Malaysia experienced a sharp currency crisis, its banking and corporate crisis was less severe than in other crisis countries.[42] It was able to avoid defaulting on its smaller stock of short-term external debt without borrowing from the IMF. However, Malaysia was not immune from the region's broader troubles: Like other countries, a boom in local lending had fueled a general boom in local asset prices, and the country experienced a sharp recession when capital inflows dried up. Pressure on the exchange rate continued well after Malaysia let the ringgit float. In response to renewed currency pressures in the summer of 1998, the government repegged its currency to the US dollar in September 1998 and imposed draconian—and controversial—capital controls.[43]

42. The estimated fiscal cost of its banking crisis was 14 percent of its GDP, relative to 21 percent in Korea, 19 percent in Mexico, and 56 percent in Indonesia.

43. For a sympathetic view of the Malaysian controls, see Rodrik and Kaplan (2001) and Krugman (1998b). Others have argued that those controls do not explain the successful stabilization of markets and reduction in domestic interest rates, as external conditions in late 1998—the deleveraging of international investors after Russia's default and Long-Term Capital Management's troubles—eliminated the downward pressures on most East Asian currencies and asset markets. We consider the merits of capital controls in chapter 6.

Russia

Russia's crisis is unique for several reasons. First, it was the only country to experience a combined currency, banking, and sovereign debt crisis in spite of the absence of a current account deficit. Rather than going from a current account deficit to a current account balance or surplus, Russia went from an overall balanced current account—with substantial inflows from external investors offsetting substantial capital flight by local residents—to a significant surplus. Second, Russia was hardly booming before its crisis: Its debt problems emerged in the context of the prolonged economic slump associated with its transition to a market economy. Third, Russia's financial crisis, despite being a combined currency, banking, and sovereign debt crisis, did not result in further severe fall in output. The downturn was less sharp than in other episodes, and Russia's real economy started recovering in early 1999.

Russia's vulnerability had many sources:

- *an oil price shock.* Asia's crisis reduced world oil demand and the market price of oil. This had a significant impact on Russia, given its concentration in oil and energy exports.
- *persistent fiscal problems.* Revenues never matched expenditures during the transition, resulting in large fiscal deficits. Russia's precrisis government debt was not as high as some other crisis countries, but its revenues were low, and its debt stock was growing particularly rapidly.[44] Russia sold very high-yielding domestic debt securities—the GKOs—to finance its fiscal deficits.
- *a pegged exchange rate.* Russia's exchange rate peg turned high-yielding, short-term domestic-currency debt into high-yielding, short-term foreign-currency debt so long as investors got out before the peg collapsed. This resulted in a severe mismatch between Russia's actual reserves and the potential demands on them if nonresident investors in the local debt market (and domestic investors fleeing local assets) wanted to exit.

While Russia was running large fiscal deficits before its crisis, it did not experience a classic first generation–style crisis where a fiscal deficit fuels a domestic boom and inflation, which then produces an overvalued real exchange rate. The fiscal deficit occurred in the context of shrinking domestic demand and was financed by selling government debt, not print-

44. Russia's debt to GDP numbers (52 percent in 1997) did not make Russia look obviously insolvent. The debt to revenue ratio is often a better measure, though, which was above 147 percent in 1997.

ing money. This resulted in a bubble in the government debt market, not a booming domestic economy. However, Russia's precrisis equilibrium hinged on its ability to attract external inflows, largely "hot money" invested in short-term government debt, to offset ongoing capital outflows stemming from very large capital flight by domestic investors. This capital flight was one of the key elements of the Russian crisis. During the 1998 crisis, external inflows turned into outflows, and resident capital flight accelerated, triggering a race to get out of the country's government debt market and a run on the currency.

Russia's difficulties provide an interesting example of how balance sheet risks interlink. In Brazil and Turkey, the local banking system held a large part of the domestic-currency debt. Since the banks financed these positions by taking in local-currency deposits, they did not need to hedge against currency risk. The foreign investors that invested in Russia's short-term ruble debt (the famous GKOs), however, often wanted to hedge against the risk that the ruble would be devalued. Russia's private banks met this demand and sold insurance against a fall in the ruble to foreign investors. The resulting forward contracts obligated the Russian banks to sell dollars on a given date at a fixed price, even if the ruble had been devalued. Unfortunately, the banking system was in no position to take on this currency risk. In effect, the Russian government had a maturity mismatch in domestic currency, and the Russian banking system had a maturity (as well as a currency) mismatch in foreign currency, as the local banks lacked liquid dollar assets that would enable them to honor their commitment to provide dollars to external investors at a fixed price if the currency collapsed. The government of Russia imposed capital controls to protect the local banking system after its default, as the banking system was clearly unable to honor these contracts.[45]

The absence of a severe contraction in output after Russia's triple crisis has a simple explanation: Russia's banking crisis did not have an impact on output because Russian banks never were in the business of providing loans to productive corporate firms. Many of them were investment, rather than commercial, banks. And most did little more than make speculative bets on the exchange rate and the government debt market (GKOs).[46] Since Russia's banks were effectively hedge funds speculating in government paper rather than lenders of funds to real firms, most Russian firms were self-financed. The devaluation helped them more than

45. Sixty percent of Russia's government debt was in foreign currency or foreign currency–linked; the debt to GDP ratio sharply rose to over 92 percent in 1999 after the currency crisis. Before the crisis, Russian banks had a net open foreign position close to 10 percent of total deposits.

46. See Freeland (2000) for a superb account of Russia's transition and the 1998 crisis as viewed from Moscow.

the collapse of the banking system hurt them. A strong rebound in world oil prices in late 1999 and 2000 also helped: Among other things, higher oil prices made it easier for the government to balance its budget after the crisis.

Brazil

Brazil experienced two crises: one in 1998 and 1999 and a second in 2001–02. Brazil's choices in its 1998–99 crisis created the vulnerabilities that led to its 2001–02 crisis, so they are worth examining together.

Brazil's vulnerability in 1998 stemmed from features that should be familiar: A semi-fixed exchange rate (formally a crawling peg) plus inflation inertia had led to an overvalued currency; the resulting current account deficit was financed in part by FDI and also in part by increased cross-border bank borrowing; and a large fiscal deficit both contributed to the current account imbalance and led to the accumulation of domestic and external debt. The eventual collapse of Brazil's peg in 1999 should not have been a surprise: The capital flows needed to support an overvalued currency had disappeared. What makes Brazil's 1999 currency collapse interesting is that it did not lead to a banking crisis, an ensuing credit crunch, and a severe recession. Output recovered soon after Brazil's 1999 crisis.

In the summer of 1998, both Brazil's banks and firms had large maturity and currency mismatches on their balance sheets. Domestic bank deposits and bank loans were largely denominated in the local currency, but both banks and firms had taken on large amounts of cross-border debt. There is little doubt that a currency crisis in the summer of 1998 would have had a severe impact on private-sector balance sheets. However, in the months leading to the collapse of the peg, the central bank sold more than $40 billion in reserves to defend the peg. This allowed most private financial and corporate firms to hedge their currency exposure—whether by increasing their holdings of foreign assets or by paying down their external debt. The government also increased its issuance of domestic dollar-linked debt, helping banks and firms hedge against the risk of a devaluation.

However, selling the government's reserves (its key foreign-currency asset) and increasing its foreign-currency debt sharply increased the government's own currency mismatch. Brazil's devaluation, consequently, resulted in a large increase in the government's debts. In effect, Brazil bailed out its banks and corporations before the crisis by using taxpayer resources to let them hedge their currency exposure. Indeed, many banks had bet that the real would fall and obtained large profits out of the crisis. This avoided a banking/corporate crisis—a crisis that in all probability would have led to larger liquidation and output costs and required an even larger ex-post bailout.

Because a private-sector "balance sheet" crisis did not accompany Brazil's devaluation, it experienced a smaller fall in output than most of the crisis countries. Its currency did not overshoot, and it continued to run a current account deficit. To the surprise of many, Brazil's devaluation did not lead to the reemergence of inflation, thanks to the adoption of a credible inflation targeting regime.[47] Brazil took advantage of years of relative calm after 1999 until 2001 to start retiring its domestic foreign currency–denominated debts. The government balance sheet improved (both in the share of foreign currency–linked debt and the maturity of the public debt) until the 2001 Argentine crisis.[48]

But Brazil also retained significant vulnerabilities that set the stage for its 2001–02 crisis. It lost about half its foreign exchange reserves in the 1999 crisis (it started with around $70 billion in net reserves), and it was not able to replace most of those reserves in 2000 or 2001. The stock of public debt to GDP rose from 40 percent of GDP in 1997 to over 72 percent of GDP in 2002, despite a significant fiscal adjustment. The maturity and currency composition of its debt improved slightly after its crisis, but most of Brazil's debt was still indexed either to the overnight rate or the dollar. As Argentina's crisis deepened, Brazil renewed issuance of large amounts of foreign currency–linked debt to meet the demand for hedging products and, effectively, to intervene in the foreign exchange market. The combination of investor jitters following Argentina's worse-than-expected crisis and concerns about a victory of the left's presidential candidate, Luiz Inacio Lula Da Silva, resulted in a significant fall in foreign financing and the real's value. Brazil responded first by drawing on a "precautionary" credit line it had set with the IMF in 2001, and when that proved insufficient, it obtained a second major—$30 billion—IMF rescue in 2002.

The ultimate success of Brazil's decision to avoid a financial crisis in its private sector in 1998 by transferring key risks to the government remains an open question so long as Brazil's debt levels remain high. The combination of strong demand for important Brazilian exports (soybeans and iron ore) from China, low interest rates in major economies, and a sound fiscal policy by President Lula may allow domestic rates to come down and allow Brazil to both rebuild its reserves and slowly unwind its dollar debts. But the fiscal cost of the exchange rate insurance that the govern-

47. See Truman (2003) for a systematic study on the experience with inflation targeting in emerging-market economies.

48. The share of foreign currency–linked debt in public debt rose from 9 percent at the end of 1996 to 15 percent in 1998 and 24 percent in 1999. It fell to 22 percent in 2000 and rose again to 28 percent in 2001. It remained at this high level through the fall of 2002.

ment offered Brazil's private sector during the 1999 and 2002 crises and the high domestic interest rates risk contributing to some form of government debt crisis. Brazil's government debt has risen to potentially unsustainable levels—ratios of both debt to GDP and debt to revenues are high. The high external debt to exports ratio continues to be a concern as well.

Ukraine

Ukraine's 1998 crisis has many parallels with the Russian crisis. Before 1998, it maintained a pegged exchange rate and, like Russia, was able to finance its budget deficits in part by attracting external investors to buy its high-yielding local-currency debt (and was even able to issue foreign-currency debt in international markets). Its overall economic management hardly won plaudits: Like other former Soviet states, output fell during the first phase of its economic transition. Following the Russian crisis in 1998, the exchange rate peg became unsustainable, and Ukraine clearly was not going to be able to convince its external investors to refinance, at least not voluntarily, the government's maturing external debts. Ukraine tried to obtain cash relief through selective ad hoc restructurings in 1998–99, before launching a more successful comprehensive restructuring in early 2000. Ukraine's overall debt was moderate—only 40 percent of GDP—not so much because of Ukraine's fiscal virtue but because Ukraine lagged behind Russia in obtaining access to external financing, and Russia's crisis occurred before Ukraine had time to run up a large debt stock. Government debt was a relatively small share of bank assets (about 14 percent): This helped Ukraine avoid a bank holiday during its sovereign restructuring.[49]

Pakistan

Pakistan's problems were in many ways distinct from those of other emerging economies with payments crises.[50] The country was certainly heavily indebted—its 1998 public debt to GDP ratio was over 100 percent—and like many emerging economies, it had to support this debt off a low revenue base (debt was over 600 percent of revenues in 1998). It typically ran large budget deficits, and its overall economic performance was poor. However, Pakistan was not a major player in international capital

49. The corresponding shares were 31 percent in Russia, 30 percent in Pakistan, and 21 percent in Argentina. This intersectoral linkage (large share of banks' assets in government paper) is an essential link between sovereign and banking distress in many crises.

50. Many details on these two episodes can be found in IMF (February 2002), a study of the experience with four sovereign debt-restructuring cases (Pakistan, Ukraine, Russia, and Argentina).

markets: It owed most of its sovereign external debt to other governments (the Paris Club) and multilateral financial institutions. Pakistan's decision to perform a nuclear test in May 1998, and the economic crisis stemming from the ensuing sanctions, triggered its financial crisis. To stem outflows, the government froze all foreign-currency deposits, including nonresident deposits (Pakistan, like India, tried hard to attract deposits from Pakistanis working abroad), and generally tightened its extensive capital controls. Following its nuclear test, Pakistan was unable to meet its external debt payments to the Paris Club group of creditors, and the Paris Club conditioned its own restructuring on the restructuring of Pakistan's modest stock of eurobonds.

Ecuador

Ecuador has many of the typical problems of a small, heavily indebted, and poorly managed economy beset by persistent political conflict. Low government revenues (only 14.6 percent of GDP in 1997) contributed to persistent budget deficits. While Ecuador's Brady restructuring was slightly more generous than most, it still left Ecuador with a large debt hangover from the 1980s crisis. Public debt stocks were relatively high overall (60 percent of GDP in 1997) and very high (412 percent) relative to government revenues. External debt was also very high even after the Brady debt restructuring.

The combination of a large debt stock and heavy dependence on a few commodity exports left Ecuador vulnerable to external shocks. A series of such shocks hit the economy in 1998: The weather phenomenon El Nino reduced the output of Ecuador's fisheries (hurting banks based in the coastal provinces) at the same time that a fall in global oil prices reduced Ecuador's export revenues. Currency mismatches were widespread: All of the external public debt was denominated in foreign currency, banks had large net open foreign-currency exposures, and by 1997 two-thirds of the nonfinancial private-sector debts (many in nontraded sectors) were in foreign currency. The banks also lacked sufficient access to dollar liquidity to match their dollar deposits.

These external shocks pushed an economy with few buffers into a crisis: They led to a banking crisis in 1998, widespread capital flight, and sharp falls in the value of the exchange rate. A bank run in March 1999 forced the authorities to freeze bank deposits. The cost of the bank bailout (the fiscal cost of the bailout eventually amounted to more than 24 percent of GDP) added to the financial troubles of the government, which was simultaneously feeling the pinch from lower oil revenues and the increase in the real debt burden that followed the sharp depreciation of the currency. The government fell behind on domestic payments and eventually defaulted on its domestic and external debt in mid-1999. The default only added to pressures on the currency, and in desperation, the president (soon to be pushed out of power given the persistent political instability of the country) decided to phase out its local currency and dollarize, i.e. formally adopt the US dollar as its currency in 2000.[51]

Turkey

Turkey combined most of the classic sources of vulnerability:

- A quasi currency board introduced as part of a plan to use a forward-looking crawling peg exchange rate—to anchor an anti-inflation exchange rate–based stabilization program—went wrong as wage and price inertia in 2000 led to a real appreciation and a growing current account imbalance.
- The banking system bet on continued exchange rate stability and borrowed heavily from abroad, worsening the gap between the banking system's short-term foreign-currency debts and available foreign-currency liquidity.
- Severe fiscal problems led to the rapid accumulation of public debt. A large share of the government's debt took the form of very short-term treasury bills that were placed in the domestic financial system, leaving the government's debt-servicing costs vulnerable to surges in domestic interest rates.
- Hidden losses in parts of the banking system, whether from state banks used well before the crisis to provide low-cost credit to favored sectors or from shady credit practices and connected lending in private banks.

In February 2001, a public spat between the president and prime minister—as political conflicts simmered on how to deal with the banking crisis—triggered a run on the currency. In three days, Turkey lost one-third of its foreign exchange reserves as domestic and foreign investors dumped Turkish lira in a stampede to buy dollars and euros. The break in the peg triggered a banking and corporate crisis, a credit crunch, and a sharp output contraction in 2001. A new large IMF loan replenished the government's foreign reserves and allowed the banking system to repay its cross-border credit lines.

However, the combination of the exchange rate depreciation's balance sheet impact, the cost of cleaning up the banking system, and the high real rates needed to attract investors—mostly local—into the government debt market threatened to quickly generate a government debt crisis. Some of

51. See Jacome (2004) for a detailed account of Ecuador's crisis.

the increase in Turkey's debt during its 2001 crisis stemmed from the delayed realization of losses in the state banking system; another portion of the increase came from the need to recapitalize private banks that had incurred large losses speculating on the Turkish lira and the government bond market. The combination of an IMF program and an impressive fiscal adjustment avoided default in 2001 and 2002. Conditions stabilized in 2003 and 2004, but real risks remain. Debt ratios are high, particularly in relation to government revenue; the sharp primary adjustment may not be sustainable over time; and future shocks to growth and the real interest rate may make the debt dynamics unsustainable again.

Argentina

Argentina's crisis stemmed from four major vulnerabilities:

- The currency board tied the dollar to the peso, resulting in an increasingly overvalued currency as the dollar appreciated and particularly after the Brazilian real tumbled. Some of the significant overvaluation stemmed from inflationary inertia in the currency board's early years; but in the period immediately preceding the crisis, Argentina was experiencing deflation, not inflation, as a way to undo the currency overvaluation.[52]
- The external imbalances the overvalued currency created were increasingly difficult to finance. The burst of privatization in the first part of the 1990s had faded by 1998, in part because many of the best assets had been sold off. The government's external debt issuance was increasingly financing the current account deficit. Argentina's current account deficit was not large on an absolute scale but was very large in relation to the country's small export sector—the more relevant measure.
- Persistent fiscal deficits (and a partially botched social security privatization) led to an accumulation of a large stock of public debt, particularly as the economy began to shrink and interest rates rose after 1998.
- Pervasive liability dollarization produced an enormous currency mismatch. Almost all of Argentina's domestic and external government debt was denominated in dollars. Most domestic Argentine bank deposits were in dollars, and Argentine firms and households usually borrowed from the banking system in dollars. The scale of these cur-

52. See Hausmann and Velasco (2002) for an argument that Argentina's real exchange rate was not enormously overvalued. See Perry and Serven (2003) for an argument that Argentina's exchange rate was overvalued by as much as 40 percent.

> rency mismatches was so large in relation to Argentina's small export sector that it was effectively impossible for most borrowers in Argentina to hedge against exchange rate risk. The banking system's underlying currency mismatch was disguised, not eliminated, by transferring currency risk to the private and government sectors, even though the banks were formally matched, currencywise.[53]

These intrinsic vulnerabilities made it extremely difficult for Argentina to adjust to a series of unexpected external shocks. Argentina depended more than most other emerging economies on the international sovereign bond market, so it was hurt more than most by the Russian shock in 1998. External bonds were both more difficult and more costly to issue. Global commodity prices were weak, and the country's terms of trade worsened. Brazil's 1999 devaluation made Brazil's products more competitive than Argentina's in the markets of Europe, the United States, and Buenos Aires. New FDI tended to go to Brazil rather than Argentina. The appreciation of the US dollar from 1998 to 2001 resulted in a nominal and real appreciation of the peso relative to Argentina's other trading partners. The 175 basis point increase in US short-term interest rates from mid-1999 to mid-2000 also hurt when the Argentine economy was contracting.[54]

It slowly became clear that Argentina was unable to adjust to these shocks. Its macroeconomic hands were tied: It could not adjust its currency peg without bankrupting many firms and the government, it lacked an independent monetary policy, and its high existing debts left it unable to run a countercyclical fiscal policy. Adjusting to these shocks through deflation was slow and painful: Labor markets were relatively rigid, and the domestic regulatory regime of many utilities allowed them to index their prices to the dollar, introducing another rigidity into the economy. Domestic deflation effectively increased the real burden of domestic dollar debts: Firms that had borrowed in dollars but sold domestically to Argentines saw their domestic revenues fall while their debt load stayed constant.[55] Most real investment headed toward sectors sheltered from external competition (and often from deflation because of dollar-indexed pricing), such as energy utilities and telecoms, not toward the traded sectors that needed to grow to help Argentina reduce its underlying currency

---

53. Goldstein and Turner (2004) have developed a new measure of currency mismatches that includes mismatches from domestic liability dollarization. According to this indicator, Argentina had the largest currency mismatch among all emerging-market economies.

54. See Mussa (2002b) for a systematic analysis of the Argentine crisis and the role the IMF played in this crisis.

55. Roubini (2001a) noted that real depreciation through domestic price adjustment produces the same increase in the real debt burden of foreign-currency debt as real depreciation through a fall in the nominal exchange rate. However, domestic prices tend to adjust more slowly, and thus the increase in real debt burdens occurs more gradually.

mismatch and external imbalance. And the coalition government that emerged from the 1999 election was fragile with a weak and indecisive leader in President Fernando de la Rua. Thus, the government's macro and structural reform program was only partially enacted.

Consequently, the real exchange rate adjustment needed as capital inflows faltered came slowly, through a painful process of domestic deflation, which increased the real burden of servicing the government's hard-currency debt even as the economy stalled and then slipped backwards. Adjusting fiscal policy more to prevent falling revenues and rising debt-servicing costs from generating a bigger deficit eventually became economically, socially, and politically unsustainable. Devaluation and default became unavoidable.[56]

It is hard to say that Argentina experienced a "sudden stop" in international capital flows because of fickle international markets. Rather, Argentina's ability to access international markets gradually eroded from 1999 on, when external investors first declined to provide new financing as Argentina went through the slow process of deflation and then sought to reduce their exposure. However, Argentina's reliance on long-term bond finance made it difficult for many external investors to run quickly. The "sudden stop" in Argentina, if there was one, came when domestic residents were no longer willing to keep their savings in Argentina and started pulling their savings out of the domestic banking system in mass in mid-2001.

Argentina's maturity mismatch is worth exploring in some depth, in part because standard measures that compared short-term external debt to reserves did not capture it. While Argentina's government debt had a relatively long average maturity, at least by the standards of most emerging markets, a large debt stock meant that every year Argentina needed to refinance a certain fraction of its existing debt. Most of the central bank's reserves were pledged to back the currency in circulation through the currency board and were not available to help the government cover its maturing long-term bonds. Argentina's international short-term debt to reserves ratio consequently overstated the reserves that were actually available to cover the government's maturing external debts.

The international debt to reserve ratio also did not take into account the potential demands for foreign exchange that could arise from a dollarized domestic banking system. Argentina's banks held a large number of dollar deposits and, as is typically the case, the banking system's dollar loans—

56. The real depreciation associated with floating threatened to dramatically increase the real burden of firms' dollar debt, household's mortgages, and dollar-denominated utility contracts. Clearly these contracts needed to be renegotiated in some manner. Argentina opted for an across-the-board redenomination of all domestic contracts into pesos (pesification), and the government defaulted on its remaining international debts. Most firms also defaulted on their international debt and entered into negotiations with their creditors. These steps are discussed in later chapters.

its assets—were longer-term and less liquid than its liabilities. The ability of Argentina's central bank to act as a lender of last resort was limited because most of its reserves were pledged to back the currency. The central bank was aware of this risk: It had insisted that the banks maintain significant liquid dollar reserves, and had arranged a "contingent repo line" that would allow the banks to "repo" or sell their holdings of Argentina's international sovereign bonds to a consortium of international banks to obtain dollars (cash) in the event of a run. These defenses, however, did not prove to be robust. When the government had difficulty rolling over its external debt, it turned—not surprisingly—to the banking system for emergency liquidity, eroding the bank's liquidity buffer. The contingent credit line proved to be a double-edged sword. The government was concerned that its use would be counterproductive, as drawing on it could be interpreted as a signal of trouble,[57] and it did not provide anywhere near enough liquidity to assure payment to most depositors in the event of a generalized run.[58]

Uruguay

Uruguay had many of the same vulnerabilities as Argentina, as well as the disadvantage of being in a bad "neighborhood": During its 2002 crisis, both its large neighbors—Brazil and Argentina—were experiencing financial difficulties. Uruguay maintained a fixed peg before its crisis—a peg that was unsustainable following the collapse of Argentina's currency board and the sharp fall in the Brazilian real. Uruguay's banking system was heavily dollarized. The country's banks had taken in dollar deposits from both Argentines and Uruguayans, but neither the banks nor the Uruguayan government held enough liquid dollar assets to be able to assure payment to all depositors in the event of a run. Uruguay's banks had a smaller exposure to the Uruguayan government than Argentine banks had to the Argentine government. They also held a larger share of their assets abroad. These comparative strengths were not enough to avoid a run: Argentine citizens started pulling their money out of Uruguay's banks in mass after bank deposits in Argentina were frozen, and Uruguayans

57. The size of the repo line also shrunk dramatically during the summer of 2002. Only certain bonds were eligible to be "repoed" through the facility. Argentina retired many of those bonds through the Brady restructuring for eurobond exchanges and retired many more in the megaswap. Poor coordination between the central bank and the ministry of finance contributed to Argentina's inability to make sure that the new bonds it issued in the megaswap were eligible to be repoed. Consequently, this facility was not able to provide significant emergency liquidity in late 2001. Argentina did draw on part of this facility in the summer of 2001 when it secured the augmentation of its IMF package.

58. See Lagos (2002) and IMF (October 2003) for a more detailed account of Argentina's crisis.

started to pull their own deposits out as well. As in Argentina, financial dollarization created extensive currency mismatches: Banks generally lent in dollars to both local firms and the government, and the real burden of these debts increased sharply after the devaluation. The usual combination of a currency crisis, banking distress, and a credit crunch combined with a sharp recession in Uruguay's largest trading partner to produce a large output contraction in 2002.

Uruguay entered its crisis with a slightly lower debt to GDP ratio than Argentina, but its debt was still substantial, and it swelled rapidly after the devaluation.[59] The central bank clearly lacked the reserves needed either to cover the government's financing needs or to act as a lender of last resort to Uruguay's financial system, forcing Uruguay to seek very large financial support from the IMF and, eventually, to restructure the government's external debt.

Conclusions

The weaknesses that gave rise to last decade's currency, financial, corporate, banking, and sovereign debt crises have not disappeared from the world economy.

Many emerging economies have significant government debt burdens and large financing needs. The list of countries with large debts includes those that have already experienced a crisis, notably Argentina, Brazil, Turkey, and Uruguay, as well as those that have, to date, avoided crises. However countries with high levels of debt—like Jamaica with a public debt to GDP ratio in excess of 150 percent—and with an increasing public debt ratio (like Colombia with a ratio in excess of 50 percent of GDP), a large fiscal deficit, growing domestic and external financing needs, and uncertain political ability to make the adjustments needed to stabilize their debt ratios are intrinsically vulnerable.[60] Lebanon remains a crisis waiting to happen.[61] Even a number of former transition economies in central Europe are slowly building imbalances that could create medium-term vulnerabilities: the Czech Republic, Croatia, Poland, and Hungary

59. The public debt ratio to GDP rose to a very high level increasing from 37 percent of GDP in 2001 to 76 percent in 2002 and from 191 percent of revenues in 2001 to 381 percent in 2002.

60. See Arbelaez, Guerra, and Roubini (2005) for an analysis of debt sustainability in Colombia.

61. Lebanon recently showed some signs of stabilization due to both to a French-led bailout package and, in all probability, a reallocation of Middle Eastern savings away from the United States to local financial centers after September 11, 2001. However, its extraordinary debt burden, fixed exchange rate, and dependence on domestic banks to finance the government still leave it exceptionally vulnerable, particularly as its government appears unable to generate the significant primary adjustment needed to stabilize its debt to GDP ratio.

all have fiscal and current account deficits. While these economies' public and external debt stock ratios are not very large yet, they are increasing rapidly and are increasingly being financed in ways that create future vulnerabilities.

Maturity and currency mismatches remain endemic in emerging markets. Emerging markets are defined in many ways by the difficulties they face in borrowing long term in the local currency and thus by the heavy use of either a foreign currency in financial contracts or very short-term domestic-currency borrowing. Whether the predominance of financial contracts denominated in a foreign currency is a product of hard to eliminate "original sin" or something that can be altered through sustained implementation of sound policies, it remains an important source of vulnerability in emerging markets (Goldstein and Turner 2004). Countries with relatively high debt burdens and significant maturity and currency mismatches on their balance sheets are constantly at risk of slipping into crisis.[62]

There are fewer fixed pegs in emerging economies, but those that remain are vulnerable. The Dominican Republic provides the most recent example of the dynamics associated with the collapse of a fixed rate peg in countries with extensive liability dollarization: The currency adjustment aggravated the country's banking crisis (originally triggered by widespread fraud) and led to a sharp sudden increase in the public debt ratio. Floating no doubt helps emerging economies navigate shocks if the float is reasonably free; but pressure on a float, including pressure stemming from the need to hedge foreign-currency debt, clearly risks leading to exchange rate moves that push those actors that are unable to hedge their foreign-currency exposure (including the government) into bankruptcy.

Even the fast-growing superstars of the emerging world—India and China—have significant vulnerabilities. Both have pegged or heavily managed exchange rates and weak banking systems. India has relied on its domestic financial system to finance large, persistent fiscal deficits. Public debt comprises over a third of the assets of the banking system; as in Argentina, Turkey, Ecuador, and Russia, bank financing of public deficits risks eventually destroying the banking system. China's debt levels would increase sharply, should the banking system's losses ever be formally recognized: Nonperforming loans are officially estimated to be about 42 percent of GDP and are likely to be significantly larger. Both countries also have important strengths: little external debt, large stocks of reserves, and vibrant economies. Their strong external position mitigates their domestic financial weaknesses. Both countries also have relatively closed capital accounts, which has limited the risk of domestic capital flight triggering a run on the banks and the currency. However, success-

62. See Rogoff, Reinhart, and Savastano (2003) for an analysis of how high debt ratios lead to "debt intolerance" and eventually default.

fully transitioning from closed to more open financial systems poses real challenges for both countries.

No doubt, emerging economies find it more difficult than advanced economies to borrow in ways that provide a country with more time to adjust to a range of shocks—including shifts in investor sentiment—without falling into a crisis. A history of financial and monetary instability—perhaps supplemented by structure—makes it harder for many, though not all, emerging economies to borrow in their own currency for long terms.[63] The solution here is simple: Countries that cannot borrow in ways that provide a cushion against a crisis need to borrow less.

Crises and runs—whether on banks, governments, countries, or currencies—stem from a combination of policy vulnerabilities, financial vulnerabilities, and investor behavior. The risk of a crisis increases along with the size of the borrower's existing debt, particularly its stock of short-term debt, and its need to take on new debt to cover ongoing deficits. So long as these vulnerabilities are present, unexpected domestic political developments, worse than expected economic data, a crisis in a neighboring country, or any of the myriad potential shocks all can trigger financial trouble. The withdrawal of some short-term creditors may lead others to want to pull out as well.

The risk of a reversal in capital flows cannot be separated from the strength of country's economic policies, just as the impact of a sudden swing in capital flows depends on how well an economy is prepared to withstand such pressures. The risk is not so much that a run will bring down a fundamentally sound economy. Weaknesses obscured when global markets are more forgiving are still weaknesses. Rather the risk is of a run overwhelming a country with real but potentially correctable problems, leaving it—and its creditors—worse off.

63. See Eichengreen, Hausmann, and Panizza (2002) for the idea that imperfections in capital markets make it impossible for emerging-market economies to borrow abroad long term in their own currency (the "original sin" hypothesis) and Goldstein and Turner (2004) for a challenge to the argument that external liability dollarization is structural and irreversible.

3

Analytical Literature on Crisis Resolution

The debate on emerging-market crises resembles the debate on car accidents. Do car accidents occur because of bad luck, because of a random accident causing pile-ups on the highway, or because of reckless driving? Does the existence of car insurance encourage bad driving? If so, should we then ban car insurance or somehow limit it? Once an accident occurs, should we avoid sending an ambulance to help a reckless driver or perhaps just provide less medical insurance to strengthen the incentives for others to drive safely? Similarly, are emerging-market crises the product of bad luck (unexpected shocks), accidents in other emerging economies that cause the financial equivalent of a pile-up (contagion), or reckless policies in debtor countries and reckless lending by their creditors? Do IMF bailouts reduce the incentives for strong policies in emerging economies and sound investment decisions by creditors? If so, should the size and frequency of IMF bailouts be limited to encourage borrowers and lenders to adopt more prudent policies? Once a crisis occurs, how should policymakers resolve it? What should be the right mix of official support (bailouts), policy conditionality (adjustment), and coordinated rollovers or debt restructurings (bail ins)?

This chapter reviews the analytical models developed to answer these questions. Most models address one of the two core debates on crisis resolution: Does a debt restructuring need to be painful in order to create incentives for a country to pay rather than walk away from its debts, or do barriers to a restructuring just impose unwelcome costs when an unexpected shock makes a restructuring unavoidable? Does an international

Box 3.1 Defining moral hazard

Adverse selection and moral hazard are the two main market failures associated with the presence of insurance. Insurance companies worry that their client base will be biased toward those most at risk: A person who knows that he or she is sick has a particularly strong incentive to buy health insurance. This is the problem of *adverse selection*. Insurance companies also worry about that purchasing insurance will change the incentives of their clients: Car insurance can lead to more reckless driving, thus increasing the amount the insurance company has to pay out; fire insurance can lead homeowners to take fewer precautions. The risk that insurance will reduce incentives for prudent behavior by lowering expected losses is called *moral hazard*. Both adverse selection and moral hazard derive from *asymmetric information* (the insurer cannot fully observe the nature and behavior of the insured) and give rise to potential market failures—concerns about adverse selection and moral hazard can prevent mutually beneficial trade and contractual agreements from taking place.

Moral hazard enters the debate over how to respond to international financial crises in at least two ways. First, a lender has trouble monitoring how a borrower spends borrowed funds after making the loan, just as an insurance company has difficulty monitoring the behavior of its clients after it writes an insurance policy. The risk that a borrower will take out a loan that it has no intention of repaying is often called debtor moral hazard—it is analogous to a homeowner buying insurance and then setting fire to his home to collect on the policy. Debtor moral hazard arises in a game with just two parties—the borrower and the lender. A third party is not needed. Second, IMF lending to protect against the risk of a run can be thought of as a form of insurance: It protects both the borrower and its creditors from the risk of a run leading to an avoidable default. The implicit insurance associated with IMF lending, like the implicit insurance that emergency lending by domestic central banks create, therefore potentially could change the incentives of both the country, which is protected against the risk of running out of funds (debtor moral hazard), and its creditors, who are protected against the risk of a default (creditor moral hazard).

In practice, the IMF has a much greater capacity to assure that its lending does not distort the debtor's incentives than it does to assure that its lending does not distort the creditors' incentives. So long as IMF loans have to be repaid in full, a debtor that takes such a loan to repay its private debts is not reducing its debt burden or the amount of effort that it will ultimately have to make to repay its debts. Moreover, IMF loans are conditional on the debtor making the effort to assure repayment to the IMF (and in most cases to other creditors as well).[1] The availability of an international lender might lead

(box 3.1 continues next page)

source of emergency liquidity help stop the international analogue to a bank run from devastating basically sound economies, or does it lead countries to adopt poor policies and lenders to make imprudent loans in the anticipation of a bailout?

Many models lend themselves to extreme conclusions. Models that show how liquidity runs cause crises often conclude that the IMF needs to be transformed into a true international lender of last resort that can supply liquidity in unlimited quantities. Models that focus on the risk that countries and their creditors act recklessly because of the IMF's insurance against a default (the moral hazard problem) often conclude that the IMF's capacity to lend large sums should be curtailed, if not eliminated

Box 3.1 *(continued)*

the debtor to delay making the effort to service its debts or to rely more on short-term debt than it otherwise would, but it should not make it easier for the debtor to take out debts that it has no intention of repaying.

The presence of "liquidity" insurance is more likely to influence creditors' decisions: So long as creditors expect to be fully paid, no matter what, through IMF lending, they will be more willing than they should be to lend to a debtor pursuing risky policies. Consequently, the availability of "liquidity insurance" may make creditors more willing to finance a debtor that has too much short-term debt and is therefore vulnerable to a run: investing in high-risk projects that could also generate large losses or not currently running the kind of fiscal policy that provides strong assurances of its future payment capacity. Obviously, debtor and creditor moral hazard are interlinked: Without reckless lending by creditors, the debtor would not be able to obtain the financing needed to pursue reckless policies.

Finally, it is worth distinguishing between international moral hazard—the risk that IMF lending will reduce incentives for good debtor policy and for international creditors to insist that sovereign borrowers follow sound policies or to lend too freely to a country's banks—and domestic moral hazard, which is created by the various types of insurance that most sovereign governments provide to the domestic financial system. The two can be related: In some cases, international support may be necessary for the debtor country's government to be able to honor its domestic guarantees.[2] But domestic moral hazard is also possible and pervasive in the absence of any international support. For example, taxpayers can be stuck with large losses if the expectation that taxpayers will protect depositors from all losses leads depositors to keep their funds in banks that are making reckless loans.

1. Of course, this presumes that the IMF can enforce the debtor's promise to change its policies. In practice, this is an issue, and the IMF's main stick is refusing to provide the balance of a tranched loan or make a new one.

2. Even when governments have declared ex ante that they will not guarantee private claims, they are often nonetheless forced to take responsibility when the time comes. Chile in the early 1980s was a case in point. Korea's guarantee of cross-border bank liabilities in late 1997 is another example from the Asian crisis. Turkey is a more recent case: During the November-December 2000 turmoil in its markets, it decided to guarantee all bank liabilities, including the cross-border ones.

(see box 3.1 on moral hazard). It is important to understand these perspectives—and the key assumptions that lead to these extreme conclusions. But we believe that neither the evidence nor a close read of the literature supports such extreme remedies. Rather, policymakers need to find the right trade-off between the different considerations in various canonical analytical models.

Consequently, we are drawn to models that introduce ways of evaluating trade-offs rather than those that push toward extreme solutions. We don't think the theoretical case for either abolishing the IMF to eliminate the risk of moral hazard or making the IMF a true lender of last resort to eliminate the risk of runs trumps the pragmatic case for providing partial insurance that can stop some but not all runs without providing so much protection as to create incentives for bad policies. The need for insurance against the risk of a run deepening a crisis is real, even if that risk cannot be divorced from a country's policies. The chance of runs devastating sound economies is slim. But the risk of runs pushing a country willing to make the reforms needed to assure its medium-term sustainability into immediate default is real. The advantage of an international source of emergency liquidity, though, has to be balanced against the risk of the presence of this "insurance" against a deeper crisis leading countries to follow poorer policies in the expectation of a bailout. This suggests that the optimal policy response is state contingent: The appropriate size and form of bailouts or bail-ins depends on whether a country is closer to being insolvent rather than just illiquid.

Similarly, an efficient regime for responding to crises should make default and the subsequent debt restructuring neither too easy nor too costly. On one hand, debt contracts must be difficult to renegotiate to create an incentive for a sovereign borrower to make an effort to pay and to avoid "opportunistic defaults." On the other hand, restructuring should not be so costly that difficulties reaching agreement with creditors prevent a country from taking needed action to address a problem marked by true "inability to pay," or add excessively to the cost of unavoidable restructurings.

This chapter is organized into four broad sections. The first summarizes four competing views on the fundamental causes of debt crises in emerging economies. The second examines models that imagine a world without the IMF or similar source of emergency financing. These models help understand how the difficulties of enforcing a contract with a sovereign shape international debt markets. The third section introduces models that add a third party—most easily conceptualized as the IMF—to the equation, whether to sanction restructurings that stem from a country's inability to pay or to provide emergency liquidity to prevent runs or both. The fourth section examines whether the IMF's lending practices that keep its insurance "partial" also crimp its effectiveness.

Four Approaches to Crisis Resolution

Four major conceptual lenses have been used to analyze emerging-market crises. Each of these lenses offers a different interpretation of core policy challenges in a crisis.

- The first set of models suggests that a country may not be able to service its debts in full and on time because of pure "inability to pay." Adverse shocks—a negative terms-of-trade shock like a fall in the price of oil or of the country's other exports—can leave a country that is making a serious effort to pay unable to do so. Alternatively, a country may have borrowed for investments with lower-than-expected returns, thus leading to low economic growth. If insolvency stems from "bad luck," the process for restructuring the country's debt to reduce it to a level consistent with its real ability to pay should be fast and orderly. Unnecessary liquidation costs need not be added to the unavoidable costs deriving from lower-than-expected returns. It follows from this perspective that legal reform that makes restructuring less costly is good for both the debtor and its creditors.

- The second set emphasizes how the difficulty of writing enforceable contracts on a sovereign government creates a potential "unwillingness to pay" problem. A sovereign that has the ability to pay may refuse to do so and default "opportunistically." This is a particular risk with sovereign borrowing because a sovereign borrower, unlike a firm, enjoys considerable effective protection from litigation, as will be discussed in chapter 8. Moreover, any country could in principle reduce its consumption and spending to mobilize the resources to service its external debts; thus all defaults are strategic or opportunistic. The core policy challenge, from this point of view, is to make sure that a sovereign debt restructuring is costly so that a sovereign has an incentive to honor its debts. It follows that legal reform—such as an international bankruptcy court—or even IMF-sanctioned debt suspensions that make restructuring less costly would be a mistake. Such reforms would reduce capital flows to emerging markets and increase the cost of borrowing for debtors who intend to pay.

- A third set of models emphasizes the risk of a run on the sovereign's or country's debt. It emphasizes the similarity between emerging-market economies and banks, as both tend to finance long-term investments with shorter-term borrowing, and highlights the risk that a self-fulfilling run triggered by investors' panic could drive a solvent country into default. The core policy challenge, from this point of view, is to prevent a run from forcing a solvent country into an avoidable bankruptcy, as the "bankruptcy costs" of default disrupt a basically successful economy. It follows that steps to transform the IMF into an international lender of last resort (ILOLR) able to lend in sufficient quantities to stop a run could help avoid crises.[1]

- A fourth set emphasizes how "insurance" can create incentives for taking on too much risk. IMF lending is a form of insurance and can en-

1. Some have suggested that IMF-sanctioned payment standstills could offer an equally effective solution to a run. However, a payment standstill is only equivalent to a lender of last resort if there are no doubts about the debtor's solvency, and creditors are not risk averse. In practice, those who worry most about the risk of a run tend to emphasize the need for an international lender of last resort, while those who worry most about moral hazard advocate IMF-sanctioned payment standstills.

courage reckless policies in emerging economies (debtor moral hazard) and reckless lending by creditors in industrial countries (creditor moral hazard). Just as the literature on sovereign runs draws heavily on bank runs, the literature on sovereign moral hazard draws heavily on models that highlight the risk of domestic deposit insurance leading depositors to keep their money in banks that gamble on high-risk, high-reward investments.[2] The risk of moral hazard implies that even effective efforts to reduce the cost of a crisis may be inefficient if they distort incentives in ways that lead others to get into trouble.

Finally, some approaches combine different lenses to develop unique explanations for sovereign debt crises. For example, the standard model of external debt considers international borrowing as beneficial: Such borrowing finances investment at home and helps smooth consumption in the face of temporary shocks. However, some authors suggest that international borrowing *by governments* may be more bad than good. The ability to borrow from abroad will exacerbate a political bias toward budget deficits and an intrinsic tendency to accumulate too much debt. In the standard model, the inability to enforce debt contracts leads to too little international borrowing. However, in models with a political bias toward deficits, existing debt contracts provide the sovereign with access to too much international credit. Overborrowing either leads to a costly default or simply creates an excessive debt burden that crimps the economy's potential and leaves it vulnerable to external shocks.

The policy recommendations that emerge from these different lenses are often in conflict, and not just in obvious ways. For example, those concerned about the risk that an ILOLR presence could create moral hazard in potential crisis countries often suggest that the solution is to make payments suspensions easier and less costly. The country's ability to bail in its creditors in the event of a run then substitutes for an international lender bailing the country out. Yet while making debt suspensions easier may reduce the moral hazard distortions that expectations of a bailout create, it may exacerbate the "unwillingness to pay" problem—creating another type of moral hazard.

Each of these models help understand the choices the official sector faces in a crisis, yet no one model offers a complete picture of the policy options. If sovereign default were too easy, it would be too frequent—but there is little evidence that sovereigns currently find default too easy and too painless and thus opt for it too quickly. If sovereign default is too costly and painful, both debtors and creditors may lose value relative to a regime where debts can be renegotiated with limited costs when a debtor

2. Thus, two conceptually separate types of moral hazard matter in sovereign debt—one exists even in the absence of an ILOLR and is the pure "unwillingness to pay" problem; the other is the distortions in debtor (and creditor) behavior that bailout expectations generate.

is unable to pay.[3] If the risk of opportunistic default stops beneficial international capital flows, steps that make default easier lead to further unwanted falls in capital flows. But if access to international borrowing fuels internal biases—like a tendency to run excessive budget deficits—making default easier may stop governments from borrowing funds they never should be borrowing in the first place.

A crisis country's ability to borrow from the IMF to avoid a bad outcome is a form of insurance that risks generating moral hazard. But this risk balances against the risk of the failure to provide emergency liquidity resulting in a "run," which would assure a disruptive default. Such a default is not only damaging to the crisis country but also can spill over and damage other economies. Moreover, the risk of a run can undermine incentives for reform if policymakers conclude that a run will lead to default well before the country starts receiving credit for any policy reforms.[4] Not providing any insurance avoids the risk of moral hazard but can be costly in other ways. Moreover, there are ways, other than getting rid of all insurance, to limit the risk of an insurance policy distorting incentives.

Crisis Resolution in IMF's Absence

Most attempts to analyze a world without the IMF look at motives and incentives of the two main players in the international debt market: a debtor country that borrows abroad and its international creditors. Most models implicitly assume that the borrower is a sovereign government and that it only has international creditors—for simplicity's sake, domestic residents are assumed not to participate in the international debt market. Chapters 6 and 7 discuss the issues created in the more realistic case where a sovereign borrows from both its own citizens and foreigners and may assign different priority to repayment of domestic and external debt.[5]

3. This need to reduce bankruptcy cost is behind proposals for legal reform such as an international bankruptcy court for sovereigns (the IMF's sovereign debt restructuring mechanism [SDRM] proposal) or a contractual approach to debt restructuring (see Eichengreen and Portes [1995] for an early argument in favor of such collective action clauses). This debate on statutory versus contractual approaches to debt restructuring will be discussed in detail in chapter 8.

4. Also, as discussed later, IMF support has an international public good component: It may limit disruptive contagion and may induce the appropriate type of policy adjustment for the country and the system as a whole.

5. Private-sector agents of the debtor country that are also borrowing from private international creditors could also be added. But, for the time being, the important issues related to the debt-servicing difficulties of private-sector borrowers are not discussed. Some of the analysis on how to address liquidity and fundamental runs on a sovereign also applies to a cross-border run on domestic banks (and even domestic bank runs), since both a bail-in and a bailout can resolve such a run. A well-established domestic bankruptcy regime provides

Debt Problems and Their Resolution

Does Inability or Unwillingness to Pay Cause Crises?

Why does a sovereign borrower experience difficulty paying its international debts? One broad answer is bad external shocks: These shocks are exogenous—that is, they are the product of changes in the domestic or international environment that are beyond the control of the sovereign borrower. Bad luck that lowers the ex post return on investments made with borrowed funds and leads to low growth and unexpected shocks to the borrowers' terms of trade are both examples of bad "states of nature" that can make a country unable to service its debts. For example, a government that depends on taxing oil exports to generate the revenue it needs to pay its external debt may experience difficulties when the oil price falls.

Another broad answer is unwillingness to pay. A sovereign may opportunistically default both in good and bad states of the world. When economic conditions in a country are good, the sovereign may decide that the conditions would be even better if it did not have to repay its external creditors. When economic conditions are bad, the sovereign may decide it can make economic conditions somewhat better if it did not repay its external debt. Or perhaps a sovereign debtor uses a foreign loan to finance consumption rather than investment and then decides to default when weak economic performance makes the cost of servicing the debt higher than expected.

This unwillingness to pay is a general problem associated with all lending. After a loan is made, the creditor cannot control the debtor's actions and may have difficulty monitoring the borrower's behavior to assure that the loan is being used for its intended purpose. However, theorists of sovereign borrowing and lending often argue that the risk of opportunistic default is higher in the sovereign context because foreign creditors have few effective remedies against a sovereign that chooses not to honor its debt contracts. If creditors cannot protect themselves against the risk of opportunistic default, cross-border lending would be too little: Creditors would have no way of knowing ex ante whether a debtor intended to pay and thus would be unwilling to lend to some creditworthy borrowers. The difficulty in taking legal action against a sovereign is sometimes characterized as a product of the legal doctrine of sovereign immunity but, as will be discussed in chapter 8, it is a more a product of the difficulty of en-

---

the basic framework for addressing the debt problems of private firms. But there are several caveats: (1) Often debtor governments assume/guarantee the external liabilities of private borrowers, like in the case of banks in Asia or Turkey most recently; and (2) the policy decision of the government can directly (capital controls) and indirectly (tax levies, regulations, and weak policies) affect private debtors' ability to pay. This is what Tirole (2002) refers to as the dual-agency problem. Resolving a crisis triggered by problems of private-sector debtors is discussed in the last section of this chapter and in more detail in chapter 6.

forcing a judgment against a sovereign. Most sovereigns are not immune from litigation, but it is still hard to use litigation to force payment.[6]

Consequently, the central paradox addressed in much of the literature on sovereign debt is why any sovereign would ever want to service its debts once it has borrowed, given the difficulty in seizing its assets if the sovereign default breaks the debt contract.[7] This literature (starting with Eaton and Gersovitz [1981], Sachs [1984], and surveyed in Eaton and Fernandez [1995]) identified two potential reasons why sovereign debtors have an incentive to pay, and thus creditors would have an incentive to lend. The first is "reputational" costs. A sovereign may be better off in the short run if it opts not to pay, but it loses in the long run because creditors won't lend to it again if it defaults (i.e., the sovereign is cut off from international capital markets as a punishment for default). The second is the "punishment" costs that creditors can impose immediately after a default. Michael Dooley and Sujata Verma (2001) emphasize the loss of output deriving from default; others postulate that the cost comes from trade sanctions. Thus, penalties are necessary to sustain international lending to emerging markets when lenders cannot distinguish between default due to inability to pay and default due to unwillingness to pay (opportunistic default).[8]

A key question that emerges from the 1980s literature on sovereign debt crises is whether the reputational costs of default (cut off from international capital markets) are large enough to create a world where opportunistic sovereign defaults do not dominate. The answer is a qualified yes: There are sufficient incentives for good behavior to make it unattractive, in theory, for a sovereign with the ability to pay to refuse to do so. The precise combination of costs needed, however, remains a subject of dispute. Jeremy Bulow and Kenneth Rogoff (1989a) argued that "reputation" alone

6. Through the 1930s, a sovereign benefited from complete immunity from litigation, though not complete immunity from "gunboat diplomacy." After World War II, the doctrine of sovereign immunity started to erode, and a sovereign no longer enjoys absolute immunity in its commercial activities. Sovereigns that borrow abroad usually waive sovereign immunity. However, it remains difficult to enforce a judgment against a sovereign even if it waives formal immunity (Buchheit 2000b).

7. Indeed the sovereign debt literature starts from the logical assumption that defaults are always due to unwillingness rather than inability to pay. In fact, with enough adjustment (cut in consumption and/or increase in taxes), any sovereign borrower should be able in principle to service its debts. Thus, inability to pay is effectively a form of unwillingness to pay: When the costs of servicing the debt (in terms of reduction in consumption and increased effort to produce) are greater than the benefits, a sovereign will decide to default rather than exert the effort to service the debt. See Sachs and Cooper (1985).

8. In the optimal contract, default sanctions are not always imposed. Rather, the sanctions are imposed only when there is an opportunistic default arising from an unwillingness to pay, while sanctions are waived if there is a true inability to pay (whether from a run that requires a rescheduling or from a shock that requires debt reduction). If lenders cannot distinguish between the two with a high degree of certainty, they will impose sanctions in all cases, and the maximum sustainable amount of foreign debt is lower.

was insufficient to sustain incentives for payment: The costs of being cut off from international borrowing are not sufficient to make repayment more attractive than borrowing the funds, putting them into an international interest-bearing asset, and using the invested funds as a buffer against future shocks. Other—trade or output—costs of default are needed to prevent opportunistic default as long as the defaulter is not cut off from international lending (rather than borrowing) after default.[9] The subsequent literature on whether being cut off from capital markets is sufficient to support an equilibrium without opportunistic default is vast: Some recent contributions come to different conclusions than Bulow and Rogoff (1989a) and suggest that reputation can be a key incentive for payment (Kletzer and Wright 2000; Wright 2001a, 2001b).

If the value a debtor places on its reputation for paying is not enough to sustain incentives to pay, breaking debt contracts needs to be costly in order to give rise to the "punishment costs" to deter opportunistic default. Many (like Dooley 2000) who are concerned about reforms that would make sovereign default too easy stress this need: They caution that any change that gives a sovereign more legal protection could enhance the temptation to default. Making the restructuring process more orderly, and by implication less painful, would result in less lending to emerging economies—and penalize emerging economies that do intend to pay with higher borrowing costs. Ironically, if default is too easy, capital flows to emerging markets could shrink, thus hurting debtors. Consequently, contracts need to be rigid, and change in payment terms should be difficult and costly.

On one hand, debt restructuring must be difficult enough to make an opportunistic default costly. On the other, rigid contracts create problems if a shock—a sharp fall in the price of the debtor's exports or a run that requires the debtor to suspend payments—leaves the debtor truly unable to pay. In these latter cases, the ability to restructure the debt contract *ex post* is clearly advantageous to all: The debtor truly cannot pay, and any added costs associated with default and restructuring hurt both the debtor and its creditors. But the ability to change a contract ex post in the event of bad luck usually requires putting mechanisms in place *ex ante* that would make all debt renegotiations less costly. Consequently, procedures designed to make it difficult to renegotiate contracts to deter opportunistic defaults become a problem when the debtor truly finds itself in a position where it cannot pay, either because of insolvency or illiquidity.

In other terms, an efficient international debt workout mechanism needs to trade off two objectives: Workouts should not be too costly, as de-

9. Whether a defaulter can lend (or accumulate foreign assets after a default) is an open issue and depends on whether the creditors can seize such assets.

fault may at times be due to the inability to pay, and restructuring can thus benefit both the debtor and its creditors, without being so easy that a debtor is strongly tempted to default opportunistically.[10]

Should Debt Contracts Be Linked to the Debtor's Ability to Pay?

Classic debt contracts—which commit the debtor to pay the contracted interest and principal independently of the return on the investment—fail to match the debtor's legal payment obligations to its payment capacity. In contrast, debt contracts ideally would be written so that payments are state-contingent. If the borrower and lender agree ex ante how to adjust payments in the event of negative shocks, there is no need to renegotiate the contracts ex post, should a shock occur. Payments would automatically be higher in good states of the world (when output and growth are high) and lower in bad states of the world (recession and low growth), reducing the chance of debt-servicing difficulties in bad states of the world. Indeed many authors—including most recently Shiller (2003), Caballero (2003), and Borensztein and Mauro (2002)—have highlighted the advantages of introducing state-contingent debt into international debt markets.

However, these contracts generally pose two broad types of problems. First, it is difficult to specify all potential shocks and contingencies in a contract. Some shocks that reduce the debtor's ability to pay would not be covered in the contract, and conversely, a debtor might cheat and claim that an exogenous shock is causing debt-servicing problems that are really due to an unwillingness to pay.

Second, like all forms of insurance, writing contracts that insure against specific contingencies risks changing the debtor's incentives. For example, a debt contract that makes payments contingent on GDP may create incentives to incorrectly measure certain GDP items and to understate GDP. More generally, a debtor that issued GDP-based bonds would be partially insured against a lower-than-expected growth and arguably would have less incentive to adopt policies that increased growth. However, this argument should not be overstated: It would be a difficult for a debtor to obtain full insurance against a fall in GDP, and if the insurance is only partial, the debtor's incentives are better aligned with its creditors.

10. During the recent discussion about the development of an international bankruptcy regime for sovereigns, the IMF suggested three ways of preventing a sovereign that defaulted opportunistically from obtaining legal protection. In the IMF's initial proposal, legal protection would be conditional to an IMF assessment that the country has an unsustainable debt position. In the second iteration of the proposal, a majority of creditors would vote on whether to grant the debtor protection from litigation. In the final proposal, the IMF did not provide any protection for the debtor, arguing that legal action was already difficult, and the capacity to force a minority to accept the final restructuring terms would be sufficient to deter most litigation. This is discussed in chapter 8.

A more realistic example of potential moral hazard comes from contracts that offer insurance against an oil price shock. Oil is an internationally traded commodity: It would be hard for a debtor to understate the oil price to lower its payments. However, a country that has market power could follow policies that lead to overproduction of oil, knowing that it was fully insured against falls in oil prices. Here, too, the obvious solution is to make the insurance partial—or to provide insurance against oil price shocks only to countries that are too small to influence global prices.[11]

Such contracts have not caught on inertia for another reason. Market participants know how to trade standard debt contracts and argue that contracts that make payments state-contingent would be illiquid. At least initially, the market would charge a "hard-to-trade" premium on top of an "insurance" premium for a form of debt that protects against bad shocks. To date, debtors generally have not been willing to pay the premium the market demands for this kind of contracts.

Emerging-market countries that desire a greater amount of risk sharing can take another approach: financing current account deficits with equity (both FDI and portfolio equity) rather than debt. By definition, equity is state-contingent: Profits, earnings, and dividends paid to foreign equity holders are greater in good times and lower in bad times. While a government, unlike a private firm, cannot directly issue equity, it may be able to raise external financing by privatizing state-owned enterprises and other real public assets.[12]

Should Default Be Easier to Discourage Overborrowing?

The standard analytical approach to thinking about international debt starts from the assumption that cross-border borrowing and lending is

11. Note that, in addition to a debt contract linked to GDP or export prices, one could achieve some more state-contingent real debt payments, if debt contracts were denominated in domestic currency rather than foreign currency. A variant of the moral hazard argument then explains why most emerging-market economies are unable to borrow long term in their own currency in international markets (the "original sin" hypothesis"): Unexpected inflation and depreciation by the debtor could wipe out the real value of this debt. Analogously, one can argue that any debt contract has some partial equity-like state-contingent features as default and restructuring allow the debtor to renegotiate the terms of the contract if negative shocks reduce the ability to pay; in this context, legal innovations such as collective action clauses make this renegotiation less costly and make debt more state-contingent than otherwise. But, again, some have presented concerns about a form of moral hazard—i.e., unwillingness to pay—as a caution against excessively easy terms for recontracting debt instruments.

12. Care, though, must be taken not to guarantee investors in privatized companies a return independent of local economic conditions. Argentina, for example, let the owners of privatized utilities price in dollars and increase their prices in line with US inflation—in theory, insulating investors from both domestic deflation and a nominal depreciation.

good: It facilitates the flow of capital from capital-rich to capital-poor countries when profitable investment opportunities in a country are greater than its national savings, it provides opportunities for portfolio diversification, and it may let countries borrow to smooth consumption in the face of temporary adverse shocks (such as wars and recessions). The key risk, from this point of view, is that difficulties in enforcing an international financial contract will lead to too little international borrowing and lending.

A growing number of theorists, however, are making the opposite argument. Sovereign borrowers do not always have benevolent incentives. Rather, sovereigns—specifically domestic policymakers who can borrow on behalf of the people of the country—may have incentives to overborrow. Policymakers may be "corrupt" or "malevolent" and have incentives to borrow to live well today and transfer the debt burden to future policymakers and taxpayers.[13] For example, in models of two-party competition, a government that inherits an underindebted country will borrow today—indeed, it will overborrow today—to finance benefits that flow to its constituents, since the cost of the borrowing may be born not by the party in power but by the opposition if a partisan change in government occurs in the future. Access to international finance can exacerbate this distortion, since there is a smaller risk that large deficits will drive up interest rates and crowd out domestic investment.[14]

From this point of view, the problem with sovereign debt is not that there is too little borrowing but rather too much of it. Sovereign governments have an inherent bias toward deficits and taking on too much debt. The ability to borrow internationally only fuels this bias and helps governments take on more debt than they should. Some governments will default rather than adjust to pay for their inherited debt, while others will be hit by adverse shocks and be unable to pay.

Bulow (2002) has made an interesting but radical argument: It should be made legally easier for a sovereign to default in order to make it harder for a sovereign with less-than-benevolent motives to borrow. Bulow specifically proposes to allow sovereign debtors to borrow only in their own legal jurisdictions, where sovereign immunity is close to full. Since emerging markets would have trouble issuing local-law debt to foreign investors, this reform aims to severely restrict the ability of "reckless" sov-

13. See similar views in Bulow and Rogoff (1990), Bulow (2002), and Rogoff (1999, 2003a). Rogoff (2003b), however, recently tempered his past concerns about debtor moral hazard and the distortionary effects of IMF lending.

14. See Alesina and Tabellini (1990). Corsetti and Roubini (1997) show that the political bias toward budget deficits and debt accumulation is exacerbated when policymakers can borrow in international capital markets, as the distortionary costs of deficits in closed economies are reduced.

ereign debtors to borrow internationally to finance bad policies.[15] Only good and responsible sovereign policymakers would be able to convince foreign investors to lend them in securities issued in domestic jurisdictions.[16] In this view, the partial legal protection offered to creditors in international jurisdictions exacerbates the bias of emerging-market policymakers toward budget deficits and debt accumulation.

Bulow thus argues that the risks of excessive debt accumulation are so severe that the world would be better off if most sovereign debtors were unable to borrow from international investors. But since a sovereign benefits from effective immunity from having its assets seized even when it borrows abroad, it is not obvious that reducing international creditor rights would, more than marginally, affect the sovereign incentives to default. Thus, even if the deficit bias and overborrowing arguments are assumed to be correct, Bulow's proposed solution would not be binding and would fail to reduce this overborrowing bias. Of course, transitioning to this new world would also be difficult: Those emerging economies that already have large stocks of debt want to find ways to lower their borrowing costs and reduce their current debt burden, not increase it.

Care, though, must to be taken to avoid imposing a cure that is worse than the suspected disease. Some sovereigns may tend to run excessive deficits, overborrow, and eventually default.[17] However, responsible international borrowing also provides many benefits to governments: Economic theory suggests that investment spending (including productive public investment) could be optimally financed with borrowing rather than current taxes (the "golden rule" of public investment financing). Also, external borrowing provides one way for responsible sovereigns to smooth the effects of external shocks that hit a typical emerging-market economy's fiscal balance (terms-of-trade shocks, changes in international li-

15. Bulow assumes that only international sovereign borrowing causes debt crises. This argument is not terribly convincing. Both cross-border bank borrowing (which may indirectly be a form of sovereign borrowing, if there is an expectation that the sovereign will guarantee payment on the debt in bad states of the world) and domestic debt have been more common sources of financial difficulty. Moreover, restricting the ability of a sovereign to borrow internationally will have a limited effect so long as the ability of the private sector to borrow internationally is not restricted (Corsetti and Roubini 1997). As discussed in chapter 2, the sovereign will borrow at home, and the private sector will in turn borrow from abroad to indirectly finance the sovereign's borrowing needs.

16. This theoretical perspective has an interesting application to the debate on international bankruptcy regimes. In Bulow's view, an international bankruptcy court that is designed in a way that the relative power of the debtor makes it easier for a sovereign to default and restructure its debts has the advantage of sharply reducing the amount of international capital lending to emerging-market sovereign debtors.

17. See Rogoff, Reinhart, and Savastano (2003) for the "debt intolerance" hypothesis—i.e., the view that emerging-market economies with high debt levels due to a history of deficit are more likely to "resolve" such a debt problem through default rather than fiscal adjustment.

quidity and risk aversion, and global business cycles). Borrowing to sustain spending and avoid procyclical fiscal adjustment can make sense in the face of a temporary shock (even if distinguishing between temporary and permanent shocks may not be easy in practice, and many emerging economies lack the credibility needed to borrow countercyclically). Thus, offering external investors the protection of a local governing law to eliminate the ability of sovereigns to borrow is a draconian solution to a real problem.

Is Litigation the Real Cost of External Default?

Creditors holding defaulted international bonds generally cannot take effective legal action against a sovereign debtor (see chapter 8 for detailed discussion). Nonetheless, most emerging-market economies have not defaulted opportunistically. Turkey, Brazil, and Uruguay are all committed to primary surpluses of over 4 percent of their GDP to avoid a default: Ecuador currently is running a primary surplus of over 5 percent after its default. Sovereign debtors have not taken the decision to default lightly. If anything, they are biased toward postponing default and delaying a restructuring, given the concerns about the economic costs of such defaults (Krueger 2001a, 2001b). Part of the explanation is that sovereign borrowers (and their political leaders) do value their reputation and believe that an opportunistic default would damage their capacity to borrow in the future (and their political future in the case of leaders).

The integration of domestic and international markets has increased the immediate economic cost of sovereign default (further discussed in chapter 8). A sovereign that defaults on its international debt usually calls into question both its ability and commitment to honor its domestic debts—and to backstop the domestic banking system. Consequently, domestic residents and international investors in local-currency assets often "punish" a sovereign for defaulting on its external debt through runs on the local banking system and on the currency. Thus, default typically is "not" an easy or painless option even when a sovereign benefits from substantial legal protection. Many emerging-market governments who inherit large debts from their predecessors—including debts that arguably stem more from overborrowing rather than from healthy investment in the future—still have tried to pay these debts rather than default.

Crises of Creditor Coordination

Self-Fulfilling Liquidity Runs

The models discussed so far have emphasized debtor behavior and focused on the difference between debt-servicing difficulties stemming from unanticipated economic shocks and from an unwillingness to pay—or perhaps an unwillingness to try to withstand possible economic shocks. Another set of models highlights how problems of creditor coordination can create debt-servicing problems. In these models, the fact that the debtor has multiple creditors is important—the incentive of each creditor to leave the others with the bill for any bad outcome can create avoidable problems for the debtor. An obvious example is the case of a panic-driven creditor "liquidity run" (see Sachs [1984] and many other models of self-fulfilling runs).[18] If a creditor believes that the others will not roll over their short-term debts, it is rational for that creditor to withdraw its financing—by refusing to roll over maturing debts—before other creditors do, even if the debtor is solvent in the long term.

The only necessary condition for a run is short-term debt in excess of the sovereign's liquid assets. A run can occur both in good states, where external conditions leave the debtor solvent, and in bad states. Runs also can occur both when the debtor is making strong policy efforts and when the debtor's policies leave something to be desired. In other terms, liquidity runs can occur both in a world where opportunistic default is a risk and in a world where there is no debtor moral hazard and where all debtors can be assumed to try hard to avoid default.[19]

Consider the case where moral hazard is not a problem: Bad states of "nature" are the only source of debt-servicing difficulties. Suppose the debtor is capable of paying its debts in full in good but not in bad states. A key insight from the domestic literature on bank runs (such as Diamond and Dybvig [1983] for a model of bank runs and Sachs, Tornell, and Velasco [1996a, 1996b] and Chang and Velasco [2001] for liquidity runs in an open economy) is that liquidity runs are costly in both cases. In good states, a run on a debtor whose short-term debts exceed liquid assets causes a solvent debtor to default. However, even in bad states a run makes the impact of the unavoidable bad shock worse than it needs to be. In these cases, debt reduction is unavoidable, but the run generates *additional*, avoidable bankruptcy costs on top of the real costs of the bad shocks. Aggregate losses would be minimized if all creditors rolled over their short-term claims and then all creditors accepted a reduction in their claims linked to the real unavoidable economic cost due to bad shocks.

18. Many of these open-economy models of bank or debt runs (such as Chang and Velasco [2001] and Cole and Kehoe [1996]) are international variants of the Diamond and Dybvig (1983) and Bryant (1980) models of bank runs. But see also Kindleberger (1970) for a classic study of panics, manias, and bubbles from a historical perspective.

19. Models of both self-fulfilling currency crises and liquidity runs imply that fundamentals have to be weak, but not too weak, to put an economy in a region where multiple equilibria, as opposed to a certain crisis (if fundamentals are very poor) or a certain noncrisis (if fundamentals are very strong), can occur. In currency crisis models the range of fundamental variables that can put an economy in a vulnerable region is varied, but in liquidity run models the condition for the economy to be in a multiple equilibria region usually occurs when the stock of liquid assets is lower than the stock of claims that can be rolled off in a run.

The desire of each individual creditor to get out before taking losses drains the sovereign's limited liquidity and increases the total cost of the restructuring.[20]

Do Creditors' Efforts to Protect Themselves from Opportunistic Default Increase the Risk of Runs?

Coordination failures and self-fulfilling runs also can occur when debtor moral hazard is an issue, and debtors do not intrinsically have an incentive to make a full economic effort to avoid default. Indeed, one interesting strand of the theoretical literature highlights how steps that creditors take to limit the debtor's incentive to follow poor policies have the side-effect of making the debtor more vulnerable to output-reducing liquidity runs.

Olivier Jeanne (2000a, 2000b) argues that creditors do not know at the time they lend whether a debtor government's fiscal policies will be prudent or profligate. International investors want to keep the government on a short leash, so they lend only for short terms.[21] The risk that creditors will run if the government opts for undisciplined fiscal policies, in turn, creates the needed incentives for the debtor to be fiscally responsible. The disciplining role of short-term debt, however, makes a debtor that does not maintain sufficient liquid assets to cover all its short-term debts vulnerable to a run. Similarly, in the Kumar, Masson, and Miller (2000) model, issuing short-term debt allows the debtor to signal its commitment to fiscal discipline: Since creditors cannot perfectly observe the debtor's policies, they need a debtor to signal its commitment. In equilibrium, the risk of a run that short-term debt creates increases the debtor's policy effort by making poor policies more costly to the debtor. However, in this model, a debtor with sound policies is still vulnerable to a self-fulfilling run. "Sunspots" (random and unpredictable events) can still trigger panic-driven runs even in good states. Thus, their model introduces a trade-off between the disciplining role of short-term debt and its role in increasing the probability of self-fulfilling runs.

A number of policy implications result from the insight that the risk of illiquidity from short-term debt emerges naturally as part of the market's

20. As shown by Allen and Gale (2000a) in a model of fundamentals-based bank runs, even if one rules out the pure self-fulfilling equilibria and thus real fundamental shocks trigger a bank crisis, in equilibrium a fundamental run will occur, and it will trigger extra and avoidable liquidation costs. See Chui, Gai, and Haldane (2000) for a model of self-fulfilling runs where poor fundamentals play an important role in triggering the run. See also Corsetti, Guimaraes, and Roubini (2003) for a fundamental run in a model where the debt crisis in an open economy can go from illiquidity to insolvency on a continuous spectrum.

21. Similarly, borrowing in foreign currency is also a commitment device as it prevents the borrower from wiping out the real value of the debt via inflation, currency depreciation, or both.

response to the risk of opportunistic default. One way to reduce the risk of a liquidity run is to lengthen the maturity of the borrower's debt. However, policy recommendations such as "avoid borrowing at short-term maturities" beg the question why in equilibrium does short-term debt emerge in the first place. Models like those by Jeanne (2000b) suggest that if maturity lengthening is forced on emerging markets by, for example, making rollover options mandatory in external debt contracts, then the flow of capital to emerging markets will shrink: Creditors may be willing to lend only if they can use short-term debt as a disciplinary device to reduce the debtor's temptation to follow poor policies. One implication of the Kumar, Masson, and Miller (2000) model is that an IMF capable of fully protecting a debtor against the risk of a run is not optimal, since the risk of a costly run is needed for short-term debt to create incentives for the debtor to sustain sound policies.

Can Runs Be Resolved Without an IMF Loan?

Problems with creditor coordination—such as a liquidity run—provide one of the main theoretical justifications for creating an international institution able to supply emerging markets with large amounts of foreign currency. Lending can help the debtor and its creditors avoid unnecessary "bankruptcy" costs in the event of a self-fulfilling run on a sound debtor. The case for an international body as an international lender of last resort therefore hinges on the assumption that creditor coordination failures cannot be easily resolved in the absence of a rescue loan from an institution like the IMF.[22] "Bankruptcy" and the resulting debt restructuring are costlier solutions to a debtor's liquidity problems than a large loan.[23]

What are the potential coordination problems that could make a restructuring costly? Remember that if the debtor is solvent and could pay its debts in full over time, the best solution is a voluntary rollover of all short-term debt. This avoids the cost of sovereign "bankruptcy." If a run occurs when the debtor is insolvent and there is a need to write down debts, the optimal approach is for creditors to agree to take an immediate haircut and thus avoid the additional liquidation costs deriving from a "disorderly" debt restructuring.

22. There is debate on whether IMF is a true ILOLR. Formally, the IMF resources are limited and the potential run in an open economy very large; thus, the IMF may not be able to be a true ILOLR (Jeanne and Wyplosz 2001). See Fischer (1999) for a case in favor of the IMF as an ILOLR.

23. See Sachs (1995) for an argument in favor of an ILOLR along such lines. Indeed, in the Diamond-Dybvig model, a full ILOLR liquidity support or even a government guarantee of deposits—deposit insurance—is able to prevent self-fulfilling bank runs. See also Jeanne (2000b), who shows that global welfare is increased through ILOLR intervention. But moral hazard from the existence of an ILOLR is finessed in most ILOLR models such as Jeanne and Wyplosz (2001).

Of course, if "bankruptcy" is costly to the debtor and is a risk in a world that lacks an ILOLR or a close substitute, then the debtor has an incentive to take steps to protect itself from the risk of a liquidity run. Consequently, it is worth looking both at the ex ante steps a debtor could take to avoid a run in the first place and the ex post solutions that the debtor would have to turn to in a world that lacked an institution like the IMF. Options include: (1) holding enough liquidity (foreign reserves) to avoid a run; (2) securing liquidity or a private bailout loan; (3) negotiated agreements with creditors to roll over short-term debts; and (4) unilateral payments suspensions/standstills.

Holding More Reserves (or Borrowing Less). One way to eliminate the risk of a run is to keep liquid foreign-currency reserves on hand well in excess of the sovereign's short-term debt, a form of "self-insurance." Korea and other East Asian countries, for example, responded to their 1997 crisis by running large balance-of-payment surpluses and building up a large reserve "war chest." Unfortunately, holding reserves has a cost: The yield on reserve assets like US treasuries is well below the average cost of an emerging-market bond. Building up reserves either requires running current account surpluses—exporting more than the country imports—or "banking" the proceeds of international borrowing and absorbing the interest rate differential between the emerging economies' cost of funds and the return on reserve assets.

Another option (discussed in chapter 6) is for a debtor to purchase in advance the right to borrow reserves from a consortium of private banks: The fee that the borrower pays to maintain access to such contingent lines obviously indicates the cost of securing access to such reserve assets, and the cost of borrowing from such facilities determines their cost if accessed.[24] Note also that debt rollover options—another form of insurance—if appropriately priced in the market, are just another variant of saying that countries should not borrow too much at short-term maturities.

Private Lender of Last Resort. Securing emergency liquidity from a private lender would appear to be the best way to deal with a liquidity run. In absolute terms, there is plenty of international liquidity (liquid assets) that the markets can provide, since even the largest emerging markets are small relative to the size of global capital markets.[25] However, in the real

24. As will be discussed in chapter 6, the market currently is not willing to supply such contingent credit facilities on terms that emerging markets find more attractive than, say, holding an equivalent quantity of reserves. International banks have discovered that it is risky to commit to provide emergency liquidity to a country when other market participants are pulling out (and market spreads are going up).

25. Brazil's total public debt stock is smaller than the United States' 2003 budget deficit.

world, the needed liquidity might not be available even to a solvent borrower. Most of the world's liquidity is not available in a crisis: Investors in US treasuries are not suddenly going to reallocate more of their portfolio to emerging markets during times of stress. Indeed, the amount of money available for unsecured lending to emerging-market sovereigns is likely to fall in a crisis. Moreover, no individual market participant may have enough liquidity (or be willing to put all of its capital at risk on a single large bet) to provide the needed liquidity alone. Each individual lender may be willing to supply a fraction of the needed liquidity but only if it is confident that other creditors are willing to do so as well. This is a classic coordination problem: The absence of a private actor large enough to internalize the coordination problems will block the private provision of crisis liquidity.

The difficulties in putting together a coalition of willing private lenders to act as a lender of last resort are augmented when there is uncertainty about the country's fundamentals. No private lender—particularly those that lack security, the protection of legal seniority, or both—wants to lend to a country that is not truly solvent. Conditioning the liquidity on policy reform is one way of reducing this risk, for which creditors would be required to not only coordinate the provision of emergency liquidity but also to reach an agreement on the macro conditions that accompany the lending and determine how best to enforce these conditions.

These institutional impediments make it difficult for emerging markets to access emergency liquidity from private markets in times of crisis. An emerging market that would be solvent if it implemented needed policy reforms may not be able to tap the global pool of liquidity by offering slightly higher interest rates. Investors that are not already familiar with emerging economies would be as likely to be scared away by the higher interest rate as to put their money in.

Negotiated Extension of Maturities. A debtor that cannot obtain an emergency loan from a consortium of private lenders can look to its existing creditors for emergency financial support and negotiate a rollover arrangement with them to avoid a unilateral suspension of payments.[26] Unfortunately, the same problems that lead to a run in the first place make agreement on a voluntary rollover difficult: Each individual creditor would prefer to exit while others roll over their claims. Moreover, if creditors seriously doubt the debtor's solvency, they have a strong incentive to exit if they can—particularly because of the difficulty in linking the

26. Here, ex post rollover arrangements—i.e., negotiated during an incipient crisis—are considered. There may also be room for ex ante rollover arrangements, such as a rollover option, that are systematically included in loan contracts; the case for these rollover options is considered in chapters 6 and 9.

rollover to policy changes in the debtor country. If agreement on a rollover cannot be reached, the debtor is forced to default and incur the socially inefficient costs of bankruptcy. Both approaches have problems.

Payments Suspension. A final option is for the debtor to impose a unilateral payments suspension—and then to renegotiate its maturing debt contracts. This solves the creditor coordination problem: No creditor can run. Indeed, one of the more surprising conclusions of the theoretical literature on bank runs is that a "bank holiday" can solve the bank run problem as effectively as a lender of last resort. So long as the run is a "pure panic," the bank's solvency is not in question, and creditors are not risk averse. This conclusion can obviously be applied to a run on a sovereign: If a pure panic were to lead to a run on a solvent debtor, creditors should be indifferent between a debt standstill and a rescue loan from an institution like the IMF, which provides sufficient liquidity to cover all near-term payments.

This raises two issues: First, how strong is the argument that a standstill offers as effective a solution to a liquidity run as an international lender? Second, if a debtor may need to unilaterally suspend payments in the event of a run, how can creditors be protected against the risk that a debtor may unilaterally and opportunistically reduce its debts? Both issues are taken up in the next section.

IMF, Crises of Creditor Coordination, and Moral Hazard

IMF as a Source of Emergency Liquidity

One of the main arguments in favor of an ILOLR is that a liquidity run risks prompting avoidable output losses. A domestic lender of last resort cannot provide the liquidity support needed to avoid a run on foreign currency–denominated claims: Domestic monetary authorities can print domestic currency at will but not foreign currency.[27] So long as the private

27. Some caveats are necessary here. In a fixed-rate regime, local-currency liquid claims can roll off and be claims against the central bank reserves. This is why the risk of a liquidity run is larger in a fixed than in a flexible exchange rate regime. Liquidity runs can also occur in a fully dollarized economy, particularly if the dollarized country lacks foreign-currency reserves in the absence of a central bank. Of course, while capital flight by local-currency claims can be addressed through the provision of local-currency liquidity by a domestic lender of last resort in a flexible (or semiflexible) exchange rate regime, the effectiveness of such a domestic lender of last resort is often limited. Such liquidity provision may lead to a free fall of the currency value. For example, Ecuador's attempts to save its banks via liquidity provision in 1998–99 led to a collapse of an already floating exchange rate and eventually to the decision to dollarize in 2000.

provision of emergency liquidity or a payments suspension cannot resolve at a low cost the coordination failures that lead to runs, international emergency liquidity support to illiquid but solvent sovereigns leaves all parties better off.[28]

The availability of an international institution that can lend to address coordination problems is in some ways providing a global public good, and not just helping to avoid a bad outcome in the crisis country. A crisis in a systemically important country could trigger crises elsewhere (contagion): Consequently, liquidity support from the IMF or a similar institution could play the same role as a domestic lender of last resort (or deposit insurance) in avoiding the spread of bank runs.[29] Even in the absence of financial contagion, a large fall in output in a major country will reduce global output, as the crisis country imports less and as its exchange rate collapse puts pressure on other exchange rates. Finally, international liquidity support not only can encourage policy adjustment but also is presumably the right kind of adjustment and reform both for the crisis country and the international system as a whole.

The case for an international lender able to provide a "full bailout" that stops a run has to be assessed relative to the alternative policy of a "full bail-in"—a combination of broad debt standstills/suspension, capital controls, and other measures to lock in all investors who are rushing to the door.[30] Why do supporters of standstills prefer them to liquidity support even in liquidity cases? For two main reasons:[31] First, official liquidity support may lead to a new form of moral hazard—that is, imprudent behavior by the debtor and its creditors in the expectation of an official bailout. Second, the official creditors may provide emergency liquidity by mistake to an unsustainable and insolvent sovereign. The typical response to a sovereign as well as a bank run has been to supply emergency liquidity, not to declare a quick standstill.

In certain theoretical models, moreover, a full bail-in solves the coordination failure that causes the run as efficiently as a full bailout. Indeed, in pure liquidity cases, the threat of a full bail-in is *sufficient* to rule out the

---

28. See Sachs (1995) for an argument in favor of an ILOLR along such lines. Indeed, in the Diamond-Dybvig (1983) model, a full lender-of-last-resort liquidity support or even a government guarantee of deposits—deposit insurance—is able to prevent self-fulfilling bank runs. See also Jeanne (2000b), who shows that global welfare is increased through ILOLR intervention.

29. See Gorton and Winton (2002) for a recent survey of contagion in bank crises. Goodhart and Huang (2000) show that an ILOLR can prevent international bank runs (contagion), but their model does not consider the issue of moral hazard, which is discussed later.

30. Such standstills are the international equivalent of bank holidays in the case of a run on a solvent bank. A credible bank holiday avoids the collective action problem (the sequential service constraint or "first-come-first-served" rule) that triggers the run in the first place.

31. See chapter 6 for a more detailed discussion.

bad equilibrium: The threat alone, so long as it is credible, is sufficient to stop the run and maintain the good, "no run" equilibrium. Since no run actually occurs, the debtor does not actually ever need to implement the threat of suspending payments.[32] Similarly in theory, the presence of a lender of last resort that promises to provide sufficient liquidity to stop the run prevents the bad run equilibrium. If all creditors know that, if and when a run occurs, the debtor will introduce standstills, capital controls, or both, and the incentive to run will disappear.

This conceptual equivalence of the full bail-in and full bailout solutions, however, hinges on two key assumptions—(1) there is no uncertainty about the debtor's solvency, and (2) creditors are not risk averse.

- First, the theoretical "equivalence" of a "bank holiday" solution (i.e., a standstill) and an ILOLR only holds in the extreme case where the bank is perfectly solvent, and the only problem the bank faces is illiquidity. If there is some chance that the bank is not solvent, a depositor is better off getting out first rather than being locked in with a bank holiday. Similarly, a sovereign's creditors are indifferent between getting out and being locked in only if the sovereign too is perfectly solvent. As discussed in chapter 2, most actual cases are not ones of pure illiquidity: creditors usually doubt the sovereign's ability to make the adjustments needed to assure its solvency. If there is some uncertainty about the country's willingness to take action to assure its solvency, bail-ins and bailouts cease to be equivalent.[33]
- Second, even in theory, if creditors are risk averse, the equivalence of a full bail-in and full bailout breaks down. Risk-averse creditors—particularly if they doubt the country's fundamental solvency—will react to the expectation or threat of a bail-in by rushing out. Consequently, the threat of a standstill is not enough to stop the run, and the debtor likely will have to implement a standstill, and the cost of the standstill risks reducing the debtor's welfare, leading to financial losses for investors, or both. Indeed, the fundamental problem with any attempt to force creditors to supply emergency liquidity by stretching out their claims is that the expectation of such an approach may accelerate the crisis, as risk-averse creditors rush to get out before the expected suspension. Indeed, in the extreme, fears that a debtor will suspend payments could even trigger a crisis that would have not otherwise oc-

32. Indeed, Diamond and Dybvig (1983) suggest that a temporary debt suspension (bank holiday) is the optimal policy to prevent multiple-equilibria runs.

33. Indeed, in the bank run literature, in addition to models of panic-driven runs, such as Diamond and Dybvig (1983), there are also many models of bank runs and crises driven by fundamentals (see, for example, Allen and Gale [2000a], Jacklin and Bhattacharya [1988], Gorton [1987]).

curred.[34] This point is familiar from economic theory: "Unexpected" capital controls may prevent a speculative attack and run on a currency, but "anticipated" ones can accelerate the attack.

The analogy between a run on a bank and that on a sovereign also is not perfect. Demand deposits in excess of available liquid reserves characterize a stylized bank. All demand depositors have the right to withdraw their funds from a bank at any given moment. At least in theory, the bank holiday can be lifted without any fundamental restructuring of the depositors' claims, so long as the bank is confident that demand depositors will not run after the holiday is lifted. A sovereign payments suspension, however, typically requires a comprehensive debt restructuring before payments can be resumed. Short-term debts that fall due during the payments suspension have to be either paid in full when the standstill ends or restructured. In most cases, the debtor will also want to reschedule payments that are coming due in the near future.

The risk that coordination problems could complicate even a necessary debt restructuring process creates additional uncertainty. As discussed earlier, creditors have an incentive to make sure that it is not too easy to change the terms of a contract in order to avoid debtor moral hazard, yet this creates a risk that both the debtor and the creditor will take losses when a restructuring is in both their interests. The greater the uncertainty and the larger the potential for the restructuring process itself to generate losses, the stronger the incentive to run before the imposition of a sovereign standstill.[35]

Will a Debtor Use a Run to Walk Away from Its Debts?

There is a risk that a debtor may stop payments not just to deal with pure liquidity runs but also to reduce its debt payments after failing to make a real effort to pay. This is all the more true if the line between a liquidity and a solvency crisis is not clear and if a country experiences a run in part because of doubts about its willingness to take the actions needed to assure its future solvency. A debtor may conclude that if it's going to have

34. One can argue that hair-trigger runs by creditors are the response of creditors who want shorter maturities so they can get out at par at the first sign a debtor's policy effort is lagging. Indeed, as Jeanne (2000a) and Jeanne and Wyplosz (2001) suggest, the maturity of external debt is endogenous and may serve as a disciplining mechanism. However, if debtors believe that the short maturities that creditors want to discipline the debtor create a countervailing risk of liquidity crises that are too costly to them, debtors also have an incentive to pay more to lengthen their debt maturity.

35. The stylized model of a "painless" bank holiday that avoids any need for a deposit restructuring also may be somewhat unrealistic. Deposit restructurings have followed many bank holidays when banks were in fundamental distress.

to suspend payments because of a run anyway, it might as well also seek additional debt relief and thus opportunistically default. The costs of a restructuring strengthen incentives for creditors to run in anticipation of a standstill and increase the risk of the "bankruptcy costs" of a standstill leading to a loss of output that may tip the scales of a crisis from illiquidity to insolvency.

At the same time, making the debt restructuring process easier so that standstills are a more attractive solution to the problem of a run risks making it easier for an opportunistic debtor to obtain agreement on a restructuring that reduces its debts. Easy resort to standstills could exacerbate the risk of debtor moral hazard and lead, in equilibrium, to lower capital flows to emerging markets. Models that introduce the risk of debtor moral hazard alongside the risk of liquidity runs typically argue that the costs of renegotiating contracts should not be too low, even if large "renegotiation" costs complicate the resolution of liquidity runs. In Dooley and Verma (2001), a debtor's incentives to take actions to maintain its solvency hinge on the costs of "bankruptcy." In Kumar, Masson, and Miller (2000), default needs to be costly to provide the "punishment mechanisms" that create the incentive for the debtor's ongoing policy effort. Thus, paradoxically, while standstills are usually recommended as a way to resolve the problem of moral hazard deriving from the existence of IMF liquidity support, they may exacerbate the other moral hazard problem, since steps to make standstills less costly could make opportunistic default more attractive.

Should the IMF Sanction Standstills Rather than Provide Emergency Loans?

Most calls for debt suspensions/standstills as a solution to debt runs have come from policy circles, not academics. However, some recent studies have assessed analytically the case for IMF-sanctioned debt standstills.[36] The basic idea is simple: The IMF would give its nod only to debtors that imposed a standstill for the right reasons, and the IMF's blessing would reduce either the legal consequences or the economic cost of such debt suspensions.

Prasanna Gai, Simon Hayes, and Hyun Song Shin (2002) concluded that officially sanctioned standstills may not reduce ex ante lending to emerging markets as long as the IMF can distinguish between a debt-servicing problem triggered by random negative shocks and one triggered by an opportunistic default. The IMF's ability to distinguish among different types of crises effectively substitutes for market discipline. The result makes sense. If private creditors can be reassured that standstills will be

36. Related studies have considered analytically the case for and against an international bankruptcy court and collective action clauses; chapter 8 will consider these arguments, where statutory and contractual approaches to debt restructurings are analyzed.

imposed only if "bad luck" prevents a debtor that is making a strong effort to pay from servicing its debt or in case of pure runs, then lending to emerging markets should not be reduced ex ante. At the same time, if the official sector can distinguish between unwillingness and inability to pay, a lender of last resort may still provide a better solution to liquidity crises if the imposition of a standstill risks triggering a broader run—a risk not captured in their model.

Hyun Song Shin (2001) and Benjamin Martin and Adrian Penalver (2003) study the effects of standstills and forced rollovers on debt's maturity structure and pricing. Since standstills reduce the liquidity of short-term debt, they lead ex ante to higher short-term interest rates. In the context of these models, however, standstills also reduce long-term interest rates as orderly, IMF-sanctioned standstills increase recovery values in case of default. Shin (2001) argues that IMF-sanctioned standstills could even lead to a fall in both short-term and long-term interest rates if standstills solve creditor coordination problems and reduce the risk of destructive runs.

One implication of these studies is that IMF-sanctioned standstills will lead creditors to lengthen the maturity of their lending. A standstill penalizes short-term debt relative to long-term debt, unlike a lender of last resort, which rewards short-term debt. However, the conclusion that standstills will lead to a reduction of long rates, an overall fall in the yield curve, and maturity lengthening strongly depends on the assumption that standstills cannot be used for opportunistic defaults. Moreover, if there is any risk that standstills will lead to losses, creditors will have incentives to lend in ways that allow them to get out fast, ahead of the standstill.

Gai and Shin (2002) examined whether IMF-sanctioned standstills should trigger a rush to the exits. In their model, an orderly standstill has two effects. On one hand, investors concerned about the loss of liquidity in the case of a standstill will tend to shorten the maturity of their debt holdings so that they can rush to the exits more quickly. On the other hand, an orderly standstill increases recovery values in the case of a crisis, which favors investors who hold longer-term, rather than shorter-term, debt. These authors' calibration results show that the relative strength of these two effects depends on the standstill's nature: If a standstill is short and significantly increases recovery values, the second effect dominates—average debt duration increases, and the probability of a crisis is reduced. The rush to the exits dominates when standstills last longer and have a smaller impact on recovery values.

However, none of these analytical models provides a systematic comparison of the benefits and costs of standstills relative to solutions based on emergency liquidity. Rather, they tend to compare disorderly unilateral debt suspensions only with more orderly IMF-sanctioned standstills. Realistic models of standstills that can be compared in terms of their normative implications with realistic models of catalytic official finance remain to be developed.

International Lender of Last Resort and Moral Hazard

An international lender of last resort effectively provides a form of insurance—liquidity insurance—to sovereign countries. A large body of literature has explored how insurance influences the behavior of the beneficiaries, specifically how the insurance that reduces the cost of risky behavior may perversely make it more likely. The benefits of an international source of emergency liquidity, including the ability to avoid self-fulfilling crises, have to be balanced against the risk of the provision of emergency liquidity distorting the incentives facing debtor countries and the creditors who lend to them.

Will International Lending of Last Resort Create Moral Hazard?

Before looking at models that examine how the existence of an official creditor could affect the strategic game between private creditors and sovereign debtors,[37] it is worth reviewing, once again, how deposit insurance and a domestic lender of last resort affect a bank's incentives. These models have obvious parallels to the sovereign case.

In the Diamond-Dybvig model (1983), banks are vulnerable to panic-driven runs without a domestic lender of last resort. Yet other models highlight how the existence of a lender of last resort—or more commonly, mispriced deposit insurance that eliminates the risk of a run—creates moral hazard. The incentives of the bank's owners are not necessarily aligned with the interests of the bank's depositors or the source of the deposit insurance. If the banks lack sufficient capital, the bank's owners have an incentive to "gamble for redemption" by making risky loans. If the risky loans succeed, the bank's owners win. If they fail, the owners do not lose much. The bank's capital is already gone. Since the deposits are insured, the "insurer"—in this case, the domestic government—bears any additional losses. Thus, liquidity support, which reduces the risk of losses by depositors, risks creating moral hazard even if it prevents liquidity runs. In the domestic context, such distortions can be reduced by "incentive compatible deposit insurance" (i.e., appropriately priced deposit insurance) and by regulating and supervising the banks that benefit from access to the lender of last resort. The central bank or the regulatory authority also has the power to seize the bank, change its management, restructure it, merge it with other banks, or even liquidate it—all of which should strengthen incentives for responsible bank management.

It is worth noting that the case for a domestic lender of last resort hinges, in part, on its (usually the central bank) ability to distinguish more

37. See Bulow and Rogoff (1988c); Rogoff (1999); Wells (1993); Klimenko (2001); Bhattacharya and Detragiache (1994); Spiegel (1996); Paasche and Zin (2001); Kumar, Masson, and Miller (2000); Dooley and Verma (2001); and Corsetti, Guimaraes, and Roubini (2003).

effectively than depositors between runs on insolvent institutions and those on illiquid institutions. Since small bank depositors generally have difficulty monitoring the balance sheet of a bank, such an information asymmetry is not an unreasonable assumption.[38]

Much of this analysis also applies in the international context. The existence of an ILOLR could distort the incentives of international creditors, who, like insured depositors, would not discipline a debtor pursuing risky policies by denying it financing. Creditors could lend in the expectation that the availability of liquidity from an ILOLR will allow their loans to be repaid, no matter what. The existence of an ILOLR only distorts the incentives of the debtor if international liquidity support is implicitly or explicitly subsidized. Then, a sovereign debtor may have an incentive to take out an international loan to finance the analogue of a gamble for redemption rather than face the immediate loss of entering into sovereign bankruptcy. If this gamble fails, the costs are born not by the debtor—which is already close to bankruptcy—but rather either by the crisis lender (if their claims are not senior) or by existing long-term lenders (who cannot get out and might have to take larger losses to assure the repayment of senior IMF lending).

Moral hazard could be a larger problem in the international than the domestic context for two reasons. First, a domestic regulator/lender of last resort has powers that are not available to an international regulator/lender of last resort. Sovereign debtors cannot be seized, merged, or closed down after a crisis:[39] An international lender cannot regulate sovereigns in the same way a domestic lender can regulate banks to assure that the banks maintain prudent policies.[40] Second, the argument that official creditors have an informational advantage and are better able to distinguish illiquidity from insolvency is not as strong as the argument that a domestic lender of last resort has access to information that a typical depositor

38. In the domestic context of a bank run, Wallace (1988) showed that a policy of tightening caps on deposit withdrawals as a run starts (a form of payment suspension) is superior to a policy stopping the run by providing complete deposit insurance (a form of emergency lending) if the lender of last resort does not have superior information on the nature of the run. In Wallace's model, the central bank, not the bank experiencing the run, imposes the deposit standstills: Since the central bank is assumed to be benevolent, this analysis fails to provide insights into the risk that a standstill might exacerbate debtor moral hazard.

39. Historically this seizure solution to sovereign debt problems was actually available. In previous centuries, when "gunboat diplomacy" was the rule, creditor governments could take over defaulting sovereign countries and seize their assets, or tax authorities or customs, to ensure the servicing of external debts.

40. In the corporate finance jargon of Tirole's (2002) analysis, the problem faced by both corporate and sovereign debtors are the limits to pledgeable income that can be used as effective collateral for borrowing. Sovereignty makes this problem even more serious for sovereign borrowers.

lacks. Many of the investors in the international sovereign debt market are quite sophisticated. There is a broad theoretical argument that bail-ins are better than bailouts if the official sector lacks an informational advantage.[41] On the other hand, the argument that an informational advantage is needed for there to be a case for bailout can itself be questioned: Runs on illiquid but solvent countries may stem from market imperfections other than a lack of information (for example, the forced unwinding of leveraged positions), or the official sector may have an intrinsic advantage in monitoring a country's policy effort through its conditionality even if it has access to the same information as other creditors.

Strategic Game Between a Sovereign, Its Private Creditors, and Official Lenders

The classic model of the sovereign debt market as a strategic game between sovereign debtors, their private creditors, and the official sector examined how the presence of official creditors influenced negotiations between sovereign debtors and private creditors on how much to reduce external debt. The IMF no longer lends to encourage a debtor in default to strike a deal with its creditors (apart from the indirect effects of an IMF "lending into arrears" policy). But this model can easily be extended to examine how an official lender can help a debtor avoid a restructuring in liquidity runs, so it is worth examining in some detail.

In Bulow and Rogoff's (1988c) model, private creditors know that official creditors care about international trade flows and cannot credibly commit not to be involved in debt restructuring negotiations. In their model, official lending during the negotiations allows the debtor to offer a better deal to creditors than would otherwise have been possible. Sovereign debtors expect the official sector to allow them to offer their private creditors a better deal should they default. This means that, in equilibrium, private creditors charge sovereign debtors lower loan spreads than they would have in the absence of such official creditors. Thus, the exis-

41. A number of studies have examined the case for an ILOLR when the IMF lacks perfect information on the nature of the crisis and may not be able to distinguish crises due to pure panic runs from those due to insolvency or distinguish unwillingness to pay from inability to pay. In general, the case for IMF intervention is diluted if the IMF cannot precisely distinguish between those two types of crises. Ghosal and Miller (2002) show that if the official creditor cannot assess the nature of the crisis (insolvency versus opportunistic default), there is a case for "constructive ambiguity"—i.e., official liquidity support should be provided with probability less than one. Gai, Hayes, and Shin (2001) find that the IMF's role is more likely to be beneficial if the IMF can make an accurate assessment of the country's policy efforts. Spiegel (2001) argues that the IMF's inability to distinguish runs caused by "sunspots" from those caused by "fundamental insolvency" provides an argument for lending at high "penalty" rates, since under certain conditions penalty rates can help distinguish the illiquid from the insolvent borrowers.

tence of official creditors that lend into a debt restructuring increases the moral hazard distortion in sovereign lending—creditors lend too much at too low a price, and debtors borrow more than they should.[42] Similarly, the large-scale provision of official financing to provide a sovereign with the liquidity needed to pay claims with a short-residual maturity should, by application of the Bulow-Rogoff model, be anticipated in advance and could lead to overborrowing and overlending.

Two caveats are needed here. First, the impact of IMF lending to avoid any debt restructuring in a liquidity crisis is clearer on short-term rather than on long-term claims. Since long-term claims cannot exit quickly on the back of official lending, creditors holding longer-term claims only unambiguously gain if the bailout works. Argentina's long-term bondholders are in the process of discovering that official lending that backs a failed program can dilute the value of their claims: The official sector is effectively senior and typically gets paid before long-term bondholders, who may have to take a larger haircut to assure full payment of the IMF (the greater haircut on long-term bonds "pays" for the losses created when short-term creditors were able to exit an insolvent debtor at par before the default).

Second, the Bulow-Rogoff model has only three players: the sovereign debtor, its external creditors, and the official sector. The benefits of official lending go either to the debtor or to its external creditors. In reality, other players also have a stake in the game. Adding more parties to the game creates the possibility that these parties, rather than private external creditors, will gain from the official lending. For example, if official liquidity is used to provide liquidity to domestic banks facing a run on their dollar deposits, the gains from official lending may flow to domestic bank depositors rather than to the sovereign's long-term creditors. If a default still takes place, the sovereign debtor's long-term external creditors may need to take a larger haircut to bring it back into solvency while the sovereign

42. Wells (1993) analyzes how the presence of an official creditor affects the bargaining between a sovereign debtor and its private creditors in an asymmetric information debt reduction game. An IMF policy of "lending into arrears" is more efficient than one of "no lending into arrears." The former policy leads to more efficient bargaining as delay times are reduced, and the benefits of IMF transfers go to the debtor. In Wells (1993) the IMF is an exogenous source of funding rather than a strategic player in the game. Klimenko (2001) shows that the debtor country's market power in trade affects its bargaining power in debt restructuring games involving official and private creditors. Also, he shows that if the official lender is a strategic player rather than a passive source of funds, the debtor is better off in a "lending into arrears" regime—not because its bargaining power increases relative to the private creditor but rather because its power increases relative to the IMF. Variants of the games where the IMF is a passive provider of funds rather than a strategic player are in the papers on the "debt buyback" debate (Bulow and Rogoff 1991, Sachs 1989a) where the controversial issue was whether debtors or creditors obtain most of the surplus deriving from IMF-financed debt buyback schemes. See Cline (1995) for a survey of this debate.

debtor is still repaying the IMF loans it took out to support the domestic banking system.[43]

Both these scenarios slightly modify the Bulow-Rogoff framework by adding a fourth group, thus qualifying the framework's strong conclusion—namely that official lending benefits private external creditors. In the first scenario, external creditors are effectively divided into two groups—those with short-term claims and those with long-term claims—with potentially divergent interests. In the second scenario, domestic creditors are added to the mix. The Bulow-Rogoff model nonetheless provides a useful baseline for analysis, as it highlights how *anticipated* official-sector lending will influence the strategic game between a sovereign debtor and its various heterogeneous creditors.

Other models of sovereign crises have also highlighted the risk that IMF intervention could distort the market. For example, in the Dooley-Verma (2001) model, anticipated and unconditional lending (insurance) by official creditors leads to moral hazard and makes also crises more costly: It subsidizes capital inflows before the crisis and intensifies capital account reversal and output losses once a crisis occurs.

IMF Lending May Not Lead to Moral Hazard

There is little doubt that there is a trade-off between the potentially valuable role an institution like the IMF can play in limiting the risk of panic-driven runs leading to avoidable defaults and the risk of the expectations of such lending encouraging risky policies and risky lending. Earlier, two reasons were noted why moral hazard could potentially be a greater concern in the international rather than in the domestic context: The IMF lacks the regulatory authority of a domestic central bank, and the IMF's information advantage over international investors is likely to be smaller than a domestic central bank's information advantage over domestic depositors. However, the arguments that the IMF's presence inherently distorts a debtor's incentives to adopt sound policies have three caveats.

- IMF conditionality offers a potential solution to debtor moral hazard. If IMF lending is conditional on policy changes/increased effort and if the IMF can effectively monitor the country's adherence to its promises, then IMF lending can avoid runs while IMF conditionality ensures good effort. The fact that the debtor ultimately has to make the full effort needed to repay its original loans should limit its incentives to overborrow: Creditors may get off scot-free in a crisis without dis-

43. Of course, this result assumes that domestic current and future taxpayers don't bear the costs of bailing out the domestic depositors. The exact allocations of benefits and losses among different agents depends on assumptions about the strategic strength of different players once official finance is provided.

torting overall flows so long as the debtor does not have any incentives to overborrow.

- IMF lending creates debtor moral hazard only if it has a subsidy component. If the IMF lends to a sovereign at the appropriate risk-adjusted rate, it will not engender moral hazard. It is the debtor country—not international taxpayers—that ultimately has to pay the costs of adopting risky policies: Risky policies early on means more adjustment later on to repay the IMF in full. Since IMF lending is "preferred" and paid ahead of the sovereign's other cross-border debt, the fact that the IMF lends at below-market rates does not imply that IMF lending is subsidized.[44]
- Recent theoretical work suggests that the risk of runs, in some conditions, can undermine a debtor's incentive to exert additional effort to improve its policies (Corsetti, Roubini, and Guimaraes 2003). This work will be reviewed in more detail later, but the basic intuition is simple: Without official support, a liquidity run will assure an immediate default, and policymakers will have no incentive to make policy reforms that will generate only benefits over time. The debtor's "policy effort" needs official support to have a chance of succeeding.

Finally there is a broader argument: The IMF has not created widespread moral hazard because it is not an ILOLR able to lend in large enough quantities to protect all debtors and their creditors from the risk of default. A domestic lender of last resort is usually able to protect all bank depositors from the risk of any losses. However, most international bailouts, as will be discussed in chapter 4, have been partial, not full. Long-term creditors in particular have little reason to believe that IMF lending will allow them to exit and plenty of reason to pay close attention to the debtor's policies.

Partial bailouts can be thought of as a form of partial insurance: They do not fully protect either the debtor or its entire body of creditors from a bad outcome. Just as a homeowner whose fire insurance policy carries a large deductible still has incentives not to take actions that put his house at greater risk, creditors who lend to a sovereign that has access only to "partial" liquidity insurance have different incentives than creditors who lend to one that has "full" liquidity insurance. Indeed, one of the strongest critiques of IMF lending is not that it is so effective at limiting the risk of runs that it gives rise to moral hazard but rather that partial lending is so

44. Thus, often-heard arguments (IFIAC 2000, for example) that IMF lending is a US taxpayer subsidy to emerging-market borrowers are substantially flawed as they do not recognize that IMF's *seniority* is consistent with its lending at below market rates without providing any subsidy to the sovereign borrower. Indeed, if the IMF is senior in the repayment order, its loans are less risky, and thus, it can lend fairly at below market rates.

ineffective at stopping runs that it is not worth providing. The next section takes up this topic.

Importance of the Risk of Moral Hazard in Practice

Moral hazard is inherent in all forms of insurance. The core issue is not whether IMF lending has the potential to introduce moral hazard, since it would clearly create moral hazard by lending in unlimited quantities to overindebted countries without demanding any policy reforms. The real issue is how important the distortion is in practice and whether the steps the IMF takes to limit the risk of moral hazard—limiting its lending and conditioning its lending on strong policy efforts—are able to minimize the risk of moral hazard without undermining the effectiveness of IMF lending.

Views on the analytical and practical importance of moral hazard distortions in international capital flows differ radically. Some, such as Calomiris (1998); Schwartz (1998); Dooley (2000); and Chinn, Dooley, and Shrestha (1999), believe that such distortions are important. Others, such as Summers (2000b), Zhang (1999), Truman (2002), and Mussa (2002a), think that the importance of such distortions has been overstated.[45] The issue is obviously one of quantitative degree rather than absolutes.

Two empirical issues exist in assessing the case for a large official provider of international liquidity: Does IMF finance include an implicit/explicit subsidy component? What is the empirical evidence that the expectations of IMF bailouts have distorted overall capital flows toward emerging economies, by leading either to too much overall lending to emerging economies or to too much lending to particularly risky emerging economies? Relatively little work has been done on the first question, but the existing research has rather strong conclusions: IMF lending has a very small subsidy element. Olivier Jeanne and Jeromin Zettelmeyer (2001) show that the domestic taxpayers in the debtor country—not the IMF or international financial institutions (i.e., the international taxpayers) or the country's other creditors—pay the costs of official support packages. Their best estimate is that the subsidy component of IMF lending, under realistic scenarios, is very small. The fact that domestic taxpayers bear the cost of crisis lending, in turn, limits the incentive for debtors to pursue risky policies.[46]

45. Corsetti, Pesenti, and Roubini (1999a, 1999b) and Burnside, Eichenbaum, and Rebelo (2000) model and stress that the distortions deriving from debtors' government bailout guarantees of the private (financial and nonfinancial) sector, rather than IMF bailouts, as the most important source of moral hazard in recent crisis episodes.

46. Of course, a short-sighted government that may not be in power in the future may follow reckless policies, then borrow from the IMF and thus shift the domestic burden of imprudent fiscal policy to future governments and taxpayers. But again, there is no international subsidy here—only a domestic redistribution of the costs of servicing IMF loans.

The effect expectations of IMF lending had on flows to emerging markets in the 1990s are hard to test, in part because it is generally hard to determine what drives capital flows to emerging economies.[47] Formal and systematic evidence on these issues is scarce. Xioaming Zhang (1999) did not find evidence that the Mexican bailout led to the significant reduction in sovereign spreads before the Asian crisis. Spreads on emerging-market debt fell after Mexico's rescue, but so did spreads on high-risk corporate bonds that clearly would not benefit from an IMF bailout. Timothy Lane and Steven Phillips (2000) found that it is difficult to detect evidence of moral hazard in market reactions to various IMF policy announcements and so failed to find evidence that would suggest that moral hazard has recently been on the rise. Steven Kamin (2002) did not find evidence that moral hazard has significantly distorted overall flows to emerging markets.

Dell'Ariccia, Schnabel, and Zettelmeyer (2002) examined how sovereign spreads reacted to the Russian crisis. They find partial, and mixed, evidence of moral hazard. The widening spread that occurred after Russia's default could be interpreted as evidence that the market had priced in a strong expectation that sufficient official support would be available to avoid major sovereign defaults. The "surprise" that Russia was allowed to default led market participants to reassess the scale of potential official support available to all emerging economies, leading to a widening of all sovereign spreads. Other studies (Sarno and Taylor 1999, Chang 2000, Spadafora 2001) also present evidence that is consistent with the existence of creditors' moral hazard.

It is also worth reviewing more circumstantial evidence of moral hazard. Little anecdotal evidence suggests that the expectations of large-scale IMF support that emerged after the Mexican bailout fueled the large increase in bank lending to Asia. This is possibly because Mexico was considered a special case due to its proximity to the United States. But it seems more likely that international banks and other investors simply believed in the Asian miracle and lent because they did not think Asian countries would need to be bailed out.

More anecdotal evidence suggests that investors may have expected large official support packages for certain systemically important countries, notably Russia in 1998, Brazil in 1998–99, and Turkey in 2000–03. Market participants certainly referred to Russia as a "moral hazard play" in 1998. Russia was considered too nuclear to fail, and the expectation of official support may have made the markets more willing to finance Russia than they otherwise would have been in 1997 and the first part of 1998.[48] This argument, though, cuts both ways: Investors who made the

47. See Roubini (2000) for a more detailed discussion of these arguments.

48. See, among others, Rubin and Weisberg (2003, 278): "I argued providing money [to Russia] under these circumstances would create an immense moral hazard problem. I had lived in the markets, and could feel people taking advantage of the situation."

moral hazard play in Russia ended up taking large losses and presumably learned a lesson.

More recently, spreads on Turkish external bonds arguably have been significantly lower than those of similarly rated sovereigns or of borrowers with comparable fiscal deficits and debt levels. This could be the result of expectations that Turkey is too strategically important to fail.[49] Spreads certainly widened significantly in March 2003, when the Turkish parliament failed to approve the deployment of US troops on its territory, and Turkey lost $6 billion in grants (which potentially could support a larger loan package). Spreads then came down when the United States provided $1 billion in aid for Turkey, in part because the markets perceived this as a signal of the United States' continued support for Turkey.

Despite circumstantial evidence that moral hazard has influenced investment decisions in Russia and to a lesser extent in Turkey, broader evidence of moral hazard seems lacking:

- The large official support packages that were extended to Asian countries in 1997–98, the large support package to Brazil in 1998, and the more recent series of large packages for many major Latin American countries (Argentina, Brazil, Uruguay, and Ecuador) did not trigger a wave of fresh lending to emerging economies. Net capital flows to emerging economies (particularly debt flows) collapsed after the Asian and Russian crises. Flows started to recover in 2003 but remain well below their 1996–97 peak.[50]

- Similarly, it is difficult to find evidence that the expectation of official support systematically has prompted emerging economies to undertake riskier policies. If anything, the evidence suggests the opposite. Mexico adopted much more prudent policies after its 1995 bailout and managed to navigate the 2000 election without experiencing a financial crisis. The Asian-crisis countries have dramatically increased their holdings of reserves while paying down their short-term debt, making it less likely that they will need to turn to the IMF again. Even with IMF support, the cost of recent financial crises has been severe.

49. Turkey's dollar-denominated international bonds trade differently than many other bonds because domestic Turkish banks are major holders of such instruments. This does not, however, refute the moral hazard hypothesis: Turkish banks may be willing to hold Turkey's bonds in part because they—not international investors—believe the country is too important to fail.

50. This assessment is based on the Institute of International Finance (IIF) data on capital flows in emerging markets through the end of 2003. Medium- to long term nonbank lending to emerging markets peaked—after sharply rising in the early 1990s—in 1997 to a level above $80 billion and was down to about $10 billion in 2003. Overall net private flows to emerging markets (including both bank and nonbank equity and debt flows) fell through 2002 and staged only a modest recovery in 2003. The compression in the Emerging Market Bond Index spreads in 2003 and high returns to the asset class led to a renewed interest in the emerging-market sovereign bond asset class in 2003, but net new financing has been modest so far, apart from a prefunding spike in early 2004 driven by the compression in borrowing costs.

In summary, the empirical evidence does not suggest that IMF lending, in its current form, has created widespread moral hazard. The subsidy component in IMF lending is small. Available studies do not find strong evidence that the expectation of IMF lending has significantly altered overall capital flows to emerging markets or spreads. The high cost of crises even with IMF support suggests that countries have few incentives to follow policies that may lead to currency, banking, and financial crises and possible default just because of the expectation of an IMF bailout.[51]

However, expectations of IMF support may have played a significant role in creditors' decisions to lend in some cases (Russia in 1998 and Turkey more recently). Moreover, while a sovereign may not purposely follow reckless policies to get IMF support, its expectations of IMF support may, at the margin, lead it to delay taking steps to get its house in order. More likely, though, delay stems from the difficult political economy of reform, not expectations of bailouts. Incentives abound for myopic policymaking that have nothing to with the IMF.

Do Partial Bailouts Ever Work?

Case Against Partial Bailouts

The existing analytical literature has emphasized the limitations of any "partial" solution to a sovereign financial crisis and instead has emphasized the need to adopt radical "corner" solutions—either a complete suspension of payments and of currency convertibility or the provision of enough liquidity to assure full payment of all short-term claims. According to this line of argument, supplying large but still limited amounts of liquidity (a partial bailout) won't stop the run, because creditors still have an incentive to get out before other creditors exhaust the debtor's limited supply of liquidity. A similar critique can be made of "partial" standstills: Restructuring one set of claims won't work, as locking in one set of creditors in a "partial" bail-in will lead other groups of creditors to run. If you suspend payments on the sovereign's external debt, domestic bank depositors may pull their funds out of the bank and seek to move them abroad. To be effective at ruling out a bad equilibrium, a standstill and the following restructuring need to be broad and comprehensive, and all potential channels for exiting need to be closed off.

Influential observers (Paul Krugman, for example) consequently have argued that the best solutions to liquidity crises are "corner" solutions: Half-measures don't work, and to stop runs the IMF needs to either become an ILOLR with enough resources to engineer a full bailout or, at the

51. A side implication of this observation is that Bulow's (2002) aversion toward lending by the IMF and IFIs on the grounds that IMF lending will be a source of strategic gaming between debtors and private creditors does not have strong factual basis.

other extreme, start relying on broad standstills that bail in[52] all investors. The theoretical work of Zettelmeyer (1999) and Jeanne and Zettelmeyer (2001) support the Krugman hypothesis. Their model of self-fulfilling runs stemming from a shortage of liquidity shows that partial bailouts (or partial bail-ins for that matter) are bound to fail: The "bad" equilibrium cannot be ruled out and creditors still have an incentive to run if official lending fails to eliminate the gap between the resources the debtor has on hand and those needed to cover all potential short-term claims. Ilan Goldfajn and Rodrigo Valdes (1999) make a similar point. Marcus Miller and Lei Zhang (2000) argue that debt standstills are preferable to liquidity support—since IMF funds are limited, it cannot credibly commit to provide enough money to stop a run.

Case for Partial Bailouts

In reality, however, partial bailouts and bail-ins have succeeded in some, though not in all, cases. Mexico is the most famous example of large-scale official lending without any debt restructuring, yet even in Mexico, the combined IMF and US government bailout was partial. Official lending was sufficient to cover the government's short-term debts but not to have "financed" a broad-based run out of the banking system. Korea's bail-in was also partial: The agreement to roll over short-term interbank claims, even when supplemented by official lending, failed to provide Korea with the amount of liquidity that would have been needed had domestic bank depositors sought to move their funds offshore en masse. Empirically, the combination of adjustment, financing, and targeted rollover agreements/ debt restructuring has succeeded in restoring confidence, even in the absence of sufficient financing, to avoid a bad equilibrium if everyone decided to run. While partial solutions may not work in the context of traditional theoretical models of multiple equilibria, they do seem to work in practice at least some of the time.[53]

52. A full bail-in requires doing far more than suspending external debt payments: All domestic residents and foreign investors also need to be prevented from trying to turn their local assets into foreign assets.

53. It is worth noting that the middle solutions that have worked best have been those with the most financing, such as Mexico in 1995. The initial Korean package in early December 1997 did not stop the run or prevent the crisis from deepening in part because the amount of financing available was too limited, relative to the country's maturing short-term claims—though policy uncertainty before the presidential elections also played a role. Korea's crisis was resolved only when a restructuring of maturing debts effectively increased the amount of funds that were on the table by adding a private contribution to the official lending package. Initial disbursements in cases like Indonesia were much smaller than in Korea, and one can thus argue that the limited disbursements may have contributed to the deepening of the crisis, though policy and political problems also were more serious in Indonesia. These cases are discussed in detail in the next chapter.

A set of recently developed models help close the gap between the existing theoretical analysis, which supports the "corner" solutions, and existing experience, which suggests that "middle" solutions can be successful. Giancarlo Corsetti, Bernardo Guimaraes, and Nouriel Roubini (2003) and Morris and Shin (2003) formally analyze whether partial catalytic finance (a partial bailout) can work when a crisis may be a combination of liquidity and weak fundamentals. These models provide an analytic demonstration of how catalytic IMF financing could work to stop an incipient run, in part because these new models allow for a more sophisticated understanding of the causes of a run.

In classic multiple-equilibria models, the possibility of a self-fulfilling run cannot be ruled out completely so long as the sovereign faces a financing gap. The economy always risks ending up in the bad equilibrium if not enough liquidity is available to pay everyone in the event of a rush to the exits. Limited official lending is not enough to avoid the bad equilibrium. Moreover, nothing (apart from random events, formally "sunspots") can nail down the probability that the economy will end up in the bad as opposed to the good equilibrium: The country's policy actions do not play a role in determining whether the country's creditors decide to run or stay in. Consequently, the economy is as likely to end up in one equilibrium or the other. In the new models, the state of economic fundamentals, the amount of official financing, and the amount of policy effort a sovereign exerts all play a role in determining whether or not a run happens: the better the fundamentals and the more the official support and the policy effort, the lower the risk of a run.

The Corsetti, Guimaraes, and Roubini (2003) model has a number of innovative features. Both fundamentals, including a debtor's policy action and the creditors' actions (speculation), can contribute to a sovereign debt crisis. As in Franklin Allen and Douglas Gale's model of bank runs (2000a), crises occur along a spectrum that goes from pure illiquidity to insolvency. This offers a more realistic description of crises than models that follow Diamond and Dybvig (1983). Such models ignore or downplay either the role of macroeconomic shocks or the risk that the country may be fundamentally insolvent in triggering a run. Unlike many of the models that draw on the classic Diamond and Dybvig model, which tends to downplay the issue of moral hazard, the Corsetti, Guimaraes, and Roubini (2003) model allows for the risks of both a run and moral hazard. Moreover, it is possible to perform a positive and normative comparative statics analysis of the trade-off between moral hazard from official support and the risk of a run. In contrast, in typical multiple-equilibria models, nothing—only random "sunspots"—pins down whether the good (no-run) or bad (run) equilibrium will occur.

The Corsetti, Guimaraes, and Roubini (2003) model also presents a more realistic description of the market than models that assume all creditors have access to the same information and will want to take the exact same portfolio position. This model draws on the literature on global games (Carlsson and van Damme 1993, Morris and Shin 1998), so the state of the economy and speculative activity are not common knowledge among all parties, and the game has a single unique equilibrium (rather than multiple). Since signals are noisy, and different players have access to different information on the true state of the country's economic fundamentals, not all players will follow the same choice (to run or not).[54] Finally, Corsetti, Guimaraes, and Roubini (2003) model the role of official financial institutions as that of large players in the market, whose actions can influence the behavior of other market participants depending on the relative informational advantage that such large players may or may not have compared with private investors.[55]

Many of the new analytical insights in this model stem from the impact IMF lending can have on other market participants. The IMF is assumed to seek to lend to illiquid, but not to insolvent, countries: In the model, the IMF makes mistakes but is still more likely to provide liquidity to cases where a liquidity run causes the crisis than to cases of insolvency. IMF lending therefore provides a signal to the market: A better-informed IMF reduces the aggressiveness of private speculators and lowers the likelihood of a crisis.[56] The IMF has a stronger impact on market behavior if it can strategically signal its position to the market—for example, if it can move before private investors. An IMF with sufficiently precise information can induce "strong herding behavior"—that is, private funds' managers disregard their private information and make their portfolio conditional on the IMF move, rolling over their debt if the IMF makes liquidity available to the country while pulling out funds if it does not. This body of work helps to shed light on the channels that allow "catalytic financing" to work. The bottom-line conclusion is consistent with common sense. Catalytic financing can help when the country's fundamentals are sound but not when the macroeconomic outlook is hopelessly weak.[57]

54. Vives and Rochet (2002) used a global games model to study domestic lenders of last resort. They find that regulating banks to protect their liquidity and solvency can avoid runs in the absence of a lender of last resort. However, the steps the banks have to take to protect themselves have a high cost—money that otherwise would be invested has to be used to protect the bank from runs. Emergency liquidity support, along with prudential regulation, is socially optimal: Liquidity support allows the banks to avoid the runs without lowering their investment below optimal levels.

55. See also Corsetti et al. (2004) and Corsetti, Pesenti, and Roubini (2002) on the role of large players (in this case private players such as large hedge funds) in triggering currency crises.

56. Corsetti et al. (2004) and Dasgupta (1999) examined the impact of a different large player's action—a speculator à la Soros—on the behavior and aggressiveness of other market investors in a currency-crisis model.

57. Morris and Shin (2003) reach similar conclusions on the potential success of the IMF's catalytic approach in a stylized one-period model. The empirical work of Cottarelli and Giannini (2002), Corsetti and Roubini (2004), and Mody and Saravia (2003) lends support to

Less intuitively, the Corsetti-Guimaraes-Roubini (2003) model introduces the possibility that official liquidity assistance can be necessary, under some circumstances, for well-intentioned governments to undertake appropriate policy reforms. IMF liquidity assistance helps to shield the country from self-fulfilling speculative runs and limits the risk of a run leading to a costly crisis and to the bankruptcy costs of default before policymakers accrue any gains from their reforms. Consequently, providing the government with insurance against the risk of a run lets the IMF raise the expected gains from reforms, making policy reforms more attractive. This directly challenges the conventional wisdom that official finance exacerbates the debtor moral hazard problem, since the presence of official insurance lowers the cost of bad policies and leads to riskier policies.

Other recent studies have contributed to one's understanding of the policy trade-offs between liquidity and moral hazard. Haldane et al. (2002) present a model that allows for fundamentals-driven runs. While these authors discuss moral hazard, they do not model the trade-off between moral hazard and the risk of a run.

More work needs to be done in this area of alternative crisis resolution approaches to formally address the choices policymakers face—for example, a systematic comparison of catalytic financing and standstills has not been done. Introducing opportunistic default in these models would also lead to a more complex analysis of the relative benefits of alternative crisis resolution tools. More work could also be done to resolve crises that are characterized by simultaneous runs on the government's own debt and the country's domestic banks. This leads to the next area in the new literature on crisis resolution: how to address crises triggered by private-sector, rather than public-sector, financial vulnerabilities.

Resolving Crises Triggered by Private-Sector External Borrowing

Until now, the analysis of crisis resolution has been conducted under the assumption that the borrowing debtor is a unified agent, either a country or a sovereign. This fiction enormously simplifies the analysis but increasingly limits its utility. As chapter 2 illustrated, vulnerabilities in the private sector, not public sector, triggered some emerging-market crises.[58] Other crises stem in part from the government's domestic borrowing.

---

the argument that the catalytic approach is more likely to be successful in cases where fundamentals are not too weak—i.e., in cases where the combination of policy adjustment and official finance are more likely to restore investors' confidence and prevent a disruptive run. Hovaguimian (2003) provides a more skeptical view of the success of catalytic finance.

58. One important caveat here is that private-sector vulnerabilities may, at times, be due to distortions that government policies trigger. Authors such as Corsetti, Pesenti, and Roubini (1999a, 1999b), among others, have advanced this "moral hazard" interpretation of crises, linked to the government's implicit and explicit bailout guarantees of the private sector.

Emerging markets often experience linked currency and banking crises, or even combined currency, banking, corporate debt, and sovereign debt crises.[59]

Ideally, it would be possible to conceptualize emerging economies not as countries borrowing from abroad but rather as more complex economies where firms, banks, and the government all borrow externally and also domestically, in foreign—and possibly domestic—currency. Such an approach would disaggregate "the emerging-market borrower" into more than a single agent. While a large and growing analytical literature now examines how vulnerabilities that arise from private-sector borrowing can give rise to external payments crises (see chapter 2), much less analytical work tries specifically to analyze the appropriate international response to emerging-market crises that originate in the private sector.

In principle one could argue that private-sector crises could be addressed without any public-sector intervention, either by domestic authorities or by the IFIs. Well-functioning bankruptcy regimes provide the basic framework for private debtors and their creditors to renegotiate their debts, and if such a regime is in place, the resolution of private crises may not raise any policy issues. However, leaving the resolution of private crises to private borrowers and their creditors may not be optimal for a number of important reasons. First, macroeconomic shocks—particularly currency crises—often lead to systemic, rather than individual, crises, either in the banking or the corporate sector. A systemic crisis leaves most banks—or a very large number of firms—in financial difficulty. Institutions, like bankruptcy courts, that work well for solving the financial difficulties of a single firm may break down when a country's entire private sector faces the need for a debt restructuring (Hoelscher and Quintyn 2003). Second, the government's role in protecting bank depositors from losses almost inevitably involves it in the resolution of a systemic crisis, since large losses in the corporate sector almost always lead to large losses in the banking sector. A concerted effort to solve these crises with government intervention may be either necessary or impossible to avoid.

Most intriguingly, private-sector borrowing also risks causing "self-fulfilling" crises. Jeanne and Zettelmeyer (2002) have modeled the easiest such crisis to characterize it: A run triggers a currency crisis, and the currency crisis in turn triggers the insolvency of borrowers who have taken out foreign currency loans. Private borrowers that would have been solvent but for the run are forced into bankruptcy, triggering a broad crisis.

Jeanne and Zettelmeyer show that domestic monetary policy alone cannot prevent a run if foreign-currency borrowing is extensive. Moreover, if the government's reserves are limited, an ILOLR can potentially help to

59. See Allen et al. (2002) and chapter 2 for an examination of the reasons why emerging-market crises snowball through different sectors.

avoid the broader crisis. The international lender can lend a fiscally solvent government the liquidity it needs to avert a private-sector crisis (Jeanne and Zettelmeyer 2002). International support allows the government to support domestic banks and firms that are "conditionally solvent"—that is, banks and firms that would be solvent but for the overshooting of the exchange rate—and thus avert a severe crisis. Broadly speaking, international liquidity support to a government that, in turn, supports the private-sector balance sheets makes sense only if the private entities are solvent and if international liquidity can potentially prevent a disruptive run, a fall in asset prices, or both from triggering a broader crisis (see Allen et al. 2002).

International intervention to help the authorities in emerging economies solve "private-sector crises"—typically bank runs—also raises complicated issues of moral hazard. International lending could increase "domestic" moral hazard: If the private sector expects that the government will intervene to protect private-sector lenders and borrowers, and if necessary, the official sector will provide the liquidity the government may need to be able to make good on its guarantees, the private sector has an incentive to take on more risk. Domestic moral hazard from implicit or explicit domestic bailout guarantees would be a concern even in a world without an IMF, but the issue becomes more complex when the IMF is providing the financing needed for the government to make good on its domestic guarantees, including a guarantee to sustain a particular exchange rate. Indeed, Douglas Gale and Xavier Vives (2001) suggest that dollarization could help to make a government's commitment not to provide emergency liquidity to the banking system credible, helping to get rid of moral hazard. In these models, dollarization makes sense as long as the bankruptcy costs that follow from the absence of a domestic lender of last resort are low. Obviously, the availability of international liquidity would undermine the ability of dollarization to help eliminate domestic moral hazard even as it helps limit the risk that dollarization—or the more common use of the dollar to denominate local bank deposits—could increase the number of disruptive domestic bank runs.

The analytical literature on how to resolve systemic crises that originate in private-sector vulnerabilities is still in its infancy. However, such crises may be common in the future, given growing financial integration and the vulnerabilities that informal dollarization creates in many emerging economies. This area should attract greater analytical effort.

Policy Implications and Suggestions for Further Research

The analytical literature helps to frame the debate on the core issue confronting policymakers of finding the right mix of conditional official support (bailouts), policy adjustments, and bail-ins to resolve a crisis. Different theoretical traditions look at the sovereign debt market and see different risks. One tradition looks at the sovereign debt market—or cross-border lending more generally—and focuses on the difficulty in enforcing a contract against a sovereign given the incentive for opportunistic default. This tradition worries about the risk of difficulties in enforcing a debt contract resulting in too little lending, at too high a price. It focuses on the need to create incentives for debtors to honor their commitments and warns against any official intervention that reduces the cost of default. Others argue that sovereign borrowers have too much access to international credit—credit that helps policymakers with poor incentives accumulate dangerous levels of debt too rapidly. The proposed solution: Make sovereign default easier, so credit is harder to find. Another tradition looks at emerging economies and focuses on their vulnerability to external shocks: Debt problems stem from contracts that leave payments fixed even as external events reduce a country's capacity to pay. Steps that reduce the debt restructuring costs after an external shock reduces a debtor's ability to pay could facilitate more efficient crisis resolution.

Another tradition focuses on the risk that problems of creditor coordination will give rise to market failures and lead either to a run on the sovereign's debt or, more broadly, a run on a country's foreign-currency reserves. If such runs are a risk, one potential solution is to make payments suspensions and debt restructurings easier. Another solution is to provide the international liquidity needed to stop the run. The provision of enough liquidity can eliminate the risk of a self-fulfilling crisis pushing the country into a bad equilibrium—typically an avoidable default by a solvent debtor. In theory a payments standstill can stop a run as effectively as a lender of last resort, but the conditions required for this to be true hardly seem relevant in the sovereign context; also, standstills may exacerbate the moral hazard from opportunistic defaults. Thus, liquidity support rather than a standstill may be the more appropriate way to address liquidity runs.

Another tradition highlights the risk that the provision of insurance against a liquidity crisis may introduce distortions of its own into the market, specifically moral hazard from bailout expectations. An ILOLR cannot regulate a sovereign in the same way a domestic central bank regulates the domestic banking system. More broadly, the official sector's presence inherently changes the dynamics of the strategic interaction between sovereign borrowers and their lenders. One solution would be to not provide any liquidity insurance at all; this eliminates moral hazard but at the price of making liquidity problems harder to resolve. The more common solution, in practice, has been to provide only partial insurance. The IMF lends in limited quantities and makes its lending conditional on policy adjustments by the debtor. In some cases, the IMF also has made its lending conditional on creditors' willingness to restructure their claims—a means of limiting creditor moral hazard. The debtor's policy adjustment acts as a kind of copayment that limits the risk of this insurance distorting the borrowers' incentives, just as any change in the servicing profile of creditors' claims reduces the risk of the insurance altering creditors' incentives.

All these models illuminate the challenge of developing an efficient policy for responding to crises in emerging economies. However, one of the weaknesses of the theoretical literature on international crisis resolution is that it tends to overemphasize the extreme cases. A sovereign debtor is either perfectly solvent and facing liquidity difficulties solely because of a creditor panic or insolvent regardless of any policy changes it might implement. The only effective solution to a liquidity crisis is either full liquidity insurance from an ILOLR or a total suspension of currency convertibility and sovereign payments. The only way to avoid creditor and debtor moral hazard is to avoid the provision of any IMF liquidity insurance. Any lending to a country after it defaults will be captured by international creditors or will reduce incentives for sound debtor policies ex ante. The policy prescriptions that emerge from the models that stress only one dimension of these trade-offs tend to be policies that are at the corners.

The analytical literature on crisis resolution, consequently, has provided relatively few tools to assess the policy trade-offs created by a world where the sovereign benefits from partial rather than full liquidity insurance and where most cases fall somewhere between pure illiquidity and pure insolvency. Some new models do allow for a run to exacerbate fundamental problems and for fundamental weaknesses to contribute to the source of runs. Some such models have interesting results. For example, Corsetti, Guimaraes, and Roubini (2003) illuminates why partial—or catalytic—IMF financing could work. Significant but not unlimited financing from a large player like the IMF can influence the position that other players in the market take and induce policymakers to undertake costly and risky policy adjustments.

Existing models of international crises suffer from a second set of weaknesses. They tend to assume a world that is defined by a single debtor (either a country or the sovereign), its external private creditors, and the official sector. These models yield important insights, and parsimonious models of international crises that simplify in order to clarify, no doubt, have immense advantages. But there are advantages also in developing analytical models that seek to identify more clearly the circumstances when the government, by providing hard-currency liquidity to local private entities, can avoid a broader crisis and the circumstances when such intervention is unwarranted. More effort should also be made to analyze the complex interaction between external default and domestic financial difficulty, which has characterized recent sovereign crises (most notably in Argentina). Models that imagine the emerging-market debtor as a single entity and look only at how the presence of an actor like the IMF affects the strategic game between the sovereign and its external creditors offer limited insight into the domestic financial fallout of external default.[60]

We don't think the theoretical critique of partial IMF lending is sufficiently compelling to suggest that the IMF cannot play a constructive role in crisis resolution. Analytical models can help to identify the circumstances when the IMF's insurance, combined with policy adjustments by the debtor and sometimes with a restructuring that changes the profile of creditor claims on the country, can be effective. But the gaps in most existing models—notably their portrayal of the emerging-market debtor as a single entity—also suggest that the results of any model need to be interpreted with caution.

The next chapter examines the world's growing experience with emerging-market crises, both to assess whether limited IMF lending will work and when a debt restructuring is a necessary part of the solution to a country's financial difficulties. Chapter 6 picks up many of the themes of the latter part of this chapter as it examines how to address problems characterized in part by a shortage of liquidity. Chapter 7 returns to many of the themes in the first part of this chapter as it examines how different claims on a sovereign debtor should be treated in a comprehensive debt restructuring.

60. Chapter 6 discusses in more detail the issue of how to resolve crises originating from vulnerabilities in the private sector.

4

Experience with Bailouts and Bail-ins

The financial crises of the last decade—as described in chapter 2—typically resulted in a gap between the foreign exchange the crisis country needed to cover its current account deficit, payments on maturing debts and predicted domestic capital flight, and the foreign exchange that the country had on hand or could be expected to raise in private markets. In the face of such external financing gaps, crisis resolution has three core elements:

- policy adjustments, whether a change in the exchange rate regime or in other macroeconomic policies;
- official financial support, whether from IMF rescue loans—loosely speaking "bailouts"—or the rescheduling of debts owed to bilateral creditors; and
- bail-ins or debt restructurings.

This chapter provides an overview of actual experience with bailouts and bail-ins, starting with Mexico's 1995 crisis.[1] The first section assesses the success of official support packages—bailouts. The second section reviews experience with the restructuring of debts owed to private creditors (i.e., bail-ins), ranking bail-ins from most voluntary to most coercive.[2] The

1. See the comprehensive studies by Sachs (1989b, 1990) and Cline (1995) on the 1980s debt crisis and its resolution.

2. Table 2.1b provides a summary of recent experience with crisis resolution, paying attention to topics such as capital controls, domestic bank holidays, and scale of domestic macroeconomic adjustment that are not covered in detail in this chapter. Tables 4.1 and 4.2 in this chapter provide a more detailed review of major bailouts. Appendix table A.1 (at the end of

chapter then highlights the lessons that can be drawn from recent experience, whether lessons for the use of official financing, bond restructurings, or restructuring of bank claims.

Recent experience suggests, at least to us, that no one approach is likely to succeed in all circumstances. The challenge of crisis resolution is finding the right set of tools to address an individual crisis. That conclusion, however, begs the question of how best to map different tools to different crises. Here too, we think that the growing body of experience with bailouts, bond restructurings, and bank reschedulings is starting to suggest answers.

The success of official bailouts can be judged, in part, by the speed with which the country can repay the loan. Other definitions of success are of course possible, but the capacity to repay the official sector is a decent proxy for both the country's broader return to economic and financial health and the success of the IMF's policy conditionality.[3] Judged on this basis, the most successful bailouts were provided to countries that had comparatively small debt levels and had the ability to make needed policy adjustments. These bailouts generally were provided to countries that encountered trouble as they were moving off a fixed—or heavily managed—exchange rate regime. It is still too early to judge the success of the IMF's recent experiments with providing large bailout packages to countries that have quite substantial debt levels—far above the levels of past success stories. Recent crisis countries have committed to making quite significant policy adjustments to offset their poor starting positions. They generally have delivered on these commitments, but adjustment alone has not been sufficient to put them in a position to repay the IMF quickly.

It is harder to find a single measure to gauge the success of efforts to obtain crisis financing from the country's private creditors. Success requires convincing private creditors to contribute, whether by deferring payments or by agreeing to reduce their claims on the crisis country. But it also requires that the private creditors' contribution not come at the expense of other goals—including preventing a sharp fall in output or digging the country into a deeper financial hole.

Recent experience with debt restructurings supports three general conclusions. First, bonds—including those that lack collective action clauses—can be restructured in a wide range of circumstances. Bond exchanges are necessary to clean up after a catastrophic default but also can be used to avoid default by deferring payments, as a country takes steps to stabilize its economy. Second, voluntary is not always better. In crisis conditions,

---

this book) provides comprehensive data on the official sector's exposure in different crises. Appendix table A.3 summarizes the main features of recent bail-ins.

3. There is a high empirical correlation between the speed with which a crisis country repays the IMF and the return to economic growth and financial stability of the country.

creditors left to their own devices either want to get out no matter what or demand a very high premium to "voluntarily" extend their exposure. Completely voluntary bank rollover arrangements have not prevented banks from cutting back their exposure, and completely voluntary bond exchanges have provided short-term debt relief on terms that have increased concerns about long-term solvency. Third, the official sector has an important role to play in the restructuring of debts owed to private creditors. Official action can catalyze private creditors to organize to overcome their coordination problems, reinforcing incentives to participate in a cooperative solution and increasing the cost of pulling out. The official sector is the actor best positioned to take a broad interest in the overall success of a complex restructuring. It could ensure that the various steps required for financial rehabilitation—including, among others, the restructuring of external bonds, Paris Club debt, and domestic debt—combine with the debtor's own efforts to improve its policies to produce a coherent whole.

Experience with Official Financing

IMF Lending Norms and Facilities

Before presenting the data on the size of IMF rescue packages and our assessment of the success of such bailouts, it is useful to briefly review the IMF's lending tools. The IMF has several lending facilities, each designed to meet—at least in theory—specific financing needs. Crisis lending to major emerging economies typically is done either through the IMF's main lending window—so-called stand-by arrangements (SBAs)—or through a special facility designed to provide very large amounts of financing for a very short term in the event of sudden capital outflows—the supplemental reserve facility (SRF). The IMF also has facilities for providing concessional, long-term lending to the poorest countries, but these facilities are not relevant to this discussion.

The financial terms of an SBA and an SRF have important differences. A borrowing country is expected to start repaying an SBA after two and a quarter years and finish after four years; a borrowing country *has* to start repaying an SBA after three and a quarter years and finish after five years. Countries initially were expected to start repaying SRF loans in a year and complete repayment in one and a half years and were obligated to start repaying in two years and finish in two and a half years. However, the maturity of the SRF was slightly extended recently: Countries are now expected to repay in two to two and a half years and *have* to repay in three years. All SRF loans carry a substantial surcharge (3 to 5 percentage points); SBAs that exceed normal access limits also carry special surcharges. In broad terms, countries are expected to repay an SRF more quickly than an SBA and to pay a "penalty" interest rate that encourages early repayment.

The IMF assesses the size of an IMF loan in relation to a country's IMF quota. Quotas, in turn, are based on the size of the country's financial contribution to the IMF. Countries with large quotas usually—but not necessarily—have larger economies than those with smaller quotas. A country normally can borrow up to 100 percent of its IMF quota in a year and 300 percent over three years. Anything more is considered exceptional.[4] There is a presumption that access above the IMF standard lending limits should be provided through the SRF. But exceptional financing can also be provided on "stand-by" terms.

The SRF was not created until after the Mexican, Thai, and Indonesian crises. It was used for the first time in Korea in 1997 and subsequently in Brazil, Argentina, Turkey, and Uruguay (though only a tiny fraction of Uruguay's loan was on SRF terms). Korea and Brazil (after 1999) were both able to repay the IMF relatively quickly. However, large amounts of financing increasingly have been provided through packages that combine SBA and SRF loans (Argentina, Turkey, and Brazil), in part because of growing concerns that the large payment spikes associated with the SRF could impede regaining market access.[5] Moreover, in Argentina, Turkey, and Brazil, payments on the country's initial SRF loans were effectively refinanced with new SBAs. This turned the initial two-and-a-half-year loan into a much longer five- to seven-year loan.

4. Country quotas are based on anachronistic, historical factors and often do not reflect the current economic size or potential financing needs of a crisis country. For example, Korea's quota was historically very small relative to its economic size. Consequently, Korea's emergency financial support package during its 1997–98 crisis was much larger relative to its quota than to its GDP. Reforming IMF quotas to better reflect the current relative size, importance, and potential borrowing needs of different countries is extremely contentious. Quota size is related to voting rights in the IMF—countries with a larger quota have a greater effective say and voting share in the IMF's Executive Board. The 1998 quota increase provided the IMF with more resources but had only a marginal impact on the relative standing of different members. The IMF also has access to special credit lines from some of its main contributors for additional resources, on top of the committed capital or quotas, to address severe global financial turmoil. The General Agreements on Borrowing (GAB) was introduced in 1962 and the New Agreements on Borrowing (NAB) in 1998; they are only rarely activated.

5. In 1998 the IMF introduced another tool for exceptional financing, the contingent credit line (CCL). The CCL stressed ex ante rather than ex post conditionality. In theory, countries that prequalified for IMF support with sound and transparent macroeconomic and financial policies and data transparency could qualify for a CCL, which provided access to relatively large IMF resources in case of contagion, with relatively minimal conditionality. However, no member country ever applied for a CCL, despite a number of reforms since 1998 to make it more appealing, so this facility was phased out in 2003. The IMF also has facilities to provide subsidized ("concessional") lending to very poor countries (enhanced structural adjustment facility or ESAF, now called poverty reduction and growth facility, or PRGF) as well as facilities to provide multiyear lending at slow repayment rates to countries with serious structural problems or in transition to a market economy (the extended fund facility, or EFF).

The mechanics of IMF lending are of obvious interest to IMF insiders. But why should the broader world care about the IMF's crisis financing facilities? The answer is simple: IMF lending facilities embody a theory about the appropriate use of IMF funds and consequently help to provide a basis for assessing the success of large IMF lending packages. For example, the SRF was built around the theory that larger loans—counterintuitively—could be repaid more rapidly than smaller loans, so exceptional levels of financing should be provided for shorter periods rather than normal financing. This is, in part, to assure that the IMF's funds "revolve"—that large amounts of money are not tied up in one country for a long time. The analogy to a domestic lender of last resort also influenced the SRF's design: Mobilizing overwhelming financial force would not only quickly stop capital outflows from the crisis country but also catalyze the rapid resumption of capital inflows. The quick return of market confidence, in turn, would allow the IMF to be repaid quickly.

Countries that borrow large sums but cannot repay the IMF quickly—whether because the IMF initially offered more generous repayment terms or because the initial loan had to be refinanced with a new loan—consequently are a rebuke to the theory that large amounts of money should be provided only for short terms. Slow repayment may indicate that the theory behind the SRF is wrong and that large sums cannot be repaid more quickly than small sums. Or it may indicate that the theory only works if IMF lends to the right set of countries.

One brief but important note: While the IMF measures the size of its loan in relation to a country's quota and denominates its loans in its own unit of account (special drawing right, or SDR), few others do the same. Private loans—and the bilateral loans that sometimes accompany IMF lending—are usually denominated in dollars, euros, or yen. To facilitate comparison with these financing sources, we have generally converted IMF loans into dollars. Also while the IMF defines "exceptional" lending in relation to a country's quota, we have generally opted to look at how much money the IMF is providing relative to a country's GDP or gross national income (GNI).

Size of IMF's Crisis Lending

The headlines announcing a new multibillion dollar IMF bailout—sometimes backed by additional "bilateral" financing from major countries—often paint a misleading picture of the amount of money the IMF, along with bilateral creditors, actually makes available to a crisis country. In some successful cases, confidence was reestablished relatively quickly, and the country did not have to draw on its entire package. In some less successful cases, the amount of financing actually provided fell well short of the amount promised—whether because the country failed to meet its policy commitments or because the combination of policy adjustment and financing failed to calm the markets, and the country defaulted before all available funds had been disbursed. Moreover, the desire to produce an impressive headline number has led to financing packages that include money from sources whose actual commitment was far weaker and less well-defined than the IMF's commitment. Bilateral commitments can be available for disbursement alongside IMF funds (first line of defense, as in Mexico, Thailand,[6] and Brazil in 1998–99) or can be available only if conditions are worse than expected and if the debtor country reaches a supplemental agreement with countries providing the extra financing (second line of defense, as in Indonesia and Korea).

The headline commitments and the actual disbursements in major recent IMF programs are summarized in table 4.1.[7] Only in Turkey and the most recent Brazil program have actual disbursements been close to the announced headline commitment.

A number of variables other than size are relevant for assessing a bailout's impact. A meaningful difference exists between countries that can repay their bailout loans quickly and those that cannot. A difference also exists between financing a temporary and a permanent fall in private exposure to the crisis country. In the worst-case scenario, the official sector finances a permanent fall in private-sector exposure to the crisis country and in turn is left with long-term exposure of its own to the crisis country.

"Catalytic" Lending and Rapid Repayments?

The typical case for large-scale official financing is that a large rescue loan is needed for a short period to stop a liquidity run. No effort is needed to seek explicit commitments from private creditors to maintain their exposure. Rather, the combination of financing and adjustment is expected to lead private creditors and investors to conclude that they should keep their money in the crisis country. This is the "catalytic" approach to crisis resolution.

Both relatively rapid repayment of the IMF and a fairly rapid halt to the fall in private-sector exposure should mark a successful "catalytic case." Table 4.2 and figures 4.1 to 4.3 show how quickly various crisis countries have been able to repay their IMF and bilateral loans. Tables 4.3 and 4.4 show changes in the exposure of private external creditors—both international banks and international bondholders—during recent crises. A full accounting would also look at changes in the financial claims of domestic residents, but such data are not available on a cross-country basis.

6. The United States did not participate in Thailand's bilateral financing package.

7. Table A.1 at the end of the book provides more data with the exposure to the crisis countries of all official creditors, not just the IMF but also the multilateral development banks (MDBs) and bilateral creditors.

Table 4.1 IMF and bilateral first- and second-line financing
(billions of dollars, percent of GDP in parentheses)

Country	IMF plus bilateral commitment	Peak disbursement	IMF commitment	IMF disbursement	Bilateral commitment	Bilateral disbursement
Mexico (1995)	38.9 (9.6)	27.6 (6.8)	18.9 (4.6)	15.8 (3.9)	20.0 (5.0)	13.5 (3.3)
Thailand[a] (1997)	14.0 (7.7)	11.2 (6.2)	4.0 (2.2)	3.5 (1.9)	10.0 (5.5)	8.8 (4.8)
Indonesia (1997)	26.3 (11.6)	10.8 (4.7)	11.3 (5.0)	10.8 (4.7)	15.0 (6.6)	0
Korea (1997)	40.9 (7.7)	19.4 (3.7)	20.9 (4.0)	19.4 (3.7)	20.0 (3.8)	0
Russia[b] (1998)	15.1 (3.5)	5.1 (1.2)	15.1 (3.5)	5.1 (1.2)	0	0
Brazil (1998–99)	32.9 (4.1)	17.5 (2.2)	18.4 (2.3)	13.3 (1.6)	14.5 (1.8)	9.5 (1.2)
Turkey (1999–2002)	33.8 (17.0)	23.1 (11.6)	33.8 (17.0)	23.1 (11.6)	0	0
Argentina (2000–01)	23.1 (8.1)	13.7 (4.8)	22.1 (7.8)	12.7 (4.5)	1.0 (0.4)	1.0 (0.4)
Uruguay[c] (2002)	2.7 (14.5)	2.2 (11.8)	2.7 (14.5)	2.2 (11.8)	1.5 (8.0)	1.5 (8.0)
Brazil (2001–02)	35.1 (6.9)	30.1 (5.9)	35.1 (6.9)	30.1 (5.9)	0	0

a. Bilateral data for Thailand were available only on an annual basis.

b. Russia had already drawn on the IMF to support its overall transition, and it had $14.2 billion in outstanding IMF loans when it received the additional $15.1 billion commitment. If Russia had obtained the full new 1998 crisis package, total exposure could have reached $29.3 billion, or around 7.5 percent of precrisis GDP.

c. Uruguay's bilateral loan was a four-day bridge to an augmented IMF program.

Note: Peak disbursement is not necessarily the sum of IMF and bilateral peaks. In some cases, IMF disbursements helped pay back bilateral financing, so the peaks came at different points in time. Data on bilateral financing are quarterly. Bilateral financing provided through the restructuring of Paris Club debt is excluded from these totals.

Sources: International Monetary Fund, www.imf.org/external/fin.htm, for financial data; Moody's Investor Services for GDP data; US Treasury for Mexico and Brazil's bilateral financing data; World Bank *Global Development Finance* for Thailand's bilateral data; and authors' calculations.

Mexico, Korea, and Brazil in 1999 fit the typology for a successful "catalytic" case reasonably well. Mexico fits nearly perfectly. After three years, Mexico had almost completely repaid its rescue loan, bank loans were only a little below precrisis levels, and Mexico's stock of outstanding bonds had gone up. Korea and Brazil also fit the basic typology reasonably well. Both were able to repay the IMF quickly, and in both cases, private creditors stopped pulling funds out relatively quickly. However, both countries also succeeded only after important mid-course correc-

Table 4.2. Rate of IMF (and bilateral first-line) loan disbursement and repayment
(billions of dollars, percent of GDP in parentheses)

Country	Peak disburse-ment	Quarters to reach peak	Quarters to repay half the peak disbursement	Precrisis external debt (percent of GDP)	Precrisis fiscal debt (percent of GDP)
Mexico	27.6 (6.8)	4	9	34	31
Thailand	11.2 (6.2)	12	17[a]	60	5
Indonesia	10.8 (4.7)	13	—	43	24
Korea	19.4 (3.7)	4	8	32	12
Russia	5.1 (1.2)	2	4	35	52
Brazil (1998–99)	17.5 (2.2)	3	7	25	40
Turkey (2000–02)	23.1 (11.6)	13	—	57	56
Argentina	13.7 (4.8)	4	—	51	45
Uruguay	2.1 (11.3)	8[b]	—	81	38
Brazil (2001–02)	30.1 (5.9)	9	—	44	65

— = The country has not yet repaid half its loan.

a. Thailand's IMF exposure peaked after nine quarters, and it repaid half of that exposure after 17 quarters. At that point in time, it had not repaid half its bilateral lending. However, we do not have data indicating Thailand's bilateral repayments after the end of 2001.

b. Debt levels are still rising.

Sources: IMF and bilateral first-line lending data are from IMF and the US Treasury; debt data are from Moody's Investor Service (apart from Mexico's precrisis debt data, which are from the IMF). Moody's debt numbers for Brazil are higher than other sources. The IMF, drawing on the government of Brazil's own definition of its debt, reports lower debt levels for Brazil: 35 percent in 1997 and 49 percent in 2000.

tions. As will be discussed in detail later, Korea had to supplement official support with a rescheduling of its interbank debts to obtain the time it needed to recover. Brazil's success came only after it managed to exit from its peg with less disruption than most expected, and it too actively monitored interbank rollovers after exiting from its peg. Nonetheless, the basic pattern was the same as in Mexico: Large IMF disbursements—complemented by commitments from private creditors—let the country avoid default, and large repayments to the IMF followed in relatively short order.

Figure 4.1 IMF and BIS loans outstanding

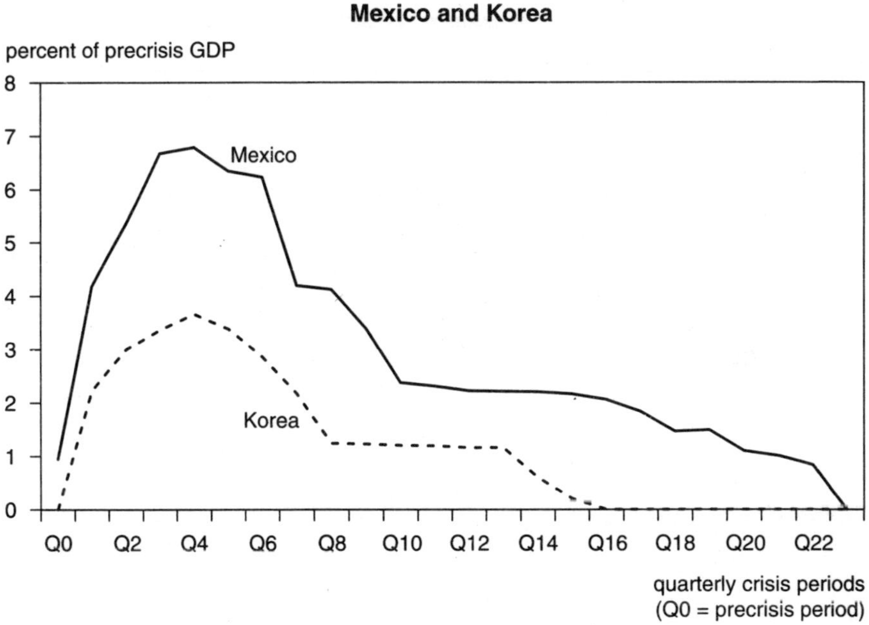

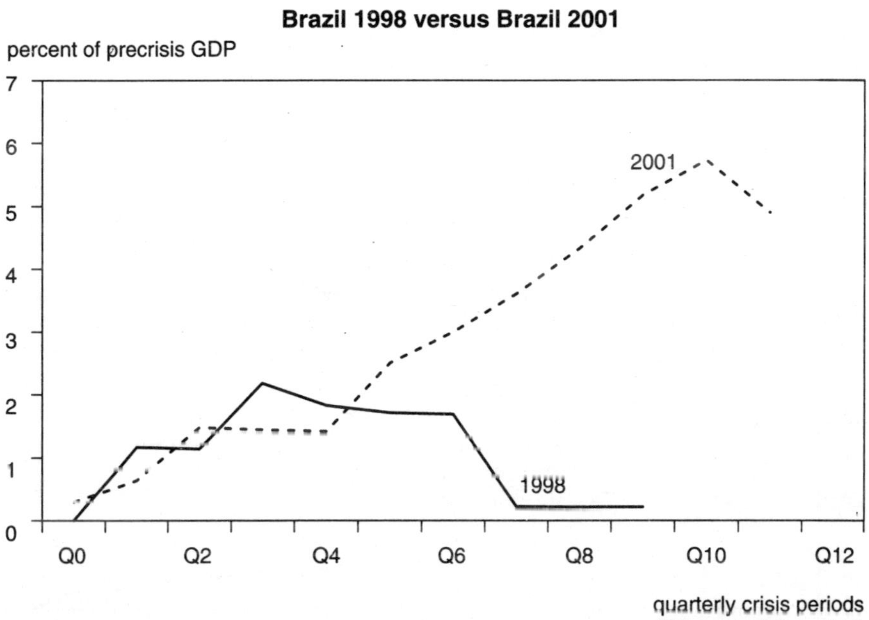

Source: Data from International Monetary Fund, US Treasury, and Moody's Investor Service; authors' calculations.

Figure 4.2 IMF and ESF loans outstanding

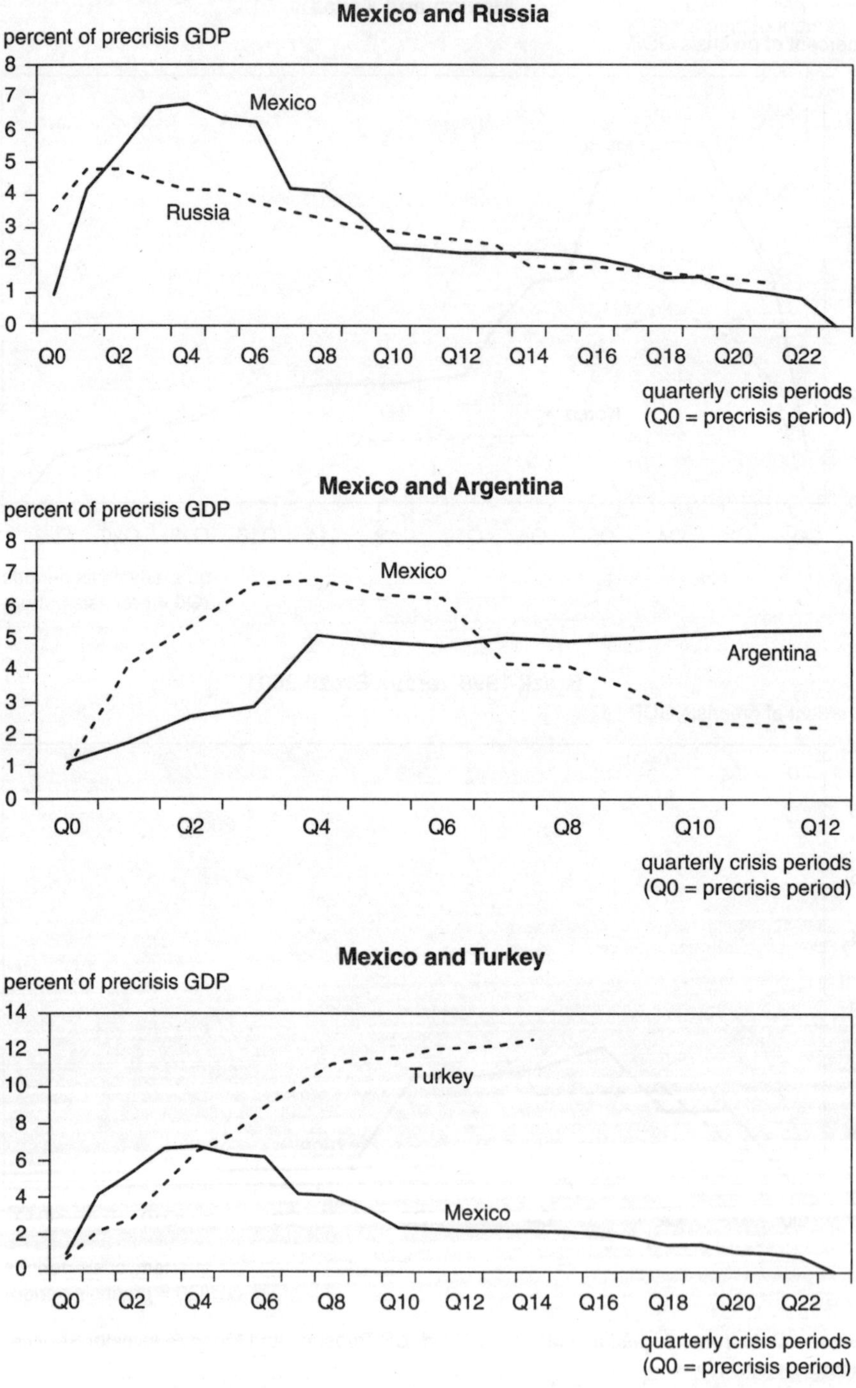

Figure 4.2 IMF and ESF loans outstanding *(continued)*

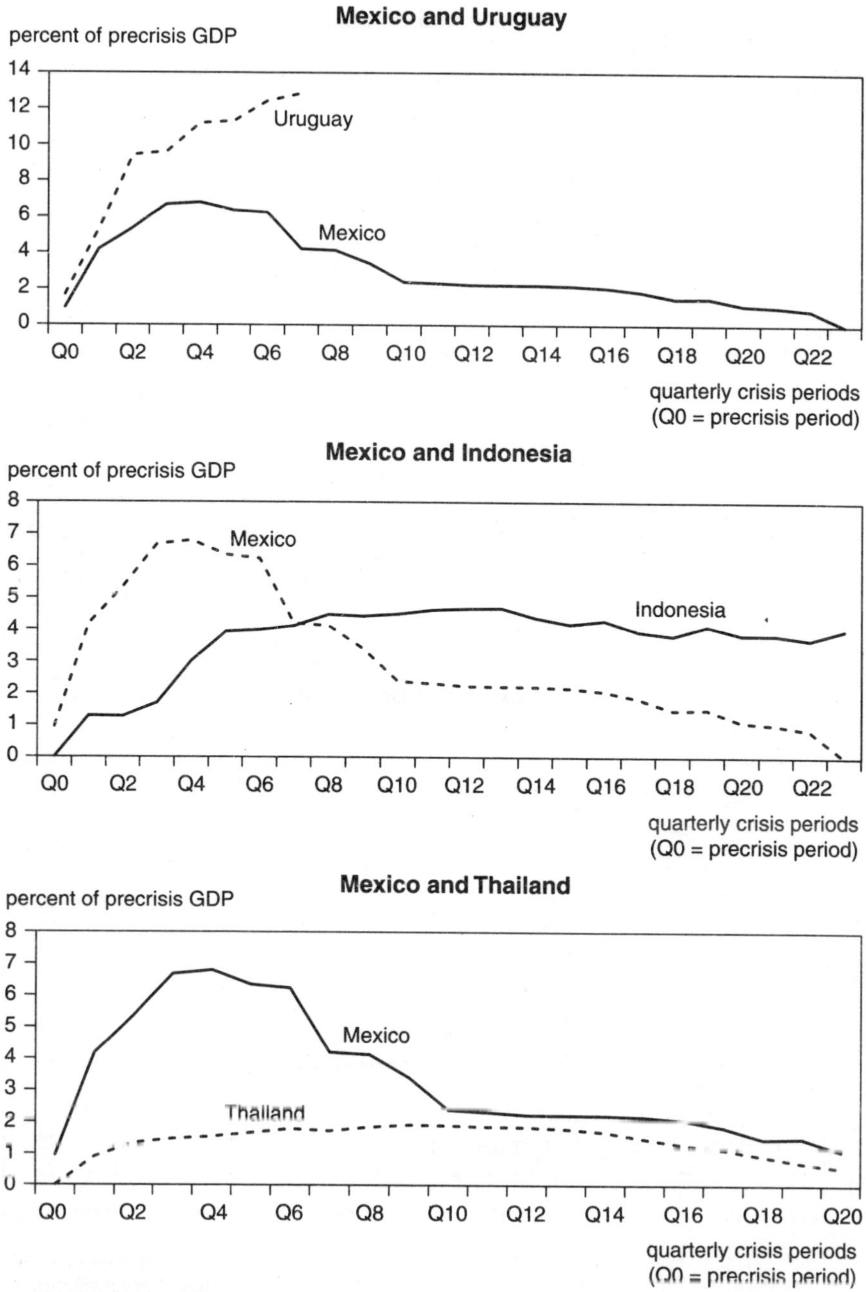

ESF = Exchange Stabilization Fund

Source: Data from International Monetary Fund, US Treasury, and Moody's Investor Service; authors' calculations.

Figure 4.3 IMF and bilateral loans outstanding

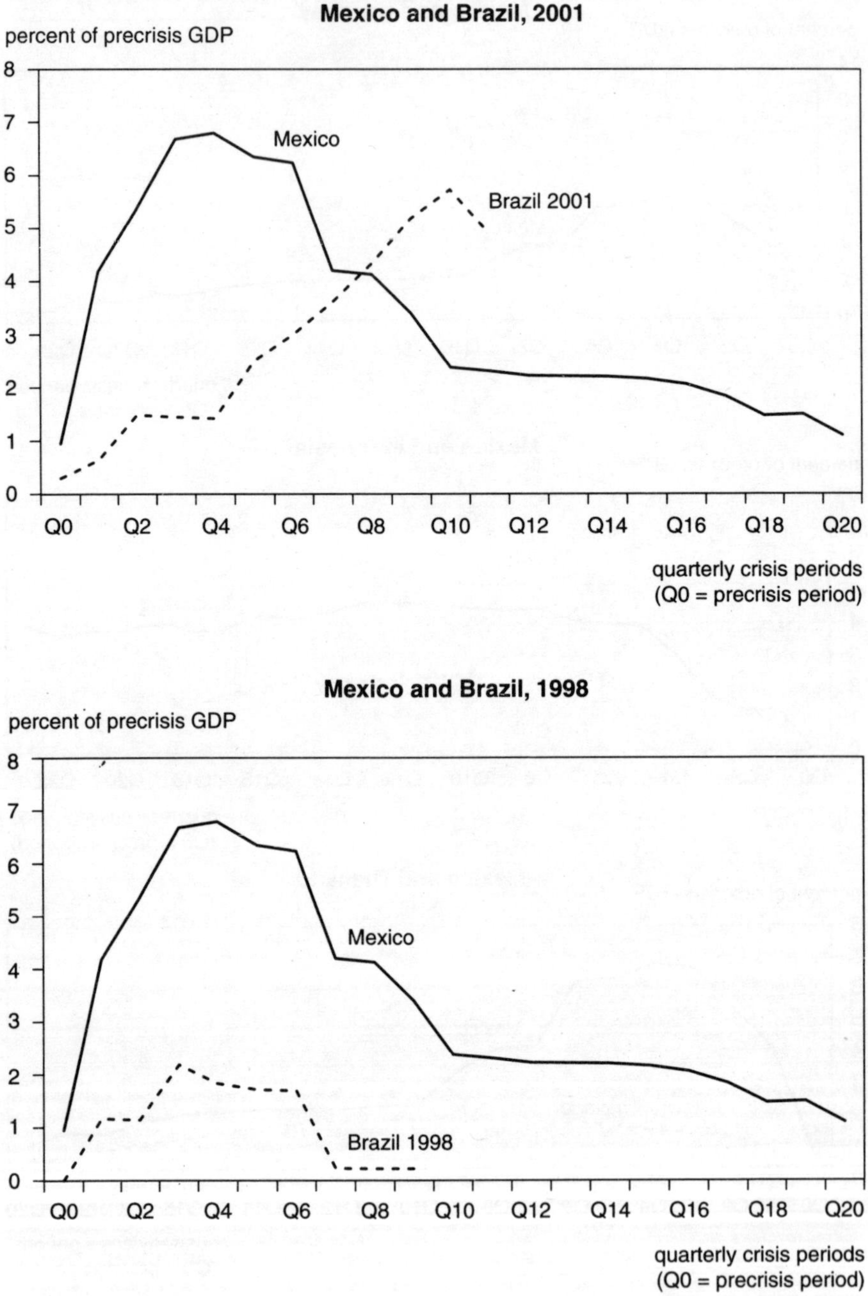

Source: Data from International Monetary Fund, US Treasury, and Moody's Investor Service; authors' calculations.

Table 4.3 Changes in IMF/bilateral exposure and international bank claims on crisis countries (billions of dollars)

Country	Net disbursements			Net change in external bank exposure		
	After one year	After two years	After three years	After one year	After two years	After three years
Mexico[a]	23.8	12.9	5.2	–7.3	–4.5	–3.3
Thailand[b]	2.8	3.3	3.3	–15.7	–30.0	–40.4
Indonesia	3.9	9.5	10.7	–8.3	–13.8	–18.3
Korea	16.8	10.8	6.0	–28.9	–36.9	–43.2
Russia	2.5	–1.1	–3.7	–24.1	–31.4	–38.9
Brazil (1998)[a]	17.5	1.8	3.7	–22.4	–17.5	–14.9
Turkey	11.2	20.2	22.1	–8.3	–12.5	–10.1
Argentina	8.9	9.3	10.5	–13.4	–40.7[c]	–44.3[c]
Uruguay	1.6	2.3	n.a.	–1.9	–2.5	n.a.
Brazil (2001)	10.8	26.2	n.a.	–7.0	–18.0	n.a.

n.a. = not available

a. Includes bilateral financing.

b. Thailand received additional bilateral financing, but this financing is not included because of a lack of quarterly data on bilateral disbursements and repayments.

c. Break in series with pesification; last observation from end of 2001.

Note: In Argentina, the international bank statistics include some of the dollar-denominated operations of foreign-owned local banks. Also Brazil started drawing on a precautionary facility with the IMF in 2001 as Argentina's crisis intensified; the scale of pressure on Brazil intensified significantly in 2002.

Sources: Data are from Bank for International Settlements, www.bis.org/statistics/hisstat8.htm (table 8, total foreign claims); US Treasury; and International Monetary Fund.

Rapid repayment in these cases was not a product of small rescue loans. IMF and US bilateral lending to Mexico totaled 6.8 percent of its precrisis GDP, IMF lending to Korea was 3.7 percent of GDP, IMF and bilateral lending to Brazil in 1998–99 was 2.2 percent of GDP (the total commitment to Brazil was closer to 4 percent of GDP, but not all was disbursed). While the amount lent to these countries was not as large in proportion to precrisis GDP as recent lending to Turkey, Uruguay, and Brazil in 2002–03, it was larger than the amounts provided in many other cases.

Rapid repayment seems primarily to have been the product of lending to the right countries. All three countries (Mexico, Korea, and Brazil) had relatively low precrisis debt to GDP levels. Both fiscal and external debt levels were manageable before the crisis and generally remained manageable after the crisis shock. All three had made policy mistakes that had drained the government's foreign-currency liquidity—notably hanging on to pegged or heavily managed exchange rates for too long. But all three

Table 4.4 Changes in IMF/bilateral exposure and in international debt securities outstanding (billions of dollars)

Country	Net disbursements			Net change in bond exposure		
	After one year	After two years	After three years	After one year	After two years	After three years
Mexico	23.8	12.9	5.2	2.3	15.3	23.7
Thailand	2.8	3.3	3.3	0.0	1.4	0.9
Indonesia	3.9	9.5	10.7	4.0	3.4	–1.2
Korea	16.8	10.8	6.0	7.6	4.8	4.7
Russia	2.5	–1.1	–3.7	5.9	4.9	3.1
Brazil (1998)	17.5	1.8	3.7	0.0	10.1	21.4
Turkey	11.2	20.2	22.1	–0.5	0.8	4.1
Argentina	8.9	9.3	10.5	15.2	14.6	16.7
Uruguay	1.6	2.3	n.a.	0.4	0.5	n.a.
Brazil (2001)	10.8	26.2	n.a.	10.9	17.0	n.a.

n.a. = not available

Note: International debt securities outstanding can go up as a result of Brady-to-eurobond exchanges, which are relevant for both Mexico and Brazil. The data series does not include outstanding Brady bonds. International debt securities outstanding can also increase as a result of the exchange of domestic debt for international bonds. This is relevant for Russia, which exchanged GKOs for eurobonds in June 1998, and for Argentina, which exchanged domestic bonds for eurobonds in the megaswap.

Sources: Data are from Bank for International Settlements, www.bis.org/statistics/secstats.htm (table 15B, bonds and notes); US Treasury; and International Monetary Fund.

also were, with reasonable adjustments, effectively solvent. Brazil in 1998–99, though, is a less clear-cut case than Mexico and Korea. Its comparatively small export base created a high debt-to-exports ratio, and the crisis shock pushed its government debt stock toward potentially troublesome levels.[8]

Cases of Slow Repayment, Default, or Both

In other cases, large initial loans failed to create—or to create as rapidly as initially envisioned—conditions that allowed for the rapid repayment of the IMF's initial loan. In most of these cases, the exposure of private creditors to the crisis country did not stabilize—or it stabilized at a low level

8. Brazil's debt-to-GDP ratio sharply increased after 1999, but so did the primary balance. The primary balance went from approximately zero in the first Cardoso administration (1995–98) to a significant surplus above 3 percent of GDP in the second Cardoso administration (1999–2002). The increase in Brazil's debt—and the substantial stock of both foreign-currency and short-term debt—left Brazil vulnerable to further difficulties. For more details, see the discussion on Brazil in chapter 2.

and then failed to rebound strongly. These "slow repayment" cases are worth a bit more scrutiny, in part because the causes of slower-than-expected repayment differed substantially.

Thailand and Indonesia

In Thailand and Indonesia, substantial amounts of official financing were made available but still fell well short of the amounts needed to cover all maturing short-term external debt. These programs were truly catalytic: The hope was that the available financing, combined with policy adjustments—monetary tightening following a float plus various structural changes to address weaknesses in the private sector—would combine to restore the confidence of the external creditors of Thai and Indonesian banks and firms. In neither case did the approach work as planned. Domestic balance sheet weaknesses were larger than anyone anticipated, and the needed restructuring of the domestic financial and corporate sectors ended up taking a long time and proved more costly than initially expected.

IMF lending failed—for a host of reasons—to stop the rolloff of external lending in both Thailand and Indonesia. These two cases nonetheless have important differences. Thailand had dug itself into a deep financial hole before its crisis by financing large current account deficits with short-term external debt—a topic covered in chapter 2. Its $46 billion stock of short-term external bank debt was enormous, both absolutely and relative to Thailand's economy.[9] The Thais often complain that they did not receive as much financial support as other countries, in part because the United States did not contribute to Thailand's bilateral support package. It is true that Thailand received a comparatively small IMF loan—$4 billion, or a little over 2 percent of its precrisis GDP. But a $10 billion commitment from other Asian economies and commitments from the World Bank and the Asian Development Bank augmented the IMF loan, and the overall amount of financing made available to Thailand by the end of 1998 (6.3 percent of precrisis GDP) was not significantly smaller than that made available to Mexico. Thailand's real problem was that it simply had much more short-term external debt than most countries.

Thailand's IMF program did succeed at stabilizing domestic financial conditions fairly rapidly, particularly after a new government took control in November 1997: Domestic bank depositors by and large did not flee; domestic financial conditions stabilized in the course of 1998; Thailand avoided a burst of inflation following its devaluation; and bank and corporate restructuring proceeded more rapidly than in Indonesia, though not as rapidly as in Korea. But domestic stabilization did not halt the

9. The overvalued baht overstated the true size of Thailand's economy, when expressed in dollar terms. Consequently, even the ratio of short-term debt to precrisis GDP was extremely high—25 percent. This ratio actually understated the extent of Thailand's debt problems.

exodus of external creditors. Table 4.3 shows that Thailand's external bank claims fell by $35 billion between mid-1996 and mid-1999. A more complete measure of external exposure over a slightly longer time frame tells the same story: Total external claims on Thai banks, firms, and the government fell from $102.2 billion at the end of 1996 to $45.9 billion at the end of 2000 (World Bank's *Global Development Finance* 2003). Thailand's large current account surplus after 1997, not official lending, financed most of this $56 billion fall in private external exposure. Between end-1996 and end-2000, Thailand ran a $41.2 billion cumulative current account surplus.

Thailand's IMF program effectively tided it over until its precrisis current account deficit turned into a large postcrisis current account surplus that allowed it to pay back a large share of the external debts it had built up in the boom years. After 2000, Thailand had little trouble repaying the IMF out of its ongoing current account surplus.

Indonesia experienced a more dramatic and persistent collapse in output than Thailand. The combination of Indonesian firms scrambling for foreign exchange to pay their debts and Indonesian citizens withdrawing money from the domestic banking system in order to move their savings abroad led to a dramatic fall in the exchange rate. While Thailand was by and large able to avoid a domestic bank run, Indonesia was not, in part because initial bank closures were handled poorly.

But Indonesia's difficulties had deeper reasons. The country clearly needed to be willing to dismantle the tight nexus between the state, Suharto's family, and a set of well-connected businessmen in order to qualify for international help. The international community was reluctant to help Suharto unless he showed real commitment to reform. Yet any reform was sure to disrupt established business patterns. Suharto's regime had been around for a long time. As the economic and financial crisis deepened, many wealthy Indonesians with ties to the Suharto regime decided to hedge their bets and move more of their savings abroad. Creditors who had lent to firms closely tied to Suharto also had strong cause to get out if they could. The combination of the international community's reluctance to support Suharto unless he demonstrated clear commitment to change and the desire of Indonesia's elite to hedge against the risk of real change made resolving Indonesia's crisis unusually difficult.

Indonesia ended up receiving a significant amount of external support. But relatively little of that support came during the fall of 1997, the peak of Indonesia's crisis. Most of the assistance came as part of a program to help pick up the pieces during the course of 1998 and 1999. Table 4.3 also shows that Indonesia experienced a smaller fall in private exposure than Thailand. However, this smaller rolloff illustrates the difficulties of relying solely on the changes in the exposure of external creditors to assess the success of IMF programs. The most likely explanation for the smaller rolloff is that the more dramatic collapse in output and enormous fall in the exchange rate left fewer debtors in a position to repay. Only after financial conditions stabilized did the external exposure to Indonesia start to fall rapidly. As in Thailand, the fall in private exposure exceeded the financing the IMF made available. The combination of the exchange rate depreciation and a sharp reduction in domestic output turned precrisis current account deficits into large postcrisis current account surpluses, and the foreign exchange these surpluses generated, in turn, helped to finance an orderly unwinding of the country's external debts. The substantial restructuring of interbank claims as well as the external debt of corporate borrowers needed to unwind the imbalances built up in the boom are covered in detail later.

Russia

Russia is an unusual case. The IMF program in the summer of 1998 obviously failed to avoid a default. However, Russia could still repay its 1998 IMF loan quite quickly, for two reasons. First, the amount of new IMF financing in the course of 1998 was quite small. Russia received only the first installment of its IMF loan, since the IMF cut off further financing after it became clear that limited financing and lukewarm (at best) implementation of fiscal reform had failed to calm the markets. IMF exposure only increased from around $13 billion to around $19 billion in the course of 1998 (an increase of $6 billion, or 1.5 percent of Russia's precrisis GDP). Second, Russia's default and devaluation proved to be more damaging to the world and far less damaging to Russia than most expected.[10]

One key reason for the limited impact of Russia's sovereign default on its domestic economy is that Russia's small domestic banking system played little role in financing private business. Wiping out Russian banks had little economic impact, particularly because most domestic deposits in failed banks were just transferred to a large state bank—Sberbank. The positive impact of the devaluation on economic activity, as Russian production displaced imports, more than offset any negative impacts from a weak banking system. Finally, the loss of access to financial markets had the salutary effect of forcing Russia—and particularly the government of Russia—to live within its means. The combination of the economic rebound, lower debt payments to private creditors, improved fiscal policy, and above all a bit of good luck—a surge in oil prices—allowed Russia to start repaying the IMF relatively quickly.[11]

10. Russia's default precipitated widespread contagion, in part because many leveraged international investors had taken out large bets on Russia.

11. Russia owed around $14 billion to the IMF even before it encountered financial difficulties in 1998 as a result of the IMF financing to support Russia's transition. Our assessment focuses on how quickly Russia was able to bring its IMF debt levels back down to precrisis levels. By 2001, Russia had made net repayments back to the IMF well in excess of the additional funds it received in 1998.

Argentina

The January 2001 IMF program (the *Blindaje* or shield) provided enough money to cover all of the sovereign's financing needs in the first quarter of 2001. But even this substantial financing package (roughly $15 billion, or 5.4 percent of GDP) would have worked only if Argentina were able to raise some funds from the markets in the remainder of that year.[12] When it became clear that the initial program was not working—the economy continued to shrink, external private creditors were not willing to provide additional financing, and a domestic bank run started adding pressure on reserves—the program was augmented by a bit more than $8 billion in the fall of 2001. This brought the IMF's total commitment to $23.8 billion (8.2 percent of GDP). The augmented program, however, collapsed before all these funds were disbursed. In December, Argentina was forced first to declare a bank holiday (the *Corralito* and then *Corralon*), then to default on its external debt and finally to devalue.

The IMF program did not primarily finance the repayment of Argentina's international sovereign bonds: Data from the World Bank's *Global Development Finance* indicate that public and publicly guaranteed external debt to private creditors—largely sovereign bonds—fell by only $2 billion in 2001.[13] In this case, however, the small reported fall is somewhat misleading: There is little doubt that domestic purchases of international sovereign bonds, notably $3 billion by Argentina's pension funds, offset payments on international bonds held abroad in excess of $2 billion.[14] Moreover, Argentina had grown accustomed to financing interest payments on its existing bonds by selling yet more bonds, so its inability to place new bonds no doubt added to its financial troubles. Yet the $9 billion in net lending from the IMF in 2001, the $10.6 billion fall in Argentina's reserves, and a similar but harder-to-track fall in the banking system's own reserves did not primarily finance the repayment of international bonds. A domestic deposit run of roughly $16 billion and a substantial fall in international banks' lending to Argentina's banks and private firms were far more important sources of pressure. Argentina's difficulties in accessing international markets no doubt contributed to the run by other creditors,

12. The initial program included a series of commitments by Argentina's domestic creditors (banks and pension funds) to provide additional financing. These commitments are discussed in detail later.

13. Public and publicly guaranteed external debt owed to private creditors fell from $66.1 billion to $64.1 billion (World Bank's *Global Development Finance* 2003). Technically, the domestic holdings of international bonds are not external debt, but many countries do not track who holds their international bonds and report all international bonds as external debt.

14. The government of Argentina estimated that $5.5 billion of its maturing bonds in 2001 were held externally. Net payments to external creditors of $5.5 billion and net domestic issuance of "international bonds" of $3.5 billion would produce the fall of $2 billion reported in World Bank's *Global Development Finance*. Around $1 billion of the government of Argentina's short-term also was held externally.

but maturing international bonds were not the primary source of financial pressure on Argentina.

After default and devaluation, Argentina began to generate substantial current account surpluses. These surpluses have allowed it to pay interest and some principal on its loans to the IMF and the MDBs and, after the first part of 2002, to begin to rebuild its reserves. However, it is clear that Argentina could not—and would not—repay the IMF and the MDBs in full on time—a fact that was recognized in Argentina's 2003 IMF program. Argentina is clearly a case where catalytic financing failed: The IMF loan helped to finance a permanent capital outflow, and the IMF was left with long-term exposure to a financially weak country.

Turkey

Turkey's government so far has been able to raise the financing it needs to avoid default despite its large debt load and substantial annual borrowing. The Turkish lira has stabilized, the economy has started to grow again, and Turkey has generally delivered the large primary surpluses it promised. However, Turkey is not in a position to repay the IMF according to schedule. The IMF lent Turkey almost $10 billion in 2001 and $9 billion in 2002. The IMF's total lending to Turkey—$23 billion, or over 11 percent of Turkey's precrisis GDP—is far more than what the IMF and the United States lent to Mexico in 1995. While Mexico was making substantial net payments back to the IMF and the United States in the second and third years of its crisis, Turkey has yet to start to make significant payments. Turkey therefore falls in a different class than Mexico, Brazil, and Korea.

IMF lending to Turkey effectively financed two things. First, the IMF was indirectly helping Turkey to finance its large budget deficits—a nominal deficit of 16 percent of GDP in 2001 and 14 percent of GDP in 2002. Large deficits meant that Turkey's overall government debt was growing rapidly.[15] The sums worked only if existing domestic creditors rolled over their debts and provided the government with some new financing, and the IMF provided the additional external financing needed to sustain large ongoing budget deficits. The IMF typically lends money to a country's central bank, not to its government, but in this case the central bank acted as an intermediary, and the money the IMF provided was clearly used to provide noninflationary financing for the government.[16] Second, the in-

15. These high nominal deficits were the result of the burst of inflation after the collapse of the peg in 2001; real, inflation-adjusted deficits were significant but much lower.

16. An increase in the government's external debt is consistent with either growing reserves or a fall in the private sector's external debt—as the external inflows that finance the government's ongoing budget deficit also provided foreign exchange that can either be saved in reserves or finance net repayment of private debts. In 2001, there were large net payments on the private-sector external debts. In 2002, more of the inflow from the IMF was saved as reserves.

flow of foreign exchange from the government's external borrowing made it possible for the external creditors of Turkey's banking system to reduce their exposure without triggering a crisis. Directly and indirectly, the foreign exchange that the IMF provided to the government of Turkey provided the foreign currency that Turkey's banks needed to repay the cross-border loans that they had taken out before the crisis to finance their bets on high-yielding Turkish treasury bills. In 2001, $10 billion from the IMF was matched by a $10 billion fall in external bank lending to Turkey. External creditors stopped pulling funds out in 2002. This allowed the $9 billion in the IMF lending in 2002 to finance an increase in Turkey's reserves.

Turkey's initial 2001 IMF program was based on extremely optimistic assumptions about Turkey's ability to repay the IMF quickly, though it should have been clear all along that Turkey had at best a need for medium-term—not short-term—financing. Turkey's high initial debt levels, large stock of short-term domestic debt, and high domestic real interest rates implied that growing debt levels would accompany a program based on disinflation and real fiscal adjustment. If all went well, the large increase in the government's debt stock that the IMF helped to finance would not generate future problems. With time, interest rates would come down, lowering the budget deficit and reducing Turkey's annual financing need. A growing economy would, over time, reduce Turkey's debt-to-GDP ratio, as it started to occur in 2003. Turkey eventually would be able to not only finance its ongoing budget deficits on its own but also raise the funds to repay the IMF. Any realistic assessment would have suggested that Turkey's fiscal stabilization was not going to happen quickly.

Turkey's finances have now improved, in part because the perception that it is now too strategically important to fail helped to lower the real interest rate it has to pay on its debts. Turkey has done its part as well, running a significant primary surplus and keeping inflation under control. Falling real interest rates on Turkey's domestic debt translate quickly into a smaller budget deficit, so it is possible that Turkey may be able to raise the financing it needs in 2004 without additional official support. Turkey, though, has the ability to tap into an $8.5 billion medium- to long-term loan from the US government in 2004, should it choose to do so to limit the amount of debt that it needs to place domestically. Alternatively, Turkey might tap this loan to help repay the IMF.

Turkey is scheduled to repay the IMF $8.9 billion in 2005 and an additional $10.3 billion in 2006. These payments, though, will probably be deferred. It will be surprising if Turkey is able to make large repayments before 2007 or 2008, or even later. Since large-scale IMF disbursements started at the end of 2000, and the pace of IMF lending picked up in 2001, when all is said and done and assuming no further crisis occurs, the IMF is likely to have provided Turkey with a large six- to seven-year loan, not a large two- to three-year loan.

Brazil and Uruguay

It is still too early to make a definitive assessment of the success of recent IMF programs in Brazil and Uruguay. Both countries have recovered financially from their crises, but they certainly risk not being in a position to repay the IMF rapidly. Both have received large amounts of financing: Disbursements to date are 10.1 percent of Uruguay's precrisis GDP and 5.2 percent of Brazil's precrisis GDP. Brazil's debt levels increased substantially between 1998 and 2002, so both countries now have substantially higher debt levels than in the "quick repayment" cases of Mexico, Korea, and Brazil in 1998–99.

Brazil's commitment to fiscal adjustment has been impressive, and financial conditions have stabilized. In 2002, in contrast, the IMF loan and an IMF-approved fall in Brazil's own reserves effectively permitted a large rolloff of bank loans as international banks desired to sharply reduce their exposure to Brazil.[17] However, this has had a price: Brazil's net reserves remain small, particularly in relation to the short-term external debt of Brazil's private sector and the government's own domestic dollar-linked debts. Brazil's low reserves, in turn, make it difficult for it to repay the IMF quickly without putting its own financial health at risk, even though domestic financial conditions have stabilized and external creditors have stopped pulling money out of Brazil.

Uruguay will be discussed in more detail later, since it combined large-scale IMF financing to stop a run by both external (largely Argentine) and domestic depositors with a debt exchange to extend the maturity of its government's bonded debt. But even after its bond exchange, Uruguay's high overall debt levels, its high rates of domestic dollarization, and its small net reserves call into question its capacity to repay the IMF quickly.

Experience with Bail-in Policies: Rollover Arrangements and Debt Exchanges

The announcement of an official rescue package lays out the official sector's entire commitment at one point in time—though, in some cases, this commitment is increased as the crisis intensifies. In principle, this makes it easy to calculate the resources that the official sector has put on the table to help resolve recent emerging-market crises. Summing up official com-

17. The Bank for International Settlements (BIS) reports that consolidated bank claims on Brazil fell from $142 billion at the end of 2001 to $103 billion at the end of 2002—a fall of $39 billion. Brazil's net reserves fell by about $12 billion during this period while the IMF's exposure increased by $12.5 billion. Thus, the IMF's "catalytic" lending helped Brazil finance the exit of international banks without having its own (gross) reserves fall too much. The bank rolloff stopped in 2003, when Brazil's new government demonstrated its commitment to maintain a credible fiscal policy.

mitments, though, is not enough. As the previous section emphasized, a full assessment of the role official lending has played in crisis resolution requires looking at the share of the official sector's "commitment" that was actually disbursed, the scale of private outflows that this official lending has helped finance, and the speed with which the country was able to repay the IMF. Yet despite these difficulties, chalking up official crisis lending is still far easier than chalking up the various private financial contributions to crisis resolution. Private contributions are not always announced with the IMF lending package.

Dimensions of Bail-in Policies

Assessing Contributions from Private Creditors

A consensus definition of a private-creditor commitment to crisis resolution does not exist. Some commitments announced at the time of the initial program have been vaporware. Some real commitments were made only when the crisis intensified and thus were not part of the original program. Some private financial contributions have been entirely involuntary—the country just stopped paying and obtained financing from arrears until agreement was reached on a restructuring. Others were obtained after negotiations or through a "voluntary" exchange where creditors agreed to make concessions to avoid a worse outcome. Some creditors agreed to only a temporary delay in payment—though they may take a loss if they sell their claim in the secondary market. Others have agreed to a deep restructuring or a significant haircut on their principal's face value. This diversity complicates any survey of efforts to obtain crisis financing from private creditors.

Mexico defines one extreme. A $39 billion commitment from the official sector meant that all investors who wanted to exit from the infamous short-term dollar-linked government debt (tesobonos) could do so.[18] Recent sovereign defaults—Russia in August 1998, Ecuador in the fall of 1999, and Argentina at the end of 2001—clearly define the other extreme. Private creditors of these countries were "bailed in" most forcefully, as the debtor country first unilaterally extended the maturity of their debts by stopping payments and then often obtained outright debt reduction from its creditors in a restructuring before resuming payments on the restructured claims. However, a number of cases fall between a "full" bailout and a "full" bail-in.

18. About $19 billion of this consisted of the IMF program, and the other $20 billion came from the US Treasury's Exchange Stabilization Fund (ESF); see Rubin and Weisberg (2003) for a behind-the-scenes tale of how the US Treasury decided to use the ESF to support Mexico after the Republican Congress balked at its initial plan to have the US government guarantee a large loan to Mexico.

Crisis countries have convinced their external creditors to commit to maintaining their exposure to the country and—often with official-sector support—also put in place systems to monitor whether claims were, in fact, being rolled over. If the goal of the monitoring is nothing more than to provide creditors with the comfort that the actions of other creditors will be monitored, this can be very close to encouraging entirely voluntary refinancing of maturing loans. But when the commitment to roll over claims is stronger, a rollover agreement effectively becomes a rescheduling that extends the maturity of short-term claims. In other cases, a sovereign has asked its bondholders to agree to extend the maturity of their bonds in order to avoid the risk of outright default.

Five issues warrant further discussion before recent private contributions are assessed: the different roles the official sector can play in different cases; the complexities in a crisis that arise from the external borrowing of a country's private debtors; the difficulties in distinguishing between financing provided truly voluntarily to a crisis country and that provided as the result of coercive approaches; the importance of separating out the contributions domestic and foreign creditors made; and the importance of distinguishing between changes in an investment's market value and those in its financial terms.

Official Sector's Role

Debt restructurings are a part of borrowing and lending; they would occur in the absence of any official-sector intervention. We are interested in those cases where the debt restructuring is part of a broader crisis resolution strategy supported by the official sector. Possible roles for the official sector include the following:

- providing the country with some financing while leaving it up to the country to determine how to raise the remainder of the needed financing. In some cases, this is a sign that the country's problems are not severe, and it should need only a modest amount of financial support if it makes appropriate policy adjustments. In other cases, a large loan lets the country make near-term payments, in the hope that continuing to pay and policy adjustments will combine to make it possible for the country to regain access to market financing ("catalytic finance").
- linking official financing to the country's "voluntary" debt management operations. Voluntary swaps—like new issuance—are part of a well-functioning government's normal financial activity. This approach is very similar to allowing the country to determine how best to raise the financing it needs to supplement its official loan.
- linking the availability of official financing to the development of a system to monitor the rollover of private debts.

- linking the availability of official financing to reserve floors that commit the country to maintaining a high level of reserves. Reserve floors are a part of all IMF programs. If the floor is set at a level that allows substantial payments, then the IMF is allowing the country to borrow its funds to make payments to other creditors. But if the reserve floor is set at a high level, then it can preclude the use of the country's own reserves or reserves borrowed from the markets to make debt payments, effectively forcing the country to seek a restructuring.
- linking the availability of official financing to a debt restructuring in cases where the debt path has been assessed to be unsustainable. This is not the same as telling a country to default: In principle, the country could reach agreement with its creditors before a formal default.
- arm-twisting creditors to participate in a rollover arrangement or debt restructuring. The official sector generally has leverage over the debtor, not the debtor's creditors. However, the official sector sometimes can exert leverage directly over certain types of creditors—particularly banks. The official sector usually stops short of telling banks what to do. Nonetheless, major governments can make it clear that it is in the banks' collective interest to cooperate to avoid default by agreeing to roll over their exposure ("moral sausion").

In the first two cases, the IMF is not demanding that private creditors do anything that they would not want to do—and private financing that the country raises is part of a purely voluntary commercial transaction. We would not consider the financing raised in such operations to be a concession from private creditors to help the country through a crisis.

Restructuring Private-Sector Debts in Systemic Crises

The rolloff of a country's private-sector unguaranteed external debts can be a major source of pressure on a country's reserves and the source of a capital account crisis. A currency crisis is often the cause of the simultaneous distress of large segments of the financial and private corporate sectors, which can trigger a liquidity run on the private sector's cross-border short-term liabilities or create difficulties in servicing long-term foreign currency–denominated debt. In other cases—notably Argentina and Russia—the financial chaos that accompanied the sovereign's own financial crisis combined with a currency crisis to make it impossible for many private debtors to service their external debts. Debt-servicing problems of individual private-sector borrowers—a bank, another financial institution, or a nonfinancial corporation—are part of a well-functioning market economy. Yet there clearly is a difference between isolated financial difficulties in some firms and economywide difficulties in nearly all private firms. In these systemic crises, efforts to secure the "restructurings" of the external debts of a country's private-sector borrowers are often a crucial part of a program for resolving a countrywide financial crisis. It therefore seems reasonable to include these restructurings as private creditors' contributions to crisis resolution.

Voluntary Versus Coercive Debt Exchanges

The line between a normal, voluntary market transaction—issuing a new bond or a voluntary debt exchange—and an involuntary concession to avert a crisis is not always clear. Some debt exchanges done in the context of an IMF program occur at market rates and are "catalytic" in spirit. They rely on the combination of official financing and adjustment to convince creditors to participate in the exchange on an altogether voluntary basis. Other debt exchanges are done at below market rates to avoid an imminent default, as creditors agree to accept less than full value to avoid a worse outcome. These transactions—and indeed all exchange involving the sovereign's external debt—are voluntary in some loose sense. The sovereign has no legal means to force external creditors holding claims governed by external law to give up their claims—though creditors also lack the legal ability to force a sovereign to make payments. Creditors who accept deep haircuts, in a sense, do so "voluntarily": They prefer a deep haircut and the voluntary resumption of payments on the new debt to continuing to hold debt that the sovereign debtor is not willing (or able) to pay.

However, for our purposes, distinguishing completely "voluntary" transactions that offer a market return from those "voluntary" transactions that are done to avoid a worse outcome is important.[19] Three features mark a completely voluntary transaction:

- The debtor pays the market interest rate on the new debt: A creditor is indifferent between holding the original claim and the new claim. Market value is not lost.
- The debtor intends to make full payments on all of its debt. Creditors who opt out of the debt exchange will be paid as their claims come due.
- The debtor does not pressure regulated domestic institutions to participate in the deal, and international authorities also do not pressure external institutions to participate.

Domestic Versus Foreign Debt

Efforts to mobilize crisis financing traditionally have focused on obtaining financing from external sources. In the 1980s, foreign bank creditors of

19. Indeed, credit rating agencies define debt restructurings made under the shadow of a debt default (and at below market rates)—cases such as Pakistan, Ukraine, and Uruguay—as default episodes.

sovereigns were generally bailed in, as their syndicated loans were temporarily rolled over (sometimes with new money to facilitate the repayment of interest), restructured, and then eventually converted into Brady bonds. In the 1990s, both interbank claims and external bonded debt were restructured to complement IMF financing.

Over time, however, it has become more common to include the restructuring of domestic debt—for the time being, the term "domestic" is being used to mean debt that a crisis country's residents hold. So a bond denominated in foreign currency and governed by a foreign country's law would count as domestic debt—as part of the private sector's contribution to crisis resolution. This reflects two trends. First, emerging-market governments have more leverage over domestic creditors and often believe that commitments from domestic banks and pension funds are the easiest way to meet pressure from the IMF's membership to demonstrate private-sector involvement. Second, the blurred line between domestic and external debt—a key theme of chapter 2—means that domestic debts increasingly do put pressure on a country's reserves. If domestic residents do not roll over their short-term debts denominated in foreign currency, or if they pull their foreign currency–denominated deposits out of the banking system, the resulting capital outflows can put pressure on the government's foreign-currency reserves.

The relative treatment of domestic and external debts in a restructuring is taken up in more depth in chapter 7. It is still necessary, though, to lay out the reasons why we have opted *not* to consider commitments by domestic residents in the same way as commitments from external creditors, even though the line dividing domestic from external is not always clear-cut.

- First, restructuring domestic debt does not necessarily address the concerns that bailing out external creditors will lead to moral hazard, since a domestic restructuring can free up resources for the repayment of external creditors. An expectation that IMF lending would be combined with a domestic debt restructuring to reduce domestic pressures on reserves while external creditors would have more time to exit would tend to encourage, not discourage, external creditors to lend to risky countries.

- Second, the restructuring of sovereign debt held by domestic residents—or a freeze on government-guaranteed bank deposits—can be thought of as a tax on certain kinds of domestic financial assets (a capital levy). Domestic residents are typically asked to contribute to crisis resolution in many ways: Taxes are increased, government spending is cut, an economic contraction reduces real incomes and imports, and devaluation reduces the external value of domestic wages and domestic financial assets denominated in the local currency. The fall in domestic welfare from these steps is as much a part of the domestic adjustment effort as the domestic debt restructuring. Counting only the domestic debt restructuring hardly seems fair.

Changes in Secondary Market Prices Don't Count

The market value of a country's long-term international bonds typically falls in a crisis and rises if the country recovers. Similarly, the market value of many other securities—domestic debts and domestic stocks—will almost certainly fall in a crisis. The secondary market value of traded securities is certainly an important indicator of a country's financial and economic health. Investors who buy high and sell low also no doubt take losses. However, a country's contractual obligation to pay is independent of the value the market assigns to that commitment. Brazil has to pay just as much on its bonds at the end of 2003, when the market valued its bonds at close to par, as in 2002, when Brazil's bonds traded well below par value. In order to reduce the payments burden on the country, a restructuring needs to change the country's financial commitment to pay. As sovereign debt lawyer Lee Buchheit (2000b, 18) has noted, "A sovereign does not pay the net present value of its debts; it pays the gross dollar amounts of those claims as they fall due."

Foreign direct investors may also take losses in a crisis, particularly if they have not invested in the country's export sector. A crisis-induced contraction is not an ideal economic climate for any investor, and a foreign direct investor is—unless the firm hedges—taking on local-currency exposure with its investment. Consequently, the value of foreign direct investment (FDI) often falls as the crisis country's currency falls. FDI is an attractive way for an emerging economy to finance current account deficits precisely because it provides automatic risk sharing: Payments on traditional debt contracts are independent of economic conditions, but the return on equity investment like FDI is directly correlated with economic conditions. However, we do not believe that changes in the market value of foreign firms' local investments should be considered a contribution to crisis resolution any more than changes in the market value of long-term bonds.

Nonetheless, every rule calls for a few exceptions. A firm's contractual relationship with the government largely defines the return on some direct investments. Renegotiating such contracts to reduce the country's payment obligation has obvious similarities to renegotiating debt contracts and can be considered one way private investors do contribute to crisis resolution. For example, the foreign owners of privatized Argentine utilities had the contractual right to index their price to dollars. Like holders of dollar-denominated bonds, they were contractually protected from the risk of devaluation. Since Argentina clearly could not honor the original contractual terms after its currency board collapsed, sharing the "downside" required breaking the underlying contract—whether unilaterally or through negotiation.[20]

Real World Example

These definitional issues are not simply a question of semantics. Argentina's large debt exchange in the summer of 2001 illustrates the implications these definitional issues have both for our survey and in the real world.

Argentina's IMF package in December 2000 included a headline private-sector involvement (PSI) component of almost $20 billion. This was largely a cosmetic effort to show that the private sector was being "involved," since there was little real commitment of private money. Argentina largely was promising to continue with business as usual: domestic pension funds that had been buying large amounts of government bonds for some time would continue to do so, domestic banks promised to continue to roll over their short-term treasury bills (letes) at market rates, and the government of Argentina promised to continue its long-standing policy of actively managing its public-sector debt by engaging in various market-based debt swaps.[21]

As pressure intensified, Argentina decided to undertake a major sovereign debt exchange in June 2001—the so-called megaswap—to provide the government some needed cash flow relief through market-based voluntary "liability management." The megaswap clearly was an integral part of Argentina's approach to obtain private financing to supplement IMF financing. However, it is harder to assess whether or not the megaswap represents a contribution by Argentina's external creditors to crisis resolution. While the exchange was aimed at Argentina's international bonds—defined as bonds governed by an external governing law—many of them were held by domestic banks and pension funds. In economic

20. Argentina pesified utility tariffs and then froze the tariffs at precrisis levels even though inflation increased substantially in the year after Argentina's devaluation. There is little doubt that this imposed significant losses on both the equity investors in Argentina's utility sector and on the domestic and foreign creditors that had lent to the privatized utilities. It is worth noting that some losses to the owners of Argentina's utilities would have happened even if the government did not take any action. Once the currency collapsed in Argentina, most users would have not been able to pay tariff rates linked to the dollar (these rates tripled as the currency went from 1:1 to over 3:1). The downward renegotiation of Argentina's utility tariffs was inevitable, though tariffs did not need to be frozen in nominal peso terms and thus reduced in real terms. The apportionment of the losses associated with Argentina's banking crisis among depositors, taxpayers, and the banks owners (often foreign banks) raises even more complex issues, which are covered in chapter 7.

21. Also, there was less to the promises by local banks and pension funds than met the eye. The pension funds promised nothing more than the continuation of their existing policy of investing 50 percent of the new "inflows" coming in the pension system in the government's debt. The banks left the rate on their rollover of short-term government debt undefined. When conditions deteriorated in the summer of 2001, the banks demanded such a high rate that Argentina concluded it was better off just repaying the banks.

terms, debts held by local residents should be considered domestic debt even if a foreign law governs the debt contract. Moreover, domestic investors subject to pressure from the government of Argentina accounted for a disproportionate share of the bonds that participated in the exchange. Domestic residents accounted for over 80 percent of the $30 billion of bonds that opted for the exchange.

There is little doubt that those creditors who agreed to participate in Argentina's June 2001 megaswap did so under the cloud of adverse economic conditions, and domestic banks and pension funds were under substantial pressure to participate in the exchange. This gave the exchange a somewhat less-than-voluntary tinge. But participating creditors also were fully compensated for any concessions they made: The bonds offered in the exchange carried market interest rates and offered investors an equal market value (or net present value neutrality) as their old bonds in the secondary market. Otherwise, no external investor would have participated in the exchange.[22] Indeed, the high market rate on this large transaction only fueled serious concerns about Argentina's future debt sustainability.[23]

All in all, this exchange was a private contribution to crisis resolution only in the loosest sense, as external creditors did very little to help Argentina despite the large headline size of the transaction. Most of the financing the exchange provided came from domestic investors—whose forbearance, along with new money raised in other transactions, helped the government sustain payments on its external debt for a few months longer. Those external investors who participated in the swap did so on a fully voluntary basis—the government had no ability to twist the arms of its external creditors—and received a market rate on their new bonds.[24]

22. Equal market value means that the market value of the new instrument was equal to the market value of the old instrument on the day of the exchange. External investors holding the same instrument as domestic investors also may opt to participate in the deal if they think that domestic investors will go along with the deal, because "secondary" market trading is likely to be focused on the new instrument, rather than on the small old orphan instrument.

23. See the exchange between Mussa (2002a) and Cline (2002) on whether the megaswap was too costly; chapter 6 discusses this issue in more detail. Cline argues that the swap exchanged old bonds valued well below par for new bonds also valued well below par, so the high market yield on the new bonds did not necessarily imply a much larger debt burden than on the old bonds. Mussa, however, is right to note that offering market rates on a fully voluntary deal implied a substantial increase in the long-term debt burden of a country that was at least close to insolvency. Evaluated at an appropriate discount factor, the net present value of the new stream of payments was much larger than that of the old instruments.

24. In November 2001—only a few months after the megaswap—Argentina restructured for a second time those international bonds held by Argentine pension funds, banks, and other institutional investors. International bonds held domestically with a face value of nearly $55 billion were restructured into new "guaranteed loans" governed by domestic Argentine law. The new loans preserved face value but had a coupon that was capped at 7 percent, and Ar-

Private Creditors' Contribution to Crisis Resolution

Appendix table A.2 shows changes in private exposure in the major financial crises of the last decade, and appendix table A.3 provides an overview of rollover arrangements and debt exchanges where private creditors' have contributed to the resolution of major financial crises over the last decade. Appendix table A.3 is a summary of the amount of PSI, so to speak, in recent crises. All of the restructurings were either done in the context of an IMF program or, if they were done while the country was formally off-track with the IMF, were ratified in a subsequent IMF program. Almost all also involved the sovereign's external debts—though sometimes the sovereign only incurred the debt after it guaranteed the external debt of private banks. In a few cases, the restructuring of the unguaranteed external debts of private banks and firms is also discussed.

Appendix table A.3 presents these restructurings chronologically. However, the following discussion ranks the restructuring in order of increasing coerciveness and greater financial losses. This helps facilitate analysis of different techniques for securing contributions from private creditors. Of course, any classification is partly arbitrary. Any given episode or bail-in tool could be ranked slightly above or below another one.

Full Bailouts

As discussed earlier, Mexico provides the clearest episode of a bailout with no bail-in, as sufficient financing was provided to allow Mexico to pay off its entire stock of maturing tesobonos. Efforts to explore a voluntary exchange offer to extend the maturities of the tesobonos did not go anywhere. But even with the very large official support package, the overall financing picture worked only if a broad swath of private investors was willing to maintain, voluntarily, its existing exposure to Mexico.[25] Rubin and Weisberg (2003, 13) noted "Even that [$30 billion, enough to cover all tesobonos] might not be enough, taking into account other government debt, the external debt of Mexican banks, and the potential for capital flight as domestic holders of pesos converted them in dollars." Silent contributions from investors who voluntarily maintain their sav-

gentina pledged to the revenue from its financial transactions tax to back these loans. At the time, Argentina intended to do a second exchange to restructure its remaining international bonds. To no one's surprise, however, Argentina was unable to carry out the second exchange before falling into default. Some of these "guaranteed loans" were subsequently pesified—i.e., changed from dollars to pesos. Other holders of these loans—mostly pension funds that challenged the pesification—seem likely to be forced to go back to their original bonds. This transaction was much more coercive than the megaswap and failed to attract any significant external participation.

25. The central bank of Mexico did advance US dollars to its banking system to help manage the pressure on the banking system's liquidity from the rolloff of external and domestic dollar liabilities.

ings in the crisis country are vital in most cases, even though they are not formal commitments by creditors to help the country through difficult times.

Catalytic Financing

It is relatively common for an IMF program to provide substantial upfront financing and to hope that paying those debts coming due in the near term will help the country regain the confidence of its creditors and raise private financing at a later date.[26] If the initial disbursements and associated policy reforms fail to slow the pace of private outflows, the country can seek either additional official financing or direct commitments from its private creditors. The success of various catalytic IMF programs has already been discussed.

Requiring the Country to Raise New Money: Romania

IMF programs have occasionally included commitments by the crisis country to raise new money from the private markets. Often, the official sector initially requests the country to restructure a maturing payment but then drops the request in the face of opposition from the crisis country. The IMF would then let the country pay its maturing debt and instead accept a commitment to raise money in the future to offset the payment. Romania is the most obvious example. In 1999, the Romanian government used its dwindling reserves to pay a $720 million maturing bond just before the conclusion of its negotiations with the IMF. The subsequent IMF program included a requirement that Romania raise $600 million—80 percent of the $720 million payment—to replenish its reserves. However, Romania was not in a position to quickly raise $600 million at reasonable interest rates, and the IMF was not willing to cut off its financing just because the markets were not willing to lend to the country on sustainable terms. In the end, the IMF waived the program' private financing (PSI) requirement, and greater-than-expected current account adjustment let the country replenish its reserves.

Voluntary Debt Exchange: Russia, Argentina, and Turkey

As part of its IMF program, a country is committed to do voluntary market-based swaps at market rates to reprofile part of its debt. The country's creditors can get paid and exit if they are not satisfied with the rate the country offers in the swap; there is no commitment on their part. Russia, for example, tried to convince external investors in its short-term, domestic treasury-bill market to give up their very high-yielding ruble-denominated

26. See Corsetti, Guimaraes, and Roubini (2003), and Morris and Shin (2003) for an analytical formalization of IMF's catalytic finance.

treasury bills (GKOs) in return for protection from exchange rate risk by swapping into longer-term eurobonds in July 1998. However, participation in this exchange was relatively low.[27]

Turkey and Argentina, in contrast, targeted domestic investors. In June 2001, Turkey exchanged about $8 billion of short-term Turkish lira debt, mostly held by domestic banks and residents, into longer-term dollar and lira debt. Argentina, as discussed earlier, completed a megaswap in June 2001, which extended the maturity of around $15 billion of government debt and capitalized all interest payments on another $15 billion of long-term debt. Even though only 20 percent of the participants in Argentina's swap were external investors, 20 percent of $30 billion is not a small number. Both Turkey and Argentina's swaps occurred at current market rates and were therefore quite expensive, but both also included some degree of implicit moral suasion to encourage domestic investors to go for the swap. Domestic investors were also aware that not accepting a deal risked leading to more coercive outcomes.

In our judgment, all of these exchanges took place at market rates and primarily attracted the participation of domestic investors. They consequently do not meet our criteria for a financial contribution from private external creditors. The rollover arrangements and debt exchanges that followed were more coercive and, when successful, generally resulted in private creditors giving up payment today in order to avoid a worse outcome tomorrow—not just to gain a higher rate of return. Consequently, the more coercive rollover arrangements and debt exchanges generally meet our criteria.

Voluntary Bank Rollover Arrangements: Brazil and Turkey

Brazil (in 1999 and 2002) and Turkey (in 2002) asked external banks to agree to maintain either their interbank credit lines or their existing trade credits and set up systems to monitor rollover rates.

In 1998 Brazil started to collect data on rollover rates from its domestic banks and to share that data with the IMF. However, it opposed any effort to go beyond data collection and directly encourage its international bank creditors to maintain their cross-border exposure.[28] This effort, however,

27. Over $30 billion in GKOs were eligible for the exchange and only $4.4 billion participated. Moreover, only one-third of the participants were foreigners. Most external investors preferred to take their chances on higher-yielding GKOs. This did not prove to be a good bet. The new eurobonds carried a rich 12.75 percent coupon and yielded 15 percent at the time of the exchange. Moreover, Russia did not default on these bonds during its crisis. One of the bonds that emerged from this exchange—the Russian Federation 28—traded at $1.60 on the dollar at the end of February 2004.

28. Bank exposure sharply fell in the second half of 1998 as expectations of a currency crisis increased. The initial monitoring agreement was very soft and had no binding element whatsoever.

took on a different cast after Brazil devalued in early 1999. As part of its modified IMF program, Brazil obtained an informal agreement in March 1999 with the major international banks to maintain their interbank exposure. The IMF also monitored bank exposure on a daily basis. This agreement, however, only required banks to maintain their February 1999 exposure levels.[29] Since a large share—roughly 50 percent—of international bank exposure had rolled off between the summer of 1998 and February 1999, this was not a terribly demanding commitment. The banks had already reduced their exposure substantially. Still, the banks did broadly honor their February commitment.

Brazil's 2002 IMF program did not require the country to approach its bank creditors to obtain a commitment not to reduce their exposure. Brazil nonetheless decided to ask US and other international banks not reduce their interbank exposure and trade credits before the presidential elections. The Brazilian government reached an informal agreement—though one with little effective enforcement—that the banks would maintain some types of exposure through the election. This agreement did not involve any IMF monitoring and had little impact: It was even milder than the 1999 rollover agreement.

Turkey's program required the country to approach its banks and seek their commitment to maintain interbank exposure. Turkey did obtain soft commitments and set up a system though its own central bank to monitor changes in interbank lines. However, the United States was opposed to any attempt to twist banks' arms. Official creditors proved unwilling to put any direct pressure on creditor banks (mostly US and German banks) or to "punish" Turkey for the rolloff of bank lines by reducing IMF disbursements. This effort was a failure: About two-thirds of the monitored interbank positions rolled off during 2001. Turkey's experience indicates that a rollover of interbank exposure only works with true commitment and real consequences for either the country or its creditors if the rollover rate is low: It is not enough just to put in place a system for monitoring daily positions.

Bank Rollover Arrangements/Reschedulings: Korea and Indonesia

Successful agreements to roll over interbank claims can be hardened into formal agreements to convert interbank lines into longer term bonds. Korea converted $22 billion of short-term interbank claims into one- to three-year bonds fully guaranteed by the Korean government. These bonds carried a significant spread over the London Interbank Offered Rate (about 270 basis points)—though this was less than the "market"

29. The new agreement was also fairly soft. The banks did not enter into a legally binding commitment, and the statements emerging from various meetings with the banks used different wording to describe the banks' commitment. For more details, see IMF (September 2000e).

spread in the late-1997 crisis period. Indonesia's restructuring managed to reschedule $6 billion in interbank debts in two separate deals. In March 1998, Indonesia offered to exchange those interbank debts maturing before March 1999 for new claims that had a full guarantee from the central bank of Indonesia. As part of the rescheduling, the banks also committed to maintain their aggregate exposure to Indonesian banks at April 1998 levels for a year. While $2.8 billion participated in the exchange, it was still a lower-than-expected figure. The rolloff of trade credits and other positions continued. A second exchange offer was made in March 1999 for debt maturing between April 1999 and December 2001, and $3.2 billion of $3.6 billion in eligible debt participated.[30]

The Korean agreement had both voluntary and coercive elements. When Korea first sought a rollover arrangement, it lacked enough foreign exchange reserves to continue to honor its guarantee of the Korean banks' interbank debts. The threat of default was real. After $10 billion or so in IMF lending failed to stop the run, the US government—and the governments of other countries with major international banks—concluded that further IMF lending would occur only if the banks agreed not to pull their funds out. The G-10 governments actively encouraged the banks to get together to discuss a coordinated rollover of their claims. Calls were placed from the US treasury secretary to the heads of major international banks (Rubin and Weisberg 2003, Blustein 2001). Moreover, inviting the banks to the New York Federal Reserve in late December 1997 also sent a clear signal—though the Federal Reserve and others stopped short of explicitly telling the banks what to do. Korea's experience contrasts directly with Turkey's rollover, when every attempt was made to distance the US government from even attempting to monitor rollover rates.

This agreement also had important voluntary aspects. The bank coordinating committee monitored rollovers, with help from the IMF and the G-10, to assure individual creditors that their forbearance would not finance others' exit. Official action tried to catalyze a private market solution to the creditor coordination problem that created the run. Agreement on the rollover and the subsequent rescheduling was reached in a semiconsensual process. The banks got their principal back with a lag of between one and three years, and the interest rate on the rescheduled claim, while below high crisis spreads, was only a bit above precrisis spreads on Korean debt (IMF September 2000e). Given that the banks were trading up to the sovereign in terms of the guarantee of their claims, and the sovereign in this case was clearly a better credit risk than the original bank, the terms were favorable to the creditors. International banks that lent even to a low-quality Korean bank ended up with a claim on the Korean

30. Bank Indonesia drew on a series of contingent credit lines (mostly from Japanese banks) to obtain additional hard-currency liquidity during the 1997 crisis. These credits were directly to the sovereign, and they generally have been restructured when they have come due.

government, and Korean taxpayers made up any gap between the Korean bank's domestic assets and overall liabilities.

The official sector was less involved in negotiating the agreement to restructure Indonesia's interbank credit lines. Interbank lines were less central to Indonesia's problems. Moreover, the negotiations of the bank rollover started only well after Indonesia had sunk into deep crisis: A Korean-type deal that averted a total collapse to the benefit of the crisis country and its creditors alike was not on the table. Indonesia's bank rescheduling was less about avoiding a bad outcome and more about cleaning up the financial mess that results when an economy and a financial system implode. Many international banks still decided that it was in their interest to extend the maturity of their loans to Indonesian banks in return for a sovereign guarantee rather than risk holding on to their original loan and not being paid.

Maturity-Extending Bond Exchanges: Pakistan, Ukraine, and Uruguay

In all of these cases, the sovereign's external bonds were restructured through an exchange offer under the implicit threat of default. The country generally was able to stay current on all or most of its obligations (one of Ukraine's bonds technically came due before the exchange was completed). The exchange pushed out maturities but maintained the face value of the restructured bonds and carried a substantial coupon—typically the precrisis coupon, though in Ukraine's case the coupon was reduced—but from an unusually high starting level. Yet these restructurings had a clear coercive component: Bondholders were being asked to accept a new bond with a market value of less than 100 cents on the dollar instead of receiving full payment at the time of maturity—something that makes financial sense only if there is a threat of default. Creditors who bought the bonds in the primary market and then sold after the restructuring took losses, though the bonds could increase in price if the country's prospects improved. Creditors who bought the bonds at the low preexchange price experienced immediate mark-to-market gains.[31]

Coercive Restructurings of Claims on Private Borrowers: Thailand, Indonesia, and Argentina

The policy tools for resolving systemic crises that arise from private firms' borrowing differ from those for resolving a sovereign crisis. Absent a guarantee that makes a private problem a sovereign obligation, the sovereign can encourage a private restructuring, often by providing some form of subsidy to a successful restructuring, or it can impose capital controls that prohibit payments of the private sector's unrestructured external debt. Some countries, like Indonesia, have called for a pause in private

31. Appendix table A.3 provides the details of these bond restructurings.

payments because the private external debt of firms was at the center of the countries' financial difficulties. A surge in demand for foreign exchange from firms desperate for foreign currency to meet a surge in repayments put pressure both on reserves and the exchange rate. Otherwise, outright controls on private-debt payments have generally been imposed only in the context of a sovereign default.

Both Thailand and Indonesia experienced systemic crises that stemmed primarily from the external borrowing of private banks and firms. In both cases, the external debt of the banking system was treated differently than that of finance companies or private firms. External creditors who lent to the Thai banking system were generally paid in full. External creditors of the Indonesian banking system that did not exit in 1997 or early 1998 were able to obtain a full government guarantee in return for extending the maturity of their claims. In broad terms, those who lent to Indonesia's commercial banks ended up being paid in full but not on time. Other external creditors generally have done less well. Thailand suspended payments on the external liabilities of 56 restructured finance companies. To be sure, this accounted for only $4 billion of Thailand's external debt—a relatively small amount (6 percent) of the total. Roughly half of the treated claims (creditors holding claims on the 40 finance companies closed in the second stage of the crisis) were converted into five-year maturity claims on the main state-owned bank at an interest rate of 2 percent. Despite the low interest rate, this restructuring was relatively generous: Creditors with claims on bankrupt finance companies obtained claims on a state-owned bank backed by a solvent government. The other half of these claims (those on the 16 finance companies closed in the first stage of the crisis) received only the proceeds from the auction of the assets of failed financial institutions.

Indonesian firms had substantially more external debt—$66 billion—than Indonesian banks ($17 billion). After the rupiah went into a free fall in 1997–98 and the economy suffered a severe recession, most Indonesian firms that were not affiliates of large multinational companies stopped servicing their external debts. When the government called for a pause in external debt service of private firms in January 1998, it largely was ratifying the status quo—most firms had already stopped paying at this stage, and the government lacked the ability to stop those that wanted to pay from continuing to do so.[32] Payments were suspended on an estimated $25 billion of debt.[33] Indonesia sought to put in place a framework

32. Because domestic banks were the largest creditors of Indonesia's bankrupt firms—and because the banks themselves were insolvent and under government control—it was effectively impossible to restructure the corporate system without also restructuring the banking system.

33. About half of the external debt of the Indonesian corporate sector was that of the local subsidiaries of multinational corporations. Most of this amount was regularly serviced. It was the debt of domestic Indonesian corporations that went into arrears.

for restructuring the external debt of its private firms. The resulting Jakarta Initiative—an agreement reached only after long negotiations among the World Bank, the IMF, the Asian Development Bank, Indonesia, and its external creditors—provided, at least in principle, a framework for the restructuring of Indonesia's corporate debts, both domestic and external.[34] However, the need to coordinate an external restructuring with the restructuring of the firms' domestic debts, the lack of an appropriately functioning judicial system, and delays in approving and implementing a new domestic insolvency regime all contributed to a very protracted and slow process. External creditors were not bailed out here: The case-by-case restructuring of these loans certainly did result in significant losses for many external banks that lent directly to Indonesian firms. Indeed, the absence of a strong judicial system willing to transfer ownership to foreign creditors probably resulted in larger losses than would have otherwise been the case.

Argentina's private firms, including those that lacked any export revenues, borrowed heavily in dollars from external creditors and fell into default after the peso was devalued. The imposition of controls on the repayment of private debts accompanied the sovereign default, but most firms were bankrupt and in no position to pay to begin with anyway. These controls have been loosened and no longer impede payments. Most major firms are currently engaged in negotiations with their creditors on restructuring terms, but, by the end of 2003, only a few had reached agreement with their creditors. Argentina did not offer guarantees, exchange rate subsidies, or other inducements to facilitate the external restructuring.

Sovereign Default: Ecuador, Russia, and Argentina

Sovereign default cases can be divided into those where the sovereign default occurred because an initial, catalytic program failed (Russia and Argentina) and those where a sovereign default occurred in the absence of an IMF program (Ecuador).[35] Russia defaulted on $14 billion in domestic-law, domestic-currency debt—the famous GKOs (short-term treasury bills) and OFZs (federal bonds)—and on $32 billion of Soviet-era hard-currency debt—interest arrears notes (Ians), restructured principal notes (Prins),

34. One component of the Jakarta Initiative was a proposal to provide unsubsidized exchange rate insurance to companies that reached agreement with their creditors on the restructuring. However, the insurance was offered at a point when the exchange rate was heavily depreciated and few worried about further depreciation. Without any explicit subsidy, this insurance did not prove to be popular and failed to catalyze the restructuring process.

35. At the time of the default in the summer of 1999, Ecuador did not have an IMF program in place. It did sign a letter of intent with the IMF in September 1999, but the negotiations on stand-by dragged until April 2000. Ecuador consequently had an IMF program at the time of its sovereign debt exchange in August 2000.

and past-due interest bonds (PDIs).[36] The GKOs were restructured in 1999, while the Ians, Prins and PDIs (also called London Club debt) were restructured into eurobonds in 2000. Ecuador defaulted on one of its Brady bonds in September 1999 and on all $6 billion of its Brady bonds and eurobonds by end-1999. These debts were restructured into roughly $4 billion in new eurobonds in mid-2000. However, it is misleading to compare just the face value of the old and new bonds: Ecuador's old bonds were collaterized and carried a low floating-rate coupon, and the new bonds are uncollateralized and carry a relatively high fixed coupon—though the high coupon was phased in through a step-up structure.[37] The government of Argentina defaulted on $47 billion in external debt owed to private (foreign) creditors in early 2002.[38] These restructurings are discussed in more detail in the section that draws lessons from recent bond restructurings.

Capital Controls

Capital controls can be used to prohibit residents' payments on external debt. They also can be used to restrict the ability of investors holding local assets to buy foreign currency or to move their funds abroad. These kinds of controls lock in domestic and external investors alike but tend to have a bigger impact on local investors since local residents own most domestic financial assets. Because capital controls prevent investors from moving funds outside the country and thereby put pressure either on reserves or the exchange rate, they can be considered a way of forcing private investors to contribute to crisis resolution. The controls do not necessarily

36. These treasury bills were worth substantially more before Russia devalued the ruble. For details of the restructuring of Russia's Ians and Prins, see Sturzenegger (2002).

37. Ecuador's exchange had two components. Its short maturity eurobonds and its uncollateralized Brady bond (the PDI bond) were restructured into a new eurobond in a complicated formula that favored holders of the short-maturity eurobond. Holders of the eurobonds agreed to maturity extension but no reduction in face value or coupon, while holders of the PDI did a bit more. The collateralized Brady bonds were restructured into a new long-maturity eurobond with a step-up coupon. The face value of the new bonds was substantially reduced. However, much of the apparent fall in face value stemmed from the early release of the collateral: Bondholders agreed to write off future collateralized principal payments in exchange for immediate access to the collateral locked in in the Brady structure. Assessing the debt relief in this exchange therefore requires comparing the uncollaterized payments on Ecuador's Brady bonds against the payments on Ecuador's new eurobonds rather than comparing the face value of the old bonds against that of the new bonds.

38. As discussed earlier, some of Argentina's eurobonds were held domestically. Argentina first converted these international-law bonds into dollar-denominated domestic-law loans, and then converted these loans into peso-denominated instruments in the pesification process. However, some domestic investors did not accept pesification. Argentina recently indicated that investors who did not accept pesification would get their original bonds back and participate in the external restructuring. This has increased the amount of international bonds outstanding and the size of Argentina's default.

stop payment but do stop investors from converting local payments into foreign currency.[39]

Capital controls have been used in a number of crises. Thailand unsuccessfully introduced controls to defend an overvalued exchange rate in early 1997. Malaysia introduced capital controls on September 1, 1998, only after its currency substantially depreciated. Such controls did not imply a default on private-sector claims but severely restricted—albeit temporarily—domestic investors' ability to shift from domestic to foreign assets and foreign investors' ability to exit from their existing financial investments in Malaysia. Russia sharply tightened its controls in 1998. Ukraine avoided outright default in 1998 but also tightened its controls after its devaluation. Argentina introduced new capital controls in 2001, at the time of the sovereign payments default. These controls, as discussed earlier, blocked private firms from making payments on their external debt, though many of them in any case would not have been able to pay following the devaluation. They also sought to limit the capital flight and associated exchange rate depreciation that followed the sovereign default.[40]

These differences are important. Thailand introduced controls to avoid any currency depreciation when it had a large current account deficit. Its controls failed but did make it harder for external investors (banks and hedge funds) to bet that the currency would depreciate and even forced some foreign investors to close out their short positions.[41] However, local investors still had incentives to convert their local currency into foreign currency before the almost inevitable devaluation. Malaysia introduced draconian controls only after the ringgit had already substantially depreciated, with the objective of stopping further depreciation while it introduced a looser monetary policy. Malaysia's new exchange rate peg—introduced in September 1998—held, and the country subsequently converted the controls into an exit tax that was then reduced. Its controls now have been largely eliminated.

Malaysia's actual experience does not clearly support either proponents or opponents of controls. Malaysia's controls seem to have been more ef-

39. Capital controls are discussed last even though they are clearly less coercive than defaults, in part because controls directed at supporting a given exchange rate stand a bit apart from steps that lead directly to a restructuring of external payments. However, it should be noted that controls limiting the ability of residents to purchase foreign assets are quite different from those that prohibit private firms from making external debt payments and thus lead to default. Chapter 6 discusses in more detail the merits of capital controls.

40. Pakistan has never liberalized its capital account, and it maintained widespread capital controls during its sovereign restructuring. However, any tightening of its controls stemmed not from its relatively small sovereign restructuring but by the need to limit capital flight following its nuclear tests and the subsequent imposition of economic sanctions.

41. See Blustein (2001) for a complete account.

fective than many expected—circumvention was limited, and the exchange rate peg held. On the other hand, it is quite possible that the ringgit would have stabilized even in the absence of the decision to repeg it and to introduce exchange controls. Pressures on all Asian exchange rates subsided significantly in the fall of 1998. Domestic interest rates fell by as much in countries like Korea and Thailand between September and December 1998 as in Malaysia.[42] Indeed, one can argue that the primary impact of the peg was to prevent Malaysia's ringgit from appreciating like other Asian currencies during the fall of 1998. The long-term impact of the controls is also hard to assess. The controls did not stop Malaysia from honoring its external debts and had little impact on its ability to borrow on the international bond market. The controls presumably have had a greater impact on Malaysia's ability to attract domestic portfolio investment since they did lock portfolio investment in the country for a time and may have made Malaysia a less attractive location for FDI.

Exchange controls have also been employed following disorderly exits from exchange rate pegs that led to sovereign default, notably in Russia and Argentina. Imposing controls neither prevented further depreciation of either the Argentine peso or the Russian ruble nor stopped capital flight.

In Argentina and Russia, imposing capital controls in the midst of a deep crisis did not prevent further depreciation in the nominal exchange rate. This is not terribly surprising. Given the sharp increase in the demand for foreign currency and the panic that accompanies sovereign default and highly illiquid foreign exchange markets, it would have been unrealistic to expect that controls alone would have stopped the fall of the Russian ruble and Argentine peso. However, both the depreciation and the scale of capital flight could have been larger in the absence of the controls.[43] In Russia's case, the skills firms had developed in skirting precrisis controls may have limited the practical impact of the tighter post-

42. Renewed policy credibility and strong current account adjustment played a role in reducing speculative pressures. Capital-market developments also played a role. After the Russian default and the ensuing Long Term Capital Management crisis, a number of highly leveraged institutions had to unwind large speculative short positions, reducing pressure on many Asian currencies. In particular, the sharp appreciation of the yen in October 1998 led to massive losses to hedge funds and other leveraged players who had shorted the yen and played the carry-trade game against Asian currencies. Most of the large "macro" hedge funds and some of the proprietary trading desks of international financial institutions subsequently scaled back their operations, leading to an overall reduction in the scale of speculative positions. One can argue that Malaysia's controls were effective in part because they were not severely tested.

43. As part of its default, Russia imposed controls that prohibited private payments on external debts in order to protect its banking system. However, the banks would not have paid, with or without controls, and any counterfactual would need to factor in the disruptions inherently associated with the failure of banks to meet their external obligations.

default controls.[44] In Argentina's case, the controls—along with significant central bank intervention and high interest rates on performing central bank paper—seem to have played some role in helping to stabilize the peso following the default.[45] While the controls did not stop all capital flight, they did lock the peso cash flow generated by Argentina's regulated utilities into the domestic financial system and thus removed at least one potential source of pressure on the exchange rate.[46]

Our analysis has not assessed how systemic banking crises that often accompany a sovereign debt or a currency crisis have been resolved. Systematic deposit freezes did take place in Ecuador and Argentina. More limited bank holidays and deposit restrictions were also introduced in Uruguay and Pakistan (in the latter case as a consequence of previous banking crises) to stem bank runs. While bank holidays are not formally controls on capital movement, they are a means of limiting pressure on the capital account: It is hard to move funds abroad if those funds cannot be withdrawn from the banking system. Consequently, a bank holiday can substitute for formal capital controls.

Finally, it should be noted that most countries did not introduce comprehensive capital controls during their crises—Mexico, Korea, Indonesia, Brazil, Turkey, and Uruguay all avoided major capital account restrictions.[47] Thailand flirted with controls before its devaluation but did not impose controls afterward. Only in cases of outright default have widespread capital controls and domestic deposit freezes been the norm. Of course, policies that "involve" private creditors by limiting payments on some forms of external debt—by a voluntary agreement if possible, by default if not—do restrict capital flows. However, restrictions both on the movement of portfolio flows across borders and to the ability of nondis-

44. Capital controls rarely prevent further depreciation in the exchange rate for several reasons: Capital controls are difficult to enforce; the hedging and speculative demand for foreign currency is large after a currency and debt crisis; and the foreign exchange market is thin in a crisis so it only takes a small surge in demand for foreign exchange to produce a sharp nominal depreciation.

45. Even in a sovereign default, the sovereign may remain current on some set of its debts. Argentina, for example, defaulted on its external foreign currency–denominated sovereign bonds and both froze and pesified most dollar-denominated bank deposits. However, the government continued to pay the low interest rate on its restructured and pesified "guaranteed loan." On top of this, the central bank began issuing new, performing peso debt. But the amounts of this "performing" central bank paper were small in relation to the overall amount of nonperforming sovereign debt.

46. The regulated utilities generally were not paying any of their debts, so they were generating positive cash balances in pesos, even though they could not increase their prices in line with inflation after their contracts were "pesified."

47. Some countries, such as Brazil, have some ongoing capital account restrictions, as their capital account regime is not fully liberalized yet.

tressed private firms to make their external debt payments generally have been avoided.

Lessons for the Official Sector

This section highlights the lessons that the official sector should take from this body of experience, both for the provision of official financing and for attempts to link official financing to commitments from private creditors. The following sections pull out more specific and technical lessons from recent bond and bank restructurings.

Lessons for Provision of Official Financing

Large-scale financing works better when debt levels are low and the country's commitment to reform is credible. Large official loans buttressed by policy reforms—and in some cases by efforts to encourage the rollover of private claims—were most successful in Mexico, Korea, and Brazil in 1999. All three countries experienced relatively rapid economic recovery, either regained market access (Mexico and Brazil) or saw their external debt stabilize at a lower level (Korea), and were able to repay the IMF and—in the cases of Mexico and Brazil—their bilateral creditors relatively rapidly. These three countries went into their crises with lower debt levels than other crisis countries and were willing and able to implement needed policy changes. In other cases, the commitment of even large amounts of financing did not prevent a default (Russia and Argentina). A combination of larger initial debts, rigid exchange rates, and poor policy performance—especially on the fiscal side—prevented catalytic IMF financing from generating the quick turnaround in market confidence needed to allow the country to finance ongoing deficits in the market.[48] The success of some recent cases of large-scale financing (Turkey, Brazil, and Uruguay) remains open to question. Exceptional support and policy adjustment have so far prevented default (but with a coercive debt reprofiling in Uruguay), but debt levels are high, and the political feasibility of maintaining large primary surpluses remains uncertain.

Large loans to countries with large debt levels are unlikely to be repaid quickly. Providing exceptional financing to countries with high debt levels exposes the IMF to large financial risks, even when the country is committed to making significant fiscal-policy adjustments. In the worst

48. For the IMF's own assessment of its recent programs, see IMF (July 2002a). For a comprehensive assessment of the official sector's role in crisis management, see Frankel and Roubini (2003).

cases, as in Argentina, the program may fail completely. Widespread default precludes rapidly raising funds to repay the IMF, and even in the best case, the threat that the country may default on the IMF may push the IMF into defensive lending. However, recent experience suggests that even in cases where IMF lending and the country's own efforts avoid default, relatively heavily indebted countries may not be in a position to obtain access to private financing on the scale needed to both cover their ongoing financing needs and repay the IMF quickly (Brazil, Turkey, and Uruguay). Here, the IMF is effectively lending for the medium and long terms, not the short term. Large loans to heavily indebted countries imply that the IMF will have a very large exposure to a small set of borrowers for some time, leaving the IMF's finances at risk, should conditions (domestic or external) turn sour.

Rollover arrangements can complement "catalytic" financing. In two success stories—Korea and Brazil in 1999—large IMF lending was supported—after a lag—by commitments from bank creditors to roll over their interbank exposures. These programs blurred the line between a pure "catalytic" approach, which provides financing to reassure investors so they won't want to exit, and more coercive bail-ins, since the commitments to roll over exposure themselves blurred the line between forced maintenance of exposure and a voluntary commitment. Such a strategy's success, however, depends on the circumstances. Argentina tried to supplement "catalytic" financing with a soft and relatively voluntary bail-in of domestic creditors (it targeted domestic creditors because it believed that they would be most inclined to voluntarily commit to maintaining their exposure and provide new financing). However, Argentina's overall finances were unsustainable, and this approach failed miserably.

Lessons from Efforts to Bail In Private Creditors

Linking IMF financing to a country's ability to raise new money does not work. The sovereign loses leverage over its creditors once it decides to make a payment. It may be able to raise new financing (on reasonable terms) from private creditors after making a payment, but it also may not. Strong policies alone are not enough to guarantee the quick resumption of market access. It is therefore dangerous to link IMF financing directly to a country's capacity to raise new private financing, as the Romanian experience suggests. The official sector, in practice, has been unwilling to penalize by cutting official financing a country that is unable to raise market financing. The lesson here is simple: Let bygones be bygones. Either seek a restructuring before the payment is made or let the country operate with a lower level of reserves and decide for itself when it is in a position to raise new money from the markets without the pressure of IMF program timelines.[49]

Bonds as well as bank loans can be restructured. The mechanics of a bond restructuring differ from those of a bank restructuring. Bond exchanges typically reprofile either the country's entire stock of bonded debt or a significant chunk of it, while it is often possible to reschedule bank claims as they come due. Other differences are overstated: Bond exchanges can be used to push out maturities, just as bank loans coming due can be rescheduled to provide a country with breathing space. Bonds also can be restructured before default. Indeed, depending on the maturity profile of its bonded debt, the debtor even may have more time to take preemptive action with bonds, typically long-term instruments, than with bank loans.

The official sector can play a constructive role in helping private creditors overcome coordination problems. Official prompting was necessary for the banks to get together and agree first to roll over and then to reschedule Korea's interbank debts. The resulting coordinated rollover and rescheduling was better for both the banks and Korea than outright default—yet outright default was the most likely outcome if the official sector had refused to intervene.

Official intervention is always controversial. But supplementing catalytic financing with efforts to encourage private creditors to coordinate and roll over their exposure has worked in the right conditions. If a coordinated rollover that avoids immediate default would serve the collective interests of the creditors, the crisis country, and the G-7 governments, it is reasonable for G-7 countries to actively encourage the debtor and its creditors to come to an agreement. Government intervention here is not telling creditors where to invest so much as indicating to creditors who already have invested in a country that they can either act individually and assure default or act collectively and avoid default.

The official sector needs to back rollover arrangements. The official sector took an active role in putting Korea's rollover arrangement in place.

49. Romania ultimately bore most of the consequences of its decision to deplete its reserves by paying rather than restructuring its external debt. Even with IMF support, the subsequent reserve buildup required deep domestic adjustment in 1999 and early 2000, as a sharp output contraction led to a sharp import contraction. On the other hand, Romania's payment record helped it maintain a high credit rating and ultimately regain market access at favorable spreads. Romania, though, is also unique. It had very little remaining private debt after making the large payment in 1999. In other cases, the costs of paying short-term debts may be born in part by creditors holding longer-term claims rather than the country itself. Longer-term creditors gain from holding a claim on a country with a solid payment record but can also lose out if the country is unable to sustain payments over time, as they are left holding claims on a country that has fewer reserves.

Phone calls were placed to the heads of the major banks, making it clear that the alternative to cooperation was a default: Additional official financing to Korea would be forthcoming only if there were an effective rollover arrangement. The official sector's role in Brazil's March 1999 rollover arrangement was less active but still important. Brazil's agreement was purely voluntary. The agreement itself did not contain sanctions for a bank that drew down its exposure. However, the official sector's concern with the overall success of the rollover created the risk of a large rolloff leading the IMF to ask Brazil to seek stronger commitments from the banks. In contrast, the official sector clearly indicated that its role in Turkey was only to help the government collect information. In the absence of any real threat of individual or collective sanction, first US banks and then some European ones sought to significantly reduce their exposure.

Monitoring alone may sometimes have an impact, and putting in place a monitoring system also creates the infrastructure, should the official sector decide to insist on a firmer commitment at a later point in time. Yet effective monitoring agreements have been backed by clear understanding that the country will lose access to official financing, the official sector will ratchet up direct pressure on the banks, or default is likely if the banks do not roll over their claims.

Voluntary is not always better: Too little debt relief can prove costly. The official sector has tended to give catalytic financing a chance and, if that does not work, to let the country try a market-based rescheduling that alleviates short-term liquidity concerns as the country adjusts to address debt sustainability concerns. An additional restructuring is always possible if initial assumptions prove to be too optimistic. Caution, and a desire to protect the debtor's long-run reputation, suggests that it is better to err on the side of being generous than to encourage the debtor to seek a significant haircut from its private creditors. This can work. In Korea, maturity extension was sufficient to restore sustainability.

However, a decision to rely entirely on a market exchange at high crisis rates to extend maturities also can be costly. The rate the market charges on more voluntary deals can increase concerns about solvency, and the risk that the country may need to default/restructure again can be a drag on economic performance (the debt overhang problem). In two particular cases, the initial restructuring terms failed to provide the basis for a long-term recovery and instead prolonged the country's financial difficulty. Ukraine's 1998 and 1999 restructurings carried a high price tag (Sturzenegger 2002, 35–37) and created a new spike in debt service in 2000 and 2001 that made financial recovery difficult. Argentina engaged in a series of transactions in the course of 2001 that failed to provide sufficient debt relief—indeed, the June megaswap only produced a bigger and expensive long-term hole.[50] In a third case, that of Russia, low participation rates limited the impact of Russia's voluntary GKO-for-eurobond swap. But had more participated, the outcome likely would not have been positive. Russia would have been left with a much bigger stock of high-coupon, dollar-denominated debt. Since Russia's exchange rate needed further adjustment, this additional burden of dollar debt likely would have been unsustainable after the ruble depreciated.

Preserving a bond's face value has real advantages, but only if the country can afford it. Many countries have sought to restructure their bonds by offering a new instrument that carries the same face value, around a 10 percent coupon and a longer maturity (Pakistan, Ukraine, and Uruguay). Such terms usually imply net present value losses for investors at the height of the crisis. But they also provide investors with a substantial upside, should the country recover, since the new instrument should trade around par.

These terms also offer important advantages to the crisis country. The country is offering its creditors a new instrument that looks a lot like a standard emerging-market bond, something that generally helps make it easier to convince creditors to participate in an exchange. Above all, such terms can avoid extensive fights about priority—the topic of chapter 7—because participating creditors are not being asked to make major concessions. Instruments held by domestic banks need not be exempted from this kind of restructuring, for example, to avoid a potential source of conflict on inter-creditor equity.

On the other hand, not all countries can afford such generous terms. Such a restructuring would probably have been insufficient to save Argentina, given its large currency mismatch and the overvaluation of its currency. We also have concerns, explored in more detail later, about the terms of Ecuador and Uruguay's restructuring.

The official sector needs to help coordinate the debtor's overall restructuring. It is unrealistic to believe that sovereign debt crises can be left entirely to the "market" to resolve, if for no other reason than the IMF, the World Bank, and Paris Club creditors (bilateral creditors) all usually have exposure to the crisis country. This reason creates a need, at a minimum, to coordinate the restructuring of the crisis country's debts to private creditors with the restructuring of the country's Paris Club debts and the provision of IMF and World Bank financing, which, if nothing else, may be needed to refinance the international financial institutions' existing exposure. These topics are discussed in depth in chapter 7. However, the official sector's role should go beyond protecting its narrow interests as one of many creditors of the crisis country. It also needs to actively coordinate

---

50. Chapter 6 provides a fuller accounting of the cost of this swap in the discussion of the use of voluntary exchanges as a tool for reducing pressure on reserves during crises.

the overall restructuring and to make sure the overall restructuring terms, in conjunction with the debtor's own policy changes, lay the basis for the return to sustainability. This implies that the IMF ought to play two roles.

Debtors tend to systematically resist making major policy shifts—a devaluation and a debt restructuring both have political costs—and often would rather take on new debt, whether from the official sector or the domestic banking system.[51] The IMF has to be honest and firm about the need for a change in policies, including the need to change the exchange rate regime and to initiate a restructuring, and be prepared to withhold financial support when a debt restructuring is necessary. Relying on voluntary solutions can be especially dangerous in these circumstances, as the country's management may have incentives to strike costly deals to buy time to avoid taking necessary but politically damaging steps. This is a key lesson from Argentina: No one was willing to take responsibility for making the decision to devalue and seek a coercive restructuring. However, continued official support for Argentina's policy of trying to pay the debt and to avoid devaluation through fiscal adjustment promises and increasingly desperate voluntary debt exchanges progressively sapped the country's resilience, making the unavoidable default more costly.

There is an important but subtle distinction between providing a country with financing only if it is willing to seek a debt restructuring and telling a country to default. Conditioning new financing on a debt restructuring is not quite the same as insisting on a default: Ideally, the country will be able to reach agreement with its creditors on a cooperative restructuring that avoids formal default. The IMF cannot stop a country from running down its own reserves to sustain its debt payments, though in some cases the IMF should signal that nonpayment would be preferable to running down reserves to delay initiating an inevitable restructuring. Such linkages should not be controversial in principle. The official sector, like any creditor providing new financing or restructuring its own debt, can condition its money on a range of policy actions. There is no reason why one of those policy actions could not be a debt restructuring if it is needed to restore sustainability. Rhetoric against forcing countries to default is specious: The official sector cannot force a sovereign to change its policies; it can only indicate the conditions under which it is prepared to provide its financing. The decision to withhold such support can trigger a country that lacks own resources to change its currency regime and seek a restructuring, but the official sector is not forcing the default so much as indicating that it is unwilling to use its funds to avoid a devaluation, default, or both.[52]

51. The collapse of a peg systematically leads to the sacking of the economy minister or, in cases like Argentina, to more radical political crises. Defaults are also politically painful.

52. The IMF's Articles of Agreement let each country choose its own currency regime. However, the IMF is under no obligation to support unsustainable exchange rate regimes with large loans.

In the event that a country has to seek a comprehensive debt restructuring, the IMF is unquestionably the actor best positioned to develop a framework that guides the overall restructuring. The IMF has leverage because of its capacity to provide new financing during a restructuring, and it is organized so that it has the capacity to use its leverage to pursue objectives other than maximizing its own private returns. No private agent is as well-positioned to condition its financing on changes in economic policies that can, over time, restore debt sustainability and lay the foundation for renewed growth. Moreover, it is difficult to see how private agents with disparate and at times competing interests could come together to negotiate macroeconomic policy conditionality—especially if that conditionality is linked to the provision of new money. Since the initiation of a comprehensive debt restructuring is usually highly disruptive and risks triggering the collapse of domestic asset prices and secondary runs, the IMF should plan in advance and be prepared to support a strategy that minimizes these costs. This is another lesson from Argentina: The official sector was unwilling to plan for a default and, for a host of complex reasons, unwilling to provide Argentina with effective policy guidance or financial support during the crucial period that followed the default and devaluation.

To be sure, IMF incentives are also not perfect. The IMF may act more like a creditor seeking to maximize its own repayment chances rather than like an impartial bankruptcy judge overseeing a complex restructuring (though history suggests the IMF usually tends to act less like a creditor and more like the representative of a coalition of governments). But other parties' incentives in the debt restructuring process are also less than pure. A debtor country's government, as discussed earlier, may have a political interest in delay, when the overall interest of the country would be better served by taking the painful steps to restore sustainability quickly. Each group of private creditors cares more about the terms of its own deal than those of the overall restructuring. The fees and commissions of the debtor's private financial adviser hinge on a successful deal with the debtor's private creditors—they could care less if that deal fails to provide the basis for overall sustainability or shifts a disproportionate burden onto other creditor groups. No disinterested party has leverage over a sovereign, and of all the interested parties, the IMF is the one best situated to take a broad view of the restructuring process.

Lessons from Bond Restructurings

Bonds have been restructured before default (Pakistan, Uruguay, and Ukraine). Bonds have been restructured after an extended period of default (Ecuador, Russia's securitized London Club debt and GKOs/OFZs).

Bonds held primarily by sophisticated institutional investors have been restructured (Ecuador, Russia's London Club debt). Bonds narrowly held by a few wealthy individuals and the domestic banking system have been restructured (Pakistan). Bonds that were spread among literally thousands of bondholders have been restructured (Ukraine and Uruguay had bonds that had been sold to many retail investors in Europe). Bond restructurings have extended maturities without lowering coupons (Pakistan and Uruguay), have extended maturities and reduced coupons while maintaining face value (Ukraine), and have provided face value debt reduction (Ecuador, Russia's London Club debt restructuring and GKOs/OFZs). Ecuador, Pakistan, and Ukraine all obtained participation rates above 95 percent in their exchange, and Uruguay obtained a participation rate above 90 percent.[53] Clearly, bond restructurings are possible in a wide range of circumstances.

Collective action clauses help but are not necessary. Policymakers and academics alike identified two reasons why the absence of collective action clauses in New York–law and German-law bonds could make these bonds difficult to restructure. First, New York–law bonds lacked the provisions typically found in English-law bonds that identified a process for calling a meeting of bondholders to work out restructuring terms. Since the holders of "bearer" bonds were anonymous, and bondholders could be widely dispersed and difficult to track, this was a source of particular concern. Second, many New York–law bonds required the unanimous consent of all bondholders to change the bonds' financial terms. The absence of provisions allowing a supermajority to amend a bond's financial terms gave a minority of bondholders the legal right to decline to participate in the restructuring and then litigate for better terms (see, among others, Eichengreen and Portes 1995).

However, collective action clauses have not proved to be necessary for a successful bond restructuring. Pakistan, Ecuador, and Uruguay all have conducted successful exchange offers without bondholder meetings. All "sounded out" the market to determine restructuring terms that would attract widespread participation but did so informally. Pakistan, notably, had bonds that allowed it to call a meeting and opted *not* to, in large part

53. Debtors usually have gone to great lengths to let "sleepy" holdouts that did not meet the original exchange deadline go into the original restructuring deal late, further minimizing their exposure to litigation. However, a debtor that already has convinced most creditors to enter into the deal does have an incentive to avoid the costs of litigation by buying out a small number of holdouts rather than facing a potential court fight. Ecuador, for example, was able to deaccelerate its remaining "orphan" Brady bonds and then "cure" its default by making relatively small interest payments on them. Ecuador's lawyer argues that holding an illiquid instrument that pays a trivial coupon and that cannot be accelerated in the event of default is a particularly cruel form of punishment for an international investor.

because it was afraid that bondholders might come together at the meeting and decide not to accept its restructuring terms.[54] Countries whose bonds lack collective action clauses have also found creative ways to limit the risk of holdouts—holding out means holding on to an instrument that most other investors opted to leave behind for new bonded claims. For example, the legal advisers for Ecuador and Uruguay made use of provisions in New York–law bonds that allowed the amendment of the bonds' *nonfinancial* terms as a surrogate for collective action clauses. Bondholders who agreed to participate in the exchange agreed, as their last act as holders of the old bond, to vote to change the old bond's nonfinancial terms in order to make holding out less attractive—such amendments are known as "exit consents" (Buchheit and Gulati 2000). This made holding out less financially attractive and reduced the risk of holdouts stopping payments on the new bonds.

While clauses that allow the amendment of a bond's financial terms are not necessary, they are certainly useful. Ukraine demonstrated how amendment provisions could be used in the context of a broader exchange offer. Four of Ukraine's five bonds contained majority action clauses, so Ukraine made a proxy vote in favor of amending the bond's financial terms a condition for participation in its exchange. It then called a formal meeting to amend the bond's terms. Other sovereigns are likely to similarly use their clauses: Bondholder meetings are out, exchange offers are in.

Finally, one country—Russia—avoided the difficulties associated with a bond restructuring by excluding its eurobonds from its general restructuring, even though they generally had collective action clauses. International investors in Russia happened to hold large quantities of two types of debts in which the government of Russia had a particularly strong legal hand: domestic debt and a Soviet-era state bank's debt. Russia therefore decided to restructure its domestic debt—domestic Russian courts would handle any litigation—and the portion of its external debt that a Soviet-era state bank rather than the Russian Federation formally owed. The state bank lacked assets, so had Russia acted in particularly bad faith, it could have simply declared the bank bankrupt, written off its equity in the bank, and left creditors holding claims on an empty shell.

Amendment provisions are not the only reason why participation rates in recent exchanges have been high. Ukraine, Ecuador, and Russia all put a significant upfront cash payment on the table to encourage participation. Other sweeteners are also possible: Ecuador released the Brady collateral, and Russia let creditors exchange claims on a Soviet-era bank for claims on the government of Russia. Creditors usually anticipate that the new bonds, after a successful exchange, will be worth more in the sec-

54. Pakistan also opted not to use the amendment provisions in its bonds at all. It seems to have believed—falsely—that it had to choose between calling a bondholders meeting to amend its bonds and an exchange offer. Its collective action clauses did provide a fallback option if the exchange failed.

ondary market than the old bonds. Recent restructuring deals have systematically provided mark-to-market gains to investors: Twenty percent for Ukraine, 32 percent for Russian Prins and 18 percent for Russian Ians, 3.5 percent for Pakistani bonds, and averaging over 30 percent for Ecuador's different bonds.[55]

Finally, many investors value liquidity—the capacity to trade in and out of a bond. Liquidity requires an active secondary market, and after a successful exchange, trading moves to the new instrument. The holdouts are stuck with a small and often illiquid orphan bond. Early concerns that bondholders would prove more inclined to litigate than regulated banks discounted the value bondholders place on liquidity and how this would reduce incentives to hold out. Investors that do not specialize in litigation are often inclined to accept an offer if they believe other investors will accept it, simply because they value the ability to easily trade out of their position.[56]

Multi-instrument exchange offers have emerged as a key mechanism for coordinating the restructuring of international sovereign bonds. Exchange offers have become the restructuring vehicle of choice. In part, this simply has made a virtue out of a necessity. Brady bonds lacked language describing a realistic process for amending the bond's financial terms. This pushed debtors to use exchange offers, which allowed the

55. A definitional issue is important at this stage. It is often said that restructuring deals imply net present value (NPV) losses for investors, i.e., they are not NPV neutral. But the term NPV loss is imprecise. Before a restructuring deal, the current price of the bond is often low and the spread high, if the country is deemed to be unable to pay its original debt in full and on time—both principal and interest. The discounted value of such a stream of debt payments—discounted at the current market yield—gives the current (low) market price of the bond. Starting from this baseline, a restructuring that stretches cash flows into the future and/or reduces such cash flows will provide, by definition, an NPV loss if the discount rate (the market yield on the claim) stays constant. But the market yield and the spread on the new claims do not have to be necessarily the same. A restructuring deal that improves ability and willingness to pay should reduce market yields and spreads. If such reduction in yields does occur, even a restructuring that would be NPV negative at fixed yields can provide a mark-to-market gain (in the form of a higher price for the new claims relative to the pre-deal market price for the old claims). Such a mark-to-market gain can—and has—occurred even in cases that reduced the face value of the original claims significantly, so long as the fall in market spreads that followed the deal was large enough to compensate for the reduced face value. For example, investors obtained mark-to-market gains in spite of significant face value haircuts in Ecuador and Russia. Thus, deals that look ex ante to be NPV negative may actually be characterized by significant ex post NPV (or mark-to-market) gains.

56. Local financial institutions—including local banks owned by foreigners (Banco Citi in Argentina, for example)—are often major holders of a sovereign's international bonds. Such local financial institutions are unlikely to hold out and fight, given their ongoing relationship with the sovereign. International banks have to weigh the benefits of their ongoing relationship with the sovereign—benefits that include the fees and commission from ongoing and future underwriting of a country's bonds and the franchise value of their commercial banking operations in the debtor country—against the gains of litigation.

debtor to issue new bonds in return for the old ones tendered in the exchange. Bondholders either could hold on to an old bond in default with its pleasing but unenforceable language promising that there would never be another restructuring or could accept the new bond and get paid.

Exchange offers also provide important advantages for both the debtor and the creditor when the debtor needs to restructure multiple instruments:

- The debtor is not obligated to go forward with an exchange if participation falls below the threshold the debtor and its advisers have set. Consequently, the debtor gets to see before going forward how many bondholders have accepted the overall deal and, more important, how many bondholders have declined to participate and are potential holdouts. If participation levels are too low and the risk from holdouts too high, the debtor can pull the offer from the table. Debtors had this right in the 1980s too: They would not go forward with a restructuring of syndicated bank loans that failed to provide "critical mass."
- A multi-instrument exchange also provides creditors with information about the terms being offered to other bonds. Creditors can assess the restructuring terms offered to similar instruments and the payments profile that would result from a successful exchange before deciding whether to agree to restructure their particular instrument.

Indeed, in many ways, the investment bank advisers who help the debtor develop its exchange offer have assumed many of the coordination functions performed by bondholders advisory committees in the 19th century and by bank advisory committees in the 1980s. The advisers' experience and knowledge of the market help the debtor develop restructuring terms that match investor preferences. A debtor that has placed bonds with retail investors generally asks the same financial institutions/advisers that convinced the retail investors to purchase the sovereign bonds in the first place to convince them to accept the terms of an exchange offer.

Litigation has played a small role in recent bond restructurings, but that may change with Argentina. Chapter 8 discusses the reasons why litigation against a sovereign is difficult even though sovereigns lack the formal protection of an international bankruptcy regime. Two points are key. First, it is hard to collect on litigation by seizing a sovereign's reserves or other assets. Rather, potential litigants generally opt out of a restructuring deal and then the holdouts try to hold up payments on the new bond. Second, holding out and litigating makes sense only if the *risk-adjusted discounted net* value of holding the original claim is greater than that of the new claim. To date, the combination of relatively attractive exchange offers and the difficulty of collecting on litigation generally has deterred holdouts. Litigation is costly, the outcome of litigation is uncertain, and the final payoff may occur years after a prolonged period of litigation. Vulture creditors who buy debt at deeply distressed prices in the secondary market are usually more interested in the mark-to-market gains from a successful exchange than in holding out and litigating. The infamous Elliot, the fund that successfully sued Peru, accepted Ecuador's exchange offer rather that pursuing a more risky holdout strategy.

Holders of one of Ecuador's collateralized Brady bonds did accelerate their claim after default out of concern that Ecuador would try to treat eurobonds and perhaps uncollateralized Brady bonds more favorably than collateralized Brady bonds. But they took no further legal action once Ecuador stopped payments on all its bonds. These bondholders sought to broaden the restructuring to provide a more equitable deal, not to secure a more favorable deal for themselves at the expense of other bondholders.

It seems likely, though, that litigation will play a larger role in Argentina. Argentina has remained in default longer, is seeking more relief from its bondholders than other crisis countries, and has plenty of small "orphan" bonds that lack collective action clauses among the 98 international bonds that it is not paying. Some small investors have initiated litigation on their own, as has one large player that bought a controlling stake in a single bond issue. More ominously, the courts have certified one class action lawsuit against Argentina. At some point, the balance will tip, and rather than refraining from litigation, most bondholders will conclude that they also should seek to obtain a judgment against Argentina if for no other reason than most other creditors also have judgments against it.

Comprehensive bond restructurings work better than piecemeal restructurings. One issue that arises in a restructuring is whether to adopt a *piecemeal* or *comprehensive* approach to the restructuring. In a piecemeal approach, each claim is restructured as it comes due, and the debtor goes through a series of small restructurings. A comprehensive restructuring, in contrast, seeks to restructure the complete set of bonded securities at one time.

Ukraine initially tried the piecemeal approach. However, this approach suffered from numerous problems. Creditors did not want to agree to extend the maturity of their individual instruments beyond early 2001, as they worried that they would be in the "payment shadow" of a large bond maturing in 2001. Because there was no hope that a piecemeal restructuring of relatively small instruments could significantly change the overall debt profile, creditors focused on extracting as much cash out of the debtor as possible while maintaining their position, should a subsequent restructuring prove necessary. Indeed, several claims were rolled over for very short terms at interest rates of nearly 20 percent. These efforts at market-friendly individual restructuring only made Ukraine's debt-servicing problem worse: Ukraine was paying high interest rates only to create a huge spike in payments in 2001. It was able to exit from its crisis only when it recognized that a comprehensive restructuring of its bonded debt was necessary in the first half of 2000.

Russia, as discussed earlier, stands out as the only country that was able to exclude a significant share of its external debt—its Russian-era eurobonds—from a comprehensive restructuring. Russia's eurobond stock was not that large, no bonds were maturing in the near term, and Russia wanted to "preserve" the purity of its Russian-era eurobonds to facilitate new borrowing. However Russia was able to carry this strategy out only because its London Club debt was technically an obligation of a Soviet-era state bank, Vnesheconombank, not the Russian Federation. Creditors holding the Soviet-era debt (London Club debt) could sue only to stop further payments by Vnesheconombank, not further payments by the Russian Federation.[57]

Restructuring terms have not necessarily ensured medium-term debt sustainability. Sustainability has two components. First, the overall debt burden has to be consistent with the country's overall capacity to make payments. This is the standard definition of sustainability. Second, the payments profile on the debt structure has to be consistent with the country's likely capacity to access market financing. After all, many of the countries that got into trouble did so primarily because a large fraction of their total debt was coming due in the near term and the country found it difficult to raise the financing it needed.[58] A restructuring can produce a sustainable debt profile without reducing the face value of the debt, so long as the coupon on the new debt is consistent with the debtor's payments capacity, the restructuring eliminates payments humps by pushing out maturities, and the debtor takes advantage of the respite from market pressure to implement reforms to increase its long-term payment capacity. Conversely, debt reduction does not guarantee a sustainable debt profile, particularly if a lower face value is offset by higher coupon payments.

Creditors want the debtor to agree to the highest level of debt service consistent with the debtor's ongoing financial viability. They want to challenge the debtor, but it is also not in their long-term interest to reach agreement on a payments profile that the debtor cannot sustain. Unfortunately, several recent debt restructurings have not obviously succeeded in

57. Some of the same creditors owned Russian-era eurobonds and Soviet-era London Club debt, reducing the incentive for the holders of the Soviet-era debt to broaden the restructuring to include Russian-era debt.

58. Some have argued that a solvent sovereign should always be able to raise new financing. However, long-term creditors want assurance that short-term payment problems will not destroy the value of their investment before they are willing to supply long-term financing. Consequently, there is good reason to believe a potentially solvent sovereign would have difficulty raising new long-term financing if it faced a near-term spike in payments that might result in default.

restoring medium-term debt sustainability. The ability of some debtors to service their new obligations often depends on favorable economic results (high growth), sustained implementation of demanding adjustments, and some good luck (the absence of commodity price shocks and favorable global capital market conditions).

- The restructurings in Russia and Ukraine appear to be successes. Even though progress on economic reform has been limited, Ukraine's core problem was that its entire public debt stock was coming due in a 16-month period rather than being too high relative to its ability to pay it (it is estimated to be slightly above 30 percent of GDP at the end of 2003, down from 48 percent in 1999). Russia had too much debt (especially relative to its public revenues, a 147 percent ratio in 1997), in particular too much short-term debt that carried very high real interest rates. However, the London Club and GKO restructurings wiped out a large fraction of Russia's debt and eliminated the risk of a series of bad domestic debt auctions leading its debt burden to spiral out of control. Improved economic policies, renewed growth, and high prices of oil and metals have dramatically strengthened the fiscal deficit and debt position of both sovereigns: Russia's public debt to GDP ratio is estimated to have fallen to 32 percent (and the debt-to-revenue ratio to 80 percent) in 2003, and its fiscal balance is in a surplus. Both Ukrainian and Russian bonds traded in 2003 and 2004 at levels that suggested the markets believe their debt burden is sustainable. Both countries could access the market if they wanted to.

- Pakistan's overall debt is not sustainable—its overall public debt levels remain high (83 percent of GDP in 2003), particularly in relation to the government's anemic revenues (debt to revenue was over 500 percent in 2003). But blame should be placed on the unwillingness of official bilateral creditors to consider debt reduction, not on the terms of the 1999 bond restructuring. The amount of external bonded debt is too small relative to claims held by official creditors to drive overall debt sustainability.

- Ecuador's medium-term sustainability is an open question: Its public debt-to-GDP ratio has fallen (but troubling signs indicate that this decline may be because inflation has led to a real overvaluation), and the public debt-to-revenue ratio remains very high.[59] Even with rapidly rising dollar GDP, high oil prices, and a decent primary surplus, Ecuador has had difficulty avoiding domestic payment arrears and staying current on its Paris Club debt. The coupon on Ecuador's large

59. Some market analysts also were concerned that Ecuador's deal would keep the country in a state of likely insolvency; see Goldman Sachs, *Emerging-Market Daily Comment*, July 1998, 2000.

eurobond will continue to increase until 2006.[60] Further restructuring could be difficult to avoid if fiscal adjustment slips while oil prices remain high or if oil prices slip while fiscal adjustment remains high. It is disturbing that after a combined restructuring of its Paris Club debt and external bonded debt, Ecuador remains at best on the cusp of sustainability.[61]

- Uruguay's debt-to-GDP ratio remains extremely high after its restructuring (it was estimated to be above 90 percent of GDP at end-2003), and the initial maturity-extending debt restructuring risks not being sufficient to provide enduring sustainability. The official sector is filling near-term financing gaps, but medium-term sustainability requires both sustained policy adjustment and a bit of good luck. A new restructuring that would reduce the face value and coupon of Uruguay's bonds cannot be ruled out.[62]

The terms of the domestic and external debt restructuring usually differ. Whether domestic and external debt should be restructured simultaneously and on similar terms is a controversial issue. It will be discussed in more depth in chapter 7. Two lessons, though, emerge clearly from recent experience. First, most sovereign debtors in deep trouble end up restructuring both domestic and external debt. Second, the timing, terms, and conditions of the domestic and external debt restructurings usually differ. Only Uruguay has sought to restructure both its external and domestic bonded debt on similar terms in a single exchange. The fact that Uruguay was only seeking maturity extension, not debt reduction or a reduction in interest rates, no doubt made it easier to treat all creditors similarly.

Lessons from Restructuring of Bank Claims

Sharp falls in international bank lending to crisis countries have often been the most important source of pressure on a crisis country's reserves. This is as true in recent crises in Argentina and Brazil as it was in East Asia, even though the recent Latin American crises are typically thought to be primarily "sovereign" crises. Banks that lend short-term can run much faster than long-term creditors. Since the total stock of international bank claims

60. After 2006, the coupon will have stepped up to a level where the ongoing burden of the new debt stock is basically equal to the ongoing burden on Ecuador's old debt stock (the exact comparison hinges on assumptions for the London Interbank Offered Rate (LIBOR); the new debt has a fixed rate while some of the old debt carried a floating rate).

61. Ecuador's per capita GDP did not allow it to qualify for HIPC (heavily indebted poor country) relief from the Paris Club back in 2000, even though its debt-to-exports ratio and debt-to-government revenue ratio are both well above HIPC criteria for significant debt reduction.

62. Debt data are from Moody's Investor Service (2003); end of 2003 data are estimates.

on emerging markets dwarfs the total stock of internationally traded sovereign bonds, it is not surprising that—before Argentina—the total size of bank restructurings dwarfed that of bond restructurings. Rollover arrangements in Korea, Indonesia, Brazil, and Turkey easily covered well over $50 billion in bank loans—even if Turkey's unsuccessful rollover is excluded. The bonded debt restructured in Ukraine, Ecuador, Pakistan, and Uruguay totaled only around $12 billion.[63] What lessons should be learned from the interbank rollover agreements of the last decade?

Costs of failure need to be clear. Korea is both the most successful example of a bank rollover arrangement and the case with the highest costs of failure. Korea's reserves had been nearly exhausted by the end of 1997: The alternative to a rollover was a default. There was no possibility of the banks reducing their exposure by another $10 billion and Korea learning to live with $10 billion less in reserves. Neither Brazil (in 1999) nor Turkey (in 2001) was out of reserves when they asked their interbank creditors to maintain their exposure. The cost of Turkey's failed rollover was something more diffuse and less tangible than outright default. Turkey ended up with both fewer reserves and fewer external debts of its banks. The fall in reserves meant that the country's remaining private creditors and its new official creditors had claims on a riskier country.

Key banks need to take ownership of the rollover. The informal institutions for coordinating the rollover of bank claims that were put in place in the 1980s have not disappeared entirely. Once the official sector made clear that a rollover was necessary, the bankers could call on the network of contacts made in the 1980s to quickly put in place mechanisms for coordination. This was particularly important in Korea since there was little time to obtain the commitment of the necessary banks and to put in place the needed monitoring system. The support of major banks—and some key individuals—can also make a difference. The bankers know each other and can encourage others to roll over their claims, reducing the need for outright official intervention. The support of key banks can demonstrate that agreeing to the rollover has a sound commercial reason.

The support of major banks also helps for another reason: The ultimate success of the rollover may depend on the major banks' ability—and willingness—to convince their clients to agree to the rollover as well. One reason why Turkey's rollover failed is that the major international banks were not willing to make such an effort. International banks argued that

63. There have also been a number of restructurings of long-term bank loans that have been partially securitized. Russia's London Club restructuring is the prime example. Russia was restructuring a long-term syndicated bank loan, and several banks held a significant share of the loan. But about half of the bank loans also had been securitized before the restructuring and sold to classic "bond market" investors. Consequently, this restructuring has characteristics of both a bank and a bond restructuring.

many credit lines that appeared to be "cross-border" lines were in fact the by-product of services that the banks offered to investors, not actual bank exposure. An investor wanting exposure to the local Turkish market might deposit dollars in a New York bank, the New York bank would then lend dollars to its Turkish branch, and the local bank would sell the dollars and invest in the lira overnight market. The profits (or losses) on this chain of transactions would all go back to the New York investor. The bank in effect was only providing the service of converting the dollars into lira and investing the lira in the local market.[64] International banks argued that they could not control the rolloff decisions of such investors—often highly speculative hedge funds—but it also seems unlikely that they seriously tried. The difficulties with informal institutions for coordination among banks, which were apparent in Turkey, suggest that over time more formal institutions for coordination—such as rollover options in bank loans—may become more necessary.

Adjustment alone does not guarantee success. Both Brazil and Turkey generally delivered on their commitments to policy reform. Brazil's international banks had reduced their exposure substantially in 1998 before the agreement in 1999. It is possible that they had reduced their exposure to a level that they were comfortable with and would have maintained their exposure at that level, even absent the monitored rollover agreement so long as Brazil delivered on its policy commitments. However, any significant slippages on Brazil's fiscal adjustment would have likely led to a significant additional rolloff in 1999. Turkey's 2001 devaluation—and perhaps the scale of the fiscal losses that the government of Turkey was assuming as a result of the domestic bank bailout—was more of a surprise. International banks had less time to reduce their exposure before the agreement and had more exposure to Turkey than they wanted. Consequently, they continued to cut back on their exposure to Turkey throughout 2001, even though Turkey, by and large, delivered on its promises of fiscal reform.

Government guarantees of interbank lines have been widespread. In theory, interbank lines are an obligation that one bank owes to another. They are not claims on the government's reserves. The bank that takes out a cross-border loan should maintain sufficient hard-currency reserves of its own to limit the risk of a run.[65] In practice, most governments step in

64. Rob Kahn of Citigroup brought this point to our attention.

65. Without implicit access to the government's reserves to limit liquidity risks, it would be hard for emerging-market banks to make money by borrowing short-term money from international banks to lend to their domestic clients. Without "liquidity insurance" from the government, emerging-market banks financing themselves from abroad would have to maintain large and costly buffers of liquid reserves. This undermines profitability: A large share of the funds the bank is borrowing from abroad at a premium over LIBOR has to be invested in low-yielding US treasuries.

and offer a full government guarantee to all cross-border interbank lines at the early stages of a crisis. Full guarantees of cross-border interbank positions were provided in Thailand, Korea, Indonesia, and Turkey to stop—not always successfully—a cross-border run. Until such guarantees are no longer the norm, however, the short-term debts of the banks have to be considered a major potential drain on the government's reserves. The issues about the use of such guarantees are discussed further in chapter 6.

Anticipated forced rollovers may bring the bank run forward. The risk of the country imposing a semivoluntary rollover agreement before it has exhausted its reserves can make cross-border lenders more inclined to flee at an early stage. This is a well-known perverse side-effect of anticipated capital controls, debt suspensions, or bank holidays. Such measures—if unexpected—may successfully lock in international investors, but if they are expected, they may lead creditors and investors to take flight earlier. This perverse effect was at work in Brazil in 1998. International banks remembered their experience in Korea. When the pressure on Brazil increased, rumors that a similar coercive rollover would be imposed on interbank lines in Brazil—as well as concerns that capital controls such as those recently imposed by Russia and Malaysia may also be applied in Brazil—contributed to the large fall in this cross-border exposure in 1998. International banks reduced their exposure to Brazil by 30 to 50 percent before they committed to maintain exposure at February 1999 levels. Of course, it is hard to separate a reduction in cross-border exposure that stems solely from fears of a coerced rollover or capital controls and a reduction that stems from fears that the country will just run out of reserves—it makes sense for a risk-averse bank to get out, if it can, in either case.

A rollover agreement does not prevent banks from reducing their overall exposure. Modern financial markets provide banks with a number of ways to hedge against the risk of losses on the debts that have been caught up in a rollover arrangement. A couple of examples are illustrative. First, international banks often have local affiliates. Even if the international bank's cross-border exposure is frozen, its local affiliates can reduce their local lending to shrink the bank's overall exposure. For example, major international banks have encouraged their local Brazilian operations to reduce their exposure to government debt during times of stress. Second, derivatives can be used to reduce exposure. For example, international banks shorted the external debt of the country—especially the highly liquid C-bond—to hedge against losses in Brazil. The purchase of a credit default swap, a derivative that provides insurance against the risk of a sovereign default, would have the same effect.

Not all hedges, however, are created equal. The crisis country would much rather have the international bank hedge by shorting the sovereign's long-term international debt or by buying a creditor default swap than by asking its local bank to cut its own exposure. If a local affiliate sells its local government bonds and purchases dollars, its activities are generating capital outflows that offset the bank's international commitment. An international bank, in contrast, can only short a country's debt if another investor agrees to go along. Demand for a short can put pressure on the secondary-market price of the country's debt, but moves in the secondary-market price of long-term international bonds do not directly result in any outflows from the country.[66]

Conclusions

Newspaper headlines can paint a deceiving picture of how recent crises have been resolved. The decision to provide a country with a large rescue package is usually front page news, but the amount of financing actually provided is not. Few casual observers of the international financial system know that Russia received only $5 billion of its $20 billion rescue package in the summer of 1998, or that, thanks to an unexpected rebound in oil prices, it was able to pay this loan back surprisingly quickly. Similarly, Russia's default was front-page news, while the details of the restructuring agreement it reached with its creditors were confined to investment newsletters. If the amount of financing the IMF actually provided is compared with the financial terms of Russia's debt restructuring, there is little doubt that private creditors contributed far more "emergency financing" to Russia than the IMF.

This is but one example of how bail-ins have been an important component of crisis resolution in emerging-market crises in the last decade. The fact that Korea's bank creditors were called to roll over their debts after an initial burst of IMF financing failed to stop the run is relatively well known. The lower-profile restructuring of $6.4 billion in interbank claims in Indonesia—and default and subsequent slow restructuring of roughly $15 billion in hard-to-track bank loans to Indonesian firms—is often left out of the story of Indonesia's crisis. Yet the total amount of financing these restructurings provided exceeds the $10 billion that Indonesia received from the IMF and even the $14 billion that Indonesia received from the IMF and the MDBs combined. More recently, the maturity of $5.5 billion of Uruguay's bond debt was combined with a $3 billion IMF loan that effectively bailed out the domestic banking system. In some cases, like Korea and, we hope, Uruguay, a restructuring played a key role

66. Obviously, there would be an impact on the capital account if the bank were able to go short only because a local investor took the long position. A credit default swap sold by an international bank to an international investor is different from a credit default swap sold by a local bank to an international investor. More broadly, movements in the secondary-market price of international debt can be correlated with other outflows that do put direct pressure on reserves.

in averting a deeper financial collapse. In other cases, a restructuring was necessary to clean up the mess that resulted when an initial IMF loan failed to avoid a deep collapse.

Of course, private creditors have not contributed as significantly to the resolution of all recent crises. Mexico's external creditors were not asked to do anything in 1995. More recently, Brazil and Turkey's external creditors have been let almost entirely off the hook even as the official sector has supplied enormous amounts of financing. Argentina is seeking major concessions from its external creditors after its default, but its program initially was built around a large IMF loan and financial commitments from "captive" domestic financial institutions—not around any commitment from Argentina's external creditors.

If the first lesson of experience is that private creditors have been more involved in the resolution of recent crises than many think, the second lesson is that there is no one way to "involve" private creditors in financial crises. The cases reviewed in this chapter demonstrate how hard it would have been to apply any mechanical rules to obtain greater contributions from private creditors. A different subset of private creditors held different claims on a different set of local actors in each case. The country's chances for carrying out a preemptive restructuring to avoid a default varied, as did the techniques used to execute the restructuring.

While the cases in this chapter make clear that bail-ins can play a role alongside official financing in resolving emerging-market crises, there clearly has been a strong tendency to steer away from heavy-handed efforts to involve private creditors at the early stages of most crises. The first step in the official sector's response to almost every crisis has been to provide official financing as the crisis country undertakes policy adjustments and to hope this combination convinces private creditors to stop pulling money out. More coercive approaches were adopted only if policy adjustment and official financing did not work. Bail-ins have been tools of later resort, if not of last resort.

This approach reflects the preference of most crisis countries not to take steps that would jeopardize their future market access, as well as concerns that the use of coercive approaches in systemically important countries would trigger domestic runs, contagion, and jeopardize the flow of market financing to emerging economies. It also reflects the real uncertainties that confront policymakers: Is a country simply illiquid or is its illiquidity a symptom of deeper insolvency? Are policymakers in the crisis country truly committed to making policy adjustments? How will markets respond to the proposed combination of policy adjustments and official financing? In the face of these uncertainties, the IMF and its major shareholders have been reluctant to deny some countries liquidity solely on their judgment about the strength of the countries' financial position. It is far better to provide the country with some money and let the market decide whether the country has to seek a restructuring.

Any decision to seek a debt restructuring does risk making the country's difficulties worse, at least in the near term. Consequently, it often makes sense to see if credible policy adjustments supported by official financing can spare a country the risks of a restructuring. However, the preference to keep the hope of avoiding a restructuring alive also reflects a bias toward giving catalytic financing a chance, even when the odds of success are low. In chapter 9, we return to this problem and argue that the standard sequencing of catalytic financing first and then a restructuring if catalytic financing fails does not always offer the most effective response to a country's crisis. In some circumstances, it may be more effective to initiate a restructuring early on, particularly if the restructuring of some problematic claims can be combined with an IMF loan that seeks to prevent the restructuring from triggering a broader run. No one solution is right for all crises.

5

Official Policy Toward Crisis Resolution

This chapter examines the official policy statements that have outlined the G-7 and the IMF's intended approach to emerging-market financial crises. These statements address both sides of the official sector's policy: The first is the financial resources that the IMF, sometimes in conjunction with others, makes available to emerging-market economies willing to accept the IMF's policy conditions. The second is the treatment of private creditors' claims on the crisis country.

Before reviewing the evolution of policy, however, it is worth asking a basic question: Why issue policy statements outlining the official sector's intended approach? After all, one official-sector policy could be to avoid any such statements. Market participants and emerging economies could infer the official sector's response to future crises from its responses to previous crises. Even though writers—and perhaps readers—of G-7 and the International Monetary and Financial Committee (IMFC) communiqués certainly would welcome a policy of not issuing policy statements, such an approach is unrealistic. The official sector intervenes in the market by providing financial support to countries in distress, creating a corresponding need to outline the criteria that guide its decisions. In principle, clear policy statements could help the governments of emerging economies and private investors alike make more sensible economic and financial decisions.

The motivation for issuing a policy statement varies. Some statements try to reconcile the official sector's actual response to the most recent crisis with the existing policy. Others try to signal to investors and emerging economies alike that future crises will be handled differently than the most recent one. Take two examples: After Mexico's bailout, many in the G-7 wanted to signal strongly that large bailouts should not always be expected. Conversely, after Russia's default, great care was taken to signal that official financing was still available to countries more committed to policy reforms.[1] Policy statements also have called for institutional changes to make future crises easier to resolve—changes in the way the IMF lends as well as in the legal terms used in sovereign debt contracts.

Two major themes emerge from this chapter. First, the constant restatement of policy toward emerging-market crises reflects the absence of a deep consensus within the G-7 and the official sector on the right way to respond to crises. The United States often has a different position than the United Kingdom, let alone continental Europeans. Indeed, the United Kingdom has often been closer to France and Germany than the United States.[2] Central banks, who have a seat at the G-7 but generally not on the IMF board, often have a different point of view than G-7 finance ministries.[3] The finance ministries themselves are often uncomfortable with the decisions they made in the heat of the last crisis. Second, the official sector has been much more willing to say that it *intends* to adopt a new approach to crisis resolution than to actually adopt one. Calls for less IMF lending have not led to any reduction in IMF lending.

The official sector's policy toward emerging-market financial crises can be divided into four stages.

- Stage 1 was defined by the fallout from Mexico's bailout. It was marked by the 1995 Halifax G-7 communiqué, the 1996 Report of the G-10 Deputies on Sovereign Liquidity Crises, and the decision in 1997 to create an IMF facility to provide large amounts of financing for relatively short periods.
- Stage 2 was defined by the crises in Asia and Russia. The key policy themes are apparent in the reports the short-lived G-22 issued in the fall of 1998, but the resulting policy is best reflected in the G-7's proposals to reform the international financial architecture in the summer of 1999.
- Stage 3 was marked by a period of comparative calm in international financial markets, ongoing debates over how to implement the policy

1. The G-22's report, for example, emphasized that the principles laid out for debt restructurings were not "an agenda for addressing the problems currently being experienced in any emerging markets" (Group of 22 1998a, vi).

2. See "From Bail-out to Bail-in," *The Economist*, March 27, 1999, to get a flavor of the debate between the US and the European members of the G-7 during the tail end of the Clinton administration. See Rubin and Weisberg (2003, 24–25) for the G-7 debate over Mexico

3. The Bank of England and the Bank of Canada, for example, have supported tighter limits on IMF lending than their respective finance ministries.

outlined in 1999, and a push to reform the IMF's lending facilities. It culminated in the IMFC's adoption of the Prague framework in the fall of 2000.

- Stage 4 reflects the impact of the Bush administration and a new IMF management team led by Horst Köhler and Anne Krueger on the policy debate. This discussion centered around the development of an international bankruptcy regime and the need, at least in principle, to limit access to IMF financing. The April 2002 G-7 action plan offers the strongest statement of this policy approach.

This chapter discusses the forces that shaped each stage in the evolution of official policy.

Reaction to Mexico's Bailout

Mexico was the first of the "capital account" crises of the 1990s. Its payment difficulties stemmed from its short-term domestic dollar-linked debt (tesobonos), not long-term syndicated international bank loans. Just as the source of financial pressure differed, so did the official sector's policy response. The norm during the 1980s was to call together a committee of bankers to begin restructuring negotiations. Mexico did not summon the holders of tesobonos to the central bank to renegotiate their terms, in part because international bankers were no longer the only or necessarily the biggest players. Attempts to organize a voluntary exchange never went anywhere. Rather, the United States and the IMF provided Mexico with large loans to pay off maturing tesobonos. The size of the Mexican bailout broke new ground for both the United States—which used the exchange stabilization fund (ESF) to loan $20 billion to Mexico—and the IMF—which offered more money (about $18 billion) to Mexico than it had to any previous country.

Mexico was a success: It repaid the United States ahead of schedule, regained market access quickly, rebuilt the reserves it had blown defending an overvalued exchange rate peg, and generally pursued prudent macroeconomic policies. However, many in the G-7 were still uncomfortable.

- The US Treasury was uncomfortable making large bilateral loans to avoid financial meltdowns in emerging economies. The Clinton administration wanted to multilateralize the financing of crisis countries, which meant mobilizing new resources to augment the IMF's lending capacity.
- Many Europeans were uncomfortable with the size of the IMF's lending to Mexico and with the precedent of bailing out holders of traded securities. The Europeans worried that the IMF was being used to help

a US neighbor and to protect both the US investors who had bought tesobonos and the US banks that had lent to the Mexican banks to play the tesobono market. Many in Europe wanted to return to traditional lending limits and to signal that sovereign bonds and other traded securities would be restructured in future crises. Most US policymakers also supported work on bond restructuring: They defended the Mexican bailout as a pragmatic response to unique circumstances, not as a model for all future crises.

Consequently, a desire to make large IMF loans easier to provide coexisted alongside a sense that the official sector had done too much and private-sector investors too little in Mexico. These two sentiments informed the two major policy statements that emerged following Mexico's bailout: the G-7 communiqué at the Halifax Summit in the summer of 1995 and the 1996 report of the G-10 deputies on sovereign liquidity crises.

The Halifax communiqué emphasized the need to equip the official sector with new tools to manage the pressures that came with greater financial integration. It called for "adequate multilateral financial mechanisms" that could be "brought to bear *on a scale and with the timeliness* required to overcome the consequences of external shocks that may arise from the increased mobility of international capital" with conditionality "to quickly restore market confidence and access to private-sector money"(Group of Seven 1995, 5). The communiqué specifically suggested three reforms to expand the IMF's capacity to respond to Mexican-style crises:

- a new emergency financing mechanism to provide "high upfront access and faster procedures to access Fund resources" when IMF lending exceeded normal access levels. This led immediately to procedures to speed up IMF decision making and eventually to the creation of the supplemental reserve facility (SRF) in 1997.
- doubling the resources available through the backup credit line that the G-10 countries provide the IMF[4]
- an IMF quota review to increase the IMF's lending capacity. When the US Congress finally approved an increase in the US IMF quota in the fall of 1990, the IMF's resources increased by roughly 50 percent.

The communiqué noted that even an expanded IMF financing capacity "may not be sufficient in all cases" and coyly mentioned "other mechanisms that might usefully be considered in situations of crisis" (Group of Seven 1995, 5). The unwillingness to talk more explicitly about debt restructuring reflected both Mexico's delicate position in the early summer

4. The new arrangements to borrow (NAB) augmented the general arrangements to borrow (GAB).

of 1995 and a desire to avoid repeating the seemingly endless cycle of debt renegotiation that had marked the 1980s. It is striking, particularly in light of later communiqués, how little attention was placed on debt sustainability in defining the circumstances appropriate for exceptional levels of IMF financing. The communiqué instead emphasized the need to ward off contagion. Large-scale financing was justified for problems that could pose a "significant threat to the stability of the world's increasingly integrated financial system" (Group of Seven 1995, 5).

The 1996 report of the G-10 deputies on sovereign liquidity crises—more commonly called the Rey Report—focused on the need to facilitate the restructuring of bonded debt, given that sufficient official financing might not be made available to resolve all crises.[5] The deputies rejected calls, made most notably by Jeffrey Sachs (1995), for an international bankruptcy court. They instead drew on a recommendation Barry Eichengreen and Richard Portes made and encouraged market participants to include collective action clauses—contractual provisions that could facilitate a debt restructuring—in future sovereign bond contracts. The deputies assumed that the collective interest of bondholders in limiting the risk of holdout litigation would lead the market to adopt such provisions on its own: The report did call for the official sector to take steps to encourage the introduction of such clauses.[6] Finally, the G-10 deputies suggested that the IMF should be prepared to lend into arrears on bonded debt. The IMF could signal its approval of a debtor country's decision to seek a bond restructuring by continuing to lend even if the country was not paying on its bonded debt (the IMF had adopted a policy of lending into arrears on bank debt in the 1980s to put pressure on commercial banks to agree to restructure their syndicated bank loans).

Several aspects of the G-10 report are striking in light of the subsequent debate. The G-10 explored the role of a bond restructuring in resolving *sovereign liquidity* crises. The title of the report did not hint at the subsequent policy of emphasizing debt restructuring in cases closer to insolvency and IMF lending in true liquidity crises. Nor did the report hint at vulnerabilities stemming from the external borrowing of a country's private banks and firms even though such vulnerabilities would give rise to the Asian crisis. Indeed, the report emphasized the need to exclude cross-border bank lending from a restructuring to facilitate commerce. Finally the report focused on the legal obstacles to restructuring international sovereign bonds, even though domestic tesobonos, not international bonds, had precipitated Mexico's crisis. The G-10 report responded as much to the general shift in cross-border sovereign financing from syndicated bank loans to international bonds as to Mexico's specific crisis.

5. The G-10 report is named after Belgian Deputy Central Bank Governor Jean-Jacques Rey, who chaired the deputies committee.

6. Peter Kenen (2001) has emphasized this weakness in the Rey Report.

In 1997, the IMF took up the G-7's 1995 call to create a facility better suited for the provision of unusually large amounts of IMF financing but for shorter terms. The United States and others argued that capital account crises could be resolved most efficiently by providing large amounts of financing—"Powell Doctrine" financing—to catalyze a quick turnaround in market confidence. The IMF did not agree to create a facility for crisis of confidence (the SRF) until 1997, but it makes sense to think of its creation as part of the official sector's overall response to Mexico. The IMF's normal access limits did not apply to the facility, but its other terms were more demanding: The country paid higher interest and had to repay faster than normal—after only two and a half years.

The debate over how to respond to emerging-market crises died down in early 1997. The communiqué of the 1997 G-7 summit in Denver is notable for how little attention it devoted to global finance. The G-7 heads of state and finance ministers, like most private forecasters, failed to anticipate the Asian financial crisis. Thailand's specific troubles were not a surprise, but the impact Thailand's crisis had on the broader region was. Given the importance of short-term bank lines in the Asian crisis, perhaps it is not surprising that central banks—and above all the Bank for International Settlements (BIS)—did far better than finance ministries at anticipating Asia's vulnerability (BIS 1997).

Reform of the International Financial Architecture

In 1995, Mexican-style crises seemed to be the exception, avoidable if countries recognized the need to avoid Mexico's policy mistakes. However, by the end of 1998, a number of major Asian emerging economies, Russia, and Brazil had experienced sharp crises. Official policy also needed to adapt to a world that seemed to be marked by a higher risk of crisis and to reflect the emergence of crises clearly stemming from excessive private-sector, rather than public-sector, external borrowing.

The official sector's response included an intensified push to provide the IMF with additional quota resources, an effort to specify more clearly when large-scale IMF support was appropriate, and a much stronger emphasis on obtaining financial contributions from the crisis country's private creditors.

When Is Large-Scale IMF Support Appropriate?

Once Russia's default and the long-term capital management (LTCM) crisis convinced the US Congress to agree to a quota increase, the need to define the circumstances when the IMF should mobilize its expanded lending capacity became more urgent. Four ideas had currency in G-7 circles. Large-scale support is appropriate in these circumstances:

- when a country is a victim of external contagion. Countries judged to have sound policies should be insulated from turbulence in global markets.
- if a country is not intervening heavily to defend a fixed exchange rate (Rubin 1999). Official support should be reserved for countries that have let their exchange rates float or that have an "institutionalized commitment" to exchange rate stability, such as a currency board or participation in the European exchange rate mechanism.[7]
- for illiquid but not insolvent countries
- only if private creditors are also contributing to crisis resolution. Those concerned about moral hazard wanted a "private" copayment to go with the official sector's liquidity insurance to prevent such insurance from distorting market outcomes.

Of course, some argued that large-scale support was never appropriate and that the IMF should return to its traditional lending limits. However, the United States rejected such proposals outright, and other finance ministries also probably would have rejected them.

Policy statements consequently reflected, sometimes quite softly, a mix of the four ideas. For example, the Cologne statement echoed US Treasury Secretary Robert Rubin's earlier calls for the IMF not to finance countries intervening heavily to defend fixed exchange rates. The G-7's call for a contingent credit facility implicitly accepted the need to protect countries running sound policies from contagion.[8]

However, consensus was not possible either on the proposition that financing should be provided to illiquid but still solvent countries or on the proposition that official financing should always be linked with efforts to secure private-sector cofinancing. Many in Europe—and some in the United States—were uncomfortable with the suggestion that the private

7. Frankel (1999) provides a critique of the hypothesis that exchange rate regimes at the corner—namely a float and hard pegs like currency board or outright dollarization—are intrinsically more stable. Frankel does not dispute the correlation between countries with soft pegs and crises in the 1990s but argues that the reason why soft pegs were linked to a crisis is simply that most emerging economies had some form of soft peg at the time.

8. Some G-7 countries had reservations, but rather than opposing the idea they sought to make sure the bar to access contingent financing was kept high. In the end, no country ever applied for the contingent credit line (CCL) that the IMF created in 1999. Countries that might have qualified were concerned that the markets would interpret their decision to apply as a sign of a hidden weakness rather than of strength. The advantages of qualifying were not overwhelming. Countries that qualified for a contingent line did not get automatic access to financing, and most countries believed—correctly—that they would be able to obtain access to crisis financing through traditional facilities. The IMF eliminated the CCL in 2003.

creditors of illiquid but not insolvent countries would be bailed out in full. They believed that private creditors should be asked to agree to roll over short-term claims, stretch out the maturity of their claims, or otherwise contribute financially to the resolution of liquidity problems as well as solvency crises. But US policymakers were equally uncomfortable with European efforts to rule out the provision of large-scale financing in liquidity cases in the absence of a corresponding financial commitment from private creditors. They argued that in practice, it was often difficult to arrange a private contribution without taking coercive steps that might fuel a broader panic—a panic that could well push the country into insolvency.

Policy statements therefore had to find ways of bridging the gap between the United States' desire to maintain the option of providing large IMF rescue loans and the European desire to tie the amount of official financing more closely to financial commitments from private creditors. For example, the Cologne statement emphasized the need to find ways, if possible, for private creditors to contribute to crisis financing but also clearly left open the option of providing large IMF loans—so long as the country was not intervening heavily to defend a given exchange rate.

Private-Sector Involvement

Birmingham G-7 Communiqué: Summer 1998

The call for greater involvement of private creditors emerged out of a sense—most notable in the statements of US Treasury Secretary Robert Rubin—that private lenders had lent to Asian borrowers (typically banks and private firms) without thoroughly assessing the risks associated with their lending (Rubin and Weisberg 2003, 257–58). Moreover, Korea's interbank rollover arrangement provided a model for how private creditors could contribute constructively to resolving emerging-market financial crises, though it was not clear if this model was replicable.[9] "Catalytic financing" from the IMF and the G-7 had played a smaller role in the resolution of the Asian crisis than in Mexico, and the restructuring of the debt Asian banks and firms owed to external creditors had played a bigger role.

The Birmingham communiqué in the spring of 1998 signaled the official sector's continued willingness to look to private creditors for crisis financing. "Ensuring that the private sector takes responsibility for its lending decisions" was one of the five areas where the Birmingham communiqué indicated action was needed to strengthen the architecture of the global financial system (Group of Seven 1998a, 3).

> We also need approaches to ensure that the private sector is involved in crisis resolution, and bears the cost as well as the rewards of its lending decisions. . . . There

9. Chapter 4 provided the details of the treatment of external claims on Korean, Thai, and Indonesian banks; Thai finance companies; and Indonesian firms.

> will always be pressure in the event of a crisis to act quickly to stabilize the situation. We need to find ways in which this can be done without implicitly insuring debts to the private sector (Group of Seven 1998a, 18–19).

It was not clear, however, how calls for "all exposed institutions in the private sector" to "bear some costs" would be implemented, other than by IMF lending to countries that are in arrears on their debt to private creditors after a payments standstill (Group of Seven 1998a, 19).

G-22 Report: Fall 1998

The G-22 brought major emerging economies together with the G-7 countries to discuss, among other topics, crisis resolution. The resulting report (Group of 22 1998a) was only partially successful. Much of it did little more than broaden the consensus that supported the core conclusions of the G-10 deputies report (Group of 10 1996). It did, however, add calls for strengthened national bankruptcy regimes and improved deposit insurance to limit "domestic" sources of moral hazard to the G-10's focus on bond restructuring.

The core of the G-22 report built on the Rey Report's call for the IMF to signal its willingness to lend into arrears on bonded debt and on the G-7's suggestion that IMF lending in the context of a standstill might help stabilize a crisis country without letting private investors off the hook. The G-22 consequently laid out a model for crisis resolution where a restructuring of the debt a country owed to its private creditors, rather than IMF financing, provided the bulk of crisis financing. The IMF's primary role in this framework was to develop the macroeconomic policies the country would adopt during the restructuring. By lending to support those policies, it also would implicitly signal that the debtor's decision to seek a restructuring reflected the lack of realistic alternatives. However, the G-22 did not outline the criteria that the IMF would use to determine that there was no reasonable alternative other than a debt restructuring. The overarching assumption was that debt-restructuring cases would be "exceptional" and that catalytic financing and adjustment would remain the norm.

In retrospect, the G-22 report is also notable for its optimistic belief—one typical of the late 1990s—that financial innovation could solve most problems. The G-22 called for legal innovation to improve sovereign debt contracts. It called for greater use of private contingent credit facilities—facilities that let a country buy in advance the right to borrow from a group of private banks during a liquidity crisis. It called for innovative financial contracts that would provide a greater degree of risk sharing between the country and its creditors, such as bonds with payments linked to the oil price or to GDP growth. Unfortunately, the official sector's call for financial innovation came at a time of financial retrenchment in the private sector. No G-22 country that used New York law for its sovereign bonds subsequently decided to use clauses. The market for bonds with a higher degree of risk sharing never developed. The number of countries with contingent credit facilities slowly sank from three to zero: Indonesia drew on its credit lines in its 1997 and 1998 crises; Mexico drew on its facility in 1998 to the displeasure of its creditors; and Argentina, after renewing its facility in 1999 with the help of an enhancement from the Inter-American Development Bank, drew on the remainder of its facility just before defaulting in late 2001. Well before Argentina, though, the banks concluded that they had initially underpriced these facilities, and the market for such facilities dried up.

Cologne G-7 Communiqué: Summer 1999

The Cologne communiqué responded to the challenge set out in the Birmingham communiqué. It set out a framework that outlined how the official sector intended to involve the private sector in crisis resolution.

The principles in the Cologne framework accurately described the trade-offs those in the official sector acutely felt. However, because the principles that were to guide official policy were in tension, they offered relatively little concrete guidance to market participants. Official action should neither "undermine the obligation of countries to meet their debts in full and on time" nor undermine the principle that "market discipline will only work if creditors bear the consequences of the risk that they take." The official sector would balance the contribution "reducing net debt payments to the private sector" could make toward meeting a country's immediate financing needs against the impact that measures to reduce payments could have on "the country's own ability to attract new private capital flows, as well as the potential impact on other countries." One principle, however, was not balanced by an offsetting principle. It indicated, "No one category of private creditors should be regarded as inherently privileged relative to others in a similar position. When both are material, claims of bondholders should not be viewed as senior to claims of banks" (Group of Seven 1999, 45a–d). While this statement lagged behind the Paris Club's decision to ask Pakistan to seek a comparable restructuring of its eurobonds, it accurately foreshadowed the official sector's subsequent willingness to force Ecuador to seek a restructuring of its bonded debt.

Cologne also laid out a comprehensive set of options for "involving" private creditors. The list of options extended well beyond lending into arrears. It included steps the official sector could take when it wanted both to "involve" private creditors *and* to help the country avoid the disruption of a formal default. Some proposed options were quite soft: a road show to explain the program, efforts to "seek" (not to obtain) voluntary commitments of support, and a commitment to raise new funds from private markets. The G-7 indicated that no single option was right for all cases, rather "the appropriate role for private creditors, if any, and the policy approaches needed to induce private creditors to play this role will vary depending on the circumstances of the case (Group of Seven 1999, 46). But Cologne also provided private markets with hints to help them assess when a given option was most likely. The right approach would depend on "the country's underlying capacity to pay," "its access to the markets," and "the nature of outstanding debt instruments." The words "liquidity" and "solvency" were never explicitly used, but the framework clearly reflected the United States' basic belief that different approaches should be used in liquidity than in solvency cases. Sovereign arrears and extensive controls on private payments, for example, were appropriate in the event of insolvency but risky in the event of illiquidity.

Cologne balanced a clear desire to find a way for private creditors to play a greater role in resolving all crises with an unwillingness to precommit to any given approach to securing private financial commitments. The United States neither wanted to rule out the large loan used successfully in Mexico nor signal that large bailouts without any bail-ins would be the norm. The United States neither wanted to rule out a decision to seek an interbank rollover as in Korea nor signal that an effort to call the banks would be a component of all future IMF programs. Secretary Rubin did not want to make statements that would not stand up to the strain of an actual crisis (Rubin and Weisberg 2003). Cologne consequently can be criticized for keeping all options on the table. However, it did try to lay out the principles and considerations to guide the G-7 in responding to a specific crisis.

The Debate Fractures

Cologne did not end the debate on how to respond to crises. Rather, the debate veered in several directions.

The United States pushed to "operationalize" the Cologne framework by spelling out in more detail how the IMF should apply Cologne's broad principles. G-7 calls for the IMF to "put strong emphasis on medium-term financial sustainability" (Group of Seven 2000, annex 2) reflected concerns that the IMF was paying too much attention to implementing a rule requiring that 80 percent of debts coming due during the period of the IMF program be restructured and not enough attention to the impact of the restructuring terms on the crisis country's financial health.[10] The G-7 also called for the IMF to do more to implement the Paris Club principle of comparability of treatment. The United States' emphasis on cases where

10. For example, in 1998 and 1999, Ukraine's restructuring terms had deferred payment on 80 percent of the debt coming due, but payments had only been deferred by a year, and the restructuring carried an implied interest rate of nearly 20 percent. Retroactive application of the 80/20 rule also led the IMF to impose a requirement that Romania raise 80 percent of the amount Romania paid to retire a large eurobond just before its IMF program. Both episodes are covered in more detail in chapter 4.

there was a consensus that a restructuring was necessary—Ecuador being the prime example—also reflected a desire to avoid "relitigating" the broad debate on the need to link all IMF lending to efforts to involve private creditors.

The IMF staff argued that Cologne fell short of providing the IMF with the policy guidance it needed to develop a workable framework. In particular, it failed to spell out how decisions about IMF lending should be linked to the decision about whether, and how, to obtain crisis financing from private creditors. The IMF's proposed framework highlighted two possible approaches toward crisis resolution. The first approach focused on the ability of "strong adjustment programs and Fund support" to catalyze "private-sector involvement." Here, the Fund staff implicitly adopted a loose definition of private-sector involvement: So long as the private creditors and investors decided to return to the crisis country at a later date, they were "involved," even if they were pulling out funds at the time of the crisis. The second approach focused on the need to take "concerted" action to secure private-sector involvement, whether a concerted interbank rollover or a bond restructuring. Catalyzing the future return of private creditors was appropriate when "financing needs were relatively small"—Fundspeak for a country that did not need much money—or when financing needs were large but the country has "good prospects for regaining market access in the near future" (IMF September 2000a). Concerted action was needed when an early restoration of market access was judged to be unrealistic or when the country's debt burden was unsustainable.

The IMF's framework implicitly lumped Korea—where a concerted rollover arrangement for interbank credits had helped to resolve what in retrospect was primarily a problem of illiquidity—with Russia, where unilateral default and subsequent restructuring resulted in a different kind of concerted restructuring. The IMF's willingness to combine these two kinds of restructurings reflected the IMF staff's belief that the opportunity to work cooperatively with creditors on a restructuring that avoided default would be increasingly rare.[11] Korea was a rare exception, not a model for future crises. The real choice was more between a large IMF bailout and a highly disruptive default, a default that would likely need to be accompanied by "additional measures"—a euphemism for capital controls—to contain capital outflows (IMF September 2000a). While Cologne sought to expand the set of possible policy options by highlighting the wide range of steps that might be taken to involve private creditors, the IMF's proposed framework sought to pare down the list of policy options to only two.

The IMF, above all, hoped to find a way to limit G-7 carping about the provision of large rescue packages. To the IMF, it often seemed that the G-7 consensus was to call on the IMF to find a way to help the country

11. This skepticism is found, for example, in the IMF's July 2002 paper discussing possible reforms to IMF lending facilities (IMF July 2002a).

and to avoid bailing out any creditors—and then to criticize it for failing to do the impossible.

Others in the official sector were more interested in asking whether the IMF should be in the bailout business at all. For example, a paper from the Bank of England and the Bank of Canada—circulated in private early in 2000 and then posted in public—called for sharply scaling back IMF lending and relying on officially sanctioned payments standstills to solve liquidity crises (Haldane and Kruger 2001). The debate this paper triggered is worth examining because the rules the Bank of England and Bank of Canada proposed offered a clear alternative to the constrained discretion the United States advocated.

Advocates of rules argued that without a rule limiting official financing, the official sector would always be pushed to lend more than optimal in the heat of a crisis. They also noted that even large loans had proven ineffective in some cases. The United States—joined by the IMF staff—argued that standstills were too blunt a tool to address liquidity crises. The stabilizing standstill postulated in theory was likely to be highly destabilizing in practice. Stopping a run on the sovereign's external debt by suspending sovereign payments—or even by suspending payments on cross-border interbank credit lines—is fairly easy to do. However, stopping payments risks triggering both cross-border contagion and additional runs inside the crisis country, as a suspension of sovereign or cross-border payments can lead to a rush to take funds out of domestic banks and move them abroad. Stopping the broader run requires a much more comprehensive suspension of currency convertibility. This debate is fleshed out in chapter 6.

The call to let standstills replace large-scale official lending failed to attract the support of most European finance ministries, let alone the United States. Yet many European governments that did not want to make standstills the standard response to crisis resolution wanted another rule: The IMF should make sure that the private sector was "always" involved in crisis resolution. The underlying logic of this position was simple: the larger the amount of official financing, the larger the need to take action to limit the associated distortion. Most healthcare plans include a small payment for each visit to the doctor to discourage overuse of medical facilities. IMF lending is a form of "insurance" and could distort incentives for sound risk assessment by private creditors if not matched by some sort of private-sector "copayment." Two suggestions were put forward to provide substance to this rule. One emphasized that large-scale official financing always should be accompanied by commitments on the part of some private creditor groups not to pull their funds out. The other put less emphasis on obtaining matching commitments from private creditors and instead argued that IMF programs should always leave a financing gap that the country would be expected to work with its private creditors to fill.

The United States was unwilling to accept either suggestion. A rule tying IMF financing to confidence-destroying steps to lock in (some) private creditors would make it harder for countries to regain the confidence of private investors and creditors.[12] Rather than being reassured by the news that a country was approaching the IMF for help, creditors would worry that they would be locked in and so would run faster. In the domestic context, the lender of last resort rarely conditions its liquidity support on the imposition of a partial bank holiday. A commitment not to meet all of a country's financing needs risked systematically underfinancing IMF programs.[13] A domestic lender of last resort can stop runs, because it promises to provide enough financing to let any depositor leave: This promise, in turn, means that few depositors want to leave.[14] Inside the US Treasury, there was a strong belief that the United States' willingness to provide a very large loan had been one of the keys to the success of Mexico's bailout. A principle of the "Rubin doctrine of international finance" that Treasury staff gave Robert Rubin at his departure was: "Money is no substitute for strong policy, but there are times when it is more costly to provide too little money than to provide too much" (Rubin and Weisberg 2003, 251).

IMF Reform

During his tenure as Treasury Secretary, Lawrence Summers put particular emphasis on reforming the IMF's lending facilities. His proposed reforms did not seek to change dramatically the way the IMF lends to emerging economies. Rather, Summers called on the IMF to reform its lending facilities to reflect its core financial fire fighting mission.

Summers suggested that the IMF phase out facilities that provided longer-term financing to emerging-market economies and rely on three core facilities: standby arrangements for countries that did not face capital account crises, the SRF for capital account crises, and the CCL to protect countries with sound policies from the risk of contagion. Summers also proposed raising the charge on all IMF lending, making the lending terms of the CCL more attractive to encourage countries to apply for it

12. Chapter 6 examines the conditions when steps to lock in some creditors might be combined with official financing to encourage other creditors and investors to maintain their exposure to the crisis country. Official financing can, in some circumstances, complement a debt restructuring.

13. The proposal to leave part of the country's financing need for private creditors to fill assumed that financing "gaps" could be determined with a high degree of precision. This can be questioned. A lot of judgment goes into estimating the size of the gap, since the gap depends on the estimated rollover rate on maturing financial claims as well as the scale of capital outflows by private creditors and investors. IMF programs always project a gap equal to the IMF's lending in order to show a fully financed program, but the financing gap forecast has a large margin of error.

14. See Jeanne and Wyplosz (2001) for an analytical formalization of this idea.

and introducing an expectation that IMF loans should be paid in advance, if possible. Not all of these reforms were adopted, but the IMF generally did move in the direction Summers suggested. For example, the IMF board decided to impose a surcharge that increased alongwith the size of a country's IMF loan.

Summers' proposals echoed, albeit very softly, some of the calls of the Meltzer Commission (IFIAC 2000),[15] though his reforms were no doubt intended in part to ward off calls for more radical change. However, Summers' proposed reforms also left the IMF with substantial flexibility. The SRF was clearly intended to be the main vehicle for providing large IMF loans, but nothing formally prevented the IMF from providing large loans on more generous standby terms.

Prague Framework

By the fall of 2000 it was clear that these debates had run their course. Agreement to radically change policy was not possible. At the fall 2000 IMFC meeting, a synthesis of the IMF's proposed framework and previous G-7 statements provided the basis for a new compromise policy. The Prague framework suggests three possible responses to crises:

- "In some cases, the combination of catalytic official financing and policy adjustment should allow the country to regain full market access quickly." Think Mexico. But that statement also indicated that Mexican-style responses also should not be the norm: "Reliance on the catalytic approach at high levels of access presumes substantial justification, both in terms of its likely effectiveness and the risks of alternative approaches."
- "In other cases emphasis should be placed on encouraging voluntary approaches, as needed, to overcome creditor coordination problems." Think Korea or Brazil—countries that sought to monitor the rollover of interbank claims (and in Korea's case, stretch out maturities) as they undertook policy changes.
- "In yet other cases, the early restoration of full market access . . . may be judged unrealistic, and a broader spectrum of actions by private creditors, including comprehensive debt restructuring, may be warranted. . . . this includes the possibility that, in certain extreme cases, a

15. Peter Kenen (2001) summarized the Meltzer Commission's recommendations succinctly: "The Meltzer Report recommends that the IMF transform itself into an ILOLR [international lender of last resort]. It should limit itself to making very short-term loans, base its lending decisions exclusively on preconditions aimed chiefly at appraising the soundness of its member countries' banks, and do little else." The proposed term structure for IMF loans—120 days with one rollover—was particularly unrealistic.

temporary payments suspension or standstill may be unavoidable." (IMF September 2000b, 22). Think Ecuador and Ukraine.

While Prague did articulate the range of responses available to the official sector, like previous statements, it offered relatively little guidance to market participants seeking to know where the official sector would draw the line between those crisis best addressed through catalytic and probably large-scale official financing, perhaps supplemented by efforts to coordinate some groups of private creditors, and those crises best addressed through a debt restructuring.[16]

Prague effectively ended the debate on trying to "involve private creditors" in crisis resolution. The basic policy dilemma that ran throughout this debate was never really resolved. It was easy to see how private creditors could be coerced into providing crisis financing if the official sector made obtaining private financing its primary objective. It was hard to see how the steps required to assure the provision of crisis financing from private creditors who, left on their own, were inclined to cut and run, could be reconciled with the official sector's other objectives. The official sector's primary goal was always to limit the economic impact of the crisis, not to involve private creditors—and key players believed that there often was a trade-off between these two objectives.

Views of Emerging Economies and Private Sector

The debate on private-sector involvement primarily was a debate among the G-7 and G-10 over the appropriate use of the funds they provided the IMF. Particularly after the G-22's demise, emerging economies often felt excluded from the debate.

Many major emerging economies—Brazil, Argentina, and Mexico in particular—wanted the debate to go away. They believed that the core problem in the international financial system was the collapse of private capital flows to emerging economies after 1998, not the difficulty in getting private creditors to contribute to crisis financing. In their view, talk of "involving private creditors" inhibited the resumption of capital flows. They did not believe that concerns about moral hazard warranted restricting the IMF's ability to be able to provide Mexican-style liquidity support. Some Asian emerging economies had a more positive view of efforts to "involve" private creditors. They believed that international banks and market speculators shared responsibility for Asia's financial difficulties and that painful

16. Despite its limitations, the Prague framework did say far more about the options available to the IMF in a crisis than the IMFC had been willing to say. Back in 1998, the whole topic was considered too sensitive to discuss clearly. The IMFC could only agree to call on the IMF "to study further the use of market-based mechanisms to cope with the risk of sudden changes in investor sentiment" (IMF October 1998, 3).

policy adjustments inside Asia should be matched by efforts to rope in the Asian economies' private creditors. Korea in particular believed the active role the G-7 had played in encouraging banks to roll over their exposure was central to the successful resolution of its financial difficulties.

The private financial community's views also varied. In general, the private sector—or at least the Institute for International Finance (IIF), which claimed to speak on behalf of the private financial community—welcomed large "catalytic" financial packages. The IIF also lauded the rollover arrangements in Korea and Brazil as examples of the success possible when the official sector collaborated with private creditors.[17]

However, an important minority in the private sector believed that large-scale official financing was distorting the market and that the uncertainty official intervention created offset any benefits (Porzecanski 2002). Large official packages let short-term creditors—often banks—exit. But they do not allow long-term investors, like bondholders, to get out. No doubt, long-term creditors, like the crisis country's citizens, benefit if the rescue works. The country avoids a broad default, and the market value of the country's bonds recovers. However, long-term creditors can be left worse off if an IMF rescue fails to resolve the crisis, as the need to pay back preferred creditors like the IMF can reduce the resources available for other creditors. Critics of large rescue loans often argue that such loans bail out the bond market, but in reality—as argued in chapter 4—they typically do far more to bail out international banks and other short-term investors.

The largest differences between the official sector and private creditors, though, arose over the restructuring of international sovereign bonds (Gopinath 1999; "When Lenders Should Be Losers," *The Economist*, March 27, 1999). Some in the markets believed that bonds, and in particular the Brady bonds that emerged from the 1980s debt crisis, should be "preferred" instruments and insulated from restructuring. The 1996 call for collective action clauses by the G-10 deputies signaled that the official sector did not share this belief, but their call for clauses hardly attracted the attention of most in the market.[18] Nor, for that matter, did Asia's crisis.

---

17. In some ways, central banks, some of which also functioned as bank supervisors, were more uncomfortable with these arrangements than the major international banks. Once a large private bank decided to maintain its exposure, it had a self-interest in encouraging other banks to do so as well. Bank supervisors worried about the risk of encouraging the major international banks to roll over their exposure to a country that subsequently was unable to pay, exposing the banks they supervised to substantial losses.

18. The IIF—the leading group of private creditors—issued a report of its own in 1996 arguing against the G-10 deputies' call for the use of collective action clauses in international sovereign bonds. It subsequently softened its position and only opposed efforts to force the markets to adopt collective action clauses. It is clear, though, that the IIF did not do much to encourage voluntary change either. It did not, for example, highlight that many dollar-denominated bonds in the major indices were governed by English law and therefore already had clauses.

Asian governments had not issued many international sovereign bonds before their crisis and paid the bonds that they had issued.

The bond restructuring debate heated up only in 1999, after three events combined to grab the market's attention. First, many major institutional investors held Russia's defaulted London Club debt, which had been securitized and traded like a bond. Second, the Paris Club asked Pakistan in early 1999 to seek to restructure its bonds by the end of 1999 (one of its bonds matured in December 1999). Third, Ecuador decided in the fall of 1999 not to make payments on some of its external bonds, in part because the official sector made it clear that Ecuador's bonds would have to be part of the broader financial restructuring the country clearly needed. Since Ecuador's bonds—unlike Pakistan's—were in the leading index of emerging-market debt, Ecuador's default had a particularly strong impact on the market.[19]

Two basic responses emerged from the markets. Some objected to the very idea of a coercive bond restructuring. Voluntary exchanges at market rates were fine, but the IMF should not condition its lending on a bond restructuring—and the Paris Club should not link the restructuring of debts owed to Paris Club creditors on a "comparable" restructuring by bondholders.[20] Such linkages were described as "forcing a country to default." The most dire warnings from the private sector have aged every bit as poorly as certain official policy statements: Claims that any restructuring of sovereign bonds would destroy the market are difficult to square with the sustained rally in emerging-market debt from 1999 to 2003.[21] Others accepted that bonds would need to be restructured but argued that the process of restructuring left much to be desired. This seemed to echo the official sector's own long-standing interest in improving the bond re-

19. See Currie (1998), Brainard (1999), Caplen (2000), and Hubbard (2000) for accounts of these bond restructurings, written largely from the point of view of investors in emerging-market debt securities. An unnamed emerging-market banker was quoted by Currie as stating, "A sovereign Eurobond default now could be cataclysmic," though he also noted that this was, in part, because of unsettled market conditions after Russia's default.

20. IIF (1999a, 5–6) publicly argued that "private investors and creditors . . . do not seek to be bailed out by the official sector" and "no category of private financing, including Eurobonds and Brady bonds, should be automatically exempt from restructuring." However, the IIF also argued vehemently against restructuring Ecuador's bonds (particularly its Brady bonds), even though Chase Research noted that Ecuador's 1999 interest bill was 12 percent of GDP at a time when Ecuador lacked market access. See Dallara (1999) and IIF (1999b).

21. These returns were all the more impressive considering that one of the largest issuers of sovereign bonds—Argentina—defaulted on its international bonds at the end of 2001. New bond issuance slowed following Russia's London Club restructuring and Ecuador's restructuring—but it is not obvious that this was a bad thing, given the rising levels of indebtedness in many emerging-market sovereigns. See IMF (October 2003) for a more extensive discussion of current debt levels in emerging economies.

structuring process. However, the convergence was more apparent than real. The official sector worried about the risk of holdout litigation. Market participants were concerned with another set of issues: the debtor's ability to pick and choose whom to pay (and not to pay), and the debtor's apparent preference to avoid negotiating directly with a committee of bondholders and instead to rely on their investment bank advisers to set the terms for a unilateral exchange offer.[22]

Chapters 7 and 8 take up the details of the restructuring process. It is worth noting, though, that responding to private-sector complaints posed a dilemma for the official sector. On one hand, many in the markets argued that the official sector had been too involved in cases like Pakistan and Ecuador and that it was wrong for the IMF to condition its program on a bond restructuring. On the other hand, addressing bondholder concerns about the way countries like Ecuador and Russia went about their restructuring would have required the IMF to become more involved in the restructuring process. For example, Ecuador's initial decision to pay its uncollateralized Brady bonds, not to pay its collateralized Brady bonds, and to seek to withhold its eurobonds from the restructuring went down poorly with international investors. While the decision to exclude the eurobonds was reversed after holders of Brady bonds threatened legal action, Ecuador's actions left a bitter taste in the mouths of most bondholders. However, avoiding this mistake would have required the IMF to go beyond indicating that Ecuador needed to restructure if it wanted access to official financing and to start giving concrete advice on the right way to go about a restructuring.

A New Administration, a New Policy?

A series of changes occurred in 2001. The Bush administration replaced the Clinton administration. Stanley Fischer retired from the IMF, and Anne Krueger joined Horst Köhler at the top of the IMF. This completed the turnover of the team that had gone through Mexico and Asia together.

This section examines the subsequent effort to forge a new policy toward financial crises. The first part focuses on the Bush administration's policy statements. The second discusses how the Bush administration's

22. The private sector is far from homogenous. The "buy" side—the institutional investors that are the main purchasers of emerging-market securities in the United States—doubted that the major "sell" side—investment banks that advised emerging markets on new issuance and debt exchanges—would adequately represent the "buy" side's interest. The fact that many large US commercial banks active in the 1980s debt restructuring had become, over time, the largest players on the "sell" side of the bond market (JP Morgan, Citibank through Salomon) only heightened "buy side" suspicions.

new policy preferences were reflected in the G-7 and the IMF's policy statements.[23]

US Policy Statements

Many in the Bush administration's economic policy team came into office believing that official action to "stabilize" emerging-market crises—like other forms of government intervention in private markets—was a mistake.[24] The best way to limit the risk of official action distorting private markets was to limit official lending, not to offset IMF loans with steps to lock in certain groups of private creditors. John Taylor (2001a, 4) put it simply: "In order to reduce bailouts of private investors it is necessary to limit the use of official resources, especially in cases where debt sustainability is in question." He qualified this statement by noting that any change needed to be gradual, but the clear emphasis was on "[moving] in the direction of less reliance on large official finance packages." US Treasury Secretary O'Neill emphasized that the risk of contagion should not be overstated in order to provide a rationale for official intervention (O'Neill 2001). The Bush administration also signaled that it would refrain from trying to coordinate the behavior of private creditors. Active participation by the US government in Korean-style rollover arrangements repeatedly was ruled out (Taylor 2001a and 2001b).

The Bush administration's unwillingness to articulate a "framework" that laid out how the official sector should respond to a range of crises was indicative of its deeper differences with the Clinton administration. Crises in Mexico, Asia, and Russia had led the Clinton administration's foreign economic policy team to conclude that the US government could not stand by if a financial crisis threatened a major ally or threatened to trigger widespread financial chaos. The United States, the rest of the G-7, and the IMF would need to be involved in finding constructive solutions. Moreover, the Clinton administration believed that official intervention

23. Between 1996 and September 1998, the IMF increased its outstanding credit by $31 billion in response to the crises in Asia, Russia, and Brazil. Since September 2000, the IMF has increased its outstanding credit by $49 billion in response to crises in Turkey and a series of Latin American economies. IMF loans to Turkey, Argentina, Brazil, and Uruguay, as discussed in chapter 4, were all quite large in relation to these countries' GDP.

24. Suskind (2004, 173) noted, "Many conservative economists, including Larry Lindsey [the head of the National Economic Council] felt the international lending of the Clinton era had placed too much of taxpayers money at risk and done more harm than good . . . the Rubin and Summers gravy train, they felt, had created a moral hazard problem, a situation in which developing countries were encouraged to make bad decisions because they knew the IMF would bail them out." The position of President George W. Bush is a little less clear. As governor of Texas, he strongly supported the 1995 loan to Mexico. Suskind reports that President Bush supported the decision to lend to Argentina in the summer of 2001 but has not delivered a major policy speech outlining his approach to the IMF.

could at times correct for private market failures. International institutions were needed to stabilize the international economy, just as domestic institutions—like a central bank able to supply emergency liquidity—were needed to stabilize the domestic economy. The policy challenge was how best to limit the risk of inevitable official intervention distorting global capital flows.

The Bush Treasury's emphasis on limiting official involvement contributed to its other policy initiative: the development of new institutions for sovereign debt restructuring. Changing sovereign debt contracts—or the adoption of a new international treaty to create a sovereign bankruptcy regime by statute—would enable a country to address its financial problems directly with its creditors, with minimum official involvement. Taylor (2001a, 4) noted: "The official sector should not encourage countries to default on their debts, though we recognize that restructurings can and will happen in certain cases. . . . It is therefore important to develop some kind of international insolvency mechanisms to ensure that if and when restructuring occurs, it does so in an orderly matter that treats creditors fairly, *reducing the scope for arbitrary, unpredictable official action.*" This topic is covered in depth in chapter 8. It is nonetheless worth noting that Taylor based his case for an international bankruptcy mechanism on the need to reduce the distortions official action created, not on the need to eliminate the market failures from the uncoordinated actions of private creditors.

The Bush Treasury's rhetorical emphasis on limits, however, was hard to square with the Bush administration's decision to support large augmentations to the financial support packages provided to Argentina and Turkey in 2001 and its support for large new programs for Brazil and Uruguay.[25] The Bush administration put forward a number of arguments to demonstrate how these large loans were consistent with its stated policy of limiting access to IMF financing. The need to change market expectations meant that limits needed to be introduced gradually. Opposition to any IMF quota increase would limit, over time, the IMF's overall lending capacity. A policy of not providing bilateral support further limited available official financing.

These arguments, though, did not stand serious scrutiny. The 1998 quota increase had expanded the IMF's lending capacity to roughly $200 billion, reducing the need for supplemental lending from bilateral creditors. IMF programs to Turkey and Uruguay were larger in relation to GDP than the combined sums the IMF and the United States provided to Mexico. The

25. The Bush administration joined with others in the G-7 to insist that a substantial fraction of IMF lending to Argentina, Turkey, and Brazil be provided on SRF terms. However, the Bush administration and the G-7 were more effective at insisting that the IMF use the SRF than they were at insisting that the IMF lend only to countries that had a realistic chance of repaying a large loan quickly. Argentina, Turkey, and Brazil all were not in a position to repay their SRF loans when they came due, and new longer-term standby loans were provided to refinance the initial SRF loan.

IMF alone provided more money to Brazil in 2002 and 2003 than the IMF and a group of bilateral lenders provided in 1998 and 1999. The Bush administration also was unable to avoid bilateral lending. It used the ESF for a very short–term bridge loan to Uruguay. If Turkey would allow the United States to use its territory to invade Iraq, the United States was willing to dip into the ESF to provide a loan to Turkey, which would "bridge" not to an IMF program but to a formal congressional approval of a loan guarantee.[26]

G-7 and IMF Policy Statements

The G-7 and the IMFC policy statements in 2001 were forgettable. In April 2002, though, the Bush administration convinced the G-7 to issue a one-page action plan outlining a new approach to emerging-market financial crises. The action plan focused heavily on the need to introduce collective action clauses into debt contracts. But it also indicated that "we [the G-7] are prepared to *limit* official lending to normal access levels except when circumstances justify an exception." In case anyone missed the message, the statement went on to conclude: "It is becoming clearer that official sector support is being *limited*. *Limiting* official sector lending and developing private sector lending are essential parts of our action plan" (Group of 7 2002).

However, this statement only widened the gap between the G-7's tough rhetoric and its actual lending decisions. Indeed, flights of fancy all around marked the spring of 2002. The G-7 was indulging in calls for limits on IMF lending even as it was backing large loans to Uruguay and Brazil, and the IMF was indulging in calls for a new treaty setting out bankruptcy law long after it was clear that key G-7 countries were not on board.

One indication that the G-7 was not prepared, in reality, to reduce access levels came at the IMF board meeting. The IMF staff suggested a range of procedural hurdles to the provision of exceptional levels of access. However, none of the proposals that had real bite—such as amending the IMF articles to require a supermajority rather than a majority of

26. The Bush administration argued that its use of the ESF has been consistent with its policy of avoiding bilateral financing for financial crises, since Uruguay's loan was paid back almost immediately and since bilateral financing was offered to Turkey only to deal with the specific economic costs Turkey would incur as a result of a war in Iraq. The US offer to provide Turkey with a $6 billion grant (which could be used in part to help cover the cost of a guarantee for a larger amount of low-interest rate loans) died when the Turkish parliament voted against authorizing the use of Turkish territory for military operations against Iraq. However, in September 2003 the United States and Turkey reached agreement in principle to use $1 billion from the United States to back a more modest but still substantial $8.5 billion low-interest rate loan to Turkey. As of July 2004, Turkey has not drawn on this loan, but it still clearly ended the policy of saying "no" to bilateral money. The Clinton administration had initially proposed bailing out Mexico with a loan guarantee as well. It only turned to the ESF after Republicans in Congress decided to oppose the loan guarantee.

the board to support large loans, requiring the activation of the NAB for part of the program's financing, or charging IMF members a surcharge to compensate the IMF for the financial risks associated with large loans—generated widespread support among the IMF's key member countries.[27] In the end, the IMF board agreed only on the need for relatively minor changes to improve the IMF's internal information flow and risk assessment along with automatic *ex post* evaluation of large IMF programs.[28]

The IMF also developed a new—and long overdue—template for debt sustainability analysis that tried to address some of the analytical weaknesses that had tended to make previous sustainability assessments too optimistic. However, it was becoming increasingly clear that improved debt sustainability analysis alone would not make it any easier to determine who should get access to large IMF loans. Better stress testing did not suddenly allow debt sustainability analysis to determine, mechanically, the right size for an IMF loan or help the IMF assess whether a crisis country will be able to maintain the policy adjustments needed to keep its debt levels from rising. Improved analysis coincided with an increase in the IMF's exposure to countries with both large debt levels and risky debt profiles.

The fall 2002 IMFC communiqué started the process of bringing official policy statements closer in line with reality. Rather than calling for limits that the international community was not prepared to implement, this communiqué called only for more "clearly defined criteria" to justify exceptional access and "strengthened procedures" to help the IMF board assess the risks associated with large-scale lending (IMF September 2002a).[29] The April 2003 G-7 statement also adopted a more sober tone. It called only for "greater discipline in the provision of official finance"(Group of Seven 2003a).

Conclusions

The official sector's core challenge has been how best to adapt to the changes in private international capital markets that developed in the early 1990s. The official sector's policy should be judged on both how

27. Drawing on the NAB requires the approval of 80 percent of the NAB's contributors, so requiring NAB's activation would make large-scale lending more difficult. The CFR Task Force Report (1999) suggested that the IMF provide exceptional financing only in the event of "systemic" crises and that NAB finance all such lending.

28. Specifically, the IMF staff needs to provide the board with rigorous debt sustainability analysis and a formal assessment of the risks to the IMF's financial position. See IMF (July 2002a) and IMF (January 2003b).

29. The 2003 decision to push the SRF's repayment expectations and repayment obligations back—full repayment is required after three rather than two and a half years—offers additional evidence of the G-7's growing realism.

well it responded to developments in the market and how well its efforts to signal its policy provided useful signals to private markets.

The official sector's record on providing emerging-economy borrowers and their creditors with advance warning of policy change is mixed.

- Halifax (1995) accurately signaled the G-7's desire to expand the IMF's lending capacity, in part to avoid institutionalizing heavy reliance on US bilateral financing. This was reflected in the leading role the IMF took in Asia.
- Birmingham (1998) underscored a new focus on finding ways to respond to crises that did not "insure" payment of private claims—a shift apparent in the subsequent work of both the G-7 and G-22. In the end, the effort to find ways to convince private creditors to provide crisis financing alongside the IMF floundered on the difficulties inherent in roping in creditors without insisting the country take coercive steps—like threatening default—that ran the risk of triggering a broader crisis.
- Cologne (1999) foreshadowed the official sector's willingness to insist that sovereign bonds would need to be restructured. However, its signal that official financing should not be used to support pegged exchange rates was a bit at odds with the subsequent provision of significant support to Turkey, while the country maintained a pegged currency regime.
- Prague (2000) never explicitly indicated how severe a country's problems needed to be to rule out an approach based on catalytic financing. Nonetheless, its suggestion that "exceptionally" large financial support require particularly strong justification is hard to square with subsequent decisions in Turkey, and Argentina. Both received significant amounts of official support to avoid a debt restructuring despite doubts about their solvency.
- If Argentina and Turkey are hard to square with the spirit of Prague, they are even harder to square with the spirit of calls for new limits. Neither the Bush administration nor the G-7 has backed talk of limits with a real willingness to scale back official financing.

In many ways, the biggest surprise is how well official policy statements in 1995 and 1996 charted out the official sector's subsequent policy course. Mexico demonstrated that the combination of modern financial technology, capital account liberalization, and the issuance of short-term debt could combine to generate very large capital outflows. This has proven true time and time again. Policy weaknesses sometimes overlooked in good times can give rise to fears that lead to large outflows when the mood shifts. The G-7 and other stewards of global financial order responded by developing the IMF's capacity to lend larger sums to the crisis country to help prevent a devastating collapse. This required expanding the resources available to the IMF. At the same time, the stewards of global financial order have sought to make some types of debt easier to restructure, whether out of a desire to develop an alternative to large bailouts or out of recognition that even rescues comparable in size to the loan given to Mexico will not always be sufficient to avoid a debt restructuring. The G-10 started calling for collective action clauses in 1996, though little happened until the Bush administration made the introduction of collective action clauses an overarching policy priority.

Yet the basic approach to emerging-market crises laid out in 1995 and 1996 also continues to be a source of deep discomfort. The Clinton administration did not believe that it was credible for the official sector to step aside and let the country and its creditors sort out the crisis without any official-sector involvement. Instead, Clinton-era policymakers sought to find ways to limit the risk of official action distorting market incentives. The Bush administration believed this framework implied too active a role for the official sector. However, the Bush administration's stated long-term intention to limit official financing—an intention the G-7 has endorsed—has not resulted in any reduction in the amount of money the G-7 wants the IMF to put on the table in actual crises.

6

Responding to Liquidity Shortages

The question of mobilizing a large IMF loan to supply foreign currency to a crisis country is the most controversial issue in crisis resolution. Critics say large bailouts do little more than insulate countries from the consequences of their policy mistakes and investors from their bad investment decisions. Proponents say that large rescue packages have saved countries with only temporary problems the pain of an avoidable default and prevented cascading crises like the one in Argentina. Successful rescues limit contagion and even spur better policies in many emerging markets.

Unless a country acts with unusual foresight and seeks help early on, the alternative to a large rescue package is usually a temporary halt in payments. The standstill can be on payments of government debt, on interbank payments, on depositors' ability to take funds out of the banks, on domestic and international investors' ability to convert domestic currency into foreign currency (capital and exchange controls), or a combination of some or all of them. Also, a narrow standstill could risk triggering runs elsewhere, leading the country to eventually impose a broader standstill that includes most debt payments, withdrawals from the banking system, and currency convertibility.

Chapters 3, 4, and 5 touched on the core debate between mobilizing a rescue loan and imposing a standstill. However, the debate is far from settled, either in theory or in practice. This chapter therefore tries to synthesize the insights from various models with lessons from recent experience to broadly assess the options for responding to crises marked in part by a liquidity shortage.

A liquidity shortage can arise in a range of contexts. Some countries that run low on reserves have little overall debt, correctable problems, and strong prospects for regaining market access if their short-run liquidity needs are addressed. Other countries that run low on reserves have economic problems that are more difficult to fix, yet the country may not be insolvent if it can implement needed policy changes—and avoid the economic shock that usually accompanies default. Finally, a scramble to secure the country's remaining liquidity is also a problem in a country close to insolvency: It makes the unavoidable restructuring more costly. Since liquidity shortages arise in a broad range of circumstances, a core argument of this chapter is that different solutions may be needed for different "liquidity" problems.

This chapter has three sections. The first examines the debate on whether to mobilize a large official loan to meet a surge in demand for foreign currency, whether to impose a standstill on payments, or whether to combine a partial standstill and a rescue loan. It pays particular attention to the difficulties that arise in a world where the amount of emergency official liquidity is too small to cover all potential sources of demand for liquidity. While the theoretical debate generally has focused on assessing the choice between a lender of last resort (a full bailout) and a complete standstill on all payments (a full bail-in), most real-world cases require choosing among a partial bailout, a partial bail-in, or some combination of a bailout and a bail-in.

The second section looks at the complexities created when the financial difficulties of private borrowers, not those of the government, lead to pressure on the country's reserves. In addition to discussing the complexities associated with banking and corporate crises, this section discusses the pros and cons of exchange and capital controls.

The third section turns to proposals to find an alternative to both official rescue loans and standstills. This section begins with a discussion of possible private-sector substitutes for IMF lending, whether private lenders of last resort, contingent credit lines, or voluntary debt swaps. It then examines calls to use public guarantees or other "enhancements" to induce private emergency financing. The chapter concludes with proposals to "contractualize" standstills by writing rollover options into debt contracts and with proposals to replace official loans to crisis countries with official intervention to support the secondary market value of emerging economies' bonds.

When Is Official Liquidity Support Warranted?

Choosing Between Official Financing, Payments Standstill, and Consensual Rescheduling of Maturing Claims

A country facing a sudden surge in foreign-currency payments that exceeds its own reserves has three broad choices: It can seek a large official loan to meet the surge in demand, it can suspend payments and break its contractual promise to pay on time and in full, or it can convince its creditors not to demand payment immediately.

If the crisis is truly acute, drawing down reserves or adjusting policies to reduce financing needs may not be viable options. Reserves may be exhausted, and a depreciated exchange rate or fiscal tightening may not generate the needed foreign currency in the short time available. The official sector's basic choices mirror those of the crisis country: It can supply a large rescue loan, it can signal its approval of the country's decision to impose a standstill (usually by lending into arrears to that country), or it can help the country convince its creditors not to demand payment.

Theoreticians of sovereign debt crises have emphasized the analogy between a sovereign financial crisis and a bank run and have examined the choice between a lender of last resort and a standstill in responding to a "run." In a pure run on a solvent country, a large loan that guarantees payment to everyone is sufficient to stop the run. But a standstill on all payments that locks all creditors in has the same result: Once everyone is expected to be locked in, no one has any further incentive to run because, in the model, the only reason for the run in the first place was a fear that others might run first, not doubts about the country's solvency. These models therefore tend to support responding to liquidity crises with "corner-type" solutions—either a loan large enough to cover all short-term claims or a comprehensive standstill is preferable to a partial bailout.

However, the counterintuitive conclusion of these models—that creditors are equally happy with a standstill that forces all of them to maintain their exposure to the crisis country or with a lender of last resort that provides enough financing so that all creditors can get out if they want to—only holds in the absence of doubt about the country's long-term solvency. In most real crises, of course, creditors are jittery, feel that they lack perfect information, harbor doubts about the country's solvency, and would rather be bailed out—or allowed to exit—than be forced to stay in. Models that have examined how doubts about solvency can trigger a run on a country's liquidity have come to another conclusion. "Catalytic" financing—a bailout that is not large enough to assure that everyone can get out if they want to—can work, but only if the loan is made to a country whose policy problems are not too severe. In these models, the combination of access to additional official financing and policy changes can avoid a panic and a complete run. The additional money on the table allows the country's least committed creditors to leave without giving rise to fears among the country's remaining creditors that the country will run out of reserves before its policy reforms take hold.

These formal models—already discussed in detail in chapter 3—provide important insights into crises. They also necessarily paint a simplified picture of emerging-market crises. Most models imagine a world with one debtor, either the government or the country, that has a single set of external creditors. In reality, an emerging economy is composed of multiple debtors—the sovereign government, the country's banks and other financial institutions, and the country's firms and households—all of which obtain financing from many different creditors, both at home and abroad. Moreover, anyone holding a local currency–denominated financial asset can put pressure on the country's reserves or the exchange rate, should they opt to shift their savings from local financial assets to foreign assets.

In this messy and complex world, most realistic policy options will address only one of many potential sources of pressure on the country's reserves. Even the biggest bailouts are not large enough to let all potential creditors and investors—including domestic residents who have invested their savings in the country's banking system—to exit, particularly if everyone wants to exit at the same time. A rescue loan sufficient to cover all the sovereign's maturing short-term debts, for example, works only if bailing out the sovereign—and indirectly its creditors—leads the country's other creditors (those who lent to banks and firms) and investors (those holding local financial assets) to renew their loans and keep their savings in local assets. This is one reason why appropriate policy adjustments almost always need to accompany a rescue loan: Financial stability still hinges on convincing a range of creditors and investors that they want to continue to hold financial claims on the crisis country.

Similarly, most actual standstills are far messier than the stabilizing standstill postulated in many models, in part because the standstills assumed in models rarely cover all potential sources of pressure on the country's reserves. No proposal to use a standstill to address a liquidity shortage should be considered complete unless it specifies which claims should be caught in the standstill, why a standstill on one set of claims won't trigger a broader run on other claims, and what steps need to be taken to allow the standstill to be lifted. For example, a standstill that stops payments on the sovereign's short-term debt works only if it does not trigger a broader run, whether by the banking system's external or domestic creditors or simply by all those holding the local currency. This is one reason why a country facing payments difficulties is far better off if it can convince its creditors with maturing debts to agree to defer payments rather than just unilaterally announcing it has stopped payments. Announcing an agreement on a restructuring is less likely to trigger a broader run than announcing a unilateral payments moratorium. Yet a negotiated restructuring that averts default is not always possible: Almost every creditor would rather be the last to get out rather than the first to agree to defer payments.

This discussion on the resolution of liquidity shortages raises another important point: A crisis country's exchange rate regime will shape both its choices in a crisis and the choices facing the official sector. After all, most emerging economies have few more important prices than the price at which domestic financial assets can be traded for—presumably—much safer foreign financial assets. In the absence of exchange controls, a fixed exchange rate increases the scope of potential pressure on the country's reserves in a crisis: The government's promise to trade local currency for foreign currency at a fixed price turns all liquid, domestic-currency financial assets into a claim on the country's reserves. A domestic bank depositor, for example, can withdraw domestic currency from a bank and then convert it into foreign currency at a fixed rate. If the country runs out of reserves, it either has to break its promise to maintain a fixed exchange rate or impose a bank holiday or exchange controls that try to lock savings in the country.

If the country's currency floats—and if domestic debts are denominated in domestic currency—the country's central bank can always lend the government the local currency it needs to pay its debts and provide the local currency liquidity the banks need to avoid a bank holiday. But vast injections of local currency into the economy to settle maturing local currency–denominated debts also put tremendous pressure on the exchange rate. The government, in turn, usually intervenes to limit the exchange rate fall, putting pressure on the government's reserves. The core problem remains: If domestic residents—and external investors who have bought local financial assets—lose confidence and want to trade en masse their local financial assets for external assets, a financial crisis may be unavoidable.[1]

Advantages of Rescue Loans

The pros and cons of large-scale financing and those of a standstill are in many ways mirror images. The core advantage of large-scale financing is that it avoids the cost associated with standstills. The core advantage of a standstill is that it avoids the distortions associated with large-scale official lending. It is therefore difficult to discuss one option in isolation.

The fundamental advantage of a large rescue loan is simple: It limits the risk that a payments standstill would transform a potentially temporary problem—the immediate shortage of liquidity—into a deeper, more permanent problem. The conceptual argument was discussed in chapter 3. The inability to honor contractual commitments has to be costly to create incentives for a country to make a real effort to pay its debt. However, if the country has the capacity to pay its debt over time and only faces a temporary shortage of liquidity, then bankruptcy costs are a problem. Penalizing a country for running out of reserves even if it has the long-term capacity to pay its debt in full (with policy adjustments) could leave both the country and its creditors worse off since the "costs of bankruptcy" themselves might be large enough to make it impossible for the country to pay its debt over time.

1. Still, liquidity runs are more severe under fixed rates than under flexible rates. Fixed exchange rates turn all short-term liquid assets denominated in the local currency into a potential claim on scarce reserves. But if the country's currency is floating, then only short-term foreign-currency debts are a direct claim on reserves.

The key risk of sovereign bankruptcy is not creditor litigation. As will be discussed in detail in chapter 8, the sheer difficulty of taking effective legal action against a sovereign usually provides the sovereign substantial protection from the risk of creditors being able to seize its remaining reserves or other assets. A sovereign government that runs out of reserves and has to restructure its foreign-currency debt—or a sovereign that cannot supply the domestic banks with the foreign currency they need to cover their maturing debts—faces a more immediate risk of the sovereign restructuring triggering a broader run and a cascading crisis of confidence. Depositors may start to pull their savings out of the banking system and transfer them abroad. Those holding local currency or a financial asset denominated in the local currency may rush to sell their local currency for foreign currency.

A rescue loan on a scale sufficient to allow a troubled government to pay its maturing foreign-currency debts not only avoids default on the specific debts that are causing the country's immediate payment problems but also can help convince a wide range of other investors with claims on the country not to run. For example, the financing that enabled Mexico to honor its short-term tesobonos increased the confidence of domestic depositors in the banking system and thus reduced the risk of a domestic bank run immediately resulting in a broader, deeper crisis.[2] A standstill on tesobono payments, in contrast, would have increased the risk of domestic Mexican bank depositors running, thus widening the crisis.

Official financing has a second advantage: The expectation that a rescue package, rather than a standstill, will meet the pressure on foreign exchange reserves can reduce the risk of runs developing in the first place. If creditors holding short-term claims anticipate that the country will impose a standstill, they may try to get out before the standstill is imposed—particularly if a standstill risks leading to a change in government or if there is uncertainty about the policies the country will adopt after it freezes payments. Economic theory indicates that anticipated payments suspensions—like anticipated capital controls—will accelerate the onset of pressure. Indeed, expectations of a standstill may actually trigger a run that would not have otherwise occurred. This argument should not be pushed too far—if a creditor holding a maturing claim believes the country's policies are unsustainable, then it will want to get out even in the absence of any expectations of a quick standstill. Still, interbank creditors to

2. During Mexico's crisis, the Bank of Mexico did make some dollar loans to domestic banks that needed to pay maturing dollar claims. However, domestic depositors by and large did not flee, even though the banking system incurred large losses as a result of the devaluation. Protecting bank depositors from losses required a costly government bailout. The fact that the government of Mexico was able to avoid default on its existing debt made its promise to honor the new debt it placed with the banks as part of the bank bailout more credible. Bank solvency crises are often much easier to resolve than a bank run, so long as the government itself is solvent and taxpayers can pay for the cost of the bank bailout over time.

Brazil probably ran faster than they otherwise would have because of memories of Korea and the capital controls in Malaysia and Russia. Argentina's bank depositors probably were jumpier than average in 2001 because of the country's history of resorting to deposit freezes in the 1980s.

Official financing has a third advantage. Policymakers have few incentives to improve their policies if they are sure that a run will push the country into default before any policy reforms yield dividends. Liquidity insurance that protects against the risk of a run thus increases the incentive to improve policies.[3] One of the prime criticisms of official assistance is that countries may be more willing to run risky policies if they expect an official bailout. However, this argument is too simple: Once a country has got into trouble, official support may be needed for it to be willing to make a last ditch investment in good policies. For example, the liquidity assistance provided to Brazil in 2002 gave the newly elected government the hope that a run would not devastate the country before the new government had a chance to demonstrate its fiscal credibility and may have therefore contributed to the incentives for the new government to maintain large primary surpluses. Once a sovereign government decides it cannot avoid the costs associated with breaking its basic contractual commitment to pay on time, it may decide that there is little additional cost to failing to make a good faith effort to improve its policies and breaking the implied commitment to seek to repay in full at a later date.

Finally, official financing can reduce the risk of the crisis extending to other countries. Investors caught in a standstill have a strong incentive to reduce their exposure to other potentially risky countries. If other countries have not built up reserve stocks that protect them from such a risk, investor jitters following a crisis in one country could trigger self-fulfilling crises elsewhere. This contagion risk is correlated with the size of the initial crisis country. The larger the country, the greater the probability that a wide range of investors will have exposure to that country: Nothing leads to a broad reassessment of risks like actual losses. Moreover, a large country is far more likely to trigger investor losses on a scale that triggers disruptions in a range of financial markets. (See box 2.2 for a more detailed discussion of "wake-up call" and "common creditor" channels for contagion.)

Advantages of Standstills

The main argument in favor of payments standstills is that they avoid the distortions associated with official lending. In theory, official lending distorts the incentives of both the debtor, who may run riskier policies expecting official lending to protect it from a subsequent crisis, and its creditors. In practice, the risk of official lending distorting creditors' incentives is a greater concern. The debtor never really gets off the hook: Rescue loans

3. For a formal model, see Corsetti, Guimaraes, and Roubini (2003).

normally come with painful conditionality, the debtor has to pay its rescue loan back, and as discussed earlier, official financing can strengthen incentives for reforms when crisis conditions could otherwise have led policymakers to throw in the towel. Private creditors with short-term claims, in contrast, have the option of getting out without taking any losses if they do not renew their claims. Long-term creditors cannot get out on the back of official financing: They are locked in until the day the loan or bond matures. Of course, a successful IMF loan that helps a country through a short-term crisis is likely to increase the secondary-market value of long-term debt. Expectations of official lending could lead creditors, or at least those that lend for short terms, to lend too freely to countries with risky policies or with simply too much debt, thereby making crises more likely.

The risk of creditor moral hazard is mitigated in part by the fact that most rescue loans fail to provide anywhere near enough liquidity to protect even all short-term creditors from losses, as events in Thailand, Indonesia, Russia, and Argentina have demonstrated. The country may fail to deliver reform and thus fail to get all of the promised official financing. Or even if it delivers, the amount of official financing available may simply be insufficient to pay everyone in the event of a broad run.[4]

Some creditors with short-term debt (including creditors holding what were originally long-term claims that are close to maturity) may get out before the rescue fails, but creditors who cannot get out because they hold long-term debt or who bet wrong and opt not to get out may end up taking bigger losses. Senior IMF loans typically are repaid even after a country defaults, and the priority accorded to payments to the IMF and other senior creditors may imply larger losses for the country's remaining junior creditors (see chapter 7).

However, these qualifications do not alter the core reality: The surest way to eliminate all risks of moral hazard is to simply stop providing liquidity insurance to emerging economies and instead to rely on standstills to address a wide range of their financial difficulties.[5] Emergency official lending can spare a country the pain of default only by providing enough financing to give some creditors with maturing debts the option of exiting. Some may not exercise that option and choose to renew their exposure, but others will likely opt to get out.

Ironically, the official sector's steps to limit the risk of moral hazard—delivering official support in tranches tied to policy reforms to control debtor moral hazard and limiting the overall amount of funds put on the

4. Apart from a few well-known moral hazard plays (Russia in 1997 and early 1998 and Turkey from 2001 on), there is little evidence that expectations of future bailouts systematically distort risk spreads or flows. See chapter 3 for a detailed discussion and references.

5. Creditors have many other reasons to prefer short-term lending that offers the prospect of getting out at par. Even without official lending, the country's own reserves provide short-term creditors with some degree of protection.

table—lead to a second critique of official lending: The partial bailouts needed to limit the risk of moral hazard simply don't work. Unless the official sector is prepared to throw caution to the wind and make sufficient upfront financing to assure that everyone who wants to get out can, a standstill may offer a more effective solution to liquidity problems. A domestic lender of last resort lends all that is needed to stop the run, while the IMF risks putting enough money on the table to allow some creditors to exit but not enough to stop the run. Since the chances of a partial bailout allowing the country to avoid some kind of standstill are slim, the country would be better off to simply impose a standstill early on, before running through an IMF loan.

This critique has a grain of truth: The amount of money that the official sector initially put on the table in both Uruguay and Korea failed to stop bank runs. Uruguay stopped its run only by getting a much bigger loan, and Korea did so only by convincing its creditors to postpone payment on maturing interbank loans. However, the criticism of official financing is too pessimistic. In the right conditions, official financing backed by policy reforms has catalyzed the voluntary rollover of private debts, stabilized the country's finances, and left the country in a position to repay the IMF relatively quickly. Mexico in 1995 and Brazil in 1999 are examples.

Finally, relying on payments freezes to address liquidity as well as solvency crises avoids the risk of the official sector diagnosing a country's problems incorrectly and will treat what is truly a permanent problem of insolvency (too much debt) as a temporary problem of illiquidity. Lending significant sums to a country that should have been declared insolvent from the start, or that cannot make the policy changes needed to assure its long-run solvency, has a range of costs. The fact that some creditors could get out using IMF funds weakens incentives for sound risk assessment—to the detriment of the international financial system. Backing a failed strategy damages the IMF's credibility, leaves it with lots of exposure to a country that is in no position to repay the IMF quickly, and may thus put the IMF's resources at risk. This lending typically does not lead to financial losses, but it does reduce the money that the IMF has available to lend to countries facing truly short-term problems. Finally, it leaves the country itself worse off: After exhausting the IMF's lending capacity and willingness to avoid a payments standstill and a restructuring, the country will not be able to borrow additional IMF reserves to limit the risk of a broader financial collapse as the country goes through its restructuring. Backing the wrong strategy has a large opportunity cost.

Is It Riskier to Provide Too Much Financing or Too Little?

It is easy to say that the provision of official "liquidity" is the right response to a "liquidity" crisis. It is much harder to answer the question of how much liquidity is needed.

Both lending too little and too much can be risky. Small loans may fail to reassure investors that the country's finances are strong enough to withstand the withdrawal of credit by those least committed to the country. If large capital outflows overwhelm a small loan while a large loan can stop, or at least slow, the run and give the country a chance to improve its policies, then the large loan may be less of a risk than the small loan. This is not just a theoretical proposition: The data presented in chapter 4 show that some large loans have been paid back quickly—indeed, more quickly than some smaller loans.

However, lending large sums to a country with substantial debt is always risky. Even an extremely large loan is not enough to guarantee success, since the potential demand for foreign exchange—including that from domestic residents seeking to flee—is usually more than the financing the official sector can reasonably provide. Moreover, the most effective way to address concerns about a liquidity shortage is to provide large amounts of money to the country quickly. But this response risks providing the country with large amounts of financing before it has time to show its ability to implement the policies needed to improve its long-term solvency. A large loan can fail because even it may not be big enough, because the country is unable to sustain the implementation of needed policies, or because the country simply was in deeper trouble than initially believed. A failed large loan leaves both the country and the official sector in a worse position than a failed small loan. Argentina is a prime example.

Obviously a balance has to be struck here. The key challenge is providing enough liquidity—relative to the potential sources of drain—to catalyze a positive solution, without exposing the official sector to too much risk should everything go wrong. The less money that is provided upfront, the easier it is to shift approaches quickly if the provision of liquidity, plus adjustment, fails to convince the needed number of investors to stay in. If an initial burst of "catalytic" financing fails, the country can shift approaches and impose a standstill on the remaining claims before running up a large debt to the IMF and other official lenders. On the other hand, the possibility of the official sector shifting approaches makes it harder for small amounts of money to achieve the desired result. If creditors conclude that the initial loan doesn't provide the country with enough money to have a chance of working, they have every incentive to get out while they still can.[6]

A comparison between official lending to Mexico in 1995 and Russia in 1998 is instructive. Mexico's rescue package was large enough to cover a substantial fraction of near-term pressures, so a very large fraction of the loan was made available to Mexico immediately. In Russia, catalytic fi-

6. If the country has substantial reserves when it approaches the IMF, then the IMF can set the reserve floors in the IMF program to allow the country to spend a significant fraction of its own reserves. The IMF effectively authorizes a country to spend its own money to finance a surge in demand for foreign currency. Subsequent IMF financing can then allow the country to rebuild its reserves if it meets program conditions.

nancing was tried without as much conviction. Less money was made available, with more tranching and a greater willingness to move quickly toward a restructuring if an initial round of financing—and lack of credible policy adjustment—failed to produce signs of quick improvement.[7]

The nature of the country's payments difficulties, the country's debt profile, and the risk of a restructuring triggering a broader run will all combine to determine whether a strategy of "official lending and adjustment to avoid *any* debt restructuring or payment holiday" is a worthwhile bet. The amount of financing needed to give such a strategy a fighting chance also depends in part on the nature of the country's financial difficulties. If only one actor in the economy is experiencing financial difficulties, for example the government, then enough money could be provided to cover that actor's near-term debts. But such a loan would not be enough to meet the additional demand for foreign exchange from private firms unable to roll over their debts or from the banking system if depositors pulled their savings out of local banks en masse. It would also not cover all government debt payments over a longer time frame.

Combining Official Financing with a Coordinated Rollover

When policy credibility is lacking, investors lack complete information about the country's true financial health, the country's economic conditions are uncertain, and official lending does not provide enough money to protect everyone from losses, risk-averse investors may still prefer to withdraw rather than roll over their investments. Even if the official sector provides substantial support, the basic collective action problem remains: If one creditor stays in and all the others run, the one that stays in risks incurring losses. In some cases, combining official financing with a coordinated rollover of some classes of claims may be more effective than official financing alone.

Korea is the obvious example.[8] The country faced a large spike of payments on its interbank credits at the end of 1997. An initial $10 billion from the IMF and other official creditors failed to stop the run. One pol-

7. The fact that the Duma could not deliver on promised fiscal adjustment made the decision to cut off Russia's IMF financing easier. However, the program could have still failed to engender the needed improvement in confidence even if the Duma had shown more willingness to make reforms, given the sheer scale of maturing GKOs that needed to be refinanced and the need for interest rates on GKOs to fall quickly to avoid a debt trap. The IMF program did not provide anywhere near enough financing to cover all maturing GKOs.

8. Blustein (2001) provides a detailed account of Korea's crisis. IMF officials recognized the risk of the initial IMF loan being too small to stop the run. They initially had expected the bilateral component of the IMF program to be part of the "first line" of defense and to be disbursed alongside the IMF financing, not "second line" and available only in the event of undefined contingencies. The two-month period of Korea's crisis also coincided with an election and significant uncertainty about the direction of policy.

icy option would have been to increase the amount of official financing available. Another would have been to leave Korea alone to address its problems without any help from the IMF or G-7. The latter option would have forced Korea to declare a unilateral standstill on the payment of its external bank debt. Neither option seems preferable to the option that was actually adopted—combining official financing with official help in organizing a semivoluntary rollover agreement.

Korea was lucky: A relatively small and homogenous group of creditors accounted for most of the debt falling due in late 1997 and early 1998. These are precisely the conditions when a coordinated rollover supplemented with official financing is most likely to be effective. Many argue that it is possible to negotiate a targeted rescheduling with a consortium of international banks but not with more widely held bonded debt. We would not be so sure. Some traded securities are relatively narrowly held. Plus, examples abound of debt exchanges that have successfully extended the maturity of traded securities. Conversely, the rescheduling of interbank lines may be becoming more difficult: In Turkey, the major international banks often acted as intermediaries for hedge funds and other investors who wanted to play the Turkish interbank market for high overnight yields while retaining the option of getting out fast.

A targeted attempt to coordinate the rollover or rescheduling of a single set of claims is quite different from a general standstill on all payments. Any attempt to defer payments on some claims can have two effects on other creditors and investors. On one hand, changing short-term to long-term debt reduces demand on the country's reserves. On the other hand, the need to seek a coercive restructuring itself is a negative signal that risks triggering a broader run.

In Korea, a negotiated standstill on external bank payments reassured, not spooked, other investors. A negotiated standstill reduced the risk of a more disruptive unilateral moratorium on payments, and the rollover agreement was part of a broader package of official lending and policy reform. Other partial bank holidays have had the opposite impact. Argentina imposed a partial bank holiday on domestic bank deposits at the end of 2001 (a freeze on sight deposits). Its holiday was unilaterally imposed—though it is difficult to see how Argentina would have negotiated with millions of small depositors—and was not combined with the announcement of a credible path through its financial difficulties. Not surprisingly, bank depositors scrambled to find other ways to get out.

Liquidity Difficulties That Signal Risk of Future Insolvency

Many liquidity crises stem in part from incipient solvency problems. Difficulty rolling over debts creates an immediate shortage of liquidity, yet growing debt levels may also imply the need to increase the primary fiscal balance or to let the exchange rate fall to improve long-term solvency. The country is not insolvent if it can deliver sufficient, sustained policy reform, but it is not in trouble solely because of liquidity difficulties either.

Both are the most common type of crises and the most difficult to address. One option is to provide significant amounts of official financing to solve the liquidity problem. However, this transfers onto the official sector much of the risk of the sovereign not being able to deliver the needed policy adjustments. Another option is to reschedule sovereign claims coming due at a normal—that is, precrisis—interest rate (a truly voluntary swap at market rates would aggravate concerns about future solvency as discussed later). Private creditors retain their exposure to the underlying risk and will take losses if the country fails to deliver needed policy improvements or is subject to an unanticipated shock. But the terms of the debt restructuring also leave creditors with a substantial upside if the country does recover. Pakistan, Ukraine, and more recently, Uruguay have followed this broad strategy.

A forced extension of maturities carries with it two risks. One, if many creditors refuse to participate in the restructuring, the sovereign may be forced into an unwanted default.[9] Two, a forced change in the terms of the sovereign's own debt also risks triggering a broader run. Even successful efforts to force private creditors to defer some payment can lead to the emergence of other potential drains on reserves.

Are Targeted Debt Reschedulings Inequitable?

Any approach that singles out one set of claims for a rescheduling while providing financing to reassure other creditors and investors is inherently inequitable. Different sources of pressure on the country's foreign-currency reserves are treated differently: Some creditors and investors are paid in full if they want to exit while others are told that they need to reschedule their claims (Group of 22 1998a).

Concerns about inequities can be minimized if it is clear that one set of claims—tesobonos in Mexico, GKO payments in Russia, and interbank lines in Korea—accounts for the vast bulk of the pressure on a country's foreign-currency reserves. Concerns about equity—along with concerns about triggering a broader loss of confidence—are also mitigated if the restructuring does not ask too much from those creditors who are the focus of the rescheduling. Asking one set of creditors to reschedule their claims to solve a short-term liquidity crunch is one thing, but asking them to make deep concessions to improve the country's solvency when other creditors are not is quite another.

9. Schelling (1960) famously noted that threats—in this case the threat to default if creditors do not agree to a restructuring—are costly if they fail, while bribes are costly if they succeed.

Risks of Gradual Escalation

One approach to crisis management would be to try various options in sequence: First provide catalytic financing; if that does not work, organize some form of rollover; and if that too does not work, suspend payments and move toward more formal restructuring. This policy of gradual escalation would assure that every country gets a chance to see if it can avoid a restructuring with an initial official loan, even if that IMF conditional loan approach may have little chance of success.

Another approach would be to make an initial judgment about the likely success of pure catalytic lending and—if such probability is low enough—make the provision of liquidity contingent on the country's ability to negotiate a debt rescheduling—effectively a targeted payments standstill—with a set of its private creditors. Access to official financing can be made contingent on the country's ability to convince its interbank creditors to roll over their claims or contingent on the country's ability to execute a bond exchange that pushes out the maturity of its bonded debt. Making official support contingent on a targeted restructuring from the beginning, however, requires that the official sector make an upfront judgment about the likely success of catalytic financing—a judgment that is sure to be controversial and that the IMF may occasionally get wrong.

If the amount of official financing put on the table is too small—relative to the likely sources of demand for foreign currency—to have a realistic chance of stopping the run, it makes sense to move immediately to organizing a voluntary rollover or maturity-extending exchange. For example, Korea would have been better off if it had moved more quickly to seek a rollover, as the amount of money on the table in Korea was too small to have a realistic chance of stopping the run. Similarly, if the country's debt levels and policy track record combine to raise substantial concerns about the country's capacity to sustain the improved policies required for long-term solvency, a maturity-extending or reducing debt exchange should be part of a country's program from the start. In both cases, though, official lending is still needed, since the debt restructuring is likely to address only one of many potential sources of demand for foreign exchange.

Case for Pragmatism

We are pragmatists who believe the best approach to any crisis characterized in part by a liquidity shortage will hinge in part on the "facts on the ground." Details like how much is coming due when, whether the claims creating the most trouble are bank loans or traded securities, who holds the claims, what the potential is for negotiating a voluntary rollover to provide time to reach agreement on rescheduling terms, and the risk of a concerted rollover of one set of claims triggering a run elsewhere all will help to determine the viability of different policy approaches.

We are pragmatists also in a second sense. One single approach does not make sense for all the circumstances when a liquidity shortage can arise. Lending too little can be self-defeating if it fails to stop the run. But the risk of lending too little has to be weighed against the risk of lending too much to the wrong countries—a risk that is particularly acute if large sums are needed before the country can show its commitment to improve its creditworthiness.

Standstills pose practical difficulties of their own—difficulties sometimes glossed over by their most vocal proponents. Which claims should be caught in the standstill? What will prevent a standstill on one set of claims from triggering a broader run? What steps need to be taken to allow the standstill to be lifted? It is far easier to imagine a quick exit from a targeted standstill that is followed by a quick agreement on a rescheduling (Korea exited from its interbank rollover arrangement in less than three months) than from a broad standstill (look at Argentina). At the same time, a narrow standstill risks triggering a broader run and ultimately failing to solve the crisis.

Finally, it is a mistake to think that a series of small and incremental steps offers the best way to avoid a bad outcome. Most approaches have the best chance of working when they are embraced early on, with enough conviction to be given a real chance to work.

Private-Sector Financial Difficulties

The easiest liquidity crisis to conceptualize is one where the sovereign itself lacks sufficient reserves to repay all of its maturing debts and barring a rescue, will be forced to suspend payments on its own debt. However, repayment of the sovereign's own debt is only one potential source of demand on the country's reserves. A shortage of foreign-currency liquidity can also arise under these conditions:

- the banking system is unable to roll over its external debts, and the government is unable to lend the banking system the hard currency it needs to make payments.
- domestic bank deposits are denominated in a foreign currency, and the banking sector itself lacks sufficient stocks of foreign currency to cover a surge in withdrawals.
- the corporate sector is unable to roll over its external debts, and firms in distress cannot buy the foreign exchange they need at a price they can afford in the market.

- domestic bank depositors pull their domestic-currency deposits out of the banking system and seek to convert all their holdings of domestic currency into foreign currency, causing the price of the domestic currency to fall and leading to pressure to intervene.
- more generally, investors are unwilling to hold domestic assets at the existing interest rates, and their desire to shift into foreign assets puts pressure on the exchange rate.

Such imbalances between the supply of and demand for foreign currency can arise if a private sector–driven boom leads to financial difficulties, as was the case in Asia. But such imbalances can also arise if a sovereign crisis leads investors and creditors to lose confidence in the financial assets of the country's private sector. A bailout and a standstill remain the basic options, but the standstill has to cover transactions between private borrowers and their creditors and/or those private citizens looking to sell their local currency and buy foreign currency.

External-Bank Liquidity Crises

Banking crises are common in emerging-market economies. Such crises have many potential causes. A lending/credit boom—often fueled in part by poor bank supervision and other microeconomic distortions such as implicit guarantees—can lead to overlending and large loan losses when economic conditions turn sour. Exchange rate changes can result in large losses if the banking system itself has a currency mismatch or if the banks passed on their currency risk by lending in foreign currency to debtors that lack foreign-currency revenue. Heavy exposure to an overindebted sovereign also can push the banking system into crisis.

Developing and implementing a coherent strategy for addressing a severe banking crisis is difficult. Some form of "triage" is often needed to determine which banks are insolvent and need to be closed, merged with healthy banks, or both; which banks should be kept open but placed under temporary government control/tight supervision ("intervened" in the language of banking crises); and which are basically solvent and should continue to operate under their current management.[10] To avoid passing losses onto depositors, the government often needs to recapitalize the banking system, usually by giving the banks government bonds to make up for their nonperforming assets.

Restructuring the banking system's assets and closing bad institutions, though, is rarely enough. Steps also need to be taken to stop a run from

10. A complete discussion of the issues that arise in the resolution of banking crises is beyond the scope of this book. See Group of 22 (1998b) and Hoelscher and Quintyn (2003) for a detailed discussion.

draining the banking system of liquidity. Banks are, by definition, in the business of maturity transformation and cannot withstand a sudden withdrawal of either deposits or cross-border lines. If a significant fraction of bank liabilities—domestic deposits as well as cross-border lines—are denominated in a foreign currency, then the banks' need for liquidity usually translates into pressure on the country's foreign-currency reserves.

A sovereign almost always tries to stop a run by guaranteeing the banking system's foreign-currency debts.[11] If the guarantee fails to stop the run, then the sovereign needs to come up with sufficient foreign currency to honor its guarantee. If it cannot, then the sovereign either has to renege on its guarantee, leaving the banking system unable to honor its debts, or has to impose a standstill on the banks' foreign-currency liabilities.

The widespread use of government guarantees for cross-border interbank lines no doubt makes these kinds of crises easier to resolve. Even if the guarantee does not stop the run, the fact that the country's external creditors now have claim on the government makes it easier to negotiate a rollover arrangement or debt rescheduling. Rather than, say, 100 banks renegotiating their claims on 20 banks of different credit quality, they can simply negotiate with the government. This makes it easier to reach a negotiated agreement with the banking system's external creditors. The risk of a unilateral suspension of payments on the banks' external liabilities triggering a domestic bank run provides the crisis country's government with a strong incentive to use a guarantee to facilitate a voluntary agreement.

However, the widespread use of guarantees for interbank lines is quite troubling. Providing emergency liquidity to allow small domestic depositors, who lack the capacity to assess the creditworthiness of a complex financial institution, to exit without taking losses is one thing. Protecting sophisticated international banks from losses is quite another. The expectation that interbank lines, at worse, will become claims on the government may make international banks too willing to lend to shaky banks, and the easy availability of external financing can contribute to poor domestic lending decisions. Such guarantees are particularly pernicious when restoring the banking system's solvency may require a large taxpayer-financed bailout as well as the provision of emergency liquidity.[12]

11. South Korea, Indonesia, and Turkey all issued such guarantees at the early stages of their respective crises. Thailand guaranteed payment on cross-border lending to commercial banks but not on cross-border lending to Thai finance companies.

12. The provision of emergency liquidity to the banking system does not necessarily result in losses for taxpayers. So long as the central bank is supplying liquidity only to solvent banks, the emergency loan from the central bank just covers a temporary liquidity shortage. The bank retains enough good assets to assure full repayment of all creditors, including the central bank. However, it is often difficult to sort good banks from bad banks at the height of a crisis. In many cases, the government is less interested in trying to sort out good banks from bad banks than in protecting domestic depositors—and often the

But coming up with an alternative approach to cross-border bank runs is difficult. Most governments try to stop a run with a blanket guarantee and consider alternative policy approaches only if the guarantee fails to stop the run. Once such a guarantee is extended, the IMF is loath to make revoking the guarantee a condition for its lending. It would be better if governments issued guarantees to the banking system's external creditors only in exchange for a commitment to roll over maturing claims or even a formal rescheduling. But even here creditors are protected from outright losses if they lent to a bad bank, so long as the government can make good on its promises. Passing losses onto the banking system's external creditors requires locking in short-term bank creditors at an early stage of the crisis (or at least not guaranteeing the banking system's longer-term liabilities), some form of triage, and then forcing external creditors that lent to banks that either have to be closed or taken over by the government (intervened) to take outright losses.[13]

Eliminating expectations that the government will guarantee the repayment of cross-border interbank loans in a crisis, though, is likely to be next to impossible. Consequently, emerging-market economies need to regulate their banking system's external borrowing extremely tightly. Indeed, the unusual risks associated with external borrowing may justify imposing high reserve requirements (effectively a tax) on external borrowing. Such reserve requirements not only discourage external borrowing but also have the added virtue of creating a liquidity buffer that the banks can draw on before they turn to the government for emergency support.

Systemic Corporate Crises

A systemic corporate rollover and financial crisis poses much more difficult conceptual questions. The sovereign could guarantee full payment of private firms' maturing short-term external debts to stop a run on such claims.[14] Fortunately, such an approach is rarely followed. An outright

banks' external creditors—from any losses. If the bank's assets are not sufficient to cover its liabilities, protecting the bank's creditors—domestic depositors and external creditors alike—from losses requires a taxpayer-financed bailout. This is typically done by giving the banks a government bond (a new asset) to make up for any gap between their existing assets and their liabilities. A recent estimate put the cost of a banking crisis at roughly 20 percent of GDP in Mexico, Korea, and Ecuador; 30 to 35 percent of GDP in Thailand and Turkey; and a staggering 50 percent of GDP in Indonesia, though these numbers may fall if these countries succeed in recovering more value from the portfolio of bad loans the government assumed during the crisis (Hoelscher and Quintyn 2003).

13. This is what happened to external lenders to Thailand's finance companies, as discussed in chapter 4. Lenders to Thailand's commercial banks, however, received a full guarantee.

14. In the 1980s debt crisis, Latin American sovereigns often were forced to assume the external debts of private firms—often state firms—to facilitate negotiations with external-bank creditors.

bailout of firms is hardly a good option: Firms are not regulated like banks, so expectations of a government bailout would make firms too willing to lower their financing costs by borrowing from abroad in foreign currency for short terms.[15] Another option is to indirectly bail out firms by selling the sovereign's foreign exchange reserves to meet the surge in demand from firms, thereby reducing pressure on the exchange rate. Here, the domestic banking system effectively does the triage between healthy and sick firms: A healthy firm with maturing short-term foreign-currency debt ought to be able to obtain the domestic loan to purchase external reserves in the open market more easily than a sick firm. Yet another approach is to let nature take its course. Demand for foreign currency to repay external debts will put pressure on the exchange rate, and eventually, the exchange rate will fall to a point where firms stop trying to pay. Firms with foreign-currency debts are forced into bankruptcy. This approach avoids a corporate bailout, but it has costs of its own—particularly if many firms have similar problems. The result can be a systemic crisis in the corporate sector.

Even if the government initially stands back and avoids helping firms with heavy foreign-currency debts, it is unlikely to be able to stay out of resolving a systemic corporate crisis for long. Firms that cannot pay their foreign currency–denominated debts to external creditors typically also stop paying their domestic debts, and a crisis that stems initially from firms' difficulties in repaying their external debts quickly leads to large losses for the domestic banking system.[16] In many cases, local firms have borrowed in foreign currency directly from the local banks, not just from foreign creditors. The ensuing banking crisis ends up drawing the government into the corporate restructuring process: As part of the process of recapitalizing the banking system, the government may take over either the banks or the banks' bad loans. In truly severe crises, this leaves the government—along with foreign lenders—as the theoretical owner of most local private firms. The resulting restructuring process is often extremely slow: Many firms remain formally bankrupt for a long time, with substantial economic costs.[17]

Finally, the sovereign can encourage voluntary corporate debt restructurings that keep firms that are unable to refinance their maturing exter-

15. Conversely, banking crises could be addressed like corporate crises, and the sovereign could refrain from guaranteeing the foreign-currency liabilities of all the banks and instead leave each individual bank to stand on its own feet. To our knowledge, such an approach has not been tried in any actual case.

16. Thailand, Indonesia, and Argentina are all examples.

17. Bankruptcy regimes in emerging economies are seldom strong, and few can handle the stress created if most of the economy's productive assets are under the supervision of a bankruptcy court. Local courts—and local legislatures—are often reluctant to allow foreign creditors to use bankruptcy proceedings to assume equity control over local firms that borrowed from abroad. Indonesia is the prime example.

nal debts out of bankruptcy. If the debt causing trouble is owed to external creditors, then the government has two broad options. It could offer a subsidy to encourage restructurings—for example, by offering exchange insurance to firms that reach agreement with their creditors[18]—or the government could impose controls that preclude private firms' repayment of unrestructured external debts. Both are ways of providing firms with breathing space without providing an outright sovereign guarantee.

Either a coordinated restructuring of corporate debts or a broad suspension of corporate payments, though, raises more difficulties than a sovereign payments suspension. It is inherently difficult to reconcile the need for a collective solution that reflects the reality that many firms have similar financial problems stemming from a common problem—often too much short-term foreign-currency debt—and the need for a solution that also reflects the different financial positions of different firms. Controls that temporarily prohibit all foreign-currency payments, for example, will favor those who are unable to pay at the expense of those who retain the capacity to service their debts.

Consequently, a central issue in corporate "liquidity" crises is whether to take a case-by-case approach where each firm negotiates individually with its domestic and external creditors (possibly under an umbrella of common rules) or to take a centralized across-the-board approach where the central government largely decides the restructuring guidelines.[19] A firm-by-firm approach will provide debt relief appropriate to each individual firm. However, the negotiating process takes time—rapid agreement on a rollover can be hard to get in a systemic corporate financial crisis, and without an agreement, most firms will fall into formal insolvency. Across-the-board solutions can avoid the delays associated with case-by-case negotiations and may make sense when many debtors suffer from the same problems.[20]

The same issues arise if, as is often the case, the problem is not so much a shortage of liquidity but the systemic insolvency of a wide range of

---

18. Exchange rate insurance can be, in principle, either subsidized or unsubsidized. Exchange rate insurance, if subsidized, is more likely to encourage rapid agreement on a restructuring. The cost of the subsidized insurance has to be weighted against the probability that the insurance will help a country avoid a systemic crisis and the expected cost of the systemic crisis. In the worst case, firms that would have survived in any case take advantage of the subsidized insurance, while the country is still left with most of the costs of a systemic crisis.

19. An approach based on out-of-court individual debt renegotiation under the aegis of a set of broad principles is often called the "London approach." The London approach was created in part because English bankruptcy law was not well suited to "in court" debt reorganization, so the Bank of England encouraged out-of-court corporate reorganization for firms that could avoid liquidation. Indonesia took a similar approach with its Jakarta Initiative; Korea did the same for the restructuring of the *chaebols*.

20. Stiglitz (2002) is among the most prominent advocates of an across-the-board solution.

firms. Indeed, the line between a systemic liquidity crisis and a systemic solvency crisis is very fuzzy: If many firms have borrowed in foreign currency, then a large currency depreciation is likely to leave all firms illiquid, in the sense that they are unable to refinance their maturing foreign currency–denominated debts, and many firms become insolvent as well. Some firms may be fine with just a temporary rescheduling, others will need to restructure both their operations and debts, and still others may need to be liquidated immediately.[21]

Here too there is a long-standing debate between the advantages of letting each firm and its creditors negotiate the right solution for the individual firm and the advantages of an across-the-board solution. The obvious advantage of a solution crafted to each individual firm has to be weighed against the sheer difficulty of renegotiating the debts of many firms at the same time and against the costs of letting many firms languish in bankruptcy for an extended period. An across-the-board solution is likely to have more advantages and fewer costs if dollar-denominated debt has created problems for many small local firms (and households); the advantages of a perfect triage have to be weighed against the logistical complexity of a case-by-case restructuring of thousands of small loans.

Across-the-board solutions to systemic solvency crises are certainly far easier to apply to domestic debts. Argentina, for example, imposed an across-the-board restructuring of domestic dollar-denominated debts when it pesified domestic dollar loans—leaving firms that had borrowed externally to renegotiate their foreign debts with their external creditors.[22] A crisis country can create a uniform framework for restructuring firms' external debt, but it cannot unilaterally change the terms of external debt contracts. Such an across-the-board restructuring seems to be close to what Joseph Stiglitz (2002) had in mind when he called for a "super Chapter 11" to facilitate corporate debt restructurings when firms are subject to common macroeconomic shocks, though Stiglitz's proposal would have also

21. If payments are temporarily deferred, firms that have deeper problems are likely to eventually fall into default and go through bankruptcy. However, deferring payments temporarily rather than liquidating the firms immediately is still costly. The firms' owners have an incentive to run the firms into the ground (asset stripping) during the temporary standstill—minimizing their losses while increasing the losses of the firms' creditors. On the other hand, there are also incentives problems if most firms, including the merely illiquid ones, are allowed simply to go bankrupt. Creditors usually do not want to take over operational control of a broad set of firms—monitoring the behavior of existing management is difficult—and even if creditors do want to assume control of the firm, the process of transferring control from existing management to creditors is usually slow. At various points in time during a protracted period of bankruptcy, the incentives of the management and of the firms' creditors will not be perfectly aligned.

22. The need for some form of across-the-board solution in Argentina is hard to argue with, given the scale of the country's domestic-currency mismatch. Whether "asymmetric pesification" provided the appropriate solution—or provided too large a subsidy to certain debtors at taxpayers' expense—is a more difficult question that is explored in chapter 7.

provided protection from litigation from external creditors holding unrestructured claims.[23]

Exchange Rate Crises and Capital Controls

Exchange rate crises arise when investors—residents and nonresidents alike—are unwilling to hold financial assets denominated in domestic currency at the prevailing interest rates. For example, domestic depositors pulling local currency–denominated deposits out of the banking system in a run often want to flee to the safety of foreign assets. The emergency liquidity (domestic currency) that the central bank supplies to the banks quickly translates into pressure on the exchange rate.

The government has four basic options to reequilibrate demand for domestic and foreign financial assets. First, the sovereign can let the exchange rate fall—with potentially devastating consequences for those who have borrowed in foreign currency. Second, the sovereign can intervene in the foreign exchange market, by selling either its reserves or domestic debt denominated in foreign currency. Third, the central bank can raise short-term interest rates to make domestic currency–denominated financial assets more attractive than foreign assets (assuming that domestic debtors can afford to pay the higher rates). Finally, the government can impose capital and exchange controls that prohibit the purchase of foreign exchange with domestic financial assets.[24]

Exchange controls have to be evaluated against the other policy options. They can be used in different circumstances:

- to defend an overvalued exchange rate, defined simply as an exchange rate that requires continued net capital inflows because it is consistent with a current account deficit (Thailand). The goal is often to force investors to close out short positions that have been financed by borrowing local currency from the banking system, thus defending the exchange rate without raising domestic interest rates.
- to prevent an already depreciated exchange rate from overshooting on the downside in the absence of a payments standstill on either the sovereign's external debt or the private sector's external debt (Malaysia). Here, controls are an alternative to raising local interest rates

23. The external creditors of Argentine firms have exercised considerable forbearance and generally have not sought to obtain operational control of firms that are not paying their debt. Neither bondholders nor the major international banks particularly want the headaches associated with running politically unpopular Argentine utilities.

24. If a bank run is contributing to the imbalance in the foreign exchange market, the sovereign could also declare a bank holiday. Limiting access to domestic currency limits the number of people who can convert domestic currency into foreign currency.

to defend the already depreciated exchange rate or to selling foreign exchange reserves to limit the depreciation.

- imposed in conjunction with a payments standstill on government, banks, and firms' external debts (Argentina and Russia) to prevent an already depreciated exchange rate from falling further and causing excessive overshooting that exacerbates balance sheet effects. It is less clear that controls substitute for higher domestic interest rates here: Neither the government nor the banking system may be honoring their short-term debt.

The use of exchange controls to defend an overvalued exchange rate is typically a bad idea. Such an exchange rate requires continued capital inflows from abroad to cover an ongoing current account deficit, and limiting the ability of existing investors to get out is not the best way to attract additional investment. Moreover, controls do not eliminate investors' basic incentive to get out before a possible devaluation.

The use of controls to prevent an already depreciated exchange rate from depreciating further raises more difficult issues. Excessive exchange rate overshooting is costly if the country has extensive foreign-currency debts. The orthodox response, raising domestic interest rates, is also costly if the economy has a large stock of short-term debts. If short-term interest rates have to stay high for an extended period, the high short-term rates could drive many banks or firms into insolvency, further undermining confidence. The fact that the exchange rate has already adjusted before the imposition of controls is important, since the current account surplus associated with the depreciated exchange rate should eventually generate pressures for appreciation, and thus provides a potential exit strategy. But using controls to limit the ability of private citizens seeking to exchange their domestic currency for foreign currency (both foreigners and domestic citizens) in a private market transaction is obviously an extreme, and potentially costly, step.

Malaysia famously introduced such exchange controls simply to obtain additional monetary policy flexibility even though it was not experiencing congruent external payment difficulties. More commonly, countries have introduced controls to stem pressure on the exchange rate after a sovereign default (see chapter 4).

There is good reason to be suspicious of capital controls. The temptation to impose controls to substitute for important policy adjustments—including letting the exchange rate adjust—is real. Thailand's use of controls to protect the overvalued baht is a case in point. Controls inherently give rise to the potential for corruption. At the same time, a religious prohibition against capital and exchange controls in all circumstances is neither realistic nor desirable, especially when sovereign debt suspensions and standstills are already used as part of the crisis resolution process.

Countries with both a large stock of debt indexed to short-term interest rates and a large stock of debt denominated in foreign currency will find the trade-off between tight money and a depreciated exchange rate more acute than advanced economies that have large stocks of long-term fixed-rate domestic-currency debt. Most countries will try to use all possible tools to stabilize their exchange rate after a sovereign default. Countries that have already integrated into the global market are right to shy away from using controls. However, exchange and capital controls have to remain options in extreme circumstances.

Alternative Approaches to Liquidity Crises

The choice between an official bailout and a standstill that locks in creditors is stark. One requires large-scale official intervention in the market. The other requires that the crisis country violate its contractual commitments and negotiate a rescheduling with its creditors. A number of proposals seek ways either to mobilize private funds for countries facing liquidity crises or to make it easier to suspend payments, at least temporarily, without violating contractual commitments. These proposals seek to make the choice between liquidity support and a standstill less black and white—although we argue that none succeeds at offering a true alternative. Proposals to avoid direct loans to the crisis country and instead to prop up the price of emerging-market debt to limit contagion are also considered.

A Private Lender of Last Resort?

Many have asked why the private sector cannot provide crisis liquidity to countries that are illiquid but not insolvent. Mobilizing private funds avoids not only the need for a large loan from the IMF or the G-7 but also the need for a standstill. Private emergency lending also has precedent. Consortiums of private US banks—usually organized by JP Morgan—provided lender-of-last-resort support to other US banks during a financial crisis before the creation of the Federal Reserve System.

Theoretically, it is possible to argue that private-sector initiatives to bail out emerging economies have not emerged because of the availability of official financing. However, it is far more likely that official lending has emerged because private investors have not been able to mobilize the necessary crisis liquidity.[25] The difficulties with a private lender of last resort

25. Similarly, the creation of the Federal Reserve System was in part the result of the realization that private lenders-of-last-resort solutions in domestic financial crises had serious limitations.

are well known. First, every creditor would rather flee and have another creditor put up the needed liquidity, creating a collective action problem. Second, risk-averse investors often would rather flee than increase their exposure if the debtor's solvency is even partly in doubt. Indeed, the risk management programs of most financial institutions lead them to reduce their exposure in a crisis—not to lend into a crisis. Third, no private agent is large enough, patient enough, and risk-neutral enough to be willing to provide large-scale support to a crisis country at interest rates that do not exacerbate the country's financial distress. No existing private agent is large enough to internalize the collective action problem. The emergence of a private lender of last resort is extremely unlikely.

Voluntary Debt Swaps in Crises

If a country has lost access to capital markets, one way to reduce pressure on reserves is to perform a voluntary debt swap to stretch out the maturity of debt coming due in the near term. This reduces the country's immediate need for cash. As discussed in chapter 4, a voluntary swap can be performed at current market yields without the threat of default: The market value of the new bonds offered in the exchange has to equal or exceed the value of the old bonds. Voluntary debt swaps (and debt buybacks) are standard debt management tools, often used in lieu of new issuance. For example, Mexico, Brazil, and many other countries have conducted voluntary "Brady bond for eurobond swaps" in recent years to lower their debt service costs during normal market conditions, when spreads are not very high. However, voluntary debt swaps take on a different character in crisis conditions, when spreads are very high.

Voluntary swaps conducted during crisis conditions typically have severe economic costs: Short-run cash flow relief is expensive when market spreads are high. A country may buy time but at the price of making its long-term debt problems substantially worse. A country that tries to reprofile its debt at high crisis rates risks making the same mistake as an individual who, facing difficulties servicing a mortgage that was taken out when interest rates were low, decides to refinance the mortgage at much higher interest rates in order to obtain a few years of debt-service relief. The probability of the sovereign being able to service in full and on time the new, expensive debt created in the swap is likely to be very low.[26] In

26. The most significant example of a voluntary swap under crisis conditions is Argentina's summer 2001 "megaswap." Chapter 4 covers this transaction in some detail. Note here that the $30 billion exchange provided Argentina with short-run debt relief but only in exchange for unrealistic promises to pay more on its debt in the future. Consequently, the exchange was quickly followed by an intensification of Argentina's crisis. At the time of the megaswap, the spread on Argentina's debt was about 950 bps, and Argentine debt yielded over 15 percent. The country reduced its undiscounted debt payments by $12 billion in the five years after the deal by promising to make future, undiscounted debt payments of $56 billion.

crisis conditions, an exchange that pushes out maturities without worsening the country's long-term sustainability will be necessarily somewhat coercive.

Guarantees and Enhancements

A number of proposals have been made to mobilize emergency liquidity from private creditors by providing an official guarantee for private crisis lending, by otherwise extending the official sector's preferred status to private lending, or by making it possible for private creditors to obtain collateral to back their crisis lending. Gerald Corrigan's (2000) call for the official sector to move away from large official loans—sometimes combined with coercive efforts to involve private creditors—and instead to use enhancements to mobilize private funds in a crisis is typical of these kinds of proposals. Private creditors could provide crisis liquidity if they had access to the same preference in repayment given to official creditors or if the official sector found other ways to "enhance" private lending.

These proposals generally have the same basic advantages and disadvantages of an IMF loan, as they generally use the official sector in some way to make it attractive for private lenders to provide funds when they otherwise would be unwilling to lend. Nonetheless, there are differences between proposals that seek to mobilize private funds with a full guarantee from the official sector (or a G-7 country), a partial official-sector guarantee, and by pledging collateral to back private lending.

Full Guarantee. One easy way to mobilize crisis lending from the private sector is to provide a full guarantee: If the country cannot pay, the official sector picks up the tab.[27] A fully guaranteed loan is simply a less transparent official bailout. The private sector puts up the money only in name. A cynic might also note that the investment banks would earn fees on guaranteed loans that they do not on IMF loans—and even a small fee on a $10 billion guaranteed bond issue is real money.

If the country's future debt burden is calculated by discounting the new debt at the high crisis rates, the exchange did not increase the country's debt burden. However, from the country's point of view, it does not make sense to discount long-term debt at a rate of 15 percent—a rate that implies almost certain default on long-term debt. If the "before" and "after" cash flows are compared using "normal" discount rates, the megaswap clearly increased the net present value (NPV) of Argentina's debt. At a discount of 12 percent, this increase in the NPV of debt was $5 billion; at a discount rate of 7 percent the increase in the NPV of debt was about $15 billion.

27. The IMF's Articles of Agreement do not allow it to guarantee payment on a sovereign's external debt. The IMF can only lend to help a country buy collateral. The World Bank, the other multilateral development banks (MDBs), and any of the G-7 countries, in contrast, can guarantee payments on a sovereign's external debt.

Partial Guarantee. Partial guarantees are just what their name suggests—loans that the official sector backs partially, not fully. The key question is whether a partial guarantee can successfully mobilize the foreign currency the country needs in a liquidity crisis. In most cases, the answer is no.

The market typically prices and values partially guaranteed instruments as being the combination of two components: a guaranteed loan, which is valued as G-7 or World Bank risk, and an unguaranteed loan, which is valued as pure country risk.[28] The guaranteed portion of the loan provides a financial benefit to the debtor, since the guarantee lets a risky country borrow at a risk-free rate. But apart from this subsidy, blending a guaranteed and an unguaranteed bond does not create any extra value. Indeed, the markets usually value such an instrument as being worth slightly less than a separate World Bank bond and a separate unguaranteed country bond.[29] A $3 billion guarantee for a $6 billion bond is very similar to being able to borrow $3 billion from the official sector and $3 billion from private creditors.

Various proposals have been made to create partial guarantees that produce "more bang for the buck." However, arguments that these structures, unlike a simple partial guarantee, can exploit market inefficiencies and create value are not fully convincing. In most cases, proponents of these guarantees argue that while the official guarantee is formally and legally limited to only part of the cash flow (say a rolling interest payment), the "halo" of that guarantee will fall on the entire loan and lower the spread on the uncollateralized component of the loan. The market will believe that the debtor is less inclined to default on even the unguaranteed payments.

Simple structures that combine a clearly guaranteed and a clearly unguaranteed payment stream have failed to produce this kind of "halo." For example, the market did not assign a halo to the uncollateralized portion of a Brady bond. Financial engineers also have experimented with more complex structures designed to convince investors that the amount of de facto protection the limited guarantee provides far exceeds the size of the formal guarantee. In general, these experiments have not worked well.

28. The so called stripped spread of the bond should be equal to the spread on uncollateralized or unguaranteed instruments.

29. While Brady bonds are not formally guaranteed, the "Brady" collateral acts as a form of de facto guarantee on the repayment of Brady bond principal. A classic collateralized Brady combines a fully collateralized principal payment (since the payment is backed by a 30-year treasury) and a largely uncollateralized interest payment stream. Collateralized Bradies have been disappearing from the market, however, because the market prefers "pure" country risk, and it is advantageous to the country to retire the Brady bonds in a "Brady bond for eurobond" swap.

No structure is more ingenious than a rolling reinstatable guarantee. In this structure, the World Bank guaranteed the first payment (or first two payments) of the bond. If the country made the first payment, the guarantee rolled to the next payment. If the country could not pay the guaranteed tranche, the World Bank would pay, and the country would have a brief period to repay the World Bank. So long as the country could come up with the funds to repay the World Bank, the guarantee was "reinstated" and rolled to the next payment. The idea was simple: The country would not want to default on the World Bank, so the guarantee would almost certainly roll over and eventually cover the full bond. While the World Bank formally guaranteed only the first payment, the "halo" of the guarantee would extend to the entire instrument.[30]

In practice, the market found this structure hard to understand. Bonds issued with rolling reinstatable guarantees were valued more like a single guaranteed bond and a series of unguaranteed bonds than like a series of payments all of which benefited from a World Bank guarantee. This structure was used to help countries facing a temporary (or so it was argued) widening in the market spread on their bonds to place bonds at a more reasonable price, not raise funds at the height of a crisis.

More important, Argentina—one of three countries to experiment with this structure—put the rolling reinstatable guarantees to test in its default. Argentina missed the guaranteed payment on its rolling reinstatable bond; the World Bank made that payment; and Argentina, in turn, owed the World Bank the money it had paid on the guarantee. That was the easy part. The hard part was deciding whether to pay the World Bank back in time to allow the guarantee to be "reinstated" and then "roll" on to the next payment. Argentina opted *not* to pay the Bank within the period required for the guarantee to roll. This ended any chance of the guarantee being "reinstated" and assured that the formally unguaranteed tranches would not be protected. This was within Argentina and the World Bank's rights, but it also destroyed any chance of convincing the market that the structure would confer a "halo" in similar future deals of this type.

Indeed, Argentina's crisis powerfully highlighted the real risks associated with reinstatable guarantees. In a crisis, the official sector and the country have to decide whether the "halo" is real: Ambiguity has no room. Either the bond benefits from just the partial guarantee and the un-

30. Had this structure worked as advertised, the combined instrument would be worth more than the sum of its parts (unlike a Brady bond). But even here, the structure is not really creating value. Rather, the structure is effectively transferring value from other unguaranteed bonds to the holders of the partially guaranteed bond. The holders of the nonguaranteed part of the partially guaranteed loan benefit because their claim is being given seniority relative to other nonguaranteed claims. Chapter 8 argues that it is usually more efficient to provide seniority explicitly rather than through clever financial engineering.

guaranteed parts are restructured, or the entire bond is paid.[31] Had Argentina honored its partially guaranteed bond in full, it effectively would have ended up with more senior debt. In some sense, it would be in the worst of all worlds. It would have paid a higher ex ante rate for borrowing through this complex structure than for borrowing directly from the multilateral development banks (MDBs), yet ex post it would have treated the bond like other low-cost MDB debt. As it turned out, the creditors that believed in the bond's structure lost out rather than Argentina.

Fully or Partially Guaranteed Debt Exchange or Swap. Guarantees and other enhancements also can be used to encourage participation in a voluntary debt swap—both swaps that seek to extend the maturity of the country's debt and swaps that aim both to solve short-run liquidity problems and to reduce the country's debt burden. The most famous example is the Brady plan. Official lending was made available to help countries purchase the collateral (long-term US treasury bonds) used to "enhance" the Brady bonds offered in exchange for debt reduction (not all countries borrowed from the official sector to buy the needed collateral—for example, Brazil paid for the collateral out of its own reserves).

The need to break the impasse that had prolonged the 1980s debt crisis may have justified the subsidy inherent in such lending. But most proposals for partial guarantees are not designed to end a period of prolonged default but rather to support voluntary debt swaps that would help a country avoid immediate default. For example, the US Treasury called for the IMF to use $3 billion of Argentina's augmented August 2001 IMF loan to support a deal that would restore Argentina's debt sustainability.

As discussed earlier, the core problem with market-based voluntary swaps in crisis periods is that paying crisis interest rates to defer payments is very expensive. Enhancements potentially offer a way out of this bind—a subsidy from an official lender can make the exchange more affordable to the country. However, there is no free lunch. A partially guaranteed swap—barring the use of a structure like a rolling reinstatable guarantee that tries to create leverage out of fuzzy complexity—is like a partially guaranteed new issue. The exchange can be broken down into two components: a voluntary exchange of old debt for new, guaranteed debt and a voluntary exchange of old debt for new, more expensive, unguaranteed debt.

The easiest way to understand the guaranteed component of such exchanges is to compare it with taking out an IMF or World Bank loan to fi-

31. Technically, Argentina could have honored the bond in full with the rolling reinstatable guarantee either by paying the instrument in full and never calling on the MDB guarantee or by taking out a long term loan from the World Bank in time to pay the short term obligation that Argentina incurred from the Bank after it called on the guarantee. If the Bank had made additional funds available quickly, the guarantee would have been reinstated and rolled to the next payment.

nance the repurchase of existing market debt at a discount, since the same basic analysis applies. If the country's existing debt trades at a deep discount in the market, trading market debt for official debt (whether through a swap or an outright buyback) lets the country reduce its existing debt stock at the margin. For example, the $3 billion made available to Argentina in the summer of 2001 could have bought back either roughly $4 billion of short-term debt (which traded at around 75 cents on the dollar) or $6 billion of long-term debt (which traded at around 50 cents)—so Argentina could have reduced its overall debt stock by between $1 billion and $3 billion and slightly reduced its overall coupon payments as well. The government of Argentina had about $95 billion of traded debt at the time. Reducing that debt to $92 billion would not have made Argentina's debt any more sustainable.[32]

A bigger buyback obviously could have had a bigger impact, but it creates another problem: A large voluntary buyback is likely to drive up the market price of the country's debt, reducing the amount of debt relief possible in a voluntary exchange.[33] Any increase in the market prices reduces the debtor's gains from a large buyback financed by official lending, as creditors capture more of the benefit of official lending. Embedding the exchange of existing debt for new, guaranteed debt in a bigger transaction that has a large unguaranteed component also cannot increase the transaction's size. However, the conditions when exchanging existing debt for new, guaranteed debt is attractive (the existing debt trades at a deep discount) are precisely the conditions when exchanging existing debt for new,

32. Formally, the NPV benefit for the country would have been the difference between the interest rate on the retired debt relative to the interest rate on the IMF loan times the amount of the IMF loan. Borrowing $10 billion from the IMF at 4 percent to retire debt yielding 15 percent only implies NPV benefit of $1.1 billion, practically nothing compared to Argentina's overall external debt of over $100 billion.

33. Bulow and Rogoff (1988a, 1988b, 1989b) provided the classic critique of using official resources to finance debt buybacks. They argued that the buyback increased the residual value of the remaining debt, so the gains from official enhancements went to the country's remaining creditors rather than the debtor. The exact distribution of gains depends on a range of assumptions. For the academic debate on the "debt buyback boondoggle," see the exchange between Sachs (1989, 1990) and Rogoff and Bulow. Rogoff and Bulow formally critiqued using official resources to buy back the debt of a country that is already in default: Higher market prices on the country's remaining debt implied that the subsequent debt restructuring would result in a higher future debt burden. The analysis is slightly different if the country is already paying its debt. So long as the country ends up paying its debt, the country's debt burden is fixed by contract and independent of the price the market assigns to its debt. In order to realize any gains from a low market price, the country has to default and restructure. Ironically, if junior creditors conclude that an exchange financed with senior debt is unlikely to provide enough relief to let the country avoid default, the exchange may not have much of an impact on the debt's secondary-market prices: Fears about subordination and the risk of larger losses in the event of a default will trump the impact of adding a new buyer to the market.

unguaranteed debt is unattractive, because of the high rate creditors will demand in any voluntary transaction.

Whether the buyback is large or small, using senior debt to retire junior debt makes the country's debt stock more rigid. This is important: Replacing debt that can be reduced in a restructuring with debt that cannot will leave both the country and its remaining junior creditors worse off if the buyback/guaranteed exchange fails to provide enough relief to allow the country to avoid default. In general, attempts to use financial engineering to find a solution to severe debt-servicing problems are futile—and often harmful. Using official resources to make a transaction that tries to improve the country's debt sustainability on truly voluntary terms is inefficient and very costly: Only a coercive debt restructuring can provide the meaningful debt relief to restore sustainability.

Secured Lending. Others have proposed raising crisis financing by issuing sovereign bonds backed by some form of security—be it oil or other export revenues. Martin Feldstein (1999, 2000), for example, suggested that Korea raise crisis liquidity by issuing bonds backed by export revenues.

These proposals suffer from four problems:

- The sovereign that does not impose exchange controls has no claim on the export revenues of private firms and therefore cannot pledge those revenues to back a sovereign bond issue. Exchange controls can include a "surrender" requirement that forces private firms with export revenues to sell the foreign exchange they earn to the government, but once such controls are lifted, private firms are under no obligation to turn their export revenues over to the government. Indeed, the firm may well have pledged its export earnings to back its own debt, in which case the government has to buy the foreign exchange in the market to make its own debt payments.
- If high-risk emerging-market economies could easily borrow on a secured basis, they almost certainly would use their ability to issue secured debt to lower their overall borrowing costs—not as an emergency source of crisis liquidity. The key limit on "securitization" is that the sovereign's basic asset is domestic tax revenue—an asset that hardly can be pledged credibly to creditors.[34]
- Some sovereigns do have access to foreign currency that they could pledge to back a bond issue, including transfers from a state oil company, taxes on the export of petroleum/other products, or the interna-

34. Argentina pledged the revenue from its financial-transactions tax to back a "guaranteed loan" in one of its final efforts to avoid default. In practice, however, this structure failed to protect investors from losses—the loans were either pesified or the holders were forced to give up the guaranteed loan and take the original global bonds.

tional receivables of a state-owned telecom company. But even here there are limits. For example, a country could unilaterally cut its petroleum export tax, leaving its creditors with less security. Full protection requires complex financial engineering, which diverts revenues through an offshore account that the creditors have access to before the sovereign gets its hands on the money.

- Most fundamentally, new secured debt should reduce the value of existing unsecured debt. Sovereign debt contracts typically contain negative pledge clauses—provisions that say the sovereign cannot give security to new debt unless it gives security to all existing debt as well—to protect existing creditors against such a risk. It is often possible to engineer around such provisions. But the basic risk that these provisions were designed to protect against remains: Barring an increase in the country's payment capacity, new secured debt should decrease the value of the country's long-term unsecured debt.

Pledging revenue streams or collateral to create a security interest has a negative impact on claims (whether private or official) that are not given access to the pledged collateral or revenue.[35] Some creditors gain, but typically at the expense of other creditors. The debtor's ability to pay is usually not increased simply because it has taken out a secured loan. There is no free lunch.

A pledge of security can create value in certain circumstances. For example, in the event of a liquidity run, securitized lending—like official lending—may improve welfare by avoiding a default created by a run

35. In general, the analytical literature on securitized credit (see, for example, Klapper 2000 for a review) finds that secured loans occur at the expense of unsecured loans—pledging collateral or providing seniority to one lender subordinates the claims of other creditors. Secured lending may have a rationale if there are informational asymmetries. For example, the borrower may not be able to credibly "signal" to potential lenders that its likelihood of defaulting is lower than the one perceived by the market; then, pledging collateral in exchange for such lending may help signal that default is not likely. Secured lending can also help address other agency problems. Jensen and Meckling (1976) show that collateral controls for the risk of the debtor engaging in asset substitution—i.e., borrowing to invest in riskier assets than the creditor anticipates. However, it is not obvious that "collateral" helps address the problems inherent in sovereign borrowing and lending. For example, a highly indebted sovereign who is likely and willing to default and is currently unable to borrow more may use the enhancement or collateral to receive new nondefaultable loans. But rather than signaling the sovereign's greater capacity to pay all loans, the pledge of collateral may simply transfer value from existing unsecured loans, as collateral (the sovereign/country's assets) that previously was available for all creditors is pledged to back the new secured loans. If the country ends up defaulting, unsecured creditors receive even less than they otherwise would have. Rather than correcting an information asymmetry, the use of collateral can allow the sovereign to transfer assets to a select group of favored creditors or to gamble for resurrection.

that fundamentals do not justify. Here pledging security to raise new money offsets a creditor coordination failure. However, given the difficulties in securitizing sovereign revenue streams, it is not at all obvious that "securitization" offers a better model for resolving sovereign liquidity crises than the existing model of IMF lending. Indeed, the IMF's ability to lend on the strength of its preferred status creates a tool that can be mobilized more quickly and used to help a wider range of countries than would be possible if the only way of mobilizing emergency liquidity was through a pledge of security. Moreover, IMF lending also comes with conditionality that, in principle, should increase the debtor's ability to pay all creditors. In contrast, a debtor's ability to find assets to create a security interest may be independent of its commitment to making needed policy changes.

In sum, the proposals to mobilize private financing in liquidity crises generally are less effective and a less transparent means of mobilizing crisis liquidity than a plain old IMF loan. Most have the same basic effect on the country's finances—they give the country access to a new asset (the foreign exchange raised by the debt issue) and create an offsetting liability that the country promises to pay before it makes other payments. Raising the funds on private markets is not a virtue, if the downside risks remain with the official sector or if the money comes solely on the strength of a pledge of security.

Private Contingent Credit Lines

Another approach to obtaining crisis liquidity is to buy the liquidity in advance of a crisis, a form of ex ante insurance. Countries can buy the right to borrow from a group of banks in the event of trouble. The particular details of a contingent credit line (CCL) can vary, but the easiest CCL to understand gives a government the right to borrow a defined amount at a fixed interest rate from a group of banks at a time and place of the government's choosing. The banks receive a fee in return. CCLs can be thought of as a substitute for reserves. Instead of holding reserves "on balance sheet," CCLs provide "off balance sheet" reserves. The fee the banks charge can be compared with the cost of holding reserves—typically the difference between the country's cost of funds and the risk-free interest rate it earns on the reserve holdings.

Unfortunately, the actual experience with private CCLs has been dismal, and such facilities hardly offer a viable substitute for official lending. Back in 1997, three countries—Indonesia, Mexico, and Argentina—had access to private CCLs. All three countries eventually drew on their credit lines, and in no case was the experience a happy one for the country or for its bankers.

- During its 1997 crisis, Indonesia drew on a series of private CCLs that it had arranged with a group of largely Japanese banks. But the resources the private credit lines provided were too small to stop the stampede to the exits and thus failed to help Indonesia ward off its crisis. As these credit lines have come due, Indonesia has generally rescheduled the maturing principal, given its precarious finances.

- Mexico drew on its facility in 1998. The banks were eager to get the fees during the emerging-market financing boom in 1996 and 1997, and Mexico bought the right to borrow at a rate that proved attractive when spreads rose across the board after the Russian default. But when Mexico drew on its facility, the banks cried foul because it was able to borrow at a rate well below the prevailing market rate, and the banks that marked to market had to book losses. The banks subsequently concluded that it was too risky to offer a country the option of borrowing at a fixed price and that any subsequent facility should carry a variable interest rate—making the facility less attractive to the country.

- Argentina's credit line was intended to provide liquidity to the banking system rather than to help the sovereign raise money. Argentina's central bank bought the right to sell (with a promise to repurchase) the banking system's holdings of Argentina's international bonds in return for cash. However, this facility failed to work as designed when Argentina's banking system experienced severe stress in 2001. Argentina feared that drawing on the facility would trigger the bank run the facility was meant to deter. The banks were quite keen to get out of this commitment as Argentina's finances deteriorated. When Argentina's megaswap retired many of the bonds that were eligible to be "repoed" for cash, it effectively reduced the size of the facility. In the end, the credit line was too small to provide the sums Argentina needed. Argentina did draw on the credit line in September 2001, but it opted not to obtain the maximum possible sum. It obtained $1.5 billion from private creditors and an additional $1 billion from World Bank and Inter-American Development Bank enhancements that were part of the facility.

The amount of additional financing that these facilities provide in a crisis is hard to assess: The banks will take steps to hedge the risks associated with their commitment to lend to the crisis country. Some hedges—like shorting the country's external debt—put pressure on secondary-market prices but do not directly result in pressure on the country's reserves. Other potential hedges, such as reducing the local exposure of the banks' affiliates in the debtor country, can put pressure on the country's reserves. One virtue of the official sector is that it does not seek to hedge its crisis lending and truly provides net new financing.

Rollover Options

Another proposal seeks to make a standstill less costly by embedding in the debt contract an option to roll over maturing foreign-currency payments. The universal debt rollover options at penalty rates (UDROPs) that Willem Buiter and Anne Sibert (1999) proposed would give the debtor the ability to roll over maturing foreign-currency debts at a penalty rate defined in the contract. All foreign currency-denominated debt contracts, whether domestic or external, public or private, would need to contain such options. In the event of a rush to the exits and other self-fulfilling runs, such an option might prevent bad equilibria from ever occurring in the first place. Also if the debtor invoked the option, the cooling off period could provide the debtor time to convince creditors that the country's problems are addressed and that they should not decide to exit when the option expires. The debtor would also receive six months of protection from litigation. In Buiter and Sibert's proposal, the option would be exercised at the sole discretion of the individual debtor. Peter Kenen (2001) has proposed that the rollover options should be written to give the country's government or the central bank the ability to activate them, including those in private debt contracts. This would assure that the rollover option was only exercised in a coordinated effort to resolve a systemic crisis.

Rollover options have obvious appeal: The global financial system would be safer if more debtors bought more protection against the risk of a run, whether by paying more to borrow for longer terms or by buying options that give the debtor the contractual right to roll over a claim at a penalty rate. However, it is unrealistic to think that rollover options alone would make a broad standstill an attractive substitute for official lending.

A "contractualized" comprehensive payments standstill is still a comprehensive payments standstill, with all its downsides. The contractual right to defer payments on foreign currency-denominated debts won't stop a run out of the domestic currency or the domestic banking system, won't define the policies that the country needs to take in the interim, and won't prevent creditors holding foreign currency-denominated claims from running the moment the "contractual" standstill ends. One country's decision to invoke its rollover option could lead to a run out of other risky countries. Contractualizing the standstill does avoid the risk of litigation, but legal risks are typically the least of the debtor's concerns (see chapter 8). Rollover options might make the whole process less disruptive, more orderly, and generally less risky but probably not by that much.

Moreover, rollover options seem unlikely to ever be made truly universal. Even if—a big if—regulation in the international financial centers could assure that all cross-border lending carried such provisions, it is not at all obvious how such provisions could be inserted into all domestic debt contracts. Yet domestic debts denominated in foreign currency are often as important a source of difficulty as international debts, and regulators in the major international financial system have no way to force sovereign countries to include such provisions in their domestic debts. The options would be needed not only in the government's domestic foreign currency-denominated debt but also, presumably, in foreign currency-denominated domestic bank deposits.

In our view, the early proponents of rollover options aimed too high. It makes more sense to insert rollover options into cross-border, interbank credits than into all foreign-currency debts in order to make a comprehensive standstill less disruptive. The goal of such rollover options would have to be narrower: They would likely do little more than provide an organized framework for the crisis country's government, the borrowing banks, and the creditor banks to negotiate a formal rescheduling. Suppose a country like Korea had included such provisions in its cross-border debt. It could have invoked the rollover options in December 1997. This would have avoided the need for the official sector to play as active a role as it did in encouraging the banks that lent to Korea to participate in its coordinated rollover arrangement. A "cooling-off" period would not have solved Korea's crisis on its own but might have provided the time Korea needed to negotiate a formal rescheduling.

Rollover options could play this role if they were in all interbank claims on the crisis country and, as Kenen suggests, if the central bank could exercise the rollover option in a crisis. This would deal with a real problem in the international financial system—the difficulty of getting external bank creditors to roll over their claims in a crisis and the resulting pressure for the government to offer an across-the-board guarantee at the first sign of serious trouble.

However, the difficulties in putting such provisions in just interbank contracts should not be underestimated. The right to defer payments unilaterally is a much more profound change in a contract than the ability to amend a contract's financial terms through a supermajority vote. Putting clauses into bonds governed by New York law seems to have hardly affected the sovereign bond market, but rollover options clearly would change the interbank market. The length of the rollover effectively becomes the minimum maturity of any debt contract. A very small difference exists between a six-month claim with the option to be rolled over for another six months and a one-year claim, apart from subtle asset pricing differences associated with the value of an option rather than an obligation. Debtors and creditors often have good reason to prefer short-term claims (Jeanne 1999). Attempts to use regulation to lengthen maturities "forcibly" will lead to a shortening of the original maturity of the debt, a higher price, a reduction in the amount of lending available to emerging-market debtors, or all three. Lenders would no doubt have stronger incentives to pull their loans out early, before the rollover option was invoked.

Inserting such provisions into cross-border debt contracts would require a serious, concerted regulatory push. Such rollover options could be introduced either from the creditor's side—as a result of a coordinated push from G-10 regulators—or from the borrower's side. Both raise real difficulties. Borrowing-country regulators tend to be loath to introduce provisions that make it harder for their local banks to access international markets. G-10 regulators would worry that the expanded use of rollover options would make it harder for the banks they regulate to protect their own financial health by pulling out quickly, even if they were good for the system.[36]

It also would be necessary to decide if such options needed to be included in cross-border bank credits among banks located in advanced economies or just in credit extended to counterparties in emerging economies. Putting the options only in debt to emerging economies requires a consensus definition of an emerging economy and risks introducing a regulatory discontinuity in the market. The impact of putting such options in all cross-border debt might be small if individual banks, not the crisis country's central bank, exercised such options. Markets would assume that such options would be unlikely to be used for credits among banks in advanced economies.

Realistically, the official sector is unlikely to be willing to make an effort for a change that, at the end of the day, offers only a partial solution to a country's liquidity problems. The official sector will then have to rely on ad hoc attempts to convince cross-border bank creditors to roll over their claims on the crisis country if the official sector does not make sufficient liquidity available to stop a cross-border run.

Financing the IMF Through a Tax on Cross-Border Exposure

Edwin Truman (2001) has suggested a different way of easing the trade-off between IMF liquidity support and a private debt restructuring or a standstill: augmenting the IMF's current resources through a new tax on all cross-border financial exposure.[37] The debtors and creditors that would benefit from the expanded IMF liquidity insurance would, in a sense, prepay for this protection. Put differently, the official sector should have access to more resources—even after the IMF's 1998 quota increase—to "help backstop cross-border finance in times of crisis," but the resources should be raised by a targeted tax on the "beneficiaries" of IMF lending.

36. A host of additional technical difficulties would also need to be overcome. What constitutes a cross-border credit? Should such options be included just in cross-border credits among banks or also in credits extended to finance companies or even standard firms?

37. Formally, Truman proposed the creation of an international financial stability fund (IFSF). The IFSF would be a revolving trust fund administered by the IMF. The disbursement of loans from the trust fund would be linked to IMF-supported adjustment programs.

Some of the details of Truman's proposal can be questioned. Truman imposes a small tax on all cross-border exposure, including cross-border lending between industrial countries. Such borrowers and lenders do not benefit as directly from IMF liquidity protection as do emerging-market borrowers and lenders, though they benefit indirectly when the IMF intervenes to avert emerging-market crises that could give rise to systemic crises. Truman also does not tax domestic borrowing and lending denominated in foreign currency. However, as we have argued, both foreign currency-denominated domestic bank deposits and foreign currency–denominated domestic government debt can give rise to substantial pressure on an emerging economy's reserves. IMF loans frequently have been used to meet the financing needs created when domestic bank depositors want to pull out of the domestic banking system and move their funds abroad, yet domestic depositors are not being asked to pay the tax that helps augment the IMF's lending capacity.

Politics, though, is the biggest obstacle to increasing the amount the IMF could lend by imposing a user fee on global finance. Countries—the United States in particular—are unlikely to agree on imposing a global tax to finance a multilateral financial institution. The power to raise funds through taxation is a power that sovereign states have guarded jealously. National governments prefer to keep multilateral institutions on a short leash and financially dependent on national governments. Truman's proposal implies the existence of a global supranational authority with a willingness to pay global taxes to support multilateral financial institutions that provide global public goods. Such a global authority does not exist today.

Intervening to Support the Bond Market, Not Crisis Countries

Classic IMF lending provides financing directly to the crisis country. A number of proposals have been made to use official financing not to lend directly to the country but rather to buy in the secondary market either the country's own debt or the debt of other emerging economies. These proposals typically are designed to limit asset-market contagion, as a crisis in one emerging market often leads to a sharp fall in the market value of the financial assets of other emerging markets.

Guillermo Calvo (2002) has proposed using official funds during a panic to smooth out the excessive overshooting of the price of a broad index of emerging-market debt. A crisis in one country can trigger a contagious fall in the price of the long-term debt of other emerging-market borrowers, leading to sharp increases in the borrowing costs of emerging markets that need to finance current account and fiscal deficit, refinance existing debt, or both. However, this proposal has many shortcomings:

- First, experience with most price-stabilization schemes—be it currencies or commodity prices—is not encouraging. If the fund were to keep the price of emerging-market debt above its medium-term equilibrium value, then this fund would lose money and eventually go bankrupt (like most commodity-stabilization schemes).

- Second, the fund would purchase the debt of all the countries that are part of an emerging-market debt index and consequently, indirectly support countries that deserve support (victims of contagion) and those that don't (i.e., those whose spreads have rationally increased because of changes in the market's perceptions of their fundamentals). The fund would provide support to those countries that are robust enough to survive without any assistance, to those that are beyond the point of no return but whose debt remains in an index, and to those where financing might make a difference.
- Third, supporting countries based on their weight in a bond index favors those that have financed themselves by issuing international sovereign bonds relative to those that have done so in other ways (bank lending and foreign direct investment). There is no reason to believe that countries that rely heavily on international bonds are particularly deserving of support.
- Fourth, supporting the secondary-market price of bonds does not actually provide any financing to emerging economies. Emerging economies benefit only indirectly. The large war chest that would be needed to intervene heavily to support a sovereign bond index almost certainly would generate more bang per buck if it were used to lend directly to crisis countries.

Lerrick and Meltzer (2001) have suggested that the official sector should intervene to support the secondary-market price of the debt of the crisis country—buying the debt at its fundamental value—rather than to support a broad emerging-market index. Their basic motivation, however, is similar: Supporting the secondary-market price of the crisis country's debt helps avoid the contagion generated when large falls in the secondary-market price of a major debtor disrupts the broader debt market.[38] Lerrick and Meltzer argue that their proposal would both reduce the risk of contagion from prolonged undershooting in the market price of the crisis country's debt and help to reduce the debt of insolvent sovereign debtors.

However, the idea of spending large amounts of official funds to prop up the price of a crisis country's sovereign debt is far-fetched at best and

38. Proponents of the efficient markets hypothesis would argue that the distress of a creditor, absent any information indicating weakness in the debtor, should not lead to a substantial change in asset prices, as other investors should step in to buy the asset. However, other investors may have difficulty determining whether the fall in prices reflects the fact that some investors have access to new, private information about the fundamentals of other countries or that it is a bargain because a leveraged investor has to unload its portfolio.

outright harmful at worst. Buying debt in the secondary market provides a buyer for investors who cannot sell their bonds in the market but does not provide new foreign-currency reserves to the crisis country. Yet volatility in the secondary-market price of a country's long-term debt is a bigger problem for investors than for the country. The real problem for a country comes when it runs out of cash to pay maturing claims: A crisis country needs access to foreign currency, rather than a slightly higher secondary-market price for its long-term debt.

Lerrick and Meltzer's proposal also exposes the official sector to much larger risks than the current practice of lending directly to the crisis country. If the official sector offers to buy the crisis country's debt at too high a price, it could end up spending far more buying debt in the secondary market than it now lends to the crisis country. The authors claim that the official sector could offer to buy bonds at a price that is low enough to limit the risk to the official sector yet high enough to ensure that falls in the price of the crisis countries' bonds would not trigger widespread contagion. Reality may be quite different. Figuring out the fundamental value of the debt of a distressed sovereign is hardly an easy task. The observed volatility in the market price of sovereign bonds reflects the fundamental difficulties in finding the correct price of such debt as much as the tendency of markets to overshoot. For example, Lerrick and Meltzer suggested a floor of 60 cents on the dollar for Argentina's international sovereign bonds. Consequently, the IMF might have spent up to $54 billion to buy Argentina's $90 billion or so in outstanding international sovereign bonds—bonds that the market has priced between 25 and 30 cents after Argentina's default. These prices suggest that the official sector would have bought assets worth between $30 billion and $36 billion for $54 billion, while investors whose claims, after default, were worth 30 cents on the dollar would have sold them to the IMF for 60 cents on the dollar, a net gain of $20 billion plus. This would have been the mother of all bailouts. The distortions associated with buying investors out at a generous price would be much larger than those associated with the $13 billion that the IMF actually provided to Argentina.[39]

Paradoxically, implementation of this proposal risks providing the biggest bailouts to insolvent—rather than illiquid—countries. The official sec-

39. Lerrick and Meltzer's (2001, 4) argument that the IMF faced little risk even if all investors had exercised their option to sell at 60 cents on the dollar—"the IMF group would hold $90 billion in claims as security to $54 billion in loans that would be redeemed in a short time frame by the new creditworthy Argentine economy"—was reckless. How would Argentina repay "in a short time frame" $54 billion in loans after it had already exhausted most of its reserves? How could defaulted bonds now worth as little as $30 billion (a price that reflects the market's current assessment of Argentina's capacity to pay) be used to repay a debt of $54 billion? Would the IMF renegotiate the bonds it held as security after the default, effectively determining the country's future debt burden, and then try to sell the resulting new bonds onto the market? Or would the IMF agree to retire the $90 billion in bonded debt in exchange for Argentina paying the $54 billion in loans?

tor is likely to end up with the country's debt only if it sets the price too high—for example, when it overestimates the country's underlying solvency. The authors' goal is to eliminate the moral hazard associated with traditional IMF bailouts, but their proposal risks creating a monster of much greater moral hazard proportions.

The desire to come up with alternatives to large bailouts—or risky standstills—in liquidity crises is understandable. Unfortunately, most of the proposed solutions are likely to be ineffective. Some would be altogether pernicious.

What Is the Right Policy?

Large official rescue packages or some form of standstill and debt rescheduling do not have a true alternative. Private bailouts do not exist for good reasons. Indeed, modern risk management tools probably have made it less likely that the large banks will ever lend into a crisis.[40] Guarantees are typically a less transparent and effective way of providing a bailout than a direct official loan with conditionality. Voluntary debt swaps at high rates during crises worsen debt sustainability, even when enhanced with official resources. Contractualizing standstills with rollover options might help but does not change the fact that the country has had to invoke its standstill clause. Supporting the secondary-market price of emerging-market debt rather than supporting the country is an inefficient and wasteful—and possibly very risky—use of official funds. The core policy choice is likely to remain one among the provision of large amounts of official resources to help the country meet a surge in foreign-currency demand, a coercive restructuring that limits the rollover of private claims, and a combination of financing and steps to lock in some sets of private-sector creditors.

We do not believe that a single approach makes sense for all crises. Managing crises effectively means trading off different risks. The closer a crisis to a clear illiquidity case, the greater the benefits of avoiding the economic costs associated with a standstill and the smaller the risk of official lending generating substantial moral hazard. If the IMF and the G-7 are willing to put enough money on the table for "catalytic" official financing to have a realistic chance of working, then the risk of official lending may be smaller than the risk of seeking a restructuring triggering a broader run. A comprehensive standstill would not have provided the right solution in Mexico in 1995 or in Brazil in 1999.

Proponents of standstills often seem more interested in limiting official financing than in offering the country facing a liquidity shortage a credi-

40. International banks reduced exposure to Argentina during 2001 and to Brazil before its 2002 elections.

ble path through the crisis. A standstill offers a solution to a liquidity problem only if it is possible to specify what set of claims will be caught in the standstill, how the country can exit the standstill, and how to manage the risk of the standstill leading the crisis to snowball. A limited standstill risks spooking other investors and broadening the run. Preemptively freezing all payments shuts down the financial system and much of the private economy.

At the same time, the right approach is not always to provide large amounts of official financing in the absence of any private debt restructuring. The official sector has to be able to distinguish between temporary and permanent problems and to be willing to deny "catalytic" financing to countries where there is a significant risk that the problem is not just a temporary liquidity shortage. The official sector, though, has tended to do the opposite and to think that more Mexican-style liquidity crises are out there than there really are. The IMF's principals—the G-7 and other countries that provide most of the IMF's usable resources—have political, geostrategic, military, and financial interests that create pressure for bailouts that avoid, or at last postpone, nasty crises in geopolitical allies and systemically important countries. Their agents—the IMF's management and staff—often have a similar bias toward treating large cases as liquidity cases, both because the IMF is at times "captive" to the wishes of client countries and because the IMF itself does not want to be blamed for forcing a country into a debt restructuring.

There are cases where neither a full bailout of all creditors with claims coming due is appropriate nor immediate debt reduction is the right approach. Many countries face pressure on their reserves that stem in part from concerns that overall debt levels have increased to the point where there are substantial questions about the country's solvency, even though the country may not be insolvent if it can deliver the needed policy effort. These countries have a liquidity problem, but they also typically need to meet their liquidity needs with medium-term rather than short-term financing. These countries will need to restructure some of their debts. Such a restructuring will have a better chance of working if it is combined with official lending, which can limit the risk of restructuring one set of claims triggering secondary runs that will immediately push the country into insolvency. This approach was followed in Ukraine and more recently in Uruguay—and might have been tried in Argentina at the end of 2000 or early in 2001.

These preferences imply that the official sector's role should vary in different crises. But if its response varies in ways that the markets cannot predict or understand, then official policy action will be a source of uncertainty in the market. Therefore, the best way of addressing this risk is to strive to respond similarly to similar kinds of crises, not to insist that the official sector respond to different crises in the same way.

7

Seniority of Sovereign Debts

A formal insolvency regime typically sets out, in general terms, how different types of claims on a distressed private firm will be treated in a restructuring and the order of payment in the event of outright liquidation. Bankruptcy law usually indicates that equity is junior to debt: Debt gets paid first, and if debt cannot be paid, debtholders may take control of the firm. Back taxes get paid ahead of most private debts. Different kinds of debts may have different levels of priority—for example, debts backed by collateral are treated better than unsecured debts. These rules tell a firm's creditors where their claims stand in the pecking order.

In contrast, no formal rules of priority lay out how different types of claims on a distressed sovereign will be treated. Nor does a court have the power to force a sovereign government to respect any rules of priority.[1] The difficulties of taking effective legal action against a sovereign—discussed in depth in chapter 8—can give the sovereign the ability to discriminate in favor of some classes of claims. Different creditors will argue that their claims should be given priority. As a result, the relative standing of various claims on a sovereign government is often ambiguous. The priority that the sovereign opts to grant different types of debt may not match creditors' prior expectations.

1. In some countries, certain public entities are subject to an insolvency regime. Municipalities in the United States, for example, are subject to Chapter 9 of the US bankruptcy code. Municipal bankruptcy regimes may even explicitly declare that public employee wages and some public expenditures are senior to financial liabilities. US states are not subject to an insolvency regime. However, some state laws may set out the relative seniority of various claims. Here, too, some spending items linked to the provision of public services may have formal priority over debt claims.

Priority can be absolute or relative. Absolute priority means that claims at the top get paid in full, those in the middle get paid in part, and those at the bottom get nothing. Relative priority assures only those at the top of the priority structure better treatment than those at the bottom. Nobody may get paid in full. In corporate bankruptcy, the rules of absolute priority—the ranking of claims in the event of liquidation—determines the bargaining power of different participants during the restructuring negotiations, and thus drive the relative priority accorded to different claims. No comparable rules of absolute priority cast a shadow over a sovereign restructuring. Since a sovereign in default usually is unable to grant absolute priority to many—if any—creditors, the debate is usually over relative priority.

Most sovereigns do respect a number of informal rules, avoiding total chaos. The priority traditionally granted to creditors like the IMF, the World Bank, and other multilateral development banks (MDBs) is almost always respected, in part because these international financial institutions (IFIs) usually refinance their maturing debt rather than demand full payment after a default. In some cases the IMF may go beyond simply refinancing its existing debt and provide new debtor-in-possession (DIP) financing during a crisis.[2] Different external-law bonds are usually treated roughly equally: The structure and payment mechanics of a typical international bond make it hard for a sovereign to restructure one bond issue while sparing another. However, these informal rules still leave plenty of sources of contention. Should the sovereign's debt to private external creditors be treated better, or worse, than its debt to other governments? Should the sovereign's external bonded debt be treated differently than its external bank loans? Should foreign-currency debts held by domestic creditors be treated better or worse than, or the same as, those held by external creditors? Should debt held by domestic banks be treated on different terms in a restructuring? Should the IOUs from pension and wage arrears be treated better, or worse, than other domestic debts?

This chapter examines the current debate about the relative treatment of various types of sovereign debt—a debate that can be interpreted as arguments about the priority structure that a bankrupt sovereign should put in place in the absence of any binding, formal rules of priority. It is divided into three broad sections. The first defends both the informal priority currently given to IFI debt and the principle that Paris Club creditors should condition their restructuring on a "comparable" restructuring of debts owed to private creditors.

The second section discusses the most difficult and controversial issue in most sovereign restructurings: the relative treatment of domestic and external debt.

---

2. The term "debtor-in-possession (DIP) financing" comes from Chapter 11 of the US bankruptcy code.

The third section examines proposals to introduce a more formal priority structure into the sovereign debt market, whether to limit the risk of debt dilution or to make debt restructurings more orderly. We conclude that it is not possible to develop an enforceable system that substantially improves on the status quo.

Our focus on the issue of priority reflects our sense that the debate on sovereign debt restructuring has been framed too narrowly. Too much attention has been placed on the potential of the shift from syndicated bank loans to international bonds to give rise to new forms of collective action problems. Too little attention has been placed on the far bigger issue of deciding who is in and who is out of the restructuring. It is worth noting that proposals to create an international bankruptcy mechanism for sovereigns—discussed in depth in chapter 8—would not necessarily clarify the relative seniority of different claims on a sovereign. The IMF's proposal, for example, did not cover domestic debt and allowed a sovereign to leave some unsecured external debt out of its restructuring.

We have little doubt that difficulties in reaching agreement on the priority that should be given to different classes of debt are likely to be a far more important impediment to the rapid resolution of a severe sovereign debt crisis than holdout litigation. But we also believe that the obstacles to creating a formal priority structure—and then forcing a sovereign to abide by it—are almost certainly too large to overcome. The real challenge is finding ways to make the current ad hoc and informal priority regime work better. Here, as elsewhere, we believe that incremental steps—more flexible Paris Club restructuring terms for middle-income countries and greater understanding of the case for restructuring domestic and external debt on different terms—is more likely to tangibly improve the debt restructuring "architecture" than more radical reforms.

Relative Treatment of Different Sovereign Claims

A sovereign "bankruptcy" is distinguished by the diversity of different claims on the sovereign's resources as well as by the absence of any authority that has the power to supervise the restructuring. The various potential claims on a distressed sovereign are worth reviewing in detail.

Direct Sovereign Debt Obligations, External and Domestic. External creditors often include private-sector creditors (banks, bondholders, and others), other governments (Paris Club members and others), and multilateral creditors (such as the IFIs). Domestic banks and pension funds are often important domestic creditors. Debts owed to multilateral creditors traditionally have been given priority. Some form of collateral may back—either fully or partially—some external debt, but most external debt is likely to be unsecured.

Contingent Liabilities. The banking system typically is the most significant source of such implicit liabilities. This is true even in the absence of a system of deposit insurance formally backing the banking system, as the government typically guarantees most bank liabilities in a crisis. The implicit liabilities deriving from pay-as-you-go social security systems can also be important. Retirees promised a retirement benefit in return for the social security taxes they paid while working have a clear claim on the sovereign's future tax resources.

Arrears on Wages, Pensions, and Social Payments. A sovereign often stops paying its workers and pensioners in full before falling into broad-based default. Ecuador, for example, stopped paying teachers and policemen before it stopped paying its external debt, and Argentina started paying workers with quasi-currencies before it stopped making debt payments. After the default, those who were not paid in full before the default usually want the money that they are owed.

All these financial claims compete with one another and with other "stakeholders" for a share of a sovereign government's ongoing revenues. Creditors cannot force a sovereign that has defaulted to cut domestic spending, to raise taxes, or to devote all of its revenues to service its debts. Consequently, the treatment that a sovereign should grant to debt service relative to other spending priorities—defense, police, education, and pensions—is among its key decisions following a default.

The diversity of claims on the sovereign makes deciding who gets paid and who does not, and who takes a large haircut and who takes a smaller haircut, intrinsically difficult. Still, a bankrupt sovereign does need to reach agreement with all those holding financial claims to end its crisis, and the terms of these agreements will create—at least ex post—a de facto priority structure.

International Financial Institutions

A sovereign typically pays debts owed to the IFIs even if it is not servicing its other external debts. The effective seniority of IMF and MDB claims is not a matter of legal right. Formally, IMF and World Bank loans are just like any of the sovereign's other unsecured debt. However, sovereigns typically have paid the IFIs even when they are not paying other unsecured creditors, giving the IFIs effective "preferred creditor status." Bilateral official creditors have always respected the IFIs' preferred position: Indeed, the historical willingness of bilateral creditors to restructure their claims in order to assure payment to the IFIs has been central to the conception of the IFIs' preferred status. A sovereign's desire to maintain its future access to emergency financing and a good working relationship with the other governments that provide the IMF with its financing provides a powerful incentive to follow the convention of paying the IMF even if the sovereign defaults on its other debts.

A number of private investors, however, are questioning the "preferred" status of the IFIs. Argentina, for example, owes a substantial sum to the IMF and the MDBs, and private creditors ask why all unsecured external creditors, including the IMF and the World Bank, shouldn't take a haircut when the sovereign cannot pay.[3] Some argue that the risk of losses would discipline the IMF and prevent it from making large loans to risky countries.

These arguments should be rejected. The IMF is not as a private lender seeking profitable lending opportunities, but a public institution responsible for stabilizing the international financial system. The IMF's preferred status is central to it ability to perform its two key roles in the international financial system: It acts as a proxy for a true lender of last resort, lending significant sums to countries facing a temporary liquidity problem, and as a proxy for a sovereign bankruptcy court by providing new financing to a sovereign undergoing a restructuring. In both cases its financing is tied to an agreement with the crisis country's government on a framework for policy changes, which effectively lays out the country's plan for emerging from distress.

The IMF's preferred status lets it lend when private creditors will not, even though it has to guard against losing the taxpayers' funds it manages. A classic domestic lender of last resort lends against collateral. A sovereign government, in contrast, typically has limited ability to offer collateral: Its core asset is some combination of its commitment to future fiscal adjustment and its commitment to buy foreign exchange that the rest of the economy will generate in the future. The priority granted to the IMF provides it with the security needed to lend large quantities at reasonable rates against such intangible assets.

Without effective seniority, the IMF would have to act more like a private lender and pay more attention to maintaining a diverse portfolio, severely crimping its ability to lend large sums to major emerging economies.[4] It would need to lend to a sovereign at high market rates in order to avoid systematically losing money[5] and would be less able to put

3. Argentina owes about $40 billion to the IMF, the World Bank, and the Inter-American Development Bank. It owes between $80 billion and $90 billion to international bondholders, but domestic investors hold a large share of Argentina's international bonds. International investors truly hold perhaps only $40 billion to $50 billion. The complexities of Argentina's restructuring are discussed in detail later.

4. No private lender would be willing to have its exposure exclusively in relatively high-risk debtors such as Turkey, Brazil, Argentina, and Uruguay without some assurance that its debts would be given priority. Five countries currently account for 86 percent of the IMF's nonconcessional lending.

5. The IMF's Articles of Agreement require it to lend on terms that do not put its resources at risk.

money in when other creditors are pulling money out. Since we believe, as discussed in chapter 6, that there is a need for an international source of emergency liquidity—appropriately priced and linked to appropriate policy adjustments—we also believe that payments to the IMF need to continue to be given priority over payments to other external creditors.

The IMF performs a second role in the international financial system. During a sovereign debt restructuring, an IMF program acts as a surrogate—sometimes an imperfect surrogate—for the supervision that a bankruptcy judge provides during a corporate reorganization. Sovereign bankruptcy certainly is very different from corporate bankruptcy, and the IMF's role also clearly differs in many ways from that of a bankruptcy judge. The IMF has leverage because it lends, not because it can put an end to a "reorganization" process and either push the country into liquidation or force a change in the country's "management." Consequently, the IMF will have, unlike a bankruptcy judge, its own money on the line in the crisis country. If the IMF did not have money—or the ability to put additional money—on the line, then it would not have had the ability to influence the policies adopted by a sovereign government in default. Classically, senior lenders care the least about a borrower's policies: The lender's seniority assures it payment no matter what (Gelpern 2004). The IMF, in contrast, should use the leverage created by its preferred status to perform its public policy role of laying out a framework for the country's macroeconomic policies after a default.

The economic argument for the preferred status of IMF lending to a country undergoing a debt reorganization therefore parallels in part the economic argument for giving seniority to "new money" in bankruptcy. Granting seniority to new financing is necessary if a distressed firm is to remain viable during its reorganization. So long as the firm is worth more as an ongoing entity than if it were to be liquidated, such seniority serves the interest of existing creditors. IMF financing also can help to reduce the fall in output following default, helping other creditors.[6] But the analogy to DIP financing actually understates the case for providing the IMF with seniority. IMF financing is important because access to new money not only can avoid larger falls in output but also provides the hook that lets the international community shape the policies of a sovereign government in distress or default.[7]

6. See IMF (January 2003b) for a discussion of the role IMF financing and an IMF program could play in a sovereign debt restructuring. It is striking that the IMF has not sought to play this role in Argentina.

7. The argument for the seniority of MDB lending is more complicated, since most MDB loans are not provided during financial distress. The general argument for MDB seniority rests on the need to find a way to finance, at low cost, the development of very poor countries. The MDBs can only lend to risky countries at low rates, for long terms, and on an unsecured basis because of the priority that is traditionally given to the repayment of this debt.

Eliminating the IMF's preferred creditor status would do far more harm than good, but private creditors are right to note that the IMF has not always played its role in the international financial system well. Argentina is a case in point. In 2001, the IMF provided emergency liquidity support to a country that, in our judgment, was too indebted to have a reasonable chance of avoiding a restructuring. Argentina's need to repay, over time, the additional IFI debt it took on in the course of 2001 no doubt reduces, at the margins, the amount that the country's other external creditors can expect to recover in a restructuring. Of course, successful rescues also help a country's long-term creditors. Without its preferred status, the IMF would not have lent as much to Argentina. But it also would not have lent as much to Brazil, Turkey, and Uruguay.

In Argentina, the IMF also has had difficulty in performing its second role in the international financial system: defining a macroeconomic program for a country in default. Argentina's fall 2003 agreement with the IMF did not define the amount of primary fiscal adjustment Argentina needs to do beyond 2004 to repay all its creditors. Rather, the program left the job of negotiating Argentina's fiscal adjustment path to Argentina's private creditors. The funds Argentina owes the IMF have hamstrung the IMF and no doubt diminished its leverage. The IMF's major shareholders who—at least in 2003—did not always back the IMF in its negotiations with Argentina have also weakened the IMF's leverage. Eliminating the IMF's preferred status would not solve these problems. Rather the solution is to find ways for the IMF to use more effectively the leverage that comes from its ability to lend when others will not.

The burden that priority payments to the IFIs places on a distressed debtor should not be exaggerated. The IMF and MDBs typically are repaid in full only because they are patient enough to allow a country many years to recover before demanding repayment. They may even provide new money to cover interest payments in some cases.[8] This is another way the IFIs do not act like private lenders. Private lenders lend for short terms so that they have the option of getting out if conditions turn sour. The IMF's short-term lending is repaid only if the borrowing country is in decent economic and financial shape. Of course, defensive lending to reduce the risk of the debtor defaulting on the IMF—and also on the MDBs, because an IMF program is a prerequisite for MDB lending—is hardly ideal. It ties up the IMF's balance sheet and can lead to watered-down policy conditionality, reducing both the IMF's credibility and its ability to lend to

8. IMF resources are at risk of default in the present system. A few countries, such as Sudan, have defaulted on their IMF lending, though this happens rarely. The heavily indebted poor countries (HIPC) process allows very poor countries to reduce their debt to multilateral lenders (IMF and World Bank) as well as their bilateral debt. Middle income countries are expected to pay the IMF and World Bank back in full over time, even if they default on their private debts—and, in general, they do. Russia is a case in point.

other countries. The IMF is effectively "bailed in" if its short-term catalytic lending fails, as its short-term loans are rolled over to avoid formal arrears. Rather than getting absolute priority, the IMF and other IFIs often have to struggle to convince the crisis country to continue to pay interest on the country's multilateral debt.

Paris Club Debt and Private External Debt

The major bilateral creditor countries—OECD countries like the United States, Japan, the United Kingdom, and France—meet regularly in Paris to coordinate the restructuring of their debts to debtor countries. These bilateral creditors are commonly called Paris Club creditors.[9] A debtor seeking to restructure the debt it owes Paris Club creditors is asked to seek a "comparable" restructuring from its other external creditors—be they bilateral creditors that are not part of the Paris Club or private lenders. Not surprisingly, the Paris Club has been a lightning rod for complaints about the official sector's bail-in policies—in part because Paris Club creditors had significant exposure in the initial bond restructuring cases of Pakistan, Russia, and Ecuador.[10]

Private creditors accuse the Paris Club of being secretive, arbitrary, unfair, politically biased, and unwilling to even talk to private investors (IIF 1999b, Caplen 2000, and Booth 2001). These complaints can be separated into two critiques. One critique argues that the Paris Club should not ask a debtor to seek a comparable restructuring of the debtor's outstanding international bonds in order to facilitate the development of private capital markets. A second critique calls on the Paris Club to do a better job of coordinating its restructuring with private debt restructuring. The first critique is wrong. The second has a grain of truth but is also based on a number of misconceptions.

Why should the Paris Club condition its restructuring on a comparable restructuring by other external creditors, including private creditors? The answer is simple: so as not to subordinate its taxpayers' claims to those of other creditors and, in the process, subsidize payments to bondholders or other groups of creditors. The bilateral creditors who meet in the Paris Club do not lend to other sovereigns on the expectation that their debts would be systematically subordinated to the sovereign's other external debt, apart from debts owed to the IFIs. When most private lending to emerging-market sovereigns came from banks, the Paris Club conditioned its restructuring on the debtor's willingness to seek a comparable

9. See Reiffel (2003) for a detailed history and analysis of the Paris Club and its procedures.

10. The Paris Club also had significant exposure in Indonesia, but bondholders did not. Indonesia's creditors—largely Japanese banks—did not protest the Paris Club's requirement that Indonesia seek a comparable rescheduling of their claims. Indonesia's bonded debt was judged de minimis, and the Paris Club did not insist that it be included in the restructuring.

restructuring of its external bank loans. The banks met in a club of their own—the London Club (which often meets in New York, despite its name)—to coordinate their own restructuring. Bonds were typically left out of these restructurings because the country's bonded debt was too small to be worth the trouble (bonds were considered *de minimis*), not because the Paris Club agreed to give these claims priority. As international banks got out of the business of providing medium- and long-term sovereign financing and as sovereigns turned to the bond market to raise money, continuation of long-standing Paris Club policy implied that the Paris Club would ask countries to seek to restructure their bonded debt on comparable terms. The markets could and should have expected it.[11]

The argument that comparability is illegitimate because political rather than strict commercial considerations motivate official bilateral lending lacks merit. Some bilateral lending certainly has been motivated as much by a desire to aid a country as to be paid back with a profit. Other bilateral loans really are not even foreign aid so much as export subsidies. But even in private-sector lending, the obligation to repay is independent of the reasons the lender made the loan. A financial conglomerate that makes a loan to win investment-banking business still has a valid claim. The interest rate the US government charges on its bilateral lending is intended to reflect the risk of the taxpayer not being repaid, not the costs of systematically subsidizing bondholders.[12]

The fact that Paris Club creditors have legitimate reasons for insisting that a sovereign in distress treat all unsecured external debt comparably does not mean that they always have the leverage to assure that all such debt will in fact be treated comparably. Indeed, sovereign debtors often stop paying official bilateral creditors well before they stop paying private creditors, effectively treating Paris Club debt as junior debt. Strategic nonpayment on Paris Club debts often helps a sovereign pay private creditors in full and on time. For example, Nigeria accumulated over $23 billion of arrears to the Paris Club in the 1990s while paying its Brady bonds and other bonds in full.[13] Ecuador was able to issue a new eurobond in 1997, when it was in arrears to the Paris Club. Sovereign debtors know that going into arrears to bilateral creditors has few immediate consequences. As a rule, bilateral lenders do not litigate to recover payment. However,

11. Some in the markets thought that the perceived difficulty of restructuring bonds would lead the Paris Club to exempt bonds from Paris Club conditionality.

12. After the credit reform, the charge is set in the Interagency Country Risk Assessment (ICRAS) process.

13. Former Nigerian President Sani Abacha and his clan are reported to have $2 billion in their private accounts ("Sani Disposition," *The Economist*, September 7, 2000); he and other Nigerian insiders are rumored to hold a substantial sum of Nigeria's external sovereign debt in his private accounts. Nigeria's long-standing desire to pay its private debt while not paying bilateral debt was not simply the product of its belief in the sanctity of private contracts.

most countries eventually find that they cannot finance themselves indefinitely by running arrears to the Paris Club. When a country approaches the IMF for financing, the Paris Club creditors—who also have the most votes on the IMF Executive Board—can insist that any IMF lending take place only in the context of a general restructuring of all the country's external debt.

Implementing the Paris Club's policy of linking its own restructuring to a comparable restructuring by other external creditors raises a host of difficult practical questions. How can two sets of creditors reach agreement with the debtor on terms that treat both sets "comparably" while also recognizing their distinct preferences? This question does not just arise between the Paris Club and private creditors or even just in sovereign restructurings. Different groups of creditors in a corporate restructuring may also have different preferences and want different restructuring terms. In a wide range of restructurings, banks and retail investors put a higher premium on preserving the face value of their claims than professional money managers, who care more about the bond's market value than its face value.

Private creditors' complaints that the Paris Club initially did not make great efforts to explain how it went about assessing comparability have merit, but a number of misconceptions have complicated the debate on the relative treatment of Paris Club debt and private bonds. The first misconception is that different restructuring terms imply the absence of comparability. In some cases, private creditors have agreed to reduce the face value of their claims while Paris Club creditors have not. However, different terms can reflect the need to craft restructuring terms to match the preferences of different creditors—not discriminatory treatment. For example, private creditors considered par Brady bonds (no face value debt reduction, low coupon) "comparable" to discount Brady bonds (face value debt reduction, higher coupon) in Brady restructurings.[14]

A need to minimize the budgetary costs that Paris Club creditors incur in a debt restructuring heavily (almost certainly too heavily) drives the

14. Private-sector representatives often ask for reverse comparability, with the Paris Club matching private-sector debt reduction if the private sector restructures before the Paris Club. Private creditors, of course, are free to hold up their own agreement on the sovereign until the sovereign is able to reach agreement with the Paris Club on terms that the Paris Club accepts and that private creditors judge comparable. Private creditors, however, have been unwilling to delay a deal with mark-to-market gains to increase their leverage vis-à-vis the Paris Club. In any case such tactics would be unproductive. The Paris Club has different preferences and constraints than private creditors, and it should not agree to debt reduction simply because private creditors are willing to do it. As a matter of policy, Paris Club creditors should not agree to restructuring terms unless they are confident of getting the necessary budget funds to pay for the restructuring and budget funds are too scarce to be allocated solely on the basis of the amount of debt relief private creditors provide. Rather budget funds should be allocated on the basis of broader public policy objectives (including helping the world's poorest).

club's preferences. The accounting and budget rules for Paris Club debt restructuring usually do not require that its creditors discount future cash flows at market rates. Paris Club creditors often can avoid taking a budgetary charge even when they reschedule claims at relatively low interest rates for very long terms, because they can use a discount rate on the new claims that does not reflect an objective assessment of the expected probability of repayment. Consequently, Paris Club creditors have an institutional preference for the equivalent of the "par" option. Apart from a few exceptions, the Paris Club generally does not provide debt reduction for middle-income countries.[15] However, few private creditors would prefer the terms of a typical Paris Club debt restructuring to those of the private deal, even when the Paris Club does not agree to debt reduction. When valued at market discount rates, Paris Club restructuring terms usually imply significant reduction in the NPV of the creditors' claims.[16]

Moreover, Paris Club loans include a series of features not present in private debt contracts. Paris Club debts effectively have an embedded option that allows the debtor to roll over principal and capitalize interest at its own discretion—since the debtor can stop paying these debts with little consequence. Paris Club creditors do not litigate and never panic. A private debt contract with no legal enforcement rights and similar embedded options would trade at a deep discount. These features imply that a Paris Club restructuring can be comparable to a private debt restructuring even when the terms differ—no private creditor would be willing to provide credit to a sovereign at the terms, risk features, and spreads that official bilateral creditors provide.

The second misconception is that private creditors in Russia and Ecuador restructured their debts on substantially more generous terms than the Paris Club. The relative treatment of Paris Club and private debts can be assessed in different ways: Private creditors, not surprisingly, have tended to emphasize those ways of looking at comparability most favorable to their arguments. In Russia, holders of Soviet-era external debt (restructured in the London Club) did agree to do more than the Paris Club. However, comparability needs to be assessed by looking at how Russia treated all of its external private debts, including its Russian-era eurobonds. Since the high-coupon eurobonds were altogether excluded from the restructuring, the overall treatment of Russia's private external debt was comparable to that of Russia's Paris Club debt. In Ecuador, a fair assessment of comparability requires looking at all the terms of the restructuring—cash sweeteners, maturity, coupon, and the treatment of collat-

15. Poland, Egypt, and former Yugoslavia are the most notable examples.

16. Paris Club creditors' preferences often reflect the projected budgetary cost of the restructuring, which differ from calculations of the NPV using market rates. Paris Club agreements are commitments to restructure on the proposed terms, but the actual execution of the restructuring depends on each country's budget rules.

eral—not just the face value of Ecuador's new bonds. Once adjustments are made for the debt reduction that stemmed solely from the early release of collateral on two of Ecuador's Brady bonds, it is not obvious that uncollateralized private creditors offered more debt relief than Paris Club creditors. For example, the holders of Ecuador's 2002 and 2004 eurobonds were able to trade their existing claims at par for new high-coupon eurobonds maturing in 2012.[17] Private creditors tend to overlook cases like Pakistan, where the terms of the private restructuring were more favorable than those of the Paris Club restructuring. The Paris Club has been firm in insisting on the principle of comparability but flexible in interpreting its precise meaning.

Nonetheless, real differences—some of which are quite technical—make it difficult to coordinate the Paris Club and private restructurings:

- The Paris Club typically restructures only those payments coming due during the country's IMF program (in Paris Club terminology, the "consolidation period"). This can result in a series of restructurings of Paris Club claims rather than a comprehensive restructuring of the entire stock of Paris Club debt, which tries to address the country's problems once and for all. The Paris Club agrees to a comprehensive restructuring of a country's entire debt stock only after the country has completed a three-year IMF program. Private-sector debt restructurings, in contrast, typically restructure the entire "stock" in a single restructuring to avoid repeat restructurings. While bank restructurings in the 1980s often were implicitly conditioned on the completion of an IMF program, bondholders generally have made an IMF program a condition for the execution of their restructuring.
- There are no well-understood rules on how to allocate available near-term cash flow among different creditor groups. The Paris Club's flow rescheduling model requires the country to allocate cash flows among creditors in proportion to the amounts they have coming due during the IMF program period. Paris Club creditors use this method to apportion payments among themselves. They turn to this method most naturally for apportioning payments between Paris Club and private creditors. This method tends to favor creditors with large arrears (often Paris Club creditors, because countries typically go into arrears on Paris Club debt before private debt) or with principal payments coming due during the consolidation period. Private creditors do not

17. Holders of uncollateralized Brady bonds did not get as good a deal as holders of the 2002 and 2004 eurobonds, and holders of the uncollateralized portion of partially collateralized Brady bonds did agree to substantially alter the profile of their uncollateralized payments to Ecuador's benefit. However, all arrears on bonded debt were also settled in cash, while arrears to the Paris Club were settled in large part with new debt.

necessarily follow a similar rule. They often base restructuring terms on aggregate amounts outstanding, not the amount coming due.

- Paris Club processes are built around an assumption that the Paris Club restructuring precedes the restructuring of the debts of both other bilateral and private creditors. The Paris Club uses its rules to decide what share of the sovereign's near-term cash flow it should take, leaving the remainder for other creditors to divvy up among themselves using their own rules. This process breaks down when private bondholders restructure before the Paris Club, as has been the case in some recent restructurings.[18]
- The Paris Club has its own arcane system for according informal seniority within the Paris Club in order to facilitate new lending. A country's initial restructuring sets a cutoff date, and in theory lending after the cutoff date is senior to old lending in the event of future payments difficulties. This can become a problem if a country ends up going back to the Paris Club, because the original cutoff date does not change. Private creditors do not have a comparable system or any comparable complications. (In the 1980s, "new money" that bank creditors provided was initially kept out of the restructuring, but over time this practice disappeared.)

There is value in improving dialogue between the Paris Club and private creditors, so that both groups better understand how the other operates and the sources of their different preferences. Indeed, the Paris Club has been taking steps to increase its transparency, after private creditors correctly pointed out that it was difficult to find information on how the Paris Club operates or on the amount of debt a country owed to Paris Club creditors.[19] However, the need to improve coordination does not mean that the Paris Club creditors should accept private demands to ne-

18. The difficulties in allocating near-term cash flows are a manifestation of the general difficulties created when one major group of creditors does a "flow" restructuring—i.e., it only restructures those claims coming due in a defined period (Paris Club creditors do not accelerate their claims)—and another group of creditors does a "stock" restructuring—i.e., it restructures the entire stock of outstanding debt. The prorated distribution of cash flows according to claims coming due in the consolidation period works reasonably well if all creditors are doing flow restructurings but less well if one creditor group is restructuring the entire stock. In practice, the Paris Club has been willing to interpret this rule flexibly.

19. The Paris Club set up a Web site, www.clubdeparis.org, that provides information about its activities, rules, upcoming cases, and claims being restructured. The Paris Club (or another international body) could do more—for example, a more systematic registry of all Paris Club bilateral claims might be useful to investors. Certain Paris Club procedures are arcane, and the flexibility that is consistent with Paris Club procedure—changing cutoff dates, for example—is not always obvious. More public information about its procedures and rules might help everyone avoid misunderstandings.

gotiate restructuring terms on a case-by-case basis with a committee of private creditors.

The inherent difficulty in negotiations between governments and private financial firms means that there is a high risk of the "negotiations" resulting in a slower and more contentious process without necessarily producing substantially different outcomes.[20] Unless private creditors want to lobby their legislatures for budget funding to pay for debt concessions, general Paris Club policies will dictate the club's restructuring terms. Most restructurings follow the basic Paris Club procedures: normal terms (i.e., substantial maturity extension at favorable interest rates but no debt reduction) for middle-income countries, Houston terms for poorer countries, and HIPC terms for those that qualify for it. It takes a political decision to provide a high-profile country with special treatment.[21] The Paris Club is not a formal organization so much as an ad hoc group of rotating creditors, with rules and procedures to enable relatively low-level technical experts to handle a large number of cases reasonably efficiently. It is not currently set up for high-profile negotiations with private creditors.[22]

This is not to say that the Paris Club's specific practices do not need to change. For example, it is worth discussing how to better balance "flow" and "stock" considerations in allocating available near-term cash flows among various creditor groups.[23] There is a case for favoring creditors who have been discriminated against before the restructuring and thus favoring those with large arrears (typically the Paris Club). There is also a case for providing more cash to creditors who place the highest value on cash (market creditors) and who are most willing to agree to real debt reduction in return for higher upfront cash payments.

The standard market critique that the Paris Club is a political wild card whose actions cannot be predicted, ironically, is not the strongest critique of the club. The Paris Club's biggest problem is that its restructuring terms

20. Once the IMF defines the amount available for debt service and rules are agreed upon on the distribution of upfront cash, restructuring terms cannot be in sharp contrast to comparability and medium-term sustainability.

21. Special considerations were made for countries such as Poland, Egypt, and Serbia. Key creditors have already committed to give Iraq special treatment.

22. France hosts the club and by convention both chairs its meetings and provides its secretariat, but the French secretariat cannot speak for all Paris Club creditors. Private creditors would need to negotiate with the individual governments that make up the Paris Club, barring a major reorganization.

23. We believe a widely understood rule—like some variant of the proportionality principle used in recent cases—would ultimately provide a more predictable and fair distribution of the burden than a formal negotiating process, given the Paris Club's need to operate with a framework defined by established rules and principles. All groups of creditors would need to reach an informal understanding that both Paris Club and private claims are rescheduled and/or paid in cash in proportion to the outstanding claims of both groups, either the overall amount outstanding or the portion of claims coming due in a defined period.

are too predictable and fail to take the specific circumstances of the country sufficiently into account. Paris Club rules reserve outright debt reduction—which requires scarce budget resources—for the poorest countries. Middle-income countries get substantial cash flow relief but no debt reduction. The absence of deep debt reduction from holders of either Ecuador or Russia's external bonded debt undermined private-sector complaints about the absence of Paris Club debt reduction in either country.[24] Argentina, however, is seeking deep debt reduction from its private creditors. Since Paris Club exposure in Argentina is small, the absence of outright reduction by Paris Club creditors won't undermine the country's overall solvency, but it still highlights how general rules can result in suboptimal outcomes in specific cases. Fortunately, the G-7 has recognized that the Paris Club may need to be more flexible in some middle-income countries (Serbia and Iraq are obvious examples) and has called on it to rely less on preset terms and more on debt sustainability analysis to figure out how much relief a country truly needs (Group of Seven 2003b). It remains to be seen how the Paris Club will use this new flexibility—and whether private creditors will push the Paris Club toward restructuring terms that help them more than the crisis country.

Domestic Versus External Debt

The treatment of domestic debt is often the most contentious issue in a sovereign debt crisis. Sovereigns facing a deep crisis, like Argentina now or Ecuador in 1999, rarely leave either domestic or external claims entirely out of a restructuring. Consequently, the substantive policy issue is whether these two categories of debt should be restructured on similar terms or domestic debt should be given some priority.

What Is "Domestic" Debt?

The absence of a simple definition of the difference between domestic and external debt is one sign of the complexity of this issue. The standard economic definition is based on the principle of residency. External debt is any debt held by a foreign resident, regardless of debt instrument's governing law or currency of denomination. A local-law, ruble-denominated Russian treasury bill held by foreign investors, consequently, counts as external debt. Conversely, a dollar-denominated, New York–law eurobond held by a Turkish bank should be considered as domestic debt. Another economic definition uses the currency of denomination to define the difference between domestic and external debt.

24. External investors who bought Russia's domestic GKOs clearly did take substantial losses.

The legal definition, in contrast, focuses on governing law. Domestic debt is defined as debt governed by domestic law, regardless of whether the debt is denominated in local or foreign currency or whether a foreign or domestic resident holds it. Conversely, debt governed by foreign law is defined as foreign debt, even if a domestic resident holds it. Phrases like "domestic banks hold lots of the country's external debt" implicitly rely on governing law to define what constitutes external debt (IMF August 2002).

In most countries, domestic residents still hold a larger fraction of the domestic-law debt than foreigners, and nonresidents still hold a larger fraction of the foreign-law debt. As markets become more integrated, however, foreigners are increasingly investing in domestic-law debt and domestic residents are increasingly buying the country's foreign-law debt. The banking systems of Turkey and Lebanon hold a substantial fraction of these countries' New York-law eurobonds—as did Argentina's banking system before the November 2001 eurobonds-for-guaranteed-domestic-loans swap. In other cases—the United States today and Russia in 1998—foreign investors hold large quantities of a country's local-law, local-currency debt.[25]

The difference between the legal and economic definitions of domestic and external debt can complicate the discussion of the relative treatment of domestic and external creditors. If foreign investors hold the country's external-law debt, and domestic investors hold the domestic-law debt, it is technically easy to offer different restructuring terms to holders of domestic and external debt. Payments on domestic-law debt are usually made inside the crisis country and are harder for holders of foreign-law debt to stop. If both domestic and foreign residents hold the same external-debt instrument, offering different terms to residents and nonresidents is more difficult.[26] It typically requires a multistep process. Argentina's November 2001 "bonds for loans" swap, for example, was designed to appeal to domestic holders of the country's eurobonds (foreign investors typically could not hold a domestic-law loan). Once most domestic residents exchanged their foreign-law bonds for a new domestic instrument, it was possible to treat the new domestic instruments differently than the original bonds.

---

25. In practice, it is difficult to track who holds a sovereign's external-law bonds. Many countries simplify the calculation of their country's external debt by just assuming that all external-law bonds are held externally. As a result, the reported external debt of some countries exceeds the amount that nonresident investors truly hold. This was particularly true with Argentina.

26. The sovereign often does have the ability to offer different terms to external and domestic investors if they both hold the same domestic debt instrument—e.g., Russia offered international investors holding its GKOs different terms than domestic investors. The legal leverage of external investors in domestic debt markets varies dramatically from country to country.

To simplify the discussion of the relative treatment of domestic and external debt, we assume that residents hold all domestically issued debt and nonresidents hold all foreign-issued debt—that is, there is no difference between the economic and the legal definition of external debt. We recognize that this is only a rough approximation of a much more complex reality.

Treatment of Local-Currency Debt

Local-currency debt is subject to devaluation risk on top of default risk, as well as the risk of exchange controls restricting an investor's ability to convert local-currency payments into foreign currency. Either a sharp currency devaluation or an unexpected burst of inflation is likely to reduce the real value of fixed-rate domestic-currency debt in the event of a crisis, even in the absence of a debt restructuring. Consequently, a "comparable" restructuring of domestic-currency and foreign-currency debt usually implies offering different terms to holders of domestic-currency and foreign-currency debt. However, even if local-currency debt has to be restructured on terms that take into account the risk of further devaluation or future inflation, the question remains whether domestic-currency claims should be restructured on terms that differ substantially from those offered to external investors holding foreign-currency claims. Here the issue for domestically held local-currency debt and domestically held foreign-currency debt is the same.

Equal Treatment for Domestic and Foreign Debt?

Treating all the sovereign government's unsecured creditors equally has obvious intuitive appeal. The underlying logic that justifies attempts to treat Paris Club and private external debt "comparably" seems to apply to the treatment of domestic and external debt as well. Why should unsecured external creditors agree to subordinate their claims to those of unsecured domestic creditors?

Two economic arguments potentially justify discriminating in favor of domestic debt. First, the "pain" of the domestic debt restructuring is part of the overall pain domestic residents bear in a crisis, and the restructuring process should aim to balance the overall domestic adjustment effort with the restructuring of external claims on the country. Domestic residents feel the pain associated with economic contraction, falling real incomes, and fiscal tightening while foreign creditors do not. Consequently, greater concessions from foreign creditors can be consistent with a balanced allocation of the overall "pain" between domestic residents and external creditors. The second argument is more direct: The local banking system often holds domestic debts disproportionately, and a domestic debt restructuring that leads to a banking crisis typically reduces the value that external creditors can expect to receive.

The first argument highlights the need to distinguish between the adjustment effort *foreign investors* and *domestic agents* make, not between the relative treatment of foreign and domestic creditors. The domestic residents in a crisis country would bear a substantial burden even in the unlikely event that their financial claims on the government were not restructured. Domestic fiscal adjustment requires an increase in taxes and cuts in public spending and services. Higher direct taxes (such as income taxes) and indirect taxes (such as consumption/sales taxes) and reductions in public salaries, public pensions, and public services all result in lower income for domestic residents. Also, residents mostly bear the falls in output, employment, and consumption needed to improve the country's external balance. Falls in the local-currency value of a wide range of real and financial assets, such as equity and real estate, also tend to have a bigger impact on residents than nonresidents, because residents typically hold more such assets than foreign investors.[27]

In most cases, however, the financial claims of domestic residents also are restructured. A government that can no longer act as a lender of last resort to the banking system often has to freeze deposits, turn short-term deposits into long-term bonds, implement capital controls and otherwise restrict access to domestic financial assets. Frozen deposits and other domestic debts are often restructured in ways that imply a fall in their real value. Indeed, reductions in the real value of domestic debts can be thought of as just another way of taxing residents. The tax—formally called a capital levy—is imposed on the value of financial assets rather than on current income or spending.

Assessing whether domestic residents and foreign investors are making a "comparable" contribution to crisis resolution therefore requires looking beyond the relative treatment of domestic and external debt and examining the many other ways in which domestic residents contribute to crisis resolution. Of course, there is no single, unitary domestic agent that bears all domestic costs. The distribution of the domestic adjustment burden among domestic taxpayers, domestic beneficiaries of public spending, and domestic holders of financial assets is usually at least as contentious as the relative treatment of external and domestic debt. Conceptually, though, it is still possible to separate the adjustment costs domestic agents bear from the concessions foreign investors make.

A truly *insolvent* country cannot pay its foreign debt in spite of making the maximum feasible domestic adjustment. Foreign investors, therefore, have to bear the full residual burden to restore solvency. The improvement

27. The real value of other local currency–denominated financial assets (like those a debt contract creates between two citizens) can also fall, though a fall in the real value of private contracts can benefit debtors even as it hurts creditors.

in the country's fiscal position that can be generated by reducing the value of domestic public debt—effectively a tax on financial wealth—should be thought of as part of the maximum feasible domestic adjustment. Just as other types of domestic adjustment have limits, so does the amount of adjustment that can come from a haircut on the domestic debt. From this point of view, the ideal debt restructuring process would start by determining how much domestic pain/adjustment is economically necessary—as well as how much is politically/socially feasible—to put the country back on a sustainable growth and fiscal path. This in turn would determine the debt relief needed from external creditors. The discussion about domestic debt restructuring should be part of the internal debate over who within the society should bear the needed domestic adjustment cost, not part of the discussion over external debt restructuring terms.

It is worth noting that domestic debt reduction has only a limited impact on the economy's overall capacity to generate the foreign exchange for external debt service. Payment of the government's external debt requires (1) that the economy as a whole generate the needed foreign currency and (2) that the government raise enough money domestically to buy this foreign currency. A haircut on domestic debt would reduce domestic financial wealth, leading to lower consumption and imports. However, this is a very indirect way of generating the needed external adjustment. Of course, smaller domestic debt payments mean that the debtor can use more tax revenue to purchase the foreign exchange needed to make external debt payments. But large domestic haircuts may lower the amount of domestic fiscal adjustment that is politically sustainable even as those haircuts reduce domestic financial claims on that fiscal surplus. Domestic residents who have taken large financial haircuts on their domestic debts may not be willing to accept additional sacrifices (higher taxes/lower government services) to pay foreign creditors (see box 7.1 for an elaboration).

Difficulties That Domestic Banks Create

The argument that a domestic debt restructuring is a form of domestic taxation that redistributes domestic resources within the economy and therefore should be considered a form of domestic adjustment hinges on rather abstract questions of equity. The banking sector's heavy domestic debt holdings more commonly justify the different treatment of domestic and external debt.

Banks are almost always highly leveraged: A bank's owners put up capital, and the bank takes in short-term deposits and invests the resulting funds in longer-term financial assets. The mismatch between a bank's promise to return depositors their funds on demand and its longer-term and often illiquid assets adds to the financial fragility inherent in a high degree of leverage. If the value of the financial assets the bank holds falls

Box 7.1 Different haircuts for domestic and external creditors

Consider the following illustrative and hypothetical example. A government has a debt-to-GDP ratio of 100 percent, with domestic creditors holding one half and foreign creditors the other half. This debt is unsustainable, and the country formally defaults. At the time of default, the country was not running a primary surplus. All agree the government needs to tighten its belt, but it cannot achieve a primary surplus of more than 4 percent of GDP. All also agree that the long-run growth rate of the economy will be 3 percent and that the long-run real interest rate will be 11 percent. The differential between the real interest rate and the growth rate is 8 percent (11 percent minus 3 percent), which—in conjunction with a primary balance of 4 percent—implies that the debt-to-GDP ratio should be reduced to 50 percent.

One solution would be to cut everyone's debt in half, so that of the 50 percent of GDP in new debt, one half is held domestically and the other half externally (scenario 1). The domestic haircut is a form of taxation—a capital levy—that is imposed on domestic financial assets. Suppose that domestic investors, who are also taxpayers, decide that they would prefer to spread their losses over time (scenario 2).[1] They consequently agree to pay higher taxes to produce a larger surplus to avoid reducing the face value of the debt they hold. If foreigners take the same haircut as before, the country's debt-to-GDP ratio falls from 100 to 75 percent. Domestic investors still hold debt worth 50 percent of GDP, while foreigners now hold debt equal to 25 percent of GDP. The primary balance required to stabilize the debt ratio is higher, since the debt level is higher—6 percent of GDP. Formally, scenarios 1 and 2 treat both domestic and external investors the same, even though the second scenario does not impose a haircut on domestic creditors. In both cases, foreigners hold debt equal to 25 percent of GDP after the restructuring, and 2 percent of GDP is allocated to service this external debt. Domestic investors are also agreeing to the same losses: A large domestic haircut implies that the full burden of domestic adjustment is being born upfront in the form of a capital levy

(box 7.1 continues next page)

a little, then bank capital can be written down and depositors can be kept whole without any injection of taxpayer funds. If the fall in the value of the bank's assets exceeds bank capital, in theory, depositors need to take a haircut. Yet they rarely do. Banks play a key role in the payments system, and an uncontrolled bank run triggered by fears of losses among depositors is economically devastating. Consequently, the government almost always steps in to protect bank depositors from losses in the event of a systemic crisis, even in the absence of formal deposit insurance.

Governments typically bail out banks by giving them—perhaps in exchange for a portion of the banks' equity—a government bond of sufficient value to balance the banks' liabilities and assets. These long-term bonds are a way of protecting deposits from losses by shifting the losses onto future taxpayers. If the domestic banking system holds a large amount of domestic debt and the government wants to protect depositors from losses, a haircut on domestic debt implies the issuance of more domestic debt to bail out the banks. Consequently, imposing an equal haircut on foreign bonds and the domestic bonds held by local financial institutions only increases the amount of new domestic debt that the government will have to issue to fi-

Box 7.1 *(continued)*

while a larger primary surplus implies that the same loss is spread over time.[2] The size of the primary balance devoted to service the foreign debt determines the size of the foreign haircut, regardless of how domestic losses are allocated over time.

Let us take the discussion a step further. Suppose that foreign creditors convince the country that a 50 percent haircut on their debt is too much, and the country agrees to impose a proportional haircut of 25 percent on both foreign and domestic creditors. The debt ratio then falls to 75 percent: Foreign creditors hold debt equal to 37.5 percent of GDP, as do domestic creditors. A primary balance of 6 percent of GDP is now required to sustain the higher debt burden that emerges from a smaller haircut (scenario 3). Relative to scenario 2, the country is running the same 6 percent primary balance, and external creditors are taking a smaller haircut. This is possible because domestic investors are in effect agreeing to accept larger losses. Half of the 6 percent primary balance, or 3 percent of GDP, is devoted to servicing the foreign debt, relative to only 2 percent of GDP in the previous two scenarios. In scenarios 2 and 3, the country is running a 6 percent of GDP primary balance, but the 6 percent primary balance in the second scenario was predicated on the need to spread the *domestic* losses in the first scenario over time, not on the need to do more domestic adjustment to service external debt.

1. Here we assume that the average domestic creditor is equivalent to the average domestic taxpayer. This is true on average, but individual differences imply only some domestic redistribution.

2. On an NPV basis, a 50 percent haircut and a primary balance that increases from 0 to 4 percent leads to an equivalent loss to domestic residents as a primary balance goes from 0 to 6 percent and no haircut.

nance the bank bailout. Reducing the value of banks' holdings of domestic government bonds—so long as explicit or implicit government deposit insurance fully backs the banks—provides almost no debt reduction for the government.[28] If depositors cannot take losses and bank capital is exhausted, then taxpayers have to bear the burden of bailing out the banks.

In theory, the effective haircut that foreign investors suffer is equal in the following two scenarios:

- Foreign investors are discriminated against in the debt restructuring and receive worse terms than domestic banks holding the same bonds;
- Foreign investors are not discriminated against, and both domestic banks and foreign investors receive the same terms, but a much higher average haircut is required since the resulting bank bailout will re-

28. The same argument holds if the haircut is imposed on the government debt holdings of pension funds whose benefits are defined. Unless the government wants and can impose a capital levy on the workers who are entitled to these assets, any haircut on these claims will become another liability for the government.

quire the government to issue new debt to protect bank depositors from losses.

The advantages appearing to treat all creditors the same and then recapitalizing the banking system have to be balanced against the advantages of avoiding the bankruptcy costs associated with a systemic bank restructuring. Restructuring all debts avoids protecting both wealthy domestic holders of domestic debts and the banks' equity owners from the pain of a restructuring. However, pushing the entire banking system into insolvency through a comprehensive restructuring is also costly. Restructuring all debt on equal terms increases the odds of a deposit run.[29] It is easier for the government to tell depositors not to worry if banks' debts are being excluded than to explain that it will issue more debt to make up any losses in the banking system from a debt restructuring.

One could certainly argue that domestic depositors should bear some of the burden in a sovereign debt crisis and that the government should improve its own solvency by imposing a capital levy on the financial wealth of all bank depositors. While domestic debt is rarely restructured on the same terms as external debt, domestic debt is usually restructured in severe crises, and bank depositors often take losses. Deposit freezes, forced conversion of foreign-currency deposits into local-currency deposits (pesification) and of deposits into longer-term bonds (at a market value well below par), and caps on the interest rates provided to frozen deposits are all ways of imposing a haircut on bank deposits.

The choice between imposing a tax on bank depositors and asking external creditors for additional debt relief illustrates well the basic arguments for giving more favorable treatment to domestic debts. Bank depositors are likely to see their real incomes fall no matter what as domestic output falls and may also bear most of the burden of the tax increases and spending cuts needed to improve the government's fiscal position. As long as the amount of pain that domestic agents, including bank depositors, are willing to take is limited, only the country's nonresident creditors can bear the residual adjustment burden. Of course, this creates problems when there is a large gap between the amount of "pain" domestic agents

29. From an intertemporal perspective, a country's ability to service its defaulted external debt is independent of whether the depositors accept a capital levy or not. A haircut or capital levy on deposits results in immediate losses for domestic residents. If there is no deposit haircut, then the banks will have to be recapitalized with recapitalization bonds that have to be serviced over time through higher taxes/revenues. From an intertemporal point of view, the domestic burden of an immediate capital levy on deposits should be equal to the discounted value of the higher future taxes needed to pay for bank recapitalization (leaving aside distribution effects). Consequently, external creditors should not necessarily care how the country decides to resolve the insolvency of its banking system. If the average taxpayer is also the average depositor, this intertemporal shift of the burden has no domestic distributional consequences. Realistically, some redistribution of wealth will occur in the two alternative scenarios, as individual depositors may differ from the average taxpayer.

are willing to bear—whether through more fiscal adjustment or a deeper domestic debt restructuring—and that international investors are willing to accept. Unless the two sides reach agreement on how to apportion the economic loss, no deal is possible. Deals where creditors pretend that they will be paid what they think they deserve at some point in the future and where debtors pretend that these payments can be made without any additional adjustment carry a high risk of sowing the seeds for future trouble.

The final balance between domestic adjustment of all sorts and external debt relief will reflect the economic, political, and legal leverage of all parties in the process. Chapter 8 emphasizes that the legal leverage of external creditors is limited so long as the debtor is willing to incur the economic costs (loss of external market access and difficulty attracting new domestic as well as external investment) of prolonged default. Domestic creditors may not have greater legal leverage but typically do have greater political leverage: Any elected government is likely to prefer prolonged external default to a prolonged domestic bank holiday. Domestic creditors also are a far more likely source of new financing than external creditors. Finally, domestic creditors often—though not always—have less diversified portfolios than the average international investor.[30] They consequently often have a greater stake in the outcome of the restructuring.[31] The equilibrium between domestic and external adjustment—and the relative priority attached to paying different sets of claims—will reflect the government's perception of the relative costs and benefits of all these factors.

A Real World Example: Argentina

Argentina offers a concrete example of many of the issues already discussed.

- *blurring the lines between domestic and external debt before the crisis.* Argentina entered its crisis with a relatively large stock of external-law bonds and a relatively small stock of domestic-law debt. Domestic banks, pension funds, and individual Argentines were large holders of Argentina's external-law bonds. During its crisis, Argentina con-

30. An investor holding a diversified portfolio of emerging-market debt can absorb large losses at one point in time in one emerging-market economy without necessarily taking overall losses. Indeed, studies (such as a recent one by Klingen, Weder, and Zettelmeyer 2004) suggest that over long horizons, emerging-market investors receive on average returns equal to a risk-free rate asset such as US Treasury bonds. In 2001, returns on the emerging-market bond index (EMBI) were positive despite Argentina's default.

31. There are cases, though, where some external investors have a less diversified portfolio than some domestic investors. A retail Italian investor that put—unwisely—all its savings into Argentine bonds may have more "Argentine" exposure than a wealthy Argentine with a large offshore bank account, of which only a small proportion was invested in Argentina's external debt.

verted much of its external-law debt into domestic-law debt through a "eurobonds for guaranteed loans" swap and added to its domestic-law debt by issuing new compensation bonds (Bodens) to make up for the banks' losses. Domestic investors, however, are estimated to hold at least 40 percent of Argentina's remaining external-law bonds.

- *difficulties assessing equity: When should the clock start?* During the latter part of 2000 and throughout 2001, Argentina could not raise funds abroad. However, it could still place significant quantities of new external-law bonds with its domestic banks and pension funds. Funds raised domestically—along with IMF lending—helped to finance interest payments as well as the repayment of maturing principal on the portion of Argentina's external-law debt that was held abroad. Domestic residents were effectively forced to increase their exposure to the government of Argentina even as international bondholders were reducing their exposure. After Argentina's default, however, the domestic debt holders that accepted the restructuring terms implicit in the "pesification" have been paid while the external-law bonds remain in default. External creditors can complain that Argentina has given preference to domestic debt after its default; domestic creditors can legitimately respond that Argentina's crisis started well before its external default and that the "clock" should have started ticking when funds raised domestically were used to pay external creditors.

- *limiting the banking system's losses after a sovereign default.* Argentina's crisis was so severe that it was impossible to protect bank depositors from any losses. After Argentina's default, its domestic-law debt, including the guaranteed loans that were created in a "bonds for domestic loans" swap only weeks before, was redenominated from dollars into pesos by government decree. Even though domestic bank deposits were converted into pesos at a relatively favorable 1 to 1.4 peso exchange rate and then indexed for inflation, depositors clearly have taken losses. Those who kept their claims in the banking system after the deposit freeze was lifted now have a deposit worth about 60 cents rather than a dollar—and those who pulled their funds out at the height of the crisis often took larger losses. Yet there is also little doubt that Argentina has put a higher priority on resolving its domestic banking crisis than on resolving its external-debt crisis and has sought to limit the scale of losses domestic depositors have borne. The banks' domestic debts have been serviced according to the new restructuring terms while other debt has remained in default. The government also has issued new debt (Bodens) to avoid the need for depositors to take larger losses as a result of Argentina's household and corporate debt crisis.

- *the difficulty in solving a debt problem by default if domestic banks hold large amounts of debt.* Ironically, while the government of Argentina defaulted in part because it had too much debt, its default has resulted in an increase in its overall debt stock. Since Argentina's debts have increased by more than its capacity to pay, it has divided its debt into two categories—one group that has been given priority and another that has not. Argentina paid the IFIs, the banks' pesified guaranteed loans (before being restructured twice, these claims were international bonds) as well as the new Bodens thoroughout its crisis. It has been in default on bonds held by external investors and by Argentina's pension funds since early 2002. (An exchange offer for these bonds is expected in the fall of 2004.)

- *the difficulties in resolving a systemic banking crisis.* Argentina had both a sovereign crisis and as a result of its private firms' extensive dollar-denominated debts, a systemic corporate crisis. Argentina moved preemptively to solve its domestic corporate payments crisis by converting domestic bank loans into pesos at a favorable 1 to 1 exchange rate. The gap between the 1 to 1 conversion rate on banks' loans and the 1 to 1.4 conversion rate on deposits initially resulted in large paper losses in the banking system, but the government subsequently picked up most of the tab by giving the banks new bonds to compensate them for their losses in this "asymmetric pesification." Many have criticized the asymmetric pesification. However, those who blame pesification or asymmetric pesification for the financial chaos of the crisis are confusing cause with effect. Almost all Argentine households and firms had more dollar debt than they could pay following the devaluation. Systemic corporate and banking crises are always costly, and the restructuring process itself is almost always politicized. Large financial losses need to be apportioned among important domestic constituencies: domestic depositors, domestic taxpayers, beneficiaries of government spending, domestic banks, and domestic businesses.[32]

The last point is worth exploring in more depth, because the cost of Argentina's domestic banking and corporate crisis has dramatically increased Argentina's debt stock. There are two distinct issues. First, could a different way of resolving Argentina's domestic crisis have reduced the overall losses associated with its crisis? Second, could losses have been allocated in a different way, so that Argentina's taxpayers—and perhaps its external creditors—picked up a smaller tab?

In our view, the large losses of Argentina's banking system—losses that the banks' owners, bank depositors, or taxpayers had to absorb—are not primarily the result of pesification or even the asymmetries of the pesification process. Any banking system that has lent to domestic borrowers in dollars—or another external currency—takes large losses in the event

32. In Argentina, external investors owned many local banks and local utilities with large dollar debts—a fact that would have complicated any process for resolving the country's domestic crisis.

of a major currency depreciation. Argentina had a particularly large problem because its domestic dollar debts were unusually large and its export sector was unusually small (Goldstein and Turner 2004). It is, of course, impossible to know for sure if the losses from pesification are larger, smaller, or equal to the losses that would have occurred if dollar claims had remained in dollars and been restructured. Yet there is good reason to believe that keeping all bank loans in dollars would have been as costly, in aggregate.

Indeed, if all domestic loans had been kept in dollars and the peso/dollar exchange had still fallen from 1 to 3 (or even a bit less), almost all the financial assets of the banking system—loans to the government, provinces, households, and firms—would have fallen into default.[33] This would have put immeasurable strain on the banking system, the domestic bankruptcy system, and many small firms and households. The resulting restructuring process would have been both lengthy and costly. Individual debt renegotiation is slow: Large domestic Argentine firms who borrowed from abroad and thus did not benefit from pesification generally were still in default at the end of 2003—two years after the crisis. Moreover, it is unrealistic to believe that the government would not have been drawn into the process of renegotiating household mortgage and small business loans. Some across-the-board solution was clearly needed for small borrowers, and deciding who should get how much relief—and who should bear the associated costs—would have been politically paralyzing even if the debts had initially remained in dollars.

Another option would have been to keep domestic loans in dollars but to reduce all dollar debts by a fixed percentage. This option, however, is not all that different from pesification. One to one pesification is similar to a two-thirds haircut of the face value of all domestic dollar debts. Argentina could have kept debts in dollars and imposed a smaller haircut. However, there is no guarantee that this would have reduced overall losses.[34] In the face of a deep recession, less debt relief would have implied some additional firms and households could not service their debts.[35] The

33. Pesification prevented domestic loans to the government and provinces from falling into default, though the new debt carries a low interest rate. Households, consumers, and small businesses whose debts were pesified are generally paying on their peso debt. Argentina's banking system still has problems—the yield on government debt is low, and probably below the average long-run cost Argentine banks will need to pay on their deposits. Many big Argentine firms also remain in default. They cannot resume payments on their domestic debts before reaching agreement on restructuring terms with their external creditors.

34. Pesifying both domestic loans and deposits at a 1 to 1.4 rate would have reduced the size of the across-the-board haircut—and probably resulted in a higher ratio of nonperforming loans. Pesifying both domestic loans and deposits at a 1 to 1 rate would have provided borrowers the same relief but imposed bigger losses on bank depositors.

35. Remember that the revenues of domestic firms without export revenues increased in line with the growth of nominal domestic GDP, so pesification did not necessarily reduce the real value of their debts by two-thirds.

marginal cost of pushing additional households and firms into bankruptcy should not be underestimated: Bankruptcy itself is costly, and an unresolved debt overhang can destroy value. Some firms that paid their pesified debts in full—and effectively paid their original dollar debts in part—would not have paid anything at all for an extended period. Providing debt relief through one to one pesification produced winners and losers (sometimes arbitrarily); it was done in a haphazard way and like all across-the-board solutions, provided some debtors with more relief than they needed and others with less. However, the scale of Argentina's domestic debt problem was such that it is not clear that any alternative solution would have reduced the overall size of the financial loss—though undoubtedly it could have produced a different set of winners and losers.[36]

The second question is the distribution of the resulting loss. It is hard to see how more of the loss could be passed on to the Argentine banks' owners. The restructuring process effectively wiped out all of the banking system's existing capital and inflicted large losses on the banks' owners (often major international banks).[37] The government has had to issue new bonds to the banks to offset the losses created by the asymmetries in the pesification process precisely because foreign bank owners otherwise would have walked away, leaving the government in control of almost the entire banking system. If providing less debt relief to domestic debtors would have led only to larger losses from nonperforming loans, as we have argued, then reducing the costs that taxpayers picked up would have required shifting more of the costs on to domestic depositors. The "asymmetric" part of asymmetric pesification was a way of limiting the domestic

36. Indeed, the Argentine pesification was not substantially different from the US decision to repudiate the gold clause when the country went off the gold peg in 1931, and the dollar depreciated against gold by two-thirds. The US Supreme Court upheld the repudiation of the gold clause in 1935. Without such repudiation, large segments of the corporate and business sectors whose debts were contractually linked to the value of gold would have gone bankrupt. Argentina "dedollarized" its domestic debts, and the United States "degoldized" its domestic debts. See Kroszner (1998) for more details.

37. The overall impact of the steps Argentina has taken to restructure its banking system on the interest of the banks' foreign owners is complicated, since some steps helped the banks' owners and hurt others. While the asymmetries in pesification initially imposed large losses on the banks' owners, but the banks subsequently have been largely, though not yet fully, compensated for the effects of asymmetric pesification. Some banks are probably better off with pesified deposits, a performing pesified loan, and a compensation bond than a nonperforming, dollar loan, and dollar deposits. Foreign-owned banks may have been hurt more by the freeze on utility tariffs, which has damaged the financial health of many of their most important clients, than by asymmetric pesification plus compensation. Moreover, the government's overall approach to the resolution of the banking crisis undoubtedly has had a large and often unexpected impact on the competitive position and balance sheets of different banks. The government has not used the crisis to close, consolidate, intervene, or otherwise restructure a number of publicly owned banks that went into the crisis in poor financial condition, and bank regulators have not forced the closure of weak, domestically owned private banks.

depositors' losses by having taxpayers pick up the difference between the conversion rate on bank deposits and bank loans. Asymmetric pesification is not all that different from reducing all dollar deposits by a smaller percentage than all bank loans, with taxpayers making up the difference.

Politically, though, it seems unlikely that it would have been possible to increase the losses borne by domestic bank depositors through a different domestic bank restructuring process. Most bank depositors do not believe that they are the beneficiaries of Argentina's system of assigning priority. Rather, they believe that they have taken unwarranted losses because the banks failed to honor their dollar deposits in full. This highlights our broader argument: If Argentina had kept the bank deposits in dollars (or converted dollar deposits into peso deposits fully indexed to the dollar), depositors would have borne fewer upfront losses while the government of Argentina would have had an even larger bank bailout bill. Rather than taking losses upfront, Argentines would have spread the banking system's losses over time, through higher taxes and less government spending to pay for the bank bailout. On the other hand, had the banks not been recapitalized through the compensation process and had depositors taken a larger haircut, depositors would have less financial wealth, the government of Argentina would have a smaller domestic debt stock, and Argentina would have less need to either reduce government services or increase taxes to pay its debts.

External creditors argue that they—and not future Argentine taxpayers—are currently being asked to pay some of the cost of the bank bailout: Argentina is asking external creditors to agree to a large haircut to make Argentina's debt stock compatible with its current fiscal effort. This argument has a grain of truth but also makes a number of assumptions that should be laid out explicitly. A larger deposit haircut helps external creditors only if there is no offsetting reduction in the size of the primary surplus that Argentines are willing to run. Less domestic debt and the same primary adjustment imply that more of the primary adjustment would be available to provide the fiscal resources (though not the foreign exchange) needed to support a higher level of external debt service. However, it is entirely possible that a bigger domestic haircut would result in a reduction in Argentina's political willingness to adjust, a smaller primary surplus, and no more resources for external debt service.

Concluding Remarks on Domestic Debt

A sensible system of priorities should recognize that domestic and external debt have a number of important economic differences and that this may call for different—and sometimes better—treatment of certain domestic financial claims. Domestic debt restructuring is effectively a tax on one kind of domestic financial wealth and should be considered part of the internal adjustment the debtor needs to make to restore itself to solvency, not part of the external debt restructuring. However, our argument for treating domestic debt differently from external debt is not an argument that the debtor should avoid making any domestic adjustments. The overall domestic adjustment effort that the bankrupt country makes and the concessions external creditors provide should be balanced. A bankrupt sovereign that pushed all the costs on its external creditors to avoid any domestic adjustment would obviously fail to provide the needed balance. The case for treating domestic debt better is that domestic residents are adjusting in other ways, not that external creditors should spare a crisis country's residents from any painful domestic adjustment.

The economic case for treating domestic debt differently than external debt is particularly persuasive if the financial system holds a large share of the domestic debt. The economic disruption associated with the total collapse of the domestic financial system is well worth avoiding. However, there are also limits to how much the sovereign can favor the domestic banking system. Domestic debts often need to be rescheduled to address liquidity problems, and if the domestic debt stock is large, then domestic holders of government debt also will likely need to accept a reduction in their financial wealth as part of the overall domestic adjustment required to restore sustainability. If domestic banks hold all the government's debt, then it is obvious that domestic debt the banks hold cannot be fully protected from losses.

Arguments in Favor of a Formal Debt Seniority Regime

The uncertainties about the relative priority accorded to different claims on a sovereign in the current sovereign debt restructuring process—uncertainties that are obvious in Argentina—have prompted a number of calls to develop a clearer system of priorities for sovereign claims.[38] Proponents of reform argue that a set of more defined priorities would improve on the current nonregime in several ways:

- First, the ambiguity in the current system makes it much harder to rapidly reach agreement on a needed debt restructuring. The system of priorities in a bankruptcy regime makes both the debt restructuring more orderly ex post and the relative treatment of different claims more predictable ex ante (Gelpern, 2004). In the absence of an agreed, enforceable system of priorities, different groups of creditors and the debtor have to agree (whether explicitly or by default) on the relative priority that should be given to different sets of claims before they can negotiate actual financial terms.

38. See Zettelmeyer (2003) and Gelpern (2004) for thoughtful discussions of seniority issues.

- Second, the current system risks encouraging hard-to-restructure debt contracts. Creditors can game the system by hoping the debtor will give informal priority to instruments that are legally hard to restructure.[39] Providing formal seniority to the various sovereign debt claims might allow the development of instruments that make debt restructuring less messy (Zettelmeyer 2003).

- Third, the lack of a formal seniority structure in sovereign debt can distort the sovereign's incentive to manage its debt wisely (Bolton 2003, Bolton and Skeel 2003, Paasche and Zin 2001). The absence of a first to lend, first to be paid—or first in time—priority structure can lead to sovereign overborrowing. The first creditor who lends to a sovereign debtor would prefer that the sovereign not take on any more debt, thus assuring that the initial creditor would have an exclusive claim on the sovereign's debt-servicing capability. Additional loans from other creditors dilute the value of the first creditor's claim unless every new loan results in an equal increase in the debtor's overall ability to pay. The first lender will anticipate this risk and therefore charge the sovereign more, while later creditors will charge less than they should because they can appropriate some of the sovereign's debt-servicing capacity from earlier creditors. The lender's inability to control later borrowing imposes an externality on earlier borrowing. If earlier claims had greater seniority than later claims, the spread on the initial debt would be lower and that on later debt would be higher. This would reduce a sovereign's incentives to overborrow.

Obstacles to the Creation of a More Defined System of Priorities

Difficulty in agreeing on the relative priority that should be given to different claims on the sovereign is certainly a major impediment to rapid agreement on a restructuring. Yet the conceptual and practical obstacles to creating an explicit seniority system for sovereign debt are profound.

Diversity of Sovereign Debt

The main obstacle is the sheer breadth and complexity of the financial claims on the sovereign and more broadly, the number of "stakeholders" that have an economic interest in how the sovereign's difficulties are resolved. Ranking the seniority of all the explicit claims on the sovereign (domestic and external debt and within external debt, the claims of dif-

39. The best example of this may be Nigeria's Brady bonds, which have several features that would make Nigeria usually vulnerable to the risk of litigation, should it default on its Brady bonds. On the other hand, Nigeria traditionally has had other reasons to pay its Brady bonds while running arrears to the Paris Club. Wealthy Nigerians, including former President Abacha's family, reportedly had large holdings of Nigeria's Brady bonds.

ferent groups of private and official creditors) is itself a daunting task. However, ranking explicit claims is not enough. There would still be a need to figure out the relative seniority of explicit and implicit debt—such as pension claims and guaranteed deposits—as well as the priority to be given to paying debt relative to supporting government spending and keeping taxes from rising. Specifying in advance the right balance between increasing taxes, reducing government spending, reducing current and future pension liabilities, imposing losses on depositors, reducing domestic debt, reducing external debt held by private creditors, and reducing external debt held by official—bilateral and multilateral—creditors is next to impossible.

The existence of so many creditors, claimants, and stakeholders makes the resolution of any sovereign debt and financial crisis eminently a political process that does not lend itself to simple legal rules. This is particularly true for ranking the sovereign's domestic liabilities, which, as discussed, can involve choosing between paying police salaries and paying bank depositors.

Is a Seniority System Enforceable?

A related issue is the enforceability of any formal seniority scheme. In the corporate context, a bankruptcy judge can use the power of the state to prevent discriminatory payments to junior claimants and can exercise considerable control over the distressed debtor's assets. No one has similar power over a sovereign in distress. As discussed in the next chapter, the difficulty in initiating successful litigation against a sovereign provides it with substantial freedom of action. This potentially includes the freedom to ignore a formal seniority scheme. The difficulties in enforcing a formal system of debt seniority are particularly acute with respect to domestic debts.

The inability to liquidate a sovereign and distribute the proceeds from liquidation according to defined rules of *absolute* priority is not the crucial barrier to the creation of a system of sovereign priorities. The bigger barrier is the absence of a supranational power that can enforce a system of *relative* priorities (Gelpern 2004). Domestic bankruptcy law can set out a priority structure for semisovereign public entities, including subnational governments that, like a sovereign, cannot be liquidated. US law allows creditors to seek a court order forcing a municipal debtor to increase taxes to fund debt service, even if this has been very hard to do in practice. However, there is a difference between a municipal debtor that is subject to national law and a sovereign.[40] Sovereign countries have a degree of independence that exceeds the legal independence of US states, and US states, unlike US municipalities, are not subject to federal bankruptcy law.

40. Black's Law Dictionary (6th ed., 1990) defines sovereignty as a "supreme, absolute and uncontrollable power by which any independent state is governed."

A sovereign not subject to external enforcement might nonetheless conclude that following an established system of priorities is in its own interest. Sovereigns do care about their reputation and failing to follow a generally accepted seniority system would likely damage their future ability to borrow. Sovereigns, for example, have found it in their interest to pay the IMF and World Bank even when this has required sacrifices, in part because of the reputational costs of trying to change the "rules of the game." If the formal ranking were enshrined in national laws, then a national court might be able to issue an enforceable legal order that stopped discriminatory payments to junior creditors if more senior creditors were not being paid. Of course, such a remedy would be effective only if the sovereign were making payments to more junior domestic debt holders. Senior creditors have few remedies if the debtor simply refuses to pay anyone. Finally, official creditors that currently lend to a sovereign in distress on the strength of their preferred status—notably the IMF—could use the leverage that comes from their new lending to strengthen incentives to respect a defined system of priorities. The IMF might be willing to lend into arrears if the country had defaulted on its debts but not if the country also "defaulted" on the established system of priorities.

Proposals for a More Defined System of Sovereign Priorities

Most proposals to make the priority given to different sovereign debts more explicit set aside the relative treatment of external and domestic debt and of private and official debt and instead focus on the creation of an explicit seniority regime for the sovereign's private external debt. This focus makes it much easier to define and enforce a clear system of priorities even as the more limited coverage limits the impact the new system of priorities would have on the restructuring process. A number of these suggestions warrant further examination.

Bolton-Skeel Proposal: First to Lend, First to Be Paid

Patrick Bolton and David Skeel (2003) have proposed the creation of a simple system of seniority where debt issued earlier would be senior to debt issued later. This "first-in-time" priority system would eliminate the incentives sovereigns have to dilute their capacity to pay existing debt by taking on additional debt. Such a proposal would no doubt achieve its intended objective of hindering overborrowing.

However, this particular proposal has shortcomings. First, it would fundamentally change the way sovereign debt trades in the secondary market. The date of issuance would matter more than the bond's residual maturity. This means, for example, that a new five-year bond would be worth less (because of its lower position in the pecking order) than a ten-year bond that was issued five years ago and that has a residual maturity of five years. This would make constructing a sovereign yield curve difficult, since the standard yield curve implicitly assumes that all bonds that make up the curve have the same priority. Other technical issues to consider include the treatment of debt issued in voluntary debt exchanges for outstanding long-maturity debt. No doubt the markets could adjust to these new rules, but it may not be easy.

Second, junior creditors who are lending at a later point in time would have a strong incentive to find other ways of protecting themselves from losses. Markets adapt (Lipsworth and Nystedt 2001). Junior creditors may insist that their claims carry a short maturity. A first-in-time priority rule risks creating a bifurcated sovereign debt market, with some long-term senior debt that benefits from formal priority, some very short-term junior debt, and perhaps very little in between. Consequently, giving formal seniority risks creating incentives to increase the use of forms of debt that make rollover/liquidity crisis more likely.

Third, making the new system work would likely require additional rules. The first-in-time priority rule would have exceptions. For example, as will be discussed in detail in the next chapter, most bankruptcy regimes granted seniority to new financing to facilitate the operational and financial adjustments required by a distressed debtor that is undergoing a financial reorganization. Since the IMF performs an analogous role in the sovereign context, presumably it would continue to receive some form of priority. Indeed, the denial of IMF financing would likely be central to the enforcement of priorities in a world of sovereign states.

Moreover, other rules may be needed to protect the intent of the priority structure. For example, some bankruptcy regimes require that firms in the "zone of insolvency" be managed to protect the interest of senior creditors and even give them a claim on payments made to more junior creditors just before a formal bankruptcy declaration. The sovereign world has a similar problem. A country that runs down its reserves to pay short-maturity junior debt just before default effectively damages—by depleting its reserves—the interest of its long-term creditors in the process. However, so long as the sovereign has not missed a payment before formal default, the formal seniority granted to long-term debt issued far in the past offers creditors no protection against this risk. Taking steps to limit the risk of the sovereign acting against the interest of its senior, long-term creditors could require introducing an additional layer of complexity. A regime that did not limit the risk of a sovereign fully depleting its reserves by making payments to junior creditors before default would still work but with less effective protection for senior creditors.[41]

41. The same basic argument could be extended to other uses of the sovereign's reserves. Intervention in the foreign exchange market, for example, could deplete sovereign reserves before default, damaging the interest of long-term creditors—as could lender-of-last-resort lending to the domestic banking system facing a run out of dollar deposits.

Finally, a first-in-time rule makes it cheaper for a policymaker that inherits a low debt load to engage in a borrowing binge.[42] Consequently, a policymaker with a bias toward fiscal irresponsibility would have a strong incentive to issue as much cheap debt as possible early on. (Bolton and Skeel would give all debt issued in a given year the same priority.) At the limit, overborrowing would be accelerated rather than reduced. Problems with time consistency are an even bigger obstacle for other proposals to limit sovereign overborrowing. For example, some have suggested that a sovereign should commit to an upper limit on its debt stock (either absolute or a share of GDP) to lower borrowing costs. If the promise not to borrow above a limit actually lowered current borrowing costs, it might just encourage those policymakers to borrow more upfront (Zettelmeyer 2003). Realistically, though, there is no way to prevent later policymakers from exceeding the proposed limit.

Soros Proposal: International Deposit Insurance Agency

Other proposals would provide seniority to part of the external debt issued by a sovereign in order to limit the risk of a liquidity crisis. For example, George Soros (1998; "Avoiding a Breakdown: Asia's Crisis Demands a Rethink of International Regulation," *Financial Times*, December 3, 1997) proposed the creation of an international deposit insurance agency that would insure international investors' claims against default. Soros aims to reduce the risk of investor panics generating self-fulfilling crises of confidence. Fully insured claims would not have any incentive to run. To reduce the risk of moral hazard, Soros suggests that the amount of insurable claims be capped. The IMF would set the ceiling on insured borrowing, and debtor countries would pay the cost of this insurance scheme through an insurance fee.

This proposal has a number of problems.[43] If the insurance fee is actuarially fair and there are no informational failures, then the cost of issuing insured debt would not differ from that of issuing uninsured debt. A fully insured bond would be riskless and have no spread relative to other riskless international bonds. However, the insurance fee should be equal to the spread of that country's uninsured debt. Including the insurance fee, the cost of external borrowing for the country would remain the same.[44]

42. In the Alesina and Tabellini (1990) model of excessive deficits and debt, for example, the sovereign overborrows because a government that may not be in power in the future discounts the welfare of future taxpayers/generations too much.

43. See also Eichengreen (1999) for a thoughtful discussion.

44. If market prices are different from actuarially fair prices, then the debtor may gain or lose. Differences in the relative knowledge or ignorance about fundamental risks between the debtor and market providers of insurance may be a channel through which value is created. But one has to rely on externalities or informational failure to make such an argument.

Of course, setting the right fee structure would be difficult, and there could well be an implicit subsidy. The IMF also would have to protect against the risk that politically important countries would use their leverage to obtain a higher borrowing limit than their fundamentals warrant.[45]

The desire to limit the risk of runs motivated Soros' proposal for the international equivalent of deposit insurance. However, to truly eliminate the risk of runs, a debtor would have to be precluded from issuing uninsured debt in excess of the cap that was set on its insured debt. Uninsured claims would continue to have strong incentives to run.[46] Such debt might be more expensive to issue, and thus countries may issue less of it. Creditors, however, also would have strong incentives to make sure that they had the option to exit from such "uninsured" lending quickly and thus to lend only for relatively short terms. There is no guarantee that the risk of liquidity runs would be reduced—insured claims would not run, but uninsured claims would have strong incentives to get out quickly.

Soros suggested that one benefit of his proposal is that the explicit insurance provided to some claims would make it easier to deny a bailout to those claims that lacked insurance. However, this is not obvious. If letting the country default on its uninsured claims risked a deep crisis in a politically important ally—or risked triggering contagion to other countries that had issued large amounts of uninsured debt—in practice, the IMF or the G-7 might step in and bail out a country having difficulties with its uninsured debt.

The Soros proposal does try to provide seniority in a clear and transparent way and to charge a fair fee for the provision of insurance. Many other proposals to provide sovereign debt with some form of seniority through credit enhancements (collateral, guarantees, or other forms of insurance) are less transparent. These proposals are usually motivated by a desire to help a sovereign that is having difficulty placing unsecured external bonds—whether because of a run, growing doubts about its fundamentals, or unsettled global market conditions—raise additional external financing without generating the appearance of a bailout. They often use partial credit guarantees from the World Bank or other MDBs to engineer a class of semipreferred sovereign debt. These proposals, discussed in

45. A number of other difficult questions would also need to be addressed. For example, the rolloff of cross-border bank lines has been a major source of pressure on the sovereign's own reserves, as most sovereigns step in and protect the banks during a crisis. If the deposit insurance applied only to the sovereign's external borrowing, it would not stop all runs. If private banks were eligible, the insured loan would either need to be explicitly guaranteed by the sovereign, which would assume responsibility for supervising the bank, or the international deposit insurance agency would need to assume some regulatory functions.

46. This shortcoming is common to all proposals that guarantee (or provide collateral for) some claims on a sovereign but not others: Claims that are not guaranteed or enhanced still have an incentive to run.

chapter 6, can be viewed as proposals to introduce a more defined seniority system into a sovereign's external debt in order to help it raise money in times of distress.

If relative seniority has to be provided, it should be done transparently through a conditional IMF loan or a full guarantee from another preferred creditor. However, attempts to create implicit seniority hierarchies through clever financial engineering add more uncertainty into an already uncertain restructuring process.

Gelpern Proposal: Pick Your Own Priority Scheme

Anna Gelpern (2004) has proposed that sovereigns could choose their own system of priorities and make it public by enshrining it in domestic law or private contracts. Some US states have set through a democratic process—either state law or the state's constitutions—a clear structure of payment priorities. These priority systems usually grant absolute priority to some forms of public spending, such as public services and public employees' wages. Should a restructuring be necessary, creditors would negotiate over the tax receipts left over after these payments are made. Countries could, if they wished, create a similar priority regime. This reform would be a step in the direction of clarifying the priority various claims on the sovereign would have in the event of a restructuring. Gelpern does not recommend any particular set of priorities, only that a sovereign define in advance the priorities it thinks would be appropriate.

But even this modest reform may be very hard to implement. First, the number of stakeholders and claims that have to be ranked in a comprehensive priority structure is so large and complex that it may not be possible to set out a simple and efficient set of priorities. The contract setting out priorities may be impossible to write—particularly given all the contingencies that it might need to address explicitly. A simpler priority scheme may not be substantially more efficient than the current system, as many key disputes will not be resolved ex ante. Second, any self-chosen priority regime may not be time-consistent and enforceable. The country may conclude that it is not in its interests to follow its articulated priority structure in the heat of a crisis. The banking system, for example, may hold a large share of the country's junior claims, and following its articulated priority structure would therefore have substantial costs. The credibility of any self-chosen priority regimes will remain in doubt, since a country can always default on its self-chosen priorities. Third, a sovereign default and restructuring is more complex than even the restructuring of a US state's debts. Subnational entities, even sovereign states, usually don't issue their own currency, back their banking systems through deposit insurance, have large implicit liabilities from massive social security obligations for all their citizens (local public employee pension schemes are often fully funded), or have the ability to impose capital controls to limit tax-evading capital flight. The priority structures of US states have not been tested by an actual restructuring—and may never be. The US government would probably not let a state like California default.

Incentives for a country to follow its own system of priorities could be strengthened by denying IMF lending to a country that does not follow its own system. But IMF enforcement has its own difficulties. The IMF's own prior exposure constrains its leverage—denying IMF financing to a sovereign that has defaulted on its own priority structure could result in a default on the IMF. Even setting aside the IMF's interests as a creditor, it may be better off using its limited leverage to improve a country's macroeconomic policy framework rather than forcing a country to stick to its priority structure. The details of the priority structure will likely be contested, and the IMF may even conclude, for example, that protecting the country's banking system is more important than religiously following any preexisting priority structure. The international community's interest, writ broadly, would be better served by helping the country recover rather than punish it for failing to live up to its self-defined system of priorities.[47]

Still, Gelpern's proposal has greater merit and fewer costs than proposals for more radical reform. It could force a sovereign to make its priorities in default explicit, and once priorities are made explicit, the reputational cost of defaulting on an articulated priority structure would be increased. Too many high-risk sovereigns prefer to think that default is unthinkable and that no contingency plan for a default is needed. Yet even if sovereigns are expected to lay out its intended system of priorities, the risk of a sovereign concluding that it is not in its interest to follow its self-chosen priority regime is real.

Conclusion

The absence of well-defined rules of priority clearly is a source of uncertainty for investors following a sovereign default. Sovereigns have substantial—though certainly not unlimited—freedom to determine ex post the priority structure that is in their interest. Investors who base investment decisions on the types of debt instruments that were favored in the previous restructurings will often be disappointed. Since holding patterns vary, the type of instruments that get relative priority also tends to vary. Look at the difference between Russia and Argentina's external bonds. Russia paid external bonds issued after the fall of the Soviet Union in full and on time even as it nearly wiped out the real value of its domestic debt and obtained significant concessions from holders of its Soviet-era exter-

47. Gelpern (2004) in the end recommends only that sovereigns be encouraged to lay out their own priority structures and that the IMF report on the sovereigns' adherence to their self-selected structures as part of its surveillance process.

nal debt. Argentina more or less has proposed doing the opposite. It is seeking a larger haircut from its external bondholders than it imposed—through a series of restructurings—on the domestic-law debt held by its banking system.

The core question in the debate on sovereign priorities is whether it is possible to develop a system that both can be enforced and substantially improves on the status quo. We are skeptical.

The current system has its own logic and its own norms. Experienced market participants know that the IFIs have effective priority as a result of the IFIs' role as providers of new money in a crisis and that this priority is sustained in part because the IFIs are typically willing to roll over their positions for some time. Savvy market participants also know that a sovereign is likely to go into arrears on Paris Club debt before it suspends payments on its privately held debt, since the risk of enforcement actions from Paris Club creditors is negligible. Long-term syndicated bank loans and international sovereign bonds are both likely to be restructured if the sovereign has significant amounts of bonds and loans outstanding. It is hard for a sovereign seeking deep debt reduction to exclude some of its international bonds entirely from the restructuring—one bond issue has no reason to agree to voluntarily subordinate itself to another bond issue. Claims to collateral are likely to be respected. Short-term external debt—including the claims of international banks on local private banks, which are more often than not implicit liabilities of a sovereign—lacks formal seniority but can often get out before the restructuring.

The biggest uncertainties arise as a result of domestically held debt—including foreign-law debt held domestically. The current rules of the game reflect the self-interest of sovereign governments. A government in default will almost always take action to limit the losses depositors bear. The gymnastics that Argentina went through to create a subset of performing domestic debt out of an initial debt stock that was heavy on international bonds are a case in point. Incentives to favor domestic debt are further strengthened by an expectation that it will be easier to regain access to domestic rather than international markets. A restructuring regime that grants the sovereign substantial discretion will almost always result in preferential treatment of debt held by banks or in the creation of performing bank recapitalization bonds to limit the size of any haircut on depositors. This is not bad: We have tried to show that treating the domestic debt restructuring as part of the broad domestic negotiation about how to apportion the burden of domestic adjustment has economic and political logic.

Even if these broad norms are followed, there is no shortage of residual uncertainty. However, a much clearer priority regime may not be possible to design or feasible to enforce, given the scale and complexity of the financial claims on a sovereign and the difficulties forcing a *sovereign* government to follow a priority structure, if it does not believe it reflects its interests. Even radical institutional change, such as the creation of an international bankruptcy regime, might not create a very precise system of sovereign priorities. It is hard to write rules sufficiently precise to avoid the need for interpretation, or rules that creditors would not contest the through the courts.[48]

What really matters is whether relative priority can be assessed ex ante with some reasonable degree of predictability and without an excessively large number of surprises. The current nonsystem could be codified over time. Yet even a real effort to make the existing rules of the game more explicit is unlikely to result in a true system of priorities that defines the relative treatment of all financial claims on the sovereign. Sovereign commitments to constrain their own freedom of action are only credible to a point. The current regime has costs, but its current fuzziness and ambiguity also may be inherent to any regime that deals with sovereign borrowers.

48. See Tarullo (2001) and Gelpern (2004) for the argument that any formal regime would need the authority to make new rules.

8

Legal Reform

Former US Treasury Secretary Paul O'Neill's fall 2001 call for an international bankruptcy court reinvigorated the debate on the best process for restructuring sovereign debts. O'Neill's call was surprising for many reasons: It came from an administration otherwise not noted for its warmth toward international organizations; it seemed at odds with the US Treasury's earlier warnings against official actions that might "encourage default;" and it seemed to reverse long-standing US skepticism toward the creation of an international bankruptcy court.

When the US Treasury did not follow through with a plan outlining what O'Neill had in mind, the IMF's First Deputy Managing Director Anne Krueger (2001a) filled the void. In her November 2001 speech she proposed amending the IMF's Articles of Agreement to provide a sovereign with bankruptcy-style protection from its creditors. In April 2002, in response to criticism that her initial proposal gave the IMF too large a role in granting legal protection, she proposed letting a supermajority of creditors vote to grant the debtor legal protection (Krueger 2002a). However, the US Treasury's enthusiasm for radical reform quickly waned. At the April 2002 conference where Anne Krueger laid out her revised proposals, US Treasury Undersecretary John Taylor called for immediate action to introduce new contractual provisions into sovereign debt contracts—an old idea embraced with new vigor. The IMF's proposals, according to Taylor, offered a fruitful agenda for academic research (Paul Blustein, "IMF Crisis Plan Torpedoed: Treasury Official Rejects Proposal A Day After It Is Advanced," *Washington Post*, April 3, 2002).

The implicit message in Taylor's speech was clear. As was often the case, O'Neill was at odds with the rest of the Bush administration. It was not much of a surprise when the new US treasury secretary, John Snow, signaled that the United States would not support the IMF's proposed blueprint for a sovereign bankruptcy regime. Attention shifted to calls to create a code of conduct that might make it easier for a sovereign debtor to reach agreement with its creditors. The conclusion, at least for the time being, of the political debate over the IMF's bankruptcy proposal—the sovereign debt restructuring mechanism (SDRM) in IMF acronymese—does not make it any less important to understand the issues that arise when a sovereign needs to restructure its debt. The debate over a code of conduct and the right set of contractual changes continues. Calls to create an "international bankruptcy regime" for sovereigns could come back if litigation impedes Argentina's inherently difficult restructuring.

There is a case for reform, but it is more modest than the proponents—and opponents—of either clauses or an international bankruptcy regime usually indicate. Letting a supermajority of creditors vote to change the terms of a sovereign bond—or a series of sovereign bonds—would make it somewhat easier for a sovereign to get out of default or to restructure before falling into default. However, supermajority voting will *not* make default substantially less costly to a sovereign, make a sovereign more willing to opt to restructure, or make it easy for the IMF to refuse requests for official support.

Specifically, we argue the following:

- A de facto—though not de jure—Chapter 11 debt reorganization process for sovereigns' international debt already exists.[1] Sovereigns are not firms. They cannot be liquidated. Debt does not usually become equity following default.[2] "Control" remains in the hands of the sovereign's management—its government—rather than the sovereign's creditors.[3] Litigation cannot easily or quickly shear off the country's

1. Chapter 11 is the portion of US bankruptcy law that governs the reorganization of a debtor that is worth more as an ongoing business; Chapter 7 governs the liquidation of a firm.

2. If a sovereign owns equity in local firms, it can use the "equity" it holds in a state-owned firm to retire some of its debts. Such debt-for-equity swaps were common in the 1980s, though the amounts were small. A sovereign also can issue state-contingent bonds that have "equity-like" features (e.g., GDP-linked bonds). Such bonds would have payments that vary in line with economic conditions, sharing some of the upside and the downside with bond investors. This idea was discussed in chapter 3.

3. Fortunately, or to some unfortunately, "gunboat diplomacy" to take over a deadbeat sovereign and seize its taxes and custom revenues is no longer an option for creditors, unlike in the 19th century. On the other hand, a tool some debtors used to deal with creditors in the past—beheading them—also is currently not available (see Rogoff, Reinhart, and Savastano 2003) for this latter historical curiosum). The increasing difficulty in seizing the assets of a bankrupt sovereign parallels the evolution of corporate bankruptcy regimes, which have also generally evolved over time to favor a firm's reorganization and rehabilitation rather than its immediate liquidation.

sovereign assets to the benefit of its creditors. That sounds a lot like Chapter 11. Sovereign debt restructuring even has something close to debtor-in-possession (DIP) financing—such financing comes from the international financial institutions (IFIs) rather than private creditors.

- Default is costly even though sovereigns currently enjoy substantial effective protection from litigation. It is, quite appropriately, hard to take legal action to seize a country's liquid financial assets, notably its international reserves, after a sovereign defaults on international bonds. Rather default typically leads to a sharp loss of confidence in all of the country's other financial assets—the sovereign's local debt, the local currency, and local bank deposits indirectly backed by the sovereign. These runs are far more likely to trigger a severe loss in output after a sovereign default than litigation.
- The existing process for restructuring the sovereign's external debt is not ideal. The existing stock of New York–law debt that requires unanimity to change the bond's key financial terms makes restructuring more difficult than it should be. The absence of majority-restructuring provisions in many sovereign debt contracts makes holdout strategies viable for a limited number of bondholders. Payments to holdouts are a tax on the restructuring that follows a default, not a tax on default. Of course, making it more expensive to get out of default indirectly makes it more expensive to enter into default. But the benefits of an indirect tax that *may* deter opportunistic defaults are smaller than the disadvantages of legal provisions that make it harder for a sovereign to reach agreement on a restructuring, resume payments, and escape from default.

This chapter is organized into four sections. The first discusses the problems that arise in a sovereign debt restructuring. The second examines proposals for changing the terms of sovereign debt contracts and proposals for creating a supranational bankruptcy regime for sovereigns, focusing in particular on the IMF's plan. The third section looks at calls to create a code of conduct for sovereign debt restructurings and attempts to mandate the use of creditors' committees. The final section evaluates the potential for legal reform to transform the sovereign restructuring process dramatically.

Potential Obstacles to Sovereign Debt Restructuring

As discussed in chapter 4, the absence of an international bankruptcy court has not prevented Ecuador, Ukraine, Pakistan, and Uruguay from restructuring their international sovereign bonds or prevented Russia from restructuring its Soviet-era syndicated bank debt. The absence of collective action clauses also has not been an insurmountable barrier to a restructuring: Ecuador restructured its bonds, which lacked clauses, after its default, and Uruguay even managed to preemptively restructure bonds that lacked clauses in order to avoid a default. The current process for restructuring sovereign bonds can be made to work in a range of circumstances. The case for legal reform has to be that reform can improve on the existing process—not that it is needed to do a restructuring.

Existing Debt Restructuring Process

It can be difficult to determine whether a sovereign government is truly unable to pay or is simply unwilling to make the needed adjustments. At a certain point, though, the debate over willingness to pay and ability to pay becomes moot (discussed in chapter 3). A sovereign that lacks market access will run out of the cash and be unable to pay its maturing debts. Since a sovereign in default cannot be shut down and its assets cannot be distributed among its various creditors, some form of financial reorganization is the only alternative to a prolonged default.

The need to restructure the claims that many creditors hold, in turn, creates a potential collective action problem. Every individual creditor would be better off if it got paid in full while other creditors bore the burden of the restructuring. Potential difficulties with collective action arise with the restructuring of a single bond, since each individual bondholder would prefer to be paid in full while other bondholders agreed to a restructuring. But they also arise at other levels. The holders of a specific bond issue may seek to convince the debtor to exclude their bond from its overall restructuring or may decide not to agree to a restructuring that holders of other bond issues accept and then litigate for full payment. Different groups of creditors—for example, international bondholders, domestic banks, and other governments—will seek to convince the debtor that other groups of creditors should absorb more of the necessary losses. The difficulties that a sovereign faces increase with the number of instruments and the diversity of interests holding a legal claim on the sovereign. Argentina is an extreme case: It needs to restructure 98 international bonds held by a diverse group that includes international institutional investors, domestic pension funds, and hundreds of thousands of retail investors.[4]

The documentation used in international bond contracts can make these coordination problems more difficult to solve. The law of one of four

4. Domestic residents often also buy bonds issued internationally and governed by the law of one of the world's major financial centers. They may prefer a country's international bonds to its local bonds for any of a range of reasons (the use of a foreign currency, the protection of international law, or a more liquid instrument). In countries such as Turkey, Lebanon, and Argentina before 2001, local residents are the primary market for certain international bond issues. Other countries—the United States now but also Russia before 1998—rely heavily on foreign participation in their local debt market.

places governs almost all international sovereign bonds: New York, England, Germany, and Japan. New York state and England are by far the two most important jurisdictions.[5] Japanese law is used almost exclusively for yen-denominated bonds. German law traditionally governed deutsche mark bonds, but English rather than German law increasingly governs euro-denominated bonds.

Differences between the contractual provisions used in New York–law bonds and those used in English-law bonds have been a long-standing point of concern, with many arguing that the standard "boilerplate" documentation used in New York tended to increase the risk of litigation and coordination problems. A traditional New York (and German) bond contract lacked so-called collective action clauses, while a traditional English (and Japanese) bond contract included such clauses. The contractual provisions used in New York before 2003 and England differed in two specific ways.[6] First, many, though not all, New York–law sovereign bond contracts give each individual bondholder the right to initiate litigation and allow each bondholder to keep for itself anything that it recovers from the sovereign. Such provisions increase the incentive to initiate litigation. English-law bonds, in contrast, typically require the support of bondholders who hold at least 25 percent of the bond to initiate litigation, and some English-law bonds also require that the proceeds of any litigation be distributed equally among all bondholders.[7]

Second, most traditional New York- and German-law bond contracts require the unanimous support of all creditors to change a bond's financial terms.[8] Such provisions give each individual bondholder the right to opt

5. Chapter 7 discussed the different ways of defining external debt and argued in favor of a definition based on residency. However, in the specific context of discussing the legal obstacles to a successful debt restructuring, it makes most sense to define international debt as debt governed by a foreign law.

6. The standard documentation used in New York–law bond contracts started to change in spring 2003 after Mexico's decision to introduce provisions allowing supermajority voting in New York–law bonds. Other issuers have followed Mexico's lead, but changing the composition of the existing stock of bonded debt governed by New York law will take time. For the next few years, the average New York–law bond will continue to lack clauses allowing the amendment of the bond's financial terms.

7. See IMF (June 2002b, September 2003b) for a more detailed discussion of such "majority-enforcement clauses."

8. The argument that traditional New York–law bonds lack collective action clauses is only partially correct. While payment dates and amounts can be changed only with the unanimous support of all bondholders, New York–law bonds typically contain provisions that allow the amendment of all of the bonds' terms other than the bonds' key financial terms (payment date and amount) with the support of either 50 percent or two-thirds of the outstanding holders of a debt instrument. In effect, traditional New York–law bonds contain collective action clauses but exempt the bond's key financial terms from these clauses.

out of a restructuring and then litigate to collect the bond's original payment terms in full. English- and Japanese-law bond contracts, in contrast, typically contain clauses that allow a supermajority—often 75 percent of those present at a bondholders' meeting—to amend the bond's key financial terms (Buchheit 2000b).

Difficulties of collective action, whether from a bond's legal documentation or other sources, are the primary source of the potential market failures (externalities, in economic jargon) that could hinder a successful sovereign restructuring. In some stages of the restructuring process, the existing system for sovereign debt restructuring already mitigates or limits these potential collective action problems; at other points in the process, it does not.[9] Consequently, before analyzing proposals for reform, it is worth reviewing the potential market failures that could arise in the sovereign debt restructuring process.

A Rush to Exit from the Sovereign's Own Debt. A creditor holding a claim on a sovereign government has an obvious interest in getting paid and getting out before any sovereign debt restructuring. Creditors holding debts that are about to mature are in a different position than those holding long-term debts. A debtor has a legal obligation to pay its short-term debts in full on the date the debt matures, letting its short-term creditors exit. Indeed, the maturity structure of the sovereign's debt tells creditors rather precisely where they stand in the queue to get out and makes jumping the queue impossible. A creditor holding a long-term claim can sell it only to another market participant. It thus makes sense to distinguish a rush to the exits by creditors with short-term claims from a rush to sell by creditors holding long-term claims. The former puts pressure on the debtor's reserves, the latter on asset prices.

A run on the sovereign's own debt arises when creditors lose confidence in its ability to pay because of lack of reserves, concerns about its solvency, or both. If short-term creditors believe that other creditors won't renew their claims, they have an incentive to get out if the debtor lacks sufficient reserves, even if it is solvent in the long run (Sachs 1995). Creditors with doubts about the debtor's solvency may be willing to roll over their claims if the debtor is willing to pay a high enough interest rate, but the demand for higher returns to compensate for growing perceived risks also can trigger a self-reinforcing cycle that pushes a potentially solvent sovereign into insolvency. High interest rates lead to a growing debt burden and slower growth, and the growing debt burden in turn makes creditors less willing to provide financing at the rates required for eventual solvency or makes them more inclined to get out altogether. A sovereign may find that its

9. See Buchanan (2002) for a market analyst's assessment of the existing debt restructuring process. See Krueger (2002) for the IMF's critique of the current process.

debts are growing faster than its capacity to implement additional adjustments. Moreover, even a run on an insolvent sovereign, while eminently rational from the point of view of an individual creditor, can nonetheless generate a disorderly workout that lowers creditors' collective "recovery" rate.

The solution to a rush for the exits—if no creditor is willing to step in and provide a large loan to an illiquid but potentially solvent sovereign—is simple but brutal: Seek a restructuring, and if a restructuring agreement cannot be reached quickly, then stop paying. In theory, a country should not wait until it runs out of cash to seek to restructure its debts. Waiting until the last possible moment favors a few short-term creditors but disadvantages those with long-term claims. However, a payments suspension has two potential problems:

- First, stopping sovereign payments or seeking a sovereign restructuring risks triggering a broader loss of confidence that may result in a run on the currency or the banking system. The economic distress associated with these other runs will augment the scale of the economic losses. Debtors, not surprisingly, prefer to find a source of emergency financing than to incur the cost associated with default.
- Second, stopping payments means breaching a legal contract. Creditors holding the sovereign's international debt have the right to go to a court to demand full payment. The debtor has no way to force creditors to give up their claims. It needs for its creditors to voluntarily agree to give up their old claims for new ones.

A Rush to the Courthouse (Litigation Before Restructuring). Once a payment is missed and the sovereign debtor is in default, creditors have a legal right to seek various remedies. In principle, creditors can ask the court to attach the debtor's assets. Of course, an insolvent debtor lacks enough assets to go around. This creates a potential collective action problem: The first creditor to go to court gets the asset, leaving the debtor with fewer assets to offer its remaining creditors. To limit this risk, debt contracts often contain provisions to make it possible for a wide range of creditors to initiate litigation as soon as the debtor misses payments to one of them: Cross-default provisions allow creditors to declare their claims to be in default, accelerate, and litigate for the full value of the claim, if the debtor misses a payment on *another* bond.[10] Consequently, as soon as the

10. While these provisions are common in sovereign bond contracts (which initially followed the documentation pattern of US corporate bond issues), they have proven to be a smaller problem in practice than many feared. It makes sense to rush to the courthouse only if the courthouse can seize the debtor's assets. That is typically not the case with sovereigns.

sovereign misses a payment on one bond, it runs the risk of litigation from a wide range of creditors.

In the corporate context, the risk of creditors rushing to the courts rather than working with the debtor to find a cooperative solution motivated the creation of Chapter 11 of the US bankruptcy code. Chapter 11 is designed to protect the debtor (firm) from liquidation by aggressive creditors, while it develops a restructuring plan to keep itself intact.[11]

However, the simple analogy to firms overstates a sovereign's problems. A sovereign's international creditors currently have few effective remedies to pursue in the court system:

- Creditors holding claims in default cannot ask the court to liquidate the sovereign and distribute its assets or seek to gain operational control of the sovereign debtor.
- Creditors can ask the court to seize the sovereign's international assets. But sovereigns typically don't have many assets that can be seized. (A sovereign's most important asset—its power to tax its citizens—is beyond the reach of a foreign court.) A well-advised sovereign can place its international reserves in a place where a US, UK, German, or Japanese court cannot seize them, if it takes a few relatively simple precautions. Central bank immunity remains strong.
- Creditors can ask the court to block payments on other international debts. But the debtor in default is likely to have stopped payments on all its privately held international debt anyway. No one has yet tried to challenge the payments the debtor makes to the IMF and the multilateral development banks (MDBs).

Creditors have the right to initiate litigation, but the incentive to do so is small in the absence of legal strategies that can force a sovereign to pay. A reporter recently noted, "Winning a judgment to attach the commercial assets of a deadbeat nation has been relatively easy in foreign courts, col-

11. Majority-restructuring provisions in English-law bonds also developed in response to the risk of a minority of creditors liquidating a company that the majority wanted to keep intact. Particularly with railroad companies, it rarely made sense to liquidate the company and sell off its major asset—its railway tracks. Laying tracks costs a lot of money, and the tracks were almost always worth more as railroad tracks than as scrap iron. It also did not make sense to divide the railway into parcels and sell off the parcels to different investors. Most creditors holding defaulted railroad bonds usually concluded that the value of their investment would be maximized if the railroad companies were restructured rather than liquidated. However, some creditors discovered that they could use the threat of liquidation to force the creditors who believed that the firm is worth more alive than dead to offer the creditors threatening liquidation more advantageous terms. Majority-restructuring provisions were introduced into English-law bond contracts to allow the majority to avoid having to buy off such holdouts. See Buchheit, Gulati, and Mody (2002).

lecting on such orders has been nearly impossible" (Angela Pruitt, "Nicaragua Creditor Suit Muddies Sovereign Restructurings," *Dow Jones International News*, September 29, 2003). An Argentine economist, Hernan Fardi, put it more bluntly: "Short of an invasion by troops, there's nothing plausible creditors can do to capture assets within Argentina."[12] (See box 8.1 for a more detailed discussion on Argentina.)

Free Riding (Litigation after Restructuring). If this analysis is correct, a sovereign is not likely to face a real risk of its creditors seizing its remaining reserves the day after it defaults. Yet, a sovereign that defaults on its debt still needs a good lawyer. Once it has completed a restructuring and resumed payments on its new debt, some creditors may opt out of the restructuring and seeking to use the courts to obtain full payment on their original claims. Unlike a firm, a sovereign cannot use bankruptcy law provisions that allow a supermajority of creditors to approve a restructuring agreement over the objection of a minority of similar creditors. Since every creditor has an incentive to hold out and get paid in full, in equilibrium, an exchange offer that would have otherwise been mutually beneficial to the debtor and its creditors may still fail. Too many creditors may play the holdout game (Eichengreen and Portes 1995).

The incentive to hold out and thus the scope of the potential collective action problem ultimately hinges on the creditors' ability to use the legal system to convince the debtor that it is better off paying the holdouts in full or agreeing to a favorable settlement. Since holdouts—like other creditors—have difficulty getting their hands on the sovereign's reserves, they generally have tried to get the court to stop payments on the new debt that has emerged from the restructuring. They argue that the sovereign should not be allowed to pay its new debt until all its old debt—notably that held by the holdouts, is paid in full. If the court supports the

12. Quotation from "Argentina Faces Legal Battle of Attrition Over Debt," *Reuters*, October 3, 2003. Until after World War II, most sovereigns benefited from complete immunity from litigation: A sovereign had to give its consent before it could be sued in a foreign court. In the 1950s, the United States began to adopt a more restrictive definition of sovereign immunity: Sovereigns that engaged in normal commercial transactions—those that a private firm could also do—were not immune from litigation. This practice was formalized in the 1976 US Foreign Sovereign Immunities Act and Britain's State Immunity Act of 1978. See Buchheit (2000b), and Mauro and Yafeh (2003). However, a sovereign retains considerable de facto protection. Gelpern (2004, 9–10) noted: "Importantly, even where a state may be sued and has waived immunities, collecting on a judgment is difficult. For all practical purposes, state property within its own borders is completely immune." A sovereign's external diplomatic and military assets also enjoy immunity. Moreover, the erosion of a sovereign's formal immunity has coincided with the evolution of a new norm: Sovereign default is no longer an acceptable pretext for military intervention. Creditors in the 19th century lacked legal rights, "but sometimes were able to convince their government to intervene militarily, though typically only when the bondholders' commercial interests overlapped with the government's own geostrategic interests" (Mauro and Yafeh 2003).

Box 8.1 Argentina will test the current restructuring process

Argentina is currently going through the mother of all sovereign bond restructurings. Since Argentina issued more bonds, in more jurisdictions, and in more currencies than any other emerging economy, it quite literally is likely to face just about every imaginable problem during its restructuring. Argentina is seeking to restructure 98 international bonds and 54 bonds governed by Argentine law with a reported combined face value of $87 billion.[1] Both totals dwarf the combined totals of Ecuador, Pakistan, Ukraine, and Uruguay. Moreover, Argentina is currently seeking much greater debt reduction than any of these countries sought.

The set of investors who hold Argentina's international bonds is also unusually diverse. Argentina placed a higher-than-average share of its bonds with retail investors in Europe, and domestic Argentines are estimated to hold far more of Argentina's dollar debt than US and other international investors.[2] Consequently Argentina is engaged in by far the biggest restructuring of bonds held by retail investors and is also the first sovereign to ask retail investors to agree to reduce the face value of their bonds, not just defer the repayment of the bonds' principal. The biggest surprise to date in Argentina's restructuring has been the retail investors' ability to organize themselves to participate actively in the restructuring process. Representatives of retail investors have joined institutional investors to form a single, coordinating committee. The core coordination challenge facing Argentina is developing a "menu" of restructuring terms that includes items that will appeal to retail investors (who typically want to preserve face value), domestic pension funds (who also may care about preserving face value), wealthy Argentines holding government bonds offshore, and institutional investors (who care about the bonds' current market value).

Argentina's restructuring—if it happens—undoubtedly will provide new insights into the restructuring process. So far, Argentina's experience is consistent with our core argument that a sovereign's greatest legal vulnerability comes after it completes a restructuring, not before. A number of retail creditors and one creditor that holds over 50 percent of a single bond already have initiated litigation against Argentina, but they have yet to collect much. The small investors seem to be litigating in large part out of

(box 8.1 continues next page)

holdouts, the sovereign then faces a difficult choice. It can pay the holdouts in full or stop payments on all its new debt and fall back into a broad default.

The "tax" that successful holdouts impose on a successful restructuring could fall entirely on the debtor, who has to run down its reserves or adjust more to pay the holdouts. Or the "tax" could fall on both the debtor and the majority of creditors, as a debtor who rationally anticipates the need to pay off a few holdouts has an incentive to insist that other creditors agree to a deeper restructuring. Cash used to pay off a minority in full is cash that conceivably could have been distributed to the majority without making the debtor any worse off.[13] On the other hand, the desire to

13. The question of who ends up bearing the "costs" of the holdout tax is even more complicated when the sovereign has many groups of creditors. Costs not borne by the debtor could be shared by all creditor groups or could be borne disproportionately by one group of creditors.

Box 8.1 *(continued)*

frustration. The large investor's strategy is less clear. A New York court has certified one class action lawsuit on behalf of some of Argentina's creditors, but this has yet to prompt other class action litigation. On the other hand, litigation seems likely to play a larger role in Argentina than in other cases, particularly if the restructuring drags out beyond 2004. Existing litigation already implies that Argentina will need new bonds in exchange for both its old bonds and outstanding legal judgments against it, not just for its old bonds (most other debtors have not had oustanding judgment creditors when they launched their exchange).[3] There is no shortage of small "orphan" bonds that lack collective action clauses among the 98 international bonds that Argentina is not paying, making it relatively easy for a creditor to buy a large enough position in a single bond to be able to block other investors from changing the bond's terms through exit consents. The deep debt reduction Argentina is seeking implies a low recovery value from participating in the exchange and makes litigating for the bond's full value more financially attractive. Many of Argentina's creditors are no doubt studying examples of successful litigation and considering their odds. Of course, Argentina's lawyers are also considering ways to protect the payments stream of a successful restructuring—the debtor's point of maximum legal vulnerability—from holdout litigation.

---

1. Data on Argentina's restructuring comes from the Government of Argentina's Secretariat of Finance, Ministry of Economy and Production (2003).

2. The pesification of the bonds held by the banking system reduced the share of Argentina's domestically held international bonds. However, after deciding to include the bonds held by the pension funds in the restructuring, the government of Argentina now estimates that domestic investors hold more than 40 percent of the $87 billion in debt that it is seeking to restructure. US investors are estimated to hold only around 10 percent of these bonds.

3. If some holders of a bond obtain a judgment before an exchange, they may be exempted from the bond's amendment provisions.

limit the number of holdouts also may lead the sovereign to propose, at the margins, a more generous restructuring than it otherwise would have (Gulati and Bratton 2003). Thus, the overall impact of holdouts on the majority of creditors is ambiguous.

The risk of holdout litigation could be costly to both the debtor and the majority of its creditors in another way: It could delay reaching an agreement that lets the sovereign resume payments. A sovereign that can get 90 percent of its international creditors to agree to a restructuring may be unwilling to go forward with that restructuring because the litigation risks from the remaining 10 percent are too great. Prolonging the period when the sovereign is in default, in turn, usually delays the country's recovery, hurting both the sovereign debtor and the majority of its creditors.

Nonetheless, the impact of holdouts—for good or for ill—on the current restructuring process should not be exaggerated. Sovereigns typically put forward attractive restructuring proposals because they need to attract the support of the majority of their creditors, not because they want to avoid a small number of holdouts. A sovereign that gets most of its creditors to accept its restructuring proposal has a number of defenses against the risk of holdout litigation:

- First, holding out means giving up "liquidity"—the ability to trade out of a position easily. The risk of being stuck with a small, illiquid, and difficult-to-sell instrument may deter potential holdouts.
- Second, litigation is costly, takes time, and may not succeed. No legal strategy assures full payment to a holdout that is willing to incur the legal costs required to make itself a real nuisance. The most successful recent holdout, Elliot Associates, was able to collect on its litigation against Peru only after spending four years in the courts (Moody's Investor Service 2000).
- Third, the tactic that allowed Elliot to collect against Peru—its ability to convince a Belgian court that key provisions in New York–law bank loans and sovereign bond contracts, the *pari passu* clause, prevented Peru from paying the bonds that emerged from its restructuring while its old bank loans remained in default (Buchheit and Pam 2004)—may not be available in the future. The US Treasury and the Federal Reserve Bank of New York recently filed *amicus curiae* briefs that argue that the Belgian court's order to Peru was based on a faulty interpretation of the meaning of the *pari passu* clause.[14] The US courts have yet to rule on the correct interpretation of this key provision, but creditors planning to initiate litigation on the basis of the Belgian court's decision should be aware that other courts may adopt their own interpretation of the key clause.
- Fourth, debtors that have issued New York–law bonds can take a number of steps to inhibit holdout litigation. Most New York–law bonds have provisions that allow a majority to amend the bonds' nonfinancial terms. The holders of the old bonds who are willing to participate in the exchange can, as their last act as holders of the old bonds, vote to amend the bonds' nonfinancial terms in ways that make litigation much more difficult (exit consents).[15] Felix Salmon of *Euromoney* noted,

14. See Buchheit and Pam (2003). The United States (2004), Federal Reserve Bank of New York (2004), and Clearinghouse Association LLC (2004) all filed *amicus curiae* briefs arguing against the Belgian court's interpretation of the pari passu clause.

15. Ecuador, for example, amended its bonds to eliminate the Luxembourg listing requirement and the requirements that it cancel bonds acquired by the debtor. Because Ecuador also reversed the acceleration of one of its bonds (the other bonds had not been accelerated), these changes effectively meant that the remaining bonds lacked the votes to accelerate their bonds in the event of a missed coupon payment. Since the bonds had a long maturity, any litigious creditor would have to wait a long time for the bond to generate enough arrears to make litigation worthwhile. See Buchheit and Gulati (2000) and Buchheit (2000a).

"If bondholders can be persuaded to swap into a new instrument, they can be asked as they exit the old bonds to vote to strip them of many of their key protections. Anybody remaining behind is left with an illiquid and unattractive instrument in default which will almost certainly be worth less than the new bonds that everyone else swapped into" (Salmon 2003).

- Fifth, even if the courts rule in favor of those seeking to copy Elliot's strategy, sovereign debtors will take additional steps to limit their potential vulnerability. Notably, debtors, with the support of creditors who participate in the restructuring, are likely to amend the old bonds in ways that make it harder for holders of the "old," unrestructured debt to block the payments stream on the "new" debt that emerges from the restructuring.[16] After all, neither the creditors who participate in the restructuring nor the debtor has an interest in letting holdout creditors push the debtor back into default.

Holdouts have proved, at least to date, to be a much less severe impediment to successful restructurings than the official sector feared in 1996, when the G-10 published a report that called for the adoption of collective action clauses. The number of holdouts in recent bond restructurings has been manageable. Yet, the risk of successful holdouts imposing a higher tax on future restructurings cannot be discounted entirely:

- The attractive returns some investors have obtained by holding out could inspire copycat litigation (Singh 2003). Until the courts rule otherwise, Elliot's successful strategy against Peru provides a roadmap other holdouts can follow. Nicaragua is appealing the decision of a lower Belgian court, which used the logic of the Peru-Elliot decision to rule against Nicaragua.[17] The Democratic Republic of the Congo recently settled rather than face a protracted legal battle.
- The more debt reduction the debtor needs and the lower the market value of defaulted debt, the larger the potential gains from a "hold out

16. Uruguay, for example, convinced its creditors to amend the "old bonds" waiver of sovereign immunity so that the payments streams on the new bonds were exempt from the standard waiver.

17. Nicaragua v. LNC LLP. The Belgian court that initially ruled against Elliot ruled in favor of LNC, since its original ruling in Elliot had been reversed by the Belgian Court of Appeals. Both Elliot and LNC argued that payments on the new debt could be seized to pay the old debt, since the new and old debts were "pari passu." Nicaragua is appealing. In both cases, the Belgian courts ruled on the meaning of a key phrase in New York–law bonds and used this ruling to block payments through Euroclear—a payments clearinghouse based in Belgium. Buchheit and Pam (2003, 8) noted in the context of the original ruling on Elliot that "the Belgian Court of Appeals was being asked to interpret New York law as it applied to a boilerplate provision in an unsecured New York loan agreement in the absence of any controlling (or for that matter, any) New York judicial precedents on the point."

and litigate" strategy. Litigation is more attractive if the alternative is to accept a restructuring worth 20 cents (the potential return from litigation that recovers the full value of the principal and any past due interest exceeding 500 percent) than if the restructuring is worth 50 cents (the potential return is closer to 100 percent). Unless the probability of successful litigation falls alongside the prospective returns, the risk of litigation should go up alongside the amount of debt relief the debtor is seeking. However, creditors participating in an exchange that returns only 20 cents on the dollar also have more reason to worry that the large cash payments to holdouts are cutting into their own returns and therefore have a stronger incentive to help the debtor limit its exposure to litigation.

- Sovereigns often pay a small number of holdouts in full rather than fight their claims for full repayment.[18] This is often quite rational: If the bonds have not been accelerated (or have been deaccelerated), the sovereign only has to make small coupon payments to avoid the costs of protracted litigation. However, if creditors come to expect that a small number of holdouts will be paid on relatively favorable terms, the credibility of future debtors' threats to treat holdouts roughly is undermined.

- The legal strategies of both holdout creditors and debtors will continue to evolve. Argentina is sure to attempt to protect the payments streams on its eventual restructuring from Elliot-style litigation. Potential holdout creditors similarly will attempt to protect themselves from the risk that exit consents will undermine their post-restructuring leverage. For example, a large player noted for its aggressive behavior has bought up more than 50 percent of one of Argentina's smaller New York–law bonds—enough to prevent Argentina from being able to amend the bonds' nonfinancial terms through exit consents.

In sum, ad hoc ways can limit the risk of holdouts posing substantial problems. To date these approaches have worked, but none of them is ideal.

Absence of an Agreed Priority Structure: Negotiating the Relative Treatment of Different Creditor Classes. A bankruptcy regime typically lets creditors know ex ante how they will be treated in relation to other credi-

18. Ecuador was able to deaccelerate its bonds and avoid litigation risk by clearing arrears and then continuing to pay a relatively small coupon. Indeed, paying creditors London Interbank Offered Rate (LIBOR) coupons at current interest rates could be considered a form of punishment. Holdouts would have preferred that Ecuador remained in default so that they could initiate litigation. Uruguay never defaulted, so it too needs to make coupon payments only for the time being. Debtors certainly have not always paid holdout creditors the full principal value of the creditors' claim—mitigating any expectation that a small number of holdouts will receive a generous payoff even without having to go to court.

tors holding similar types of claims (Gelpern 2004). Bankruptcy law sets out a priority structure that outlines how different types of debts will be treated, and a court makes sure that high-priority claims get more than low-priority ones. The result: Holders of different types of debt generally know how their class of claims will be treated relative to other classes, even if they do not know exactly how well they will do.

As discussed in chapter 7, however, no court or law can force a sovereign to respect a priority structure. The absence of any agreed, enforceable rules of priority is both good and bad. It certainly can make it more difficult to reach agreement. The debtor and its creditors have to agree in broad terms on how different creditor groups should be treated before they can get down to negotiating financial terms. However, the debtor's ability to favor some creditors also provides some of the lubrication that helps a sovereign function without formal bankruptcy protection. Paying some debts while in default can help limit the impact of sovereign default on the banking system and let the sovereign obtain limited new financing.

Provision of Senior New Money. Creditors have good reason not to want a sovereign to be able to raise substantial new funds after a default: Losing access to international markets after a default is a prime incentive for payment.[19] On the other hand, it may not be in the interest of the bankrupt sovereign's creditors for the sovereign to be completely unable to access any new financing. Most domestic bankruptcy laws have provisions that allow a bankrupt firm undergoing reorganization to retain access to some new credit, on the theory that access to new money ultimately leads the firm's existing creditors to recover more of their initial investment.

The difficulties in providing new money to a sovereign are arguably another type of collective action problem in a restructuring. All creditors might be better off if the debtor obtained access to limited amounts of new money to finance its ongoing operations. However, each individual creditor would prefer that the new money be used to pay down its debt rather than to increase the value of the firm (or sovereign) for all creditors. Even if the new money can only be used for the benefit of all creditors, each individual creditor would rather that another creditor put up the funds. Bankruptcy law solves this collective action problem by assuring the providers of new financing (or DIP financing) that they will be repaid before most existing debt and by preventing any individual creditor from claiming the "new money" for its exclusive benefit.

19. One of the early insights of the analytical sovereign debt literature was that a defaulted debtor may be a decent credit and could even be able to borrow again relatively rapidly. The debtor will have a reputation for not paying but may also have less debt than countries that are trying to pay all their debt. Some creditors may be willing to take a chance and lend to the country that defaulted; the loss of market access following default is not a given.

However, the current absence of private DIP financing for a sovereign may be a smaller problem than proponents of an international bankruptcy regime think:

- Bankrupt sovereigns already have access to new money. Preferred creditors—the IMF and MDBs—can provide net new financing to a sovereign that is in default on its private international creditors. This financing is functionally analogous to DIP financing, and the debtor's self-interest in maintaining access to this source of financing provides a strong incentive for it to sustain payments to preferred creditors even absent legal priority. Moreover, a sovereign that defaults on its international debt may still be able to borrow domestically.[20]
- A bankrupt sovereign may have less need to access new financing than a private firm. Firms need to carry inventory, buy parts, and otherwise borrow at least from suppliers in order to remain viable. Sovereigns can—and do—operate by matching cash receipts and cash expenditures, particularly when they are not making payments—principal and interest—on their existing debt. Arrears to government suppliers in effect may allow the government to borrow for short periods even after default.
- In some emerging economies, a sovereign guarantee is needed for private firms to access trade credit. For example, export financing agencies often require a sovereign guarantee and can be a major source of trade financing. In other economies, private banks provide trade financing without any involvement from the sovereign. So long as trade credits are exempted from capital controls, private firms may be willing to provide other private firms with trade credits—and even longer-term credit—while the sovereign is in default. If a sovereign guarantee is needed for private firms to access trade finance, an informal commitment by the sovereign to give priority to trade financing may be all that is needed.[21]
- The absence of new financing often compels the debtor to make needed policy adjustments. Given the typical fall in a government's revenue

20. The government of Argentina has incurred substantial new debts subsequent to its default, largely by issuing compensation bonds to banks and bank depositors. This is not exactly new money, since the government is not selling new debt for cash. But it certainly has resulted in new future obligations for the government. The Central Bank of Argentina did not default on the debt it issued, and it has developed a market for peso-denominated central bank paper subsequent to default.

21. Kletzer and Wright (2000) note that the postulated cost of default from a loss in access to trade financing has not been observed in practice. Argentina, for example, has sustained access to trade financing by allowing local banks to take in dollar deposits and make dollar loans only if they can demonstrate the dollar loans are being used for trade financing.

following a default—even after taking into account the interest savings—the need to match revenues and expenditures often demands real adjustment. Being forced to make sudden and procyclical adjustments in the face of a downturn may hurt the crisis country, but it is not obvious that it hurts the sovereign's creditors.

Policy Conditionality. Creditors who agree to provide a debtor with relief from its debts will want it to agree to take steps to increase its ability to pay. This requires collective action: Different creditors are likely to have different conceptions of the steps the debtor needs to take. The current system for sovereign debt restructuring generally relies on the IMF to solve this coordination problem. The debtor negotiates a set of policy reforms that often set out the broad parameters for the subsequent debt restructuring with the IMF in return for new loans or the refinancing of the IMF's existing exposure. A single entity like the IMF can reach agreement with the debtor more easily than a group of creditors with different and at times competing interests. The IMF also is far better positioned to link its financing to monitored policy commitments than private creditors.

Private creditors point out—correctly—that creditors play a larger role in commercial debt reorganizations. In part, this is because IMF conditionality is a partial substitute for private conditionality. But nothing forces private creditors to rely on IMF conditionality: External private creditors, for example, could refuse to restructure their own claims unless the debtor agrees to additional policy changes. In practice this has rarely happened, largely because of the difficulties a sovereign's disparate creditors face in coordinating their actions (it is far easier for creditors to coordinate their rhetorical demands). Coordination gets more difficult as the number of creditors go up. Plus, many creditors value the ability to trade in and out of a bond, and are unwilling to give up the ability to trade in order to make a credible commitment to link their willingness to agree to a restructuring to the debtor's ongoing compliance with its policy promises.

Rush to Default. Most potential market failures in a restructuring arise from collective action problems among creditors. However, the risk of opportunistic default stems from a different kind of market failure: the difficulty in writing an enforceable debt contract with a sovereign borrower. Just as sovereign borrowers worry that their creditors will rush to the exits at the first hint of trouble, precipitating an avoidable default, private creditors worry that a sovereign will prefer an opportunistic default to necessary policy adjustments (Dooley and Verma 2001).

As discussed in chapter 3, theoreticians of sovereign borrowing have paid great attention to this risk. Some academic models suggest that the threat of losing market access and a sovereign's desire to preserve its reputation for creditworthiness might not be enough to eliminate incentives *not* to pay. In practice, these models often paint too narrow a picture of the "reputational" costs of defaulting on international debt. An international default usually not only damages the sovereign's reputation with international investors but also hurts its domestic credibility. Opportunistic default has been rare.

Of course, any change in the existing regime for sovereign debt restructuring risks reducing a sovereign's incentive to pay, making opportunistic default more likely, and reducing capital flows to emerging markets. However, it is important not to exaggerate the role that the threat of litigation currently plays in sustaining incentives for sovereign payment. The market for sovereign bonds functions even though a creditor buying a New York–law sovereign debt contract has only limited ability to enforce the contract through the courts. Sovereign debtors already enjoy substantial effective protection from legal action following a default. It is hard to believe that the threat of holdout litigation provides much of a deterrent to default: Such litigation comes with a long lag and usually hurts the government that is trying to resume payments, which may not be the government that stopped payments.[22]

No Rush to Get Out of Default. In some ways, the real risk is not that a sovereign will rush to default—default itself remains extremely costly, despite the absence of a strong legal sanction. Rather, it is that a sovereign that has already incurred the large costs and reputational damage associated with a default will be in no particular hurry to restructure. Once the initial economic and financial shock of the default wears off, the cost of continuing to remain in default may be comparatively small. Creditors have little to fall back on but the threat of litigation, and that is not much of a threat since it is next to impossible to seize a sovereign's assets. Indeed, the sovereign's vulnerability increases, perversely, when the sovereign reaches a settlement with a majority of its creditors. A holdout then can attach the new external payments stream.

The basic incentives to get out default parallel the basic incentives not to default. Settlement with existing creditors is a prerequisite for the eventual resumption of international market access. More intangibly, resuming payments on a sovereign's external debt often contributes to the ability of a country's private firms to raise money externally. A restructuring agreement also can increase the confidence of a country's domestic residents, making domestic residents more willing to keep their savings at home. Finally, persistent default poses a problem for a country's capacity

22. It is possible that emerging-market sovereign debtors systematically overestimate their vulnerability to litigation, and, therefore, their perceived vulnerability creates a significant incentive for payment even in the absence of strong evidence that a sovereign's external creditors can take effective legal action following a default. See Sachs (2002) for an argument along these lines.

to continue to borrow from the IMF and the other IFIs. A country in default on its international sovereign bonds can continue to receive financing from the IMF for some time, but not indefinitely.

Other Runs. Stopping payments on the sovereign's own debt eliminates a direct source of pressure on its reserves. Investors can no longer "run" out of the sovereign's own debt.

However, default may trigger other runs—a run on the domestic banking system, a run on the currency, and a withdrawal of cross-border interbank credit. When a sovereign breaks its promise to pay its debts, it calls into question its ability to deliver on its other common promises, including the promises to provide a currency that offers a stable source of value and to backstop the banking system. These promises are easy to fulfill if everyone believes in the sovereign. But once confidence is gone, a sovereign is in the same position as a bank with more demand deposits than reserves. If everyone wants out, no one can get out. Markets break down, reserves are exhausted, and bank deposits and currency markets are often frozen.

Such bank runs are not simply the product of an irrational loss of confidence by depositors.[23] Most highly indebted sovereigns owe a lot of money to the local banking system: Such interlinkages can cause a sovereign crisis to spread quickly—a sovereign crisis often becomes a banking crisis, and a banking crisis often becomes a currency crisis.

Don't Forget about Politics. A default is a fairly visible signal of failed policy. A sovereign default usually results in domestic fiscal adjustment, cuts in spending and increases in income and value-added taxes, and a fall in domestic financial wealth. A domestic as well as external debt restructuring is often necessary in severe crises. Chapter 7 emphasized that a domestic debt restructuring is a capital levy—a tax on domestic savings. Not surprisingly, default often leads to political change.

The difficulty in finding a durable new government and developing political consensus around a new approach to economic policy can severely impede reaching rapid agreement on a restructuring. Indeed, the political costs of default—and the impact default has on the personal and professional reputation of policymakers—is one reason why governments delay seeking a restructuring until well after it is clear that they have no other choice.

---

23. Argentina is a case in point. Argentina ultimately was able to stop the run on its banks, in part because its central bank was willing to rediscount performing pesified bonds to supply emergency liquidity to the banks even as the government was in default on its international debt. But this improvised guarantee was clearly partial: Deposits were repaid in devalued pesos. Depositors had every reason to run. Argentina, in fact, imposed a deposit freeze (the *Corralito* and *Corralon*) before it defaulted on its international debt.

Approaches to Legal Reform

There are two dominant approaches to legal reform—contractual and statutory.[24] The contractual approach aims to change the restructuring process by changing the provisions in existing debt contracts. The statutory approach would create a body of international law to govern the restructuring of at least the sovereign's external debts—in some proposals, all of the sovereign's debt. The restructuring process outlined in the international treaty would override the provisions found in the debt contract.

Both approaches seek to address the rush to the courthouse and the free rider or holdout problem. The rush to the courthouse is either stopped through an outright stay on litigation or slowed by provisions that make it more difficult for an individual creditor to initiate and collect on litigation. The free-rider problem is addressed either through the introduction of provisions that allow a supermajority of the holders of an individual bond to make the restructuring binding on all holders of that bond or through the creation of legal capacity to hold a broader "aggregated" vote of the holders of all instruments participating in the restructuring. Many proposals also are motivated by a desire to use legal change to strengthen incentives for sovereigns with unsustainable debts to move more quickly to address their problems. Majority voting might encourage sovereigns to initiate a preemptive restructuring, and greater protection from the risk of litigation might lead sovereigns to suspend payments more quickly, stopping a rush to the exits.

While it is important to compare and contrast the statutory and contractual approaches, it would be a mistake to assume that all statutory or all contractual proposals are the same. Some contractual proposals attempt to increase the debtor's ability to address holdouts by amending the bond's financial terms; others aim to increase the creditors' leverage by imposing new reporting requirements on the debtor and by limiting the debtor's ability to amend the bond's nonfinancial terms. Some statutory proposals assign a large role to a third party—either the IMF or a new international court; others try to minimize the role of a third party and leave most decisions in the hands of the debtor and its creditors. Some would make the restructuring process more friendly to the debtor, while others would tilt the balance of power toward creditors.

Contractual Proposals

Two broad options for contractual change have been put forward: broadening the use of majority-restructuring provisions similar to those used in

24. Some have also proposed a "code of conduct" for sovereign debtors and their creditors (both before and during a debt restructuring) as a complement, not necessarily as an alternative, to a contractual or statutory approach. The code is discussed later in this chapter.

traditional English-law documentation or adopting the new clauses similar to those proposed by a group of creditor representatives. Of course, keeping traditional New York–law documentation is also an option.

Broadening the Use of Majority-Amendment Clauses. Imitating English-law practice would require, at a minimum, changing the provisions used in New York–law bonds to allow the amendment of the bond's key financial terms with a 75 percent majority vote. A broader reform would also introduce a requirement that litigation could only be initiated with the support of 25 percent of all holders of the bond, and that any proceeds from such litigation would need to be shared among all the holders of the bond.

However, adopting the key provisions used in English-law bonds does not require adopting all English-law conventions lock, stock, and barrel. Some standard English-law provisions could be modified to match New York–law conventions and reflect legitimate creditor concerns without watering down the core change. For example, to amend a bond, the bond's voting provisions could require the support of 75 percent of the outstanding principal value of the bond to change its key terms rather than the support of 75 percent of bondholders present at a meeting that meets quorum requirements. (See box 8.2 for a more detailed discussion of various types of collective action clauses).

It is also possible to give a set of key nonfinancial terms the same protection that is provided to a bond's financial terms. The ability to amend a bond's financial terms directly through a transparent vote reduces the need to rely on provisions allowing the amendment of a bond's nonfinancial terms to avoid holdouts (so-called exit consents).

Litigation-Friendly Clauses. A number of organizations representing private creditors joined together at the end of 2002 to lay out their own proposals for changing bond documentation.[25] They suggested the intro-

25. The Institute for International Finance (IIF), the Emerging Markets Traders Association (EMTA), the Emerging Markets Creditors Association (EMCA), the Securities Industry Association (SIA), The Bond Market Association (TBMA), the International Primary Markets Association (IPMA), and the International Securities Market Association (ISMA) all joined together to propose new clauses. These industry groups were motivated by a sense that the official sector's proposals, which focused on addressing the collective action problem created by holdout creditors, failed to address what creditors believed were more important problems in the restructuring process. Creditors worried that debtors would abuse exit consents, particularly if domestic creditors held a large share of a country's international bonds and argued that the creditors had difficulties establishing a satisfactory dialogue with the debtor. The decision to propose a high threshold for amending financial terms reportedly reflected both the difficulties of reaching consensus among the creditor organizations and an expectation that any "consensus" clauses would emerge from additional negotiation with the official sector. The creditors' proposals, however, may have backfired. The risk of the creditors' proposals defining New York-law documentation convention seems to have contributed to Mexico's decision to introduce its own preferred set of clauses into its New York–law bonds.

Box 8.2 More on bond documentation

Even before Mexico's 2003 decision to introduce collective action clauses into its New York-law bonds, bonds with clauses that allow a supermajority to amend the bond's key financial terms already constituted well over 20 percent of the market for dollar-denominated international sovereign bonds and around 50 percent of the smaller market for euro-denominated international sovereign bonds. A number of issuers used English law for their dollar-denominated debt, just as some issuers used New York law for their euro-denominated debt. Russia, Lithuania, Latvia, Ukraine, Pakistan, and Kazakhstan all have issued dollar-denominated bonds governed by English law that contain clauses. Argentina, Brazil, and Turkey traditionally used English law in their euro-denominated issues even as they used New York law in their dollar bonds. Colombia, Chile, Lebanon, and Mexico, in contrast, have traditionally used New York law for both their dollar- and euro-denominated debt.

Mexico's decision to introduce clauses into its New York–law documentation, however, has eroded the identification of New York governing law with the absence of collective action clauses.[1] Right now a number of "flavors" of collective action clauses are floating around. Eventually, however, the market is likely to settle on a single standard for voting provisions or perhaps on a range of accepted formulas:

- Traditional English-law documentation allows for the bond's payments terms to be amended with the support of 75 percent of those present at a bondholders' meeting that meets quorum requirements. If the quorum requirement is low and not many bondholders show up at a meeting, such provisions could allow the bond's terms to be amended with the support of less than 20 percent of the holders of the bond's outstanding principal value.

- Mexico partly followed the English-law convention of allowing 75 percent of the holders of a bond to amend its key financial terms when it introduced majority-amendment provisions into its international bonds in spring 2003. However, the 75 percent is calculated on a different basis—holders of the entire principal amount outstanding—rather than those represented at a meeting that meets quorum requirements. Bonds held directly by the debtor and bonds held by institutions where the debtor exercised equity control would be excluded from the vote. Mexico also broadened the definition of a bond's key financial terms to go beyond payment terms and dates. Any change in voting rules, governing law, jurisdiction, the pari passu provision, and the waiver of sovereign immunity also required the support of 75 percent of the holders of bond's outstanding principal value. Other terms could be amended by a two-thirds vote. Mexico did not make use of a trustee structure.[2]

(box 8.2 continues next page)

duction of provisions that would allow a supermajority to amend a bond's financial terms. However, they wanted the thresholds for the supermajority vote to be set higher than is the norm in the English-law market. The private creditor organizations proposed allowing 85 percent of the holders of a bond's outstanding principal value to amend the bond's financial terms, but only so long as no more than 10 percent of the holders of that bond objected. The support of 90 percent of the bondholders would be needed to overcome the opposition of the 10 percent. Provisions that related to the ability of creditors to sue to collect on their bonds could

Box 8.2 *(continued)*

- A few issuers have used documentation that resembles Mexico's, but increased the voting thresholds to 85 percent for key terms. Brazil initially used such documentation, but it recently reduced the voting threshold in its bonds to 75 percent.

- Uruguay's bonds have Mexican-style clauses that allow the bond's key terms to be amended with the support of 75 percent of the holders of the bond's outstanding principal value. But they also have provisions that allow for "aggregation." In the "aggregated vote," the votes of all Uruguay's outstanding external bonds are pooled and the threshold for amending the financial terms of any individual bond issue is lowered to two-thirds *so long as* 85 percent of all the holders of Uruguay's external bonds support the restructuring. The ability of one-third of the holders of a single bond issue to opt out of the "aggregated" vote protects against the risk that all of Uruguay's bondholders might gang up to impose large losses on a specific bond. Uruguay made use of a trustee structure, which makes the decision to litigate a collective rather than an individual one and assures that any proceeds from litigation are shared. The trustee is also responsible for excluding bonds directly or indirectly under the debtor's control from any vote. Uruguay's documentation also requires that Uruguay disclose the details of its economic plan and debt restructuring proposal to the trustee for distribution to all bondholders in the event of a restructuring.[3]

---

1. This identification was never perfect. Richards and Gugiatti (2003) looked closely at the terms of all New York–law bond issues to assess the impact of clauses on spreads. They found—to their surprise—that a few bonds issued prior to Mexico's seminal bond issue contained collective action clauses, apparently because these particular bond contracts had been drafted by the English offices of New York law firms. The New York–law bond issues of Egypt, Lebanon, Qatar, and Kazakhstan all contained collective action clauses (as did a small Bulgarian issue), so, nearly $12 billion in New York law–bonds contained collective action clause, even before Mexico put clauses into its own bonds. Market participants were not aware of the use of clauses in these bonds—reinforcing Richards and Gugiatti's overall argument that clauses have no impact on pricing.

2. Mexico's clauses generally followed the provisions recommended by the G-10. However, Mexico initially did not adopt the G-10's recommendation to use a trustee rather than a fiscal agent structure. Under the G-10 model, only the trustee, not the individual bondholders, would be able to initiate litigation. The trustee also would assure that the proceeds of litigation would be shared among all bondholders (Group of Ten 2002).

3. See Gelpern (2003) for a comprehensive comparison of the G-10's proposals, the proposals of industry groups, and the documentation used by Mexico and Uruguay.

not be amended at all. The voting thresholds for modifying a bond's nonfinancial terms would be raised from 67 to 75 percent, and more important, the definition of "financial terms" would be broadened. Bonds controlled directly or indirectly by the debtor would be excluded from the vote (control would be defined broadly and could include regulated financial institutions that the debtor did not directly control). In practice, provisions for amending financial terms would be tighter than those now found in English-law bonds, and provisions for amending nonfinancial terms would be tighter than those now found in New York–law bonds.

Creditor groups also proposed introducing two additional sets of contractual provisions into bond documentation. First, the documentation would require additional financial disclosure from the debtor, with the disclosure requirements increasing should the debtor fall into default. Second, the documentation would include a set of provisions that would require that the debtor pay the expenses of a committee formed to represent creditors' interest during a restructuring.

Assessment of Competing Contractual Proposals

Some proposed changes could make it easier for a debtor to avoid holdout litigation; others could make a restructuring harder—and give the creditors more leverage. The devil is really in the details: The thresholds for amending the bond's financial and nonfinancial terms, the definition of financial and nonfinancial terms,[26] and the definition of who is eligible to vote all matter.

It is possible to create bonds with collective action clauses that are harder to restructure than current New York–law bonds that lack collective action clauses. For example, the creditor groups proposed contractual changes that would make it harder to amend a bond's nonfinancial terms to encourage participation in a restructuring. However, those changes would not be balanced with provisions that would make it significantly easier to avoid holdouts by amending the bond's financial terms. A potential holdout could obtain the 10 percent needed to block a restructuring amendment without much difficulty. If the debt trades at 20 cents on the dollar, it takes only $10 million to buy a blocking $50 million position in a $500 million bond with 90 percent majority-amendment provisions and $20 million to buy a blocking $100 million face position in a $1 billion bond. Sophisticated creditors who hold less than this are not likely to initiate litigation anyway. Elliot spent $11.8 million to buy its position in Peru's sovereign debt in 1995 and ended up collecting nearly $56 million. Those interested in imitating Elliot's strategy are likely to be willing to commit similar—if not larger—sums.[27] Litigation is expensive and makes sense only if the creditor is angling for a substantial payoff.

The need to assure that any consensual restructuring has the support of the overwhelming majority of the country's creditors has to be balanced against the need to offer the debtor—and its cooperating creditors—pro-

26. Technically, bonds that grant other terms the same protection they give the bond's key financial terms often define a set of "reserve matters" (which include both the bond's financial terms and a set of key nonfinancial terms) that have a higher level of protection than all other provisions in the bond contract.

27. Indeed, the litigation currently being pursued by one large creditor, the Darts, against Argentina is based on this mode. The Darts bought a controlling stake in a single bond issue to protect against exit consents and have a large enough claim to make litigation potentially attractive.

tection against the risk of holdout litigation. A voting threshold that lets 50 percent of the holders of a bond amend the bond's financial terms probably fails to offer creditors enough protection. Conversely, the proposed voting threshold of 90 percent fails to offer the debtor sufficient protection against holdouts. Such provisions risk pushing the debtor to find less transparent means of carrying out a necessary restructuring.

In our view, provisions that allow the amendment of a bond's key terms—financial terms as well as the key nonfinancial terms—by a vote of 75 percent of the bond's outstanding principal get the balance basically right. Amending such a bond's financial terms is much easier than is now the case in a typical New York–law bond. Yet such clauses also provide creditors with more protection than current English-law documentation.

There is no evidence that introducing this kind of collective action clauses into sovereign debt contracts would reduce a sovereign's incentives to pay. Clauses that allow a bond's financial terms to be amended do not make default per se less costly. They only make it easier for the sovereign to avoid holdouts when it can put forward a restructuring proposal that the vast majority of its creditors accept. The evidence that the threat of holdouts is needed to motivate a sovereign to pay is thin. It is hard to see how English-law bonds would survive in the market if typical English-law provisions made default an attractive option for sovereigns.[28]

Marketing Bonds with Clauses

Until recently, sovereign debtors have been reluctant to change the documentation used in their New York–law bonds (or start issuing their dollar bonds governed by English law), despite repeated calls for reform from the official sector. Their reluctance has stemmed from concerns—perhaps misplaced—that the market would penalize debtors who issued with clauses and that the first debtor to initiate change would bear a disproportionate share of the costs.

This is why the early 2003 decision of Mexico—a traditional market leader—to change the documentation that it used in its New York–law bonds was crucial. The US Treasury certainly encouraged Mexico to take the lead in introducing clauses. But Mexico's decision seems to have been motivated at least as much by a desire to bring the debate on the IMF's proposed bankruptcy regime to a close and by fear that if it did not act, it would leave the field open and allow creditor groups to rewrite the standard documentation used in New York–law bonds. Mexico realized that it would be better off if it decided the type of restructuring provisions that it wanted in its bonds and made these provisions the market standard rather than taking the risk of others setting the market standard. If Mex-

28. The use of both English and New York-law documentation in both the dollar-denominated and euro-denominated debt markets has long suggested the absence of a significant price penalty for either governing law.

ico paid any premium on its path-breaking bond, it was very small. In fact, most analysts find no evidence of *any* price penalty on the initial bond. Mexico's use of clauses in subsequent bond issuance has been described as a "nonevent" (IMF September 2003a).

Most subsequent issuers followed Mexico's example and issued bonds that allow key terms to be amended with a 75 percent vote, though a few raised the threshold for amending key terms to 85 percent. Uruguay, however, went further than Mexico and introduced truly innovative "superclauses" in the bonds that emerged from its debt exchange (Salmon 2004b). Uruguay's new clauses allow aggregated voting across several bond issues (box 8.2). These provisions are probably too innovative to become the new market standard. Nonetheless, Uruguay's clauses do demonstrate how certain innovations could both provide the debtor with more protection against holdouts and offer creditors more protection against debtor abuse.[29] Broadening the voting base helps the debtor, since it takes a lot more money and commitment for a holdout to obtain 15 percent of $5 billion in bonds than to obtain 25 percent of $500 million or even $1 billion in bonds, while the higher 85 percent voting threshold for the aggregated vote offers the creditors an added level of protection.

The use of clauses that allow the amendment of a bond's financial terms now seems likely to emerge as the market standard. One of the "big three" emerging-market sovereign debtors in the world—Russia—has long used English law for its international bonds and thus issued debt with clauses. The other two members of the big three—Mexico and Brazil—are now using majority-amendment clauses in their new New York–law bonds as well.[30] Argentina will dramatically increase the stock of bonds with clauses should it complete an exchange to end its default. Chile, Colombia, Costa Rica, Guatemala, Korea, Poland, Peru, South Africa, and Venezuela have all started using clauses in their new New York–law bond issues (Taylor 2004b).

However, changing the contractual provisions used in new sovereign debt issues will not change the terms of the roughly $200 billion stock of existing international bonds that lack majority-restructuring provisions.[31]

29. See Batholomew, Stern, and Liuzza (2002) for an innovative JP Morgan Chase proposal to introduce "aggregating" clauses after a default through a two-step exchange offer.

30. Russia traditionally used English law for its dollar-denominated international bonds but did on occasion use German law for bonds denominated in deutsche marks. Brazil traditionally used New York law for its dollar-denominated bonds and English law for its euro-denominated bonds. When it first introduced clauses into its New York law bonds in 2003, Brazil used a 85 percent voting threshold. However, it has subsequently started to issue bonds with 75 percent voting threshold.

31. IMF data (September 2003a) indicate that there are $163 billion in outstanding New York–law bonds (at least $9.1 billion of which now make use of collective action clauses) and $33 billion in outstanding German-law bonds. This estimate, however, excludes the outstanding stock of Brady bonds and therefore understates the stock of existing bonds that

IMF projections suggest that if all new sovereign debt contracts included new contractual provisions allowing a supermajority to amend the bond's key financial terms, it would take a little under 10 years for 80 percent of the entire stock of external-law debt to include collective action clauses. If debt exchanges or buybacks lead the stock to turn over before it matures, the process would be more rapid.[32] The process of changing sovereign debt contracts has only just begun.[33] Most sovereign international bonds will lack provisions allowing the amendment of key financial terms for some time: This limits the ability of contractual reform to change the restructuring process immediately—for better or for worse.

Statutory Proposals

While contractual proposals seek to change the terms of individual contracts that could interfere with an orderly restructuring, statutory proposals seek to create a set of rules that would replace existing contractual provisions. Statutory proposals therefore necessarily do two things:

- establish the legal basis needed to override existing sovereign debt contracts. Since a sovereign can issue debt in a number of jurisdictions, a treaty is required to create a body of international law that would trump conflicting national law; and
- empower an existing institution (typically the IMF) or create an institution to act as a referee between the debtor and its creditors and give the referee's decisions the force of law. Some provisions in any bankruptcy regime almost certainly will require authoritative interpretation even if every effort is made to minimize the authority given to a third party.

Statutory proposals typically aim to address the same set of problems as contractual proposals—notably the free-rider problem and the rush to the courthouse. Some, however, are more ambitious and target other

lack collective action clauses. On the other hand, it also likely fails to take into account the roughly $12 billion in outstanding New York-law bonds that Richards and Gugiatti (2003) found that included collective action clauses even before Mexico's pioneering issue.

32. Because there is a long tail of very long-term bonds, it would take another nine years to increase the percentage from 80 to 90 percent, absent liability management operations or sovereign restructurings that result in more rapid turnover of long-term bonds (IMF June 2002a).

33. If the trend toward introducing sensible restructuring provisions into new debt contracts is reversed, the official sector could take a number of steps to strengthen incentives for the use of clauses or even to require their use. See Roubini and Setser (2003).

problems.[34] Patrick Bolton and David Skeel (2003) would use a statutory regime to enforce a "first issued, first paid" priority structure. Andrei Shleifer (2003) has suggested that a statutory regime should be designed to increase creditors' leverage in a sovereign restructuring. Rather than examining all proposals for sovereign bankruptcy regimes, it makes sense to focus on the IMF's SDRM proposal. This proposal both is representative of proposals that focus on protecting a sovereign debtor from holdout litigation and is more developed than most other proposals. Consequently, it is likely to continue to frame the debate. One caution: The IMF's proposal evolved over time, so in many cases, our discussion will include options that the IMF initially considered but then discarded.[35]

Stay on Litigation to Stop Creditors from Rushing to the Courthouse?

Most corporate bankruptcy regimes insist that the debtor stop payments on all its debts when it files for bankruptcy and, in turn, be provided with automatic protection from litigation (a stay on litigation). Automatic or close to automatic protection from litigation is balanced by court supervision of the debtor while it prepares its restructuring proposal. If the debtor does not reach agreement with its creditors on a restructuring proposal, the court moves to liquidate the debtor.

The IMF's initial thinking, along with most other proposals for a sovereign bankruptcy regime, loosely followed the corporate model. Anne Krueger suggested in November 2001 that the IMF be given the ability to determine whether a debtor should be given temporary legal protection. However, relying on the IMF to determine whether a debtor deserves protection raises a host of problems. Many debtors are reluctant to expand the IMF's role in the restructuring process, while creditors argue that the IMF's financial exposure makes it an interested party. They also fear that the IMF's governance structure gives it an intrinsic bias toward protecting one of its members. The obvious alternative—setting up a new international institution just to supervise sovereign restructurings—requires an extraordinary amount of effort without eliminating the IMF's broader role in the restructuring process: The two institutions would either need to coordinate with each other or risk working at cross-purposes. It would be strange, for example, for the court to deny legal protection to a debtor that the IMF believed deserved financial support.

34. See Rogoff and Zettelmeyer (2002b) for an excellent survey of proposals to create an international bankruptcy regime for sovereigns.

35. For the final version of the IMF's proposal, see IMF (April 2003). Earlier versions include IMF (November 2002 and February 2003) and Krueger (2001a, 2002a, and 2002b).

The IMF eventually concluded that an automatic stay on creditor litigation was not desirable, largely because the IMF was not planning to require that a sovereign debtor stop payment on all its debts—or even those owed to external private creditors.[36]

The IMF's final proposal focuses on creating the legal machinery for supermajority voting on the debtor's final restructuring proposal. It assumes that most debtors would not need a stay: The possibility that the debtors proposal would be approved before an individual creditor could collect through the courts would deter most litigation.[37] However, the IMF also outlines two ways a debtor could obtain additional protection from creditors immediately after default, should such protection prove necessary. First, the debtor has the option of putting a proposal for a temporary stay to a vote of its creditors. A supermajority of creditors then would determine whether to give the debtor legal protection, just as a supermajority of creditors would vote to approve the debtor's final restructuring proposal. Second, the debtor and a committee of its creditors could petition the judicial panel set up to administer the "bankruptcy" process to block disruptive litigation if such litigation threatened to disrupt the restructuring process before a creditor vote could be organized (IMF March 2003).

Supermajority Voting to Solve the Free-Rider Problem?

A statutory regime allows a single aggregated vote of the holders of all participating instruments—for the sake of simplicity, say the holders of all external sovereign bonds—to determine the success of the restructuring plan. In principle, a single "aggregated" vote would have three advantages over the bond-by-bond voting process of standard collective action clauses:

- An aggregated vote avoids the risk of a holdout obtaining a large enough position in an individual instrument to block any amendment of the bond's terms. It is a lot harder to buy up a blocking position in the debtor's entire debt stock than to buy a blocking position in a single bond issue.

36. The IMF's Sean Hagan has emphasized this point. For an extensive discussion, see IMF (February 2003).

At one point, the IMF floated a proposal that would not have provided the debtor with any formal legal protection, while it was developing its restructuring plan—implicitly recognizing that a sovereign's core assets already enjoy substantial legal protection.

37. The IMF did suggest implementing the sovereign's legal defenses with certain provisions designed to reduce creditors' incentive to initiate litigation (so-called litigation retardants).

- The capacity to override existing sovereign debt contracts would eliminate the need to wait for the existing stock of roughly $250 billion German- and New York–law sovereign debt to be retired.[38]
- The SDRM could override contractual provisions that inhibit supermajority voting in bank loans as well as bonds. It eliminates the risk that new kinds of financial instruments with difficult-to-restructure contractual terms might emerge.[39]

However, these advantages have to be weighed against the practical difficulties associated with setting up a single aggregated vote. These difficulties are worth exploring in detail.

Which Instruments Should Participate in the Aggregated Vote? Restructuring experts often note that it is far better to hold an instrument that is not part of the restructuring than to haggle for more of the debtor's limited cash flow. Not surprisingly, the key to any proposal for an "aggregated" vote is the process used to select the precise instruments that will participate in that vote.

A comparison with Uruguay's "aggregation" clauses is instructive. Uruguay's clauses allow two possible forms of voting. Each bond can be restructured though an individual vote, or all the bonds in the series *specified in the contract* can be restructured through a single aggregated vote. A statutory regime, however, needs to find another way to define the set of creditors that would participate in the aggregated vote.

There are two broad options. One is for the statute, in broad terms, to define the set of instruments that have to participate in the vote if the debtor wants to take advantage of the bankruptcy regime. The treaty that created the bankruptcy regime would set out a series of criteria to determine whether an instrument should be part of the vote, and the debtor would be required to include all instruments that meet these criteria in its restructuring proposal. Since there would inevitably be disputes, a third party would have to determine whether a given instrument had to be part of the proposal. The other option is to let the debtor select which instruments to include in the restructuring from the set of debts that meet the basic eligibility criteria. The debtor, in effect, would get to define the "series" of instruments that would participate in the aggregated vote. The first option restricts the debtor's choices if it wants to take advantage of the bankruptcy regime. The second gives the debtor substantial flexibility to craft a restructuring proposal that suits its interest. It could, for example, opt to exclude international bonds held heavily by either domestic banks or domestic pension funds from its overall restructuring.

38. To some, this is also a key disadvantage of the proposal, since investors who bought one kind of contract lose the key protections of that contract. See Galvis (2003).

39. We are indebted to Lewis Alexander for this point.

The IMF proposed letting the debtor determine which instruments would participate in the aggregated vote. The debtor was required to set out three lists of instruments that would be

- restructured through the SDRM's single aggregated vote;[40]
- restructured outside (Paris Club debt, for example, likely would be restructured in a separate process. Some domestic debts might be as well); and
- excluded from the restructuring altogether.

One Vote or Many? In most domestic bankruptcy regimes, creditors are organized into voting classes. All creditors holding claims with the same priority are put into the same class, and the bankruptcy judge assures that the restructuring terms respect these priorities. Each class votes separately on the restructuring proposal, and approval of the overall deal generally requires the approval of all creditor classes.[41] Separating creditors into classes is a way of protecting a minority of creditors with distinct interests from being abused by the majority. For example, a supermajority of unsecured creditors cannot vote in favor of a plan that strips secured creditors of their collateral and distributes the collateral among unsecured creditors.

A bankruptcy-style restructuring process for sovereigns either could set up a single vote of all participating unsecured creditors or divide creditors into different voting classes. This is a technical issue but one with immense consequences. Almost all sovereign debt is unsecured, so following the bankruptcy principle that debt with the same legal priority should be part of the same class would imply that all of the sovereign's unsecured debt should be organized into a single aggregated vote. This change to the current sovereign debt restructuring process would truly be radical. The holders of a sovereign's domestic debt, its Paris Club creditors, and holders of its international bonds and syndicated bank loans would all be part of the same vote.

Such a change poses a host of obvious problems. If Paris Club creditors held a small part of the sovereign's overall debt, a supermajority composed of private creditors alone could impose restructuring terms on them—including restructuring terms that require budgetary authoriza-

40. These instruments would have to meet certain criteria in order to be eligible to participate in the SDRM's aggregated vote: For example, they could not be governed by the crisis country's law, and they would have to be the product of a commercial contact that creates a right to payment. Secured debt and debts owed to the IFIs also would be excluded from the vote.

41. In some rare instances, a class of creditors can be forced to accept a restructuring against its will. In Chapter 11 of the US bankruptcy code, this process is referred to as cramdown. In the sovereign context, the term cramdown is often used loosely to describe any majority voting process that allows supermajority voting.

tions. For example, Argentina's private creditors might be able to cast a vote that forces the US Congress to spend money forgiving Argentina's debt. Conversely, Paris Club creditors might outvote private creditors in some instances. In the unlikely event that domestic debt was included in the bankruptcy regime, holders of domestic debt might be able to impose restructuring terms on both the Paris Club and external private creditors.

Dividing unsecured creditors into different classes offers one potential solution to these problems. Each class would vote separately, and approval of the overall deal—and presumably the resumption of payments—would require the approval of all creditor classes. However, this requires an agreed-upon process for setting up creditor classes, and it creates a risk of one class of creditors refusing the restructuring terms and blocking the overall restructuring.[42]

Another option is to limit the scope of the SDRM's aggregated vote. This assures that only relatively similar creditors participate in the vote and avoids the need to set up lots of special classes of creditors. The IMF in the end moved in this direction.[43] Domestic debt is excluded from the IMF's final SDRM proposal. The proposed treatment of the Paris Club was a bit more ambiguous, but the cleanest version of the IMF's proposal would also leave the Paris Club entirely out of the process.[44]

This makes the SDRM easier to design and operate but also limits its potential to solve many of the most vexing problems that arise in a sovereign restructuring. In many cases, more sovereign debt would need to be restructured "outside" than "inside" the IMF's proposed SDRM.

Domestic Debt

The trade-off between a narrow international bankruptcy regime that is easy to operate and a broad, complicated, intrusive and potentially more powerful international bankruptcy regime is most obvious with domestic debt. A bankruptcy regime that excludes domestic debt would not address those cases where domestic debt accounted for most short-term pressure. It also would not determine the relative priority that should be granted to domestic and external debt, let alone to different domestic claims.

---

42. Singh (2003) notes that in corporate bankruptcy, an entire creditor class sometimes has held out for a better deal. Approval of the overall deal requires the support of all classes in the United States, and it is sometimes more trouble than it is worth to cram down the overall deal on a holdout class.

43. The IMF's final proposal gave the debtor the option of dividing its unsecured external creditors into classes, if classification would facilitate reaching agreement on a restructuring. However, the debtor was under no obligation to classify its creditors. This differs fundamentally from domestic bankruptcy.

44. The IMF staff and management suggested that the Paris Club could be part of the SDRM if Paris Club creditors always received the protection of voting as a separate creditor class. However, the IMF's Executive Board generally was less inclined than IMF staff to include Paris Club debt in the SDRM.

The legal problems associated with the restructuring of domestic debt are also fundamentally different from those associated with the restructuring of international debt. Domestic debt often can be restructured by a unilateral decree that changes the debt's payment terms.[45] Legal problems arise if the constitutionality of such decrees, or other laws mandating a debt restructuring, is challenged—not from holdouts. Even if the sovereign concludes it needs its domestic creditors to accept an exchange offer, it often has substantial powers of moral suasion, particularly over domestic banks. Consequently, a new internationally supervised process for restructuring domestic debts would introduce new constraints on a sovereign's current ability to restructure domestic debt unilaterally—a much larger loss of national sovereignty than in a bankruptcy regime limited to external debts.

Including domestic debt also would unavoidably draw the IMF, a new court, or a dispute resolution body more deeply into a range of domestic political disputes. There are many more potential kinds of domestic claims on the sovereign than international claims—a point emphasized in chapter 7. Are wage arrears debt? Should arrears to pensioners be treated differently than those to the police and teachers? If the banking system collapses, are bank deposits guaranteed by the government part of the overall restructuring process? Or should they be addressed separately (and more quickly)? The bankruptcy regime's rules could well shape the terms all these groups received in the restructuring. The difficulties in deciding what constitutes domestic debt could be reduced by limiting the bankruptcy regime to domestic debts incurred as a result of the formal extension of credit to the sovereign. But no matter how "narrow" the definition of domestic debt, a regime that included domestic debt would be exponentially more complex than one limited to external debt.[46]

Mechanism to Provide New Senior Money?

Most bankruptcy regimes grant absolute priority to new financing. Creditors providing new money are among the first in line for payments if the reorganization fails and the debtor has to be liquidated. New financing is

45. Most domestic debt contracts lack provisions analogous to the collective action clauses found in English-law international bonds. Some legal analysts have even argued that introducing a contractual procedure for domestic debt restructurings might make domestic debt restructuring more difficult, since it would lay the basis for challenging the legality of a decree that superseded the contractually defined restructuring process.

46. Including domestic debt would almost certainly require dividing domestic and external debt into different classes (so-called mandatory classification). Moreover, the interests of holders of fixed-rate debt denominated in domestic currency, debt denominated in the domestic currency but indexed to inflation, debt payable in the domestic currency but indexed to a foreign currency, and domestic debts denominated in a foreign currency differ, making aggregation of all domestic debts difficult. See IMF (August 2002) for a more detailed discussion.

often called DIP financing after a provision in Chapter 11 of the US bankruptcy code.

No sovereign bankruptcy regime could grant private creditors providing new money to the sovereign the same level of protection as domestic bankruptcy regimes. Most proposals do not even try to provide new money with "absolute" priority in payments—a nebulous concept for a debtor that cannot be liquidated. Rather they just try to provide the new money with relative priority over some other external debt payments, though presumably not over payments to the IFIs.

Priority to new money can be provided in two ways. One is through explicit subordination agreements. Existing creditors legally subordinate themselves to the new money, so the creditors providing the senior funds have a legal claim on any payments made to the now-subordinated and formally junior creditors. The other way is by making the repayment of new money a requirement for a valid vote on the debtor's restructuring proposal. This is all the IMF proposed (IMF April 2003).[47] Neither option would provide external new money with priority over domestic debt payments or would prevent a debtor from falling into default on its "new money" financing if it also were not paying its other external debts. Realistically, this would not provide sufficient comfort to generate large private flows at reasonable rates.

Moreover, the IMF's existing ability to provide new money to a sovereign going through a debt restructuring weakens the case for an elaborate mechanism for the provision of private new money. Providing new money exclusively through the IMF makes it easier to link access to new financing to policy changes on the part of the debtor, helping to offset the absence of a court that can oversee a sovereign debtor's operations. Advocates of senior new private lending often are motivated more by the desire to reduce the IMF's role in the sovereign debt restructuring process rather than to fill an obvious gap in the system.[48]

Fundamental Tensions in the Design of Any Statutory Regime

The bankruptcy analogy is in many ways misleading, because the creation of a sovereign bankruptcy regime would almost certainly create a restructuring process that differs substantially from the corporate debt restructuring process. For example, the powers the judges (or their functional equivalent) sitting on an international bankruptcy court (or its equivalent)

47. In either case, the priority provided in the sovereign context is much weaker than that provided in domestic bankruptcy. Priority in domestic bankruptcy includes a priority claim on the debtor's assets if the debtor is shut down. A sovereign cannot be shut down, so a similar protection cannot be provided. Moreover, most mechanisms to provide priority do not provide effective legal remedies, should the debtor stop paying its "priority" financing.

48. For example, Steven Schwartz's (2000) proposal for private DIP financing was motivated by the need to get the IMF out of the business of lending to countries.

could exercise over a sovereign would likely be far more limited than the powers a bankruptcy court can exercise over an insolvent firm. No court is likely to ever be given the power to assume operational control of a sovereign debtor—or to transfer operational control to creditors.

The debtor's sovereignty creates a series of additional tensions that complicate the design of any new restructuring regime.

- First, no one can force a sovereign to make use of a bankruptcy regime's provisions. A sovereign always will have the option of reaching agreement with its creditors on its own, without any "court" supervision. Any bankruptcy regime has to include features that make it attractive to sovereign debtors—or risk the fate of the IMF's contingent credit line, which was discontinued after no IMF member applied to use it. The IMF's SDRM, for example, let the sovereign pick the set of instruments that would participate in the aggregated voting process without imposing substantial new constraints on a sovereign. We don't think this alone is a large enough change to upset the fundamental balance between a debtor and its creditors, which is needed for the sovereign debt market to work. However, the risk of more ambitious proposals that provide the debtor with substantially more protection altering the balance is real.
- Second, the penalties that can be imposed on a sovereign that fails to live up to bankruptcy regime's standards are limited as long as effective litigation against a sovereign debtor remains difficult. The main penalty available to the "referee" would be to lift formal bankruptcy protection—which might not be that strong a penalty. Another potential punishment for poor behavior is losing the ability to restructure through an aggregated vote. This, however, penalizes both the debtor and its creditors just when the debtor is getting its act together. Skeptics of the SDRM like Andrei Shleifer were right to note that the SDRM did not give creditors any new rights against the sovereign.[49] Giving creditors new powers and strengthening the incentive for a sovereign to seek bankruptcy protection likely would require lifting many of the de facto protections a sovereign now enjoys.

49. Shleifer (2003) argues that the US municipal bond market works—municipalities borrow at low rates, and default is rare—because the US bankruptcy regime for municipalities requires the judge decide on the basis of the best interest of the municipalities' creditors. This argument, though, puts too much emphasis on the "best interest of creditors" clause—a provision that generally has been interpreted only to require negotiations. More important, in practice, is the ability of a state government to prevent a municipality from even filing for Chapter 9. Most state governments intervene before a municipality goes belly up: States usually bail out a troubled municipality in return for significant changes in municipal administration. Municipalities, at the end of the day, are not sovereign. See McConnell and Picker (1993).

- Third, the limited power any bankruptcy court would have over a sovereign debtor would likely mean that losing access to IMF financing would remain the strongest penalty for poor debtor behavior. A country's IMF program—the primary surplus assumption and the projected real exchange rate path—almost certainly would continue to set the broad parameters for negotiations between the debtor and its creditors (unless the IMF is unable to reach agreement with the debtor on a primary surplus path, as in Argentina). Negotiations between a debtor and the majority of its creditors would continue to be shaped far more by the country's IMF program than by the presence of a sovereign bankruptcy regime able to force a minority of creditors to accept a restructuring proposal. (See IMF January 2003a.)
- Fourth, the different balance between debtor and creditor interests in national bankruptcy regimes complicates reaching agreement on any major changes. An ambitious sovereign bankruptcy regime would not necessarily emulate many features of corporate bankruptcy, but it would require consensus on the right way to apportion bargaining power between a sovereign debtor and its creditors.
- Finally, the "architects" of any new statutory regime have to strike a difficult balance between proposing an approach that seems too close to the current restructuring process to be worth the enormous effort required to ratify a new international treaty, and an approach that engenders opposition because it would radically change the current restructuring process. SDRM-lite proposals that do little more than create the legal authority to allow an aggregated supermajority vote hardly seem worth the trouble, now that Uruguay has demonstrated that clauses can do much the same thing if all the country's bonds are issued in the same jurisdiction. On the other hand, the enormous investment in new institutions, rules, and procedures required to replicate something close to Chapter 11 of the US bankruptcy code at the international level is hard to justify so long as sovereigns do not experience more severe legal problems than they have in recent restructurings.

Would a Statutory Regime Radically Change the Behavior of Either Sovereign Debtors or the IMF?

Proponents and opponents of a statutory regime often argue that granting the debtor greater legal protection, whether from litigation immediately after default or from holdout litigation following a successful deal, will transform the incentives of all players in the sovereign restructuring process. Anne Krueger argued that the SDRM would encourage sovereign debtors with truly unsustainable debts to move more quickly to stop the rush for the exits, to the gain of the debtor and the vast majority of its creditors. Creditors, in contrast, worry that a statutory proposal will strengthen the incentives of all debtors to suspend payments rather than tighten their fiscal policy belts and cut spending/raise taxes.[50] Many proponents of an international bankruptcy regime argue that its main advantage would be that it would change the IMF's own incentives, not those of debtors or private creditors. A bankruptcy regime would make the IMF—and its major shareholders—less willing to lend to countries with unsustainable debts.

All these claims should be taken with a grain of salt. The creation of a sovereign bankruptcy regime along the lines proposed by the IMF would likely have a far smaller impact than anyone would care to admit. Sovereigns already enjoy substantial protection from litigation. Aggregated voting among the sovereign's external bondholders won't eliminate the difficulties in coordinating the restructuring of external bonds and Paris Club and domestic debts. Nor will it eliminate the complexities created when domestic banks hold a large share of the sovereign's external debt. The risk of a restructuring triggering a run on the banks, a run on the local currency, or both will remain. The collapse of the domestic banking system—particularly when combined with the widespread insolvency in the corporate sector after a collapse in the exchange rate—assure that the sovereign crisis will lead to a severe fall in output, even if the sovereign has additional legal protection. Sovereign restructurings—particularly the complex restructurings requiring deep debt reduction and real concessions from many sets of creditors—won't suddenly become fast, painless, and easy.[51]

Would the SDRM, in its final form, have made a substantial difference in Argentina? The likely answer is no. Litigation by domestic bank depositors who resisted pesification and sought to obtain full payment in dollars from the domestic courts has been a far larger problem than litigation by external creditors.[52] The severe recession that followed default was the outcome of the run on the banks that led to a bank holiday, the run on the currency that led to capital and exchange controls, and the balance sheet impact of the devaluation on an economy with pervasive cur-

50. Of course, making it easier to default would also make it harder for sovereigns to obtain access to new credit. Some academics who believe that emerging markets have an intrinsic bias toward overborrowing argued that this was a reason to create a bankruptcy regime. The SDRM would make it harder for emerging-market governments with less-than-pristine reputations to overborrow. See Bulow (2002).

51. The IMF was aware that a standstill on sovereign payments would likely have been insufficient to avoid a generalized run out of the crisis country. Anne Krueger argued that capital and exchange controls and other nonmarket actions would still be needed. The IMF (February 2003) includes a sophisticated discussion of the risk of a sovereign debt restructuring triggering a domestic banking crisis. However, the SDRM proposal itself did little to address these risks.

52. Argentina's Economy Minister Roberto Lavagna has incentives to bluff, but he declared in November 2003 that investor litigation would have no effect on Argentina's restructuring proposal.

rency mismatches—not litigation from external creditors. The ability to restructure Argentina's 98 external bond instruments in a single aggregated vote would make it easier to avoid holdouts, but it would not magically produce restructuring terms acceptable to retail bondholders, domestic Argentine pension funds, and international investors. Aggregated voting won't eliminate a gulf between the maximum offer a debtor is willing to make and the minimum offer a majority of creditors say they are willing to consider.[53]

The argument that the SDRM would have led the IMF to pull the plug on Argentina earlier is no more convincing. The SDRM does not make it any easier to distinguish between temporary liquidity problems and deep problems of insolvency, or eliminate the risk of initiating a sovereign restructuring triggering a series of runs. Political pressures to avoid the financial and economic disruption that follows a default and steep falls in output would not disappear.

Codes and Committees

Codes of Conduct

Both the Banque de France (2003) and the Institute of International Finance (IIF 2003) have proposed creating a code of conduct to guide a sovereign debt restructuring. Proposals for legal reform tend to focus on ways to limit the risk of "rogue" or "holdout" creditors disrupting a restructuring, while proposals for codes tend to focus on improving the behavior of a sovereign during the restructuring. A code of conduct could be combined with contractual change, be embedded in a statutory regime, or complement the current exchange offer–based process for sovereign debt restructurings.

A code could aim to do many things. One option is a code that lays out broad general principles—transparency, good faith, fair burden-sharing, and comparability of treatment—for a sovereign restructuring. Focusing on general principles limits the risk of the code being applicable to a specific crisis but runs the risk of not being of much use either. Principles that everyone can agree on tend to be open to multiple interpretations. Attempts to provide more precise definitions of terms like "good faith" typically result in sharp disagreements.[54] Another option is a code that clari-

53. Argentina initially sought to reduce the face value of its outstanding international bonds by 75 percent, which would imply a larger haircut in net present value (NPV) terms (the discount rate the market assigns to these bonds will exceed their coupon). Argentina subsequently indicated it would improve its offer by recognizing past due interest, but as of July 2004, it is not clear whether creditors will accept this proposal.

54. Banque de France (2003) has suggested developing a code that would set out both general principles and best practices for meeting these general principles.

fies how the key parties in the restructuring—the sovereign, its private creditors, the Paris Club, the IMF, and other IFIs—should interact. This might strengthen informal norms that shape the behavior of various parties in the restructuring. However, no player now seems very keen to constrain in advance its options in a restructuring. An ambitious code might even create a neutral third party to arbitrate the disputes that arise between the debtor and its creditors. But it is hard to see how a third party could force a sovereign debtor or a dispersed group of creditors to accept its decisions; an arbitrator most likely would only make voluntary suggestions.

However, no code could

- prevent a creditor run, stop a rush to the courts by giving the sovereign formal protection against litigation, or create the ability to restructure with a majority vote. While a code could be made semibinding on a sovereign debtor, it can do no more than suggest, but not require, that creditors roll over positions. No matter how much a code might improve debtor behavior if a restructuring is needed, creditors are still likely to prefer to get out before the restructuring if they can. Similarly, a code can only suggest that creditors reward a debtor's good faith behavior by restraining from litigation. In the absence of clauses allowing restructuring through a majority vote, a code cannot bind a minority of holdouts to a restructuring deal. The classic critique of weapons nonproliferation treaties also applies to a code of creditor conduct; they bind only those that don't want to proliferate. A debtor that works cooperatively with most of its creditors may still experience difficulty from rogue creditors who are intent on using their legal leverage to extract a more favorable settlement.
- change the core preferences of different groups of creditors or the debtor. It will not remove differences between the restructuring terms amenable to institutional investors that mark to market, those amenable to retail investors, and those amenable to the Paris Club. A code similarly will not change a debtor's incentive to protect the banking system from the fallout of its decision to seek a restructuring, even if this means treating domestic and external debt differently.

Need for Balance

Proposals for a code can be broken down into codes of "good debtor conduct" and codes of "good creditor conduct." In practice, though, it is hard to trade "good conduct" by the debtor for "good conduct" by the creditors. Most proposed codes do not create a means of sanctioning bad behavior by creditors, but link the debtor's compliance with the code to access new

IMF lending.[55] Such codes therefore are often long on requirements for the debtor and short on credible commitments by creditors.[56] This, plus the inability of a code to make a commitment by most creditors binding on all creditors—creates a significant asymmetry between the demands the code makes on a debtor and the demands it places on creditors.[57] Since creditors are pushing for a code where their obligations are very limited and their ability to pursue legal action or to hold out is unhampered, there is little chance that debtors will accept their proposals.

A less ambitious, voluntary code could prove to be more useful. Debtors often do stop communicating with creditors when they stop paying. There is a sense—we think exaggerated—that there is no obvious process for going about a sovereign restructuring. Consequently, a code that tried to lay out the minimal requirements for a cooperative restructuring might improve the sovereign workout process, in part by setting out some basic expectations that even a government in the middle of an economic and political crisis should be able to follow. Such a code might even be self-enforcing since all parties have an interest in a successful restructuring. However, a code should not be expected to settle the difficult questions of how to "fairly" allocate the pain inherent in a debt restructuring across all creditors or how to strike the right balance between restructuring external debt and policy adjustments that affect the country's citizens.

A useful code could

- *emphasize disclosure*. The debtor should be expected to provide full and accurate information about its debt profile and restructuring plans to its creditors shortly after it falls into arrears. This should include publishing a full accounting (detailed and disaggregated) of

55. In theory, adherence to the code during the restructuring could be a condition for creditors' final agreement on restructuring terms. However, this raises obvious problems of time consistency. If the debtor dithers for a few years before finally getting its act together and then puts forward an acceptable proposal, creditors are unlikely to turn the proposal down just to punish the debtor for failing to live up to a code in the past.

56. The IIF (2003) code calls for disclosure of macroeconomic and financial information by the debtor, continuous consultation before a crisis, enhanced consultations with creditors during a crisis, a standing committee of creditors, a group of "wise men" to advise debtors in trouble on appropriate policies, and extended negotiations on the terms of a debt restructuring. Debtors also agree not to discriminate between domestic and external debt or between private and Paris Club claims. Yet while the IIF wants to be involved in the design of both a program's macroeconomic conditionality and the country's debt restructuring, it, unlike the IMF, is not willing to offer new money—nor are its members willing to commit to roll over their positions.

57. In the IIF's (2003) proposed code, bondholders would agree only to evaluate whether to continue to hold a bond on its own merits. Banks commit to "consider" rolling over their exposure, but recent experience suggests a bank can consider the pros and cons of rolling over its exposure and then decide to reduce it.

its outstanding debts soon after defaulting and informing creditors of any subsequent new issuance that increases its debt stock. When the debtor is ready to put forward its initial restructuring proposal, it should also provide a list of claims that would be restructured through the exchange or the initial restructuring proposal, those that would be restructured through other processes, and those that would not be restructured. It should also indicate how its overall restructuring proposal would apportion available near-term cash flow across different creditor groups, as well as how each creditor group would contribute to the creation of a viable medium-term debt profile.[58]

- *outline how to move from imminent default to a successful restructuring.* Creditors should organize themselves to provide constructive input into the restructuring process; standing committees are likely to be unrepresentative of the debtor's current creditors and therefore unlikely to help.[59] Debtors should have an obligation to consult with creditor representatives as they develop their restructuring proposal. Creditors will have the legal right to initiate litigation while the debtor is developing its restructuring proposal, though hopefully most creditors will refrain from litigating. Debtors are within their rights to seek to use their existing contractual powers—the ability to amend the financial terms of English-law bonds and to amend through exit consents the nonfinancial terms of New York–law bonds—to limit the risks holdouts pose when the exchange offer is made.
- *set realistic expectations for intercreditor equity.* No ex ante consensus on a "fair" allocation of the burden between domestic and external creditors exists. Perfect equity may not even be in the interest of external creditors: A domestic debt restructuring that triggers a bank run could ultimately result in lower recovery levels for external creditors. Private creditors are unlikely to be willing to embrace a common understanding on how to apply the Paris Club's principle of comparability. Little is gained from promising too much.
- *call for clauses in new bonds.* Bonds that emerge from the restructuring should contain clauses that allow the amendment of the bond's financial terms.

A minimal code that sets out principles that apply to all cases should not prevent a debtor from making commitments that go beyond its relatively modest requirements in return for more concrete and specific commit-

58. Uruguay's bond documentation formally requires a similar level of disclosure.

59. In relatively simple cases (e.g., limited number of instruments, rescheduling rather than debt reduction), the debtor may be able to rely on informal market soundings. In more complex cases, the debtor may need to work with different committees representing different groups of creditors.

ments from creditors. If a given creditor group is willing to roll over its claims, to put up new money, to agree not to take legal action to collect on its claims, or even to agree amongst themselves that they will take all decisions by a supermajority vote. (For example, the two-step restructuring process laid out by Bartholomew, Stern, and Luizza [2002] would commit creditors to take decisions by supermajority voting in stage one.) Then the debtor might want to match these additional creditor commitments with additional commitments of its own. On a more modest scale, a debtor might be willing to agree to pay the fees of advisors selected by a representative committee of cooperative creditors.

If the IMF determined that a modest code's disclosure requirements made sense, then the IMF could decide to link its lending to the debtor's efforts to live up to these requirements. But it would be a mistake to orient the IMF's lending during a restructuring solely toward forcing a reluctant debtor to abide by an ambitious, creditor-friendly code of conduct. The IMF has a number of goals following a default other than enforcing a code of good conduct.[60] Financing to support macroeconomic stabilization and to mitigate the loss of output immediately after a default may be a more important goal than quick agreement on an external debt restructuring. The IMF has enough difficulty securing sound macroeconomic policies from debtors in default—particularly if the crisis country already owes substantial sums to it and may default on it absent new IMF lending.[61] Consequently, the IMF is unlikely to be willing to make adherence to a code of conduct the sole criterion to determine whether it will lend to a debtor running arrears to its private creditors.

Ambitious plans to create a binding code of conduct are neither realistic nor desirable. However, a more modest code that tries only to force debtors to lay out their overall restructuring plan in a clear and transparent way could make a positive contribution to the resolution of sovereign debt crises. Such a code would try to map out more clearly the existing sovereign debt restructuring process—one based on consultation with creditors leading to an exchange offer, combined with the use of various amendment provisions to limit the risk of holdouts.

60. The IMF's current policy (IMF September 2002b) for lending into arrears requires a sovereign debtor make a "good faith effort to reach a collaborative agreement with its creditors." Formal IMF policy papers have hinted that good faith efforts often imply good faith negotiations (IMF July 2002b). In practice, though, the IMF generally has defined good faith very broadly, to the chagrin of private creditors. The IMF would be better served if it did not make promises that exceed what it is able (or willing) to deliver. The IMF should focus on encouraging a debtor to disclose both its macroeconomic program and its restructuring plans to private creditors.

61. The IMF board indicated (IMF September 2002b) that the IMF should continue to lend if negotiations broke down because creditors' demands implied greater macroeconomic adjustment than in the country's IMF program. This, of course, assumes that the country's IMF program set out an agreed, fully defined adjustment path—something that Argentina's 2003 program failed to do.

Committees

Sovereign debtors generally have not negotiated the precise financial terms of a general exchange with a creditors' committee. Instead, sovereigns have hired financial and legal advisors who have helped the debtor assess the terms that a significant fraction of creditors would accept. The country and its advisers then launch a "take-it-or-leave-it" exchange offer (Buchheit 2000a). The debtor usually indicated that it would go ahead with the exchange only if the exchange offer attracted sufficient participation (usually at least 80 or 85 percent of claims).[62]

There is no guarantee that engaging in protracted bargaining with a creditors committee will result in a more effective restructuring process. The current process lets a debtor introduce an offer that it believes will meet creditors' bottom line, and the need to attract widespread participation creates an incentive for the debtor to put forward a fair proposal. A process based on negotiations, in contrast, implies formal bargaining with a select group of creditors to gain the committee's endorsement of the debtor's proposal before launching an exchange. Given the difficulties creditors with disparate interests face taking a collective decision, formal bargaining might result in more strategic behavior, not more rapid agreement. Moreover, agreement with a committee neither guarantees that other bondholders will accept the exchange nor reduces the risk of holdouts. Changes in the market (and law) make historical comparisons difficult, but the historical record of committees is mixed. The bondholder committees in the 1930s did settle some defaults until the 1950s (Eichengreen and Portes 1995). Bank advisory committees did not necessarily produce rapid agreement in the 1980s, in part because the most reluctant bank on the advisory committee could hold up any deal.[63]

Many private creditors believe the IMF should deny financing to any debtor that refuses to negotiate exchange terms directly with a committee. This asks too much of the IMF. Exchange offers based on informal consultation and market soundings have worked: Bondholder committees have yet to prove their value. Until they do so, there is no need for the IMF to use its leverage to empower those creditors who sit on a committee. Of course, if enough bondholders give their proxy to members of a repre-

62. Russia is a partial exception. It negotiated the restructuring of its London Club debt with a bank advisory committee. "Investors" who bought the London Club debt in the secondary market were not directly represented, but the committee did include banks that had been active in the securitization of Russia's London Club debt. However, the general applicability of Russia's process remains open to question: Russia was formally restructuring syndicated bank loans, and, as discussed in chapter 4, it held an usually strong legal hand.

63. On the other hand, once agreement was reached with the bank advisory committee, the committee could help bring other banks into the restructuring. Smaller banks looked to the lead banks for cues about whether to agree to a restructuring, and lead banks put pressure on other banks to participate.

sentative creditors committee, the debtor will have to consult closely—though not necessarily formally negotiate—with the committee to be able to launch an effective exchange.

Assessing Reform Proposals

The discussion of contractual reforms highlighted the differences between various contractual proposals and endorsed collective action clauses that allow the amendment of a bond's key terms with the support of 75 percent of the holders of the bond (clauses like those Mexico used). The discussion of statutory proposals focused on the core questions that would have to be addressed in the design of a statutory regime, including the practical difficulties associated with laying the basis for an aggregated vote. We are more sympathetic to "light" statutory proposals that focus on creating the legal basis for aggregated voting rather than proposals that try to replicate all the features of Chapter 11 of the US bankruptcy law. However, until now, we have deferred explicitly evaluating the relative merits of the contractual and statutory approaches.

Any discussion of proposals to create a statutory international bankruptcy regime should acknowledge that many of the basic problems national bankruptcy regimes are designed to solve are simply not a problem in the sovereign context, at least not right now. The difficulty in seizing a sovereign's assets deters a rush to the courthouse and provides most sovereigns de facto protection from litigation while they develop their restructuring proposals. A sovereign, unlike a corporation, does not need protection from a minority of creditors who would rather liquidate than restructure. Argentina's creditors point out—not incorrectly—that Argentina has enjoyed two years of protection from its creditors even though it has not tried very hard to develop a restructuring plan. A few nuisance lawsuits by creditors who collect almost nothing won't have a major impact on the restructuring. A sovereign in default on its international debt often does have access to new money from domestic creditors and the IFIs even in the absence of a bankruptcy regime.

Conversely, most proposals to create an international bankruptcy regime would not solve some of the problems that do arise in the international context. The absence of rules laying out the relative priority of different sovereign claims does complicate reaching agreement on a sovereign restructuring. However, as discussed in chapter 7, the scale and diversity of claims on the sovereign makes designing a sensible—let alone an enforceable—set of sovereign priorities extremely difficult. The absence of a priority structure is an argument for a different kind of reform of the sovereign debt restructuring process, not an argument for clauses or the IMF's proposed bankruptcy regime.

Ultimately, the case for moving beyond collective action clauses and adopting an international bankruptcy regime hinges on the ability—or inability—of contractual change to offer an effective solution to the holdout problem. A sovereign's greatest legal vulnerability currently comes after it has reached agreement with most of its creditors and starts to resume payments, not when it is in default.

The statutory approach clearly offers a more elegant solution to the holdout problem than collective action clauses. Holdouts have not blocked recent restructurings, but the returns some recent holdouts have achieved risk inspiring additional litigation. Holdouts were a much bigger problem at the end of the series of debt restructurings that marked the 1980s than at the beginning. The gradual introduction of collective action clauses will help. But a creditor could still buy a controlling stake in an orphan bond and then keep that bond out of a restructuring that the holders of other bonds are willing to accept. An international bankruptcy regime that created a single, aggregated vote of all unsecured external bondholders would free a sovereign that gains the support of a supermajority of its external bondholders from the risk of litigation, even if it did not gain the support of a majority of the holders of each and every bond.

On the other hand, the practical difficulties in designing even a modest statutory bankruptcy regime are real. There is no easy way to determine who will be part of the aggregated vote or to define the role that the referee that oversees the vote should play in the restructuring process. The political difficulties in gaining support for a new treaty that overrides national law are at least as daunting (see "A Global Chapter 11?" *Wall Street Journal*, April 22, 2002). A modest proposal commensurate with the nature of the problems that have been observed in sovereign debt restructurings seems to offer too few gains to be worth the costs. A more ambitious proposal requires deeper and more invasive intrusions into national sovereignty than most countries are likely to find acceptable.

Signs that collective action clauses like those used by Mexico are emerging as the market norm therefore provide a strong argument against seeking statutory reform. Uruguay's new bonds demonstrate that contractual provisions even can allow an aggregated vote across a series of its New York–law bonds.[64] However, until these more innovative provisions show signs of entering a substantial share of the stock of outstanding sovereign debt, the case for contractual reform has to rest largely on the expanded use of more standard collective action clauses. Fortunately, most sovereigns—even large emerging economies like Russia and Brazil—have not issued nearly as many international bonds as Argentina. With a smaller number of

64. Many bonds are issued as part of a series—such as a medium-term note program. Rather than registering each bond in the series, a major issuer often obtains a single shelf registration and then issues a series of bonds that meet the shelf registration's basic regulatory requirements. This already "links" together the different bonds and helps to provide the basis for "aggregation." It would be more difficult to aggregate bonds that were part of different series or to write a contract aggregating New York-law, English-law, German-law, and Japanese-law bonds.

bonds, the practical difference between a single aggregated vote and an instrument-by-instrument vote starts to shrink—so long as *all* the debtor's bonds have majority-restructuring provisions.

Nonetheless, clauses will not transform the restructuring process overnight. In the next few years, relying on contractual reforms means making the existing system work. Argentina, and no doubt others, will need to rely on provisions that allow the amendment of bonds' nonfinancial terms in order to make holding out unattractive.

Conclusion

Contractual change—or a treaty creating a sovereign bankruptcy regime along the lines of the IMF proposal—would address only one of the current market failures that complicate a sovereign restructuring: the risk of holdout litigation. Letting more restructuring decisions be taken by a supermajority vote could allow debtors to spend more time finding a deal acceptable to most of its creditors and less time working with their lawyers to minimize their vulnerability to holdout litigation. However, legal reform is not well suited to addressing the host of other difficulties facing a sovereign that needs to restructure its debts. Protection from the risk of holdout litigation won't minimize the risk of a sovereign restructuring leading to costly spillovers into the rest of the economy. It won't make it any easier to prevent a sovereign debt restructuring from triggering a collapse in the banking system, particularly when local banks are the sovereign's major creditors. The diversity of claims on the sovereign will still complicate reaching rapid agreement on restructuring terms, especially when deep debt reduction is needed. Addressing the market failures created by the secondary runs that follow a sovereign default requires creative thinking—and tools other than clauses or bankruptcy-style legal protection.

The case for taking steps to limit the risk of holdouts should rest on the ability of these steps to make the restructuring process more transparent and make the outcome of the restructuring somewhat easier to predict ex ante—not on their ability to radically reform the international financial system. Efforts to provide a sovereign with more protection from litigation—either through protection immediately after a default or through protection from the risk of holdout litigation after a restructuring agreement—are unlikely to transform the incentives of the major players in the sovereign restructuring process radically. Litigation simply is not the biggest problem a bankrupt sovereign currently faces. Contractual reform is worthwhile because it would improve on the existing restructuring process at a low cost, not because it would make the sovereign restructuring process smooth and trouble-free.

9

Recommendations for Reform

The international financial system is in far from robust health. Not because the institutional architecture of the international financial system has major gaps—the hardware of the international financial system is in better shape than is commonly assumed. The tools needed to respond to a wide range of crises by and large already exist, though there is always room for improvement. It is the software of the international financial system—the policies and practices that determine how the existing toolkit is used—that is in most need of an upgrade.

The rhetoric of many key policymakers sets a goal—limiting access to IMF financing over time—that would take the international community's most effective tool for financial fire fighting off the table. That is why limiting IMF lending has remained a long-term goal, conveniently ignored in actual crises. Even a country undergoing a debt restructuring may need access to significant IMF financing. A framework based on limits alone fails to provide real answers to the challenges posed by the sputtering, but still real, integration of emerging economies into the global financial system.

The biggest problem with the current framework is not the gap between what is said and what is done or that the posited goal of limits is unrealistic even as a long-term policy objective. Rather, it is that the current policy framework has precluded serious discussion of the best use of the IMF's ability to provide substantial emergency financing to a range of emerging economies. Claiming that substantial liquidity will not be provided in the future allows the custodians of the global financial order to avoid defining the circumstances when such liquidity provision is the right policy—and when it is the wrong policy.

This is unfortunate because the biggest policy challenge the international community confronts is not developing new tools for managing international financial crises but rather finding the best way of using the existing tools. The common image of vast flows of financial capital dwarfing a small IMF is true—if the IMF's lending capacity is compared with financial flows into the United States. But this image is no longer accurate for emerging economies. The expansion of the IMF's lending capacity in 1998 coincided with a fall in capital flows to emerging economies and a shift from current account deficits to current account surpluses in many of these economies. Capital flows started to recover in 2003 but remain well below their earlier peak.

The architecture for debt restructuring is also in decent shape. Even in the absence of an international bankruptcy regime, a sovereign enjoys effective protection from its external creditors while it develops its restructuring proposal. Debt exchanges provide a viable, if not always elegant, means of restructuring international bonds and other traded securities. The continued introduction of collective action clauses into bond contracts will only make the process more effective. Bank committees, official action, and moral suasion can help coordinate the rollover of cross-border bank credits. New money during the restructuring period comes from the IMF. That is not a bad thing: The IMF, at least in principle, can use the provision of new money both to shape the policies that a country pursues while in default and to push for the rapid development of a restructuring plan.

The current approach to crisis resolution has four major problems.

- The stated framework for policy—limiting IMF lending over time—has failed to produce consistent IMF lending decisions. If actual practice, not stated intent, defined policy, then the "rule" that best describes current access policy would be: provide larger quantities of financing to more heavily indebted countries to match their larger financing needs but, if possible, do so in fits and starts to avoid appearing to provide large amounts of financing. The IMF's total lending to the major emerging economies now exceeds its total lending at the peak of the Asian, Russian, and Brazilian crises, but its loan portfolio is now in much more heavily indebted countries.[1]

1. Between the end of 1996 and the end of 1998, IMF lending to a set of 12 crisis-prone emerging economies (the major users of IMF credit, and countries that went through a debt restructuring) increased by $35.4 billion, growing from $36.6 billion to $72.0 billion. It then fell back to $46.2 billion at the end of 2000. The IMF's lending to these countries subsequently has increased by $43.8 billion, growing to $90.0 billion at the end of 2003. The average government debt ratio of the emerging economies that had borrowed heavily from the IMF, weighted by their share of the IMF's lending portfolio, rose from 45.8 percent of GDP in 1998 to 89.6 percent GDP in 2002 (debt data are from Moody's Investor Service 2003).

- The range of problems addressed by large-scale IMF lending has been expanded. Rather than providing large short-term financing in the face of a run, the IMF is now providing large medium-term—or perhaps long-term—loans to prevent large government debt loads from spiraling out of control. Mexico was able to repay most of its loan in two to three years; Turkey is scheduled to repay large chunks of its 2001–02 loan only in 2005–06 and is likely to need more time. The IMF also is effectively being called on to act as a lender of last resort to fragile, dollarized domestic banking systems. No effort has been made to explain whether these new uses of IMF financing are a necessary part of the world's effort to help emerging economies adjust to an integrated global market.
- The IMF and the G-7 have not been willing, at least for large countries, to play an active role either in inducing a change in an unsustainable exchange rate regime or in helping a country through its debt restructuring. Rather, the IMF and the G-7 have preferred to dole out their funds in a series of programs that try to catalyze the voluntary restoration of market confidence. This strategy can work when conditions are right. In other cases, though, it simply helps the country dig itself into a deeper hole—and leaves the IMF unable to help when the country does confront its debt problems.
- Too much emphasis has been placed on international sovereign bonds relative to other potential sources of financial pressure and on protection from external litigation relative to other risks that arise in a sovereign debt restructuring. Too little attention, for example, has been placed on the risk of the decision to seek a restructuring triggering a bank run or other runs on nonsovereign claims. False expectations have been created that a better process for restructuring international sovereign bonds will reduce the need for IMF lending—and the need for an active IMF role in the debt restructuring process.

Avoiding crises altogether remains a worthwhile policy goal for emerging economies and the IMF. At the same time, efforts to prevent crises are unlikely ever to be completely successful. Emerging economies often finance themselves in ways that generate an ongoing risk of crisis, whether from dependence on short-maturity debt, on foreign-currency debt, on external debt, or all three. They typically lack the deep reservoirs of credibility that sometimes enable advanced economies to follow irresponsible economic policies for a time and then make the needed adjustments gradually, without facing a deep crisis. The IMF, the G-7, and others with a stake in the health of the global financial system should expect to continue to receive calls for help—and plan accordingly.

This chapter is divided into three sections. The first expands on our argument that the core "hardware" needed for crisis resolution is largely in place. Ample room to use the existing tools better undermines the case for radical institutional reform. The second section develops our argument that weaknesses in the current "software" of crisis resolution impede effective crisis resolution. Hopes that the need for financial support to emerging economies will wither away over time are unrealistic, have masked a substantial transformation in the IMF's role in the system, and have blocked a serious discussion of how IMF financing should be used to help emerging economies adjust to an integrated global market. The final section outlines our proposed framework for crisis resolution.[2]

"Hardware" Largely in Place

The hardware of the international financial system allows a wide range of responses to a range of crises. The toolkit has gaps, but they are relatively small.

The most important tool remains the IMF's capacity to provide emerging economies with partial insurance against the risk of liquidity runs. Without the IMF, countries would have to hold more reserves, borrow much less, and impose more restrictions on domestic and external investors' ability to move capital freely across borders—and likely still experience crises. The IMF's institutionalized, multilateral lending capacity avoids the need to organize an ad hoc coalition of the financially willing each time a crisis occurs. In a world of sovereign states, international macroeconomic policy advice needs to be attached to a loan, not a threat.

IMF lending alone, though, is not enough. Debt restructurings will continue to be necessary, both to defer payments while a country takes steps to right itself and to clean up after it has fallen off the proverbial cliff. In the first instance, creditors need to give up only their right to be paid in full on the date their claim matures, not the right to be paid in full at a later date.[3] In the latter case, the country's debts must be reduced to match its reduced payments capacity. Depending on the circumstances, it may be necessary to restructure international sovereign bonds, cross-border bank lines, domestic sovereign debt, or even domestic deposits.

2. Eichengreen (2002), Fischer (2002), Kenen (2001), Eichengreen and Kletzer (2003), and Cohen and Portes (2004) have all put forward their own proposals for reforming the world's approach to crisis resolution.

3. The right financial terms for a debt restructuring depend on the country's circumstances. Neither Korea nor Ukraine had too much debt, only too much debt coming due at the end of 1997 and from 1998–2001, respectively. Consequently, a restructuring that extended maturities at a reasonable price worked in both cases. In contrast, Argentina's attempt to solve its liquidity problems in 2001 through its expensive, voluntary megaswap failed. Argentina was taking on additional debt at high interest rates at a time when it could not afford to pay all of its existing debts.

Case for Partial IMF Liquidity Insurance

Our defense of the current hardware for crisis resolution hinges on our belief that the IMF should aim to provide partial, rather than full, liquidity insurance to emerging economies. The IMF exists to provide countries with some protection against the risk of running out of reserves. The IMF's insurance, though, is partial: It lacks the capacity to provide enough funds to let everyone who has lent to major emerging economies exit. This, though, is not a bad thing. Creditors should not be protected from the risk of all losses, and debtors with poor policies should not be protected from the risk of default. Of course, the capacity to provide partial insurance to a wide range of emerging economies implies the capacity to provide close to full insurance to those economies with relatively little debt and comparatively sound policies. That also is not something to condemn. Emerging economies with a history of responsible economic management ought to be rewarded with more protection than those with a history of profligacy.

Many analytic models of crisis resolution (box 9.1) postulate a world filled with liquidity runs on otherwise sound economies or a world where official rescue loans distort all incentives for sound borrowing and sound lending (moral hazard). These models often are critical of the effectiveness of partial bailouts, or partial bail-ins. They also tend to argue that the IMF either needs to be given a lending capability commensurate with a domestic lender of last resort or must lend only small sums to avoid moral hazard. Unfortunately, these models rarely assess potential real-world trade-offs. No IMF liquidity insurance means no moral hazard, but it also could transform manageable crises into economic disasters. Yet the risk of failing to nip runs and self-fulfilling crises of confidence in the bud has to be balanced with concerns that expectations of financial help will lead countries and their creditors to take risks that make future crises more likely.

Academic analysis that explicitly models crises in ways to avoid all or nothing conclusions suggests that partial IMF insurance can work. Protecting policymakers from the risk of a run leading to a catastrophic crisis before their investment in improved policies in times of stress pays off can encourage policymakers to pursue responsible policies rather than give up. Conditional IMF lending consequently may reduce, rather than increase, debtor moral hazard. Substantial, but not unlimited, official financing can convince creditors that default does not loom even if the most risk-averse among them want to leave (Corsetti, Guimaraes, and Roubini 2003). Partial bailouts—what the IMF calls catalytic financing—can work so long as the crisis country does not start from too weak a position.

Consequently, the risk of IMF moral hazard from IMF lending can be managed in better ways than denying all emerging economies any IMF insurance. Linking IMF lending to a country's willingness to make neces-

Box 9.1 Crisis prevention

It is hard to delve into crisis resolution without developing some sense of why crises happen in the first place. Our recommendations for crisis prevention are hardly radical. It is hard to top a list that includes less debt, less risky forms of borrowing, flexible exchange rates, well-regulated banking systems, early disclosure of financial weaknesses, and a long hard slog to build institutional and financial credibility through sustained implementation of sound fiscal and monetary policies. We emphasize four items:

- *Emerging economies that cannot borrow in ways that offer insulation against the risk of crises need to borrow less.* Few buffers against financial instability are better than long-term, fixed-rate, domestic currency–denominated debt. Such debt offers insurance against a refinancing crisis, an interest rate shock, and a depreciation in the real exchange rate. Emerging economies, though, often cannot borrow long-term in their own currency—whether because of their own lack of policy credibility or imperfections in global capital markets. Short-term debt emerges in equilibrium in part because investors have an interest in keeping countries with limited credibility on a short leash. Reducing debt levels usually yields dividends in two ways: Less debt is less debt, and the country's ability to borrow in less risky fashions goes up.
- *Pay particular attention to the systemic risks that the banking sector's foreign-currency liabilities create.* Countries have accumulated massive currency mismatches in two ways. Thai banks and finance companies built up an impressive currency mismatch by extensive external borrowing that was used to finance domestic foreign currency–denominated loans, even though most domestic deposits were in the local currency. Argentina's financial system built up an equally impressive currency mismatch by taking in domestic dollar deposits and making domestic dollar loans (in an economy with a small export sector). Insisting that the banks match foreign-

(box 9.1 continues next page)

sary (and often politically painful) policy changes limits the risk of the IMF weakening incentives for sound policies. East Asian countries in particular seem to have concluded that they would rather have immense war chests of foreign exchange reserves than run the risk of having to turn to the IMF again.

The partial nature of the IMF's insurance limits the risk of diluting creditors' incentives for sound risk management. To be sure, those who lent at short maturities and who knew when to get out will have incurred fewer losses than in a world with no IMF. But the IMF never lends enough to allow all creditors to get out, and private creditors have taken large losses in several crises.[4] The roughly $10 billion in net new financing the IMF provided Argentina in 2001 paled in comparison with the government of Argentina's roughly $95 billion debt to private creditors, the Argentine bank-

4. The fact that IMF lending can finance the exit of short-term debt is one of many reasons why the IMF should be on the watch for countries that depend heavily on short-term debt—particularly if that debt is denominated in foreign currency. See Goldstein and Turner (2004) for an extensive discussion of why the IMF also should pay more attention to the currency structure of a country's debts.

Box 9.1 *(continued)*

currency assets and liabilities is not enough to protect against a systemic crisis: The banks simply pass their currency risk on to their clients. Steps that discourage the banks from taking on foreign-currency deposits in the first place—like high reserve requirements on foreign currency–denominated bank liabilities—would reduce the banks' need to match their foreign-currency liabilities with domestic foreign-currency loans.

- *Don't stuff the banking system with government paper.* Emerging markets are subject to different risks than advanced economies and cannot simply imitate bank regulation in advanced economies. Bank regulation in advanced economies traditionally has assumed that the low yields on government bonds will deter the banks from doing little more than lending to the government. Consequently, banks usually don't have to hold any capital against the risk of default on their local-government debt portfolio. However, banks in emerging economies may need to be forced to hold significant capital against their holdings of local-government debt.
- *Flexible exchange rates.* Flexible exchange rates don't suddenly turn an emerging economy into an advanced economy. They typically don't allow—at least not yet—an emerging economy to adopt a countercyclical monetary policy, even if they do facilitate the real exchange rate adjustment that is part and parcel of being an emerging economy. Flexible exchange rates do tend to remind private borrowers of the risks associated with borrowing in a foreign currency—even if they also can create pressure on governments to issue domestic debt denominated in foreign currency to help manage exchange rate pressures. Flexible exchange rates certainly don't eliminate the risk of a crisis, as Brazil discovered. But it is also hard to imagine how Brazil could have managed the shock of 2002 without the ability to let its exchange rate adjust.

ing system's $80 billion debt to its depositors, and the Argentine private sector's $50 billion debt to its external creditors (box 9.2).

The evidence does not suggest that the amount of insurance the IMF has provided to emerging economies since 1995 has systematically distorted global capital flows. A world dominated by moral hazard should be marked by large credit flows into those emerging economies that potentially could draw on a large IMF loan. That is not the current pattern of capital flows. Emerging economies are now, in aggregate, running a substantial current account surplus and lending money to the industrial economies (Martin Wolf, "A Very Dangerous Game," *Financial Times*, October 1, 2003). Those emerging-market central banks now helping to finance the large US current account and fiscal deficits through the purchase of US Treasury bonds presumably are not doing so because they expect that the rest of the G-7 will bail out the United States.

The strongest case for moral hazard has come in those specific cases where creditors' sense of risk and reward was distorted by a perception that a country was too strategically important to the G-7 to be allowed to fail. Russia's creditors bet—inaccurately—that the G-7 would provide

Box 9.2 The Argentine debt restructuring process

In Argentina, the official sector has come close to abdicating its traditional role of negotiating an economic program with the debtor that outlines, in broad terms, the official sector's assessment of what the country and its creditors need to do to restore debt sustainability. The US Treasury believes the macroeconomic parameters of an IMF program interfere with private negotiations between a sovereign debtor and its creditors. Argentina's IMF program includes a primary surplus sufficient to allow Argentina to pay the international financial institutions and its "senior" domestic debt, but the final primary surplus target—the key macroeconomic content of a country's IMF program—is expected to emerge from Argentina's "negotiations" with its private creditors. This is a new and potentially risky approach to debt restructuring, which may not work as intended.[1]

First, it requires an unprecedented degree of coordination among Argentina's private creditors. Argentina's creditors are more diverse than in other recent sovereign restructurings—German, Italian, and Japanese retail investors (or their representatives) are sitting at the table with international institutional investors, Argentine pension funds, and representatives of private Argentine investors who bought into Argentina's external debt. It will be hard for such diverse investors to negotiate both restructuring terms and the country's macroeconomic framework. In recent bond restructurings, the debtor has not negotiated restructuring terms, let alone macroeconomic policy, with its creditors, but rather launched an exchange offer after informal consultations with market participants. Argentine creditor representatives claim that the formation of an umbrella committee representing a significant fraction of the claims in default demonstrates their ability to resolve issues of creditor coordination. But forming a committee is not enough: The committee may split when real decisions have to be taken. Argentina's creditors may be able to agree among themselves that Argentina should offer more but be unable to agree on any concessions to offer Argentina.

Second, the absence of an IMF program that helps to define realistic expectations for either Argentina or its creditors is likely to reduce the chances of a successful exchange. Creditors are initially asking for 65 cents on the dollar. Market prices of around 30 cents on the dollar throughout 2003 and early 2004 probably provide a more realistic assessment of what the country may be able and willing to pay. But there remains a large gulf even between market prices and the government of Argentina's (2003) restructuring guidelines. The IMF program does not provide a benchmark that can help nudge the two sides toward a realistic agreement.

(box 9.2 continues next page)

Russia with unlimited insurance.[5] Turkey's creditors certainly are aware of the country's strategic importance. This dilemma does not have an easy solution. Rules preventing the IMF from lending large sums would not eliminate the ability of the G-7 countries—acting collectively or individually—to bail out strategically important countries on their own.

Some have suggested that IMF-sanctioned standstills offer a good across-the-board substitute for IMF loans. We disagree. In the theoretically interesting, though practically rare, case of a pure run on a perfectly solvent entity, either a lender of last resort or a standstill stops the run:

5. See Rubin and Weisberg (2003) for an account of the decision not to augment or reprogram Russia's IMF loan to avoid a default in August 1998.

Box 9.2 *(continued)*

Third, the political economy of reform is likely to be harder, not easier, if a country has to negotiate its economic program with its private creditors. Any additional adjustment can easily be portrayed as serving the interest of Argentina's creditors, not the broader interest of sustaining Argentina's economic recovery. Argentina is, not surprisingly, resisting creditors' calls for formal "negotiations." A country that has told the IMF that a primary surplus above 3 percent is politically and socially unfeasible will find it difficult to commit to more fiscal adjustment after negotiations with its creditors. The chances of a successful exchange would have been greater if Argentina had followed the model used by other sovereigns: negotiate a realistic primary surplus target with the IMF, which sets a benchmark for an exchange offer, then consult with private creditors to develop restructuring terms that appeal to different creditor groups before launching a take-it-or-leave exchange.

Fourth, the absence of an agreed-upon macroeconomic framework leaves the official sector poorly positioned to offer carrots or use sticks to get the restructuring moving. Sticks include denying Argentina access to new IMF financing. Carrots include reduction of bilateral Paris Club claims to improve the debtor's cash flow, or even net new financing to the debtor. Such intervention is not simply official meddling. The official sector has more exposure to Argentina than either European retail investors or international institutional investors. It has much to lose if the restructuring terms Argentina offers to private creditors fail to add up, or if Argentina's restructuring proposal fails, leading to a protracted stalemate that eventually hinders Argentina's recovery.

It is certainly possible that Argentina will put forward an offer that attracts widespread participation and avoids a protracted stalemate. Argentina may find creative ways to close the gap between its Dubai offer and the current market value of its debt, whether by providing some upfront cash at the time of the deal, by recognizing some past due interest, or by deciding to run a larger primary balance. The IMF and the multilateral development banks (MDBs) could even decide to take a more active role in the restructuring process, perhaps by helping Argentina finance additional upfront cash payments in return for a commitment to additional fiscal adjustment. But the official sector's "hands off" approach is one of the reasons why the Argentine default already has dragged for over two and a half years without resolution and could drag even longer.

---

1. See also Truman (2004) for views similar to ours on the crucial role of the official sector in guiding the debt restructuring process.

Creditors run only because others may. In reality, though, creditors usually harbor doubts about the debtor's ability to make the adjustments needed to assure its long-run solvency as well as concerns that other creditors will pull their funds out. They would much rather be assured by the availability of a lender of last resort than be locked in through a standstill.

Moreover, the real world is far messier than the simple picture painted in most academic models of standstills. Stopping payments on some types of debt risks triggering other kinds of runs. Suspending payments on the sovereign's external debt, for example, risks triggering a bank run, a flight out of local assets, pressure on the currency, and corporate payment difficulties. The government could limit this risk by combining a sovereign payments standstill with bank holidays and comprehensive capital controls.[6] Both bank holidays and comprehensive controls risk turning the government's financial difficulties into an economywide payment problem. Indeed, few steps are more likely to deepen the economic contraction associated with a sovereign debt restructuring than a comprehensive bank holiday. Plus, anticipation of a bank holiday or capital controls will only strengthen incentives for domestic depositors and investors to run at the first sign of trouble, making crises more difficult to manage. For countries with low levels of debt that encounter liquidity difficulties, the risk of a broad standstill exceeds the risk associated with large-scale IMF lending.

There is no compelling empirical or theoretical case for taking the option of large-scale financing entirely off the table. At the same time, it does not make sense to provide all emerging economies with the same insurance against liquidity runs or to divorce liquidity support from policy changes. A country facing liquidity pressure may be liquid if its creditors don't run and illiquid if they do but also may be solvent if it changes its policies and insolvent if it does not. Countries with too much debt or with too little capacity to pull off the needed policy adjustments should not get the same kind of insurance as less indebted economies.

Successful rescue loans—with success defined as paying the loan back relatively quickly as well as the stabilization of the crisis country—generally have come from lending to countries with both reasonable debt loads and a political commitment to make the necessary policy changes. Mexico, Korea, and Brazil in 1998 all had high levels of short-term debt but relatively low overall debt levels, and all paid the IMF back relatively quickly. Countries with higher levels of debt—whether external or public debt—generally have *not* repaid the IMF as quickly.[7] The IMF has done better when its tries to save a country with relatively low levels of debt from the full consequences of hanging on to a pegged exchange rate for too long than when it tries to save a country from the consequences of building up a large debt stock and only belatedly making the needed adjustments.

6. Such controls would limit the ability of the country's own citizens and foreign residents alike to trade local currency for foreign currency and also limit the ability of local banks and firms to obtain the foreign exchange needed to pay their international debts without authorization.

7. Chapter 4 systematically reviews the IMF's major lending commitments since Mexico. IMF programs failed (in part because of a failure to implement IMF programs) to avoid a sovereign default in Russia and to prevent systemic corporate default in Indonesia. Thailand's program was a mixed bag: Thailand avoided the bank run that devastated Indonesia but never regained the confidence of external bank creditors and had to run large current account surplus to repay its existing external debt. It is unrealistic—and undesirable—to expect the IMF to be able to avoid all mistakes. The IMF should take some risks. At the same time, .500 is a great batting average in baseball but probably not a good one for large-scale IMF lending.

Many are, understandably, uncomfortable with a process that in the end relies on the official sector's judgment—hopefully informed by sound analysis—to identify the countries that deserve large-scale IMF support to avoid a debt restructuring. But rules that insist the IMF lend the same amount to all crisis countries simply do not make sense. Neither a "never lend large sums" policy rule nor an "always lend large sums" policy rule works well across a range of crises. The first provides too little financing when a country without too much overall debt experiences temporary liquidity problems. Limiting the IMF to its current lending norm of 100 percent of quota in a year (and 300 percent over three years) assures that the IMF will not provide enough to matter, given private investors' ability to shift their financial assets out of a crisis country. The second provides too much financing when a heavily indebted country experiences trouble.[8] A country with an external debt to GDP ratio of 60 percent should not expect the same treatment as one with 30 percent, even if both experience liquidity difficulties.[9]

The idea that the IMF should lend large sums only to countries that prequalify for such support with good policies has some conceptual appeal. However, the difficulties of prequalification should not be underestimated. Defining the right set of policies for prequalification is hard. Our understanding of the policies emerging economies need is still evolving: In 1998 Argentina was considered to be something of a model for other emerging economies.[10] The countries sure to qualify for help are unlikely to need help and may never apply. Countries that do not qualify for help in advance may still be worth helping if their problems are correctable and if they are willing to commit to needed reforms.

Above all, the IMF's major shareholders are not prepared to live by such a constraining set of rules. They are under too much pressure to give countries a chance to right themselves. Turkey and Brazil (particularly in 2001–02) would not have prequalified for IMF protection under any reasonable scheme, but it is hard to believe that the G-7 would be willing to

8. Ortiz (2002) recommended that the IMF provide any country willing to make needed policy changes with a large IMF loan to help avoid a payments interruption. This would provide the country and its creditors with more certainty about the IMF's policy response, in part because Ortiz would not link such financing to efforts to convince private creditors to maintain their exposure.

9. Manasse, Roubini, and Schimmelpfennig (2003) found that emerging economies are at risk of default at substantially lower levels of debt than more advanced economies. European economies are not at risk of default with debt-to-GDP ratios of 60 percent, but most emerging economies are. Debt-to-GDP ratios of above 50 percent are sufficient to significantly increase the risk of default.

10. Argentina lacked many of the vulnerabilities of the Asian-crisis countries. Foreign banks participated heavily in its domestic financial system, the banking system was generally thought to be well-regulated, Argentina's accounts were transparent, and a currency board allegedly assured consistency between its peg and its monetary policy.

Figure 9.1 Net private debt flows to emerging markets, 1993–2004

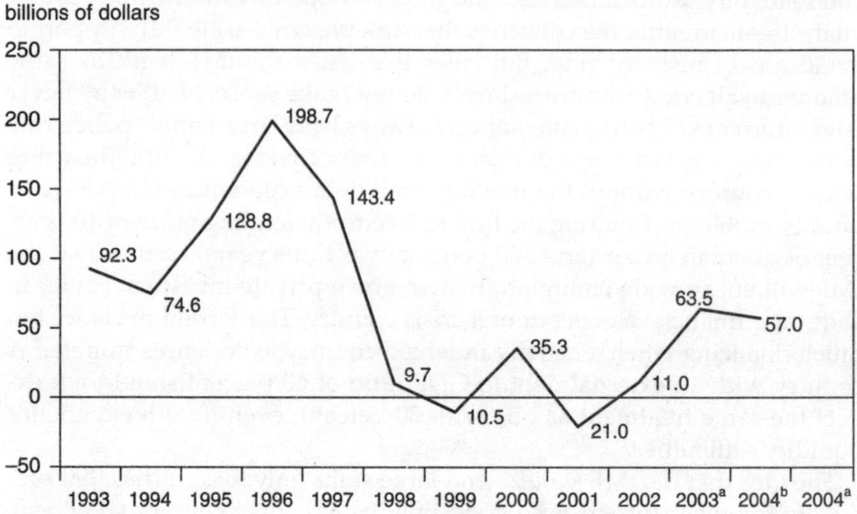

a. Estimated.
b. Forecast.
Source: Data from Institute of International Finance (various years).

stand entirely aside and let each of these countries sink or swim without any international support. No country is too big to fail, but some are likely too big or too important not to help.

Does the IMF Have the Resources It Needs?

Going into the Asian crisis, the IMF's total lending capacity was substantially smaller than the annual sum international investors lent to emerging economies.[11] The IMF's maximum lending capacity is now between \$190 billion and \$200 billion, relative to between \$130 billion and \$140 billion in 1997. Net private lending to emerging economies has picked up from the low levels of 2001 and 2002, but even with the current modest resurgence, capital flows have not returned to their 1997 levels. The estimated \$64 billion in net private debt flows to emerging economies in 2003 was both well above the 1998–2002 average of \$5 billion and well below the 1995–97 average of \$157 billion (IIF 2004) (see figure 9.1). This is not to say that capital flows cannot now overwhelm IMF lending—they clearly can. But right now this risk often stems more from the capability of do-

11. See IIF (2004) and IMF (1998). Net private credit is the sum of bank lending and other credit flows—largely bonds. The IIF estimates that the emerging economies in its data set owed \$562 billion to commercial banks, \$856 to "other private creditors" (mostly bond holders), and \$732 billion to official creditors (multilateral and bilateral) at the end of 2003.

mestic investors in emerging economies to move their savings offshore in mass than from the risk of international investors suddenly withdrawing their financing from emerging economies.

The IMF currently has the resources it needs to put enough money on the table to make a difference in most emerging-market crises. That, however, does not mean that the IMF's funds will never need to be augmented. The present pattern of global capital flows will not persist forever. As the world economy grows, as global trade continues to expand, and as some of the $500 billion in capital now flowing to the United States to finance its current account deficit starts flowing to emerging economies, the case for expanding the IMF's lending capacity will need to be reassessed. Over the medium to long term, IMF resources may need to be expanded to parallel the growth of world trade and international financial flows and the greater integration of the global economy.

The Restructuring Architecture

Three sets of concerns motivate sovereign debt theorists. Some argue that the core objective of a sovereign debt contract must be to sustain incentives for payment by penalizing sovereigns who default. Some worry more about the risk of debt contracts obstructing a helpful restructuring in the event of unexpected economic shocks, including shocks that originate in changes in capital markets' willingness to finance countries. Some others argue that the real issue is how best to discourage international investors from fueling emerging-market governments' own intrinsic biases toward deficits and overborrowing.

All three concerns are important. The expectation that payment terms can be altered too easily will inhibit lending, reduce capital flows, and increase borrowing costs. Yet a preemptive restructuring that avoids a certain default—or a restructuring that lets a country with unsustainable debts that has stopped payments get out of default in an orderly manner—can be in the interest of both the debtor and its creditors. It is particularly important that countries that can borrow only at high costs borrow for the right reasons. Yet steps to make borrowing harder and more expensive to deter future overborrowing do not help countries that already have too much debt.

Many who look at the sovereign debt market—from all three points of view—worry about the absence of any formal institutions for sovereign debt restructuring. Emerging-market sovereigns borrow at spreads that imply a significant probability of default, spreads similar to those for high-yield corporate bonds. Yet it seems, at least superficially, that the sovereign debt market lacks the institutional infrastructure—namely a bankruptcy regime—that make the high-yield corporate bond market work. Many New York–law sovereign bond contracts even lack provisions outlining an obvious process for changing the bond's payment terms. Unlike in the 19th century, standing committees of creditors are not sitting around ready to represent creditors in a sovereign restructuring.

It is important, though, not to overstate the impact of the absence of formal institutions for sovereign debt restructuring. Sovereign debtors who default on their external debt do not have to worry about the threat of liquidation, fear that their international reserves will be seized (if they take some basic precautions), or risk losing control of their domestic assets. Neither the absence of a treaty setting up an international bankruptcy regime for sovereigns nor the absence of contractual provisions spelling out how to do change a bond's payment terms has been an insurmountable obstacle to a restructuring. Multi-instrument exchange offers provide the basic technology to coordinate the restructuring of international sovereign bonds and other traded securities. Bondholders pragmatically have preferred to trade instruments that risk not being paid for new instruments that will be paid, regardless of unenforceable contractual provisions promising that a bond would never be restructured.

This is not to say that the growing use of collective action clauses that allow a supermajority of creditors to vote to amend a bond's financial terms—or the use of the "aggregating" superclauses in Uruguay's bonds—would not make sovereign bond restructurings smoother. The absence of provisions that spell out explicitly how to change a bond's payment terms often pushes a financially distressed government to use less transparent means, notably the amendment of a bond's nonfinancial terms, to herd bondholders into an exchange. Other reforms—like a code of conduct that focuses narrowly on the disclosure of the debtor's overall restructuring plan at an early stage—could strengthen the existing bond restructuring process. But these innovations would make exchange offers work better, not radically transform the existing restructuring process.

Sovereign debt theorists have overstated the role that collective action clauses play, either in creating incentives for sovereigns to honor their debts or in creating obstacles to an efficient debt restructuring. The postulated world of expensive and difficult restructurings without clauses and of quick and painless restructuring with clauses does not match the existing experience. If the absence of clauses assured virtue, Ecuador would be a model debtor. If the absence of clauses blocked any and all restructurings, Ecuador would still be in default. There is no evidence either that the presence of collective action clauses makes sovereign default an attractive option or that the absence of collective action clauses will prevent a sovereign from eventually reaching agreement with its creditors. The case for clauses is far more modest: The introduction of clauses could facilitate a cooperative restructuring in the face of adverse shocks with minimal risk of encouraging opportunistic defaults.

Criticism of the IMF's proposed sovereign debt restructuring mechanism (SDRM) also ran ahead of the relatively modest proposal that IMF management ultimately embraced.[12] The IMF bears primary responsibility for this confusion. It started by making a case for replicating Chapter 11 of the US bankruptcy code, even though many of the problems that Chapter 11 addresses in the corporate context are not problems in the sovereign context. The IMF never was able to separate its less ambitious final proposal from its sweeping initial framing of the problem. But if one sets aside the rhetoric and looks at the details, the proposed SDRM would have created a restructuring process that resembled the aggregated vote in Uruguay's new bonds far more than the court-supervised restructuring of Chapter 11 of the US bankruptcy code.

The absence of formal institutions for a debt restructuring traditionally has not been a major concern to creditors. But Argentina's prolonged default is leading creditors to lament the absence of many of the protections corporate creditors in advanced economies take for granted—protections that push a corporate creditor to put a restructuring offer on the table rather than remain in prolonged default. The solution here, though, is not to lift the informal protections that have made sovereign restructuring possible in the absence of an international bankruptcy regime. Letting creditors litigate to seize a sovereign's reserves after a default would create even stronger incentives for a sovereign to default only after running down all its reserves. In the absence of a sovereign bankruptcy regime that clearly defines the seniority of different claims on a sovereign, a creditor rushing to grab any remaining assets of the debtor would be destructive. Rather, the solution is for the IMF, backed by the G-7, to be willing to do more early on to help a country through its restructuring. The IMF should provide real money and real guidance in a real effort to avoid prolonged default.

Financial crises, though, are not caused exclusively, or even predominantly, by difficulties in making payments on a sovereign's international bonds, and crisis resolution requires more than the capacity to restructure a sovereign's international bonds. The debt restructuring architecture also needs to make it possible to restructure:

- **cross-border bank lines.** Modern risk management techniques lead international banks to limit their own risks by quickly pulling their funds out of countries at risk of crises. In the process, they have pushed more risk onto emerging economies. The withdrawal of cross-border bank credit has been a bigger source of financial pressure in most major crises than payments on international bonds.

12. The final IMF management proposal (IMF April 2003) provided the debtor with the option of seeking to convince its creditors to vote in favor of a stay on litigation and let the debtor—if it got the support of a creditors' committee—petition a dispute settlement board to block disruptive litigation before a formal vote. The IMF's December 2002 proposal resembled Uruguay's aggregating clauses more closely: It did not offer the debtor the option of calling a vote on a stay or the right to petition the dispute settlement board.

- **domestic sovereign debt**. Domestic debt often has a much shorter maturity than international sovereign bonds and thus can roll off faster. Most sovereigns have substantial capacity to restructure their own domestic debt if they need to, whether by unilateral decree or by putting pressure on domestic financial institutions to accept—voluntarily—altered terms.
- **domestic deposits**. Most countries avoid a domestic bank run by extending an outright government guarantee to the domestic banking system, giving banks government bonds to avoid losses, and by using the central bank to supply the banks with domestic currency. In extremis, though, domestic bank deposits will need to be restructured—whether through deposit freezes, mandatory "pesification" (forced currency conversion), or a mandatory exchange of deposits for longer-term bonds.

We don't think institutional change is required to be able to restructure any of these claims. Experience suggests that short-term bank lines can be rescheduled in a crisis. The informal institutions—and some of the people—that helped the big international banks survive the 1980s debt crisis remain available to help coordinate the rollover of the bank claims. The contractual provisions in domestic sovereign debt contracts have not created obstacles to recent domestic debt restructurings.

The case for institutional change here parallels that for putting collective action clauses in international bonds: Institutional change is not necessary for a restructuring but might make the existing process work better. The undeniable success in Korea has been difficult to replicate when a country is not almost out of reserves. Turkey's efforts to encourage banks to maintain their exposure in 2001 were a miserable failure. In many ways, the machinery for coordinating the rollover of bank claims in a crisis is rustier than that for restructuring traded securities.

One solution to this problem is for the official sector to insist more forcefully that the country obtain an agreement with its bank creditors to roll over their claims and to be prepared to tolerate arrears on these debts if the creditor banks do not agree. Another approach would be to modify the terms of cross-border interbank contracts to give the crisis country's central bank the right to unilaterally extend the maturity of these credits in a crisis. This is a modification of earlier proposals for rollover options (Buiter and Siebert 1999, Kenen 2001). The initial advocates of rollover options put an emphasis on making the use of such options universal in order to provide a broad "contractual" standstill in a crisis. That seeks too much. But the contractual option to defer payments into external interbank claims could be used to perform a more limited but still crucial function: providing time for the government, the borrowing banks, and the creditor banks to negotiate a formal rescheduling. Such options would replicate contractually what now is achieved informally (often with official intervention) in a successful rollover arrangement.

Make no mistake, the right to defer payments unilaterally is a much more profound change in a contract than the ability to amend a contract's financial terms through a supermajority vote. A three-month rollover option makes the shortest possible maturity of any cross-border bank credit three months and turns a three-month credit into a six-month credit. Such options will be costly and will reduce cross-border interbank lending—not a bad thing, given its risks. They certainly won't emerge voluntarily from market pressures: They will be introduced only as a result of coordinated regulatory pressure.[13] On balance, the gains of a more defined institutional framework for the renegotiation of bank claims outweigh the risk of giving banks strong incentives to reduce their exposure before the rollover options are invoked.

The current international financial system does lack tools to solve one problem: how to restructure sovereign debt held by domestic banks without triggering a domestic bank run. Unfortunately, there are no easy solutions. Advanced economies have solved the bank run problem by using the government's financial strength to protect small depositors from losses—an option that is not available to many overindebted emerging economies. One potential solution—transferring the responsibility for bailing out, supervising, and regulating the banking systems of emerging economies to a global regulator—is simply not politically feasible (Tarullo 2001). All feasible solutions are second best. The IMF already is paying more attention to the health of the banking systems of many emerging economies—a form of shadow supervision. We think it also should be more willing to help—in appropriate ways—back the domestic banking systems of sovereign debtors going through a restructuring.

Problems with Crisis Resolution "Software"

Calls for Limits Fail to Produce Consistent Lending Decisions

The current framework for deciding which countries should receive IMF liquidity insurance is not working. The G-7's stated policy goal is to limit

13. The practical obstacles to the introduction of rollover options are immense. It would be necessary to define what constitutes a cross-border creditor, to determine if such provisions need to be included in cross-border credits to finance companies or even private firms as well as to banks, and to decide if such options need to be included in cross-border bank credits among banks located in advanced economies or just in credit extended to counterparties in emerging economies. Putting the options only in credits to emerging economies requires a consensus definition of an emerging economy and risks introducing a regulatory discontinuity in the market. Putting the options in all cross-border credits would be simpler, though putting such provisions into credits among banks in the world's financial centers would generate strong resistance.

access to the IMF's traditional norms, with rare exceptions that do not need to be spelled out. Apart from Uruguay, actual lending decisions have been much closer to the policy advocated by Guillermo Ortiz, governor of the Bank of Mexico: Always provide large amounts of liquidity to try to avoid a coercive debt restructuring. Statements from both the G-7 and the International Monetary and Financial Committee (IMFC) indicate that large-scale lending should not go to countries with unsustainable debts. Yet the recent recipients of large IMF loans typically have substantially higher levels of debt than the past recipients. Current policy can be summed up, with apologies to St. Augustine, as "give me virtue but not right now."

The expectation that it will be easier to refuse in the future is not realistic: Recent large-scale lending is not just a near-term necessity created by the difficulties of weaning a fragile world off the lax lending standards of an earlier era. The pressures that led to lending to Argentina, Turkey, Uruguay, and Brazil are real and reflect the emergence of difficulties that stem from the need to finance these countries' growing stocks of debt. Larger stocks of debt will tend to lead, ceteris paribus, to the need to make larger loans to give traditional catalytic financing a chance. For all the talk of limits, more IMF money has been made available relative to crisis countries' GDP in recent crisis cases than in Mexico, Asia, or Russia. These large loans are likely to tie up a substantial portion of the IMF's lending capacity for a long time, since several are unlikely to be repaid quickly.[14] (See table 9.1.)

Recent lending decisions have broadened the IMF's role in responding to emerging-market crises almost as significantly as the Clinton administration's decision to encourage the IMF to act as a surrogate lender of last resort in Mexico in 1995. The IMF is increasingly providing medium- to long-term financing to a country that is undertaking a medium- to long-term program of fiscal adjustment, in part by sometimes financing large fiscal deficits. The IMF also has gone beyond helping countries manage a collapse of external confidence; it is now helping both to backstop domestic banking systems and to finance domestic budget deficits. Yet no effort has been made to define whether the IMF should expect to assume these roles in other crises.

This is unfortunate. After the IMF was stretched in new directions in Mexico, the United States and the rest of the G-7 developed a theory of when the new use of the IMF was appropriate, created new facilities adapted to this kind of lending, and set about expanding the resources available to the IMF so that it could play this role in future crises. No com-

14. The IMF has lent over $50 billion—roughly 25 percent of its overall lending capacity—to Turkey and Brazil. Argentina has indicated that it will not start repaying the $15.5 billion it owes the IMF until 2014 (it has offered to pay the IMF interest in the interim). Recent IMF analysis suggests that Turkey, Brazil, and Uruguay could have difficulty repaying the IMF in full when their current loans come due (IMF April 2004). Should either Turkey or Brazil slip back into crisis, the IMF's overall financial position would start to look rather precarious.

Table 9.1 IMF lending limits compared with actual lending (billions of dollars)

Country	Current limit: One year (100 percent)	Current limit: Cumulative (300 percent)	Proposed limit: One year (300 percent)	Proposed limit: Cumulative (500 percent)	Actual program: One year	Actual program: Cumu-lative	Actual program: Peak
Mexico	2.6	7.9	7.9	13.1	13.1	18.0	13.1
Thailand	0.8	2.3	2.3	3.9	2.8	3.9	3.7
Indonesia	2.0	6.1	6.1	10.2	5.0	11.3	11.3
Korea	1.1	3.2	3.2	5.4	18.9	20.8	19.4
Brazil (1998)	3.1	9.2	9.2	15.3	11.1	18.4	13.4
Russia	8.1	24.4	24.4	40.6	5.1	15.1	5.1
Argentina (September 2001)	2.8	8.3	8.3	13.8	12.7	22.1	12.7
Brazil (2001)	3.9	11.7	11.7	19.5	10.2	15.6	14.6
Brazil (2002)	3.9	11.7	11.7	19.5	22.1	29.3	22.1
Brazil (combined)	3.9	11.7	11.7	19.5	10.2	35.1	30.1
Uruguay	0.4	1.2	1.2	1.9	1.7	2.7	2.2
Turkey (2001)	1.3	4.0	4.0	6.6	11.9	20.7	16.2
Turkey (2002)	1.3	4.0	4.0	6.6	13.7	17.6	14.8
Turkey (combined)	1.3	4.0	4.0	6.6	11.9	33.8	23.1

Note: Korea's quota was unusually small and Russia's was unusually large. Turkey 2002 and Brazil 2002 partially refinanced the country's existing IMF exposure; net disbursements were smaller. Mexico, Thailand, Indonesia, Korea, Brazil 1998, and Russia are in pre-1998 quotas—current quotas would be larger.

Source: International Monetary Fund, www.imf/enternal/fin.htm, and authors' calculations.

parable effort has been made to articulate how the new uses of the IMF in countries like Turkey and Uruguay fit into a broader policy framework or whether the IMF's response to these crises should be repeated if other countries encounter similar problems.

Assessing Recent Bailouts

While the dossiers for Argentina, Turkey, Uruguay, and Brazil will not be closed until these countries repay their IMF loans, it is not too early to start asking whether the IMF should provide a similar response should other countries encounter similar trouble. Our general answer is no: The official sector's response to recent emerging-market crises should not be institutionalized. However, one important qualification is needed to this argument. The approach adopted in Uruguay—pushing the country to float early on, closing some banks and freezing some deposits while backing all remaining deposits with a credible guarantee, and restructuring the sovereign's external debt—has promise, even if we don't think Uruguay's debt levels were low enough for that approach to have made sense in this specific instance.

Argentina, of course, is the easiest case to criticize. The decision to augment the IMF's $15 billion loan to Argentina with another $8 billion loan in late summer 2001 to avoid devaluation and default was an obvious mistake (Mussa 2002b). The small augmentation of summer 2001 had no chance of working, leaving the IMF with additional exposure when Argentina collapsed and damaging the IMF's credibility inside Argentina by signaling continued IMF support for policies that failed. In our judgment, Argentina clearly had passed the point of no return and should have received additional support only if it were willing to change its exchange rate regime and initiate a needed coercive debt restructuring. Indeed, both the initial decision to lend Argentina $15 billion in January 2001 and the decision to keep lending even as Argentina missed its not terribly demanding fiscal targets in the spring of 2001 can be questioned.

No option available to Argentina in 2000 could have avoided a significant fall in output. Recognizing reality and letting the exchange rate adjust was always going to be painful. Argentina's overvalued exchange rate had masked its true debt burden. Moreover, the Argentines were not willing to make a draconian shift in policy in late 2000. Since Argentina had approached the IMF when the central bank still had substantial reserves and the government still had the ability to draw on the banking system's own liquidity to tide the government through a rough patch, the IMF's leverage was limited. Argentina almost certainly would have rejected IMF advice to act preemptively, let the peso float, and initiate a debt restructuring. Argentines committed to convertibility would have harshly criticized the IMF for the subsequent crisis. Still, the IMF should have tried more actively to initiate a shift in policies. Forcing Argentina to rely solely on its own resources to defend the currency board would have forced Argentina to abandon the currency board more quickly.

Argentina instead ended up receiving a significant loan to support an attempt to avoid both any exchange rate adjustment and meaningful debt reduction but nothing to support a transition to a sustainable real exchange rate and a more sustainable debt profile. A better policy would have used the IMF's lending capacity to limit the negative fallout from exiting the currency board and from the unavoidable debt restructuring. Such a plan would have used the IMF's funds—plus any of Argentina's own remaining reserves—to avoid a bank run and to limit the overshooting of the peso. Any plan would have needed to include the following:

- *a strategy to avoid—or contain—a domestic bank run.* The chances of creating a credible backstop would have been far higher if Argentina moved quickly. At the end of 2000, Argentina held $25 billion in reserves; the banks themselves held another $5 billion in liquid reserves in offshore accounts. Plus Argentina had substantial capacity to borrow from the IMF. Argentina could have assembled a headline package almost equal in size to $50 billion in domestic, dollar-denominated deposits.[15] Cross-border bank debt would have needed to be restruc-

15. Data from Lagos (2002) and authors' calculations.

tured, à la Korea. IMF lending also would have been available to intervene to avoid excessive exchange rate overshooting.

- *a strategy to restructure the banking sector's private lending portfolio.* Many domestic borrowers could not absorb the higher real burden on their dollar debt that would follow devaluation, and some form of across-the-board relief for small domestic borrowers was unavoidable. Unless the government planned to pass such losses onto depositors, it needed to pick up most of the tab for such relief.[16]
- *a strategy for restructuring the government's own debt.* Government debt held by Argentine banks would have needed to be treated differently than that held by external investors and the Argentine pension funds in order to avoid adding to the banking sector's weakness. Indeed, the need to compensate the banks for the losses on their private lending portfolio implied the need to take on new debt even as the government was seeking relief from its existing creditors.
- *a strategy for paying the debt that emerges from Argentina's restructuring.* Any restructuring obviously needed to be matched with domestic fiscal adjustments to enable Argentina to meet its new payments commitments. The scale and diversity of Argentina's existing debts—and the need to take on new debt as part of the banking sector's restructuring—increases the importance of clearly defining the amount of adjustment that Argentina is able to undertake, so that both Argentina and all its creditors have a clear sense of the amount of payments that Argentina can sustain.

There is no guarantee that such a policy would have produced a better outcome. But the fact that the economic collapse that accompanied Argentina's eventual default and devaluation was much deeper than necessary to bring Argentina's external accounts into some semblance of balance, which suggests that it is at least conceptually possible that an alternative policy path might have produced a smaller fall in output.

The IMF certainly would be in a stronger position to set the policy framework for the debt restructuring if it had not exhausted both its credibility and its lending capacity in 2001 trying to support the currency board. Because of its large exposure at the time of the default, the IMF has been forced to link its conditionality in 2002 and 2003 to loans that did

16. Many of the banking system's larger borrowers, notably Argentina's utilities, also would have encountered trouble. Letting the utilities continue to index their prices to the dollar would have been politically untenable (and economically unwise) after a devaluation, and a change in the utilities' pricing structure would have had to have been accompanied by a parallel negotiated restructuring of their external and domestic debts. Hopefully, these interlinked negotiations could have been completed without degenerating into the current impasse, but all parties would have had to show real flexibility.

nothing more than prevent Argentina from falling into arrears to the IMF (and other IFIs, whose lending is contingent on an IMF program). The IMF ended up settling for a program that failed to set a fiscal policy path that could guide the subsequent debt restructuring, or assure the country's overall ability to repay the IMF.[17] In theory, the absence of agreement on a fiscal adjustment path lets the bondholders negotiate directly with Argentina the amount of additional adjustment it needs to undertake to reach a settlement with its external creditors. In practice, failing to define the amount of adjustment needed to pay all of Argentina's creditors probably just increases the probability that Argentina will not be able to reach agreement with its external creditors. It is also not obvious why Argentina's bondholders—who are only one of the many sets of creditors with a claim on Argentina's fiscal effort—should be the ultimate arbitrators of Argentina's fiscal adjustment.

Turkey has received more money relative to its GDP from the IMF than Mexico received from the IMF and the US Treasury combined in 1995, despite having a substantially higher debt-to-GDP ratio than Mexico. Turkey's loan is being used in a different way than Mexico's: Turkey's IMF loan is covering a medium- to long-term, rather than a short-term, financing need.

Turkey encountered trouble at the end of 2000 when its crawling currency peg—part of an IMF-supported program to end Turkey's chronic inflation—came under pressure. The decision to provide Turkey with additional funds to bolster this peg at the end of 2000 was a mistake. Neither Turkey's government finances nor its banking system were strong enough to withstand the rigors of a peg. The peg, perversely, was creating incentives for Turkey's banking system to take on risky foreign-currency debt to finance the government—increasing Turkey's financial vulnerabilities.

Moving more quickly to a float would not have avoided Turkey's subsequent government debt crisis. The vast bulk of Turkey's $24 billion IMF credit line was disbursed after Turkey let its exchange rate float and allowed the central bank to help finance the government's large ongoing budget deficits without printing money. Consequently, the core issue raised by Turkey is the wisdom of using IMF financing to finance (indirectly) large fiscal deficits, not the wisdom of supporting pegged exchange rates. In theory, IMF help in the early stages of Turkey's fiscal adjustment program will enable Turkey to obtain the credibility needed to borrow at a lower rate in the future—the high real interest rates that led

17. The required primary surplus in Argentina's current IMF program covers interest payments to the IFIs and Argentina's "senior" domestic creditors. Argentina also has agreed to increase its primary balance to cover additional payments that emerge from its external debt restructuring. Consequently, the IMF delegated the negotiation of the final parameters of Argentina's IMF program to Argentina's bondholders.

to large fiscal deficits in 2001 and 2002 will come down over time, lowering Turkey's future borrowing need.[18]

Turkey had a true need for external financing to support this kind of program of fiscal adjustment, since the initial budget deficits exceeded what could be financed domestically. But it also needed medium-term external financing to support a slow process of fiscal consolidation at a high debt level, not short-term lending. The probability that private markets will provide the funds needed to cover Turkey's ongoing budget and current account deficits *and* the additional funds needed to repay the IMF $9 billion in 2005 and over $10 billion in 2006 is close to nil.[19]

Large-scale IMF lending to Turkey, to date, has warded off outright default and economic collapse, domestic confidence in Turkey's finances is currently strong, and it is certainly possible that Turkey will ultimately be able to repay the IMF. However, we still do not believe providing long-term financing to support a long-term fiscal consolidation program is an appropriate use of large-scale IMF financing. Judged solely on its economic and financial merits, Turkey's debt had reached a level where its IMF program should have been designed around a debt restructuring. Turkey would not have needed to move immediately to outright debt reduction: Its willingness to run a significant primary surplus would have allowed it to pay positive real interest rates on its existing debt stock, just not real interest rates of 20 to 30 percent. Turkey needed to call on its domestic banking system to trade their short-term treasury bills for longer-term debt that carried positive real interest rates. This would have required a corresponding restructuring of the short-term international bank lines that local banks had used to finance some of their bets on Turkish government debt.

This approach would be risky: Even a restructuring backed with an IMF loan can trigger a run and the potential outflows in the event of a deposit run that dwarfed the available financing. An IMF-supported domestic debt restructuring could well have produced a worse outcome than the

18. Turkey could only finance budget deficits in excess of 15 percent of GDP in 2001 and 2002 by tapping its domestic markets for new lending and then drawing on the IMF loan to provide additional new financing. Turkey's stock of government debt consequently increased substantially between 2000 and 2003. However, after rising dramatically in 2001, Turkey's debt-to-GDP ratio fell in both 2002 and 2003. Turkey's fiscal adjustment and the resumption of GDP growth both helped, but Turkey also benefited significantly from the fall in the dollar. Turkey's foreign-currency debt is largely denominated in dollars, while its economy is oriented more toward Europe. Unfortunately, many of the factors that helped Turkey in 2002 and 2003 would reverse in a crisis.

19. Turkey has received net new funds from the IMF every year since 2000. Turkey has yet to prove it can finance itself without obtaining additional official financing, let alone show that it can start to make net payments to the IMF. In late 2003, Turkey obtained a bilateral $8.5 billion guaranteed loan from the US government. Turkey has yet to draw on this loan guarantee, in part because it would commit Turkey to supporting US policy in Iraq.

approach the IMF and the G-7 actually adopted. No one should maintain that a policy of restricting IMF lending—or even a policy of restricting IMF lending to countries with large debts and large budget deficits—will be costless.

We are not so naïve as to think that lending to Turkey has been determined solely on its economic and financial merits. Turkey's commitment to democracy, strategic location, aspirations to join Europe, and longstanding alliance with the United States do give it unique geostrategic importance. However, in cases where the G-7's strategic interests require cutting a country a lot of slack, the G-7 countries themselves, not the IMF, should supply the bulk of crisis financing.

Why does this matter? After all, the G-7 countries supply most of the IMF's financing anyway. There are two reasons. First, the IMF's economic and financial credibility is eroded if its decisions are not based primarily on economic and financial criteria. Lending to Turkey through the IMF, an institution designed to treat all of its members similarly, creates an expectation that the IMF should provide less strategically important countries with similar financial problems a comparable loan. The IMF would need to be substantially expanded to be in position to comfortably lend more than 10 percent of a country's GDP for an extended period to every emerging economy with a nominal budget deficit of 15 percent of GDP and debt-to-GDP ratio of over 80 percent. Second, G-7 countries are better equipped to manage the risk that Turkey ultimately won't be able to repay on the original terms or that Turkey will eventually fall into an Argentine-style default. The IMF's funds are supposed to "revolve" and therefore to be lent and repaid quickly—not tied down in cases like Turkey.

The IMF's approach in ***Uruguay*** differed from that adopted in other recent cases. Uruguay combined large-scale support to stop a bank run with a maturity-extending restructuring of its sovereign debt.[20] A large loan from the IMF allowed the central bank to act as a lender of last resort in dollars to the banking system and therefore avoid both a domestic and external bank holiday after Argentina's own bank holiday had catalyzed a run out of Uruguay's banking system. After the run subsided, the government's own debt was restructured through a maturity-extending bond exchange. Creditors who lent to the government of Uruguay were bailed in even as the banking system was bailed out.

Uruguay is a small country, and while the IMF's loan was very large in relation to Uruguay's size, it is not large on an absolute scale. However, Uruguay is important because it raises two issues that we believe are central to defining the role the IMF should play in the future. First should the IMF provide the funds to let a central bank act as a domestic lender of last resort? Second, should it do so on a scale comparable to Uruguay when the government itself is highly indebted?

20. This is true of both precrisis and postcrisis debt-to-GDP ratios.

Our answer to the first question is a qualified yes. Avoiding a domestic bank holiday and the associated economic collapse by providing the central bank the reserves it needs to stop a domestic run can be an appropriate use of the IMF's financial capacity as the country deals with its banking crisis. The strategy of combining a restructuring that locks in those creditors that lent to the sovereign and IMF lending to augment the country's reserves so a domestic run does not undermine the sovereign restructuring can make a lot of sense.

Our answer to the second question is no. Unless the IMF is expanded, it cannot consistently lend all of its members 15 percent of their GDP to allow their central banks to act as a full lender of last resort in dollars. Uruguay could obtain such a large loan only because its economy is small, so even 15 percent of GDP was not a large absolute sum. Lending a comparable sum to Argentina, which also had a heavily dollarized banking system, would have meant lending it around $40 billion just to back the banking system—and even this sum would have fallen short of backing all bank deposits. Moreover, even if the IMF's resources were expanded so it could provide all major emerging economies loans of a comparable size, Uruguay's debt levels themselves were too high to warrant such large-scale support. Given Uruguay's high debt burden and its deep economic slump, Uruguay should have sought a bigger haircut from its creditors rather than just pushing out the maturity of its debt at precrisis interest rates during its restructuring. As in Argentina, postponing a haircut may cause greater damage than taking the bitter pill sooner.[21]

Brazil is the most difficult recent case. It received much more money from the IMF in 2001–03 than it received from the IMF and its bilateral creditors combined in 1998–99, despite entering into its current crisis with substantially more debt than in 1998–99. That is one reason why Brazil has been unable to repay the IMF as rapidly.

Brazil combines important strengths and major weaknesses. While Brazil's fiscal and external debt levels in 2002 were comparable to Argentina's before its crisis, Brazil's fundamentals were otherwise stronger than Argentina's. Brazil has run a primary surplus of 3.5 percent of GDP since the 1999 crisis, and President Luiz Inacio Lula da Silva, seeing the abyss of Argentina, decided to increase the primary surplus above 4 percent of GDP. The depreciation of the real that occurred in the course of 2002 also had brought Brazil's current account into balance. Unlike Argentina in 2000 and 2001, an overvalued currency did not understate

21. Reducing the amount of financing available and a deeper debt restructuring almost certainly would have implied a broader restructuring of domestic and external deposits than what took place. We would have tried to keep demand deposits unfrozen by backing them with a smaller bailout loan but would have frozen and then rescheduled time deposits—including those held by Argentines.

Brazil's debt burden.[22] Brazil's domestic banking system was not dollarized, so a fall in the real did not translate into debt problems for a wide range of domestic borrowers.

These strengths, the inherent risk of a domestic debt restructuring, and the likely disruption to both Brazil and the world if Brazil were to fail all combine to make the current IMF program a reasonable, though risky, bet. We think it would have been appropriate, though—given the scale of the IMF's commitment—for Brazil's external bank creditors to also have made a serious commitment to maintain their exposure.

A number of important financial weaknesses offset Brazil's strengths. Brazil's government debt is heavily indexed to short-term interest rates, so high domestic interest rates increase the government's borrowing needs and choke economic growth. Brazil never rebuilt the reserves it lost defending its exchange rate in 1998, and it lost more reserves during 2002. Reserves are now starting to rise again, but net reserves remain low for an economy of Brazil's size, particularly given Brazil's stock of short-term external debt (mostly owed by private banks and firms) and the government's stock of domestic dollar-linked debt (Credit Suisse First Boston 2003). All this combines to create an underlying dependence on borrowed reserves from the IMF.

Brazil's current government has made a real commitment to fiscal adjustment and is taking advantage of favorable financial conditions to rebuild its reserves and reduce its dollar-linked debt stock. There is hope for renewed growth in 2004—though not for quick repayment of the IMF. Brazil certainly deserves every chance to succeed.

However, should growth disappoint, fiscal adjustment slip, or international investors' willingness to look for yields wane, another crisis cannot be ruled out after 2004.[23] The emergence of new financial pressures would force both Brazil and the IMF to face a difficult choice. Would Brazil's remaining reserves—and the capacity to borrow from the IMF embedded in Brazil's current "precautionary" program—be better used to support a debt restructuring, or should both be deployed in yet another "catalytic" attempt to avoid a restructuring? Moving too fast risks forcing a country to undergo the pain of an avoidable debt restructuring, but moving too

22. However, Brazil's practice of reporting its net rather than its gross public-sector debt does understate its debt burden.

23. Growth is expected to recover in 2004, and Brazil's relatively limited external financing needs can be addressed by the recently augmented IMF program and the resources that are still available in the original $30 billion program (Brazil met all conditions to draw additional funds from the IMF at the end of 2003 but opted not to). However, the IMF's capacity to provide still more financing to help meet large external financing needs in 2005 and thereafter is limited. As a share of Brazil's GDP, the IMF's current exposure to Brazil is not anywhere near as large as it is to Uruguay or Turkey; however, as a share of the IMF's portfolio, Brazil already looms large.

slowly risks making a necessary debt restructuring more painful and disruptive. Brazil cannot continue to emerge from each crisis with higher debts and lower reserves. Brazil's government needs to deliver on its commitment to reduce Brazil's debt level over time to be in a position to continue to obtain IMF help to augment its low levels of reserves. Otherwise, a debt restructuring may become unavoidable.

Crisis Management Is Harder When Debt Stocks Are Larger

The policy dilemmas created when emerging economies with large debts encounter difficulties are real, particularly if the emerging economy's banking system is a major creditor of the sovereign. Larger debts usually translate directly or indirectly into larger needs for emergency financing. This dilemma has no easy solutions. Upping the amount the IMF lends to countries with larger debts increases the odds of success, but at some point this ceases to be a realistic policy. If the size of the IMF's insurance policy grew in relation to the size of a country's problems, IMF lending would give rise to moral hazard. Plus, lending to a country whose starting point calls into question its capacity to take on additional debt is risky, even if the IMF lends on a preferred basis.

However, not upping the size of the financing in the face of potentially bigger financing needs also is risky. Lending 10 percent of GDP to a country with a debt-to-GDP ratio of 30 percent brings more effective financial force to bear than lending 10 percent of GDP to a country with a debt-to-GDP ratio of 60, 70, or 80 percent.[24] The IMF may put enough money on the table to tie down a large share of the IMF's lending capacity, but not large enough to catalyze a clear change in market sentiment.

Neither the IMF nor its major shareholders have acquitted themselves well in the face of these dilemmas. They often have dithered rather than confronted difficult problems with decisive actions. Pressure to show progress toward the stated goal of limiting IMF lending has manifested itself in efforts to minimize the size of the IMF's initial loan. But if the initial amount is not enough, the IMF's typical response—Argentina, Turkey, and Uruguay are all examples—has been to lend more money.[25] The overall impact of drizzling out lending decisions over time may just be to di-

24. The combination of an IMF loan and US bilateral lending provided a commitment equal to 10 percent of Mexico's precrisis GDP, a little under one-third of Mexico's precrisis government debt of 31 percent. Turkey received an IMF commitment equal to 12 percent of its precrisis GDP, but that was only about one-fifth of its precrisis government debt to GDP ratio of close to 60 percent.

25. Uruguay's 2002 loan was augmented thrice, Turkey's 2000 loan was augmented twice and then superseded by a new, even bigger, loan in 2002. This new loan effectively was a third augmentation. The bilateral loan that Turkey recently received from the United States can be considered a fourth augmentation.

minish the chances of the initial IMF loan, the augmented second loan, or even a third loan catalyzing the desired change in market conditions.

The core tenet of the "Powell doctrine" of financing—to use a phrase popularized by former US Treasury Secretary Lawrence Summers—is that the chances of official intervention catalyzing a decisive shift in market sentiment increases if the full size of the official sector's commitment is put on the table from the beginning—even if disbursements are tranched to encourage adherence to policy commitments. We would add a corollary after Argentina: The chances of a debt restructuring being completed without a deep economic and financial collapse goes up if decisive action is taken early on. The country can use both its own reserves and its capacity to borrow from the IMF to prevent the restructuring from triggering a catastrophic collapse in confidence.

It's Not Just the Bond Market, Stupid![26]

To paraphrase basketball legend Bill Walton, it is important not to confuse activity with results. The price at which two international investors are willing to exchange a long-term emerging-market bond provides a visible sign of financial distress and an easy source of stories for the financial press. Wild swings in market prices matter a lot to those holding the bonds but don't always correspond to wild flows in and out of the crisis country. It is a lot harder to get real-time data on changes in banks' exposure loans, even though changes in bank exposure correlate far more closely with changes in the country's reserves. Don't get us wrong: A sustained fall in secondary-market prices usually augurs real trouble. But movements in the market price of bonds don't always mean movements of funds out of the country or don't necessarily put direct pressure on the country's reserves.

The problem with the current debate on bond restructuring is not the content of most of the proposed reforms. Many existing bond contracts do make it too easy for a minority of creditors to hold out and try to get a better deal than everyone else. The problem is that too much attention has been devoted to solving what has been, to date, a relatively small problem—siphoning attention away from other, often more important, problems.

Long-term sovereign bonds simply have not been the most common cause of international liquidity crises. Mexico, Russia, Turkey, and Brazil all turned to the IMF because of prospective difficulties in making payments on their domestic sovereign debt, not their international sovereign

26. The motto for former President Clinton's 1992 campaign was "It's the economy, stupid." The Clinton administration's economic policy went on to emphasize how the bond market would rally with deficit reduction, lowering interest rates across the board.

bonds.[27] The rolloff of short-term cross-border bank claims was a bigger source of stress in Asia, Turkey, Brazil, and even Argentina than an inability to refinance maturing international bonds. The crises in Argentina and Uruguay demonstrated how residents' willingness to shift from dollar-denominated bank deposits (local assets) to dollars and dollar assets abroad (foreign assets) can put enormous pressure on a country's reserves. Argentina, which will be remembered as the international bond crisis par excellence, lost more reserves in 2001 trying to halt a bank run than making payments on its maturing international bonds.[28] Bonds have played a bigger role in some smaller crises, but even here, the country typically confronts far more intractable problems than those posed by the absence of provisions that could limit the risk of holdouts from a sovereign bond restructuring.

The focus on bonds has deflected attention away from the risks posed by the rolloff of external bank lines, even though short-term bank lending is often a bigger problem than long-term bonds. Neither the IMF nor the G-7 seem to have seriously considered making a real commitment by the banks to maintain their exposure a part of Brazil's recent rescue package. The focus on legal obstacles to an external bond restructuring also has diverted attention from the economic and financial obstacles to a domestic sovereign debt restructuring. This is unfortunate. The domestic sovereign debt of many indebted emerging economies is growing faster than their external sovereign debt.[29] The success of future debt restructurings will likely hinge far more on finding ways to restructure domestic as well as external debt without triggering a domestic bank run than on finding ways to limit bondholder litigation.

The most promising approaches to limiting the risk of a debt restructuring triggering a bank run and a generalized flight from domestic assets require redefining how the IMF is used, not a new IMF—it is more a change in the IMF's software than a change in the system's hardware. Debt held by the banks often cannot be exempted from any restructuring, but it can be restructured on terms that lower its interest rate without necessarily reducing its face value. If the IMF has not already exhausted its

27. Mexico, Russia, Brazil (1998 and 2002), and Turkey faced difficulties because of the sovereign's domestic debt, not international bonds. The Asian-crisis countries faced difficulties because of a rolloff of cross-border bank loans to private creditors. The rolloff of bank loans was also an important factor in Brazil and Turkey; see Truman (2002, 341–46).

28. Estimating principal payments to external bondholders is not straightforward, given the large domestic holdings of the government of Argentina's international sovereign bonds. The government of Argentina estimated that roughly $6 billion was coming due on externally held bonds in 2001, and nearly all of this rolled off. This compares with the $24 billion that fled from the Argentine banking system in 2001 (authors' calculations and data from the government of Argentina and the Argentine central bank).

29. Many emerging-market economies also have less external debt than they seem to, since their domestic banks are major buyers of the governments' international bonds.

lending capacity helping the country avoid any restructuring, such a restructuring can be combined with IMF support to help convince most domestic depositors not to run (in part by demonstrating that the financing is available for some to exit). In some cases, though, this won't work. Domestic deposits will have to be frozen and depositors will have to absorb losses—either directly by an upfront haircut or indirectly by taxing domestic residents to pay off depositors over time.[30]

Of course, if emerging economies managed their public finances more prudently, they would have less need to stuff their domestic banking systems with government debt, and the debt that the banks do hold will be less risky. It would help if domestic bank regulation did not encourage domestic banks to lend to their own government. But heavily indebted sovereigns are unlikely to suddenly start regulating the banking system to protect against a sovereign default. The temptation in a crisis is always to do the opposite: to loosen bank regulation to make it attractive for the domestic banks to provide the government with the emergency financing—a form of gambling for resurrection.

IMF's Vital Role in a Debt Restructuring

The Bush administration's top economic policymakers came into office promising not to play an active role in the resolution of emerging-market crises. Their initial policy statements suggested that they would not only limit IMF lending but also let the market find its own way through a sovereign debt restructuring (Taylor 2001a, Suskind 2004). Neither the rest of the Bush administration nor the rest of the G-7 ever fully embraced this laissez-faire approach to crisis resolution. When forced to choose between letting a country slip into crisis without making any effort to help and providing a large loan, the Bush administration and other G-7 governments consistently have decided that a large loan is the lesser of two evils. Turkey, Brazil, and Argentina's 2001 augmentation are all cases in point.

However, an aversion to helping a country define a coherent strategy for a coercive debt restructuring, especially when combined with the IMF's institutional reluctance to declare a country's chosen exchange rate regime untenable,[31] still can have perverse and destructive results. As

30. See chapter 7 for a discussion of challenges created when the banking system's financial assets are claims on the government and Hoelscher and Quintyn (2003) for a comprehensive survey of systemic banking crises.

31. The IMF's Articles of Agreement give each member country the right to select their own exchange rate regime. However, the IMF is under no obligation to provide financial support to back a country's chosen exchange rate regime or even to back draconian adjustment plans designed to save the country's chosen exchange rate regime. Recent experience—Turkey and Argentina—shows that even currency boards can become unsustainable.

Argentina ran down its reserves and its capacity to borrow from the IMF even as it failed to meet its policy commitments, the probability of avoiding a complete meltdown sharply decreased. The G-7 and the IMF worried more about the risk of being implicated in the decision to abandon the currency board and to seek a coercive restructuring than about the risks of failing to support Argentina at the peak of its crisis. This was a serious mistake in Argentina and will be a mistake in other cases.

The IMF—backed by the G-7—should play an active, coordinating role rather than a hands-off role in the resolution of emerging-market debt crises. This implies helping the country develop a strategy to prevent the secondary runs triggered by the restructuring from cascading out of control and backing that strategy with new money. It also means working to make sure that all the steps required to resolve a complex crisis—the restructuring of the country's domestic debts, its international debt held by private creditors, and its debts to other governments plus the country's own policy efforts—combine to form a coherent whole.[32] Putting collective action clauses into all international sovereign bond contracts won't reduce the need for the IMF to play these active roles.

The IMF's financial exposure means that it will never be an entirely disinterested party in a sovereign restructuring. But there is no completely disinterested party with the leverage needed to play some of the supervisory roles a bankruptcy judge plays during the restructuring of a domestic firm. As the representative of the largest economies, the IMF has interests that go beyond assuring its own repayment. This gives it the authority to take action to help stabilize the international financial system. Only the IMF combines the leverage that comes from the ability to provide new money with the ability to act decisively to help define a distressed sovereign debtor's overall program for financial rehabilitation (IMF January 2003b). It is hard to imagine that a country's dispersed creditors could come together quickly and agree both to provide new financing and to link that financing to a macroeconomic policy path that would help guide the subsequent debt restructuring—particularly since the interest of different sets of creditors are not congruent.

Moving from Problems to Solutions

The core challenge of crisis resolution is not creating brand new institutions to manage international financial crises.

32. New lending from the IMF and the MDBs to refinance their existing exposure can also be thought of as a form of a restructuring.

Updated Framework for Crisis Resolution

The G-7's basic framework for crisis resolution needs to be updated to better match the existing tools of crisis resolution to the particular challenges that different crisis countries face. Many of the following principles are not new. Taken together, however, they would imply a significant change in the way the official sector handles many emerging-market crises.

Be Willing to Distinguish Between Countries and Make Hard Judgments Early On

Despite all the difficulties in distinguishing between illiquidity and insolvency—as illiquidity can be a leading indicator of insolvency—any viable framework needs to differentiate between different cases and treat different crises differently. Sorting crises into different categories is intrinsically difficult. But key decisions still need to be made upfront.

Any approach to crisis resolution should start with an assessment of the country's debt, the structure of its debt, its exchange rate regime, and more difficult, the country's forward-looking capacity to adjust its policies. Countries with too much debt coming due tomorrow, but not too much overall debt, need time to make the adjustments that will assure their solvency and allow them to regain market credibility. Countries with too much overall debt relative to their ability to increase their payments capacity—not just too much debt coming due tomorrow—need to find the best way of reducing their debt. Countries that fall in the middle need something in the middle—often maturity-extending restructurings that keep coupons low but avoid outright debt reduction. Countries with unsustainable exchange rate regimes—even a currency board—should not receive large-scale IMF financing unless they are willing to change their exchange rate regime.

Link Financing to Appropriate Policy Adjustments

Even countries whose difficulties stem more from "too much short-term debt in relation to their reserves" than from "too much overall debt relative to their long-term capacity to pay" typically need to make some policy adjustments. Pure illiquidity is rare: Cases where an illiquid country is solvent if it makes appropriate—and doable—adjustments are far more common. Even Mexico, the quintessential liquidity case, would not have remained solvent for long if it had continued to run large current account deficits as a result of an overvalued exchange rate. Moreover, IMF bailouts are partial, not total: The country still needs to demonstrate to its private creditors and its own citizens that it is taking steps to improve its creditworthiness. Countries with "too much debt relative to their long-term capacity to pay" need to take steps to increase their payments capacity even as they seek relief from their creditors. Successful crisis resolution always combines appropriate policy changes with a credible plan to deal with the debtor's short- and long-term financing needs.

Matching Financial Response to the Crisis

The three responses described below are meant to suggest that different types of financial crises in emerging economies will be resolved in different ways, just as different private-debt problems require different techniques for resolution. They should not be taken literally: there is no international lender of last resort, any bailout will be partial, and there is no perfect sovereign analogue to a Chapter 11.

- *Lender of last resort–style financing for sovereigns.* A central bank typically can supply a solvent (or potentially solvent) bank with an unlimited credit line to stop the run. The best the IMF can do is to provide enough financing to prevent immediate collapse, if some external creditors leave and some domestic residents shift their funds abroad. Financing from a surrogate lender of last resort to avoid any debt restructuring should be reserved for countries that can reasonably be expected to regain market access and repay the IMF quickly, so the IMF is not financing a permanent withdrawal in private financing. These countries typically have moderate levels of public and external debt, flexible exchange rates, and a (somewhat belated) political commitment to reform. Mexico is an example.
- *Out-of-court sovereign debt reorganizations.* A maturity-extending rescheduling of a country's external debts at sustainable interest rates (i.e., precrisis rates) is roughly analogous to an out-of-court corporate reorganization. Such reorganizations allow the firm and its creditors to avoid the cost of Chapter 11 reorganization or outright liquidation. There is a parallel for a country: Its external debts can be rescheduled to buy time for reforms that may avoid the need for deep debt reduction. This approach suits a country that may need financing for several years, while it shows that it can get its act together. Ukraine is an example.
- *Sovereign de facto "Chapter 11s" that provide significant debt reduction.* Sovereign debt reduction takes place outside the formal protections of a bankruptcy regime, in part because the difficulty in taking legal action against a sovereign has mitigated the need for formal protection. Some sovereigns, though, dig themselves into such a deep hole that getting out requires deep debt reduction. The country needs to adjust so that it no longer needs to take on new debt, and all creditors have to take large losses: There is no "given time, losses may be avoided" option. Argentina is a good example.

The lines between these responses often are a bit blurry. Korea comes closer to being a pure liquidity crisis than most after it let its exchange rate adjust, yet the approach adopted in Korea straddled the line between lender-of-last-resort financing and an out-of-court rescheduling.[33] The line between an out-of-court maturity-extending rescheduling and a sovereign Chapter 11 debt reduction also can blur. Many countries will be reluctant to seek outright debt reduction (or even a low interest rate on debt that is rescheduled for a very long time) until they give the combination of stretching out maturities and adjustment a chance to work. Uruguay is a case in point.

Large-Scale IMF Lending Can Usefully Complement a Coercive Debt Restructuring

Official financing can help limit the risk of a restructuring triggering a total panic—inherently a bad outcome—whether by helping to finance intervention to prevent extreme overshooting in the exchange rate or by helping to backstop the banking system.[34] Financial support from the IMF can help avoid steps like closing the capital account or freezing domestic bank deposits that risk expanding and deepening the crisis. In a sense, providing financing to stop a domestic run—either on the banks or the currency—while a country is seeking to push out the maturities of its external debt (bonds but external bank loans too) is analogous to restructuring the large creditors of a bank during a bank resolution while paying small depositors in full.

Large-scale lending is appropriate even in some debt reduction cases. Right now defaulting on private debt usually means losing access to significant official support as well, thus encouraging countries with too much debt to hold on for too long. One of the advantages of providing IMF debtor-in-possession (DIP) financing is that it gives the IMF leverage to define a sensible course for macroeconomic policies during the restructuring. Since the IMF is the entity best positioned to help the crisis country coordinate the different components of a complex restructuring, the IMF—backed by the G-7—needs to play an active role in crisis resolution. The disaster in Argentina shows the consequences of the G-7 and IMF's un-

33. Many firms can be insolvent (like some Korean banks and corporations) even if the government and the country as a whole are solvent. The country's aggregate capacity to generate foreign exchange may exceed its aggregate external debt service even if some major firms cannot cover their debts. Of course, if the government bails out insolvent banks and firms, it may put its own solvency at risk.

34. For example, Argentina's central bank intervened to support the peso after Argentina's default and devaluation in order to prevent an already depreciated peso from overshooting further. One year later, it was buying, not selling, dollars after the exchange rate had stabilized.

willingness to lead, manage, and use their leverage to resolve a complex crisis quickly.

Preserve IMF's De Facto Seniority

The IMF can neither finance countries like Mexico or Brazil nor take bold steps to limit the fallout from a debt restructuring without the informal priority currently given to repaying the IMF. Reducing this informal seniority would severely impair the IMF's ability to deal with crises. The IMF, though, does need to be more cognizant of the risk of a failed bailout leaving both itself and the country's long-term creditors worse off. Financing the rolloff of junior debt with senior debt before a default means a larger haircut for the country's remaining junior creditors and slow repayment of the country's senior creditors.

Don't Let Cross-Border Bank Credits Off the Hook Too Easily

More crisis countries should be encouraged to seek a monitored rollover arrangement for cross-border bank exposure, and such arrangements should be put in place well before a country is entirely out of reserves. At times, the short-term creditors of a crisis country will need to refrain from exercising their option to exit in order to give the country a better chance of emerging from its crisis. Institutional innovations like rollover options could help. But contractual innovations are not a precondition for moving more aggressively to limit the rolloff of cross-border bank credit.

Monitored commitments from the banks to roll over their claims work only if it is clear that low rollover rates will have consequences. For example, the IMF could condition its willingness to continue financing on a high participation rate in such a rollover and make a low rate a trigger to negotiate replacing the rollover arrangement with a maturity-extending rescheduling. Official pressure to encourage private creditors to roll over their short-term debts—so-called moral suasion—also should not be taken entirely off the table. In cases where lender of last resort-style financing is either impossible or undesirable and where failure to agree on a rollover that avoids default could have systemic consequences, the official sector should be willing to do everything that it can to generate a good outcome. Korea is a prime example.

Be Willing to Finance a Domestic Lender of Last Resort That Helps Backstop the Local Banking System

Few events can be as disruptive to a country's social, political, and economic fabric as the widespread collapse of the domestic banking system. Access to international reserves can help a country with a dollarized financial system avoid a deposit freeze. It also can reduce the pressure on the exchange rate associated with the central bank's provision of domestic currency in the event of a run out of local-currency deposits.

However, the IMF should support domestic lenders of last resort only in countries that are performing some form of triage during a banking run and crisis to make sure that the funds provided by the IMF are used to support the right banks. The central bank of the crisis country should not be providing liquidity to its domestic banks without also taking offsetting steps to restructure and clean up the banking system. Some banks may need to be shut down and their deposits either paid off or transferred to other banks. The equity investors in other banks may need to put up additional capital in return for liquidity support. In some cases, the needed triage may even require rescheduling some deposits while backing others in full (as in Uruguay).

No matter how the IMF resources are used, the IMF lends to a country's government, and the government retains ultimate responsibility for repayment. The IMF can finance a domestic lender of last resort if the country's government is short on international reserves but not overly indebted. Such governments have the capacity to repay all their existing debts as well as the additional debt that they are taking on in a crisis to finance a domestic lender of last resort. We are willing to go one step further and use the IMF's lending capacity to support the banking system of a country that is engaged in an early restructuring of its own debt (as in Uruguay). Here the IMF is lending largely on the strength of the priority traditionally accorded to the IMF. But the government's ultimate solvency—and capacity to repay the IMF—hinges on its ability to restructure its debt as well.

Recognize More Explicitly the IMF's Role in a Wide Range of Crises

Central bank reserves serve many functions. They back the country's domestic currency. They provide foreign currency that the central bank can lend to the domestic banking system, whether to meet demands stemming from the rolloff of external bank lines (Thailand, Indonesia, Korea, Brazil, and Turkey) or a domestic deposit run (Argentina and Uruguay). They can be sold to mop up the domestic currency that the central bank is lending to a troubled banking system (Indonesia) or a troubled government (Russia). They can be sold in the market to meet a surge in demand for foreign exchange from private firms that are having difficulty refinancing their external debt (Indonesia and Brazil). They can be lent to the country's government when it is having difficulty paying its maturing foreign currency–denominated debt (Mexico) or can be sold in the market to fund the central bank's local-currency lending to a government that is running budget deficits (Turkey).

Reserves borrowed from the IMF can be used in all these ways as well, so the IMF has a role in the resolution of a broad range of crises. The basic criteria for IMF lending, though, don't change. The IMF needs to be comfortable with how the country is using the reserves it borrows from the IMF (or how borrowing from the IMF allows the country to put more of its own reserves to use). The IMF also needs to be confident that the country will be in a position to repay the IMF relatively quickly. There is no intrinsic problem with lending the central bank's reserves to the government in the event of a run on the banking system or on the government's debt. Reserves are not just held to prevent a run on the local currency. But the bar for on-lending the reserves the central banks borrow from the IMF to finance ongoing budget deficits should be very high—as such financing needs are rarely short-term.

Lay Out a More Realistic IMF Access Policy

No one wants to bite the bullet and take the political heat associated with acknowledging that current access limits are no longer the actual norms for IMF lending to major emerging economies. No emerging economy that is part of the G-20 has been limited to 100 percent of quota in a year and 300 percent of quota over three years since Mexico.[35] These limits are so far below what a major emerging economy facing capital account pressures needs that they no longer help to assess what a reasonable amount of financial support should be. Setting higher limits for a new IMF crisis facility tailored to address the needs of major emerging economies that face higher demands for reserves during the process of financial integration (so-called capital account crises) would provide more useful guidance for the IMF. Tighter limits could be maintained for other types of lending, including concessional lending.

Specific suggestions include

- setting limits on the IMF's crisis response facility at 300 percent of quota in the first year and no more than 500 percent of quota over three years. The precise limits can be debated. The 300/500 percent limit is within the ballpark of many recent IMF programs but well below the levels of access recently granted to Turkey and Brazil. Countries should expect that they will have to repay the loan when it comes due, not just refinance it—though the option of refinancing can never be taken off the table. Realistically, countries may need a bit longer to repay than the three years provided by the IMF's current facility for large-scale lending (the supplemental reserve facility).

- authorizing the IMF to lend up to 300 percent of quota in a year/500 percent of quota over three years to countries that are engaged in an external debt restructuring. The IMF should be able to provide a significant amount of sovereign DIP financing both to countries seeking to extend the maturities of their external debt and to those seeking

35. The G-20 brings together the G-7 countries, the country holding the presidency of the European Union, and a set of the largest emerging economies to discuss global economic policy issues. Membership in the G-20 is thus a proxy for economic and financial importance. For the details on current IMF facilities, see www.imf.org/external/wp/exv/facts/howlend.htm.

debt reduction. Of course, the actual amount of financing will depend on the merits of each case: Not every country that needs a debt restructuring should receive the upper limit for DIP financing. In cases with modest capital-account pressures, the standard 100/300 percent quota should be enough.

- Providing an opt-out that allows the IMF to lend more than 300/500 percent of quota in lender of last resort–type responses to a few rare cases. The option of exceeding the new, higher limits cannot be entirely taken away, but there should be a very strong presumption that the IMF would exceed these new limits only in a very small set of cases. If access norms for emerging economies are increased, exceptional should really mean exceptional. Lending above this higher access limit should be given only to countries that can repay on time and in full; the need to refinance exceptional access should be considered *prima facie* evidence of failure. The IMF managing director should be expected to personally testify that in his or her judgment, the crisis country will be in a position to repay in full after three years and should provide documentation supporting that assessment both to the IMF Board and the public.
- The IMF's policy framework should neither deny support to small countries just because they are small and have limited "systemic" importance nor assure that all large countries that are potentially "systemic" receive support. The potential to prevent a financial crisis from cascading through the domestic economy and generating catastrophic falls in output is sufficient to justify official intervention even in the absence of a high risk of contagion. Conversely, lending large amounts to a systemically important country that has unsustainable debts is a poor use of official resources—it is better to build a firewall around the crisis country. Larger countries are likely to receive the benefit of the doubt more often than small countries, but there should be "constructive ambiguity" about how much extra help a country's size will generate.

Don't Rely on the IMF to Save Countries That Are Too Strategically Important to Fail

If the G-7 countries want to let a country of particular political or strategic importance avoid the risks of a debt restructuring, even though its debt levels suggest it is not a good candidate for an IMF bailout, the G-7 countries—either individually or collectively—should provide the additional medium-term financing the country needs. The logic is simple: The IMF is a universal institution that needs to respond similarly to countries with similar financial problems. If the G-7 wants to give a politically important country a special break, it should do so on its own dime. The IMF would presumably continue to define the country's economic plan and lend in smaller quantities. This limits the risk of the IMF's own lending capacity being tied down in long-term commitments to a few favored countries. The United States' recent willingness to provide an $8.5 billion bilateral loan to Turkey is a good first step in this direction, even if it came only after the IMF exposed itself excessively.

Graphical Presentation of Our Proposed Approach to Crisis Resolution

We are not calling for a tiered, graduated response that moves slowly through the full range of options, first giving adjustment and moderate amounts of financing a chance, then moving to some form of voluntary maturity-extending restructuring supported by a bit more money, and then letting a country move to outright debt reduction without the benefit of official support or any plan negotiated with the IMF. That is what did not work in Argentina. We are calling for a greater willingness by the IMF and its major shareholders to challenge a country's exchange rate regime—even a currency board—when it is unsustainable, a greater willingness to decide from the get go that a debt restructuring is part of the solution, and a greater willingness to put money on the table to limit the risk of the restructuring triggering a broader collapse of confidence.

Figure 9.2 illustrates how we think our proposed framework would work and highlights where we think the application of this framework would have implied significant changes in the international community's response to crises. Our proposed framework starts with an assessment of where a country stands on a spectrum from solvent but potentially illiquid to totally insolvent. The country's position on this scale would define both the amount of IMF lending and the country's approach toward its private creditors. Access can be *normal* (100 percent of quota in a year/300 percent overall), *large* for the appropriate capital account crises (300/500 percent), or *exceptional* (greater than 500 percent). Private financing may be obtained by fully *voluntary or catalytic* means, by *semi-coercive* steps to bail in creditors, like a maturity-extending debt restructuring, or by *fully coercive* steps like outright default or debt reduction. This simplifies the presentation, though it also compresses a broader spectrum of options into three boxes.

The top part of this 3x3 matrix shows how past crises were actually addressed; the bottom part shows how we believe they should have been addressed. Argentina, Uruguay, and Turkey, in our view, should have received large, not exceptional, financial packages, and this financing should have been used to limit the risks associated with a coercive debt restructuring, not to avoid any debt restructuring (unless the G-7 stepped in with junior bilateral financing). If a country like Ecuador could develop a coherent approach to its crisis, in principle it could have received additional financing to soften the impact of its restructuring. Brazil in 2001–02 poses the most difficult case. Its debt levels put it outside the bounds of a typical liquidity case. But its flexible exchange rate regime and its

Figure 9.2 Matrix formulation of crisis resolution approach

a. Actual crisis resolution

		Private financing		
		Voluntary/soft (catalytic)	**Debt rescheduling** (semi-coercive)	**Debt reduction** (after default)
Official financing	Exceptional financing (>500 percent)	**1** Mexico, Turkey, Brazil (1999), Brazil (2000), Argentina	**2** Uruguay, Korea	**3**
	Large financing for capital account crises (300/500 percent)	**4**	**5** Thailand, Indonesia	**6** Russia
	Normal financing (100/300 percent)	**7** Romania	**8** Pakistan, Ukraine	**9** Ecuador

b. Proposed new framework

		Private financing		
		Voluntary/soft (catalytic)	**Debt rescheduling** (semi-coercive)	**Debt reduction** (after default)
Official financing	Exceptional financing (>500 percent)	**1** Mexico, Brazil (1999)[a]	**2**	**3**
	Large financing for capital account crises (300/500 percent)	**4**	**5** Korea[b], Thailand, Indonesia, Brazil 2002, Turkey, Uruguay	**6** Russia, Argentina, Ecuador
	Normal financing (100/300 percent)	**7** Romania	**8** Pakistan, Ukraine	**9**

a. Allowance would be made for exceptional financing (i.e., above 500 percent) from bilateral junior loans in cases where a G-7 member considered the debtor to be strategically important.

b. Korea could have been handled as a large financing case if it had had a more reasonable quota. Its program was exceptional in size only because the quota was so small.

record-running significant primary surplus may just be enough to make a case for large or even exceptional financing in the absence of a restructuring of the government's own debt. We would have buttressed IMF lending with a concerted attempt to bail in cross-border interbank creditors.

Can the IMF Act Differently Without Institutional Reform?

An obvious criticism of our proposals is that we want the IMF to act differently but are not proposing any institutional changes that would create incentives for the IMF to act differently. The IMF sometimes may get too close to some of its members, and it has an institutional bias as a credit cooperative against pushing one of its members to do something that it does not want to do. The G-7 countries, both individually and collectively, like to be seen as trying to help rather than hurt major emerging economies and geostrategic friends and allies: The biases of the IMF's largest shareholders may also be reflected in IMF lending decisions. To return to our initial analogy, it may be hard to change the IMF's software—its lending decisions—without changing its own institutional hardware—its governance structure. Our response to the "you cannot teach an old dog new tricks" argument is three-fold.

First, a lot of proposed institutional reforms would gum up IMF decision making without necessarily generating the desired results. For example, requiring a supermajority vote to approve large-scale financing would make it more difficult for the IMF to lend large sums to risky countries. But supermajority voting also would tend to create an institutional bias against making *any* difficult decisions. We want the IMF to be more willing to make a range of difficult decisions, including the decision to link the availability of IMF financing to a country's willingness to initiate a debt restructuring.

Second, reforms that would insulate the IMF from political pressures from the G-7—such as proposals to make the IMF's Executive Board more independent of the G-7—go in the wrong direction.[36] The world is not ready for a powerful independent supranational organization divorced from national political control. IMF programs are far too invasive and embody far too many judgments about the content of good economic policy to be left purely to the technocrats. The G-7 countries need to think more systematically about the role that they want the IMF to play in the world's financial system and need to take ownership of their decisions to support large IMF loans. The IMF is not going to be more willing than its major financial contributors to make hard calls.

Third, ideas do matter. Too often, IMF financial support and a debt restructuring are presented as diametrically opposed choices. If large

36. See, for example, the proposal for an "independent and accountable IMF" in De Gregorio et al. (1999).

amounts of IMF financing make sense, a debt restructuring does not. If a debt restructuring makes sense, large IMF financing does not. Believers in lender of last resort–style financing fear that an intermediate option—out-of-court restructuring—will take Mexican-style lender-of-last-resort financing entirely off the table. Proponents of payments suspensions and debt restructurings often believe these are attractive options precisely because they would reduce the distortions introduced by IMF lending. The notion that the IMF should take a more active role—including an active financial role—in guiding a country through a debt restructuring is one that encounters substantial resistance.

There is something counterintuitive about lending potentially significant sums of new money to countries that need to seek a debt restructuring, in part because the country may already have too much debt. We think it makes sense in some cases because a country is a lot more than just the sovereign. The government of the crisis country may be at high risk of insolvency and may need both long-term financing and serious adjustments to get itself out of a deep hole. But that does not necessarily mean that there are no liquidity needs elsewhere in the economy.

Conclusion

The selection of Rodrigo Rato as the new IMF managing director is sure to focus attention—at least briefly—on the IMF's health and the state of the international financial architecture. Such an examination is needed. The IMF has quietly taken on new roles in the resolution of crises, and it is time to ask which of these roles the IMF should, and should not, be performing.

As former IMF Chief Economist Michael Mussa has suggested—paraphrasing Watergate's Deep Throat—the way to find the core issues facing the IMF is "to follow the money." A quick look at the IMF's balance sheet at the end of 2003—the $28 billion outstanding loan to Brazil, the $24 billion outstanding loan to Turkey, the $15 billion loan to Argentina, and the $10 billion loan to Indonesia—should leave little doubt that the IMF remains heavily invested in the business of providing emergency liquidity to increase the foreign exchange reserves of major emerging-market economies. Indonesia's outstanding debt to the IMF is evidence that not all large IMF loans will be repaid quickly, a lesson that Argentina is sure to reinforce. The debate over returning to the IMF's traditional lending limits was settled in practice when the Bush administration made its peace with large-scale lending in Argentina, Uruguay, Brazil, and Turkey and when the Europeans decided they wanted the IMF to lend to Brazil in the summer of 2002.

The IMF has the ability to lend quite significant quantities of money to all but the largest emerging economies, whether to help meet external debt payments that the country cannot refinance in the market, to finance a budget deficit that can no longer be financed domestically, or to prevent a restructuring from triggering a run on the banks and the currency. The IMF is big enough to matter but not so big as to guarantee that a program it backs will be a success.

This makes it all the more important to develop a sensible policy for determining who gets access to the IMF's liquidity insurance. Such a policy needs to treat countries with different problems and different debt levels differently. Liquidity insurance that saves countries with little debt from the risk of a correctable policy error—like blowing reserves defending an exchange rate peg—forcing a costly restructuring that could result in an Argentine-style meltdown is one thing. Liquidity insurance that tries to save a country that borrowed too much, built up too much debt, and now must dig itself out of a deep hole from any restructuring is quite another.

It is unrealistic to think that protection from external litigation offers a true substitute for large IMF support packages or that a better process for restructuring sovereign bonds will allow the IMF to disengage from the sovereign debt restructuring process. Bond clauses—or even the full legal protection from a statutory bankruptcy regime—should not be expected to do more than make it easier for a sovereign to avoid holdouts. They won't suddenly make it possible for the official sector to say no to requests for help or transform the management of financial crises in emerging economies. The shift from long-term bank loans to long-term bonds has not caused the wave of financial distress many emerging economies have experienced over the past 10 years. Crises are every bit as much a product of the withdrawal of short-term bank claims, the speed with which international investors can move in and out of local markets, and the sudden shifts in local residents' willingness to hold local financial assets. Provisions allowing the amendment of a bond's financial terms won't stop a cross-border bank run or be of much help if a restructuring triggers a wild rush out of the local banks or the local currency. We like bond clauses, but they are no substitute for an active IMF role in the resolution of debt crises.

Predicting future crises can be a fool's errand. But it is not a stretch to say that the IMF is likely to be forced to confront more crises of domestic confidence. Domestic debt levels in many emerging economies—not just Brazil and Turkey—are already high and often on an upward trend, and in many countries, local banks and other domestic investors hold a large share of the country's "international" bonds. Growing domestic debts often imply larger annual financing needs, both to cover budget deficits and to refinance existing debts. At some point the domestic creditors of a major emerging economy may be unwilling to continue to provide their government the financing it needs at a price it can afford.

Our core recommendation is that the decision to lend large sums always be combined with another, equally important, decision: Should the IMF's financial force be used to help a country avoid any debt restructuring or to support a debt restructuring? The logic of large packages and soft or no bail-ins when the problem is one of illiquidity versus comprehensive standstills and deep debt reduction when the problem is one of insolvency leaves many sensible options off the table. Some crises are too deep to qualify as pure liquidity cases but are not so severe as to justify a comprehensive standstill, immediate debt reduction, and all the associated economic disruption. There is room to use large IMF programs to complement a coercive debt restructuring. IMF financing can help to convince the country's other creditors and investors not to run even as the country goes about a restructuring, and the leverage that comes from provision of new money can be deployed to limit the risk of prolonged default. Even a country that gets into trouble because it has too much debt often needs more money—borrowed international reserves—along with better policies to help it get through its crisis.

Some believe that the new managing director should not focus on crisis resolution, particularly after the IMF's proposal for a new bankruptcy regime was shot down. Rather, they argue that Rato should focus on institutional reforms: increasing the representation of emerging economies at the IMF, increasing the amount of resources the IMF has available to lend, spinning off the IMF's "surveillance" from its crisis lending to strengthen crisis prevention, or even changing the IMF's own internal governance to reduce its major shareholders' influence over specific lending decisions. Many of these ideas are worth discussing, though a quest for political independence is unlikely to go further than did calls for a new international sovereign bankruptcy regime. The IMF needs to focus above all on what can and should be done to manage crises more effectively even in the absence of institutional change.

In a world where financial integration, volatile capital flows, and less than fully sound and credible economic policies make financial crises an ever-present risk, the core issue facing the IMF remains the resolution of balance-of-payments crises. Strong leadership at the top of the IMF is essential. The IMF should be accountable to its shareholders, but it should not hide behind them. Rather, it should use the persuasion power and the vast analytical tools of the institution to convince its shareholders on how best to respond to each crisis. It would help, though, if the G-7 countries that provide most of the IMF's funds were willing to go beyond the stale calls for the IMF to return to its traditional lending norms (calls forgotten in a crisis) and instead start to discuss the set of problems that they believe should—and should not—be addressed by large or even exceptionally large amounts of IMF lending. The IMF may need more financial resources in the medium term, but it needs even more urgently to decide how best to use its current resources. The IMF's existing lending capacity—along with the existing set of debt restructuring tools—offers substantial scope for creative policymaking.

Appendix A
Tables

Table A.1 Exposure of official sector, annual data (billions of dollars, percent of GDP in parentheses)

		Change in IMF exposure					Change in MDB exposure				
	Start	Yr 1	Yr 2	Yr 3	Yr 4	Yr 5	Yr 1	Yr 2	Yr 3	Yr 4	Yr 5
Mexico	1994	12.0	9.4	5.2	4.5	0.6	1.6	0.7	–0.6	0.0	–0.4
		(2.9)	(2.3)	(1.3)	(1.1)	(0.2)	(0.4)	(0.2)	(–0.2)	(0.0)	(–0.1)
Mexico[a]	1993	—	—	—	—	—	—	—	—	—	—
		—	—	—	—	—	—	—	—	—	—
Thailand	1996	2.4	3.2	3.4	3.1	1.7	0.6	1.6	2.4	2.4	2.5
		(1.3)	(1.8)	(1.9)	(1.7)	(0.9)	(0.3)	(0.9)	(1.3)	(1.3)	(1.4)
Indonesia	1996	3.0	9.1	10.2	10.8	9.1	–1.4	0.6	2.5	2.7	2.1
		(1.3)	(4.0)	(4.5)	(4.8)	(4.0)	(–0.6)	(0.3)	(1.1)	(1.2)	(0.9)
Korea	1996	11.1	16.9	6.1	5.8	0.0	4.6	9.2	10.1	9.7	9.5
		(2.1)	(3.2)	(1.2)	(1.1)	(0.0)	(0.9)	(1.8)	(1.9)	(1.9)	(1.8)
Russia	1997	6.1	2.0	–1.6	–5.8	–6.7	1.3	1.6	1.8	1.7	—
		(1.4)	(0.5)	(–0.4)	(–1.4)	(–1.6)	(0.3)	(0.4)	(0.4)	(0.4)	—
Brazil	1997	4.8	8.8	1.7	—	—	6.3	8.5	8.2	—	—
		(0.6)	(1.1)	(0.2)	—	—	(0.8)	(1.1)	(1.0)	—	—
Turkey	1999	3.3	13.2	21.2	23.2	—	0.2	0.6	1.3	—	—
		(1.8)	(7.2)	(11.5)	(12.5)	—	(0.1)	(0.3)	(0.7)	—	—
Turkey[b]	2000	9.9	17.9	19.9	—	—	0.4	1.1	—	—	—
		(5.0)	(9.0)	(10.0)	—	—	(0.2)	(0.5)	—	—	—
Argentina	2000	8.9	9.3	10.5	—	—	1.7	0.5	—	—	—
		(3.1)	(3.3)	(3.7)	—	—	(0.6)	(0.2)	—	—	—
Brazil	2000	6.6	19.1	26.5	—	—	1.2	3.0	—	—	—
		(1.3)	(3.7)	(5.2)	—	—	(0.2)	(0.6)	—	—	—
Uruguay	2001	1.6	2.3	—	—	—	0.7	—	—	—	—
		(8.9)	(12.2)	—	—	—	(3.7)	—	—	—	—

— = not available

IMF = International Monetary Fund
MDBs = multilateral development banks

a. Mexico did not receive IMF financing until early 1995, so formally 1994 is the precrisis year. However, Mexico used a large fraction of its reserves in the course of 1994 defending the peso, so 1993 data present a more accurate picture of changes in Mexico's net reserve.

b. Turkey received a modest augmentation to its existing IMF program at the end of 2000, so formally the pre-crisis year is 1999. However, the fall 2000 program was massively augmented in 2001, so starting from 2000 presents a better picture of the path of IMF lenidng.

Sources: World Bank, *Global Development Finance* (2003); IMF financial data by country, www.imf.org.

Change in bilateral exposure					Change in official exposure (sum of IMF, MDB, and bilateral exposure)					Change in net reserves				
Yr 1	**Yr 2**	**Yr 3**	**Yr 4**	**Yr 5**	**Yr 1**	**Yr 2**	**Yr 3**	**Yr 4**	**Yr 5**	**Yr 1**	**Yr 2**	**Yr 3**	**Yr 4**	**Yr 5**
10.1	1.3	–3.8	–4.3	–5.2	3.6	11.4	0.8	0.2	–4.9	–1.4	3.7	17.3	21.0	24.9
(2.5)	(0.3)	(–0.9)	(–1.1)	(–1.3)	(5.8)	(2.8)	(0.2)	(0.1)	(–1.2)	(–0.3)	(0.7)	(3.5)	(4.2)	(5.0)
—	—	—	—	—	—	—	—	—	—	–17.9	–19.3	–14.2	–0.6	3.1
—	—	—	—	—	—	—	—	—	—	(–4.4)	(–4.7)	(–3.5)	(–0.1)	(0.8)
4.3	6.0	8.8	7.9	6.3	7.3	10.9	14.7	13.3	10.4	–14.0	–12.1	–7.1	–8.8	–7.1
(2.3)	(3.3)	(4.9)	(4.3)	(3.5)	(4.0)	(6.0)	(8.1)	(7.3)	(5.7)	(–7.7)	(–6.7)	(–3.9)	(–4.8)	(–3.9)
–2.2	2.3	7.5	6.3	4.7	–0.7	12.0	20.2	19.8	15.9	–4.6	–4.6	–2.1	–0.6	–0.1
(–1.0)	(1.0)	(3.3)	(2.8)	(2.1)	(–0.3)	(5.3)	(8.9)	(8.7)	(7.0)	(–2.0)	(–2.0)	(–0.9)	(–0.3)	(–0.1)
–0.3	–1.0	1.9	1.6	0.1	15.4	25.1	18.1	17.2	9.6	–24.7	1.0	33.8	56.3	68.7
(0.0)	(–0.2)	(0.4)	(0.3)	(0.0)	(3.0)	(4.8)	(3.5)	(3.3)	(1.8)	(–4.8)	(0.2)	(6.5)	(10.8)	(13.2)
3.9	6.0	4.8	–1.9	—	11.3	9.6	4.9	–6.0	—	–11.2	–6.4	13.0	25.4	38.0
(0.9)	(1.4)	(1.1)	(–0.4)	—	(2.6)	(2.2)	(1.1)	(–1.4)	—	(–2.6)	(–1.5)	(3.0)	(5.9)	(8.9)
–0.6	–1.8	–1.0	—	—	10.4	15.5	8.9	—	—	–13.0	–24.8	–20.1	—	—
(–0.1)	(–0.2)	(–0.1)	—	—	(1.3)	(1.9)	(1.1)	—	—	(–1.6)	(–3.1)	(–2.5)	—	—
0.0	–0.7	–0.4	—	—	3.5	13.9	22.1	—	—	–4.1	–17.7	–17.4	–12.6	—
(0.0)	(–0.4)	(–0.2)	—	—	(1.9)	(7.5)	(12.0)	—	—	(–2.2)	(–9.6)	(–9.4)	(–6.8)	—
–0.7	–0.4	—	—	—	10.4	18.6	—	—	—	–13.6	–13.3	–8.4	—	—
(–0.4)	(–0.2)	—	—	—	(5.2)	(9.3)	—	—	—	(–6.8)	(–6.7)	(–4.2)	—	—
–1.0	0.4	—	—	—	9.6	10.1	—	—	—	–19.5	–23.9	–21.5	—	—
(–0.3)	(0.1)	—	—	—	(3.4)	(3.6)	—	—	—	(–6.9)	(–8.4)	(–7.6)	—	—
–1.7	–1.0	—	—	—	6.0	21.1	—	—	—	–4.1	–13.9	–9.9	—	—
(–0.3)	(–0.2)	—	—	—	(1.2)	(4.1)	—	—	—	(–0.8)	(–2.7)	(–1.9)	—	—
0.0	—	—	—	—	2.3	—	—	—	—	–4.0	–3.3	—	—	—
(–0.2)	—	—	—	—	(12.3)	—	—	—	—	(–21.4)	(–17.7)	—	—	—

Table A.2 Exposure of private creditors, annual data (billions of dollars, percent of GDP in parentheses)

Country	Start	Change in bond exposure (sum of the outstanding bonds of public and private sectors)					Change in bank exposure (sum of bank lending to public sector and short-term debts)					Change in private exposure (sum of bank and bond exposure)				
		Yr 1	Yr 2	Yr 3	Yr 4	Yr 5	Yr 1	Yr 2	Yr 3	Yr 4	Yr 5	Yr 1	Yr 2	Yr 3	Yr 4	Yr 5
Mexico	1994	3.8	13.9	13.0	15.2	19.5	–1.1	–7.8	–4.6	5.6	13.5	2.8	6.1	8.4	20.8	33.0
		(0.9)	(3.4)	(3.2)	(3.7)	(4.8)	(–0.3)	(–1.9)	(–1.1)	(1.4)	(3.3)	(0.7)	(1.5)	(2.1)	(5.1)	(8.1)
Thailand	1996	1.6	1.1	–0.2	–1.5	–3.2	–12.0	–19.8	–30.4	–45.0	–52.6	–10.4	–18.7	–30.6	–46.5	–55.8
		(0.9)	(0.6)	(–0.1)	(–0.8)	(–1.8)	(–6.6)	(–10.9)	(–16.7)	(–24.7)	(–28.9)	(–5.7)	(–10.3)	(–16.8)	(–25.6)	(–30.7)
Indonesia	1996	3.1	3.0	1.6	–0.5	–1.9	5.3	8.0	2.2	–1.3	–3.6	8.3	11.0	3.8	–1.8	–5.5
		(1.3)	(1.3)	(0.7)	(–0.2)	(–0.8)	(2.3)	(3.5)	(1.0)	(–0.6)	(–1.6)	(3.7)	(4.8)	(1.7)	(–0.8)	(–2.4)
Korea	1996	8.8	13.8	13.0	14.0	14.4	–2.6	–14.3	–15.5	–17.5	–28.7	6.3	–0.5	–2.5	–3.5	–14.3
		(1.7)	(2.6)	(2.5)	(2.7)	(2.8)	(–0.5)	(–2.7)	(–3.0)	(–3.4)	(–5.5)	(1.2)	(–0.1)	(–0.5)	(–0.7)	(–2.7)
Russia[a]	1997	11.6	11.3	31.3	30.5	—	8.9	9.9	–18.9	–13.4	—	20.5	21.2	12.4	17.2	—
		(2.7)	(2.6)	(7.3)	(7.1)	—	(2.1)	(2.3)	(–4.4)	(–3.1)	—	(4.8)	(4.9)	(2.9)	(4.0)	—
Brazil	1997	1.7	2.6	1.8	—	—	31.5	28.5	31.3	—	—	33.2	31.1	33.1	—	—
		(0.2)	(0.3)	(0.2)	—	—	(3.9)	(3.5)	(3.9)	—	—	(4.1)	(3.9)	(4.1)	—	—
Brazil[b]	1998	0.9	0.1	–4.4	—	—	–2.9	–0.2	–14.8	—	—	–2.0	–0.1	–19.2	—	—
		(0.1)	(0.0)	(–0.6)	—	—	(–0.4)	(0.0)	(–1.9)	—	—	(–0.3)	(0.0)	(–2.4)	—	—
Turkey	1999	4.9	4.1	6.1	—	—	7.9	–4.0	2.4	—	—	12.8	0.1	8.5	—	—
		(2.6)	(2.2)	(3.3)	—	—	(4.3)	(–2.2)	(1.3)	—	—	(6.9)	(0.0)	(4.6)	—	—
Argentina[c,d]	2000	–17.3	–14.1	—	—	—	–11.5	–16.6	—	—	—	–28.8	–30.7	—	—	—
		(–6.1)	(–5.0)	—	—	—	(–4.0)	(–5.9)	—	—	—	(–10.1)	(–10.8)	—	—	—
Brazil	2000	–4.5	–1.9	—	—	—	–14.7	–30.2	—	—	—	–19.2	–32.0	—	—	—
		(–0.9)	(–0.4)	—	—	—	(–2.9)	(–5.9)	—	—	—	(–3.8)	(–6.3)	—	—	—
Turkey	2000	–0.8	1.2	—	—	—	–11.9	–5.5	—	—	—	–12.7	–4.3	—	—	—
		(–0.4)	(0.6)	—	—	—	(–6.0)	(–2.8)	—	—	—	(–6.4)	(–2.2)	—	—	—
Uruguay	2001	0.2	—	—	—	—	–1.4	—	—	—	—	–1.3	—	—	—	—
		(0.9)	—	—	—	—	(–7.7)	—	—	—	—	(–6.8)	—	—	—	—

— = not available

a. Russia's exchange of London Club Soviet-era syndicated bank loans for Russian eurobonds explains the large increase in bond exposure and the large fall in bank exposure.

b. Brazil experienced large inflows in the first half of 1998 and significant outflows in the second half of 1998. In this case, annual data has its limits, since starting neither at the end of 1997 nor at the end of 1998 presents a perfect picture of Brazil's crisis.

c. World Bank *Global Development Finance* data for outstanding bank loans to Argentina's private sector in 2001 and 2002 were inconsistent with their flow numbers. The flow numbers suggest a sharp fall in exposure; the 2001 stock number suggests an increase in exposure to $21.794 billion. This seems likely to be a misprint, as it is inconsistent with other data sources as well as the flow data. We adjusted the end of 2000 stock number with 2001 and 2002 flow numbers to produce our estimate.

d. World Bank *Global Development Finance* data often includes international bonds held by domestic residents. The large fall in Argentina's stock of outstanding bonds in 2001 reflects the impact of Argentina's bonds for guaranteed loans swap, as many domestic residents swapped their holdings of Argentina's international bonds for a new domestic-law, guaranteed loan. See appendix table A.3.

Source: World Bank, *Global Development Finance* (2003).

Table A.3 Summary of past restructuring cases

Country	Time	Payments suspension	Size of restructuring	Terms	Bank loans or traded securities	Collective action/ coordination	Official-sector involvement
Korea	December 1997–March 1998	No (averted by successful rollover)	$24 billion	Commitment to roll over/ maintain exposure to Korean banks until March 31, 1998 (agreement reached on January 16); agreement to restructure $24 billion in bank loans into one-, two-, and three-year sovereign debt at 225, 250, and 275 basis points over LIBOR, reached before the March deadline. Korea's government guaranteed payments to external creditors in early December in an early attempt to stem the rolloff of bank lines	Interbank loans; efforts to monitor OTC derivatives were dropped when derivatives did not prove to be a major problem	Bank coordinating committee; daily monitoring of exposure/rollover rates (rollover rate was not 100 percent in January—some small and mid-sized banks exited)	Moral suasion of banks from central banks and finance ministries; Federal Reserve Bank of New York hosted a December 24, 1997, meeting with the banks; similar meetings held in other capitals; monitoring by G-10, central banks, and the IMF
Indonesia I	May 1998–May 1999	No (informal suspension on payments of corporate loans, not of interbank loans)	$6.4 billion, in two tranches ($2.8 billion and $3.6 billion)	Short-, medium- and long-term claims on Indonesian banks coming due between May 1998, and the end of 2000 were restructured into new instruments amortizing from 1999–2005, carrying interest rates of LIBOR plus 275 to 350 basis points (with higher interest rates on payments due at a later date), fully guaranteed by Bank Indonesia	Interbank loans; note that there was also a de facto standstill on payments by Indonesian firms to their external banks	Bank coordinating committee (Frankfurt)	IMF moral suasion; monitoring by G-10 and central banks in 1998

(table continues on next page)

Table A.3 Summary of past restructuring cases *(continued)*

Country	Time	Payments suspension	Size of restructuring	Terms	Bank loans or traded securities	Collective action/ coordination	Official-sector involvement
Ukraine I	1998–99	Yes (suspension during negotiations)	$0.63 billion (October 1998); $0.11 billion (October 1998); $0.16 billion (June 1999)	1998 (Merrill): $0.126 billion (20 percent) paid in cash; $0.504 billion rolled in 2000 zero coupon bond with yield of 20 percent.1998 (Chase): $0.027 billion paid in cash; $0.082 billion in one-year notes restructured into an amortizing instrument with final maturity in October 2000. 1999 (ING): $0.089 billion paid in cash; $0.074 billion restructured for two years at yield of 21 percent by augmenting Ukraine's deutsche mark bonds.	Traded securities (structured transactions)	Negotiations with issuers (Merrill, Chase, and ING), who placed structured transactions; limited negotiations with Merrill; intensive negotiations before 1998 deal with Chase and 1999 deal with ING	IMF reserve floor prevented it from financing repayment; IMF capped amount of debt that could be paid in cash
Indonesia II	1998–2000	No	$0.55 billion in two restructurings	1998: $0.21 billion due in 1998–99 restructured with payments into instruments with amortization from 2002–09, at same interest rate as before (LIBOR plus 87.5 basis points) 2000: $0.34 billion due between 2000 and 2002 restructured, with amortization payments from 2003–2013	Bank lines (repayment of drawings on contingent credit facilities)	Bank committee (predominantly Japanese banks)	Paris Club comparability requirement led Indonesia to seek a restructuring.

Russia I	August 1998	Yes	$33.4 billion in GKOs; $14.9 billion in OFZs; external creditors accounted for roughly $9.2 billion of the $48.8 billion total predevaluation amounts	Accounts paid into the frozen bank accounts, subsequently restructured into new, unconvertible instruments; maturing bonds exchanged for 10 percent cash and the remainder in three- to five-year bonds; conversion of ruble payments into dollars limited; in the interim, large devaluation wiped out external value of claims	Traded securities (domestic debt)	Unsatisfactory negotiations; Russia announced restructuring offer in mid-September 1998, one month after its default; Russian and external banks refused the offer, initiated protracted negotiations	No official involvement
Russia II	November 1998–July 2000	Yes; in late 1998, Russia paid the Prins, Prins paid with new bonds; banks declared formal default in January 1999; Russia missed payments on Ians in June 1999	$28.63 billion in outstanding principal on Prins and Ians and $2.80 billion in past due interest (PDI)	$28.63 billion in London Club debt exchanged into $18.19 billion of 30-year global bonds with step-up interest rates; $2.80 billion of PDI restructured into $2.53 billion 10-year global bonds and $0.27 billion in cash; there was a seven-year grace on principal on the 30-year bonds and a six-year grace on principal on the 10-year bonds; Russian Federation new obligor on debt	Traded securities: previously restructured Soviet-era bank debt (Prins and Ians) that had largely been repackaged and sold to bond investors	Bank Advisory Committee (same committee that handled previous restructuring, despite substantial change in composition of creditors); Prins and Ians, like most syndicated bank loans, lacked collective action clauses	No direct official involvement, though it was clear that this restructuring would meet Paris Club comparability requirement (Paris Club was not prepared to provide debt reduction, only debt rescheduling)
Pakistan	February–December 1999	No	$0.61 billion (three bonds)	Bonds restructured at par into a $0.62 billion 2005 bond, with four equal amortization payments from 2002 to 2005; the new bond paid an interest rate of 10 percent	Eurobonds (English law)	Ad hoc consultation; majority-amendment provisions not used	Paris Club comparability requirement forced Pakistan to seek a restructuring

(table continues on next page)

Table A.3 Summary of past restructuring cases *(continued)*

Country	Time	Payments suspension	Size of restructuring	Terms	Bank loans or traded securities	Collective action/ coordination	Official-sector involvement
Brazil	March 1999	No	Roughly $50 billion in monitored exposure from G-10 banks		Bank lines: Voluntary agreement by major banks to maintain end-February 1999 exposure for next six months		Monitoring by central banks in lender countries
Ecuador	August 1999–August 2000	Yes	$6.46 billion (six bonds) + $0.265 billion in arrears, including $3.35 billion of collateralized Brady bonds, $2.61 billion of uncollateralized Brady bonds, and $0.55 billion in eurobonds	$6.46 billion in bonds (with average interest rate of around 5.2 percent) exchanged for $3.85 billion in new bonds ($1.25 billion in 12 percent 2012 bonds and $2.6 billion in a 10 percent step-up bond maturing in 2030), $0.882 billion in collateral, and $0.143 billion in cash	Bonds (New York–law Brady bonds and eurobonds)	Comprehensive exchange offer; ad hoc consultative group initially formed but not regularly consulted; ad hoc market soundings by Ecuador adviser; amendment of financial terms precluded; use of exit consents to amend nonfinancial terms in exchange so as to encourage participation	Restructuring completed in the context of IMF program that presumed Paris Club restructuring; IMF lending into arrears
Ukraine II	January–April 2000	Yes	$1.86 billion (five bond issues maturing in 2000 and 2001); $0.74 billion in Gazprom bonds in a separate exchange	Cash settlement of accrued interest ($0.225 billion) and an exchange of old debt at par (or close to par for one bond) for 2007 bonds, with 11 percent dollar coupon, 10 percent euro coupon, and step-up amortization payments starting in 2001	Bonds (English and German laws)	Comprehensive exchange offer; intensive, coordinated effort to sell the deal and contact retail holders; amendment provisions used to cram down terms on holdouts in three bonds that had clauses	Restructuring completed before IMF program, but with IMF support (comfort letter); clear that IMF program would not provide financing needed to avoid restructuring plus IMF review of financial terms

Turkey	December 2000	No	$18.6 billion	Voluntary agreement to roll over existing exposure with monitoring by IMF	Bank loans only	Ad hoc consultation led by Deutsche Bank and Citibank	Rollover undertaken in conjunction with IMF program; IMF and Turkish authorities participated in ad hoc consultations organized by Deutsche Bank and Citibank; no G-10 central bank participation
Argentina I	November 2001	No	$41 billion in sovereign debt; $9 billion in provincial debt	Maturity extension and coupon reduction in exchange for pledge of tax revenue; international bonds held by domestic investors were exchanged for new guaranteed loans governed by domestic Argentine law; the loans were backed, in theory, by revenue from the financial transaction taxes; interest rates on the new loans were reduced to either 7 or 70 percent of their original level, and maturities were pushed out three years on all bonds maturing before 2010; holders of the guaranteed loans had the option of reclaiming their original bond if Argentina offered better terms in the planned phase 2 external exchange	Bonds (New York law)	Heavy moral suasion of local banks and pension funds, implicit threat of default	The exchange was undertaken as part of a broad commitment to seek a debt restructuring as part of the augmented IMF program; $3 billion from the IMF was in principle available to support an international exchange but was never used; the guaranteed loans issued in this exchange were later pesified

(table continues on next page)

Table A.3 Summary of past restructuring cases *(continued)*

Country	Time	Payments suspension	Size of restructuring	Terms	Bank loans or traded securities	Collective action/ coordination	Official-sector involvement
Argentina II	January–February 2002	Yes	$41 billion in sovereign debt; $9 billion in provincial debt	Forced exchange of guaranteed loans for new peso-denominated debt; creditors who accepted pesification exchanged $1 face for 1.4 pesos face; the new peso bonds paid a 2 percent coupon and an annual inflation adjustment, which was capitalized; approximately $20 billion did not accept pesification; the government is seeking to force these holders to reclaim their original bonds	Argentina-law bank loans	Default on old instruments; heavy moral suasion/regulatory forbearance for domestic banks (bank liabilities were also pesified)	No official involvement at the time of the exchange
Uruguay	April 2003	No	$5.45 billion; $3.85 billion of this was in 19 international bonds, $1.6 billion was in 46 domestic bonds; domestic investors also held some international bonds	$5.06 billion (93 percent) of bondholders elected to participate, resulting in $5.02 billion in new bonds; bondholders could elect to swap either into a bond with maturities extended by five years or into a benchmark bond; the holdouts were concentrated in the international bonds	Bonds (mostly New York law, only the $250 million Samurai bonds contained collective action clauses)	Ad hoc consultation and informal dialogue; regulatory treatment of domestic bonds strongly encouraged participation in the exchange; exit consents used in New York–law bonds; collective action clauses used with Japanese-law bonds; new bonds contain innovative "aggregation" provisions as well as 75 percent voting for amending key terms	Bond exchange was necessary to provide the financing assurances for continued IMF lending; the exchange was linked to an IMF program that provided $3 billion to halt the bank run

Argentina III	September 2003 to present	Yes	Roughly $60 billion outstanding: $50 billion principal plus $10 billion interest arrears held by international investors and roughly $20 billion in bonds held by domestic pension funds who did not accept the pesification of the guaranteed loans		Bonds (New York, English, Japanese, German, and Argentine laws)	Some bonds organized in committees, with at least three groupings: an association organized by Italian banks that represents Italian retail investors, a special purpose vehicle backed by German banks that represents $1 billion in retail investors, and a committee of institutional investors

Note: See text for explanation of acronyms.

Source: Authors' compilation.

References

Aghion, Philippe, Philippe Bacchetta, and Abhijit Banerjee. 2000. Currency Crises and Monetary Policy with Credit Constraints. Harvard University, Cambridge, MA. Photocopy.

Aghion, Philippe, Philippe Bacchetta, and Abhijit Banerjee. 2001. A Corporate Balance Sheet Approach to Currency Crises. Photocopy. www.hec.unil.ch/deep/textes/01.14.pdf.

Alesina, Alberto, and Guido Tabellini. 1990. A Positive Theory of Fiscal Deficits and Government Debt. *Review of Economic Studies* 57: 403–14.

Allen, Franklin, and Douglas Gale. 2000a. Optimal Currency Crises. New York University. Photocopy (April). www.econ.nyu.edu/user/galed/occ.pdf.

Allen, Franklin, and Douglas Gale. 2000b. *Comparing Financial Systems*. Cambridge, MA: MIT Press.

Allen, Mark, Christoph Rosenberg, Christian Keller, Brad Setser, and Nouriel Roubini. 2002. *A Balance Sheet Approach to Financial Crisis*. IMF Working Paper 02/210 (December). Washington: International Monetary Fund. www.imf.org/external/pubs/ft/wp/2002/wp02210.pdf.

Arbelaez, Maria Angelica, María Lucía Guerra, and Nouriel Roubini. Forthcoming. Debt Dynamics and Debt Sustainability in Colombia. In *Fiscal Reform in Colombia*, ed. J. Poterba. Cambridge, MA: MIT Press.

Banque de France. 2003. Toward a Code of Good Conduct on Sovereign Debt Renegotiation. Issues paper prepared by Banque de France staff. Paris: Banque de France.

Bartholomew, Ed, Ernest Stern, and Angela Liuzzi. 2002. Two-Step Sovereign Debt Restructuring. New York: JP Morgan Chase and Co. www.emta.org/keyper/barthol.pdf.

Becker, T., A. S. Richards, and T. Thaicharoen. 2003. Bond Restructuring and Moral Hazard: Are CACs Costly? *Journal of International Economics* 61: 127–61.

Berg, Andrew, Sean Hagan, Christopher Jarvis, Bernhard Steinki, Mark Stone, and Alessandro Zanello. 2003. Reestablishing a Credible Nominal Anchor after a Financial Crisis. In *Managing Financial Crises: Recent Experience and Lessons for Latin America*, ed. Charles Collyns and G. Russell Kincaid. Washington: International Monetary Fund.

Bhattacharya, Sudipto, and Enrica Detragiache. 1994. The Role of Multilateral Institutions in the Market for Sovereign Debt. *Scandinavian Journal of Economics* 96, no. 4 (December): 515–29.

BIS (Bank for International Settlements). 1997. 67th Annual Report. Chapter VI: Financial Trends in Emerging Economies. Basle: Bank for International Settlements (June 9). www.bis.org/publ/ar67c06.pdf.

Blustein, Paul. 2001. *The Chastening: Inside the Crisis That Rocked the Global Financial System and Humbled the IMF.* New York: Public Affairs.

Bolton, Patrick. 2003. Towards a Statutory Approach to Sovereign Debt Restructuring: Lessons from Corporate Bankruptcy Practice Around the World. Princeton University. Photocopy. www.princeton.edu/%7Epbolton/BankruptcyandSDRMFV.doc.pdf.

Bolton, Patrick and David Skeel. 2003. Inside the Black Box: How Should a Sovereign Bankruptcy Framework Be Structured? Princeton University. Photocopy. www.princeton.edu/~pbolton/InsidetheBlack.pdf.

Booth, Jerome. 2001. Burdens that Cannot Be Passed On. *Euromoney* (September): 341–43.

Borensztein, Eduardo R., and Paolo Mauro. 2002. *Reviving the Case for GDP-Indexed Bonds.* IMF Policy Discussion Paper 02/10 (September). Washington: International Monetary Fund.

Boughton, James. 2001. *Silent Revolution: The International Monetary Fund, 1979–1989.* Washington: International Monetary Fund.

Brainard, Lawrence. 1999. Debt Bail-Ins Floated on Unsettled Waters. Investment bank research paper. Chase International Fixed Income Research, London. Photocopy.

Bryant, John. 1980. A Model of Reserves, Bank Runs, and Deposit Insurance. *Journal of Banking and Finance* 4: 333–44.

Buchanan, Michael. 2002. A Sovereign Chapter 11—A Step Too Far. *EMEA Economics Analyst* (April 18). London: Goldman Sachs.

Buchheit, Lee. 2000a. How Ecuador Escaped the Brady Bond Trap. *International Financial Law Review* (December): 17–18.

Buchheit, Lee. 2000b. *Sovereign Debtors and Their Bondholders.* New York: Cleary, Gottlieb, Steen & Hamilton. www.unitar.org/fer/sovereign.pdf.

Buchheit, Lee, and Mitu Gulati. 2000. Exit Consents in Sovereign Bond Exchanges. *UCLA Law Review* 48 (October): 59–89.

Buchheit, Lee, and Jeremiah Pam. 2003. *The Pari Passu Clause in Sovereign Debt Instruments.* Working Paper, Harvard Law School Program on International Financial Systems (November).

Buchheit, Lee, and Jeremiah Pam. 2004. The Hunt for Pari Passu. *International Financial* Law *Review* 23, no. 2 (February): 20–26.

Buchheit, Lee, Mitu Gulati, and Ashoka Mody. 2002. *Sovereign Bonds and the Collective Will.* Georgetown Public Law Research Paper 346884. Washington: Georgetown University.

Buiter, Willem H., and Anne Sibert. 1999. *UDROP: A Small Contribution to the New International Financial Architecture.* CEPR Working Paper 2138 (May). London: Center for Economic Policy Research.

Bulow, Jeremy. 2002. First World Governments and Third World Debt. *Brookings Papers on Economic Activity 2002*, no. 1: 229–55. Washington: Brookings Institution.

Bulow, Jeremy, and Kenneth Rogoff. 1988a. Comprehensive Debt Retirement: The Bolivian Example: Comments and Discussion. *Brookings Papers on Economic Activity 1988*, no. 2: 714–15. Washington: Brookings Institution.

Bulow, Jeremy, and Kenneth Rogoff. 1988b. The Buyback Boondoggle. *Brookings Papers on Economic Activity 1988*, no. 2: 675–98. Washington: Brookings Institution.

Bulow, Jeremy, and Kenneth Rogoff. 1988c. *Multilateral Negotiations for Rescheduling Developing Country Debt: A Bargaining-Theoretic Approach.* IMF Staff Papers 35 (December): 644–57. Washington: International Monetary Fund.

Bulow, Jeremy, and Kenneth Rogoff. 1989a. A Constant Recontracting Model of Sovereign Debt. *Journal of Political Economy* 97: 155–78. www.economics.harvard.edu/~krogoff//JPE89.pdf.

Bulow, Jeremy, and Kenneth Rogoff. 1989b. Sovereign Debt: Is to Forgive to Forget? *American Economic Review* 79, no. 1 (March): 43–50.

Bulow, Jeremy, and Kenneth Rogoff. 1990. Cleaning Up Third World Debt Without Getting Taken to the Cleaners. *Journal of Economic Perspectives* 4, no. 1 (winter): 31–42.

Bulow, Jeremy, and Kenneth Rogoff. 1991. Sovereign Debt Repurchases: No Cure for Overhang. *The Quarterly Journal of Economics* 106, no. 4 (November): 1219–35.

Burnside, Craig, Martin Eichenbaum, and Sergio T. Rebelo. 1999. *Hedging and Financial Fragility in Fixed Exchange Rate Regimes*. NBER Working Paper 7143. Cambridge, MA: National Bureau of Economic Research. http://papers.nber.org/papers/w7143.pdf.

Burnside, Craig, Martin Eichenbaum, and Sergio T. Rebelo. 2000. *On the Fundamentals of Self-Fulfilling Speculative Attacks*. NBER Working Paper 7554. Cambridge, MA: National Bureau of Economic Research.

Burnside, Craig, Martin Eichenbaum, and Sergio T. Rebelo. 2001. Prospective Deficits and the Asian Currency Crisis. *Journal of Political Economy* 109, no. 6: 1155–97.

Caballero, Ricardo J. 2003. *On the International Financial Architecture: Insuring Emerging Markets*. NBER Working Paper 9570 (March). Cambridge, MA: National Bureau of Economic Research.

Calomiris, Charles. 1998. The IMF's Imprudent Role as a Lender of Last Resort. *The Cato Journal* 17: 275–95. Washington: Cato Institute.

Calvo, Guillermo. 1998. Capital Flows and Capital-Market Crises: The Simple Economics of Sudden Stops. *Journal of Applied Economics* 1, no. 1: 35–54.

Calvo, Guillermo. 1999. Contagion in Emerging Markets: When *Wall Street* Is a Carrier. Technical supplement to Understanding the Russian Virus. University of Maryland. Photocopy (May).

Calvo, Guillermo. 2002. Globalization Hazard and Delayed Reform in Emerging Markets. *Economia* 2, no. 2 (spring): 1–29.

Calvo, Guillermo, and Enrique Mendoza. 1999. *Regional Contagion and the Globalization* of *Securities Markets*. NBER Working Paper 7153 (June). Cambridge, MA: National Bureau of Economic Research.

Calvo, Guillermo, and Carmen Reinhart. 1999. When Capital Inflows Come to a Sudden Stop: Consequences and Policy Options. University of Maryland. www.puaf.umd.edu/faculty/papers/reinhart/imfbook.pdf.

Calvo, Guillermo, and Carmen Reinhart. 2002. Fear of Floating. *Quarterly Journal of Economics* 117, no. 2: 379–408.

Calvo, Guillermo, and Carlos Vegh. 1999. Inflation Stabilization. In *Handbook of Macroeconomics*, ed. J. Taylor, and M. Woodford. Amsterdam, Netherlands: North Holland.

Caplen, Brian. 2000. Paris Club Comes under Attack. *Euromoney* (September): 56–61.

Carlsson, Hans, and Eric van Damme. 1993. Global Games and Equilibrium Selection. *Econometrica* 61: 989–1018.

Cavallo, Michele, Kate Kisselev, Fabrizio Perri, and Nouriel Roubini. 2002. Exchange Rate Overshooting and the Costs of Floating. New York University. Photocopy (April).

Cespedes, Luis Felipe, Roberto Chang, and Andres Velasco. 2000. *Balance Sheets and Exchange Rate Policy*. NBER Working Paper 7840 (August). Cambridge, MA: National Bureau of Economic Research.

Chang, Ha-Joon. 2000. The Hazard of Moral Hazard: Untangling the Asian Crisis. *World Development* 28, no. 4: 775–78.

Chang, Roberto, and Andres Velasco. 1999. *Liquidity Crisis in Emerging Markets: Theory and Policy*. NBER Working Paper 7272 (July). Cambridge, MA: National Bureau of Economic Research.

Chang, Roberto, and Andres Velasco. 2001. A Model of Financial Crises in Emerging Markets. *Quarterly Journal of Economics* 116, no. 2 (May): 489–517.

Chinn, Menzie D., Michael P. Dooley, and Sona Shrestha. 1999. *Latin America and East Asia in the Context of an Insurance Model of Currency Crises*. NBER Working Paper 7092 (April). Cambridge, MA: National Bureau of Economic Research.

Chua, Amy. 2002. *World on Fire: How Exporting Free Market Democracy Breeds Ethnic Hatred and Global Instability*. New York: Doubleday.

Chui, Michael, Prasanna Gai, and Andrew Haldane. 2000. *Sovereign Liquidity Crises: Analytics and Implications for Monetary Policy*. Bank of England Working Paper 121. London: Bank of England. www.bankofengland.co.uk/workingpapers/wp121.pdf.

Claessens, Stijn, and Kristin Forbes, eds. 2001. *International Financial Contagion*. Dordrecht, Netherlands: Kluwer Academic Publishers.

Clearinghouse Association LLC. 2004. Memorandum of Amicus Curiae in Support of Motion Pursuant to CPLR 5240 to Preclude Plaintiff Judgment Creditors from Interfering with Payment to Other Creditors. EM Ltd. v. The Republic of Argentina.

Cline, William. 1995. *International Debt Reexamined*. Washington: Institute for International Economics.

Cline, William. 2002. *Private Sector Involvement in Financial Crisis Resolution: Definition, Measurement, and Implementation*. Center for Global Development Working Paper 18 (December). Washington: Center for Global Development.

Cohen, Daniel, and Richard Portes. 2004. *Dealing with Destabilizing "Market Discipline."* CEPR Working Paper 4280 (February). London: Center for Economic Policy Research.

Cole, Harold, and Patrick Kehoe. 1996. A Self-Fulfilling Model of Mexico's 1994–95 Debt Crisis. *Journal of International Economics* 41, no. 3/4 (November): 309–30.

Corrigan, E. Gerald. 2000. Two International Financial Stability Issues: Asset Price Inflation and Private Sector Participation in Financial Crisis Stabilization. *Financial Stability Review* (June): 136–41. London: Bank of England.

Corsetti, Giancarlo, and Nouriel Roubini. 1997. Politically Motivated Fiscal Deficits: Policy Issues in Closed and Open Economies. *Economics and Politics* 9, no.1 (March): 27–54.

Corsetti, Giancarlo, Bernardo Guimaraes, and Nouriel Roubini. 2003. *International Lending of Last Resort and Moral Hazard: A Model of IMF's Catalytic Finance*. NBER Working Paper 10125 (December). Cambridge, MA: National Bureau of Economic Research.

Corsetti, Giancarlo, Paolo Pesenti, and Nouriel Roubini. 1999a. Paper Tigers? A Model of the Asian Crisis. *European Economic Review* 43, no. 7: 1211–36.

Corsetti, Giancarlo, Paolo Pesenti, and Nouriel Roubini. 1999b. What Caused the Asian Currency and Financial Crisis? *Japan and the World Economy* 11, no. 3: 305–73.

Corsetti, Giancarlo, Paolo Pesenti, and Nouriel Roubini. 2002. The Role of Large Traders in Currency Crises. In *Preventing Currency Crises in Emerging Markets*, ed. Sebastian Edwards and Jeffrey Frankel. Chicago, IL: University of Chicago Press.

Corsetti, Giancarlo, Paolo Pesenti, Nouriel Roubini, and Cedric Tille. 2000. Trade and Contagious Devaluations: A Welfare-Based Approach. *Journal of International Economics* 50, no. 1: 217–41.

Corsetti, Giancarlo, Amil Dasgupta, Stephen Morris, and Hyun Song Shin. 2004. Does One Soros Make a Difference? A Theory of Currency Crises with Large and Small Traders. *Review of Economic Studies* 71, no. 1: 87–113.

Cottarelli, Carlo, and Curzio Giannini. 2002. *Bedfellows, Hostages, or Perfect Strangers? Global Capital Markets and the Catalytic Effect of IMF Crisis Lending*. Washington: International Monetary Fund.

Credit Suisse First Boston. 2003. Brazil: How to Rebuild Net Reserves. Photocopy on file with authors. September 29. Credit Suisse First Boston, New York.

Currie, Antony. 1998. Back to the Age of Defaults. *Euromoney* (December).

Dallara, Charles H. 1999. No to Burden Sharing. *The International Economy* 13, no. 6 (November/December): 44.

Dasgupta, Amil. 1999. *Social Learning with Payoff Complementarities*. New Haven, CT: Yale University.

De Gregorio, Jose, Barry Eichengreen, Takatoshi Ito, and Charles Wyplosz. 1999. *An Independent and Accountable IMF*. London: Centre for Economic Policy Research.

Dell'Ariccia, Giovanni, Isabel Schnabel, and Jeromin Zettelmeyer. 2002. *Moral Hazard and International Crisis Lending: A Test*. IMF Working Paper 02/181 (October). Washington: International Monetary Fund.

Detragiache, Enrica, and Antonio Spilimbergo. 2001. *Crises and Liquidity—Evidence and Interpretation.* IMF Working Paper 01/2. Washington: International Monetary Fund.

Diamond, Douglas, and Philip Dybvig. 1983. Bank Runs, Deposit Insurance, and Liquidity. *The Journal of Political Economy* 91, no. 3 (June): 401–19.

Dooley, Michael. 2000. *Can Output Losses Following International Financial Crises Be Avoided?* NBER Working Paper 7531. Cambridge, MA: National Bureau of Economic Research.

Dooley, Michael P., and Jeffrey A. Frankel, eds. 2003. *Managing Currency Crises in Emerging Markets.* Cambridge, MA, and Chicago, IL: National Bureau of Economic Research and University of Chicago Press.

Dooley, Michael, and Sujata Verma. 2001. *Rescue Packages and Output Losses Following Crises.* NBER Working Paper 8315 (June). Cambridge, MA: National Bureau of Economic Research.

Dornbusch, Rudiger. 2001. *A Primer on Emerging Market Crises.* NBER Working Paper 8326. Cambridge, MA: National Bureau of Economic Research.

Drazen, Allan, and Paul Masson. 1994. Credibility of Policies Versus Credibility of Policymakers. *Quarterly Journal of Economics* 109, no. 3: 735–54.

Eaton, Jonathan, and Raquel Fernandez. 1995. *Sovereign Debt.* NBER Working Paper 5131. Cambridge, MA: National Bureau of Economic Research.

Eaton, Jonathan, and Mark Gersovitz. 1981. Debt with Potential Repudiation: Theoretical and Empirical Analysis. *Review of Economic Studies* 48 (April): 284–309.

Edwards, Sebastian, and Jeffrey A. Frankel, eds. 2002. *Preventing Currency Crises in Emerging Markets.* Cambridge, MA, and Chicago, IL: National Bureau of Economic Research and The University of Chicago Press.

Eichengreen, Barry. 1999. *Toward a New International Financial Architecture.* Washington: Institute for International Economics.

Eichengreen, Barry. 2002. *Financial Crises and What to Do About Them.* Oxford: Oxford University Press.

Eichengreen, Barry. 2003. Restructuring Sovereign Debt. *Journal of Economic Perspectives* 17, no. 4: 75–98.

Eichengreen, Barry, and Kenneth Kletzer. 2003. *Crisis Resolution: Next Steps.* NBER Working Paper 10095 (November). Cambridge, MA: National Bureau of Economic Research.

Eichengreen, Barry, and Richard Portes. 1995. *Crisis? What Crisis? Orderly Workouts for Sovereign Debtors.* London: Center for Economic Policy Research.

Eichengreen, Barry, Ricardo Hausmann, and Ugo Panizza. 2003. Original Sin: The Pain, the Mystery, and the Road to Redemption. Harvard University. Photocopy (August).

Federal Reserve Bank of New York. 2004. Memorandum of Law of Amicus Curiae in Support of Defendant's Motion for an Order Pursuant to CPLR 5240 Denying Plaintiff the Use of Injunctive Relief to Prevent Payments to Other Creditors. EM Ltd. v. The Republic of Argentina.

Feldstein, Martin. 1999. *Self-Protection for Emerging Market Economies.* NBER Working Paper 6907 (January). Cambridge, MA: National Bureau of Economic Research.

Feldstein, Martin. 2000. *Aspects of Global Economic Integration: Outlook for the Future.* NBER Working Paper 7899 (September). Cambridge, MA: National Bureau of Economic Research.

Feldstein, Martin, ed. 2002. *Economic and Financial Crises in Emerging Market Economies.* Cambridge, MA, and Chicago, IL: National Bureau of Economic Research and University of Chicago Press.

Fischer, Stanley. 1999. On the Need for an International Lender of Last Resort. *Journal of Economic Perspectives* 13, no. 4: 85–104.

Fischer, Stanley. 2002. *Financial Crises and Reform of the International Financial System.* NBER Working Paper 9297 (October). Cambridge, MA: National Bureau of Economic Research.

Flood, Robert, and Peter Garber. 1984. Collapsing Exchange Rate Regimes: Some Linear Examples. *Journal of International Economics* 17: 1–13.

Frankel, Jeffrey A. 1999. No Single Currency Regime Is Right for All Countries or at All Times. *Essays in International Finance* 215. Princeton, NJ: International Finance Section, Princeton University.

Frankel, Jeffrey, and Nouriel Roubini. 2003. The Role of Industrial Country Policies in Emerging Market Crises. In *Economic and Financial Crises in Emerging Market Economies* Martin Feldstein, ed. Chicago, IL: University of Chicago Press.

Freeland, Chrystia. 2000. *Sale of the Century: Russia's Wild Ride from Communism to Capitalism.* New York: Crown Publishers.

Gai, Prasanna, and Hyun Song Shin. 2001. The Role of Sovereign Debt Standstills in Crisis Management. London, Bank of England. Photocopy.

Gai, Prasanna, and Hyun Song Shin. 2002. Debt Maturity Structure with Preemptive Creditors. London, Bank of England. Photocopy.

Gai, Prasanna, Simon Hayes, and Hyun Song Shin. 2001. *Crisis Costs and Debtor Discipline: The Efficacy of Public Policy in Sovereign Debt Crises*. Bank of England Working Paper 136. London: Bank of England. www.bankofengland.co.uk/workingpapers/wp136.pdf.

Gale, Douglas, and Xavier Vives. 2001. Dollarization, Bailouts and the Stability of the Banking System. New York University. Photocopy (July).

Galvis, Sergio. 2003. Sovereign Debt Restructurings—The Market Knows Best. *International Finance* 6, no. 1: 145–55.

Gelpern, Anna. 2003. Collective Action Shows the Way Forward. *International Financial Law Review* XXII, no. 5 (May): 15–19.

Gelpern, Anna. 2004. Building a Better Seating Chart for Sovereign Restructurings. *Emory Law Journal* 54: 1119–62.

Gertler, Mark, Simon Gilchrist, and Fabio Natalucci. 2000. External Constraints on Monetary Policy and the Financial Accelerator. New York University. Photocopy.

Ghosal, Sayantan, and Marcus Miller. 2002. Coordination Failure, Moral Hazard, and Sovereign Bankruptcy Procedures. Paper presented at the Bank of England Conference on the Role of the Official and Private Sectors in Resolving International Financial Crises, July 21, London.

Goldfajn, Ilan, and Rodrigo Valdes. 1999. Liquidity Crises and International Financial Architecture. Central Bank of Chile, Santiago. Photocopy (July).

Goldstein, Morris, and Philip Turner. 2004. *Controlling Currency Mismatches in Emerging Markets*. Washington: Institute for International Economics.

Goodhart, Charles, and Haizhou Huang. 2000. *A Simple Model of an International Lender of Last Resort*. IMF Working Paper 00/75. Washington: International Monetary Fund.

Gopinath, Deepak. 1999. Who's Afraid of the Big Bad Bail-in. *Institutional Investor* (June): 79–81.

Gorton, Gary. 1987. Bank Suspensions and Convertibility. *Journal of Political Economy* 15: 177–93.

Gorton, Gary, and Andrew Winton. 2002. *Financial Intermediation*. NBER Working Paper 8928. Cambridge, MA: National Bureau of Economic Research.

Gourinchas, Pierre-Olivier, Rodrigo Valdez, and Oscar Landerretche. 2001. *Lending Booms: Latin America and the World*. NBER Working Paper 8249 (April). Cambridge, MA: National Bureau of Economic Research.

Government of Argentina. 2003. Argentina's Restructuring Guidelines (September 22). Buenos Aires: Secretariat of Finance, Ministry of Economy and Production. www. mecon.ar.

Gray, Dale. 2002. Macro Finance: The Bigger Picture. *Risk* (June).

Group of Seven. 1995. Communiqué of the Halifax Summit. Halifax, Canada.

Group of Seven. 1996. Communiqué of the Lyons Summit. Lyons, France.

Group of Seven. 1998a. Strengthening the Architecture of the Global Financial System: Report of G-7 Finance Ministers to G-7 Heads of State or Government for Their Meeting in Birmingham. Birmingham, United Kingdom.

Group of Seven. 1998b. Conclusions of the G-7 Finance Ministers (May 9). Birmingham, United Kingdom.

Group of Seven. 1999. Strengthening the International Financial Architecture: Report of G-7 Finance Ministers to the Cologne Economic Summit. Cologne, Germany.

Group of Seven. 2000. Statement of G-7 Finance Ministers and Central Bank Governors (April 15). Washington. www.treas.gov/press/releases/ls556.htm.

Group of Seven. 2002. Statement of G-7 Finance Ministers and Central Bank Governors and Action Plan (April 20), Washington.

Group of Seven. 2003a. G-7 Action Plan Implementation (April 12), Washington.

Group of Seven. 2003b. Finance Ministers' Statements and Annex to the Deauville Communiqué: A New Paris Club Approach to Debt Restructuring (May 17), Deauville, France.

Group of 10. 1996. The Resolution of Sovereign Liquidity Crises: A Report to the Ministers and Governors. Washington: International Monetary Fund.

Group of 10. 2002. Report of the G-10 Working Group on Contractual Clauses. Washington: International Monetary Fund.

Group of 22. 1998a. Report of the Working Group on International Financial Crises. Washington: Group of 22 (Willard Group).

Group of 22. 1998b. Report of the Working Group on Strengthening Financial Systems. Washington: Group of 22.

Gulati, Mitu, and William Bratton. 2003. *Sovereign Debt Reform and the Best Interest of Creditors*. George Law And Economics Research Paper 387880. Washington: Georgetown University.

Haldane, Andrew and Mark Kruger. 2001. *The Resolution of International Financial Crises: Private Finance and Public Funds*. Bank of Canada Working Paper 2001-20 (November). Ottawa: Bank of Canada.

Haldane, Andrew, Simon Hayes, Adrian Penalver, Victoria Saporta, and Hyun Song Shin. 2002. Binding-In the Private Sector. London, Bank of England. Photocopy (August). www. bankofengland.co.uk/conferences/conf0207/bindinginps.pdf.

Hausmann, Ricardo, and Andrés Velasco. 2002. Hard Money's Soft Underbelly: Understanding the Argentine Crisis. In *Brookings Trade Forum*, ed. Susan M. Collins and Dani Rodrik. Washington: Brookings Institution Press.

Hoelscher, David S., and Marc Quintyn. 2003. *Managing Systemic Banking Crises*. IMF Occasional Paper 224. Washington: International Monetary Fund.

Hovaguimian, Catherine. 2003. The Catalytic Effect of IMF Lending: A Critical Review. *Financial Stability Review* no. 15 (December). London: Bank of England.

Hubbard, Robin. 2000. *Trying to Avoid a Plane Crash—Lessons for Sovereign Risk Analysis*. London: Chase International Fixed Income Research (February 11).

IEO (Independent Evaluation Office). 2003. Evaluation Report—IMF and Recent Capital Account Crises: Indonesia, Korea, Brazil. Washington: International Monetary Fund.

IFIAC (International Financial Institutions Advisory Commission). 2000. Report. Washington: United States Congress. www.house.gov/jec/imf/meltzer.htm.

IIF (Institute of International Finance). 1999a. *Letter to Minister Gordon Brown and Minister Tarrin*. IIF Policy Letters. Washington: Institute of International Finance (September 15). www.iif.com/data/public/icdc0999.pdf.

IIF (Institute of International Finance). 1999b. *Report of the Working Group on Financial Crises in Emerging Markets*. Washington: Institute of International Finance.

IIF (Institute of International Finance). 2003. *Code of Conduct*. Washington: Institute of International Finance.

IIF (Institute of International Finance). 2004. *Capital Flows to Emerging-Market Economies*. Washington: Institute of International Finance.

IMF (International Monetary Fund). 1997. Crisis in Asia: Regional and Global Implications. *World Economic Outlook, Interim Assessment* (December). Washington: International Monetary Fund. www.imf.org/external/pubs/ft/weo/weo1297/index.htm.

IMF (International Monetary Fund). October 1998. Communiqué of the Interim Committee of the Board of Governors (October 4). Washington: International Monetary Fund.

IMF (International Monetary Fund). September 2000a. Summing Up by the Acting Chairman: Involving the Private Sector in the Resolution of Financial Crises—Status Report. Executive Board Meeting 00/90 (September 5). Washington: International Monetary Fund.

IMF (International Monetary Fund). September 2000b. Communiqué of the International Monetary and Financial Committee of the Board of Governors (September 24). Washington: International Monetary Fund.

IMF (International Monetary Fund). September 2000c. Summing Up of the Acting Chairman. Involving the Private Sector in the Resolution of Financial Crises—Standstills—Preliminary Considerations. Washington: International Monetary Fund.

IMF (International Monetary Fund). September 2000d. IMF Board Agrees to Changes to Fund Financial Facilities. Public Information Notice no 00.79 (September 18). Washington: International Monetary Fund.

IMF (International Monetary Fund). September 2000e. Private-Sector Involvement in Crisis Prevention and Resolution: Market Views and Recent Experiences. Chapter 5 of the International Capital Markets Report (September). Washington: International Monetary Fund. www.imf.org/external/pubs/ft/icm/2000/01/eng/pdf/chap5.pdf.

IMF (International Monetary Fund). January 2001. Involving the Private Sector in the Resolution of Financial Crises—Restructuring International Sovereign Bonds. EBS/01/03. Washington: International Monetary Fund.

IMF (International Monetary Fund). February 2002. Sovereign Debt Restructuring and the Domestic Economy: Experience in Four Recent Cases. International Monetary Fund, Washington. Photocopy.

IMF (International Monetary Fund). June 2002a. Collective Action Clauses in Sovereign Bond Contracts—Encouraging Greater Use (June 6). Washington: International Monetary Fund.

IMF (International Monetary Fund). June 2002b. The Design and Effectiveness of Collective Action Clauses. SM/02/173. Washington: International Monetary Fund.

IMF (International Monetary Fund). July 2002a. Access Policy in Capital Account Crises. SM/02/246. Washington: International Monetary Fund.

IMF (International Monetary Fund). July 2002b. Fund Policy on Lending into Arrears to Private Creditors—Further Considerations on the Good Faith Criteria (July 30). Washington: International Monetary Fund.

IMF (International Monetary Fund). August 2002. Sovereign Debt Restructuring Mechanism—Further Considerations. Washington: International Monetary Fund.

IMF (International Monetary Fund). September 2002a. Communiqué of the International Monetary and Financial Committee of the Board of Governors. Washington: International Monetary Fund.

IMF (International Monetary Fund). September 2002b. IMF Board Discussion of Good Faith Criteria Under the Fund Policy of Lending into Arrears to Private Creditors. PIN 02/107 (September 24). Washington: International Monetary Fund.

IMF (International Monetary Fund). November 2002. The Design of the Sovereign Debt Restructuring Mechanism: Further Considerations. Washington: International Monetary Fund.

IMF (International Monetary Fund). January 2003a. Access Policy in Capital Account Crises—Modification to the Supplemental Reserve Facility (SRF) and Follow-Up Issues Related to Exceptional Access Policy. Washington: International Monetary Fund.

IMF (International Monetary Fund). January 2003b. Crisis Resolution in the Context of Sovereign Debt Restructuring—A Summary of Considerations. SM/03/40. Washington: International Monetary Fund.

IMF (International Monetary Fund). February 2003. Proposed Features of a Sovereign Debt Restructuring Mechanism. Washington: International Monetary Fund.

IMF (International Monetary Fund). April 2003. Report of the Managing Director to the International Monetary and Financial Committee on a Statutory Sovereign Debt Restructuring Mechanism. Washington: International Monetary Fund. www.imf.org/external/np/omd/2003/040803.htm.

IMF (International Monetary Fund). September 2003a. Progress Report to the International Monetary and Financial Committee on Crisis Resolution (September 5). Washington: International Monetary Fund.

IMF (International Monetary Fund). September 2003b. *World Economic Outlook.* Chapter III: Public Debt in Emerging Markets. Washington: International Monetary Fund.

IMF (International Monetary Fund). September 2003c. The Restructuring of Sovereign Debt—Assessing the Benefits, Risks, and Feasibility of Aggregating Claims. Washington: International Monetary Fund.

IMF (International Monetary Fund). October 2003. Lessons from the Crisis In Argentina. Washington: International Monetary Fund. www.imf.org/external/np/pdr/lessons/100803.pdf.

IMF (International Monetary Fund). January 2004. Report on Access to Fund Resources During 2003. Washington: International Monetary Fund.

IMF (International Monetary Fund). March 2004. Review of Exceptional Access Policy. Washington: International Monetary Fund.

Jacklin, Charles, and Sudipto Bhattacharya. 1988. Distinguishing Panics and Information-Based Bank Runs: Welfare and Policy Implications. *The Journal of Political Economy* 96, no. 3 (June): 568–92.

Jacome, Luis. 2004. *The Late 1990s Financial Crisis in Ecuador: Institutional Weaknesses, Fiscal Rigidities and Financial Dollarization at Work.* IMF Working Paper 04/12. Washington: International Monetary Fund.

Jeanne, Olivier. 2000a. Currency Crises: A Perspective on Recent Theoretical Developments. *Special Papers in International Economics,* no. 20. Princeton, NJ: International Finance Section, Department of Economics, Princeton University.

Jeanne, Olivier. 2000b. Foreign Currency Debt and the Global Financial Architecture. *European Economic Review* 44: 719–27.

Jeanne, Olivier, and Charles Wyplosz. 2001. *The International Lender of Last Resort—How Large Is Large Enough?* IMF Working Paper 01/76 (May). Washington: International Monetary Fund.

Jeanne, Olivier, and Jeromin Zettelmeyer. 2001. International Bailouts, Moral Hazard, and Conditionality. *Economic Policy* 16, no. 33 (October).

Jeanne, Olivier, and Jeromin Zettelmeyer. 2002. *Original Sin, Balance Sheet Crises, and the Roles of International Lending.* IMF Working Paper 02/234 (December). Washington: International Monetary Fund.

Jensen, Michael, and William Meckling. 1976. Theory of the Firm: Managerial Behavior, Agency Costs, and Ownership Structure. *Journal of Financial Economics* 3, no. 4: 305–60.

Kamin, Steven B. 2002. *Identifying the Role of Moral Hazard in International Financial Markets.* International Finance Division Discussion Paper 736. Board of Governors of the Federal Reserve System (November). www.federalreserve.gov/pubs/ifdp/2002/736/ifdp736.pdf.

Kaminsky, Graciela, and Carmen Reinhart. 1999. The Twin Crises: The Causes of Banking and Balance of Payments Problems. *American Economic Review* 89, no. 4 (June): 473–500.

Kenen, Peter B. 2001. *The International Financial Architecture: What's New? What's Missing?* Washington: Institute of International Finance.

Kindleberger, Charles P. 1970. *Manias, Panics, and Crashes: A History of Financial Crises.* Hoboken, New Jersey: John Wiley & Sons.

Klapper, Leora. 2000. *The Uniqueness of Short Term Collateralization.* World Bank Working Paper 2544. Washington: World Bank.

Kletzer, Kenneth, and Brian D. Wright. 2000. Sovereign Debt as an Intertemporal Barter. *American Economic Review* 90, no. 3: 621–39.

Klimenko, Mikhail. 2001. Trader Interdependence and the Evolution of the International Financial Institutions, Role in Rescheduling Sovereign Debt. *Journal of International Economics* 58, no. 1 (October): 177–209.

Klingen, Christoph A., Beatrice S. Weder, and Jeromin Zettelmeyer. 2004. *How Private Creditors Fared in Emerging Debt Markets, 1970–2000*. IMF Working Paper 04/13 (January). Washington: International Monetary Fund.

Kroszner, Randall. 1998. *Is It Better to Forgive Than to Receive? Repudiation of the Gold Indexation Clause in Long-Term Debt During the Great Depression*. CRSP Working Paper 481. Chicago, IL: University of Chicago.

Krueger, Anne. 2001a. International Financial Architecture for 2002: A New Approach to Sovereign Debt Restructuring. Speech at the National Economists' Club Annual Members' Dinner, American Enterprise Institute, Washington, November 26. www.imf.org/external/np/speeches/2001/112601.htm.

Krueger, Anne. 2001b. A New Approach to Sovereign Debt Restructuring. Speech at the Indian Council for Research on International Economic Relations, New Delhi, India, December 20. www.imf.org/external/np/speeches/2001/122001.htm.

Krueger, Anne. 2002a. New Approaches to Sovereign Debt Restructuring: An Update on Our Thinking. Speech at the conference on Sovereign Debt Workouts: Hopes and Hazards. Institute for International Economics, Washington, April 1. www.imf.org/external/np/speeches/2002/040102.htm.

Krueger, Anne. 2002b. *A New Approach to Sovereign Debt Restructuring*. Washington: International Monetary Fund.

Krugman, Paul. 1979. A Model of Balance of Payments Crises. *Journal of Money, Credit, and Banking* 11: 311–25.

Krugman, Paul. 1998a. What Happened to Asia? Massachusetts Institute of Technology, Cambridge, MA. Photocopy (January). http://web.mit.edu/krugman/www/DISINTER.html.

Krugman, Paul. 1998b. Saving Asia: It's Time to Get Radical. www.pkarchive.org/crises/SavingAsia.html.

Krugman, Paul. 1999. Balance Sheets, the Transfer Problem, and Financial Crises. Massachusetts Institute of Technology, Cambridge, MA. Photocopy (January). http://web.mit.edu/krugman/www/FLOOD.pdf.

Kumar, Manmohan, Paul Masson, and Marcus Miller. 2000. *Global Financial Crises: Institutions and Incentives*. IMF Working Paper 00/105. Washington: International Monetary Fund.

Lagos, Martin. 2002. The Argentine Banking Crisis 2001–2002. Report Prepared for the Argentine Bankers Association. Buenos Aires: Argentine Bankers Association (December).

Lane, Timothy D., and Steven T. Phillips. 2000. Moral Hazard: Does IMF Financing Encourage Imprudence by Borrowers and Lenders? *Economic Issues*, no. 28. Washington: International Monetary Fund.

Lerrick, Adam, and Allan Meltzer. 2001. Blueprint for an International Lender of Last Resort. Carnegie Mellon University. Photocopy (October).

Lipsworth, Gabrielle, and Jens Nystedt. 2001. *Crisis Resolution and Adaptation*. IMF Staff Papers 188. Washington: International Monetary Fund.

Manasse, Paolo, Nouriel Roubini, and Axel Schimmelpfenning. 2003. *Predicting Sovereign Debt Crises*. IMF Working Paper 03/221 (November). Washington: International Monetary Fund.

Martin, Benjamin, and Adrian Penalver. 2003. *The Effect of Payments Standstills on Yields and the Maturity Structure of International Debt*. Bank of England Working Paper 184. London: Bank of England.

Mauro, Paolo, and Yishay Yafeh. 2003. *The Corporation of Foreign Bondholders*. IMF Working Paper 03/107. Washington: International Monetary Fund.

McConnell, Michael W., and Randal Picker. 1993. When Cities Go Broke: A Conceptual Introduction to Municipal Bankruptcy. 60 *University Chicago Law Review* 425.

Mendoza, Enrique. 2001. *Credit, Prices, and Crashes: Business Cycles with a Sudden Stop.* NBER Working Paper 8338 (June). Cambridge, MA: National Bureau of Economic Research.

Mendoza, Enrique, and Cristina Arellano. 2002. *Credit Frictions and "Sudden Stops" in Small Open Economies: An Equilibrium Business Cycle Framework for Emerging-Market Crises.* NBER Working Paper 8880 (April). Cambridge, MA: National Bureau of Economic Research.

Mendoza, Enrique, and Katherine A. Smith. 2002. *Margin Calls, Trading Costs, and Asset Prices in Emerging Markets: The Financial Mechanics of the "Sudden Stop" Phenomenon.* NBER Working Paper 9286 (October). Cambridge, MA: National Bureau of Economic Research.

Miller, Marcus, and Lei Zhang. 2000. Sovereign Liquidity Crises: A Strategic Case for a Payments Standstill. *The Economic Journal* 110, no. 460 (January): 335–62.

Mody, Ashoka, and Diego Saravia. 2003. *Catalyzing Capital Flows: Do IMF-Supported Programs Work as Commitment Devices?* IMF Working Paper 03/100 (May). Washington: International Monetary Fund.

Moody's Investor Service. 2000. *How to Sue a Sovereign: The Case of Peru.* New York: Moody's Investor Service (November).

Moody's Investor Service. 2003. *Moody's Statistical Handbook: Country Credit.* New York: Moody's Investor Service (October).

Morris, Stephen, and Hyun Song Shin. 1998 Unique Equilibrium in a Model of Self-Fulfilling Currency Attacks. *The American Economic Review* 88, no. 3: 587–97.

Morris, Stephen, and Hyun Song Shin. 2003. *Catalytic Finance: When Does It Work?* Cowles Foundation Discussion Paper 1400. Yale University. http://cowles.econ.yale.edu/P/cd/d14a/d1400.pdf.

Mussa, Michael. 2002a. Reflections on Moral Hazard and Private Sector Involvement in the Resolution of Emerging-Market Financial Crises. Institute for International Economics, Washington. Photocopy (July).

Mussa, Michael. 2002b. *Argentina and the Fund: From Triumph to Tragedy.* POLICY ANALYSES IN INTERNATIONAL ECONOMICS 67. Washington: Institute for International Economics.

O'Neill, Paul H. 2001. *Excellence and the International Financial Institutions.* Detroit, MI: US Treasury (June 27).

Obstfeld, Maurice. 1986. Rational and Self-Fulfilling Balance-of-Payments Crises. *American Economic Review* 76: (March) 72–81.

Obstfeld, Maurice. 1994. The Logic of Currency Crises. *Cahiers Economiques et Monetaires* no. 43: 189–213. Paris: Banque de France.

Ortiz, Guillermo. 2002. Recent Emerging Market Crises—What Have We Learned? Per Jacobsson Lecture. Basle: Bank of International Settlements. www.perjacobsson.org/lectures/2002-ortiz.pdf

Paasche, Bernhard, and Stanley Zin. 2001. *Competition and Intervention in Sovereign Debt Markets.* NBER Working Paper 8679. Cambridge, MA: National Bureau of Economic Research.

Perry, Guillermo, and Luis Serven. 2003. *Argentina: What Went Wrong.* Washington: World Bank.

Pettis, Michael. 2001. *The Volatility Machine.* Oxford: Oxford University Press.

Porzecanski, Arturo C. 2002. *Bankruptcy Lite. The International Economy* (summer): 38–41.

Reiffel, Lex. 2003. *Restructuring Sovereign Debt: The Case for Ad Hoc Machinery.* Washington: Brookings Institution Press.

Reinhart, Carmen. 2002. Credit Ratings, Default, and Financial Crises: Evidence from Emerging Markets. *World Bank Economic Review* 16, no. 2: 151–70.

Richards, Anthony, and Mark Gugiatti. 2003. Do Collective Action Clauses Influence Bond Yields? New Evidence for Emerging Markets. *International Finance* 6, no. 3: 415–47.

Richards, Anthony, and Mark Gugiatti. 2004. *The Use of Collective Action Clauses in New York Law Bonds of Sovereign Borrowers.* Working Paper. Sydney: Reserve Bank of Australia.

Rodrik, Dani, and Ethan Kaplan. 2001. *Did the Malaysian Capital Controls Work?* NBER Working Paper 8142 (February). Cambridge, MA: National Bureau of Economic Research.

Rodrik, Dani, and Andres Velasco. 1999. *Short-Term Capital Flows*. NBER Working Paper 7364 (September). Cambridge, MA: National Bureau of Economic Research.

Rogoff, Kenneth. 1999. International Institutions for Reducing Global Financial Instability. *The Journal of Economic Perspectives* 13, no. 4 (autumn): 21–42.

Rogoff, Kenneth. 2003a. Emerging-Market Debt. What Is the Problem? Speech at the conference on Sovereign Debt Restructuring Mechanism, International Monetary Fund. January 22, Washington.

Rogoff, Kenneth. 2003b. The IMF Strikes Back. *Foreign Policy* 134 (January/February). Washington: International Food Policy Research Institute.

Rogoff, Kenneth, and Jeromin Zettelmeyer. 2002a. *Early Ideas on Sovereign Bankruptcy Reorganization: A Survey*. IMF Working Paper 02/57 (March). Washington: International Monetary Fund. www.imf.org/external/pubs/ft/wp/2002/wp0257.pdf.

Rogoff, Kenneth, and Jeromin Zettelmeyer. 2002b. *Bankruptcy Procedures for Sovereigns: A History of Ideas, 1976–2001. IMF Staff Papers* 49, no. 3: 471–507. Washington: International Monetary Fund. www.imf.org/external/pubs/ft/staffp/2002/03/pdf/rogoff.pdf.

Rogoff, Kenneth, Carmen Reinhart, and Miguel Savastano. 2003. Debt Intolerance. *Brookings Papers on Economic Activity* 1: 1–74. Washington: Brookings Institution.

Rogoff, Kenneth, Eswar Prasad, Shang-Jin Wei, and Ayhan Kose. 2003. *Effects on Financial Globalization on Developing Countries: Some Empirical Evidence*. IMF Occasional Paper 220 (September). Washington: International Monetary Fund.

Roubini, Nouriel. 2000. Bail-In, Burden-Sharing, Private-Sector Involvement (PSI) in Crisis Resolution and Constructive Engagement of the Private Sector. A Primer: Evolving Definitions, Doctrine, Practice, and Case Law. New York University. Photocopy (September). www.stern.nyu.edu/globalmacro/psipaper.pdf.

Roubini, Nouriel. 2001a. Why Should the Foreign Creditors of Argentina Take a Greater Hit/Haircut than the Domestic Ones: On the Economic Logic, Efficiency, Fairness, and Legality of "Discriminating" Between Domestic and Foreign Debt in Sovereign Debt Restructurings. New York University. Photocopy (December 14) www.stern.nyu.edu/~nroubini/asia/discriminationforeigndebt.doc.

Roubini, Nouriel. 2001b. Should Argentina Dollarize or Float? The Pros and Cons of Alternative Exchange Rate Regimes and Their Implications for Domestic and Foreign Debt Restructuring/Reduction. New York University. Photocopy (December 2) www. stern. nyu.edu/~nroubini/asia/argentinadollarization.doc.

Roubini, Nouriel. 2001c. Debt Sustainability: Theory and Application. New York University. Photocopy. www.stern.nyu.edu/globalmacro/debtsustainability.pdf.

Roubini, Nouriel. 2002a. Private-Sector Involvement in Crisis Resolution and Orderly Sovereign Debt Restructurings: The G-7/IMF Framework and the Open Unresolved Issues. New York University. Photocopy (March) www.iie.com/publications/papers/roubini-setser0303.pdf.

Roubini, Nouriel. 2002b. Do We Need a New International Bankruptcy Regime? A Discussion Paper Brookings Panel on Economic Activity (Fall). Washington: Brookings Institution. www.stern.nyu.edu/globalmacro/bankreg.doc.

Roubini, Nouriel, and Brad Setser. 2003. Improving the Sovereign Debt Restructuring Process: Problems in Restructuring, Proposed Solutions, and a Roadmap for Reform. Unpublished paper. www.iie.com/publications/papers/roubini-setser0303.pdf.

Roubini, Nouriel. 2004. Private Sector Involvement in Crisis Resolution and Mechanisms for Dealing with Sovereign Debt Problems. In *Fixing Financial Crises in the Twenty-First Century*. ed. Andrew G. Haldane. London: Routledge.

Roubini, Nouriel, and Brad Setser. 2004. The Reform of the Sovereign Debt Restructuring Process: Problems, Proposed Solutions and the Argentine Episode. *Journal of Restructuring Finance*, no. 1: 1–12.

Roubini, Nouriel and Marc Uzan, eds. 2004. *The New International Financial Architecture*, volumes 1 and 2. London: Edward Elgar Publishing Ltd. (forthcoming).

Rubin, Robert E. 1998. Statement at the Special Meeting of Finance Ministers and Central Bank Governors, April. Washington: US Treasury.

Rubin, Robert E. 1999. Remarks on the Reform of the International Financial Architecture to the School of Advanced International Studies, April 21. Washington: US Treasury.

Rubin, Robert E., and Jacob Weisberg. 2003. *In an Uncertain World: Tough Choices from Wall Street to Washington*. New York: Random House.

Sachs, Jeffrey D. 1984. Theoretical Issues in International Borrowing. *Princeton Studies in International Finance* 54. Princeton, NJ: Princeton University Press.

Sachs, Jeffrey D. 1989a. Comprehensive Debt Retirement: The Bolivian Example. *Brookings Papers on Economic Activity* 2: 706–15.

Sachs, Jeffrey D., ed. 1989b. *Foreign Debt and Economic Performance*. Chicago, IL: University of Chicago Press.

Sachs, Jeffrey D. 1990a. A Strategy for Efficient Debt Reduction. *Journal of Economic Perspectives* 4, no. 1 (winter): 19–30.

Sachs, Jeffrey D., ed. 1990b. *Developing Country Debt and Economic Performance: Country Studies—Argentina, Bolivia, Brazil, and Mexico* (volume 2). Chicago, IL: University of Chicago Press.

Sachs, Jeffrey D. 1995. Do We Need an International Lender of Last Resort? Frank D. Graham Lecture at Princeton University, April 20.

Sachs, Jeffrey D. 2002. Resolving the Debt Crisis of Low-Income Countries. *Brookings Papers on Economic Activity* 1: 1–28. Washington: Brookings Institution. www.earthinstitute.columbia.edu/about/director/pubs/BPEA_Sachs1_2002.pdf.

Sachs, Jeffrey D., and Richard Cooper. 1985. Borrowing Abroad: The Debtor's Perspective. In *International Debt and the Developing Countries*, ed. J. T. Cuddington and G. W. Smith. World Bank Symposium. Washington: World Bank.

Sachs, Jeffrey D, and Steven Radelet. 1998. *The Onset of the East Asian Financial Crisis*. NBER Working Paper 6680 (August). Cambridge, MA: National Bureau of Economic Research.

Sachs, Jeffrey D., Andres Velasco, and Aaron Tornell. 1996a. The Collapse of the Mexican Peso: What Have We Learned? *Economic Policy*, no. 22 (April): 13–64.

Sachs, Jeffrey D., Andres Velasco, and Aaron Tornell. 1996b. *Financial Crises in Emerging Markets: The Lessons from 1995*. Brookings Papers on Economic Activity 2. Washington: Brookings Institution.

Salmon, Felix. 2003. The End of the Line for Exit Consents. *Euromoney* (April).

Salmon, Felix. 2004a. Elliot Aggression Captures Low-Risk Returns. *Euromoney* (February).

Salmon, Felin. 2004b. Uruguay's Elegant Transformation. *Euromoney* (February).

Sarno, Lucio, and Mark P. Taylor. 1999. Moral Hazard, Asset Price Bubbles, Capital Flows, and the East Asian Crisis: The First Tests. *Journal of International Money and Finance* 18, no. 4: 637–57.

Schelling, Thomas. 1960. *The Strategy of Conflict*. Oxford: Oxford University Press.

Schneider, Martin, and Aaron Tornell. 2000. *Balance Sheet Effects, Bailout Guarantees, and Financial Crises*. NBER Working Paper 8060. Cambridge, MA: National Bureau of Economic Research.

Schwartz, Anna. 1998. Time to Terminate the ESF and the IMF. *Cato Institute Foreign Policy Briefing* 48 (August). Washington: Cato Institute.

Schwartz, Steven. 2000. Sovereign Debt Restructuring: A Bankruptcy Reorganization Approach. *Cornell Law Review* 86: 956–1034.

Shiller, Robert J. 2003. *The New Financial Order: Risk in the 21st Century*. Princeton, NJ: Princeton University Press.

Shin, Hyun Song. 2001. Coordination and the Term Structure of Interest Rates for Defaultable Securities. London School of Economics. Photocopy (April).

Shleifer, Andrei. 2003. *Will the Sovereign Debt Market Survive?* NBER Working Paper 9493, (February). Cambridge, MA: National Bureau of Economic Research. http://post.economics.harvard.edu/faculty/shleifer/papers/debt_NBER.pdf.

Singh, Manmohan. 2003. *Recovery Rates from Distressed Debt—Empirical Evidence from Chapter 11 Filings, International Litigation, and Recent Sovereign Debt Restructurings*. IMF Working Paper 03/161. Washington: International Monetary Fund.

Soros, George. 1998. *The Crisis of Global Capitalism*. New York: Public Affairs Press.

Spadafora, Francesco. 2001. *The Pricing of Syndicated Bank Loans to Emerging Markets: Some Further Results*. Bank of Italy Working Paper 438 (March) Rome: Bank of Italy.

Spiegel, Mark. 1996. Burden Sharing in Sovereign Debt Reduction. *Journal of Development Economics* 50 (August): 337–52.

Spiegel, Mark. 2001. *Solvency Runs, Sunspot Runs, and International Bailouts*. Working Paper 01-05. Federal Reserve Bank of San Francisco. www.frbsf.org/publications/economics/papers/2001/wp01-05bk.pdf.

Stiglitz, Joseph. 2002. *Globalization and Its Discontents*. New York: W.W. Norton & Company.

Stone, Mark R. 2000. *Large Scale Post Crisis Corporate Sector Restructuring*. Policy Discussion Paper No. 00/7 (July) Washington: International Monetary Fund.

Stone, Mark R. 2002. Corporate Sector Restructuring: The Role of Government in Times of Crisis. *Economic Issues*, no. 31 (August). Washington: International Monetary Fund.

Sturzenegger, Federico. 2002. *Default Episodes in the 1990s: Factbook and Preliminary Lessons*. Working Paper. Buenos Aires: Universidad Torcuato Di Tella.

Summers, Lawrence H. 2000a. Statement to the International Monetary and Financial Committee, April 16. Washington: US Treasury.

Summers, Lawrence H. 2000b. International Financial Crises: Causes, Prevention and Cures. *American Economic Review* 90 (May): 1–16.

Suskind, Ron. 2004. *The Price of Loyalty: George W. Bush, the White House, and the Education of Paul O'Neill*. New York: Simon and Schuster.

Tarullo, Daniel. 2001. Rules, Discretion, and Authority in International Financial Reform. *Journal of International Economic Law* 4, no. 4: 613–82.

Task Force on the Future International Financial Architecture (CFR Task Force). 1999. *Safeguarding Prosperity in a Global Financial System*. Washington: Institute for International Economics.

Taylor, John B. 2001a. Strengthening the Global Economy after September 11: The Bush Administration's Agenda. Kennedy School of Government, Harvard University, November 29. www.treas.gov/press/releases/po831.htm.

Taylor, John B. 2001b. Taylor Rules (Interview with John Taylor). *The International Economy* 15, no. 5 (September/October): 6–9.

Taylor, John B. 2002a. Grants and Sovereign Debt Restructuring: Two Key Elements of a Reform Agenda for the International Financial Institutions. Testimony before the Joint Economic Committee, February 14. www.treas.gov/press/releases/po1016.htm.

Taylor, John B. 2002b. Sovereign Debt Restructuring: A US Perspective. Remarks at a conference on Sovereign Debt Workouts: Hopes and Hazards. Institute for International Economics, Washington, April 1. www.treas.gov/press/releases/po2056.htm.

Taylor, John B. 2004a. Remarks to the IMF Conference in honor of Guillermo Calvo, April 16. Washington: International Monetary Fund. www.ustreas.gov/press/releases/js1473.htm.

Taylor, John B. 2004b. Statement Regarding the Decision by Countries to Issue Bonds with Collective Action Clauses (CACs), February 3. Washington: US Treasury. www.treas.gov/press/releases/js1144.htm.

Tirole, Jean. 2002. *Financial Crises, Liquidity and the International Monetary System*. Princeton, NJ: Princeton University Press.

Truman, Edwin M. 2001. Perspectives on External Financial Crises. Speech to the Money Marketeers of New York University, December 10.

Truman, Edwin M. 2002. Debt Restructuring, Evolution or Revolution? *Brookings Papers on Economic Activity* 1:2002: 341–46. Washington: Brookings Institution.

Truman, Edwin M. 2003. *Inflation Targeting in the World Economy*. Washington: Institute for International Economics.

Truman, Edwin M. 2004. What Next for Argentina? Washington: Institute for International Economics.

United States. 2004. Statement of Intent of the United States and Declaration of Jeanette A. Vargas in support of the Republic of Argentina's Motion Pursuant to CPLR section 5240 to Preclude Plaintiff Judgment Creditors from Interfering with Payments to Other Creditors, January 12. New York: United States Government.

Vegh, Carlos, and Amartya Lahiri. 2000. *Delaying the Inevitable: Optimal Interest Rate Policy and BOP Crises*. NBER Working Paper 7734 (June). Cambridge, MA: National Bureau of Economic Research.

Vives, Xavier, and J.C. Rochet. 2002. Coordination Failures and the Lender of Last Resort: Was Bagehot Right After All? INSEAD, Fontainebleu. Photocopy.

Wallace, Neil. 1988. Another Attempt to Explain an Illiquid Banking System: The Diamond and Dybvig Model with Sequential Servicing Taken Seriously. *Federal Reserve Bank of Minneapolis Quarterly Review* 12, no. 4: 3–16.

Wei, Shang-Jin. 2001. Domestic Crony Capitalism and International Fickle Capital: Is There a Connection? *International Finance* 4, no. 1: 15–45.

Wells, Robin. 1993. Tolerance of Arrearages: How IMF Loan Policy Can Effect Debt Reduction. *American Economic Review* 83, no. 3 (June): 621–33.

World Bank. 2003. *Global Development Finance*. Washington: World Bank.

World Bank. 2004. *Global Development Finance*. Washington: World Bank.

Wright, Mark. 2001a. Creditor Coordination and Sovereign Risk. University of Chicago. Photocopy.

Wright, Mark. 2001b. Reputations and Sovereign Debt. Stanford University. Photocopy. http://emlab.berkeley.edu/users/obstfeld/e281_sp03/wright.pdf.

Yianni, Andrew. 1999. Resolution of Sovereign Financial Crises: Evolution of the Private Sector Restructuring Process. *Financial Stability Review* 6 (June). London: Bank of England.

Zettelmeyer, Jeronim. 1999. On the Short-Run Effectiveness of Official Crisis Lending. International Monetary Fund, Washington. Photocopy (December).

Zettelmeyer, Jeromin. 2003. The Case for an Explicit Seniority Structure in Sovereign Debt. International Monetary Fund, Washington. Photocopy.

Zhang, Xioaming. 1999. *Testing for 'Moral Hazard' in Emerging Markets Lending*. Institute of International Finance Research Paper 99-1 (August). Washington: Institute of International Finance.

Glossary

Absolute priority. The rules prescribing the order of distribution of an insolvent debtor's assets. Generally, creditors at the top of the list are paid in full before creditors below them get any value.

Acceleration. Demand for full principal payment of a bond, loan, or other debt instrument. Creditors generally have the right to accelerate the bond's principal if the debtor fails to meet one of the bond's key terms. Missing a coupon payment is a common trigger for acceleration.

Aggregation. The ability to combine (aggregate) the votes of holders of different debt instruments to determine the success of a proposed debt restructuring. Most bankruptcy regimes provide for aggregated voting. For example, Uruguay's bonds also contain provisions allowing aggregated voting.

Amicus curiae. Friend of court. Amicus briefs are filed by groups that claim to have a stake in the outcome of a court's decision but are neither the plaintiff nor the defendant in the actual litigation. For example, the US government and the Federal Reserve Bank of New York filed amicus briefs in the litigation between Argentina and some of its creditors.

Bailout. Shorthand for crisis lending from official creditors like the IMF or major G-7 countries. The crisis country is expected to repay such rescue loans. In capital account crises, official lending may be used in part to help the crisis country avoid default by paying its maturing debts. Thus crisis lending bails out both the country and its creditors.

Bail-in. An arrangement where private creditors agree to roll over their maturing claims or participate in a formal debt restructuring. Such arrangements—or a unilateral payments suspension by the debtor—provide a crisis country with financial breathing space.

Bank holiday. The suspension of depositors' ability either to withdraw sight deposits on demand or to take maturing time deposits out of the banking system or both. An external bank holiday precludes payment on the banking system's maturing external debt.

Bank lines. Also interbank lines. Cross-border credits extended by one bank to another, typically short-term.

Bilateral creditors. Governments that extend credit directly to other governments. Bilateral creditors, by convention, have been willing to restructure their claims when multilateral lenders, such as the World Bank and the IMF, are paid in full.

Brady bonds. Sovereign bonds issued during the restructurings in the early 1990s that ended the 1980s debt crisis. Brady bonds were issued in exchange for restructured bank loans. Most Brady bonds were partially collateralized.

Capital controls. Restrictions on cross-border capital flows. Outflow controls can limit the ability of domestic residents and a country's existing external investors to exchange their local financial assets for external assets and/or preclude payment by local residents of their external debt. Inflow controls can limit the ability of local residents to borrow from nonresident creditors and/or restrict the ability of external investors to purchase local financial assets.

Capital levy. A tax on financial assets, as distinct from a tax on income or consumption. A domestic debt restructuring can be considered a type of capital levy.

Catalytic financing. IMF financing that, combined with policy adjustments, is expected to help generate (catalyze) new private financial flows to help meet a country's financing need. "Catalytic" programs do not provide the country with all the financing it needs; the program works only if private creditors provide additional financing.

Chapter 11. The section of the US Bankruptcy Code that governs the reorganization of a firm's debts. Chapter 11 allows a firm to continue operating even though it cannot pay its debts. Chapter 7 of the US Bankruptcy Code governs a firm's liquidation.

Collateral. Assets pledged to secure repayment of a debt. For example, some payments on collateralized Brady bonds are backed by US Treasury bonds.

Collective action clauses. Clauses in a bond contract that require—or facilitate—coordinated action by the holders of that bond. Clauses that allow the holders of a given bond to amend a bond's financial terms by a supermajority vote are sometimes called majority-restructuring clauses. The ability to vote to amend a bond's financial terms lets the holders of the bond decide collectively whether to accept the debtor's restructuring terms and makes their collective decision binding on all the holders of the bond. Clauses that require that the bond's holders act collectively to initiate litigation after a default are sometimes called majority-enforcement clauses.

Comparability/comparable treatment. The promise by a country that has secured debt relief from Paris Club (bilateral official) creditors to seek comparable relief from other creditors, whether from bilateral creditors that are not part of the Paris Club or from private creditors. The Paris Club does not ask a debtor to seek comparable relief from the IMF or the multilateral development banks.

Contagion. The transmission of difficulties in one country to other countries via economic channels (trade and financial links) or via the rational or "irrational" behavior of investors and creditors (hedging and forced selling by leveraged investors as well as herding, runs, and panics). Contagion can lead to the withdrawal of credit and capital flight as well as large moves in asset prices.

Contingent credit line (CCL). An instrument that gives a country the right, but not the obligation, to borrow from a creditor—or a group of creditors—in return for a fixed commitment fee. The creditors may be public or private. The IMF created a contingent credit line for emerging economies after the Asian crisis, but no emerging market applied for it.

Coupon. Interest payment on a bond (usually a percentage of the bond's face value).

Debt reduction. An agreement to reduce the face value of the principal of a debt instrument.

Debt rescheduling. An agreement to defer payments on a debt instrument. A debt rescheduling typically neither reduces the face value of the bond or loan nor lowers the contractual interest rate.

Debt restructuring. Any change in the contractual payments profile of a debt instrument. Debt reduction and rescheduling are variants of debt restructuring. A restructuring could aim to do little more than defer principal payments on maturing debts, without any reduction in the contractual interest rate. Alternatively, a restructuring could reduce interest payments as well as defer (or even reduce) principal payments. The loss associated with a restructuring is a function of the length of time repayment of principal is put off, the interest rate on the new debt, and the face value of the new debt instrument that emerges from the restructuring—and the discount the market assigns to this new payments profile.

Debtor-in-possession (DIP) financing. In US bankruptcy practice, senior financing provided to support a firm's ongoing operations while it undergoes a court-supervised reorganization. The name refers to the fact that the firm's management remains in control of the firm during a Chapter 11 reorganization.

Deposit freeze. The suspension of payments on bank deposits.

English-law documentation. Bonds governed by English law typically allow a supermajority of bondholders to amend the bond's financial terms, and, as a result of their use of trustees, require that bondholders act collectively to initiate litigation. Consequently, English-law documentation implies the presence of certain collective action clauses.

Eurobond. An internationally traded bond. Originally, eurobonds were dollar-denominated bonds issued outside the United States and not subject to SEC registration requirements, but over time eurobond has become the generic term for a bond issued outside the issuer's country.

Exceptional financing. IMF financing in excess of the IMF's normal lending limits of 100 percent of a quota in a year and 300 percent of quota over three years.

Global bond. An international bond that meets the registration requirements of several different jurisdictions and thus can effectively be traded globally.

Holdout. A creditor that refuses to participate in a debt exchange or other restructuring accepted by most creditors. Holdouts typically hope either to negotiate a better deal individually with the debtor or to litigate for full payment.

Illiquidity. The inability to service debts as they come due because the debtor's liquid assets are smaller than its short-term liabilities, often because a country's foreign exchange reserves are smaller than its short-term debts denominated in foreign currency. Illiquidity is distinct from insolvency, typically defined as a condition where the debtor's overall assets are insufficient to meet its overall liabilities. A liquidity crisis is one where the debtor is illiquid.

London Club. The customary process for restructuring a sovereign's debt to commercial bank creditors. There is no formal club, established membership, or fixed meeting place. The London Club is best known for its role in renegotiating syndicated bank loans to Latin American governments in the 1980s and 1990s. It also played a significant role in Russia's 1997 and 2000 restructurings, hence talk of Russia's "London Club" debt.

Majority-restructuring provisions. *See collective action clauses.*

Moral hazard. Changes in behavior induced by the availability of insurance against bad outcomes. Both creditors and debtors are susceptible to moral hazard. Creditor moral hazard is the risk of creditors' willingness to extend credit, which is influenced by the expectation that IMF (or G-7) lending will assure payment. Debtor moral hazard is the risk of a debtor borrowing expecting either to default or to be able to borrow the funds needed to pay from an insurer and therefore failing to make the ongoing effort needed for payment.

New York–law documentation. Until recently, most New York–law bonds have required the unanimous consent of all bondholders to amend the bond's financial terms (nonfinancial terms typically can be amended by a majority or supermajority vote). Consequently, New York–law documentation implies the absence of collective action clauses. However, this is changing. In 2003, a number of emerging-market issuers started issuing New York–law bonds that allow the amendment of the bond's financial terms.

Normal financing. IMF financing not exceeding 100 percent of a country's IMF quota in the first year of the borrower's economic program or 300 percent of its quota over three years.

Official sector. The term official sector covers both the major multilateral lending organizations and the major bilateral creditor countries, including the IMF, the World Bank, regional development banks, G-7, G-10, and the group of bilateral official creditors that meets in the Paris Club. Since the bilateral creditor countries are also the most influential members of the executive boards of the major multilateral institutions, there is a high degree of overlap in the official sector.

Original sin. An economic theory arguing that structural impediments in global capital markets make it difficult for emerging economies to borrow abroad in their own currencies. Countries that have to denominate their external debt in another country's currency suffer from "original sin."

Net present value (NPV). The value of a future payments stream, when future payments are discounted at an appropriate interest rate. If the discount rate is larger than the coupon rate on the instrument, the instrument's NPV will be less than its face value.

Pari passu. Of equal rank, usually applied to debt obligations. In recent years, some creditors have argued that all "pari passu" sovereign debt instruments (bonds and loans) are entitled to proportional payment where the debtor's assets are insufficient to pay all in full. The question of whether equal legal ranking includes the right to proportional payment outside bankruptcy has been litigated recently in the United States and Belgium.

Paris Club. A standing committee of major bilateral official lenders who meet in Paris to coordinate the renegotiation of official bilateral credits. The group's operations are generally governed by custom. The French finance ministry serves as the secretariat for the group. Not all official bilateral creditors are members of the Paris Club.

Policy conditionality. The policy changes that the IMF requires from a country in exchange for its financing. IMF financing is typically disbursed in portions (tranches) upon fulfillment of specific policy commitments.

Priority. The ranking of a borrower's debts. This ranking is usually determined by the order of payment in bankruptcy (*see absolute priority*). Most sovereign debts have the same legal ranking, but a sovereign may nonetheless establish informal orders of payment.

Private-sector involvement (PSI). The preferred euphemism during the late 1990s to describe the official sector's efforts to obtain emergency financing from a crisis country's private creditors. Private sector involvement could come from a consensual debt restructuring or simply from arrears on debt payments to private creditors.

Repo. Repurchase agreements. An agreement to sell a debt security (for cash), with a promise to buy the debt security back in the future.

Rollover. The renewal of existing short-term loans. In a rollover agreement, creditors promise not to pull out as their short-term credits come due. Such rollover agreements often are precursors to more formal debt restructurings. If short-term credits do not roll over, they "roll off."

Run. The withdrawal of short-term credit from a debtor or the pulling out of demand deposits from a bank. Runs are often motivated in part by concerns that the debtor will lack funds to honor all its short-term commitments and that creditors (or depositors) who do not withdraw their financing quickly risk not being paid.

Secondary market. The market for a debt security that has already been issued. Secondary-market trading among creditors does not transfer value to or from the debtor (unless, of course, the debtor participates in the market for its own debt). In the primary market, the debtor issues a new debt instrument to a set of creditors for raising funds.

Senior debt/creditor. Debt/creditor at the top of the order of payments (or the distribution of assets in bankruptcy), as opposed to junior debt/creditor. *See priority.*

Solvency. Financial condition where assets exceed liabilities. For a country, the ability to service the full contractual value of its existing debt obligations over time.

Sovereign. "Supreme, absolute and uncontrollable power by which any independent state is governed (Black's Law Dictionary 1990, 1396)." "Sovereign borrower" refers to the borrowing-country government or its agencies—i.e., borrower that is sovereign within its own territory.

Sovereign debt restructuring mechanism (SDRM). An international bankruptcy regime proposed by the management of the IMF in 2002 and 2003 that would help sovereign governments restructure their external debt.

Sovereign immunity. The legal protection granted to a sovereign borrower under international law and the laws of individual countries.

Special drawing rights (SDRs). An international reserve asset and, more importantly, the IMF's unit of account. The SDR's value is a function of a basket of US dollars, euros, Japanese yen, and pounds sterling. Since the IMF denominates its loans in SDRs, the dollar value of IMF lending varies with the changes in the dollar/SDR exchange rate. For example, one SDR was worth $1.31 in January 2001 and $1.49 in January 2004.

Standstill. A suspension of payments. A standstill may be unilaterally declared by the debtor or may result from a negotiated agreement between the debtor and its creditors.

Sudden stop. An abrupt interruption in capital inflows. A country that experiences a sudden stop will no longer be able to finance a current account deficit and may need to start running a current account surplus to finance capital outflows.

Trade credit. Short-term credit extended to facilitate the import/export of goods and services.

Tranching. Disbursing a loan in stages (tranches) to assure that the debtor lives up to its policy commitments.

Triage. Separating illiquid firms (or financial institutions) from insolvent firms (or financial institutions)—i.e., differentiating institutions that can be rehabilitated from those that should be closed down.

Voluntary debt exchange/swap. The voluntary exchange of one debt instrument for another. Creditors may voluntarily agree to make concessions in an exchange to avoid a worse outcome, such as a certain default, or they may agree to participate in an exchange to obtain a new debt instrument of equal or greater market value. There is obviously a difference between those voluntary exchanges done to avoid a worse outcome, and those done simply to obtain a market return.

Index